CONTEMPORARY LIVES

EMINEM

GRAMMY-WINNING RAPPER

ABDO
Publishing Company

CONTEMPORARY LIVES

EMINEM

GRAMMY-WINNING RAPPER

by David Aretha

CREDITS

Published by ABDO Publishing Company, PO Box 398166, Minneapolis, Minnesota 55439. Copyright © 2012 by Abdo Consulting Group, Inc. International copyrights reserved in all countries. No part of this book may be reproduced in any form without written permission from the publisher. The Essential Library™ is a trademark and logo of ABDO Publishing Company.

Printed in the United States of America,
North Mankato, Minnesota
112011
012012

 THIS BOOK CONTAINS AT LEAST 10% RECYCLED MATERIALS.

Editor: Holly Saari
Copy Editor: Amy Van Zee
Series design: Emily Love
Cover production: Kelsey Oseid and Marie Tupy
Interior production: Marie Tupy

Library of Congress Cataloging-in-Publication Data
Aretha, David.
  Eminem : Grammy-winning rapper / by David Aretha.
      p. cm. -- (Contemporary lives)
  Includes bibliographical references and index.
  ISBN 978-1-61783-323-6
  1. Eminem (Musician)--Juvenile literature. 2. Rap musicians--United States--Biography--Juvenile literature. I. Title.
  ML3930.E46A74 2012
  782.421649092--dc23
  [B]
                                    2011040468

TABLE OF CONTENTS

Eminem did not show up to the 2003 Academy Awards, even though his song "Lose Yourself" was nominated for an Oscar.

CHAPTER 1

An Oscar-Night Surprise

||||||||||||||||||||||||||||||||||||||||||||||

Marshall Mathers chose not to attend the 2003 Academy Awards ceremony in Los Angeles, California. Typically, that would not be huge news. The artist better known as Eminem does not usually hang out with movie stars. He's far more comfortable in low-key environments with the friends from his old neighborhood than at high-society, black-tie affairs.

In 2003, however, there was a good reason for Eminem to consider being there. His song "Lose Yourself" from the movie *8 Mile* was one of five nominated for an Academy Award for Music (Original Song). Eminem was asked to perform a fit-for-television version of "Lose Yourself" because of the song's R-rated lyrics, but he did not want to change the song.

Eminem did not think he could win. A hip-hop song had never before been nominated for an Academy Award, also known as an Oscar. Up against him were esteemed musicians such as U2 and Paul Simon. Eminem was also on vacation at the time of the ceremony and was not motivated enough to cut his vacation short. He expected to hear at some point that Bono from U2 or Simon had accepted the award.

THE AWARD GOES TO . . .

That evening, legendary singer Barbra Streisand was presenting the award for Eminem's category.

In the 2002 film *8 Mile*, Eminem plays the role of Jimmy "B-Rabbit" Smith. B-Rabbit is a young, aspiring rapper from the wrong side of Detroit, Michigan's, 8 Mile Road, which divides Detroit and its suburbs. His father is not around, his mother is an alcoholic, and his girlfriend becomes pregnant. Moreover, B-Rabbit is white and is considered an outsider in the mainly African-American hip-hop clubs where he is trying to make a name for himself.

Amid these problems and more, B-Rabbit gains a fan base thanks to clever and meaningful rhymes that seem to spill from his mouth with ease. He earns respect—and applause—by performing songs that speak about his own life and troubles in harsh, dark terms.

As she prepared to announce the winner of the Oscar for Music (Original Song), she said, "I'm very proud to live in a country that guarantees every citizen, including artists, the right to sing, and to say, what we believe."[1]

Streisand was noticeably surprised when she broke the seal on the envelope and announced, "The Oscar goes to Eminem."[2] The crowd was stunned as well. One of Eminem's cowriters, Luis Resto—looking conspicuous in his Detroit Pistons jersey—walked onto the stage and accepted the

gleaming award. The credit, he said, belonged to
Mathers. Resto commented,

> *It's great working with Marshall—day in, day out.*
> *He's creative. He has symphonies in his head that*
> *I'm privileged to put onto tape. . . . I think he's*
> *going to feel great about the Oscar. He's very proud*
> *[of] the song. I just don't think he expected it.*[3]

AN AWARD-WINNING MOVIE

The 2002 film *8 Mile* does not just feature
Eminem's music. It showcases him as a feature-
film actor, and it includes a story line that mirrors
his life more closely than he has admitted when
asked about the comparisons. The story of *8 Mile's*
B-Rabbit—the main character—is similar to how
Eminem grew from a boy without a true home or
father figure to an accomplished artist.

How does a troubled kid with a difficult
childhood emerge from the hip-hop scene in
Detroit, Michigan, to make it big? How does
someone with no formal musical training rhyme
the "symphonies in his head" into a microphone
with the poise of a performer who has grown

As B-Rabbit in *8 Mile*, Eminem portrayed a character who is very similar to himself.

up under a spotlight? And how does a rapper stuck right in the middle of the East Coast and West Coast rap styles form a sound all his own to become *Rolling Stone* magazine's "King of Hip-Hop" in 2011?

‖‖‖‖‖‖

Although he was born in Missouri, Marshall spent much of his childhood in the inner city of Detroit, Michigan.

CHAPTER 2

Rough Beginnings

IIIIIIIIIIIIIIIIIIIIIIIIIIIIIIIIIIIIIIIIIIIIIIIIIIIIIIIIIIIIIIIIII

Acity of 75,000 people, Saint Joseph is on the Kansas border in northwest Missouri. Saint Joseph is the birthplace of famed cowboy Jesse James, and the birth of Marshall Bruce Mathers III on October 17, 1972, eventually gave the town claim to its second well-known "outlaw."

Marshall Mathers during childhood

Marshall is the only child of Debbie Mathers and Marshall Mathers II. The two divorced when Marshall was a toddler, and he has no recollection of his father being in his life. Marshall told

60 Minutes in 2010 that he also holds no desire to meet him. He said,

> *I can't understand how [he couldn't care]. If my kids moved to the edge of the earth, I'd find them. No doubt in my mind. . . . If I had nothing, I'd find my kids. So there's no excuse.*[1]

Had he stayed in Saint Joseph, there might have never been an Eminem—at least as a rap musician. Debbie, who was a teenager when Marshall was born, shuffled from job to job. This resulted in moves between Missouri and Michigan cities, including Detroit, a growing hotbed of hip-hop. Debbie and Marshall continued to move back and forth between Michigan and Missouri, but by the time he was 12, Marshall was settled on Detroit's rugged east side.

||||||||||||||||||||||||||||||||||||||||||||||||||||||

SINGLE PARENTHOOD IN THE FAMILY |||||||||||

Eminem's mother, now known as Debbie Mathers-Briggs, was not the only single mother in Eminem's family. She, too, was the product of a poor, single-parent home. Debbie's mother, Betty Kresin, was 14 when she married for the first time. Despite being married three times, Kresin raised her five children mostly on her own, which started a pattern that would last for at least three generations.

BULLIED AND BEATEN

Because his mother moved him around so much, Marshall changed schools more times than he could remember and never seemed to fit in. Largely because he was almost always the new kid, Marshall was teased, taunted, and frequently beaten up. On October 15, 1981, a bully at Detroit's Dort Elementary School split nine-year-old Marshall's lip. The same student left Marshall with head, facial, back, and leg injuries after a separate incident in a bathroom. And in January 1982, the bully allegedly hit Marshall in the face with a snowball containing a heavy object or a chunk of ice. The incidents caused Marshall to have nightmares and be afraid of going to school.

Eminem later wrote and rapped about the incident in the 1999 song "Brain Damage." In the song, he used the name of his alleged attacker, DeAngelo Bailey. Bailey later sued Eminem, but the case was dismissed, and Bailey eventually

DETROIT'S VIOLENCE

In the 1980s, Detroit gained a reputation as the murder capital of the United States. The rise of crack cocaine during the decade spawned drug-related violence during the years Marshall was growing up near 8 Mile Road.

Before settling down in Detroit, Debbie Mathers and Marshall moved around frequently, which contributed to his poor performance in school.

admitted to bullying the rapper. Eminem sang, "He banged my head against the urinal till he broke my nose / Soaked my clothes in blood, grabbed me and choked my throat."[2] Marshall said he was frequently beaten in restrooms, in hallways, and on the way home from school. He was shoved into lockers and generally pushed around by tougher kids at rough schools.

|||||||||||||||||||||||||||||||||||||||||||||||||||||||||||

MUSIC OVER SCHOOL

Marshall was never really interested in schoolwork. A fan of rap music from the time he was in grade school, Marshall could recite tracks from the Beastie Boys and LL Cool J as if he had written the songs himself, but he could never seem to get his homework done on time. While still in school, where he was struggling in and out of class, he began finding his voice with a microphone in his hand. His uncle Ronnie, who was about the same age as Marshall, became his first strong musical influence by introducing some of the most popular rap songs to his 11-year-old nephew.

Marshall also met his rap-loving friend DeShaun Holton, known as Proof, while the two were in school, and they became inseparable best friends and rapping partners. Eminem later recalled it was around this time that he realized he wanted to be a rapper. Marshall was still trying to get through ninth grade at Lincoln High School when he began rapping on stage at neighborhood talent shows. He called himself "M&M" after his initials.

Getting bullied and moving around so frequently did nothing to help his studies. After three years of trying, Marshall had still not completed ninth grade, and in 1989, at age 17, he dropped out of Lincoln High and went to work scrubbing dishes and cooking at Gilbert's Lodge, a local restaurant, for $5.50 an hour. All the while, Marshall continued immersing himself in rap music.

|||||||||||

EMINEM'S UNCLE

Eminem has a tattoo that reads "Ronnie R.I.P." on his upper left arm. It's a tribute to his earliest influence in rap music. Ronald Polkingharn was the son of Marshall's grandmother on his mom's side. Just a few months older than Marshall, Ronnie was more like a brother than an uncle to Marshall. The two spent countless hours together.

When the movie *Breakin'* came out in 1984, Ronnie got the sound track. He and Marshall listened over and over to Ice-T's "Reckless," even though the movie's title song, "Breakin' . . . There's No Stoppin' Us" by Ollie & Jerry, was the more commercially successful track. The two boys liked the grit and the rhymes of Ice-T's song. Mesmerized by the genre, Ronnie and Marshall began belting out their own rhymes.

In 1991, Ronnie committed suicide. Eminem mentions him in several songs.

Growing up, the hip-hop group Beastie Boys was one of Mathers's favorite bands.

CHAPTER 3

Going It Alone

||||||||||||||||||||||||||||||||||||||||||||||||||||||||||||||||||||||||||||||||||||||||||||

Mathers could have ended up leading a rap group rather than becoming a successful solo artist. Growing up, he had a great deal of respect for several groups. He loved the Beastie Boys and practically wore out his copy of their album *License to Ill*. "I liked the Beastie Boys because they were themselves—

they weren't fronting," he said.[1] Mathers once saw the Beastie Boys open a concert for another of his favorite groups, Run-DMC, during the 1980s. He remembers relating to the groups' music and said, "Millions of kids around the world could relate to where they were coming from."[2] Later, others would feel the same about his music.

During his formative years, Mathers joined several bands in an effort to get started in the music business. As a young teenager, he joined the New Jacks. He and Proof dabbled in a Detroit group called Bassmint Productions. However, Mathers—still known as "M&M"—was years away from his big break.

EMINEM AND BASKETBALL

Eminem grew up in Detroit during the glory days of the Detroit Pistons of the National Basketball Association (NBA). The team won the 1989 and 1990 NBA championships and was nicknamed the "Bad Boys" for its rugged style of play. Eminem spent many hours playing hoops, and he considered trying to make a career out of it. However, his inability to stay in school—and his knack for rhyming—took his dreams in a different direction.

A NEW NAME

In 1995, Mathers changed his name. He couldn't market himself as "M&M" without copyright challenges by the popular candy company, so he changed his name to the phonetic spelling: Eminem. Around the time that he dropped out of school, "Eminem" began appearing on homemade signs that announced rap shows featuring himself and Proof, who was known as "MC Proof." (In the world of hip-hop, *MC* stands for "mic controller.") And though Eminem's following was not large, hip-hop fans in his neighborhood began to know him as an up-and-coming freestyler who could seemingly rhyme one line with any other. He was one of only a few white artists in his Detroit neighborhood, which made Eminem stand out even more.

THE HIP HOP SHOP

Beginning in 1993, home base for Eminem became the Hip Hop Shop in Detroit. The Hip Hop Shop, the brainchild of local rap fan Maurice Malone, became a popular hangout for the primarily African-American teens and young adults in the neighborhood. In the mid-1990s, every Saturday at 4:00 p.m. was open mic time at the Hip Hop Shop, and aspiring rappers took the stage to battle each other in rap. Eminem recalled,

> *Maurice was really supportive of the local scene. The Hip Hop Shop was like the Apollo—you could get booed out of there quicker than [expletive] if you weren't paying attention. It was the place if you wanted to make a name for yourself, not only in Detroit but all over the world.*[3]

The battling concept was intimidating for a first-time rapper. A battle is a war of words where only the strong survive. A battle typically consists of two artists, side by side, who take turns insulting each other before a crowd whose cheers or boos often determine the winner. The battles often become personal, offensive, and vulgar. Sometimes, the rhymes are accompanied by a background beat, but other times, the rappers perform a cappella. As

THE SHOP

Maurice Malone started the Hip Hop Shop on 7 Mile Road in 1993 in order to sell his wares, which were mostly hip-hop clothing. He was delighted in what it became. "I'm glad that the shop has had so much influence on so many successful artists," he said.[4]

Battling was how Eminem first became known as a rapper.

a freestyling competition, the routines are not to
be scripted.

Initially, Eminem had cold feet about taking the stage there, but MC Proof, who was also the host of the open mic slots, persuaded Eminem to give it a go—just once—at the Hip Hop Shop. Eminem remembered,

> He said, "Come out and see if you like it. If you don't like it, you never have to come here again." That's how I did it—I went there 20 minutes before the battle was over. This was in '95. I rapped and I got a response and it was insane. The people were jumping up and down and screaming. The heads there were like, "Proof, where did you find this dude at?"[5]

From that point, Eminem was on his way to stardom. When prominent Detroit artist D. J. Babe recalls the Hip Hop Shop, one memory jumps to mind. "The moment that sticks out for me is the infamous Eminem vs. La Peace battle," he said. "Going to that battle was actually my first time going to the shop, and Eminem was just going through everybody. They were just rapping for hours and hours."[6]

Once Eminem performed at the Hip Hop Shop, he became increasingly known throughout Detroit's hip-hop scene.

SPREADING HIS WINGS

At the time, East Coast and West Coast rap were facing off against each other. Rapper Notorious B.I.G. was the popular name in the East; Tupac Shakur ruled the West. The rivalry between the coasts was famous—and heated. But in a small building in Detroit, Eminem, Proof, and dozens of local rappers were battling right in the middle of the two coasts and borrowing liberally from each style. As for Eminem, he developed a style that was all his own.

Eminem began winning not just individual battles at the Hip Hop Shop but big contests with cash prizes. He also began getting paid for some of his appearances. He was still working at Gilbert's Lodge, and the extra cash came in handy. More than the money, he began seeing his art as a legitimate career path. Eminem was working hard

A BLEND OF EAST-WEST RAP

Eminem described his rap style like this: "The East Coast is mainly known for lyrics and style, while the West Coast is more known for beats and gangsta rap. I kinda blend it so east meets west halfway, which is the Midwest. To me, that's what it should sound like because that's where I am."[7]

on his music. It would soon pay large dividends, but not before Eminem overcame a few ups and downs.

||||||||||

Kim and Eminem had much in common upon first meeting.

CHAPTER 4

Eminem
and Kim

||||||||||||||||||||||||||||||||||||||||||||||

Eminem once said, "Hip-hop became my girl, my confidant, my best homie."[1] However, the true muse for much of his life was a vivacious, troubled woman named Kimberly Anne Scott. Kim and Eminem met in 1989 at a mutual friend's house when Eminem was 15 and Kim was 13. They hit it off instantly. The Detroit-area youngsters had been through similar struggles. They began dating, and soon they were spending most of their time together.

In 1995, the two received news that would change both of their lives forever. Kim was pregnant. Eminem had seen a lot of unmarried, teenage fathers run away at that kind of news, but he was motivated to be better than that. Eminem wanted to be a responsible father, support Kim and their child, and locate better work than his cooking and dishwashing gig at Gilbert's Lodge. Making it big in music became his mission.

On Christmas Day 1995, Hailie Jade Scott was born. Eminem was thrilled, calling it the high point of his life. He wanted to give his daughter everything he never had as a child. She became the focus of his writing efforts and the light of his life. Unfortunately, that life would not be smooth during Hailie's formative years.

||||||||||||||||||||||||||||||||||||||||||||||||||||||

FAILURE AND BREAKUP

Before Hailie's first birthday, Eminem released his first album, *Infinite*, in 1996. It was his creative work, but it would not have been possible without the help of record-producing brothers Mark and Jeff Bass in Detroit. Marky, as Mark was frequently called, had watched Eminem perform at the Hip Hop Shop and was blown away. He put all his other projects aside and began working in the studio with his new prodigy. Despite being unable to secure financial backing from a record label, Marky said, "[I] dropped everything that I was working on, borrowed $1,500 from my mother, and finished the record. When it didn't work out, it put Marshall into a real funky spin."[2]

Saying it didn't work out was an understatement. The Bass brothers were handing out cassette tapes to anyone and everyone in an attempt to get someone in the business to show interest. No one seemed to want anything to do with a white rapper whose only real music credentials came from the underground battle scene. Detroit musician Supa Emcee said,

EP AND LP

Many aspiring artists begin with an EP, a release with more than one track but not enough for a complete album. Eminem's *Slim Shady* began as an EP. It was so promising that it attracted the attention of music producers, who developed it into his first LP.

Proof, *left*, played a role in Eminem's eventual success.

"Word got around about him. A lot of people in this city with less skills were accepted, but he wasn't because of his color. He was always the underdog."[3]

Eminem even tried peddling copies of *Infinite* out of the trunk of his car. He managed to sell approximately 500 tapes. Still, his debut release had flopped, and he took the setback hard. He became depressed, and it put a strain on his relationship with Kim. The two broke up, and Kim prevented Eminem from seeing their daughter. It was one of the darkest points in Eminem's life.

After breaking up with Kim, Eminem moved in with his mother. He had been feuding with her for years over her use of prescription drugs. But under her roof again, it was Eminem who began increasing his use of such substances and alcohol. He hit bottom with a failed suicide attempt in which he overdosed on Tylenol painkillers, but threw up the pills.

|||||||||||||||||||||||||||||||||||||||||||||||||

CLIMBING BACK

In the midst of a low point, Eminem did what he does best. He put pen to paper, creating new rhymes in an effort to jump-start his career and win his way back into Kim's good graces. He and

INFINITE ||||||||||||||||||||||||||||||||||||||||||||||||||||||||||||||||||||||||||||||||||||||

Infinite was released on cassette tape and vinyl record in 1996, with only a small number of each produced. It was more than enough to satisfy the limited demand for Eminem's debut album, which no label picked up. Artists such as Proof and Eye-Kyu contributed to some of the tracks, including "It's O.K.," "Searchin'," and "Backstabber."

Proof came up with a concept for a new hip-hop group: each member would go by the name of an alternate persona—a name under which they could write and express the craziest, most shocking lyrics. The result was the group D12, and Eminem's alter ego, Slim Shady, would become a staple of his early career. Eminem said,

> When I thought of the name Slim Shady, I started thinking of a million things to rhyme with it. And that was the turning point. I realized that this alter-ego was going to become more than just shock rap."[4]

D12

When Eminem and Proof came up with the idea for D12, they wanted to create a Detroit version of the Wu-Tang Clan, a popular New York City hip-hop group. Proof wanted 12 MCs, because he planned to call the group the "Dirty Dozen." They ended up with six members, each with an alter ego. The original group members and their aliases were Eminem (Slim Shady), Proof (Dirty Harry), Bizarre (Peter S. Bizarre), Kuniva (Hannz G.), Kon Artis (Mr. Porter), and Bugz (Robert Beck). The group released its debut release, *The Underground EP*, in 1997 but did not gain acclaim until after Eminem became a successful solo artist. D12 released two albums that reached Number 1 on the *Billboard* 200: *Devil's Night* in 2001 and *D12 World* in 2004.

D12 minus Eminem

He released the demo *Slim Shady* in 1997. Eminem's career and personal life were heading in a better direction, and the best was yet to come.

|||||||||||

Eminem started thriving once he received guidance from producer Marky Bass.

CHAPTER 5
Putting It All Together

IIIIIIIIIIIIIIIIIIIIIIIIIIIIIIIIIIIIIIIIIIIIIIIIIII

As Slim Shady, Eminem could be loud and opinionated. He was crude and vulgar, rhyming about poverty, drugs, alcohol, homelessness, hate, and murder. Under the guidance of producer Marky Bass, Eminem was bursting out of the shell he had crawled into after the fast failure of *Infinite*.

Not surprisingly, his big break stemmed directly from the battle scene. Thanks to his success battling at the Hip Hop Shop, Eminem earned a trip to Los Angeles, California, to take part in the 1997 Rap Olympics, a rap battle. He was better prepared than he ever was for the Detroit battles, where his improvisational skills led to some of the best freestyle performances viewers had ever seen. In Los Angeles, Eminem rapped freestyle, but he frequently punctuated his performances with metaphors he had practiced ahead of time. He reached the finals and finished second to a rapper named Otherwize.

Eminem was crushed. However, his *Slim Shady* demo made it into the hands of well-known producer Jimmy Iovine, who was greatly impressed with Eminem. Even better news soon followed. Not only did Iovine like the demo, but he liked it so much that he passed it along to rap star and producer Dr. Dre. When Dre heard Eminem's demo, he was hooked. He believed Eminem might be a big-time rap artist in the making. "I knew it was going to be big," Dre said of Eminem's work:

> *I didn't know it was going to be this big. I didn't know it was going to be half this big. I knew people*

were going to get into him, and love him. . . . It's a perfect example of an artist coming in and taking advantage of the situation. That's what he did. He came in, and he works his [expletive] off.[1]

Dre decided that his Aftermath Entertainment— a division of Interscope—would help Eminem get to superstardom. Eminem's demo was about to become *The Slim Shady LP*.

MAJOR LABEL, MAJOR SUCCESS

Working with Dre in the studio was a turning point in Eminem's career. *Source* magazine cofounder and record-company veteran Jonathan Shecter described the creative process:

Dr. Dre, rap's greatest producer, displays a . . . mastery of his craft when he provides the musical stage upon which Eminem employs his own curiously personal writing habits. He composes his songs in bits of four or more lines, copied in tiny letters with intentional disregard for the symmetry of the page. As each new sinister couplet comes to him, he shakes his right fist quickly back and forth, in time to a rhythmic pattern known only to him. If everything fits, the message in the words and the flow of the rhyme, he'll chuckle silently to himself and scribble with even more intensity.[2]

Eminem and Dre proved to be a winning combination. Released on February 23, 1999,

DR. DRE

Dre has a place among the world's foremost rappers, and he has produced several artists who can claim the same distinction. Among his protégés are Snoop Dogg, 50 Cent, and, of course, Eminem. Dre, born Andre Young, grew up in the rough Los Angeles neighborhood of Compton. He hit it big in the mid-1980s with the gangsta rap group N.W.A.

Although Dre has influenced him, Eminem does not consider himself a West Coast rapper like Dre, and he does not necessarily follow the style that Dre made famous.

Meeting Dre proved to be a turning point in Eminem's career.

The *Slim Shady LP* debuted at Number 2 on the *Billboard* 200 chart behind the R & B group TLC's *FanMail*. It sold almost 300,000 copies in its first week on store shelves. It won the 1999 Grammy Award for Best Rap Album and would go on to be named Outstanding National Album at the Detroit Music Awards. It has since been certified quadruple-platinum, meaning 4 million copies have been sold. In 2003, it was named number 273 of the top 300 albums of all time—genre notwithstanding—by *Rolling Stone* magazine.

All of a sudden, Eminem was no longer a poor, mixed-up kid growing up on the wrong side of 8 Mile. He was a bona fide rap star. He had quickly become a favorite of rap-loving kids of all creeds and colors. In addition, he and Kim began seeing each other again, and the couple and Hailie spent time together as a family. On June 14, 1999, Eminem and Kim married.

FAME COMES WITH A PRICE

Some aspects of his rise to the top were not what Eminem envisioned them to be. Critics called his songs too vulgar and violent. In his song "I Don't Give a [Expletive]," he declared, "I'll slit

EMINEM AND KIM'S WEDDING

The marriage of Eminem and Kim on June 14, 1999, was a small celebration in Eminem's hometown of Saint Joseph, Missouri, held entirely out of the public eye. The wedding had only three guests, including Eminem's mother, Debbie Mathers-Briggs.

your [expletive] throat worse than Ron Goldman," referring to a famous murder victim.[3] In "Bonnie and Clyde," he sang, "Da-da made a nice bed for mommy at the bottom of the lake."[4] Some claimed that simply listening to Eminem's music could be harmful to young people by putting them at risk for violent behavior. Another problem with fame was Eminem's inability to go out in public without being noticed. Eminem had bleached his hair with peroxide, making it virtually impossible for him to walk through a store or mall without being recognized and pestered.

With the single "My Name Is" climbing the charts and those in charge of marketing his music eager to get him in front of his fans, Eminem was working harder than he ever had in his life. He said,

Although his rise to rap stardom was his dream, Eminem found it challenging as well.

"My Name Is" made headlines for multiple reasons. Not only did it hit the charts; it also hit the courts. Eminem's mother, Debbie Mathers-Briggs, sued her son for approximately $10 million in September 1999, claiming defamation of character. Among the lyrics was "My mom smokes more dope than I do."[6] The sides settled out of court with Eminem agreeing to pay $25,000.

Any chance there was to make money, we'd take it. Sometimes, all I had to do was show my face and maybe do a song or two. Man, I remember getting $5,000 to perform one song, which was a ton back then. We were workaholics.[5]

And his work was far from finished.

||||||||||

After the release of
The Slim Shady LP, Eminem
continued collaborating with Dre.

CHAPTER 6

The Marshall Mathers LP

||||||||||||||||||||||||||||||||||||||||||||||||||||||||||||||||||||||||

After helping Eminem record *The Slim Shady LP*, Dre asked Eminem to collaborate with him on his own 1999 release, *The Chronic 2001*. Eminem is featured on a few tracks, including "Forgot About Dre." The two then went to work on Eminem's follow-up, *The Marshall Mathers LP*, which *Rolling Stone* and *Time* magazines have called one of the greatest albums of all time.

The new album was more personal and heartfelt than its predecessor. This was not Slim Shady hurling streams of rhymes, insults, and observations. This was Marshall Mathers sharing details about his climb to fame, troubled home life, tension with his mother, and struggles with Kim. Eminem said,

> I played with the mic a lot more on The Marshall Mathers album I didn't just say my lyrics in one tone, split the verse and that was it. I learned to play with my voice. I made it do more things that I didn't really know it could do. . . . I had simply had more experience behind the mic. I was able to take the whole Slim Shady entity and just run with it on the new album.[1]

The Marshall Mathers LP was released in May 2000. One week later, it had sold 1.76 million copies, making it the fastest-selling rap album to date. It was being purchased at twice the rate of the previous record holder, Snoop Dogg's 1993 album *Doggystyle*. Eminem's album set a record for highest one-week sales by a solo artist.

NOT EVERYONE IS A FAN

If Eminem thought there was a backlash after his big-label debut the previous year, the 2000 release of *The Marshall Mathers LP* made those earlier critics seem subtle. The first single released, "The Real Slim Shady," rocketed up the charts. It reached Number 1 in the United Kingdom—a first for Eminem—and made it to Number 4 on the *Billboard* Hot 100 in the United States. The song is a harsh commentary on what Eminem believed to be phony, manufactured pop songs that were dominating the airwaves at the time. He directs stinging insults at Britney Spears, Will Smith, and Christina Aguilera. Other songs on *The Marshall Mathers LP* use vulgar and derogatory terms to describe homosexuals. The song "Kim" describes the singer choking and cutting his wife's throat. Gay rights and women's groups all over the world

MORE THAN 10 MILLION SOLD

A decade after its release, *The Marshall Mathers LP* continued to rack up sales and receive honors. In 2011, it reached certified diamond status, meaning more than 10 million copies had been sold. Nearly one-fifth of those sales occurred during the first week the LP was on the market.

were outraged. Some organized formal protests and boycotts.

||||||||||||||||||||||||||||||||||||||||||||||||||||||||

PROTEST AT THE GRAMMYS

Boycotts and protests were nothing new to Eminem by the time *The Marshall Mathers LP* was nominated for multiple awards at the 2000 Grammys. However, the protests there topped anything the controversial artist had ever experienced before. The Gay & Lesbian Alliance Against Defamation (GLAAD) came in full force. The group picketed the Grammys with signs that read "Rally Against Hate" and "Hate Set to a Groove Is Still Hate."[2] GLAAD protested the fact that the Grammys welcomed an award nominee and performer whose album used offensive terms to describe homosexuals and whose songs, in

COPYRIGHT INFRINGEMENT CLAIM ||||||||||||||||||||||||||||

Offensive lyrics were not the only controversial aspects of *The Marshall Mathers LP*. French composer Jacques Loussier filed a copyright infringement suit against Eminem and producer Dre for $10 million, claiming that the beat for "Kill You" was stolen from his composition "Pulsion." The case was eventually settled out of court.

Gay rights activists protested Eminem and his nominations at the 2000 Grammys.

the group's opinion, seemed to glorify violence against women.

Eminem got the final word, however, during a performance that came as a surprise to many. At the Grammys, Eminem performed "Stan" as a duet with legendary musician Elton John, who is gay.

After reading the lyrics to "Kim," Ontario's attorney general, Jim Flaherty, wanted Canadian border officials to keep the artist from entering the country for an October 2000 concert. "I personally don't want anyone coming to Canada," Flaherty said, "who will come here and advocate violence against women."[4] The Toronto event took place as scheduled, despite at least one media watchdog requesting a hate-crime charge against Eminem in an effort to keep him off stage.

Their song ended with an embrace between the two artists. Eminem said,

> That was history right there. He was so cool to me; he really got where I was coming from and he knew that I wasn't this straight-up homophobic dude. Elton put himself at risk by performing with me—in terms of alienating his fans who had a problem with me—and I'll always respect him for that.[3]

Although he anticipated some criticism of the album and released both clean and explicit versions of *The Marshall Mathers LP*, Eminem was surprised at the levels of outrage. He said,

Eminem shocked many people when he performed at the 2000 Grammy Awards with Elton John.

Even then I didn't believe that everything was for real. It was hard enough to realize that I was famous enough that people [cared] what I said, and even harder to believe that they'd take it all so . . . seriously.[5]

||||||||||||||||||||||||||||||||||||||||||||||||||

HIGH HONORS

While critics and protesters were speaking out against *The Marshall Mathers LP*, the album was racking up awards. It was nominated for a 2000 Grammy Award in the category of Album of the Year. It did not win that prestigious honor, but it did claim that year's Grammy for Best Rap Album. "The Real Slim Shady" also won a Grammy Award for Best Rap Solo Performance. Subsequent single releases "The Way I Am" and "Stan" also gained

ATTENDING THE 2000 GRAMMYS ||||||||||||||||||||||||||||||||||

Winning awards was the furthest thing from Eminem's mind when he got into the music business, and it has never been one of his goals. These factors played a role in his decision to not attend the 1999 Grammy Awards, when "My Name Is" won the Grammy for Best Rap Solo Performance. By the 2000 Grammys, when *The Marshall Mathers LP* was nominated for several awards, Eminem decided it was time to accept such trophies in person.

acclaim as they moved up the charts. "Stan" even reached Number 1 in Australia and the United Kingdom. Eminem was a worldwide phenomenon, for better or for worse.

||||||||||||

In 2000, Eminem appeared in court for his felony charges.

CHAPTER 7

Trouble in the Hood

Less than two weeks after *The Marshall Mathers LP* was released and months before he accepted his Grammy Awards for the album, Eminem went from sitting on top of the world to making choices that sent his life spiraling in the wrong direction. At the time, he and members of the Insane Clown Posse (ICP), a rival Detroit hip-hop act, were in the middle of a long-running feud. On one very early morning in June 2000 in Royal Oak, a Detroit suburb, Eminem was carrying an unloaded pistol and got into a heated exchange with Douglas Dail, a member of the ICP. The police arrested Eminem on a weapons charge.

That night, Eminem was at the Hot Rock Sports Bar and Music Cafe in Warren, Michigan,

RIVALING WITH THE ICP

The bad blood between Eminem and members of the ICP dated to the mid-1990s, when both Detroit-area acts were trying to make it big. At that time, Eminem reportedly handed out flyers for one of his own local shows, and on those flyers he insulted the ICP, and it did not sit well with the group.

Over the years, the rivals have traded jabs in the media and in their song lyrics. One of the ICP's songs is titled "Eminem's Mom" and contains many insults aimed at Debbie Mathers-Briggs. On the other hand, Eminem has used blow-up dolls with painted faces made to look like the ICP members, and he taunted the group by simulating lewd acts using the dolls.

Shortly after Eminem was arrested for pulling a gun on Dail in 2000, Dail's brother, William Dail, was arrested for allegedly assaulting an Eminem fan at an ICP show in Omaha, Nebraska. It seems the fan had been holding up a T-shirt supporting Eminem and throwing M&M candies at the band. As of 2011, the ICP and Eminem had put their differences behind them.

In sentencing Eminem to probation and fines for the June 2000 weapons incident in which he pulled a gun on the ICP's Douglas Dail, judge Denise Langford Morris scolded the rap star. She told him he was lucky no one had been hurt or killed. "Poor judgment is an understatement for what you did," she said.[2]

when he saw Kim kissing the bouncer. Kim told Eminem it was nothing serious, but Eminem had seen enough. This time, he pulled out an empty semiautomatic weapon. He threatened the man, John Guerra, with the 9-millimeter gun and then hit him with it.

This time, an assault arrest accompanied another weapons charge against Eminem. At a time when he should have been reveling in his success, he found himself in jail, posing for police mug shots, and making news for all the wrong reasons. "Guns are bad, I tell you," he later said. "I caught three felony charges in one weekend. And I was completely sober. No pills. Just passion."[1]

On April 23, 2001, Eminem put the incidents behind him by pleading no contest to the weapons charges, which means he would not

During his troubled times in 2000 and 2001, Eminem rejoined the group D12 and served as executive producer for the group's first album, *Devil's Night*. It is named after the illegal yet longstanding Detroit Halloween tradition of setting fire to abandoned houses. The album produced the singles "Purple Pills" and "Fight Music." It also included a hidden track (not listed on the album) by Eminem entitled "Girls."

fight the charges. In exchange, the assault charge was dropped. He paid a number of fines and fees and was placed on probation for two years. Eminem said the probation might have been the best thing for him, as it forced him to stay off the drugs he had been using. He had been taking amphetamines, barbiturates, and Ecstasy, but the terms of his probation meant he would be subjected to random drug tests. A positive test during his probation would have likely resulted in jail time. It was time for Eminem to clean up his act.

||||||||||||||||||||||||||||||||||||||||||||||||||||

BREAKING UP WITH KIM

Eminem's temper sometimes got the best of him and often led him to act rashly, and it also caused harm to those around him. His relationship with Kim had been a roller coaster before and during their marriage. The Guerra incident marked a new low for the couple, and it sent Kim further into the depression she had been battling for a long time. In July 2000, one month after the scene at the Hot Rock, Kim attempted suicide by cutting both wrists, but she survived.

At the time, Eminem was performing during the Up in Smoke tour in the Detroit suburb of Auburn Hills. He was thankful Kim's suicide attempt—like his own a few years before—had failed. It became clear to him, though, that their marriage had failed too. The following month he filed for divorce. Kim

EMINEM, FATHER FIGURE

Eminem's fathering went far beyond taking care of his own daughter, Hailie. He also took in Kim's sister's child, Alaina, when she was young and in need of a home. Moreover, he and Kim began caring for his younger half brother, Nathan, after he was taken away from Debbie Mathers-Briggs and placed in a foster home.

Kim shared custody of Hailie with Eminem once the divorce was finalized in 2001.

later filed a lawsuit trying to prevent Eminem from seeing their daughter, Hailie.

For a brief time, the couple tried to work through their problems and keep their marriage working. They dropped the divorce proceedings that December and announced they would reconcile and once more live together with Hailie. In March 2001, though, it was Kim who restarted the proceedings. Her divorce complaint cited "a breakdown of the marriage relationship . . . and . . . there remains no reasonable likelihood that the marriage can be preserved."[3]

The divorce became official in October 2001. The couple shared custody of five-year-old Hailie and Eminem was required to pay $1,000 a week in child support. Eminem insisted that caring for his daughter would always be his greatest priority. Harvey Hauer, one of Eminem's attorneys, told the *Detroit Free Press*, "It's always been Marshall's desire that whatever happened would happen in the best interest of the child."[4]

Eminem was back on his own and off drugs. He had moved past his legal troubles and seemed poised to build on the success of *The Marshall Mathers LP*. That journey would lead the Detroit rapper to one of the last places he thought he would go: Hollywood.

||||||||||

MORE TROUBLES FOR KIM

Her failed suicide attempt in 2000 and divorce from Eminem the following year were only the beginnings of a run of trouble for Kim Scott. She was sentenced to two years' probation for cocaine possession, and her probation violation for failing a mandatory drug test sent her to jail for a month.

8 Mile

8 Mile was a success in theaters.

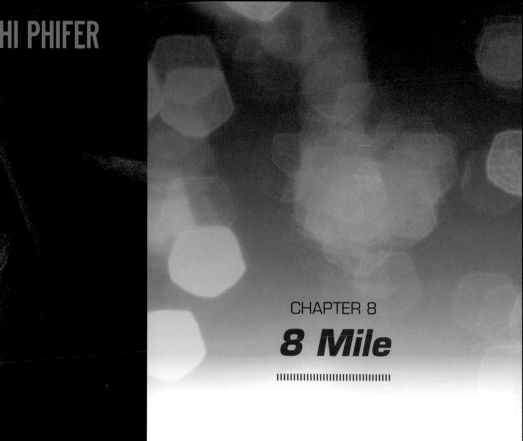

8 Mile

||||||||||||||||||||||||||||||||||||||

The story goes like this: A poor white kid growing up in Detroit's rough 8 Mile area has a knack for pulling rhymes out of his head on the spot. However, it's tough for the lone white rapper in Detroit's African-American hip-hop scene. Everyone doubts him. Fellow rappers put him down and try to keep him there.

He gets beaten up on the streets, does not see eye to eye with his struggling single mother, and has to muster all his nerve to battle on stage before a crowd just waiting to pounce on him. When he finally does, he rhymes his way to victory and blows the audience away. Sound familiar?

EM-TV

Though *8 Mile* was his silver-screen acting debut, Eminem was not a stranger to the camera by the time he starred in the 2002 film. He had already starred in several music videos, and, a year before he was approached to do the movie, he took over for Carson Daly as host of *Total Request Live* on MTV for a memorable day. The cable music network called it "EM-TV."

With the network censors on alert and bleeping out his vulgarities, Eminem began the show by starting to play a video by the Backstreet Boys, a popular boy band. He then cut it short and shouted to viewers that there would be no videos from "The Whack Street Boys," "N Stink" or "98 Disease," parodies of popular groups *NSYNC and 98 Degrees.[1] He would be picking the videos, and he started with "Guilty Conscience" by himself and Dre.

Brian Grazer, one of the *8 Mile* producers, told Eminem that he enjoyed the "EM-TV" episode. "He said that seeing me in that light made him want to work on something with me," Eminem said. "He saw that I had potential as an actor."[2]

Eminem's feature-film acting debut did not require him to do much research, because the plot for *8 Mile* could have been taken from his own life. He has held firm to his claim that the film is not a biography. Still, it's partly biographical at the very least, and no one was better prepared to handle the lead role than the man who had lived much of the plot.

||||||||||||||||||||||||||||||||||||||||||||||||||||||||||||

B·RABBIT PREVAILS

Eminem plays Jimmy "B-Rabbit" Smith, the down-on-his-luck aspiring rapper who longs to get out of his mother's trailer and away from his dead-end job as a Detroit sheet metal worker. Proof also landed a role in the film and made his movie debut as Lil' Tic. The two sat down with screenplay writer Scott Silver as he was putting some finishing touches on the script. They told him countless stories about the Detroit streets, the battle scene, and the rap rivalries they experienced while growing up in the 8 Mile area. Eminem recalled reading the script: "I remember thinking it was so close to that period of my life it was crazy. I knew it was the story I wanted to do."[3] Much of the movie

In *8 Mile*, B-Rabbit lives in a poor neighborhood, similar to how Eminem grew up.

was filmed in Detroit. Eminem and Proof were so familiar with the surroundings and the script's story line that it was easy for them to "become" their characters. The producers and director Curtis Hanson wanted Eminem to write the theme song for the movie too.

SURPRISING SUCCESS

8 Mile, which premiered on November 8, 2002, was a big success at the box office. It brought in $51 million on its opening weekend, which was more money than it cost to make the movie, and it grossed $117 million in all. Critics were generally impressed with the story line, and many of them were pleasantly surprised with Eminem's first shot at acting. His performance won him a 2003 Chicago Film Critics Association Award as Most Promising Performer. But what the critics really loved was the sound track. The first three tracks are Eminem's own, including "Lose Yourself," and he collaborated with 50 Cent and Obie Trice on a fourth. D12 also recorded a song for the sound track.

FOUR MILLION DOWNLOADS

When Eminem's "Lose Yourself" topped 4 million digital downloads in 2011, it became one of just two songs from 2002 or earlier to hit that milestone. The other was Journey's "Don't Stop Believin'" from 1981. The Journey anthem was at 4.7 million downloads when "Lose Yourself" was downloaded for the four-millionth time.

Eminem's friend Proof not only plays rapper Lil' Tic in *8 Mile*, but he also served as the inspiration for one of the lead characters, David "Future" Porter, portrayed by Mekhi Phifer. Like the real-life Proof, Porter hosts the Detroit battles in the film.

"Lose Yourself" was the movie's big winner. In addition to becoming the first rap song to ever win an Oscar, the inspirational anthem received other honors, including the 2004 award for Most Performed Song from a Motion Picture, which was awarded by the American Society of Composers, Authors, and Publishers. "Lose Yourself" became Eminem's first Number 1 hit on the *Billboard* Hot 100 in the United States. It peaked at the top spot on the charts in 24 different countries. "Lose Yourself" deviated from the mature-rated, hard-core material that had become Eminem's signature, but the release of something a little more mainstream also gained him new groups of fans who had never previously embraced his work. In August 2011, "Lose Yourself" was downloaded for the four-millionth time, putting it in rare online company.

Mekhi Phifer, *left*, Proof, *center*, and Eminem during a promotion for *8 Mile* in 2003

Eminem battling as B-Rabbit in *8 Mile*

Some in the hip-hop community called the release of a widely accepted track selling out, but Eminem does not see it that way. He said,

> *The core fans know what time it is. Know about my history and my personal connections to the history of hip-hop. To everyone else—if you loved the movie, and from there you went on to love my music, and you're 86 years old—I just want to say thank you. Hailie thanks you. Her college is paid for. As an underground artist starting out, I never wanted to sell out, but I'm sure there are fans who think I have. To them I say, I still love you. I don't feel like I made music that sold me out.*[4]

|||||||||||

Eminem performed at the 2002 Grammys, where he also received the award for Best Rap Album for *The Eminem Show*.

CHAPTER 9

Immersed
in Controversy

||||||||||||||||||||||||||||||||||||||||||||||||||||||||||||||||||||||||||||||||||||||||||

Now that *8 Mile* and "Lose Yourself" had introduced Eminem to a mainstream audience, the rapper had a larger platform on which to speak. Eminem was not at a loss for words. His 2002 release, *The Eminem Show*, produced five singles that reached the charts in the United States, the United Kingdom, or both. The album debuted at Number 1 on the *Billboard* 200, even though the leaking of illegal copies into stores and onto the Internet had caused a short first week of sales. Moreover, *The Eminem Show* became the artist's third consecutive release—in a four-year span—to win Best Rap Album at the Grammys, where it was also nominated for Album of the Year in 2003.

As usual, the album release was not without controversy. While there was not as much backlash from social groups as there was with previous releases, *The Eminem Show* rankled musical artist Moby and group Limp Bizkit, both of whom receive jabs on the album's first single release, "Without Me." During the 2002 MTV Video Music Awards, Eminem and Moby exchanged heated words in front of fans, with Eminem referring to Moby as a girl, making fun of Moby's glasses, and eventually getting booed by the crowd. On the "White America" track, Eminem directs an expletive toward Lynne Cheney, the wife of then-US vice president Dick Cheney and an outspoken critic of Eminem's violent lyrics.

Eminem and Proof, *right,* arriving at the 2002 MTV Video Music Awards

ENCORE

The Eminem Show seemed like a controversy-free release compared with his next album, *Encore,* which was released in 2004. On it, President George W. Bush was in the firing line. When an unreleased bootlegged copy of the song "We Are American" began making its rounds on the Internet before the album reached stores, the

US Secret Service said it was probing possible action over what some considered threatening lyrics: "I don't rap for dead presidents / I'd rather see the president dead."[1] Nothing came of the probe, but the controversy did not end.

It wasn't President Bush but Michael Jackson's supporters who truly lashed out against *Encore*. The video for the first single, "Just Lose It," features Eminem ridiculing Jackson. In the song, Eminem raps about "a new case of child molestation accusation" and continues, "I done touched on everything but little boys / That's not a stab at Michael / That's just a metaphor, I'm psycho."[2] Black Entertainment Television (BET) announced it would no longer air the video, although MTV continued to do so. Jackson's family members, his legions of fans, and fellow African-American entertainers called for a boycott of *Encore*. Nevertheless, *Encore* debuted at Number 1 on the *Billboard* charts. It failed to win the Grammy for Best Rap Album as Eminem's three previous albums had, but it did earn three Grammy nominations.

||||||||||||||||||||||||||||||||||||||||||||||||||||||||||||||

OFFSTAGE TROUBLES

While his albums continued to be big sellers, life in the mid-2000s was difficult for Eminem. He admitted he had been abusing Ambien, a prescription sleeping medication, and in 2005 he checked himself into a rehabilitation center to get help for his drug problem. Because of that, Eminem had to cut short his first tour in three years, which prevented him from making it to the European portion of the tour. Later that year, the *Detroit Free Press* reported that Eminem was retiring from his recording career to focus on producing. Eminem, however, told a Detroit radio station that he was uncertain whether he would be making more albums. The truth was somewhere in between, as the rapper did take a long break from the studio.

SHADY RECORDS

Eminem's break from the studio in the mid-2000s was not truly a break. Eminem was busy with his recording company, Shady Records, which he started in 1999 with his manager, Paul Rosenberg. From 2005 to 2007, Eminem helped produce four LPs for other artists—two by 50 Cent and one each by Obie Trice and Cashis.

Eminem took a break from music in 2005 to treat his drug addiction.

Eminem began a hiatus from recording in 2005, but it did not prevent him from putting out an album. On December 6, 2005, he released *Curtain Call*, a greatest-hits compilation that also includes four new tracks. One of the new songs is Eminem's duet with Elton John, "Stan," from the 2001 Grammy Awards.

Despite having told *Rolling Stone* magazine in 2004 that his romantic relationship with Kim was "pretty much out the window," Eminem and Kim remarried on January 14, 2006.[3] The couple spared no expense for the service, which was at Meadow Brook Hall in Rochester Hills, Michigan. Proof served as Eminem's best man. Hailie, their ten-year-old daughter, was the maid of honor.

But the marriage was not a sign that Eminem was ready to live a happy home life. Kim said her husband left after just 41 days. Eminem filed for divorce on April 5, 2006. And before the year was over, their second divorce was final. Kim attributed Eminem's inability to maintain a close relationship with a woman to his strained relationship with his mother. "I believe that Marshall has issues on how to express his love," she said, "and I don't think

Proof died at the age of 32.

he knows how to treat women because he wasn't treated well by his mother. He still had a lot of anger towards her."[4]

Also that year, Eminem lost his best friend, Proof. Eminem remembered what he was thinking when he first heard the news: "Not Proof. Not Proof. Not Proof."[5] On April 11, 2006, Proof was shot and killed in a nightclub on Detroit's East 8 Mile Road. "I can't even bring myself back to the place I was when I heard what happened to Proof," Eminem said. "I have never felt so much pain in my life. It's a pain that is with me to this day."[6]

||||||||||||

PROOF'S MURDER

The details of how Proof wound up with two bullets in his back and one in the back of his head at the CCC Club remain unclear. He got into an argument with Keith Bender Jr. while playing pool, and club owner Mario Etheridge, Bender's cousin, fired a gun into the air in an effort to keep things calm. Some witnesses said that Proof shot Bender, who died eight days later, and that Etheridge then shot Proof. Other witnesses reported that several people were involved in the altercation and that others fired shots. Eminem was among 2,000 people who crammed into the Fellowship Chapel on West Outer Drive for Proof's April 2006 funeral service.

Eminem went to rehab twice to kick the drug habit he had for many years.

CHAPTER 10

The Comeback Kid

|||||||||||||||||||||||||||||||||||||||||||||||||||||||||||||||||||||||||||

Eminem's drug problem, which lasted for most of the 2000s, was far more serious than his fans could have imagined. "I was the worst kind of addict, a functioning addict," he told the *New York Times* in 2009. "I was so deep into my addiction at one point that I couldn't picture myself being able to do anything without some kind of drug."[1]

After spending time in a rehabilitation clinic in 2005 while on his break from recording, Eminem began using drugs again. He said he would sometimes pop 20 pills in a day, including Ambien, pain-reliever Vicodin, and antianxiety drug Valium. One December day in 2007, he swallowed several blue pills, not knowing or caring exactly what they were. It turned out that the pills were methadone, a widely known heroin substitute. Doctors later said the drug could have killed him at that dosage.

The revelation scared him, and he checked himself into rehab again in 2008. This time, he went through the full program, meeting regularly with sponsors, doctors, and therapists. Elton John, a recovered drug addict, even offered his help to the rapper.

Beginning on April 20, 2008, Eminem began his longest drug-free stretch since he had started using as a teenager. "The deeper I got into my addiction, the tighter the lid got on my creativity," he said. "When I got sober the lid just came off. In

Eminem's "Lose Yourself" provides the pulsating background music for several recent Chrysler auto commercials. Eminem's collaboration with Chrysler began with the award-winning, two-minute commercial "Born of Fire" that aired during Super Bowl XLV in 2011. The commercial featured Eminem pointing into the camera and saying, "This is the Motor City, and this is what we do."[3] The commercial won the 2011 Emmy Award for Outstanding Commercial.

Teaming up with Eminem is not just a way for Chrysler to sell cars. The automotive giant later released a line of T-shirts reading "Imported from Detroit," with a portion of the proceeds going to benefit Eminem's Marshall Mathers Foundation, which provides funding for organizations that work with urban youth in Michigan and the United States. Paul Rosenberg, Eminem's manager and president of the Marshall Mathers Foundation, said, "The Chrysler brand and the Marshall Mathers Foundation share a parallel commitment to give back to the City of Detroit."[4]

seven months I accomplished more than I could accomplish in three or four years using drugs."[2]

RELAPSE

Eminem used his drug-free productivity to record the album *Relapse*, which recounts some of the most significant moments of his battle with pills. In "Déjà Vu," he takes listeners through the 2007 day when methadone could have killed him. In "Beautiful," a ballad he began writing during rehab, he sings—a rarity for him—and raps about the ability to come back even after hitting the bottom. "Not only is honesty one of the biggest parts of recovery," Eminem said. "I'm blessed enough to be able to have an outlet."[5]

Relapse, Eminem's first album of original material in five years, came out in May 2009 and instantly gained the Number 1 spot on the *Billboard* 200 list. It sold more than 600,000 copies in its first week. "It's hardcore, it's dark comedy, it's what Eminem has always been," said producer Dre.[6]

DIGITAL MUSIC SALES

Digital technology has significantly changed how music is purchased. Digital sales accounted for just 5 percent of revenue for Eminem's *Curtain Call: The Hits* (2005). That jumped to 16 percent for *Relapse* (2009) and to a whopping 25 percent for *Recovery* (2010).

Eminem accepted the award for Best Rap Album at the 2010 Grammys.

RECOVERY

Now that Eminem was clean and cured of the writer's block that had plagued him when he was popping pills, the hits kept coming. Less than six months after *Relapse* won Best Rap Album at the 2009 Grammy Awards, he put yet another album at the top of the charts. *Recovery*, which was released

Despite the fact that as of 2011 he had won more than a dozen Grammy Awards in his career and has been a regular performer at the Grammys and several other prominent award shows, Eminem maintains that he'd just as soon stay away from the red-carpet scene. "If it could just be about the music, I would only do the music," he said. "I don't hate the limelight, but I don't like it."[7]

in June 2010, became Eminem's sixth album to debut at Number 1. It, too, won a Grammy for Best Rap Album. His lyrics and gritty emotion earned praise along with the studio craftsmanship of Dre. Its first-week sales eclipsed 700,000, and in July 2011 it became the first album ever to be digitally downloaded one million times.

"Not Afraid," the first single, became the sixteenth song ever to debut at Number 1 on the charts. The second single, "Love the Way You Lie" featuring Rihanna, became the first track in digital music history to sell more than 300,000 copies in five weeks.

Eminem and Rihanna
performed together at the
2010 Grammy Awards.

THE FUTURE

Eminem wasn't slowing down. He and fellow Detroit rapper Royce Da 5'9" combined to form the duo Bad Meets Evil, which released its EP *Hell: The Sequel* on June 14, 2011. When the duo's single "Lighters," featuring Bruno Mars, reached the *Billboard* charts, it marked the third identity under which Marshall Mathers has put out a top-ten hit (Eminem, D12, and Bad Meets Evil). As for another Eminem solo effort, fans can take comfort in the fact that it's likely only a matter of time. Alex Da Kid, who produced Eminem's "Love the Way You Lie," said,

> *He's in a great position where [he and Dre] can make music. And whenever they feel like it, they can put it out. There's not a label telling them*

EMINEM, "KING OF HIP-HOP"

In 2011, *Rolling Stone* magazine analyzed album sales, YouTube views, and social-media popularity in an effort to crown the "King of Hip-Hop." The winner was Eminem, who beat Lil Wayne and Drake for the title. "As recently as three years ago," the magazine stated, "Eminem winning a survey like this was unthinkable; his nearly half-decade hiatus from recording made any comeback unlikely, let alone one in which he took back the charts as if he'd never left."[8]

what to do, because they've been so successful, so it's really up to him.[9]

Eminem, perhaps more than at any time in his turbulent life, had a steady hand in his own destiny.

||||||||||

TIMELINE

1972

On October 17, Eminem is born Marshall Mathers III in Saint Joseph, Missouri.

1989

Eminem drops out of Lincoln High School before completing ninth grade.

1995

Eminem's daughter, Hailie, is born on December 25.

1999

Eminem marries Kimberly Scott in Saint Joseph, Missouri, on June 14.

2000

The Slim Shady LP, wins the 1999 Grammy Award for Best Rap Album.

2000

In May, Eminem releases *The Marshall Mathers LP*, which rockets to the top of the charts and sells 1.7 million copies in its first week.

1996

Eminem releases his first solo album, *Infinite*, which is unsuccessful.

1997

Eminem meets rapper and producer Dr. Dre.

1999

In February, Eminem releases *The Slim Shady LP*, the first major-label and successful release of his career.

2000

Eminem is arrested twice in June—on a weapons charge after pulling a gun on a rival rapper and for beating a man with a gun.

2001

The Marshall Mathers LP wins Best Rap Album at the 2000 Grammys.

2001

Eminem and Kim divorce in October.

TIMELINE

2002

The Eminem Show is released.

2002

8 Mile, starring Eminem, hits theaters on November 8.

2003

Eminem's "Lose Yourself" wins an Oscar for Music (Original Song).

2006

Eminem and Kim remarry in Rochester Hills, Michigan, on January 14. Eminem files for divorce on April 5.

2008

Eminem reenters rehab in April for his drug addiction.

2009

Relapse is released.

2004	**2005**	**2005**

| *Encore* is released. | Eminem checks himself into rehab in August to beat his drug addiction. | A greatest-hits compilation, *Curtain Call*, is released on December 6. |

2010	**2010**	**2011**

| Eminem's *Relapse* wins the 2009 Grammy for Best Rap Album. | *Recovery* is released. | Eminem's *Recovery* wins the 2010 Grammy for Best Rap Album. |

GET THE SCOOP

FULL NAME

Marshall Bruce Mathers III

DATE OF BIRTH

October 17, 1972

PLACE OF BIRTH

Saint Joseph, Missouri

SELECTED ALBUMS

Infinite (1996), *The Slim Shady LP* (1999), *The Marshall Mathers LP* (2000), *The Eminem Show* (2002), *Encore* (2004), *Curtain Call* (2005), *Relapse* (2009), *Recovery* (2010)

AWARDS AND HONORS

- As of 2011, Eminem had released seven studio albums, six of which debuted at Number 1 on the *Billboard* 200 chart.

- As of 2011, he had won 13 Grammy Awards, including five for Best Rap Album.

- Eminem earned acclaim for his starring role in the 2002 feature film *8 Mile*.

- In 2003, he won the Academy Award for Music (Original Song) for "Lose Yourself," which became the first rap song ever to win the award.

- In 2011, *Rolling Stone* magazine named him the "King of Hip-Hop."

PHILANTHROPY

- Eminem began the Marshall Mathers Foundation, which helps provide funding for several Detroit-area and national charities.

- He is an active supporter of the Eight Mile Boulevard Association, which works to make a difference in the neighborhood in which Eminem grew up.

"The East Coast is mainly known for lyrics and style, while the West Coast is more known for beats and gangsta rap. I kinda blend it so east meets west halfway, which is the Midwest. To me, that's what it should sound like because that's where I am."

—EMINEM

GLOSSARY

Billboard—A music chart system used by the music-recording industry to measure record popularity.

demo—A sound recording that is meant to show off an artist to record producers.

extended play (EP)—A musical release with more than one song or track, but not enough for an album.

freestyle—To perform verses on the spot rather than from prewritten lyrics.

gangsta rap—A type of rap music with lyrics featuring the violence and drug use of urban gang life.

Grammy Award—One of several awards the National Academy of Recording Arts and Sciences presents each year to honor musical achievement.

hip-hop—A style of popular music associated with US urban culture that features rap spoken against a background of electronic music or beats.

homie—Slang for a friend; a person from one's hometown, neighborhood, or region.

long play (LP)—A musical release typically consisting of ten to 20 songs; also called an album.

MC—Standing for mic controller in the world of hip-hop; a rapper or one who controls the stage.

philanthropy—An act of charity, such as a donation, for a humanitarian or environmental purpose.

producer—Someone who oversees or provides money for a play, television show, movie, or album.

rap—A musical genre composed of rhythmic talking often accompanied by a beat.

record label—A brand or trademark related to the marketing of music videos and recordings.

track—A portion of a recording containing a single song or a piece of music.

ADDITIONAL RESOURCES

SELECTED BIBLIOGRAPHY

Bozza, Anthony. *Whatever You Say I Am: The Life and Times of Eminem*. New York: Three Rivers, 2004. Print.

Eminem. *Angry Blonde*. New York: ReganBooks, 2000. Print.

Eminem, with Sacha Jenkins. *Eminem: The Way I Am*. New York: Plume, 2009. Print.

FURTHER READINGS

Als, Hilton, and Darryl A. Turner, eds. *White Noise: The Eminem Collection*. New York: Thunder's Mouth, 2003. Print.

Hasted, Nick. *The Dark Story of Eminem*. London: Omnibus, 2011. Print.

Stubbs, David. *Cleaning out My Closet: Eminem: The Stories Behind Every Song*. New York: Thunder's Mouth, 2003. Print.

WEB SITES

To learn more about Eminem, visit ABDO Publishing Company online at **www.abdopublishing.com**. Web sites about Eminem are featured on our Book Links page. These links are routinely monitored and updated to provide the most current information available.

PLACES TO VISIT

The Grammy Museum

800 W. Olympic Boulevard, Los Angeles, CA 90015-1300
213-765-6800
www.grammymuseum.org
The Grammy Museum features exhibits related to many genres of music.

The Hip Hop Shop

5736 W. 7 Mile Road, Detroit, MI 48221
www.thehiphopshop.com
The Hip Hop Shop is the location where Eminem first started battling and first gained acclaim as a rapper in Detroit.

SOURCE NOTES

CHAPTER 1. AN OSCAR-NIGHT SURPRISE

1. "Eminem Oscar (Best Song) 2003." *YouTube.* 10 Nov. 2010. YouTube. Web. 14 Aug. 2011.

2. Ibid.

3. Ibid.

CHAPTER 2. ROUGH BEGINNINGS

1. "Eminem & Anderson Cooper: Behind the Scenes." *60 Minutes Overtime.* 10 Oct. 2010. Web. 13 Oct. 2011.

2. Corky Siemaszko. "Eminem Was Victim of Bullying as a Child; Rapper's Mother Even Sued School for Lack of Protection." *NYDailyNews.com.* NY Daily News.com, 18 Oct. 2010. Web. 17 Aug. 2011.

CHAPTER 3. GOING IT ALONE

1. Eminem, with Sacha Jenkins. *Eminem: The Way I Am.* New York: Plume, 2009. Print. 20.

2. Ibid.

3. Ibid. 25.

4. Biba Adams. "The Hip Hop Shop: A Detroit Landmark Remembered." *The Michigan Citizen.* The Michigan Citizen, 2007. Web. 23 Aug. 2011.

5. Eminem, with Sacha Jenkins. *Eminem: The Way I Am.* New York: Plume, 2009. Print. 26.

6. Biba Adams. "The Hip Hop Shop: A Detroit Landmark Remembered." *The Michigan Citizen.* The Michigan Citizen, 2007. Web. 23 Aug. 2011.

7. Anthony Bozza. *Whatever You Say I Am: The Life and Times of Eminem.* New York: Crown, 2003. *Google Book Search.* Web. 13 Oct. 2011.

CHAPTER 4. EMINEM AND KIM

1. Eminem, with Sacha Jenkins. *Eminem: The Way I Am*. New York: Plume, 2009. Print. 20.

2. Nate Cavalieri and Charles Aaron. "Before Marshall Mattered." *Spin* July 2002. *Google Book Search*. Web. 13 Oct. 2011.

3. Ibid.

4. Eminem, with Sacha Jenkins. *Eminem: The Way I Am*. New York: Plume, 2009. Print. 32.

CHAPTER 5. PUTTING IT ALL TOGETHER

1. "Dr. Dre Interview from Scratch Magazine." *Dr. Dre*. RapBasement.com, 2005. Web. 31 Aug. 2011.

2. Eminem. *Angry Blonde*. New York: ReganBooks, 2000. Print. Foreword.

3. Eminem. "I Just Don't Give a [Expletive]." *The Slim Shady LP*. Aftermath Entertainment, 1999. CD.

4. Ibid.

5. "Eminem, with Sacha Jenkins. *Eminem: The Way I Am*. New York: Plume, 2009. Print. 41.

6. Eminem. "My Name Is." *The Slim Shady LP*. Aftermath Entertainment, 1999. CD.

CHAPTER 6. *THE MARSHALL MATHERS LP*

1. Eminem. *Angry Blonde*. New York: ReganBooks, 2000. Print. 4.

2. Clinton Fein. "Rather Sad to Be GLAAD: The Eminem Controversy." *Annoy.com*. ApolloMedia Corporation, 1 Feb. 2001. Web. 3 Sep. 2011.

3. Eminem, with Sacha Jenkins. *Eminem: The Way I Am*. New York: Plume, 2009. Print. 54.

4. "Eminem vs. Canada." *ABC News*. ABC News Internet Ventures, n.d. Web. 13 Oct. 2011.

5. Eminem, with Sacha Jenkins. *Eminem: The Way I Am*. New York: Plume, 2009. Print. 49.

CHAPTER 7. TROUBLE IN THE HOOD

1. Eminem, with Sacha Jenkins. *Eminem: The Way I Am*. New York: Plume, 2009. Print. 128.

2. "Eminem Sentenced on Gun Charges." *BBC News*. BBC, 29 June 2001. Web. 5 Sep. 2011.

3. Corey Moss. "Eminem's Divorce from Kimberly Mathers Finalized." *MTV News*. MTV Networks, 10 Oct. 2001. Web. 5 Sep. 2011.

4. Ibid.

CHAPTER 8. *8 MILE*

1. "EM TV Part 1." *YouTube*. 15 Dec. 2009. YouTube. Web. 7 Sep. 2011.

2. Eminem, with Sacha Jenkins. *Eminem: The Way I Am*. New York: Plume, 2009. Print. 102.

3. Ibid.

4. Ibid.

CHAPTER 9. IMMERSED IN CONTROVERSY

1. "Secret Service Checks Eminem's 'Dead President' Lyric." *CNN Entertainment*. Cable News Network, 6 Dec. 2003. Web. 10 Sep. 2011.

2. Eminem. "Just Lose It." *Encore*. Aftermath Entertainment, 2004.

3. Touré. *Never Drank the Kool-Aid*. New York: Macmillan, 2006. Print. 33.

4. Stephen M. Silverman. "Kim Mathers: Eminem Nearly Drove Me to Suicide." *People*. Time Inc., 15 Feb. 2007. Web. 10 Sep. 2011.

5. Eminem, with Sacha Jenkins. *Eminem: The Way I Am*. New York: Plume, 2009. Print. 3.

6. Ibid.

CHAPTER 10. THE COMEBACK KID

1. Jon Pareles. "Get Clean, Come Back: Eminem's Return." *The New York Times*. The New York Times Company, 21 May 2009. Web. 11 Sep. 2011.

2. Ibid.

3. "Chrysler Born Of Fire Eminem Super Bowl Commercial FINAL." *YouTube*. 6 Feb. 2011. YouTube. Web. 11 Sep. 2011.

4. Marshall Mathers Foundation. *Eminem Gives Back to Detroit Through New Clothing Line with Chrysler*. Bloomfield Hills, MI: Marshall Mathers Foundation, 17 Mar. 2011. Web. 11 Sep. 2011.

5. Jon Pareles. "Get Clean, Come Back: Eminem's Return." *The New York Times*. The New York Times Company, 21 May 2009. Web. 11 Sep. 2011.

6. Ibid.

7. Ibid.

8. "Introducing the King of Hip-Hop." *Rolling Stone*. Rolling Stone, 15 Aug. 2011. Web. 11 Sep. 2011.

9. Jayson Rodriguez and Matt Elias. "Will Eminem Put Out Another Album Soon?" *MTV News*. MTV Networks, 19 Jan. 2011. Web. 11 Sep. 2011.

INDEX

ABOUT THE AUTHOR

Raised in Southfield, Michigan, just several blocks north of 8 Mile Road, David Aretha has authored more than 40 books for young readers and edited dozens of books on history, sports, and popular culture.

PHOTO CREDITS

Why do nations pursue such different industrial policy strategies today? The United States enforces market competition and eschews state leadership in virtually every industry. Meanwhile, French state technocrats orchestrate sectoral growth from above, and Britain bolsters firms against interference from both markets and state officials.

Political scientists generally explain industrial policy choices by interest-group preferences, but why then do groups in America always win market-oriented policies? Economists generally explain industrial policy choices by the functional needs of industry, but why then do French industries always need firm autonomy?

In *Forging Industrial Policy*, Frank Dobbin traces the evolution of nineteenth-century policies governing one of the first modernizing industries – the railroads. To organize their emergent industrial economies, nations employed principles found in political institutions. The United States used the principle of community self-determination to give municipalities responsibility for promoting railroads. France used the principle of central state supremacy to give government engineers responsibility for orchestrating rail development. Britain used the principle of individual sovereignty to guard railway entrepreneurs against interference from competitors and public officials. In consequence, nations' institutions for achieving industrial rationality and growth came to parallel their institutions for achieving political order. Today, the industrial policy strategies that emerged in the nineteenth century persist because they have shaped ideas about how industrial efficiency is achieved.

This book offers a fresh perspective on modernity that highlights the importance of meaning in rationalized institutions. It has wide-ranging implications for understanding the role of institutions and culture in all instrumental realms of life – from management to economics to science.

Forging industrial policy

Forging industrial policy

The United States, Britain, and France in the railway age

FRANK DOBBIN

CAMBRIDGE
UNIVERSITY PRESS

Published by the Press Syndicate of the University of Cambridge
The Pitt Building, Trumpington Street, Cambridge CB2 1RP
40 West 20th Street, New York, NY 10011-4211, USA
10 Stamford Road, Oakleigh, Melbourne 3166, Australia

First published 1994

Printed in the United States of America

Library of Congress Cataloging-in-Publication Data
Dobbin, Frank.
    Forging industrial policy : the United States, Britain, and France
in the railway age / Frank Dobbin.
        p. cm.
    Includes bibliographical references and index.
    ISBN 0-521-45121-3
    1. Railroads and state – United States – History – 19th century.
2. Railroads and state – Great Britain – History – 19th century.
3. Railroads and state – France – History – 19th century. I. Title.
HE2757.D63   1994
385′.068 – dc20   93-21458
                                                                 CIP

A catalog record for this book is available from the British Library

ISBN 0-521-45121-3 hardback

For my parents

Contents

Contents

Acknowledgments

I owe thanks to many. I am particularly indebted to John Meyer for unfailing and unstinting intellectual stimulation and counsel. Neil Fligstein, Robert L. Frost, Michèle Lamont, John Meyer, William Roy, and David Vogel read every sentence, and commented on most.

Several people offered helpful criticisms and suggestions on early chapter drafts: Gene Burns, Bruce Carruthers, Paul DiMaggio, Roger Friedland, Hillel Frisch, William Goode, Peter Hall, Peter Katzenstein, Suzanne Keller, Seymour Martin Lipset, Robert Liebman, Ben Schneider, Neil Smelser, Ann Swidler, Kathleen Thelen, Walter Wallace, Robert Wuthnow, Morris Zelditch Jr., and Viviana Zelizer.

For feedback and guidance at important points, and for intellectual stimulation generally, I am also grateful to James Baron, Paul DiMaggio, Ronald Jepperson, W. Richard Scott, Ann Swidler, and Viviana Zelizer.

I learned much more from the graduate students at Princeton than they learned from me. They include Terry Boychuk, Stephen Chiu, Timothy Dowd, Bai Gao, Matthew Lawson, Bing Shen, Maureen Waller, Daniel Weber, and Yan Yan. For inviting me to present early drafts in their colloquia I am grateful to David Brain (Indiana University), Ewa Morawska (University of Pennsylvania), Victor Nee (Cornell University), Nancy Bermeo (Princeton University), and Atul Kohli (Princeton University).

Thanks for material assistance go to the National Science Foundation, Princeton University's junior faculty leave program, the Center of International Studies, and the Committee on Research in the Humanities and Social Sciences at Princeton. Three department chairs in Sociology at Princeton have, over the past four years, offered what material support they could and have allowed me to teach what best suited my intellectual needs while writing this book. My thanks to Marvin Bressler, Gilbert Rozman, and Viviana Zelizer.

At Cambridge University Press, Emily Loose and Alex Holzman helped me to sharpen and focus the manuscript, and Ronald Cohen helped to make my prose intelligible.

Finally, my greatest debt is to Michèle Lamont, my companion in thought and in life. For being so much more than just a colleague, and so much more than just a mate.

1. Political culture and industrial rationality

Introduction

During the nineteenth century, each Western nation-state developed a distinct strategy for governing industry. Prevailing theories of policy-making neglect the origins of those strategies, and ultimately fail to explain why they persist through revolutions, regime changes, wars, and depressions. Functional and economic theorists who suggest that policy is driven by laws of economic efficiency cannot account for the fact that different nations show no clear pattern of convergence toward a most-efficient model. Political theorists who suggest that policies reflect the preferences of those who hold power cannot account for the fact that national industrial strategies endure under regimes with dramatically different ideologies.

Analysts use words such as "tradition" and "legacy" to explain national policy strategies, yet most theoretical frameworks privilege generalizable political and economic variables and make no place for national customs. The result is an unfortunate disjuncture between theory and empirical findings in comparative studies of policy: Whereas theory highlights universal political and economic forces, in the last analysis empirical investigations usually point to the effects of tradition. Thus in many studies, after theoretically important factors are used to explain a tiny proportion of the cross-national variance, culture and tradition are thrown in to explain the huge remaining "residual" variance. The reluctance to theorize and investigate traditions stems, I contend, from a core tenet of the modern worldview – namely that idiosyncratic traditions are relics of an earlier age that will eventually be washed away by the forces of logic and reason. A central premise of the modern worldview – that today's policy choices are governed by universal laws of interest and rationality – makes it difficult to conceive of something cultural guiding policy-making.

In this book I explore the origins of national industrial policy strat-

1

egies by charting the evolution of railway policy in the United States, France, and Britain between 1825 and 1900. My aim is to conceptualize the national traditions that shape policy-making. Two theoretical observations prompted me to take on this task. First, modern economies and the policies that support them are organized in quite different ways and show no compelling signs of convergence, yet most analysts focus attention on everything but the processes that produce and sustain these differences. Second, the few theories that do purport to explain such national differences present major flaws. National character arguments employ a peculiar form of reductionism to trace national institutional differences to collective psychological traits of unspecified origins. The new institutional/statist approaches to politics that emphasize structural inertia have generated many synonyms for continuity, but little in the way of explanation. To say that institutions persist because they are institutionalized is to define, not explain. I argue that national traditions influence policy-making by contributing to collective understandings of social order and instrumental rationality. History has produced distinct ideas about order and rationality in different nations, and modern industrial policies are organized around those ideas.

My argument is based on two simple empirical observations. First, during the nineteenth century nation-states developed institutions for organizing economic life that paralleled those they used for organizing political life. The American polity located sovereignty in a series of autonomous community governments under a weak federal structure dominated by the courts. Industrial policy situated economic sovereignty at first in community governments, which practiced active stewardship of growth, and later in an adjudicative federal structure that made Washington the referee of a free market. The French polity located sovereignty in the central state, as the only force that could orchestrate political order and hold the nation together. Industrial policy likewise located economic sovereignty in the central state, under a parallel logic that only orchestration from the center could produce economic order and further the nation's material goals. The British polity located sovereignty in elite individuals by protecting them from their neighbors, the Crown, and the state bureaucracy. Industrial policy sought to locate economic sovereignty in individual firms at first through laissez faire, and later through active protection against the intrusion of market and political forces.

Most analysts have taken the parallels between political culture and industrial culture for granted, but I contend that they contain the secret to cross-national policy variation. My contention is that different conceptions of industrial efficiency originated in the traditions of political life. As modern industrial policies were devised, extant principles of social and political order were generalized to the economic sphere.

The second empirical observation is that national industrial strategies are reproduced when nations tackle new problems. When nations face new policy dilemmas they design new institutions around the principles of existing institutions. For instance, nations that have tried to promote efficiency by stimulating price competition in the past will use this strategy to achieve efficiency in new industries. I will argue that policy approaches are reproduced because state institutions provide principles of causality that policymakers apply to new problems, and not simply because institutions give policymakers the organizational resources to repeat history. By examining policy reproduction and evolution over the first seventy-five years of the life of the railways, I explore the role of these principles of causality in policy continuity and change.

Before proceeding with the theoretical argument I review, in brief, the legacy of the national industrial policy strategies that appeared by the end of the nineteenth century. What did the different strategies look like, and how did nations' industrial strategies develop thereafter? The United States entered the twentieth century with industrial policies designed to guard economic liberties by preventing restraints of trade and enforcing price competition. Federal antitrust policy sought to preclude price fixing and combinations that would create industrial monopolies. Industry-specific regulatory agencies aimed to prevent cartels and keep price competition alive. These policies came to be associated with the idea that natural selection of firms in free markets is the mainspring of growth. Since the beginning of the twentieth century antitrust law has been expanded and fortified, and it has been used to structure industries ranging from oil to telecommunications to computers. Regulatory agencies oversee pricing and competition in such industries as electricity generation, natural gas, radio, television, and aviation. The United States' market-enforcing industrial policies contribute to the conviction that free competition will induce efficiency in virtually every economic sector.

France could hardly look different. By the close of the nineteenth century the French were working out a system of industrial governance based on public concertation of economic life. French policy aimed to guide major manufacturing and infrastructural sectors from above, on the principle that only the state can prevent self-interested entrepreneurs and market irrationalities from disrupting progress. The early twentieth century found state technocrats experimenting with mixed public-private enterprises and nationalizations. The indicative industrial planning that began in the 1950s extended the reach of state technocrats to every sector of the economy; five-year plans set sectoral goals and empowered the state to coordinate the rise of new sectors and the decline of sunset industries. French policy has been driven by the notion that a cadre of expert technocrats can guide the economy better than a hodge-podge of self-interested capitalists and better than the invisible and unthinking hand of the market.

If American policy allocated authority over economic life to markets at the end of the nineteenth century, and French policy allocated authority to technocrats, British policy allocated authority to entrepreneurial firms. Under the guise of laissez faire, Britain had encouraged cartelization and discouraged predatory mergers in order to shield small firms. The notion that the entrepreneurial spirit of the small firm was the mainspring of growth survived to shape policy in the twentieth century. The British responded to the economic crisis of the 1920s and '30s by encouraging cartelization to prevent bankruptcies. When Labour nationalized firms for ideological reasons after World War II, it preserved managerial independence from political meddling. When Britain mimicked France's industrial planning efforts in later years, attempts to promote promising sectors were bastardized into bailouts that would negate the effects of market forces on failing firms. During the 1980s the Thatcher Government returned to policies explicitly designed to locate economic authority in the firm. Twentieth-century industrial policy has guarded private initiative against interference from markets and politics to foster the profit-oriented entrepreneurialism that was identified in the last century as the source of economic dynamism.

How did the United States, France, and Britain settle on these strategies? Most political, economic, and institutional/statist approaches fail here because they take for granted the very socially constructed axioms of modernity that they should treat as objects of study. They take the modern worldview – in which behavior is oriented to economic utility maximization and to political struggles over collectivized material interests – at face value. They treat instrumental rationality as given. They objectify institutions in a way that treats the sustenance of social practices as unproblematic. They have, in essence, formalized the commonsense understandings that the modern worldview presents and turned those understandings back on modernity as analytic tools. The result is that instead of asking the big questions that stimulated the development of the social sciences in the nineteenth century – about how new social institutions and attendant conceptions of reality emerge and evolve – political, economic, and institutional/statist analysts ask questions that spring from within the modern worldview. Political analysts try to understand why one interest group or another appears to win a particular policy battle, rather than how modernity came to structure identity and action around corporate groups called nations, classes, races, and interests (but see Anderson 1983; Ruggie forthcoming; Thomas and Meyer 1984; Lipset and Rokkan 1967). Economists try to divine definitive principles of economic efficiency, rather than trying to understand how modern society came to be organized around progress and how particular conceptions of progress and efficiency emerged, as a number of economic sociologists have argued (for example, Granovetter 1985; DiMaggio and Powell 1991; Zelizer forthcoming). Institutional/statist analysts try to discern what kinds of institutionalized practices are best suited to the promulgation of particular policies, rather than trying to understand how such practices are given collective meaning and thereby sustained – how practices *become* institutions (but see Berger and Luckmann 1966; Meyer, Boli, and Thomas 1987; Scott 1992; Jepperson 1991). I call these three approaches "realist" below, to distinguish them from social constructionist approaches to the same realms. My contention is that these varieties of realism obfuscate the nature of rationality in modern settings by taking too much of the social world at face value, when they should be asking how the world got to be the way it is.

Political realism

It is a premise of democratic government that policy choices reflect the relative power of different interests in society. That idea has been at the core of the political science perspectives that explain policy choices by calculating the influence of rival groups. The interest group approach taken by pluralists (Truman 1951; Lowi 1969) and many neo-Marxists (Mills 1956; Miliband 1969) depicts policy-making as a process of conflict among competing interest groups; liberal and radical thinkers differ principally over whether the ground rules in political contests are fair. Among pluralists this approach can be traced back at least to Weber's *Economy and Society,* which discussed the rise of multifarious political clusters. Among neo-Marxists the approach can be traced back to the *Eighteenth Brumaire,* which mapped out the elite factions that struggled for control of the state under Louis Philippe. The commonsense premise of these theories – that policy decisions reflect the relative power of competing groups – so pervades academic political science that even the self-styled revolutionaries in the field treat it as a given. Rational-choice theory adds the spin that interests can be objectively assessed with mathematical models; coalitional approaches add the spin that because group interests vary over time, different factions coalesce in different moments.

This approach has offered insights into how nations choose from among *given* policy alternatives, but it fails in comparative studies. First, it fails to address the origins of those given policy alternatives (but see Bachrach and Baratz 1963; Lukes 1974). Because nations almost never choose from the same sets of options, and most often choose from mutually exclusive sets of options, understanding the origins of options is crucial. Take the issue of railway route planning. State planning was literally never considered in Britain: private planning was never considered in France. Understanding why these options did not enter political discussion is key to understanding why Britain used private planning and France used state planning, but interest group analysts have largely neglected the issue of how policy options are generated. Second, the interest approach fails to explain why a weak interest group in one country often wins a better policy outcome than its stronger counterpart in another country. Interest group analysts take it as an article of faith that the strongest group always gets its way, so that when a weak group appears to win a policy battle analysts go to great lengths to show either that the group wasn't weak, or that it didn't win. In practice, they define a group's strength by its capacity to win. Third, and perhaps most important, political realism fails to address the issue of why parallel interest groups in different countries believe very different policies to be in their interest. Railroads advocated widely divergent policies in these three countries even when their material situations would appear to have been identical. I contend that political approaches are unable to explain cross-national differences in policy because they are plagued by a form of realism that prevents them from asking how interest groups, collective problems that demand policy solutions, and actual policy alternatives are constituted.

Economic realism

The economic determinist arguments found in commonsense discourse and academic theory suggest that social systems are subject to economic laws that structure institutions. Policy institutions conform to economic laws either through macro selection processes, in which adaptive policies are reinforced, or through micro processes, in which individual-level utility maximization aggregates into collectively rational institutions. For both approaches, exogenous, universal, economic laws govern the cosmos and produce social practices. Contemporary economic theory is an exercise in discovering those laws in full detail. A central tenet is that economic reality is singular, and conforms everywhere to the same external laws. A corollary is that institutional context is not constitutive of economic life and laws, as economic sociologists are wont to argue (White 1988; Zelizer 1988). Instead, context is thought of as a set of conditional variables that have predictable effects under a general theory of the economic universe. Once the general theory is well understood, a full understanding of economic behavior and institutions devolves.

Macro approaches suggest that economic institutions, including policy, evolve toward efficient solutions and adapt efficiently to new environmental factors. In some versions, politicians and interested parties actively select efficient policy instruments, whereas in others functional requisites appear to determine policy choices. The logic-of-industrialization thesis, which has been revived in the recent development literature, suggests that each stage of economic development elicits a particular set of attendant policy and economic institutions. Alexander Gerschenkron asserts in his "late-industrializer" thesis that states respond to relative underdevelopment with certain activist policies to promote growth. Neoclassical theorists take it as an article of faith that because they coincided with growth, American market-enforcement policies reflect universal economic laws. They frequently predict convergence toward the United States' policy model. Andrew

Shonfield's political economy of modern capitalism heralded French industrial planning as the institutional model that would soon outcompete, and replace, laissez faire. These macro approaches posit that over time the most efficient policy institutions are selected either by rational agents of the state or by the invisible hand of the international market.

The new institutional economics and rational choice theory begin at the micro level to explain social institutions. Institutionalism in economic theory0links overarching economic institutions, such as industrial policies, to the utility-maximizing behavior of self-interested actors. For Douglass North (1981), political rulers maximize state revenues by creating institutions that will maximize individual income, and this is how collectively efficient policy institutions emerge. For game theorists and transaction-cost analysts, macro institutions are the manifest outcomes of micro-economic activity; thus theoretical attention is fixed at the micro level. Rational-choice theory suggests that in the aggregate, individual self-interested political behavior will eventuate in policy institutions that achieve a utilitarian compromise, that promote efficiency by maximizing the common good.

Empirically, the argument that universal economic laws structure social institutions has become increasingly difficult to sustain. When the United States followed Britain as the world's unrivaled leader in economic growth, it made sense to think that the ostensibly laissez-faire policies of these two countries reflected universal economic laws. However, the accomplishments of entirely different models of growth – found in countries as diverse as Sweden, France, and Japan – have helped to undermine that way of thinking. If dramatically different economic systems can produce comparable rates of growth, then the universe's economic laws must be broad rather than narrow; inclusive rather than exclusive. And if policies that effect cartels and make the state the arbiter of corporate success can produce growth, then the laws of economics we thought we understood must be substantially wrong. Modern societies organize much activity around the search for transcendental economic laws, believe such laws to exist, and characterize behavior as motivated by such laws. Yet, in practice, economic logic and behavior patterns vary dramatically from one context to the next. This insight dates back at least to early institutional economists, such as Thorstein Veblen (1904), who insisted that economics be an evolutionary science because economic patterns are products of history that are not overdetermined by exogenous forces. If economic laws are situational rather than transcendental, and if different sets of laws serve as adequate functional alternatives, we should be trying to understand the causes of the diversity of economic systems.

Institutional realism

The new institutional/statist perspective in political science responded to the failure of political and economic paradigms to answer the question: Why do national policy strategies persist over time? Their answer is that the inertia of state organizational structures sustains policy strategies. They subscribe to a variety of realism in which social institutions – customs, that is – have the same ontological status as skyscrapers. Social "structures" exist independently of the human actors who inhabit them. These analysts bracket the immense question of how millions of individuals achieve collective understandings of reality sufficiently coherent to motivate them to get up in the morning, staple papers together, unscrew bolts, cook hamburgers, visit post offices, and do whatever else they do to reproduce social institutions (cf. Sewell 1992). Modern state institutions are reenacted daily in all of their complexity by masses of people who share cognitive frames that give meaning to the collective project of modernity and to the minutiae of daily activity. Rather than trying to explain how these shared conceptions of reality that are the basis of customs arise, they attribute "thingness" to customs with terms like institutional equilibrium, branching, path dependence, political learning, and inertia. The result is often a descent into tautology; institutionalized practices persist because they have inertia – because they persist. An institutional approach that addresses *why* they persist promises more useful insights (for example, Jepperson 1991; DiMaggio and Powell 1991; Meyer, Boli, and Thomas 1987).

The organizational resources of states are central to these arguments. Existing resources facilitate the adoption of new policies that are isomorphic with existing policies, and thwart the implementation of policies that are fundamentally different. In the United States of the nineteenth century, for instance, the federal administration had meager organizational resources, and as a result governing strategies that required little federal coordination developed across a wide range of policy realms (Skowronek 1982). Institutionalists do not simply argue that some states have greater resources than others. They hold that states have the resources to do particular things, and that new policies that call for states to do other sorts of things tend to unravel because such policies overtax states' organizational resources (Skocpol and Finegold 1982). Studies that trace policy over long periods of time confirm that nations tend to solve new problems with familiar strategies (Krasner 1978; Zysman 1983; Ikenberry 1988), and this is taken as evidence of the ontological "thingness" of institutions.

Institutional/statist realists claim that the state's organizational features are at the heart of overtime policy continuity. One empirical quandary institutionalists do not resolve is that nation-states have grown so much in the last 150 years that they no longer resemble their former selves (Tilly 1975). The mid-nineteenth century American state, with few permanent employees outside of the post office and armed forces, quickly grew into an organizational leviathan that employs millions. Yet in the period during which the modern nation-state emerged and exploded, national policy strategies show remarkable continuity. I will argue that it is the socially constructed logics of state action, more than the organizational resources of states, that persist to produce policy continuity. In fact, states regularly create new policy instruments that require organizational resources they do not hold, but they model those policies on the principles embodied by existing policies.

Culture and meaning in modern states

Because they were developed to explain policy choices within nations, existing approaches to public policy are seldom well suited to explaining broad differences between national policy styles. That is, most theorists have started out with questions such as, "Why did the United States pass one amendment to antitrust law in 1953 and a different amendment in 1962?" The answers they have come up with shed little light on cross-national questions such as, "Why does the United States always use antitrust law to govern industries, whereas France always uses proactive state coordination?" The problem is not that it is hard to predict national policy strategies, but that existing theories don't capture what is needed to make predictions. What kinds of policies will the United States adopt to govern a new industry? Place your money on policies that enforce price competition. What are the chances that the United States will, as France sometimes does, designate the industry a "national champion" and use public monies to turn it into a monopoly? Take any odds against it.

One needs to know nothing about interest groups, micro-economic patterns, or state organizational resources to make these broad predictions. One need only grasp the logic underlying current policies to be able to guess what future policies will look like, because policies in different countries follow fundamentally different logics. They may be organized around a logic of natural selection, as in the United States, a logic of state concertation, as in France, or any number of other logics. These logics are palpable and enduring. We immediately recognize what was typically French about state railway planning and what was typically British about the state's reluctance to expropriate private lands for the railways because we comprehend these logics.

Policy analysts have not theorized nations' policy logics because the idea that national economies follow different cultural patterns is at odds with the modern worldview, in which economics, like physics, is governed by a single set of laws under one general theory. Industrial policy and other macro-economic institutions fall under that theory. Social scientists have largely embraced this idea that social reality is unitary and have undertaken the task of searching for transcendental social axioms. Ethnographers are an exception because they expect to find radically different principles of behavior in premodern societies that are not attuned to the universe's transcendental economic laws, and hence they expect to find practices and meanings that are local in origin. They begin the task of understanding social systems with an advantage that analysts of modernity lack: They know for certain that the meanings represented by premodern institutions are local fictions. When the denizens of modernity study modernity, by contrast, they presume that social institutions reflect exogenous economic laws, and hence don't treat such cultural artifacts as neoclassical theory as part of an institutionalized meaning system that shapes policy solutions and individual behavior. Instead, analysts take neoclassical theory to be true in a way that ethnographers do not take indigenous theories of the relationship between spirits and harvest outputs to be true. In recent years, the successes of economies organized on non-neoclassical lines (see Hamilton and Biggart 1988) might well have led economists to see economic theory as a belief system because those successes suggest that known economic principles are not universal. Instead, neoclassical economists defend their theories by arguing that economies not organized on market principles have been subjected to unnatural political manipulations that will be their undoing in the longrun. In short, the social sciences emerged to explain the character of modernity, and have since taken up modernity's task of uncovering the uniform social laws of the universe.

Institutionalized meaning systems

I argue that by following the lead of ethnographers, and viewing the institutionalized meanings found in modern society as products of local, social processes, we can gain a better purchase on public policy. To do so one must shift from the realist problematic, "What are the universal, rational laws of social reality?," to the constructionist problematic, "How do particular, rationalized social institutions develop in particular social contexts?" I argue that differences in rationalized meaning systems explain broad cross-national policy differences, and that rationality is essentially cultural.

There are several broad types of institutionalized meaning systems. The social sciences were born in an effort to comprehend the transformation from premodern religious meaning systems to modern, secularized, rational meaning systems. All religious meaning systems orient institutions to the service of a higher power, with an eye to the achievement of grace in the afterlife. However, systems represent the higher power and the religious ethic variously, so that social practices oriented to salvation take markedly different forms. Likewise, all rational meaning systems orient institutions to science and efficiency, with an eye to accumulation through the mastery of nature. However, systems represent the nature of rationality and the instrumental means to accumulation variously, so that social practices oriented to progress take markedly different forms. As a result, although we expect to find very different solutions to collective problems under radically different cultural systems (for example, under Muslim fundamentalism, British secular rationality, and Brazilian shamanism), it is also the case that we find very different solutions under putatively similar rationalized cultural systems.

Practices and meaning.   In religious, rationalized, mystified, and totemic societies alike, actions become customs as they are imbued with meaning. That is, actions become customary only when actors develop collective understandings of their purposes. Insofar as all social practices must be intersubjectively understood to be enacted, all practices carry meaning. Often, meaning consists of mundane, taken-for-granted relationships between means and ends that have the tone, "this is how the world works." One result is that actors often fail to recognize meaning as such because they think of collective, purposive means-ends designations as direct reflections of the nature of reality. Albert Hirschman, following Polanyi, refers to this level of meaning as the "tacit dimension" – "propositions and opinions shared by a group and so obvious to it that they are never fully or systematically articulated" as such (1977, p. 69). In modern societies, we generally deny that anything that is explicitly instrumental is also cultural.

As integrated and comprehensive meaning systems, all cultures purport to represent reality accurately and deny the existence of alternative realities. There can be only one God, or system of gods, only one general theory in physics, only one set of economic laws. The failure of social scientists to think of rationalized institutions as meaning-laden is a result of this feature of meaning systems. The problem originates in a failure of introspection. From within, it is difficult to see any cultural frame as such. It was easy for Western missionaries to see alien meaning systems as just so much superstition, but they continued to believe that their own religious system captured the essence of reality. Similarly, it is easy for students of modernity to see alien social institutions as motivated by beliefs that are social in origin ("there go those crazy French social engineers again"), but analysts have continued to believe that their *own* secular, instrumentally rational, social institutions embody the "true" nature of reality.

To explain the obvious differences among modern social systems, analysts have cordoned off instrumentally rational institutions from the realm of culture and have attributed differences to culture. The term culture, then, is reserved for institutions that are recognized by modernity to be symbolic rather than instrumental, such as the arts, religion, fashion, and education (Eisenstadt, Abitol, and Chazan 1987). Instrumental social institutions such as government, markets, firms, and science are generally treated as acultural by the social sciences. Talcott Parsons formalized this distinction for the social sciences. At the individual level, behavior is similarly partitioned into cultural and instrumental categories, and behaviors that do not appear to be self-interested are explained away by culture and norms (see Elster 1989). This general approach has led to the impoverishment of studies of culture because it has removed instrumentally rational institutions from the purview of cultural analysis. How does antitrust policy symbolize the rational universe? It is for all intents and purposes impossible to ask the question. A central paradox of modernity, then, is that a wide range of cultural forms can be found in different nations' instrumental institutions despite the fact that all of those institutions are purportedly oriented to a unitary set of economic laws. Social science has responded to this dilemma by identifying a few "cultural" institutions that cause differences in national institutional and behavioral patterns rather than by defining all institutions and behaviors as cultural and thereby problematizing rationality. Yet instrumental institutions represent means and ends in the world, and as such they are necessarily cultural.

My point is neither to challenge the modern worldview nor to propose a method for the social sciences that is so radically reflexive that it denies the capacity of modernity to study itself. I simply want to suggest that to comprehend differences among instrumentally rational cultural systems it is necessary to think of them as social phenomena. To the extent that they reflect efforts to represent the universe in rational and scientific terms, modern institutions will vary as societies settle upon different representations.

In fact, social constructionists have made these very points about a number of other rationalized realms (Berger and Luckmann 1966). Students of the nation-state have argued that it is a peculiar historical social construct that has been part and parcel of the rise of rationality, but that as a social form the modern state was in no way historically inevitable (Thomas and Meyer 1984; Anderson 1983; Sewell 1985; Ashcraft 1986; Krasner forthcoming). Institutional economists (Veblen 1904; Commons 1934) and economic sociologists (White 1988; Zelizer 1988; Granovetter 1985) have argued that patterns of rationalized economic behavior emerge for identifiable historical reasons, and then become socially constructed as efficient. The "new institutionalism" in organizations theory treats rationalized organizational policies as social constructs much as I treat state policies as social constructs (Meyer and Rowan 1977; Zucker 1977; DiMaggio and Powell 1983; Scott 1987). And constructionist sociologies of science (Bloor 1976; Wuthnow 1987; Latour 1992) treat rationalized scientific precepts as historically dependent social constructs. My approach bears strong affinities with these macro-constructionist approaches to rationalized institutions in that it makes the interpretation of subjective meaning a central component of understanding rationality.

Verstehen.   Most analysts have presumed that interpretation plays no role in the analysis of instrumental institutions because the purposes and means of those institutions are transparent. The notion that instrumental practices symbolize something seems ludicrous, because they are just there to get the job done. However, as Weber argued, the project of sociology is the "interpretive understanding of social action" and action exists only "insofar as the acting individual attaches a subjective meaning to his behavior." All action has subjective meaning, and no realm of action conforms to objective reality in a way that makes it analytically unproblematic: "In no case does [meaning] refer to an objectively 'correct' meaning or one which is 'true' in some metaphysical sense" (1978, p. 4). In other words, no type of action is intelligible in and of itself. All action is intelligible to the social scientist only through the apprehension of its subjective purpose, and of the causal relationships the actor understands to link action and purpose. Weber refers to this interpretive process as *verstehen*. My aim is to understand how different rationalized social systems came to link substantially different social processes to economic growth.

Weber contributed to our confusion about the nature of instrumental rationality by judging rational practices against an ideal-type, which suggested that they are organized around a universal set of causal relationships. His treatment of rationality contrasted sharply with his studies of religious social systems, which showed religions in all of their complexity and diversity. In fact, like Weber, most early analysts treated modernity as a unified reality.

Rationalized meaning systems

From this cultural perspective, rationality and science are the *geists* that pervade and motivate social action in the modern age. The rational universe is ordered not by overarching spiritual or mystical forces, but by a set of transcendent, disenchanted physical and social laws. The project of modern social systems is to unveil those laws and employ them to master the universe. The success of this venture, which, if we are to believe economists, is driven by an innate desire to accumulate wealth, is judged by "progress," as measured by the aggregate accumulation of goods. As progress-oriented rationality and science came to motivate human action, the bureaucracy and market replaced the church and monarchy as the central cultural loci of collective action. Like religious systems, rationalized meaning systems externalized the genesis of social order in the process of articulating general social laws. Where religious social systems posit a higher-order transformative consciousness that is essentially an incarnation of the transformative capacity of individual consciousness, rational systems posit a higher-order set of physical and social laws that rule the world in predictable ways.

The cultural systems of modern societies are thus organized around a search for the immutable physical and social laws that can enable humankind to alter the world in the name of progress. The social sciences are integral to this process, as they seek to discern the functions of complex social customs and attribute purpose even to those institutions that are not conspicuously oriented to accumulation. Rational choice approaches to norms, for instance, seek to show that although norms may serve no identifiable individual-level purpose, they do serve some higher-order rationality (see Elster 1989). Parsons' (1951; 1971) functional theory sought to show that the acknowledged symbolic, and apparently useless, institutions of modern society actually serve vital functions by producing social integration and sustaining social order. Thus, every detail of social life is envisioned in modern thought as part of a single project of furthering the accumulative mission of humankind. The modern worldview and the social sciences admit that there are nonmaterial dimensions of progress, including equity and democracy, yet they often subsume those dimensions under accumulation by suggesting, for instance, that economic liberty is an ingredient to growth (Bowles and Gintis 1986).

In brief, modernity is distinctly different from what preceded it, but it is not of a piece because the social and economic laws we believe to be "revealed" from experience are actually products of social life. Just as the deities of religious social systems assume the characteristics of the social systems they command, so do the rationalized laws of social reality tend to assume the characteristics of the social systems they govern.

The epistemology of rationalized systems.   In the quest for progress, rationalized societies employ scientific epistemology to identify uniform laws of the physical and social universe. Knowledge in all rationalized domains is governed by this epistemology – in science, in management, in economics, and in public policy. Knowledge consists of generalizations about the world that are based on empirical evidence and that take the form of cause-effect designations. These designations must be demystified, transparent, and logically consistent with existing knowledge. Empirical confirmations must follow established procedures.

The substantive laws of rational meaning systems are subject to amendment and change, because these systems stand on the claim to a method for discerning the nature of reality, rather than, as is the case with religious meaning systems, the claim to accurate substantive knowledge of the nature of reality. Thus, evidence that falsifies their cause-effect designations does not threaten rationalized meaning systems. On the contrary, disconfirmations tend to prove the utility of the method, and epistemological rules are designed to facilitate falsification. Rationality poses knowledge-building as cumulative and iterative, so that even when paradigmatic shifts sweep away all accepted knowledge in a particular realm the newly archaic wisdom is looked upon nostalgically as a necessary step on the road to enlightenment. For instance, we acknowledge that only orthodox macro-economic theory could have spawned neo-orthodox Keynesianism, and humanity had to believe the world to be flat in order to deduce that it could not possibly be. Religious systems cannot so easily withstand such disconfirmations.

Whereas epistemological principles are isomorphic across different rationalized realms, the rules of evidence vary. The natural sciences are highly formalized in that they employ clear, codified, empirical evidentiary rules. Economic theory is also highly formal, but as in mathematics the rules of evidence permit logic alone to be used to confirm theories – indeed the rules privilege logic over empirical evidence. Economic theory is also subject to constant real-world tests, so that prevailing theories can be disproven by experiences such as depressions (Hall 1989). All kinds of theories can be developed and diffused by practitioners as well as by professional theorists, but this is especially true of management theories, which are often evidenced by a single "strong" case. Because management theory is thought to be cognitively accessible to the layperson, isolated cause-effect relationships are frequently "discovered" by practitioners and diffused in charismatic treatises or through the popular press. In the natural sciences, homespun theories generally get no further than the tabloids in part because the rules of evidence are more exacting and in part because nature is not thought to be sufficiently flexible to accommodate isolated theories. Industrial-policy theory is closer, epistemologically, to management theory than to scientific theory because the general principles are considered to be cognitively accessible, so that the novice can comprehend the logic of antitrust or pro-cartel policies, for instance, and render judgments about proposed policies on the basis of commonsense canons.

Rationalized meaning – theory – in all of these realms is phenomenological in that it consists of intersubjective understandings of cause and effect. Actors generally grasp meaning from experience, whether it is the meaning of gravity (science), market competition (economics), the chain-of-command (management), or antitrust litigation (policy). We first comprehend that gravity is universal, inanimate, and demystified not through high school physics but through experience – gravity is taken to have these characteristics by everyone around us. Likewise, Americans comprehend that antitrust litigation reinforces natural selection mechanisms that produce macro-economic efficiency not through high-school civics courses but through everyday experience – antitrust is taken to have this purpose by those around us. Much of modern understanding is produced through this kind of passive social construction, in which laws of nature, economics, and so on are reflected in prescriptions for action, and are then internalized in individual cognitive structures. To say that these laws are social constructs is simply to say that they are *representations* of reality rather than reality itself. The law of gravity, as opposed to the force itself, consists of a cultural frame for representing and explaining this thing called gravity.

Vocabulary for a cultural approach to policy

An approach to policy that focuses on culture, in the form of institutionalized means-ends designations, demands a new vocabulary.

Industrial cultures. Industrial cultures are the institutionalized principles of industrial organization and economic behavior found within countries (Dyson 1983). Being cultural, they consist of practices and associated meanings. The meaning side of culture has been referred to with terms such as trope, frame, ideology, worldview, typification, collective unconscious, habitus, collective representation, toolkit, and episteme. Because I treat meanings as inseparable from the practices they are constructed around, I use "industrial culture" to refer to meaning and practice simultaneously. Being rationalized, industrial cultures share the characteristics of other rationalized systems. They are woven through different levels of action to bring coherence to those levels. They are organized around recognizable logics that have the pragmatic tenor of commonsense and are often patterned on natural analogy – as Mary Douglas (1986) argues of rationalized institutions more generally – so that where natural selection is thought to affect rationality, customs at the individual, organizational, and public policy levels will be oriented to selection processes.

Industrial policy paradigms. Industrial-policy paradigms are the institutionalized principles of policy action that reinforce industrial cultures. In Peter Hall's (1992) words, a policy paradigm is like a gestalt, in that "it structures the very way in which policy-makers see the world and their role within it." Policy paradigms consist of both practices, in the form of policies, and means-ends designations, in the form of the tenets of governmental action. They reinforce industrial cultures by creating and sustaining particular behavior patterns among economic actors, and by symbolizing those patterns as efficient. Thus American antitrust policy encourages price competition among firms, and symbolizes market competition as the source of macro-economic efficiency.

The argument

With the rise of modernity, the central endeavor of the political order was transformed from the conquest and subjugation of territories and their peoples to the conquest and subjugation of nature in the pursuit of economic growth. The political structures that were built to achieve military glory or social order through the monopolization of violence (Hintze 1975) were soon retrofitted to this goal of economic expansion. Despite their widely varying political ethics – from republican to monarchical to theological – modern nation-states came to pursue progress, so defined, single-mindedly. Empires and regimes soon came to live and die by GNP growth.

In the process of modernization, institutions that had effected political order were teleologically reinterpreted as means to economic order and progress. This occurred everywhere, but it was nowhere more evident than in Britain, where Adam Smith heralded British political traditions that had arisen for any number of historical and conjunctural reasons, but certainly not to maximize gross national product, as the ultimate cause of Britain's economic greatness. Wherever nations could call their economies successful, they linked that success to peculiar characteristics of their political orders.

Modern industrial strategies took on the character of political institutions not only because nations reinterpreted existing state characteristics as strategies for growth but also because they employed the broad means-ends designations of political culture to design economic institutions. Political cultures shaped new industrial and economic strategies principally by determining the kinds of economic and industrial *problems* nations would perceive and by delimiting the *solutions* that nations would conceive to those problems.

First, political culture influenced the sorts of events and practices nations saw as problematic – the *problems perceived*. Every political culture is organized around the sustenance of certain sorts of practices as constitutive of social order, and the repression of others as destructive of social order. For instance, in the United States and Britain, political institutions reinforced community and individual sovereignty, respectively, and guarded against the concentration of political power in the central state. In the emergent industrial economy, these countries viewed community and individual *economic* self-determination as integral to *economic* order, and guarded against the concentration of economic power in the state and in private enterprises. France, with political structures designed to achieve order by concentrating authority, perceived concentrated economic authority as a means to economic order and thus chartered huge regional railway monopolies that operated under close state supervision.

Policy-making begins when nations identify collective problems that demand public solutions. In the course of railway development, these countries identified entirely different sorts of problems. Britain saw the concentration of the industry as a problem that demanded government action: France saw inadequate concentration and coordination as a problem for the state to address. The industrial issues nations perceived to be problematic mirrored the political issues they typically perceived to be problematic, and determined the realms in which policy action would be taken. Political culture also influenced which effects of policy would be seen as problematic and hence which policies would be reworked. For instance, price homogeneity was interpreted as a failure of policy to induce competition in the United States, whereas it was read as a success of policy to stabilize the industry in Britain. The Americans took action to end price homogeneity, and the British left well enough alone.

Second, the cause-effect relationships embodied by political culture influenced the industrial policy strategies envisioned – the *solutions conceived*. For instance, in France, political order had been achieved through military absolutism and the imposition of control from the center. In Britain, order had been achieved by maximizing the autonomy of local elites who would further the public good by pursuing their own interests. As a result, when the French perceived problems of industrial order they initially thought of solutions that involved central state control. When the British perceived problems, they thought of solutions that would cause economic actors to identify their interests with collective interests. The very causal mechanisms that were symbolized as the source of political order in these countries were thus replicated in the economic realm to achieve order and growth.

The solutions used to address industrial problems were socially constructed as efficacious as they were deployed to solve new problems. For instance, New England states invented adjudicative regulatory agencies to control the behavior of firms in industries of vital interest to the public. Soon, other states adopted the same solution, and later the federal government modeled the Interstate Commerce Commission (ICC) on these state agencies. Britain established inspectorates to remedy problems in a dozen different industries, including the railways, in the second quarter of the nineteenth century. This process of reproduction contributed to the articulation of general principles of industrial order and rationality, as nations distilled the principles underlying existing policies and used them to design policy solutions to new problems.

Industrial policy solutions changed over time either when policies produced unanticipated consequences, as when government aid to railways was plundered in the United States, or when experience falsified the cause-effect designations carried by policies, as when Britain's effort to improve safety by publicizing accidents failed. In both types of situations, nations developed new policy strategies. However, once particular policies and their cause-effect designations became institutionalized, they had independent effects on future policies. Britain floundered a bit before settling on the inspectorate model of industrial governance, and eventually chose a more interventionist solution, but in its heyday the inspectorate model was used in virtually every industrial realm. The United States experimented with active state and local promotion of industry before settling on federal enforcement of price competition, but once this strategy was established it found its way into policies governing all sorts of sectors.

I argue, in general, that culture shapes how nations perceive and respond to problems and, in particular, that characteristics of political culture shaped emergent industrial policy strategies. The process was historically complex, and it was indeterminate in that each nation might have taken other paths along the way, but the effects of political culture were discernable throughout the history of railway policy. The details of what happened in each country will have to wait for subsequent chapters, but the broad outline of how industrial policy paradigms emerged can be summarized here. It is important to note, first, that the railway policy strategies I chronicle were paralleled in a number of other industries. I examine the railway industry because it emerged before modern industrial policy paradigms had been forged, because railway policy evolved alongside broad policy paradigms between 1825 and 1900, and because the industry's importance guaranteed that policymakers would generate plenty of material to be analyzed a century or more later.

Political culture

The argument begins with political culture. By 1825, each of these countries had developed a distinct political culture, comprising practices and their meanings. Political practices that had emerged for identifiable historical reasons took on meaning when ideological principles were articulated to support them, so that existing state characteristics were socially constructed as constitutive of political order. In each case, state characteristics symbolized particular positive means to political order and citizens came to think of those means as the only way to achieve order. And in each, state structure designated particular evils that threatened order. In the United States, the framers of the Constitution articulated the principle of local self-rule that had emerged in the vast, poorly integrated colonies as a theory of democratic government and sought to formalize it. Community sovereignty was the source of political order. French monarchists and republicans alike glorified the centralized institutions of the French state as the foundation of their own brands of political order, and articulated political philosophies that made centralization integral to both monarchy and democracy. Democracy, for the French, demanded a strong center to preclude the emergence of intermediate groups that might supplant the republican state in the lives of citizens. State sovereignty was the source of political order. The English Revolution supported a King-in-Parliament model of government in which every lord reigned over his own turf. British political philosophers exalted this structure as the instantiation of a minimalist theory of government and the foundation of political order and liberty. Individual sovereignty was the source of political order.

The core logic of political order was woven throughout state institutions. I argue in the coming chapters that in each nation, a single logic could be discerned that permeated such diverse state attributes as the locus of public authority, the concentration of powers, the nature of the legal system, the system of office-holding and public expertise, and public fiscal capacities.

Emergent industrial culture

National industrial strategies grew up in the railway industry around efforts to address the problems perceived in four functional areas. Nations addressed a variety of perceived problems in planning, finance, technical and managerial coordination, and pricing and competition. In each country, new industrial policies replicated, in the industrial realm, the processes and practices that had been constructed as constitutive of political order. And in each country, industrial policies prevented the processes and practices that had been constructed as destructive of political order. In the process of designing policies for growth, these countries developed cultural constructions of industrial rationality that were isomorphic with their constructions of political order. Policymakers shaped industrial institutions with the principles of social organization offered to them by a familiar world.

The United States.   In the United States, community self-rule was constitutive of political order; centralized political authority was destructive. Early rail policies were characterized by local government activism. Route planning was influenced directly by state and local governments, which actively sought to win rail service with the aim of regional growth. Governments encouraged rail construction by offering land and capital to private agents. Finance was also dominated by state and local governments, which used financial incentives to spur construction. The federal government flirted briefly with public financing of the transcontinental lines, but graft soon put an end to federal, state, and local activism. Railroads in the United States and Europe considered how to achieve technical and managerial coordination in such areas as rail gauge, time zones, safety practices, and scheduling. American governments steadfastly refused to interfere with the operation of railways; they left it to private railway owners to decide these issues. Finally, when it came to pricing and competition, American state and federal governments at first left railroaders to their own devices, but as control over the industry became increasingly concentrated, they settled on a policy of enforcing price competition as a way of guarding Americans' economic liberties against the demon of concentrated economic power. Market enforcement took the form of state and federal regulation to prevent rate discrimination, price fixing, cartelization, and the whole range of practices used by large railroads to restrain trade. By the end of the nineteenth century, state policy had become oriented to the reinforcement of market mechanisms to ensure economic liberties and effect growth, and the prevention of other forms of government meddling with economic life.

France.   In France, central state concertation of society was constitutive of political order; excessive privatism was destructive. Many in France expected the state to nationalize railroads, but fiscal constraints made that impossible. Instead, the state settled for exercising close supervision over the industry. Once the importance of railroads was recognized in France, the central state's bureaucracy assumed authority for planning the rail network. State engineers rebuffed the efforts of localities and railroaders to influence route decisions because they regarded those efforts as a potential threat to the rationality of their grand national rail scheme. Railway finance was orchestrated by the central state, which provided all of the lands and a large proportion of the capital. The state also guaranteed dividends on private capital, to attract construction funds, and in hard times took over railway construction itself to ensure progress on the network. Operating and construction standards were governed entirely by state bureaucrats, who set rates, determined management procedures, established construction specifications, engineered bridges and tunnels, and dictated carriage specifications. Pricing and competition policy was unique in France, where the state forced mergers between early independent lines to create six private regional monopolies. By creating monopolies and setting prices, the state precluded competition in the industry. In general, state policy was oriented to the central orchestration of the industry, and to preventing private self-interested railway promoters from disrupting the coherence and efficiency of the network.

Britain. In Britain, the political autonomy of individuals was constitutive of political order; domination by government or other private actors was destructive. British policy was as different from French policy as it could be. Planning was left entirely to private investors. Neither localities nor the central state presumed to meddle in private planning, except to protect landowners against unnecessary government expropriation. Railway finance was also entirely private. Parliament never once heard a proposal for public financial aid to British railways. Generally, operating procedures and construction standards were left up to the railways themselves, but the state did intervene to regulate public safety and to set third-class passenger rates in the name of protecting Britain's sovereign citizens from the excesses of concentrated capitalism. British pricing and competition policy aimed to protect firms from concentrated political authority, in the form of unwarranted state meddling in the affairs of railroads, and from concentrated economic authority, in the form of huge predatory railroads. Competition policy took the form of public interventions to prevent mergers, which aimed to maintain the autonomy of small firms, and public encouragement for cartels, which likewise aimed to stabilize entrepreneurial firms. Here, British policy differed markedly from American policy. Parliament sought to locate control over the industry in the hands of individuals, and to that end undermined market mechanisms in order to sustain firms – Britain protected firms rather than market competition.

In each country, then, industrial policy was designed to effect, in the industrial realm, processes that were thought to create order in the political realm. My ambitions in this chapter are modest. I hope to have shown that isomorphism is to be found, and to suggest that on the one hand this isomorphism is quite astounding given the diversity of institutional arrangements humanity has invented, and on the other hand it does not succumb to explanation by any of the prevailing theoretical paradigms.

To distinguish my argument from others, I have been more than a little polemical in this chapter. I do not mean to suggest that politics, economics, and institutions are epiphenomena in the modern world. Rather, I mean to suggest that these realms are more problematic than realist approaches generally concede. Economic theory makes the useful point that there are limits to what kind of behavior is rational, but real-world evidence seems to undermine the meta-theoretical presumption that one set of rules governs all economic systems. Economic analysts who study the thorny issues of how systemic logics differ, and where they come from, may be able to offer more useful insights. Political analysts are right to examine struggles among groups, but they tend to take for granted the existence of particular groups as well as groups' ideas about what is in their self-interest. Political analysts who ask how groups emerge and how they come to form preferences may be able to answer the more fundamental questions. Institutional/statist analysts are on to something when they argue that institutions reproduce themselves over time, but they have an annoying tendency to bracket the difficult question of how institutionalized constructions of reality emerge and how they influence policymaking. In the space of one volume I cannot even begin to investigate the role of institutionalized cultural meaning in these three realms. I do hope to provide some evidence that the role of meaning has been underemphasized in policy studies.

Conclusion

In sum, the cultural cause-effect designations that characterized the American, French, and British polities came to characterize their modern industrial policy strategies. This occurred as nations read reason into existing state institutions and presumed that those institutions existed to further modernity's project of progress. It also occurred as actors applied the causal logics found in the institutions around them to new problems of industrial organization. This overview has outlined early political cultures in three countries and shown that industrial cultures developed along similar lines. In no case did these parallels appear mechanistically. In each case the development of national industrial policy paradigms was an iterative and evolutionary process involving false starts, innovations, errors, and paradigm shifts. Policy paradigms continue to evolve today, and they continue to be shaped by both national and international conceptions of efficiency. In no case was today's policy paradigm overdetermined by early political culture, but in every case was its evolution conditioned by how nations had come to think about order and efficiency in the world. I hope to show in the coming chapters that the very core tenets of economic efficiency and rationality – the central ideas about how capitalism and modernity operate – are products of identifiable social and historical forces rather than of extra-societal economic precepts.

2. The United States

Introduction

In 1887, Congress established the United States' first federal regulatory agency, the Interstate Commerce Commission (ICC), and charged it with protecting the economic liberties of railway customers and railwaymen by enforcing market competition and eliminating price-fixing and rate discrimination. The principle of enforcing market mechanisms to guard economic liberties was soon extended to the rest of the economy through the Sherman Antitrust Act. And in the twentieth century, Congress established regulatory agencies in the mold of the ICC to govern a wide variety of industries. Market regulation became the distinguishing feature of American industrial policy. The new American industrial policy paradigm came to symbolize competition among free and equal firms as the mainspring of progress. A natural selection theory of economic rationality arose in which markets rewarded efficient firms with prosperity and extinguished their inefficient competitors. The concentration of power in either the state or monopolistic firms came to be seen as the greatest threat to collective efficiency and progress, because concentration threatened market processes. Direct governmental participation in industry became anathema.

By the mid-twentieth century, market regulation was the United States' primary strategy for spurring growth, but that had not always been the case. At the dawn of the new nation, state and local governments actively promoted economic growth. They invested public funds in private enterprises and in general showed little reticence to take the reins of the economy. As Seymour Martin Lipset (1963) has argued, the first Americans did not draw a sharp line between state and civil society. They plotted to stimulate economic growth in town meetings and in state legislatures, and never questioned whether it was proper for the government to involve itself in economic matters. In the United States, the foundation of political order had been sovereign local and state governments that carried out the will of the community. The basis of the economic order was to be these same governments pursuing the economic goals of the community. This first American industrial policy paradigm of "rivalistic state mercantilism" made the pursuit of economic growth through positive action a central duty of local and state governments.

That early policy paradigm was transformed as American state institutions responded to changes in the economy. In the first phase of railway policy, local, state, and federal governments offered bonuses in money or in lands to induce firms to build railways. Those incentive schemes invited corruption, and Americans responded by forswearing government activism. In the second phase of railway policy, state and federal governments installed regulatory commissions that would circumscribe the powers of monopolistic railway firms in order to guard the economic liberties of citizens at large. These new policies aimed, first and foremost, to prevent restraints of trade and protect the liberties of railway entrepreneurs and consumers. But they were also articulated in terms of a new principle of economic order based on competition and natural selection. As Congress self-consciously vested control of the railway industry in market forces, industrial culture came to symbolize the market as the source of rationality in the modern economy. In the emergent industrial policy paradigm, the federal government effected industrial efficiency by establishing the ground rules of competition and then serving as referee. But government was to refrain from guiding private economic action, because such guidance constrained economic freedom and interfered with the normal operation of markets.

Chapters 3 and 4 reveal that in other countries these taken-for-granted ideas about market efficiency, since codified in neoclassical economic theory, never emerged. In French public policy, the market was a source of disturbance and dislocation, and only state planning could rationalize economic life. In British policy, the market had disastrous effects on the entrepreneurs whose ambitions provided the stimulus for growth, and market mechanisms were sacrificed in order to protect those entrepreneurs. In each country the distinct idea about industrial rationality that evolved in the railway industry persists today.

This chapter explores how these events unfolded in the United States, and why the United States' industrial strategy was transformed from active localism to market regulation. The first section discusses the American state before the advent of the railways. The following sections chronicle the United States' responses to the four functional problems faced by railroads everywhere: planning, finance, technical and managerial coordination, and pricing and competition. At the end of each section I compare the problems American lawmakers perceived, and the solutions they conceived, with the problems and solutions that emerged in France and Britain. The purpose of organizing the chapters around four functional realms is to highlight how very differently the United States, France, and Britain responded to parallel issues of industrial organization, and to chart how those responses contributed to emergent notions of industrial rationality.

American state structure

When the colonies of the New World won freedom from British rule and regrouped to form a national government of their own at the end of the eighteenth century, they built in safeguards against the despotism they had been subjected to under the British. The Constitution maximized the independence of the existing communities and states that comprised the new nation. This was government from below. The federal government existed only to shield the autonomy of those primordial communities. As Tocqueville (1945, p. 61) saw it, self-governing localities and states predated the Constitution, and the federal government was designed to sustain a form of democracy built on town meetings and community self-rule rather than to impose an alien form of governance on the polity: "The form of the Federal government was the last to be adopted; and is in fact nothing more than a summary of those republican principles which were current in the whole community before it existed, and independently of its existence" (Tocqueville 1945, p. 61).

These two elements of the United States' polity – activist state and local governments and a passive federal superstructure that secured community self-governance – were reflected sequentially in her industrial policies. The United States' first industrial policies involved active state and local promotion of economic growth, and later policies involved passive federal structures for securing the self-determination of free economic actors.

Next, I examine the early American state characteristics that set the stage for these developments.

The locus of political authority. The new Constitution preserved the autonomy of towns and states with the logic that decision-making authority should be allocated to the lowest possible level of government. Thus the federal government held power only in the realms where local control was unworkable, such as the military, foreign policy, the mails, and interstate commerce. The regional offices of the federal government were left virtually uncoordinated, and it devolved upon political parties and the courts to oversee the administration of federal policies in the states (Skowronek 1982). By dispersing political authority throughout the states and local communities, the new Constitution sustained the participatory structure of governance that had existed before the Revolution. At the same time, it protected subcentral governments against the domination from afar that had characterized the colonial period. State and local governments controlled their own schools, planned and built their own public works, engaged their own militias, collected their own taxes, established their own courts, and organized their own legislative bodies. By allocating substantial authority to regional units, this government structure circumscribed the capacity of the central state to develop and execute domestic policies.

The concentration of powers. The tripartite federal structure was envisioned as a means to ensure that power would not accumulate in any one office of government. The Constitution's architects argued that governmental centralization was illogical and inefficient. They contended that the checks and balances of the new government would create a system in which the division of power among equals was the key to effectiveness. The United States' organic political philosophers depicted administrative centralization as a concomitant of governmental coercion and insisted that because coercion would be unknown in the United States, so would administrative centralization. Although the administrative weakness of the federal government seemed intractable by the time of Tocqueville's journey through America, some of the architects of the new nation had envisioned a much stronger central state. Alexander Hamilton's *Report on Manufactures* called for an active federal role in the economy, but the states were wary of empowering a higher authority to rule over them, and the champions of decentralization thwarted Hamilton's proposal (Miller 1959, p. 461).

State and local governments thus held extensive authority in the United States. Tocqueville argued that real power lay with the separate states and municipalities, their "legislative bodies daily encroach upon the authority of the [federal] government, and their tendency . . . is to appropriate it entirely to themselves." He suggested that the greatest threat to the survival of American government was the excessive authority that had been granted to subnational governments (1945, p. 92). Yet states and localities did not have administrative capacities to match their decision-making authority, for although the Constitution had required only that they adopt republican formats, subnational governments copied the federal government's separated powers, bicameral legislature, judicial autonomy, and shallow administrative hierarchy. This meant that subnational governments would find it difficult to administer ambitious, proactive, policy programs, and that the role of government in the United States would move away from instrumental activism and toward adjudicative formalism.

The legal system.   The separation of governmental powers and the checks and balances built into the Constitution afforded the judiciary more power in the United States than it had been given elsewhere. The courts were charged with ensuring that the administration and the legislature did not overstep their constitutional or legal bounds. Citizens who believed that the government had assumed undue powers could appeal to the courts for redress. As such the courts became the ultimate authority in the American polity. They had final say over administrative rulings and legislative decisions, and assumed the role of guarding the rights of citizens against the excesses of the state. The common law tradition contributed to this role by giving civil traditions, rather than lawmakers, the last word in matters of the law. Because executive units had no authority to use sanctions in administering the law, they came to depend on the courts for enforcing the law. The result was that enforcement was carried out by a judiciary empowered to redress breaches of the law *post hoc,* rather than by a proactive bureaucracy that could preclude breaches from occurring.

Office-holding and public expertise.   At the dawn of the railway age the United States was without a professionalized civil service. Public officials – from the president to the proverbial dog-catcher – were elected or appointed, which meant that amateur volunteers filled government posts until the civil service model of public office-holding spread across subnational governments in the twentieth century (Tolbert and Zucker 1983). Government posts were not filled from the ranks of an independent corps of career administrators whose livelihoods depended upon their integrity; they were filled by impermanent officials who produced an elaborate system of spoils and patronage.

On the one hand, the system attracted aspirants motivated solely by personal gain, and provided no checks to preclude the incumbency of such men. On the other hand, because tenure was impermanent and officials were poorly remunerated, officials had much to gain by accepting bribes and misallocating public resources and little to lose if they were turned out of office for doing so (Shefter 1977).

One corollary of this system of office-holding was that technical experts were rarely found in government offices. Other nation-states had developed technical expertise in the process of designing, building, and operating major public works projects such as bridges, turnpikes, tunnels, and canals. In the United States these enterprises were dominated by private groups, such as the groups that ran the New Jersey Turnpike (established 1804) and the Pennsylvania Turnpike (established 1806). Hence, state agencies developed little expertise in transport engineering, construction, or administration (Goodrich 1960, p. 21). The army employed a certain number of transport engineers, but these men worked on designs for the nation's private canals and turnpikes in the role of consultants to private entrepreneurs. No level of government contained a professionalized service of engineers, accountants, and administrators.

State fiscal capacities.   Whereas the federal government had weak fiscal capacities in the nineteenth century, subnational governments had substantial authority to raise and spend revenues as they saw fit. Before the railway age, states and localities had often promoted projects that would stimulate growth, in part because the nation's capital market was decentralized and local capital markets were often poorly organized. Wall Street only became the nation's center of private finance as the rail industry matured, and largely as a response to problems posed by rail finance (Chandler 1977). In the early years, the existence of competing state currencies made national financial centralization difficult to imagine. Whereas federal fiscal capacities were weak, state and local governments had access to considerable resources for regional development in their powers to raise revenues and issue bonds on their own accord (Dalzell 1987; Lipset 1963; Adams 1927). They could not always deliver on longterm commitments, but that did not stop them from promising funds.

American states and localities used their fiscal capacities, and political autonomy, to sponsor a wide range of industries in the decades after the Revolution. Special acts of incorporation offered enterprises limited liability, franchise and monopoly rights, and the right to expropriate private property (Creighton 1989; Taylor 1951). Town councils and state legislatures arranged financing for vital enterprises by requiring publicly chartered banks to provide capital, loaning public monies, guaranteeing bonds, purchasing stock, and giving outright grants (Hartz 1948). Nearly all state governments invested in banks, turnpikes, canals, and railways (Callender 1902). Massachusetts also offered bounties to the producers of hemp, rope, sailcloth, duck, and twine to benefit the shipping industry; made direct loans for the construction of textile factories; and exempted glasshouses, cotton factories, breweries, and salt and sugar houses from taxation (Handlin and Handlin 1947). Virginia's public Fund for Internal Improvements (1816), with assets that reached $40 million by 1860, undertook a wide range of public-private joint ventures (Goodrich 1949). Pennsylvania had entered into joint ventures with 150 private firms by 1844 (Hartz 1948, p. 290). In the first four decades of the century, state governments assumed a funded debt of over $200 million to underwrite private enterprises (Callender 1902, p. 114). Municipal governments were equally active. For instance, Pennsylvania localities invested $14 million in private enterprises between 1840 and 1853 alone (Lipset 1963, p. 52).

What is most striking about these early ventures, from the vantage point of the late twentieth century, is that governments were unhindered by any reticence to intervene in the economy. They did not equate the actions of town meetings and state legislatures with the uninvited meddling of the rebuffed colonial regime. Moreover, they did not recoil from providing unequal advantages to enterprises – they granted monopolies to some and offered unique incentives to others. The idea of laissez faire had no place in their debates. On the contrary, for the first three-quarters of the nineteenth century the "ferocious doctrinal consistency" that already characterized British economic thinking was nowhere to be found. "At times the degree of tutelage which state governments arrogated to themselves in Jacksonian America appears so extreme that it suggests the direct inspiration of Colbert, rather than anything that belongs to the Anglo-Saxon tradition" (Shonfield 1965, p. 302). The doctrine of laissez faire only emerged later in the century, when the growing availability of private capital negated the demand for public capital (Lipset 1963, p. 52).

American political culture. American state institutions depicted community sovereignty over political life as the means to order, and the source of liberty, by affording local governments wide-ranging authority to establish and pursue goals as they saw fit. The overarching federal structure was framed as a neutral shield against alien political intervention that operated on a cooperative model. State governments occupied an uncomfortable middle ground between self-governing localities and the disinterested federal superstructure, unsure whether to pursue activism or nonintervention. Just as state structure designated community self-rule as the source of political order, constitutional checks on federal authority suggested that the greatest menace to social order and democracy was centralized government authority. Restraints on public authority were found not only at the federal level, but also in the subcentral governments modeled after the federal state. Americans came to associate all sorts of unwanted government intervention with tyranny, and this bolstered their commitment to preventing governments from meddling in the affairs of private concerns. There was nothing wrong with government activism per se, only government activism that took the form of unsolicited intervention in private affairs. Public policy depicted concentrated *private* authority as a menace to political order as well, by means of the disestablishment of religion, curbs on "restraints of trade" in business, and the autonomy of educational governance (Rostow 1959, p. 43). In short, the social practices associated with community self-rule were constitutive of order in the United States' institutionalized political culture, and social practices associated with the concentration of authority in the central state or in private hands were destructive of order.

Railway policy

Americans gave substantial control over railway planning and finance to local and state governments, as direct representatives of the public will. However, they saw the emergence of corruption among railroad officials and public servants as evidence that direct government promotion of industry would endanger private liberties and public legitimacy, and foreswore public aid to private enterprises. This signaled the end of local activism in American industrial policy. Subsequent policies were oriented to sustaining the economic liberties of railroads and their customers. In matters of technical and managerial coordination, policy was designed to give control to private parties, acting individually or in concert, and to deny state and federal governments the capacity to dictate to railroads. Control over pricing and competition had been left in private hands, but when private actors began to dominate their peers, Americans perceived a threat to liberty and order and devised regulatory policies that would keep industry control outside of the state, but by outlawing "restraints of trade" would move it from entrepreneurs and local governments to an idealized market. Thus, after an interim period during the 1870s and 1880s when Americans had eschewed local activism but had not embraced a positive industrial policy paradigm to replace it, new federal policies contributed to the rise of a policy paradigm based on government enforcement of market mechanisms. Natural selection in government-refereed markets came to be seen as the source of economic order and economy-wide efficiency.

Planning

The first functional problem faced by proponents of railway development was planning. How would railways be planned? In particular, who should plan them? Americans saw planning and promotion as a task that belonged to private entrepreneurs and subnational governments. Governments had a right, and duty, to promote the interests of local citizens by stimulating the development of rail service.

State and local planning

In the first decades of the railway age, state and local governments provided massive direct aid to private railroads in order to influence their route decisions. In effect, states and localities made most route decisions through their promotion schemes. Local boosterism for railway aid seemed to be contagious. As one community schemed to attract a railroad, the inhabitants of neighboring villages quickly assembled and plotted to win a depot for themselves (Fisher 1947). States practiced boosterism as well. Spurred by the success of the Erie Canal, which was completed in 1825, states offered diverse financial incentives to stimulate rail construction. New York, Pennsylvania, Massachusetts, Maryland, Virginia, the Carolinas and Georgia financed railroads westward in the hope of dominating trade between the East and the new territories (Goodrich 1960, p. 2). In this process, state and local governments translated the political logic of self-rule into an industrial policy paradigm of local activism.

Railroads appeared in the United States in the aftermath of a public debate over whether the federal government should nationalize public works projects, particularly transport projects. John Quincy Adams advocated public leadership in internal improvements, and sponsored legislation to provide federal funding for a number of canal and turn-pike projects. In the 1820s, an economic recession bolstered the argument that the federal government lacked the resources to undertake internal improvements. By 1830 the enthusiasm for federal aid to canals and turnpikes had come to an end, and Andrew Jackson called on state governments to undertake improvements themselves (Cleveland and Powell 1909, p. 96).

The appearance of railway technology gave a stimulus to the practice of "rivalistic state mercantilism," which was designed to win commerce, industry, and transport facilities (Schieber 1981, p. 131). Pennsylvania legislators realized the threat that the nearly complete Erie Canal posed to Philadelphia's commerce and manufacturing in 1823 and appointed a commission to explore transport routes to Pittsburgh. The legislative committee endorsing the appointment of this commission argued:

> On the north side of Pennsylvania, before the lapse of many months, New York will have united by a canal of more than 400 miles in length the Hudson River with Lakes Champlain and Erie. On the south side of the state, Maryland and Virginia projected a noble scheme of uniting the Potowmac (sic) with the Ohio. . . . Noiseless and modest [Pennsylvania] may continue to move, but unless she awakes to a true sense of her situation, and ascends to times and circumstances, she will be deprived of the sources of public prosperity, her career of wealth will be less progressive than that of other states, and instead of regaining the high commercial rank she once held, she will be driven even from her present station in the system of the Confederacy. (quoted in Bishop 1907, p. 172)

Pennsylvanians saw it as the duty of government to sponsor the infrastructural projects necessary to produce prosperity. In their discourse they made little distinction between government and community, depicting government action as the incarnation of community will. In the minds of Pennsylvanians, the state government was the only entity that could orchestrate the capitalization of such a massive project. The history of the Erie Canal was testament to the capacity of states to undertake such projects.

A few years later, in Baltimore, a commission reporting on the route that was to become the Baltimore and Ohio railroad argued that it was incumbent upon the community to seize the opportunity to make Maryland America's gateway to the West:

> Baltimore lies 200 miles nearer to the navigable waters of the West than New York, and about 100 miles nearer to them than Philadelphia. . . . and by far the most practicable route through the ridges of Mountains that divide the Atlantic from the western waters is along the depression formed by the Potomac in its passage through them. Taking then into the estimate the advantages which these important circumstances afford to Baltimore, in regard to this immense trade, we again repeat that nothing is wanted to secure a great portion of it to our city, but a faithful application of the means within our own power. (quoted in Hungerford 1928, p. 20)

Advocates of state action depicted governments as corporate actors who could affect the public will, rather than a source of potential disruption to the free market. For them, government activism carried none of the negative connotations of British colonial rule, and none of the negative connotations of state intervention that Adam Smith had articulated – and that would come to guide later American policy. In a speech before the Massachusetts' legislature in May of 1828, the Governor argued that the state must build, or commission, railroads to the Hudson and to Providence: "Here then is a measure of encouragement to domestic industry within our own control – a system of internal improvement, opposed to no constitutional scruples, of which no interest can complain, and by which all interests will be promoted" (General Court of Massachusetts 1828, pp. 25–26). In Massachusetts and elsewhere, the litmus test for legitimate public activism was that it must produce no aggrieved party. If no private party objected to a proposal for government sponsorship, then the proposal must be in the public interest. In the end, although private concerns actually surveyed and plotted routes in the United States, subnational governments played key roles in routing decisions by providing financing.

Federal planning

In the 1860s the federal government briefly undertook a role parallel to that of subnational governments when advocates of transcontinental railroads argued that Washington must act to create lines of national interest just as local governments had acted to create lines of local interest. To ensure that cross-country railroads were feasible before committing federal resources, Congress charged the army with studying possible routes. Congress then provided land grants and loan guarantees to four transcontinental lines, to speed the development of transport links to the West. However, the congressional role in railway planning, which is discussed in the next section, was short-lived.

In sum, the principal policy problem Americans perceived in the area of railway planning concerned how to stimulate private parties to plan and undertake railway development. Policy was oriented to ensuring that communities and regions would get the rail service they desired. By contrast, the French perceived a problem with allowing local governments and private parties to participate in railway planning. How could self-interested entrepreneurs and local governments carry out the planning of a rational, coherent, network that would serve the nation? The French were concerned to see that no one but the state's expert engineers, who had the nation's interest foremost in their minds, would play a role in railway planning. Americans articulated a different logic of efficiency, in which private actors would plan and build the lines that were most needed because it was in their interest to do so. Local government participation would help draw railroads to the communities that most desired them. British policymakers were determined to allow private parties to put railroads where they pleased, without interference from local or central governments. The British were mainly concerned to ensure that railroads did not abuse public powers of expropriation by abridging private property rights unnecessarily. In short, Americans believed responsibility for planning belonged to state and local governments in conjunction with private entrepreneurs, the French believed it belonged to the central state, and the British believed it belonged exclusively to private entrepreneurs.

The solutions these governments conceived were also entirely different. American subnational governments used public incentives to influence private planning decisions and win the rail depots they coveted. The French decided as early as 1833 that state technocrats must plan the entire rail system, and from that date private parties and regional governments were denied the capacity to plan railroads. In Britain, Parliament addressed the problem of unnecessary expropriations by scrutinizing route plans carefully and interrogating railway entrepreneurs and their route engineers. By contrast, American governments passed out railway charters willy-nilly, even for duplicate "nuisance" lines designed to annoy railway barons' competitors rather than to serve public purposes (Stover 1970, p. 87). To prevent politicians from impeding private planning, American states passed general railway incorporation laws in the 1850s that would allow any thirteen persons to receive a charter without special legislative approval (Skowronek 1982, p. 135).

Finance

In the United States, the issues of planning and finance were not neatly separated, because governments influenced route planning by offering financing. Americans saw the promotion of economic growth as a natural duty of government, and states and localities pumped huge sums into private railways. That all changed because of an unresolved tension between the institutional mandate that empowered communities and the mandate that prevented governments from interfering with private activity. By empowering communities and states to act in the interest of local groups, American state structure encouraged government activism in industry. Yet, by depicting government oversight of, and intervention in, the activities of private parties as tyrannical, state institutions doomed activism to devolve into corruption. In the 1830s, Americans had perceived unwanted public intervention in private enterprise to be illicit, but they thought of unopposed government activism in growth as part and parcel of democracy. By 1870 a subtle change had occurred – there was a sense that any sort of positive government action brought corruption.

State and local aid

In the decades after railway technology was introduced in the United States, state and local governments acted quickly and decisively to win railway service. They afforded powers of eminent domain, donated rights-of-way through public lands, and aided private railways with loans, bond subscriptions, and cash donations. Where entrepreneurs willing to build local railroads could not be found, states and localities built railroads themselves. Up to 1860, every significant American line received construction aid from both states and localities (Goodrich 1960).

The public role in the financing of the Baltimore and Ohio Railroad (B & O), organized in 1827, was typical. The B & O's promoters collected $1.5 million in bond subscriptions from private investors and an additional $500,000 from the city of Baltimore. In 1828, capitalization was doubled to $3 million from private investors and $1 million from the city. The federal government refused to aid the project, and the state of Maryland initially refused assistance because it was in the midst of underwriting the construction of the competing Chesapeake and Ohio Canal and state coffers were empty. But in 1833, Maryland granted $500,000 to provide for a branch to Washington. In 1836 the B & O ran out of money and the promoters could not find new private backing. Maryland and Baltimore each agreed to provide another $3 million in bond subscriptions. The ensuing recession of 1837–39 made these bonds unsalable, and in order to ensure that construction continued, Baltimore allowed the B & O to issue $1.5 million worth of its own "railroad notes" in lieu of the payment of city dues. The first 178-mile leg from Baltimore to Cumberland was completed by 1842, and the B & O reached its western terminus, Wheeling, in 1853 aided by a $500,000 subscription from the city of Wheeling, the reinvestment of its own revenues, and the disposal of Maryland's pre-depression bonds (Goodrich 1960, pp. 80–82). This pattern of early government capitalization and repeated government capital infusions during the course of construction was characteristic.

States and localities in every region aided railway companies. Intrastate lines of minor importance sometimes received aid only from localities, but major lines usually gained the help of states as well. Municipalities in 29 states invested in railway companies; in New York alone, some 300 separate localities invested (Goodrich 1960, p. 237). Before the Civil War, state governments allotted some $300 million in cash and credit to transportation development – primarily to railroads – and local and county governments allotted more than $125 million. By 1861, states and localities had provided 30 percent of the total capital invested in railways. Between 1861 and 1890, state aid amounted to $95 million and local aid exceeded $175 million (Goodrich 1960, p. 268–270). All told, states and localities provided at least half of the capital invested in early American railways. Even these figures may underestimate the public sector contribution to railway capitalization, because railwaymen often exaggerated private contributions by watering the stock. Moreover, these figures exclude the value of publicly purchased rights-of-way and the tracts of land that Midwestern states typically granted railroads in lieu of cash.

States and localities often provided financial assistance in the form of bond guarantees in order to attract capital from London investors (Chandler 1965, p. 45; Heydinger 1954). When Massachussetts voted $4 million for the Western Rail-road in 1833, it issued the bonds in British sterling (Cleveland and Powell 1909, p. 217; Goodrich 1960, p. 128). The city of Albany also contributed to the project with public scrip in the amount of $1 million (Massachusetts Committee on Railways and Canals 1839, p. 54; 1845, p. 110). Britain's Railway Mania of the 1840s and early 1850s fueled the trend.

How did American states and localities come to invest so heavily in railway development? Regional governments held the authority to make autonomous decisions, to raise revenues independently, and to use public monies as they saw fit. In consequence, government officials took on the tasks of entrepreneurs: "The elected official replaced the individual enterpriser as the key figure in the release of capitalist energy; the public treasury, rather than private saving, became the major source of venture capital; and community purpose outweighed personal ambition in the selection of large goals for local economies" (Lively 1955, p. 81). Government intervention in industrial development was simply a matter of communities taking charge of their own futures. As Louis Hartz (1948) found in Pennsylvania, Carter Goodrich (1949) found in Virginia, and Oscar and Mary Handlin (1947) found in Massachusetts, state and local governments actively and deliberately promoted industrial development in those years without questioning the efficacy, or the propriety, of doing so. On the contrary, as late as 1871 Massachussetts' Board of Railroad Commissioners' report argued: "It now seems to be generally conceded that some provision for the construction of a certain amount of railroad facilities is, in this country at any rate, a matter of public charge" (1871, p. viii).

John Quincy Adams and Alexander Hamilton had articulated a logic of political order in which the state exercised sovereignty over the economy – a logic quite at odds with the notion of laissez faire. The early activism of subnational governments was given meaning by this logic. Economic progress was an appropriate goal of the state because it benefited all, as Adams argued in a state of the union address:

> The great object of the institution of civil government is the improvement of the condition of those who are parties to the social compact, and no government, in whatever form constituted, can accomplish the lawful ends of its institution but in proportion as it improves the conditions of those over whom it is established. Roads and canals, by multiplying and facilitating the communications and intercourse between distant regions and multitudes of men, are among the most important means of improvement . . . For the fulfillment of those duties governments are invested with power, and to the attainment of the end – the progressive improvement of the condition of the governed – the exercise of delegated powers is a duty as sacred and indispensable as the usurpation of powers not granted is criminal and odious. (quoted in Richardson 1896, V. II, p. 295).

Government activism was part and parcel of democratic political order because it embodied community self-determination, rather than menacing the polity as Britain's laissez faire rhetoric of the 1830s suggested. In 1853, Pennsylvania's Chief Justice declared that states had a duty to promote growth;

> It is a grave error to suppose that the duty of the state stops with the establishment of those institutions which are necessary to the existence of government: such as those for the administration of justice, preservation of peace, and the protection of the country from foreign enemies . . . To aid, encourage, and stimulate commerce, domestic and foreign, is a duty of the sovereign as plain and as universally recognized as any other. (quoted in Hartz 1948, p. 304)

Americans differed over whether this principle extended from local to state and federal levels of government, but they agreed among themselves that local governments had the power and duty to foster growth. In France, by contrast, republican theorists articulated a contrary theory of democratic political order in which efforts of private groups and local governments to direct the economy threatened the sovereignty of the representative, central, state.

Public promotion was not motivated by the same precept of statism found in France, where the state gave *direction* to the economy, but by a precept of public *stimulation* of private activity. States and localities aimed to induce private parties to build the railroads that would serve citizens. Although they never planned to own railroads, governments did not hesitate to build and operate roads when they could not entice private parties to build them. For instance, Pennsylvania took the lead in the development of the Main Line by providing the lion's share of the funding, but sold its interest to the Pennsylvania Railroad Company after the line was completed (Hartz 1943). In the middle of the nineteenth century, then, the United States seemed to be moving toward an industrial policy paradigm in which state and local governments helped to orchestrate financing for firms they deemed important.

Local aid scandals.   Railway boosterism sparked the imagination of every itinerant snake oil salesman and con man in the country. Men with little experience had cards printed up proclaiming themselves to be railway promoters, and went to work soliciting financing from state and local governments. Corruption and graft were soon rampant in the rail industry. Where public aid drew incompetent railroad promoters, ill-planned lines were never completed or went bankrupt soon after completion. Where aid drew outright thieves, cities found that they had been hoodwinked into providing funds to men with counterfeit credentials and forged accounts.

Railway promoters and public officials were exceptionally creative when it came to defrauding the public. First, railway promoters often won public assistance to build lines that had no chance of making money. The New York and Oswego Midland is a case in point. Its promoters won commitments of aid totaling $5.7 million from fifty scattered municipalities to build a line that zigzagged across New York, avoiding all major cities. The line was bankrupt almost as soon as it was opened, but not before its directors compensated themselves handsomely (Hartz 1943, pp. 66–77). Second, a common ploy was for the directors to disappear with public funds before laying a single railroad tie. The Northwestern Railroad Company won promises of aid from Pennsylvania localities, with the stipulation that public aid would be distributed only after private stock subscriptions were collected. The Northwestern's directors forged private subscriptions, collected the promised funds from the localities, distributed $22,000 of those funds to themselves for their own services, and voted to release their treasurer from accountability (Hartz 1943, p. 96). Third, railroads regularly watered the value of existing public stock by printing new stock certificates to distribute to their directors without collecting any capital in return. As majority shareholder of the New York Central Commodore Cornelius Vanderbilt voted himself a $20 million bonus in such unfunded stock certificates. Jay Gould increased the book value of Erie common stock from $24 million to $78 million in the eight years between 1864 and 1872 without adding any new funds or value to the railroad. The *Commercial and Financial Chronicle* found that twenty-eight American railroads had in this fashion increased their nominal capitalization from $287 million to $400 million between 1867 and 1869 alone. By 1885, Henry Poor's railroad annual estimated that one-third of railway capitalization was water (Stover 1970, p. 85). Fourth, railroads sometimes found ways to inflate the value of public stock guarantees. For instance, South Carolina authorized the sale of $1 million in state railway bonds, only to discover sometime later that $2 million had been sold by railroads. Georgia agreed to endorse first-mortgage railway bonds, and later discovered that the bonds they had in fact endorsed were second-mortgage bonds (Locklin 1954, p. 112). Fifth, railway promoters often grossly inflated the costs of construction and pocketed the public funds they claimed to have spent. Baltimore investigated the Western Maryland in 1892 and concluded that whereas the city's interest in the railroad amounted to $8.5 million, the replacement cost of the road would have been $3.5 million. The commission laid blame on Baltimore's lax accounting system (Goodrich and Segal 1953). Finally, public officials and legislators regularly took bribes, in the form of cash or rail stock, in return for political leverage. A city investigation in Baltimore found that Mayor John Lee Chapman had helped to bribe three city councilmen to vote for aid to the Western Maryland line in 1864, but the publicity did not prevent Baltimore from providing the road with another $5.7 million over the next two decades (Goodrich and Segal 1953, p. 21).

There is widespread agreement that railway aid schemes were rife with corruption because state and local governments failed to exercise administrative controls over railroads. Did they fail to exercise control because they lacked the administrative wherewithal to oversee railroads, or because they operated with a model of governance in which government intervention in private matters was tyrannical? Most of the literature is mute on this distinction – governments failed to provide oversight, whatever the reason. As Andrew Shonfield concludes of the period, "While the state governments embarked on public enterprise and public regulation of industry with a vigour that is reminiscent of the traditional French approach to economic policy, they entirely failed to equip themselves with a core of professional administrators of French quality" (1965, p. 305). Samuel O. Dunn concluded after the turn of the century, "The railway corporations had an excessive influence over politics and government which they used to the public detriment" and they had such influence largely because "civil service laws and rules did not exist or were not enforced, and practically all public officials and employés were selected, retained and dismissed for political reasons. Grafting in public office was common" (1913, p. 9).

But why did governments fail to control their own investments, and ultimately undermine public promotion of industry? Administrative incapacity played a role initially, in that American governments did not have cadres of public transport engineers and administrators who would naturally assume the task of overseeing the administration of railway aid. France did have such a cadre, and they did oversee public aid. However, the importance of political culture became clear after railway aid scandals began to appear, when policymakers refused to expand public controls and even to exercise the controls that *were* at their disposal. American political institutions had depicted unwanted government meddling in private affairs as inimical to political order and democracy, and this extended even to unwanted meddling in the affairs of publicly funded corporations. As a result, governments failed to take even the simplest of precautions. First, governments regularly neglected to exercise normal shareholder rights in the corporations they had invested in. Virginia actually passed a law forbidding majority government representation on railway company boards, regardless of the level of government investment. Between them, the state of Maryland and the city of Baltimore held the lion's share of B & O stock, but they refused to accept a majority of the voting seats on the board and never even asked to review the company's accounts (Hungerford 1928). Second, governments seldom gave directions to their representatives on railway boards, and when they did give directions their representatives frequently ignored them. For example, in 1856 three Baltimore-appointed directors of the B & O voted, against the explicit orders of the city council, for a stock-watering scheme that would give an "extra dividend" to private shareholders. The city council censured their appointees for selling their votes to the railway's directors, but did not succeed in preventing the dispersal of the "extra dividend" (Goodrich and Segal 1953, p. 29). Third, when proposals to fortify government controls were heard, they were uniformly rejected as unwarranted interference with the economic liberties of private citizens. As Massachusetts' Railroad Commissioners wrote in 1871:

> The principle upon which our government is founded, – that of least possible governmental interference and largest possible individual development, – has a strong hold on the popular mind. The public opinion of the Commonwealth unquestionably accepts with great reluctance any measure calculated to bring industrial enterprises within the influence of politics. (Massachusetts Board of Railroad Commissioners 1871, p. lx)

It was one thing to aid and abet private enterprises that promised to enrich the community, and another thing altogether to dictate how those enterprises would be run.

The result of governments' determination to keep out of the management of private concerns was that railway aid scandals swept the country like a plague. This underscored the susceptibility of office-holders to graft and bolstered the American notion that state expansion – in this case embodied by public aid to enterprise – is inescapably evil. As Governor Edmund Davis of Texas argued in 1870 of his state's efforts to protect public railway subsidies:

> Every legislature (sic) and every convention of the people since these works received subsidies, has been beset by applications (sometimes not unaccompanied by the odor of corruption) for relief from the force and effects of the contracts under which the grants were made, while the restrictions placed upon the beneficiaries of these grants to secure the safety and convenience of the people and moderate rates of fare and freight have been wholly disregarded. (quoted in Cleveland and Powell 1909, p. 232)

In other words, railways not only bribed administrators to look the other way, they bribed legislators to relieve them of the public obligations they had incurred in exchange for government aid. As long as railwaymen could purchase relief from public controls, in one way or another, regulations alone would be ineffective.

The demise of local activism.   Americans perceived the abuse of public aid to be particularly heinous because their state institutions depicted concentrated authority as a danger to the polity. In France, by contrast, the corruption of early aid to local railroads was perceived as an administrative failure that could be remedied by bureaucrats. In the United States, corruption generated tremendous publicity because it seemed to shake the very foundation of the political order. States reacted with constitutional amendments prohibiting all public investment in private enterprises. The state of New York first prohibited state aid to railways in its 1846 constitution. By the end of the 1860s,

California, Iowa, Kentucky, Kansas, Maine, Maryland, Minnesota, Nebraska, Nevada, Ohio, Oregon, Pennsylvania, and West Virginia had joined the bandwagon with constitutional provisions that enjoined their legislatures from aiding private enterprises with public bonds or with stock subscriptions. Most states also outlawed government loans and restricted local aid by decreeing that municipalities could only elect to aid railways by plebescite, and could only provide 5 percent or 10 percent of the cost of a project (Cleveland and Powell 1909, pp. 237–240).

State and local aid to railways would probably have ended even if it had not led to graft, because the same administrative weaknesses that initially invited corruption also led governments to make unrealistic financial commitments to railways (Locklin 1954, p. 108). Neither state nor local governments employed accounting staffs, who might have warned them that they were making financial commitments they would not be able to honor. The results were dramatic. Local governments in twenty-five states defaulted on their obligations to railroads. In the years after the Civil War, Pennsylvania, Maryland, Indiana, Illinois, Michigan, and Minnesota failed to make good on their obligations, and eight Southern states defaulted on Reconstruction-Era railway bonds (Cleveland and Powell 1909, p. 239). As California Governor Newton Booth lamented in 1879, "All through the Western and Southwestern States bankrupt towns and tax-ridden communities bear witness to the fact that the habit of voting subsidies was once as popular as it is now odious" (quoted in Cleveland and Powell 1909, p. 236).

The commitment to local government involvement in growth was such that in reaction to the ban on public investment in private enterprises a number of governments built railroads entirely with public funds. Most followed what Carter Goodrich (1968) has called the "state in-state out" pattern by selling or franchising the line upon completion. Earlier cases in which governments had constructed lines because they could not find willing entrepreneurs followed the same pattern. Pennsylvania operated the Philadelphia and Columbia Railroad from 1834 to 1855, when it sold the line to the Pennsylvania Railroad. North Carolina operated the Atlantic and North Carolina Railroad from the 1860s until just before World War I, when the state located a private lessee (Dunn 1913). Houston built a small line toward the Gulf in 1861 and sold it to private investors upon completion at a profit (Goodrich 1960, p. 161). Cincinnati completed construction of a railroad to Chattanooga in 1880 with $18.3 million in public bonds and promptly leased it to a private concern (Hartz 1943). Georgia's Western and Atlantic saw annual losses of $60,000 to $100,000 before it was leased to a private firm, which operated it at a profit (Dunn 1913, p. 44).

Federal promotion

The controversy over federal aid to railroads provided a forum for airing an ongoing debate over the role of the federal government in the economy. The Constitution encouraged communities to take charge of their own destinies, and the proponents of federal activism saw the nation as one community with a single interest when it came to trans-continental transport. For them, proactive federal policy was not for-bidden by the Constitution so long as it involved only positive inducements and not policies that intruded into the operations of private firms or that created hardships for some concerns in the process of creating advantages for others. The soon-to-be-infamous federal land grant schemes were designed following this logic, and they might well have initiated a new era of federal activism in the economy if they had not engendered corruption.

Early grants of federal lands.   Long before the railway land grants were made, Congress had used land grants to achieve a variety of public ends. In many minds the Constitution limited Congress's power to give away public monies, but it did not prevent Congress from giving away public lands (Sanborn 1899, p. 11). Congress rewarded soldiers from the Continental army of 1776 with land grants, and later did the same for those who fought in the War of 1812 and the war with Mexico. In the early years, Congress made land grants to private parties in lieu of payment for all sorts of public services, and from the 1830s Congress awarded new cities and towns with land grants to be used for schools, public buildings, and public works. After 1841, each new state could select 500,000 acres of land to be used for internal improvements (Sanborn 1899). More to the point, by 1850 seven million acres had been granted to promote construction of private canals and turnpikes (Stover 1970, p. 58). In the process of allocating land grants for various public purposes of unquestioned merit, Congress had made grants of lands a legitimate means for achieving public ends in the American mind. Here was a policy paradigm for sponsoring public works that seemed tailormade for railways.

Congress first promoted railway development by turning over federal lands to states, which then patented the lands to railroads. The first such grant was made to Alabama for a line from Illinois to Mobile in 1850 (Henry 1945). Over the next dozen years, Congress allotted lands to Michigan, Wisconsin, Minnesota, Iowa, Illinois, Missouri, Arkansas, Louisiana, Mississippi, Alabama, and Florida (U.S. Department of the Interior 1890). Thus far, however, Congress had evaded the question of the constitutionality of direct federal land grants to private enterprises.

The debate over the federal role.   Congress spent a decade debating the federal government's authority to patent lands to private firms before passing the first transcontinental land grant bill in 1862. Scores of bills were considered. The arguments for federal promotion of railroads centered on the national purposes that would be served by a transport link to the West. A transcontinental railroad would speed the settling of unpopulated regions, bolster military control in the territories and Western states, and create a trade link between Europe and the East (Mercer 1954). For routes traversing the unpopulated Western territories, no state government had the wherewithal to sponsor rail development single-handedly (U.S. Congressional Record 1898, pp. 37–38). Moreover, federal assistance was deemed necessary to attract the foreign capital that was considered essential to the development of transcontinental railroads (Heydinger 1954; Cleveland and Powell 1965, p. 53).

Three different proposals for federal participation in railway development were made over the course of the decade, and a fourth alternative was heard from congressmen who wanted the federal government to refrain from intervention. Proposals to give transcontinental rail transport to a single private developer, or to the federal government, were assailed because they called for concentrating control in one place. In the end, they were abandoned in favor of a proposal that would create several, competing, private lines.

First, some argued that only the federal government would be capable of orchestrating the construction of a cross-country railroad, thus Congress should undertake to build a national railroad with public funds. This proposal received scant attention because even President Buchanan argued that federal construction would result in unprecedented corruption. In his annual message dated 6 December 1858, Buchanan asserted that federal construction of a transcontinental railroad "would increase the patronage of the Executive to a dangerous extent, and introduce a system of jobbing and corruption which no vigilance on the part of the Executive could either prevent or detect" (quoted in U.S. Department of the Interior 1890, p. 33). Buchanan argued that the presidency, and by implication the polity, would be degraded by such a project.

Second, in 1851 the entrepreneur Asa Whitney proposed to build a transcontinental road privately. In return for this public service he asked Congress to sell him a sixty mile-wide swath of federal land stretching from Lake Michigan to the West Coast for ten cents an acre. Whitney and his backers argued that this proposal differed little from the federal land grants that had already been made under the auspices of the separate states, and would not involve Congress in the affairs of private enterprises. In his words, "My desire and object have been . . . to give my country this great thoroughfare for all nations without the cost of one dollar." He also contended that as guardian of the public interest, Congress would be guaranteeing that the remaining lands "held by the government would be enhanced in value more than four-fold" as a result of access to rail transport (quoted in Goodrich 1960, p. 171). Congress gave Whitney's proposal close scrutiny, but eventually rejected it for two reasons. The line would concentrate control over all transcontinental transport in the hands of a single enterprise, and this posed a threat to the economic liberties of other citizens. Moreover, the project would involve Congress in advantaging one economic actor to the detriment of others, because unlike earlier routes that received state-level land grants, the transcontinental project was coveted by a number of railway entrepreneurs (Haney 1908).

Third, and most popular, were proposals for federal land grants modeled more closely on the state-level grants, to be allocated to successful applicants for several different routes. These proposals solved the problem of concentrating too much power in the executive branch, or in the hands of a single private party, but they did not resolve the controversy over the broader federal role. The argument against land grants was that the Constitution had been designed to prevent the growth of federal powers, and the intrusion of the state into the private economy, as a means to preserve the polity. Strict constitutional constructionists argued that federal promotion of industry invited undue political influence in private affairs and thereby threatened political order. In the 1850s, Senator John Milton Niles, Democrat from Connecticut, argued that it was meddling with the Constitution to circumvent prohibitions on federal investment in private enterprise: "To say that we can get around the Constitution by granting the public lands, instead of taking the money directly out of the treasury, is certainly trifling with the judgment of this body" (U.S. Congressional Record 1897, Appendix p. 535). Opponents of federal leadership questioned whether Congress had ever had the authority to aid public works with land grants.

Land grant proponents argued that the federal government was charged with promoting the nation's interest. By acting to promote projects of national interest which could not be organized locally, Congress would be fulfilling this role. Senator Lewis Cass, Democrat from Michigan, argued in the 1850s that as custodian of the public trust Congress should act as any rational private investor would by bestowing "a portion (of public lands) for the purpose of improving the value of the rest" (Senator Cass quoted in U.S. Congressional Record 1897, Appendix p. 536; also see Sanborn 1899, pp. 27–28). By contributing to the construction of a transcontinental railroad, Congress would be helping to enrich the nation, and would at the same time increase the value of the remaining federal lands in the territories. This theme also appeared in an annual message of President Franklin Pierce (1853–1857), who said, of applications for railway land grants,

> It is not believed to be within the intent and meaning of the Constitution, that the power to dispose of the public domain, should be used otherwise than might be expected of a prudent proprietor, and therefore, that grants of land to aid in the construction of [rail] roads should be restricted to cases where it would be for the interest of the proprietor, under like circumstances, thus to contribute to the construction of these works. (U.S. Department of the Interior 1890, p. 27)

Cross-country railroads would also facilitate the federal government's undisputed roles as conveyer of the mails and provider of military protection. Land grant proponents emphasized these federal functions in their arguments: railroads would make long-distance transport faster and cheaper for the post office and the army. Any contribution of land would be more than repaid by reduced federal transport outlays. To counter narrow interpretations of Congress's constitutional powers, land grant proponents wrote bills that highlighted these functions. The Pacific bill stated that the purpose of the legislation was to "aid in the construction of a railroad and telegraph line from the Missouri River to the Pacific Ocean and to secure to the Government the use of the same for postal, military and other purposes" (U.S. Department of the Interior 1890, p. 26).

This third proposal succeeded largely because it called for several, competing, privately held lines – none with a monopoly on this vital transport route. In fact, the very first line was to be divided between two separate companies, and would connect with a series of other trunk lines for service from the Midwest to the East Coast.

The details of land grant legislation.   On 1 July 1862, Abraham Lincoln signed the Pacific Railroad Bill, chartering the Union Pacific and Central Pacific railroads to build a route from Omaha to Sacramento with the aid of land grants and federal loan guarantees. The two tracks were to meet near the California border. The bill provided land for the right-of-way and, most importantly, huge tracts of land alongside the route that the railroads could sell to recover their construction costs. The bill also gave first-mortgage loan guarantees of up to $50 million, at $16,000 to $48,000 per mile of track depending on the incline of the section. These two railroads were the only roads to receive federal financial backing.

The charters of the Northern Pacific (1864), the Atlantic and Pacific (1866), and the Texas and Pacific (1871), were substantively identical to the Pacific Railroad Bill, but for the fact that they did not include loan guarantees. Each charter provided a 200 to 400 foot right-of-way through public lands as well as checkerboard tracts alongside the route that amounted to half the acreage within either twenty or forty miles of the route (Henry 1945). The charters stipulated that where promised lands had already been sold, railroads were entitled to claim the closest federal lands that were as yet unsold – because the lands closest to the rail routes were expected to become most valuable. In the case of the first Pacific charter, the Central Pacific was to begin building from Omaha and the Union Pacific was to begin from Sacramento. To speed construction, Congress set up a rivalry in the form of a race from the two endpoints to the center, by letting the exact meeting place be determined by the speed of construction of each company. Each would win the land grants and loan guarantees that went along with the portion of track it built.

The system of administration.   In devising a scheme for aiding railways, Congress's foremost concern was to come up with a system that would prevent corruption without substantially expanding federal authority. The result was a system of administration that was carefully crafted to be both self-policing – so that new federal powers would not be needed – and invulnerable to corruption. First, lands would be turned over to railroads only after track was built to prevent promoters from absconding with federal aid. When a railroad completed a twenty-mile stretch of track, federal inspectors attended a demonstration and certified it complete and operable, after which the General Land Office deeded the adjacent lands to the railroad. Second, time limits on beginning and completing construction obviated the need for government oversight of progress. Charters called for the roads to be begun within one or two years of legislation and completed within ten to twelve years, or the right to claim federal lands would be forfeited. Third, railroads had to demonstrate that they had collected enough private capital to begin construction before they could use federal authority to expropriate the privately owned lands they would require for rights of way. This clause sought to preclude unnecessary expropriation by railways that would not be able to complete lines. Fourth, to safeguard federal loan guarantees Congress appointed five government directors to each of the twenty-member boards of the Union Pacific and Central Pacific lines. The corruption of loan aid led Congress to refuse loans to later lines, and to demand seventeen directorships on the twenty-four-member board of the last line to be chartered, the Texas and Pacific (Haney 1910, pp. 56–58 and 152–153; U.S. Congressional Globe 1862–3, p. 2749; 1863–4, p. 2327).

With these provisions, Congress established safeguards against unscrupulous and incompetent railway promoters without expanding federal control over private enterprise. The entire federal force charged with administrating the first four of the five transcontinental grants consisted of ten temporary, part-time, unpaid directors and six federally appointed railway inspectors. The paperwork associated with turning over the deeds was to be handled by the General Land Office (U.S. Congressional Globe 1862–3, p. 2749; 1863–4, p. 2327; Haney 1910, pp. 56–58). Congress had fashioned an aid scheme it believed to be immune to the corruption and graft that had invaded state-level aid to railways, but the weak link in this scheme turned out to be Congress itself.

The Credit Mobilier scandal.   Stephen Skowronek argues that the American commitment to liberalism and to a minimalist state undermined efforts late in the century to govern pricing and competition in the railway industry (1982, p. 122). It also undermined federal promotion policy by producing two kinds of scandals that would lead Americans to distrust federal leadership in economic growth. First, the absence of federal controls over loan guarantees to the first two Pacific lines enabled the infamous Credit Mobilier – an organization established to distribute the profits of the Union Pacific – to plunder federal aid. The Credit Mobilier's creative financing arrangements allowed railway directors to recoup their personal investments even before the line was completed. The promoters were soon paying themselves huge profits in undervalued Union Pacific securities. The appointment of five public directors to the board of each of the two Pacific lines, who were to report to Congress annually but who exercised no power over the lines, proved to be an inadequate check on fraud. Despite a clause that prohibited them from owning stock in the railways on whose boards they sat, the government appointees were soon accepting bribes in the form of railway stock for their cooperation. This practice went unpunished because no procedure had been established for enforcing the clause – even the actions of federally appointed directors were not subject to positive administrative controls and were constrained only by the threat of post hoc litigation (Crawford 1880).

Second, the Union Pacific bribed federal lawmakers to gain generous terms on federal aid. At the heart of the scandal was Oakes Ames, a Republican congressman from Massachusetts who served on the boards of both the Credit Mobilier and the Union Pacific. Ames used railway stock to buy the votes of at least eighteen legislators, including House Speaker James G. Blaine and Grant's two vice-presidents, Schuyler Colfax and Henry Wilson (Thompson 1983, p. 170). Lawmakers were offered Union Pacific and Credit Mobilier stock at par, which was well below real values, and immediately reaped huge profits. In many cases they paid no money up front – the initial "investment" was simply deducted from the first dividend check (Crawford 1880; McCabe 1873). In return, they backed bills that offered the Pacific line extraordinarily generous public incentives. In an 1864 amendment, Congress doubled the land to be deeded to the railway and altered the financial terms to the railways' advantage by guaranteeing second-mortgage bonds instead of first-mortgage bonds. This enabled the firms to sell first- and second-mortgage bonds to the public simultaneously (Mercer 1982, p. 255). That practice was scandalous even by the lax accounting standards of the day. The public uproar over the Credit Mobilier began in 1868 when stockholders realized that their investments had been misused and diluted, and culminated in a congressional investigation in 1872 (Trent 1981).

The demise of federal land grants.   In 1872, Congress forswore further land grants to the railways. The land grant program had represented an effort to transform the federal government into an active force in economic development along the lines sketched by Alexander Hamilton nearly a century earlier. Coming in the decade of the Civil War, the land grants coincided with a substantial increase in the size of the federal government that could have facilitated such a dynamic federal role. Yet a new and expanded federal role was not to be. The land grant experience not only put an end to the practice of railway grants but brought the notion of federal participation in economic development to an early end. It may well be that, as Margaret Thompson (1983) argues, much of what was perceived to be a new and heinous form of corruption at the federal level was in reality merely the emergence of the now-venerated political tradition we call lobbying. Nonetheless, the land grant program undermined the integrity of Congress and seemed to threaten democracy itself.

The land grant episode galvanized anti-statist sentiments by fulfilling the Constitution's prophecy that state power breeds corruption. Railway land grant history soon became a central parable of anti-statism in American political lore, and by the middle of the twentieth century the land giveaway had become part of every American high school history textbook (Henry 1945).

The move away from activism in industrial development was paralleled and supported by changes in judicial activity during the 1860s. In the courts, 1860 marked the end of a period of judicial "instrumentalism" in which court decisions were ruled by pragmatic developmentalism more than by abstract legal principles (Horwitz 1975; Scheiber 1975). Like the subnational governments, the federal courts had promoted progress with policies that supported the release of entrepreneurial energies. The switch to legal "formalism," which was based on the application of universal legal principles and the increased reliance on precedent, may have been incremental rather than revolutionary (Scheiber 1981) but either way it reinforced the change that was going on in public rail policy in these years.

In the last quarter of the nineteenth century, the public policy pendulum swung away from state leadership (Hurst 1956, p. 53). What would rise to replace activism? In the 1870s and 1880s, the United States had only a negative model of the government's role in growth. As the economist Henry Carter Adams wrote in 1886: "the present generation is without principles adequate for the guidance of public affairs. We are now passing through a period of interregnum in the authoritative control of economic and governmental principles" (1954, p. 66). Adams advocated a new sort of governmental role, in which the state would establish ground rules for business activity that would encourage entrepreneurial competitiveness and put an end to unscrupulous behavior. In Adams' model, the government was to be an assertive, if disinterested, umpire in the nation's industrial markets.

In sum, Americans at first believed that it was the duty of their local, state, and federal governments to promote industrial growth to the end of enriching the nation and serving citizens' wants. Their initial reaction was to situate sovereignty over economic matters in their representative, local, governments, just as they had conceded political sovereignty to those governments. Rivalistic activism among subnational governments was the way to achieve economic ends, and growth would be produced by this sort of rivalry. This vision of the means to economic order contrasts sharply with what we will see in France during the same years. To achieve economic order and growth in the rail industry, the French believed that the central state would have to dominate finance. If local governments or private entrepreneurs were to dominate the industry, the result would be a hopeless jumble of disorganized, poorly constructed, stretches of rail track. British finance policies were designed to achieve order and growth by locating control exclusively in the hands of private actors. If government, at any level, were to become involved in rail finance it would trespass on the liberties of individual entrepreneurs and create economic disarray. The profit-seeking behavior of multitudes of individual entrepreneurs, whose liberties were to be shielded by Parliament, would generate economic order and growth. Thus the problem Americans perceived in rail finance was how to situate control in local communities in order to allow them to pursue their own destinies, while simultaneously preventing the concentration of illicit authority in public or private hands. The problem the French perceived was how to prevent localities and private parties from gaining control of finance. The problem the British perceived was how to prevent governments from interfering with private activity.

The solutions these countries conceived also looked quite different. American and French governments alike sought to use public funds to draw private capital to the industry. But whereas American finance strategies were designed to place the industry in the hands of private entrepreneurs even when public funds outweighed private funds, French finance strategies were designed to sustain government control over railroads even when private funding dominated. Americans aimed to create a private system of railroads using public inducements. The French aimed to create a public system of railroads with the help of private capital. Britain's early finance policies were genuinely laissez faire: The state did nothing to promote or regulate private finance.

The United States' reaction to the corruption of public aid also contrasts starkly with the reaction we will see in France. What sort of a problem was this, and how would it be solved? In the United States, corruption evinced the inherent threat to political order posed by state expansion. Americans were certain that their governments had overstepped their bounds in offering aid to railroads, and forswore future government aid to enterprise. The French had the opposite reaction. For them, the misuse of public funds indicated that government controls on industry had been inadequate, and they responded by fortifying government controls over future aid. In short, although the end of public sponsorship in the United States may at first appear to have been the result of America's administrative incapacities, Americans might have responded by expanding public powers rather than by terminating sponsorship. American rivalistic statism came to an end largely because Americans believed that the only cure for corruption – expanded public controls – was worse than the disease.

Finally, American federalism contributed to the constitution of the principal interest groups interested in finance. In the United States, the main interest groups were local conglomerations of manufacturers, merchants, and farmers who joined together to promote railroads that would serve their regions. This seemed natural in the United States. But in France during these same years, the principal interest group consisted of members of a state engineering cadre that had first been established to serve the crown's military needs. During monarchical and republican regimes alike, this elite group of technocrats dominated finance debates. Their interest was to promote rail development, but to promote the establishment of a single national system that would remain under their control. In Britain, the key interest groups looked different still. In the absence of active regional governments and of autonomous state technocrats, British transport policy had spawned a sectorally based group of canal owners opposed to railway development.

Technical and managerial coordination

The third set of functional problems faced by American railroads concerned the establishment of technical and managerial standards that would facilitate interconnections, permit railroads to borrow one anothers' track and carriages for through traffic, and allow coordination of the industry. Technical standards in areas such as signaling and braking also promised to increase railway safety. Alfred Chandler (1977) argues that it was these demands for coordination, both within and among railroads, that generated the United States' managerial revolution in the late nineteenth century. In comparative perspective, the American state's reluctance to interfere with the internal operations of private enterprises had generated many of these problems of coordination in the first place. On the Continent, government control of technical standards and operating procedures had led to early standardization in most nations.

American governments' decision to leave railroads to their own devices contributed to the peculiarly privatized notion of industrial progress that emerged there. In the United States a huge national rail network grew in the absence of public coordination. The lesson Americans took from United States railway policy was not merely that progress had occurred despite government's hands-off stance, but that progress had occurred because of it. A wide range of operational and technical issues were left to private decision processes in the United States.

The first issue of technical standardization to arise in the industry was track gauge. Gauge standardization at the national level was important because wherever lines with incompatible gauges met, trains running on one track could not continue on to the other line. Passengers and freight had to be transferred from one train to another. Governments around the world realized that they could preclude this problem by stipulating a standard gauge in all railway charters. However, in the United States, neither states nor the Congress were inclined to dictate to railways, and as a result each railway was allowed to choose its own gauge. Hence, as late as 1861, half of America's total trackage was in some gauge other than the popular 4 feet 8½ inch width (Westbay 1934, p. 32). At the end of the 1860s a survey found twelve different gauge widths in use in the United States (Poor 1871). It was not until 1886 that a private organization took upon itself the task of standardizing rail gauge, and convinced operators throughout the country to undertake the massive job of recalibrating the gauge on all non-standard lines to the 4 feet 8½ inch standard and replacing the thousands of carriages and locomotives built for nonstandard gauges (Moody 1938). Governments, as investors in railroads, bore much of the cost of their own reluctance to standardize rail gauge. The problem was not that Congress and the states failed to foresee the problem of gauge diversity, but that they were intent on protecting the entrepreneur from unnecessary public meddling.

Second, American governments left it to private parties to standardize time zones in order to make railroad connections regular and predictable, and to coordinate connecting train schedules for different railroads. Because long-distance travel was time-consuming and arduous before the railway age, local control over the time produced few inconveniences because individuals seldom moved through many localities in a single day. With the rise of railways the fact that Wisconsin, for instance, had thirty-eight different time zones made transport schedules a nightmare to interpret. At one point the major railroads used fifty-four different times to run their trains. A cross-country traveler might have to change his watch twenty times. In the absence of congressional leadership, a group of over one hundred railroads formed the General Time Convention (GTC) in 1873 to coordinate scheduling. In 1874 it established the Interline Uniform Time Tables, and by 1883 it had set out the four time zones that would become the American standards (Dunlavy forthcoming: Stover 1970; Kennedy 1991). Congress was so intent 0n preserving the autonomy of regional governments that it did not give legal standing to the four time zones for another thirty-five years (Schivelbusch 1986, p. 44). After the GTC, which later became the American Railroad Association, helped to standardize time zones, it spent most of its energies coordinating connections between lines to facilitate through traffic.

Third, train drivers depended on signalmen, and later on mechanical signaling systems, to let them know whether the track ahead was clear. The thousands of different American railroad companies developed countless signaling standards, and as the system became integrated drivers were often confused by signals they were unaccustomed to. What meant "stop" on one system meant "go" on another. Tragic and costly accidents proliferated. Some states established statewide signaling standards, but this did not solve the problem for interstate traffic. Finally, in 1884 the GTC reached agreement on standard nationwide signaling procedures. Federal imposition of signaling standards had been steadfastly opposed by railwaymen, who disputed the government's right to interfere in any way with internal operations (Dunlavy forthcoming).

Fourth, Congress left decisions about the use of rudimentary safety devices, such as brakes and emergency cords, to the railroads until very late in the century. As a result, many trains operated without even the most elementary of safety appliances (Haney 1910). To take two examples, railway employees were frequently crushed when operating manual link-and-pin couplers between trains (Brandes 1976), and trains that had no brakes often met with accidents that injured passengers and employees alike. In 1868, Eli H. Janney received a patent for an automatic coupler that would permit trains to be joined without imperiling an employee, and in 1869 George Westinghouse received a patent for a dependable air brake. States tried to encourage railways to install automatic couplers and air brakes by publishing railroads' accident records alongside statistics on their use of these devices, but state legislatures were reluctant to dictate to railroads. As a result, private railroad associations encouraged their members to employ safety devices to improve the industry's safety record, and to protect the trains of firms that had installed brakes from being hit by the trains of firms that had not. Some two decades after private rail associations had taken up the cause of safety devices, Benjamin Harrison signed the Railroad Safety Appliance Act of 1893, requiring the use of brakes and automatic couplers (Haney 1910).

American governments sometimes did take action to reinforce the decisions of private associations, or to encourage public-mindedness among railroads, and in these cases they conceived solutions that were in keeping with the United States' adjudicative, noninvasive, model of governance. They aimed to locate control over economic activity in civil society to the greatest extent possible. In designing regulatory commissions, New England legislators reasoned that they could cause railways to act in the public interest by simply bringing matters of general concern to the attention of the citizenry. In 1872, Massachusetts' commissioners argued that there were "three methods and three methods only" for controlling the behavior of the railways. Railways could be governed (1) via compulsory legislation that dictated how they must operate, which smacked of tyranny; (2) through state operation, which was probably beyond the fiscal and managerial abilities of the states; or (3) "By the results gradually but inevitably brought about in this country through the agency of an enlightened public opinion making itself felt by means of discussion and popular agitation" (1872, p. clxx). Most state railway commissions thus concentrated on making the public aware of problems in the industry. In Massachusetts the commission published extensive records of accident investigations with the aim of encouraging railroads to install safety devices. Where private parties sustained damage notwithstanding these efforts, they could obtain redress either through the courts or through the arbitration of the commissions themselves. Reckless and poorly managed railroads faced the loss of business and the threat of litigation.

In short, in virtually every realm requiring managerial or technical coordination, private associations arose in the United States to take up the task. Beginning in 1855, the American Associations of Passenger Traffic Officers, Travelling Passenger Agents, and Baggage Traffic Managers were founded to coordinate through transport among lines. These groups met regularly to make arrangements for passengers and freight that made connections between different railroads. Beginning in the early 1880s, associations were established to standardize various technical aspects of the industry, including couplings, gauge, bridge construction, and brakes. These groups had names like the Air Brake Association, the Roadmasters and Maintenance of Way Association of America, the Association of Track and Structure Suppliers, the National Railway Appliances Association. In all, twenty-two different national associations were founded to coordinate and standardize railroad domains as diverse as scheduling, safety equipment, bridge construction, rates for through traffic, and signaling (Kennedy 1991, p. 146).

What issues of technical and managerial coordination were thought to belong to the public realm in the United States? At first glance it appears that no issues were considered to fall within the domain of state action. However, state and federal governments often acted to give the force of law to private-sector coordinative agreements, with the rationale that railroads that rejected private-sector agreements should not have a financial advantage over their more public-spirited competitors. Thus, governments reluctantly required the use of safety devices so that reckless railroads would not enjoy unfair advantages. Governments frequently took such actions at the behest of railroads who wanted their less public-spirited competitors to live by the same ground rules they imposed on themselves. Yet Americans did not see any of the core problems of coordination as belonging naturally to the state. Americans described government standard-setting as a threat to the political and economic liberties of private railroads. It was thought that railroads would naturally choose the technologies and operating guidelines that were most efficient, and market mechanisms would compel them to make decisions that would serve the public interest.

By contrast, the French saw myriad problems with allowing private railroads to establish their own technical and managerial guidelines. Entrepreneurs would sacrifice safety, dependability, speed, and everything else that was in the nation's interest – to cost. Market mechanisms would encourage this sort of behavior. In all technical matters, then, the French saw private decision authority as problematic because it would undermine efficiency and fail to serve the nation. British policymakers came closer to their American counterparts. They saw public controls as potentially tyrannical, but in cases where the safety and vitality of working class passengers were imperiled by the decisions of private railroads, they saw it as incumbent upon the state to establish standards.

The solutions Americans conceived to problems of coordination placed authority over the industry squarely in the private sector. States paid no attention to most matters of coordination, and when they did become involved, as in the case of safety, they aimed to inform public opinion of the ill behavior of private railroads in order to cause market mechanisms to do the job of controlling industry. By contrast, French public policy gave control over all issues of coordination to state technocrats. The French state established a standard gauge, set the national clock, established and updated signaling standards, dictated that railroads must employ air brakes and emergency cords, set construction specifications, and made managerial decisions concerning everything from rates to scheduling. From the very first years of the industry the only other solution that received serious consideration was nationaliz-ation of the railroads, which would have made the state's technocrats the direct managers of railroads rather than puppeteers. For the most part the British, like the Americans, believed that technical and man-agerial decisions should be made in the private sector, and saw state involvement as politically dangerous and economically irrational. However, when it came to protecting the working class from injury and from price gouging, the British state dictated to railroads.

In the absence of public controls, United States' railroads devised solutions themselves. In so doing they developed greater coordinative capacities than they might have otherwise (Chandler 1977). In prac-tice, then, expertise in railway administration (rate setting, scheduling, and so on) that arose in the public sector in most European nations rose in the offices of privately held railroads in the United States. One consequence was that Americans increasingly understood industrial growth to be the province of the private sector, for state action always seemed to end in corruption and the railways got along quite well without state oversight. In brief, by turning over authority for industry coordination to the private sector American state and federal govern-ments reinforced the lessons of early public promotion of railroads. Industry worked best when left alone by the state.

Pricing and competition

The issues of pricing and competition first arose in the context of efforts to protect the economic liberties of rail customers and indepen-dent railroads. The United States' widespread concern with restraints of trade was driven by a commitment to maximizing economic freedom as a means of guaranteeing political freedom (Fligstein 1990; Wilson 1980). Federal protections for economic liberty emerged in a number of realms in the late nineteenth and early twentieth centuries, driven by dramatic increases in economic concentration. The new regulations denied large firms the ability to dominate their peers by enforcing competition and by outlawing "restraints of trade." When these pol-icies coincided with rapid economic growth, they came to be seen not only as protections for economic liberties but as a positive prescription for growth. The enforcement of market mechanisms became the foun-dation of the United States' new industrial policy paradigm, as Dar-win's natural selection metaphor was applied to the industrial realm.

In this process, the United States worked out a new strategy for locating sovereignty over the economy in civil society. Although active localism had maximized community control over growth, it had been plagued by corruption. Federal regulation of markets could cede control over the economy to civil society by permitting Washington to remain above the economic fray as a neutral overseer, while containing the excesses of large private-sector economic actors. Now, policy situated control over industry outside of the central state, but in market mechanisms rather than in self-governing communities. The administrative model for governing pricing and competition came from two contemporary sources: (1) state experiences with railway regulation, and (2) the regulatory structure that had evolved within the General Land Office to govern competition for land grants. Government activism had been discredited by the experience of public efforts to finance railroads; however, government adjudication had been reinforced by the successes of these regulatory bodies.

The market-enforcement logic found in the Act to Regulate Interstate Commerce and the Sherman Antitrust Act was truly novel in the late 1880s. Earlier public policies had not been designed to affect price and service competition among railroads, or among firms in any sector. Instead, American law had supported the freedom to make contracts of all varieties, including price-fixing agreements and pooling arrangements, whereby competing firms agreed to divide business and profits among themselves. In accord with this tradition, Congress passed legislation in 1866 that legalized pooling among railroads by permitting them to share rolling stock and track (Kennedy 1991, p. 145). Although the 1866 legislation was not enforced because it conflicted with common law precepts that held such agreements to constitute restraints of trade (McCraw 1984, p. 49), it nonetheless encouraged associational behavior. By 1870 groups of regional freight agents were meeting regularly, and in full view of the public, to set common tariffs (Adams 1893, p. 152). "In 1875, Albert Fink's Southern Railway and Steamship Association reached agreement on rates for the main lines that served the South, and by the end of 1878 Fink's Eastern Trunk Line Association was setting rates for the major northern lines, east of the Mississippi River" (Chandler 1977, pp. 139–140). In those years, railroads could sign and abide by price-fixing agreements voluntarily, but they lacked the ability to force unwilling railroads to participate in pools and this caused great instability among pools (Massachusetts

Board of Railroad Commissioners 1882, p. 36). During the ensuing years Fink lobbied Congress to make cartel agreements legally binding, and had he won American industrial policy might have taken an entirely different course (Massachusetts Board of Railroad Commissioners 1878, p. 84; Chandler 1977, p. 141).

Notwithstanding Fink's lobbying failure, cartels and pools came to predominate between 1870 and 1890. As the Chamber of Commerce of the State of New York wrote in 1881, "In most instances competition is now supplanted by pooling or other forms of combination" (Massachusetts Board of Railroad Commissioners 1881, p. 30). Although Americans perceived a number of evils in the resulting concentration of economic power, they also perceived evils in proposals to use government action to restrain combinations. Most important, market enforcement had not yet been articulated as a positive theory of the role of government in industry, by which the state could guard against the evil of economic concentration while preventing the expansion of political control over firms. And the United States' industrial culture was not yet motivated by a logic of natural selection in free markets.

State regulation

The biggest railway firms – those associated with names like Cornelius Vanderbilt, Jay Gould, and Leland Stanford – quickly grew larger than state governments and soon rivaled nonpostal federal employment. Huge railroads held the fates of towns and entire regions in their hands. Neither legislators nor railway entrepreneurs had anticipated that individual railroads would become so powerful, for they had originally expected railroads to operate as public thoroughfares. They envisioned railways, like canals and turnpikes, being used by private transport companies that would pay tolls to the operators. That system had prevented monopolization in canal and turnpike transport by encouraging the establishment of competing public carriers. As D. Lardner wrote in *Railway Economy* in 1851, "It was expected that the public should be admitted to exercise the business of carriers upon [the rails], subject to certain specified regulations and by-laws. It soon became apparent, however, that . . . such a system would speedily be attended with self-destruction" (quoted in Schivelbusch 1986). Technical considerations made the use of railroads by multiple transport firms impracticable initially. First, because trains could not pass one another on railroads as could barges on canals and coaches on turnpikes, transport firms could not be allowed to use the track as they pleased. Second, because early trains had no brakes it was imperative that a single operator exercise strict controls over scheduling. When a train driver came into view of an unexpected train on the same track, as was the case when a Fitchburg train came upon a New London Northern train near Miller's Falls, Massachusetts on 11 March 1876, he was, in the words of the commission that inquired into the ensuing accident, "already too near the junction to stop his train" (Massachusetts Board of Railroad Commissioners 1877, p. 24).

In the United States, as in Britain, government resolved this problem by granting the companies that built railroads exclusive monopolies on transport over their tracks. The result was that most towns were served by a single carrier, whose scheduling and rate decisions could make or break local farmers, merchants, and industrialists. Moreover, in the context of an unregulated market, railways tried to introduce predictability by dominating competing railroads: "The issue of how to control one's competitors was paramount in the late nineteenth century" (Fligstein 1990, p. 23). The resulting railroad cartels effectively monopolized transport throughout sizeable regions.

American states identified the restraints of trade imposed by large railroads on local shippers and small railroads as an evil that threatened political order, individual liberty, and economic efficiency. Railroads represented just the kind of concentrated power that American political institutions vilified as the enemy of the polity. However, it was not obvious how American governments could remedy this situation without trespassing on other economic liberties. Instead of solving the problem by forging large regional monopolies with tightly controlled pricing structures, as France did, or by enforcing cartels that would help small independents to survive by sustaining price levels, as Britain did, American states developed policies that would prevent railroads from abusing their transport monopolies by allowing injured parties, including rail customers and independent lines, to file grievances with the state.

The first state commissions.   State governments invented the regulatory commission in the second quarter of the nineteenth century to govern banks, commercial firms, railways, and gas companies. Massachusetts set up the first of many state banking commissions in 1838. Rhode Island put together the first railway regulatory commission in

1839, and five New England states followed Rhode Island's lead by the beginning of the 1860s (Wilcox 1960, pp. 5–22; Sanders 1981). By 1886, just before passage of federal regulatory legislation, twenty-five states and territories had established railway commissions and another five had passed regulatory legislation that called for enforcement by the courts (U.S. Senate 1886, p. 655). Thus, a governing solution that had first been experimented with to constrain the behavior of banks was soon popularized and copied across a number of industrial realms.

States tried two different regulatory solutions to contain the monopolistic behavior and "unfair" practices of railroads. On the one hand, the New England states set up regulatory agencies that contained monopolistic behavior by offering aggrieved parties recourse through exposure and arbitration. On the other hand, farming states established regulatory agencies that had adjudicative mechanisms, but that also allowed governments to establish railway rates.

New England commissions. The impetus for the New England commissions was a concern that railroads were injuring shippers by charging different prices to different customers. In so doing, railroads abused the monopolies granted in their charters and broke the public trust. The case that spawned the Rhode Island commission illustrates the nature of the problem. The Boston and Providence Railroad, which had a rail monopoly between its two endpoints, also held a steamboat line that ran between Providence and New York that did not enjoy a monopoly. To increase business on its steamboat line, the B & P discounted rail rates for customers who promised to use their steamboat service on the second leg of the Boston-New York trip. By penalizing rail customers for using competing steamboat lines, the B & P put those lines at a disadvantage. Rhode Island perceived an effort to restrain trade in this practice, and established a commission to secure to all of:

> [Rhode Island's] citizens and inhabitants . . . the full and equal priv-
> ileges of the transportation of persons or property at all times, . . .
> And to enquire into any contract, understanding, or agreement, by
> which any railroad company shall attempt to transfer, or give any
> steamboat company or any steamboat, any preference over any other
> such company or boat. (quoted in Kirkland 1948, V.II p. 234)

The other New England states established railroad commissions in response to similar pricing conflicts between railroads. In 1855, Vermont appointed a commissioner after a conflict between the Vermont Central and the Rutland and Burlington, and in 1858, Maine set up a commission as the result of repeated complaints from two lines that serviced Portland and Bangor (Haney 1908; 1910; U.S. Senate 1886). The United States' anti-concentration sentiments led lawmakers to perceive a special evil in efforts by railroads to use their monopoly powers to win business.

Most industry analysts believe that unfair competitive practices arose in the first place because American governments had refused to impose controls on the railroads. It was true that the railways appeared to be abusing government-granted powers with practices designed to injure certain clients and bankrupt their competitors. But as E. M. Teagarden analyzes the situation, "Most [rate difficulties] were a result of adherence to the concept of *laissez-faire* in business activities without any real sense of social and moral responsibility or [of economic necessity resulting from varied competitive advantages or disadvantages" (1972, p. 161). Because the states had not enacted preemptory legislation, businesses engaged in activities that would have been seen as illicit anywhere: "Since there were few laws or rules guiding behavior, almost anything was possible" (Fligstein 1990, p. 13). Americans quickly branded practices that took advantage of monopoly powers conferred in public charters illicit, and sought policy solutions.

The New England commissions were designed to affect the public will largely through the use of exposure, and as a last resort through arbitration. They had the authority to investigate all sorts of complaints, to search for and expose potential problems and injustices in the industry, and to arbitrate conflicts where exposure did not remedy a problem. But the New England commissions could neither sanction railroads nor establish transport prices. Their annual reports were perhaps their most potent weapons. The reports included financial information on all operating railroads, as well as statistics on accidents, fatalities, rates, and the use of such "safety" equipment as brakes. They also published the results of special investigations of ratemaking and safety problems. In their 1871 report, for instance, the Massachusetts commissioners included a lengthy discussion of an August collision at the seaside town of Revere in which 29 people died and 57 were injured. While taking care not to assign blame directly ("The Commissioners do not understand that it in any way belongs to them to apportion responsibility"), they nonetheless made clear that the accident resulted from lax management and aggressive price competition, which brought the Eastern Railway more passengers than it could readily accommodate (Massachusetts Board of Railroad Commissioners 1872, p. cii). The manifest aim of these reports was to bring the pressure of public opinion to bear on railway operators.

Why did these commissions have such weak powers? Charles Francis Adams, director of Massachusetts' first railway commission (established 1869) and the descendant of two presidents, was the principal architect of the regulatory commission. Adams argued that railways were a new type of enterprise that enjoyed a natural monopoly over a public good that was fundamental to life and livelihood. Consequently the government had a duty to oversee railway administration. He applauded the success of the state-owned Belgian railway system, and briefly championed the French model of private franchises under strict state controls, but he eventually came to the view that those forms of railway administration were not for the United States. Adams argued that American state capacities were inadequate to effect strong positive controls over railways. The tripartite separation of federal powers and the federal-state disjuncture would make it difficult, if not impossible, for the government to effectively manage enterprises as complicated and large in scale as the railways. Better to let them manage themselves, Adams reasoned, and keep a watchful regulatory eye on them. As head of Massachusetts' railway commission and later director of the Union Pacific Railway, Adams became the United States' most vocal and prolific proponent of regulation (McCraw 1984; Adams 1887).

Adams advocated regulatory structures that were well suited to American state capacities. The growth of public powers was minimized, in Massachusetts: "The powers conferred on the commissioners hardly deserved the name; and such as they were, they were carefully hedged about with limitations against their abuse" (Adams 1893, p. 138). In accordance with the United States' anti-bureaucratic political culture the commissions comprised from one to four men, and their terms were limited to three years. In the words of the House Journal of Vermont, a one-commissioner state, the public commissions must be kept to a minimum because salaried state offices are "in all cases, an evil" (quoted in Kirkland 1948, V. II p. 234). To guard against the threat of graft and corruption inherent in all state offices, commissioners were explicitly prohibited from owning railway stock and from hearing cases involving firms in which they had an interest (U.S. Senate 1886).

The Granger commissions.   After the New England states began regulating railways in the 1850s and 1860s, a second group of states set up commissions in the 1870s and 1880s (Kennedy 1961). This time the issue was long haul-short haul discrimination. The problem was simple. Farmers who shipped produce from rural areas to cities paid higher absolute prices than did freight customers who shipped goods much longer distances between large cities. The Granger movement brought farmers together to protest these pricing practices, and won railway commissions from legislatures in the South and Midwest.

The problem of long haul-short haul discrimination arose for two reasons. First, in the railway industry the fixed costs of the roadbed and rolling stock were extremely high, whereas the marginal costs associated with increased traffic were relatively low. The industry's high fixed costs encouraged railways to discount rates below real costs on competitive routes, because every dime a railroad earned beyond the marginal cost of running a train helped it to amortize fixed costs. Thus railroads slashed prices on competitive routes to win business (Mercer 1982). Second, most railroads provided both competitive service between cities, and noncompetitive service to the isolated towns located along their routes. Railroads offset low profit margins on competitive routes by charging high rates for service to and from isolated towns where they held monopolies. Between Cincinnati and Indianapolis, for instance, there were two reasonably direct routes by the end of the 1850s and two routes that were roughly 50 percent further in miles. Even without considering the possibilities of circuitous routing, four companies could offer relatively direct freight service. All four discounted prices to win business. However, each line provided exclusive service to a number of intermediate towns, and thus could charge a premium for transport from towns like Shelbyville, Indiana and Oxford, Ohio. Railroads commonly charged more for short-distance service to isolated towns (for example, the 25-mile Shelbyville-Indianapolis route) than for long-distance service on the very same routes (for example, the 100-mile Cincinnati-Indianapolis route) (see Chandler 1956, p. 84). Americans would not have been wrong to conclude that such price-cutting on competitive routes was natural in this kind of industry. Instead, they came to see this pricing strategy as particularly sinister because it disadvantaged some shippers while advantaging others.

In effect, transport between urban nodes was subsidized by transport to and from peripheral regions. As Charles Francis Adams put it:

> The principles of free trade did not have full play: they were confined to favored localities. . . . The work of the railroad centres was done at a nominal profit, while the corporations recompensed themselves by extorting from other points where competition did not have to be met, the highest profits which business could be made to pay. (1893, p. 119)

In 1867, farmers and ranchers joined together in the National Grange of the Patrons of Husbandry to fight rate discrimination. Farmers and ranchers faced the greatest injuries from rate discrimination because they transported goods from far-flung rural areas to urban markets. Manufacturers, by contrast, were often advantaged by rate-making practices because their intercity freight was subsidized by high rural rates. By 1875 the National Grange had some 800,000 members in 20,000 local Granges, as they were called. Their single goal was to induce states to regulate railway rates so as to halt discriminatory rate-setting (Stover 1970, p. 91). Beginning in 1871, Illinois, Wisconsin, Minnesota, and Iowa established "strong" commissions with powers to directly regulate railways rates, and in most cases to set maximum rates (McCraw 1984, p. 57). Over the next two decades the Granger movement won legislation to regulate rates throughout the South and Midwest.

The adjudicative model prevails.   In the eyes of the Granger movement, the railways posed a threat not only to rural livelihood but to the polity itself. Leaders argued in stark terms that the monopoly powers exercised by railroads constituted a form of concentrated power that was inimical to American political order. An 1873 resolution passed by many granges stated,

> The history of the present railway monopoly is a history of repeated injuries and oppressions, all having in direct object the establishment of an absolute tyranny over the people of these States unequalled in any monarchy of the Old World, and having its only parallel in the history of the medieval ages, when the strong hand was the only law, and the highways of commerce were taxed by the feudal barons, who, from their strongholds, surrounded by their armies of vassals, could lay such tribute upon the traveller as their own wills alone should dictate. (quoted in Adams 1893, p. 129)

Railway practices were not merely unfair; they embodied political and economic tyranny. The Granges proposed to make states equal to this threat by reinforcing their powers to check the growth of concentrated economic authority. The Granger commissions they spearheaded were given unprecedented powers to intervene in the rate-making decisions of private railroads by adjudicating conflicts and, where that failed, by setting maximum rates.

However, railroads in the Midwest and South ignored the dictates of state commissions and continued to charge what they pleased. As C.F. Adams put it: "In the West, during the years 1872–3, if a railroad official was asked what course the companies proposed to pursue in regard to the new legislation, the usual answer was that they did not propose to pay any attention whatever to it" (1893, p. 136). Commissions indeed found that their edicts had no force. As Ohio's railroad commissioner lamented in his 1870 report:

> There is not a railroad operated in the State, either under special charter or the general law, upon which the law regulating rates is not, in some way, violated, nearly every time a regular passenger, freight, or mixed train passes over it. (quoted in Massachusetts Board of Railroad Commissioners 1871, p. clxxi)

When Iowa passed regulatory legislation that set maximum passenger and freight tariffs in March 1874, Iowa roads such as the Chicago, Burlington, & Quincy simply ignored the law and continued to charge what they had always charged (Larson 1984, p. 143).

Why did the Granger commissions uniformly fail to gain compliance? Thomas McCraw argues that the approach was irrational: "It simply made no sense for small state agencies to perform pricing functions for giant interstate corporations whose tracks crossed thousands of miles in a dozen different states" (1984, p. 57). It may have been a poor idea, but states did try to carry it out. Adams argued that the failure of the commissions resulted from the weak administrative capacities of American states, coupled with American sentiments against the expansion of state authority. First, state constitutions gave governments no administrative authority to sanction private actors who ignored their edicts. The courts were to be used to compel compliance, and although lawmakers took great pains to appoint commissioners without ties to the railroads, they could not prevent the railroads from bribing judges to overrule the commissions. Second, the states had no preexisting technical expertise in transport administration. Governors typically staffed their commissions with upstanding citizens who knew nothing about the industry. American anti-bureaucratic sentiments contributed to this problem, as Adams argued:

> The American mind is not bureaucratic . . . In America there are not many specialists, nor have the American people any great degree of faith in them. The principle that all men are created equal before the

law has been stripped of its limitations, until in the popular mind it has become a sort of cardinal article of political faith that all men are equal for all purposes. Accordingly, in making up commissions to deal with the most complicated issues arising out of our modern social and industrial organization, those in authority are very apt to conclude that one man can do the work about as well as another. (1893, pp. 132–133)

Americans' distrust of technocrats led to Granger commissions composed of community volunteers rather than publicly employed experts. Moreover, public anti-railroad sentiments ran so strong that governors could not appoint experienced railwaymen to their commissions. The result was that they established small commissions made up of upstanding but naive citizens who were easily fooled by the railroads.

The conspicuous failure of Granger commissions to bring about changes in railway rate-making led many states to abolish them in short order. However, workable solutions to the problem of rate discrimination were developed in Illinois and Massachusetts. Unlike other Granger states, Illinois recognized that it was not practical for the legislature or an administrative commission to set rates by fiat, and instead relied on an adjudicative procedure. Thus the two states' approaches were not so far apart. Massachusetts developed perhaps the most successful short haul legislation in 1871, when they made it illegal to charge more for short distance transport than for long distance transport over the same track (Kennedy 1961, p. 17; Wilcox 1960, pp. 5–22). Customers who perceived rate discrimination could appeal to the commission for redress. This clause was both popular and successful because it put an end to rate inequities without dictating rates to railroads. Within a year the major railroads had revised their price structures (Massachusetts Board of Railroad Commissioners 1872, p. xxv), and by 1885 the commissioners wrote: "No law in this State is more thoroughly enforced than this. Indeed it would be more correct to say that, instead of being enforced at all, it is universally acquiesced to and obeyed" (Massachusetts Board of Railroad Commissioners 1885, p. 49). This adjudicative model of governance was soon heralded as the only workable solution to the problem of railway regulation because it promised to remedy the problems posed by the railways without substantially enlarging state powers. By the 1880s, this model was being promoted for a federal regulatory commission that would be able to redress the failures of the Granger commissions (Kirkland 1948, V.II p. 232).

Federal regulation

An early type of conflict that the federal government was called on to remedy involved competition between railroads for federal land grants. In addressing that issue, the federal government developed a model of administration that it would later replicate to address problems associated with interstate railway rates.

Regulating land grant claims. An adjudicative model of railway governance resembling that of the New England commissions grew up in the General Land Office (GLO), as that office struggled to devise a way to deal with competing claims for federal lands. The minimalist administrative architecture of the land grants illustrated a weakness that permeated American government: No government entity was charged with custody of the public interest in the case of unforeseen contingencies. Thus, when the Union Pacific built temporary wooden culverts and bridges to speed access to federal loans, J.L. Williams, a federal appointee to the Union Pacific's board, feared that they would distribute profits from the government bonds before replacing the wood with stone (U.S. General Land Office 1868, p. 2). There was nothing in the federal legislation to stop them from doing so, and there was no public authority with the capacity to veto the practice.

The principal problem lawmakers overlooked when writing the land grants concerned competing claims for federal lands. A Railway Department emerged within the GLO, which, without any mandate from Congress to do so, evolved a quasi-judicial approach to land grant administration.

Several kinds of conflicts over federal lands emerged. First, once the railways began claiming public lands, the GLO was deluged with appeals from citizens who contended that the railways had been given title to lands that were rightly their own (Haney 1910). These claims were not easy to reconcile, because property rights were difficult to pin down in the unsettled territories (U.S. General Land Office, 1860s). Second, whenever one of the transcontinental lines intersected with a line that had received a land grant through a state government, a dispute over the lands in the vicinity of the intersection arose (Goodrich 1960). In 1871, a controversy arose between the Union Pacific Railroad Company Southern Branch and the Kansas Pacific Railway Company, over lands that both were eligible for in the vicinity of Junction City, Kansas. The GLO asked the advise of the Attorney General, who replied that the line that had first submitted a route plan had first claim to the lands (U.S. General Land Office 1870s). Third, the land grant bills called for land claims to be forfeited after a specified period of time, but railroads regularly contested GLO efforts to withdraw lands. By some estimates one half of land grant trackage was not laid before the applicable deadline (Sanborn 1899, p. 82). In 1876, the Supreme Court gave Congress the exclusive right to withdraw lands, but this did not keep railroads from appealing to the GLO for extensions (Sanborn 1899).

The Railway Department, established to deal with the rising tide of land grant disputes, is first mentioned in GLO records from the early 1870s (U.S. General Land Office 1870s). The GLO gradually developed a set of appeal mechanisms, which varied somewhat over time, that drew directly from the United States' court-centered system of legal enforcement. In France, the enforcement of railway law was turned over to the Ministry of Public Works, whose rulings were final and whose decisions were made by fiat. The GLO never decided claims by fiat. Instead, it set up a quasi-judicial framework within the agency. Both sides in a dispute were asked to present their cases before GLO officers. The officers used legal precedents to decide land claims, and frequently asked the Attorney General to interpret precedents. Parties could appeal GLO decisions to several levels within the agency before turning to the courts for satisfaction. The department also treated its own rulings as precedents in future conflicts unless those rulings were overturned by the courts (U.S. Department of the Interior 1890). In short, like the state railway commissions that regulated rate disputes, the Railway Department of the GLO fashioned a peculiarly American approach to administration in which the state would be no more than a neutral arbiter in civil matters. The Railway Department's procedures were widely accepted, and frequently utilized by railroads and by other contenders for public lands.

The GLO established this adjudicative process without the benefit of a congressional mandate, which makes the wide acceptance of the department's jurisdiction all the more striking. However, this model of governance had a long precedent in American political institutions, unlike the much maligned public-rate-setting model of the Granger states. The adjudicate model of governance had substantial legitimacy even before the GLO developed its own variant.

Comparative evidence suggests that in France and Britain as well, citizens accepted the legitimacy of familiar models of governance in new substantive realms and challenged the legitimacy of alien models. In France, railroads accepted the authority of an administrative agency that followed traditions of bureaucratic autonomy to assume proactive control over rates, technical guidelines, and operating procedures. In Britain, railroads challenged an advisory board that helped Parliament review charter proposals with the claim that it undermined representative government, but granted the railway inspectorate the power to investigate and report on accidents even before it had Parliamentary authority to do so. In short, Americans accepted an adjudicative extension of government power that reflected the court-centered system of enforcement they were accustomed to, the French accepted a proactive administrative form of authority that their state had used in the past, and the British accepted an expansion of the state's powers of inspection that was designed to locate control over the industry in informed public opinion.

Origins of the Interstate Commerce Commission. Federal regulation of pricing and competition was the next major step in the evolution of the United States' modern industrial policy paradigm. During the 1880s, regional rail monopolies, integrated railway trusts, and other sorts of combinations emerged. These rail networks practiced various kinds of rate discrimination, engaged in predatory pricing practices to bankrupt their small competitors, and discouraged market entry in the industry. Stephen Skowronek argues that the industry now appeared as a sort of Frankenstein monster: "Unintentionally but inevitably it had overpowered its sponsors at the state level, and finding no higher authority capable of providing supervision, it had become unruly and disruptive" (1982, p. 135). Americans saw the industry veering out of control as it grew, and saw abuses of concentrated power wherever they looked. The industry had become extremely competitive, and pricing practices that emerged to quell competition or to take advantage of service monopolies were soon perceived to be illicit. A number of these practices, such as asymmetrical rates for competitive and noncompetitive routes and rate agreements among competing lines, were considered to be perfectly reasonable in other countries. However, American political institutions had designated practices that appeared to concentrate great political or economic authority in the hands of a few as dangerous.

By the 1880s it was widely agreed that the states had failed to contain the powers of large-scale railroad networks. In the words of the Senate's Select Committee on Interstate Commerce:

> The committee has been impressed by the unanimity with which the witnesses examined agreed in attributing the evils most complained of to transactions which have been made possible by the lax general legislation of the several States, such as the construction of unnecessary railroads for speculative purposes, fictitious capitalization, and all the fraudulent financial schemes by which such enterprises have been notably characterized. (U.S. Senate 1886, p. 48)

B.H. Meyer of the University of Wisconsin later compared the history of corruption and abuse among American railroads with the European experience, and blamed the states for failing to adopt preemptory legislation to prevent exploitation:

> The relative promptness and thoroughness with which European countries legislated upon railway subjects saved them from some of the excesses of the evils from which we have suffered. There are probably few if any abuses connected with railways which did not manifest themselves there, but these never gained such headway, because of the greater care and thoroughness exercised in remedial and preventative legislation. (Meyer 1903, p. 18)

Citizens increasingly called for federal solutions to the problems associated with railway pricing and competition. Over the course of the decade preceding passage of the Act to Regulate Interstate Commerce (1887), Congress debated 150 bills for governing the railroads. It was torn between competing institutionalized precepts of government, which caused it to view concentrated economic powers as a threat to liberty but by the same token to view extensive state control over private life as a threat to the sovereignty of the natural civil community.

Congress never considered most of the solutions to industry concentration that other countries adopted, and I have suggested that this was because American political culture rendered interventionist federal solutions tyrannical. It never discussed the kind of public-private management found in France, or the full-scale nationalization that Belgium adopted. The most activist solution Congress considered was an adjudicative regulatory commission: The only real alternative was not to intervene at all.

Those who have studied the regulatory debates have, unanimously, followed the political realist method of reconstructing the battle lines to assess which interest group prevailed. It has been difficult to reconcile who won this struggle because over the course of the debate a number of different groups spearheaded regulation. In an early study of the conflict, Solon Buck (1913) argued that the Act to Regulate Interstate Commerce was begun by the Granger movement because state-level regulation had not fulfilled its promise. Ida Tarbell (1904) and Gerald Nash (1957) argue, on the other hand, that Eastern oilmen pushed the act through Congress, and Lee Benson (1955) suggests that New York merchants were really key. Chandler (1965) argues that both farmers and railway labor were important. Gabriel Kolko (1965) contends that railway companies themselves finally pushed regulatory legislation through Congress, after initially opposing regulation, to reduce competition in the industry. Kolko's *Railroads and Regulation* spawned a series of studies that refuted (Martin 1971; Hoogenboom and Hoogenboom 1976) or modified (Sanders 1981; Freitag 1985; Rubinson and Solokovsky 1988) his claims. This much is clear – by 1887, segments of every interested group advocated regulation. What is most interesting about the positions taken by these groups is not so much that they disagreed over *whether* to regulate railways, but that they agreed that regulation was the only possible way to govern the industry. Railroad customers who hoped to prevent price fixing advocated a regulatory agency. Railroaders who hoped to gain federal enforcement of their cartels likewise advocated a regulatory agency.

The first phase of the debate concerned whether to regulate railroads. The second phase concerned what should be regulated. What is most striking about these debates is that both sides argued that their positions were backed by the same principle of political order. Both contended that they sought to prevent the concentration of power in an entity alien to the natural political community. In the debate over *whether* to regulate, railroad customers claimed that they wanted to contain the powers of railroads, and railroads themselves initially argued that they hoped to contain state powers. In the debates over *what* to regulate, railroad customers argued that cartels should be outlawed because they concentrated economic power, and railroads argued that cartels should be enforced because they were the only preventative against amalgamations.

Arguments for regulation. For most of the 1870s the railways fought against regulation and their customers fought for it. The railways had challenged the constitutionality of state-level railway regulation, but in *Munn v. Illinois* (94 U.S. 113, 1877) the Supreme Court found that states had the power to regulate railways because they were "affected with public interest." States could set maximum transport rates, and they could set interstate rates in the absence of federal regulation. Regulatory proponents believed that the federal government held the power to regulate interstate traffic, just as states held the power to regulate intrastate traffic. Minions of the railroads argued before Congress that only states had the power to regulate commerce, and argued before state legislatures that only Congress could do so. To further confuse Congress on the issue of constitutionality, the Court reversed its stand on state-level regulation in 1886, by holding that states could not regulate shipments beyond their own borders (*Wabash, St. Louis and Pacific Railway Company v. Illinois* 118 U.S. 557, 1886).

The 1884 hearings of the Congressional Committee on Commerce brought out all of the major players in the railway regulation debate. The proponents of regulation saw railway combinations as an impending threat to economic liberty and to progress itself. Arguing the case of commercial interests was Simon Sterne – who also served as attorney for New York's Board of Trade and Transportation, member of the governor's blue ribbon commission on governmental reform, and prosecutor in the Hepburn committee investigation of the railroads in New York.

> The reason why you cannot with reference to the railway interests allow things to take care of themselves, and why legislation is necessary in relation to that great interest to insure fairness to the individual, is because railways are in their nature of a monopolistic nature. (U.S. House 1884, p. 120)

Sterne insisted that railways were qualitatively different from other enterprises because they held natural monopolies. The invisible hand of the market did not govern monopolies, hence the visible hand of regulation was needed. In 1884, Representative John Davis Long, Republican from Massachusetts, used the same argument to contend before the House that it was the duty, and constitutional right, of Congress to halt rate discrimination:

> What is the evil, then, at which we should direct legislation? It is the evil of unjust discrimination and undue preferences. . . . Shippers make complaints . . . that by favoritism on the one hand and discrimination on the other, in the form of special rates, drawbacks, private contracts, &c., they are wronged; that thereby one mercantile house is enriched at the expense of the ruin of another; that one local shipper is bolstered up and his neighbor crushed out by the malice or the interest of the railroad company, and that the natural and fair

competition of commerce and trade is destroyed by the artificial and partial preferences and discriminations of these great overriding public carriers. . . . This evil, so far as it is involved in interstate commerce, we are in duty bound to meet, and so far as that I have very little question of our constitutional power to throttle it. (U.S. Congressional Record, 48th Congress, Second Session, 1884–85, p. 43)

Railways had used their monopolies over regional transport to abridge the economic liberties of citizens. In one way or another, proponents of regulation attacked that evil (Kolko 1965). Market competition was natural and fair; monopoly was neither. Proponents of regulation made substantially the same claims that advocates of state-level regulation had made. They came down on the side of supporters of antitrust legislation, who suggested that the state had a duty to sanction practices that restrained trade in order to safeguard economic liberties (Fligstein 1990).

Economic concentration in huge trusts and cartels threatened traditional economic liberties in the minds of Americans. The huge combines that emerged from the 1880s endangered independent railway entrepreneurs as well as certain farmers, shippers, and manufacturers. They seemed unnatural to Americans, who had seldom seen firms with more than a hundred employees, and they threatened more than economic liberties. They "seemed to be mysterious mutations, the consequences of some evil tampering with the natural order of things. They were not merely economic freaks but also sinister new political forces – powers that had to be opposed in the name of American democracy" (McCraw 1984, p. 77). It was incumbent upon Congress to protect the United States from huge railroads that held the fates of farmers, industrialists, and men of commerce in their hands.

Arguments against regulation.   Opponents of regulation likewise argued that tyranny threatened the American polity, but tyranny in the form of concentrated state power. The greatest threat to economic liberty and freedom, they held, came from state expansion. They contended that the attempt to interfere with railroads was part of a broad post-bellum federal expansion that was fundamentally unconstitutional. A Mr. Depew, representing the New York Central Railroad Company, argued before the Committee on Commerce:

I have observed how the pendulum of public opinion on the question of constitutional construction has swung in the last one hundred years. We started with the old Confederation, with the idea that the absolute veto power must reside in the sovereign States. That led to such disagreements that our present Government was constructed and we had our Constitution. The ideas of Hamilton prevailed for about twenty years, and then came the school of Jefferson, which ultimated in the Kentucky resolutions of 1789, and finally in the time of the civil war the constitutional exercise of power by the government had been ciphered down to nothing. Upon that question half a million men lost their lives, and he most liberal construction of the Constitution came to be not only the ruling idea of the people but an absolute passion. That led to the grasp of power by the Federal Congress which would have astounded Jefferson and astonished even Hamilton. (U.S. House 1884, p. 26)

This grasp of power could lead only to the corruption of the government and denigration of the polity. Opponents of regulation played on American anti-concentration sentiments and the belief that statism brought graft and the disintegration of governmental integrity, a belief that had been fueled by the Credit Mobilier scandal and state and local aid scandals. Mr. Sellers testified:

I say if this entire aggregate wealth (of the railroads) is brought under the supervision and control of the Congress of the United States, it would have in a short time a corrupting and degrading influence on the Federal government, and would have a tendency to introduce a battle of usurpation greater than any done in the Supreme Court of the United States, in the reports of which I think there are many, and the time has come to call a halt and allow the corporations to be ruled by the people at home and not by the Congress of the United States. (U.S. House 1884, p. 24)

Experiences with the corruption of federal, state, and local aid to railroads fueled arguments against renewed federal intervention. The railroads now argued that any expansion of public power threatened to lead to a similar end. State interference with pricing would be particularly susceptible to graft.

Regulation opponents argued that even the current agitation for regulation represented the abuse of political leverage. The railroads took up the theme that commercial men had conspired to install railway regulation – against the wishes of the public at large and against the basic tenets of the Constitution – because they stood to profit from lower transport rates. The representative of the New York Central Railroad argued before the Committee on Commerce:

This whole agitation [for railway regulation] began . . . by a syndicate in the city of New York composed of not over thirty persons . . . If this evil [railway monopolization] was so great, if this injury was so

monstrous, if this baronial power was so tremendous, if this feuda-
tory power was so strong . . . would there not be such meetings of
citizens, such delegations of commercial bodies, such delegations
from persons in all pursuits that Washington would be filled and
Congress overwhelmed by the people coming here in their power and
stating clearly their grievances and demanding a redress for them?
Where are your delegations? Where are your petitions? Gentlemen,
open your desks – bring them out. They do not exist. (U.S. House
1884, p. 25)

Proponents of regulation responded in kind by suggesting, on the contrary, that the railways had captured control of politics and had prevented the passage of regulatory legislation in order to guard their
profits. The chairman of the committee responded: ·

I do not doubt, if the people had the power to tax others as the
railroads have, to raise money to send their representatives here, they
would be as fully represented as the railroad companies. (U.S. House
1884, p. 25)

The Credit Mobilier scandal, and the plethora of similar scandals in
other realms that plagued the Grant administration, led Americans to
believe that powerful lobbies might capture congressional votes and
subvert democracy at any moment (Thompson 1983). Every government action became suspect.

Opponents of regulation also argued that the writers of the Constitution had precluded federal regulation as part of their vigilant effort to
prevent the rise of federal tyranny. Section 8 of Article I of the Constitution reads: "The Congress shall have power . . . To regulate commerce
with foreign nations, and among the several states, and with the Indian
tribes." The railroads argued that commerce, so described, referred
only to trade conducted *between* the boundaries of sovereign states and
not to railways because they operated *within* the boundaries of sovereign states even when carrying goods from one state to another. Mr.
Sellers, representing the Philadelphia, Baltimore, and Wilmington Railroad Company, argued before the House committee that the Constitution afforded states full authority over business conducted within their
boundaries, including the business of railways and turnpikes which in
all cases exist within the boundaries of states, and contended that the
Commerce Clause applied only to control of commerce on waterways
located between states: "Commerce is commerce continued upon wa-
ters that are not within States" (U.S. House 1884, p. 11).

Sellers also contended that Congress wanted to claim for itself the powers that rightly belonged to the separate states, and thereby usurp their sovereignty. This appeared to be a direct threat to the American polity: "In the state of nature, by the law of nations . . . land within a nation is wholly under the control of that nation. It is a violation of the sovereignty of a nation to attempt to regulate anything as to its land. Now, when we formed our Constitution we recognized that as to land within a State" (U.S. House 1884, p. 16). This argument framed the movement for regulatory legislation as an effort to transform the federal government into a centralized despot that denied the regions their rightful authority to govern themselves.

Railwaymen also argued, more narrowly, that the commerce clause gave Congress the power to regulate commerce itself, but not the power to regulate common carriers. Mr. Depew of the New York Central argued: "I draw this distinction. You do not [propose to] regulate the commerce, you [propose to] regulate the carrier, and that you cannot do" (U.S. House 1884, p. 27). Mr. Sellers likewise suggested that even if one grants that Congress may regulate interstate commerce over land, "regulation as to the charges that an individual or corporation may make . . . is wholly beyond the power of Congress" (U.S. House 1884, p. 21). Proponents of regulation countered that these arguments were frivolous and made nonsense of the Constitution.

Some scholars have argued that the Constitution severely constrained Congress's ability to govern the railways. At the time, the railways did contend that the Constitution precluded regulation, as well as all of the more interventionist solutions that emerged on the Continent. Yet the Constitution by no means served as an iron cage in the realm of transport policy. Long before the railway regulation debates, Alexander Hamilton had advocated a more active federal role in the private economy, and just two decades earlier Congress had encountered little resistance to land grant legislation that made Washington a bondholder in private railroads, and included a number of controls, albeit ineffectual controls, over their management. In the decades following the establishment of the Interstate Commerce Commission, all sorts of regulatory agencies with considerably greater powers than were being proposed in the 1880s were found to be entirely consistent with the letter and intent of the Constitution. In short, federal powers to intervene in industry have been interpreted variously over time, because the Constitution's utterances about commerce and manufacturing are imprecise. But both sides in these debates believed their arguments would be most forceful if couched in terms of concern about the concentration of powers. And both sides saw the effectiveness of arguing that their opponents were trying to capture the political process for illicit purposes.

What should be regulated? The debate over *whether* to regulate soon shaded into a debate over *what* to regulate. The main debate came down to a single issue: Should Congress use regulation to outlaw cartels or to enforce their agreements? Both sides in the debate framed their arguments in the anti-concentration rhetoric that had become emblematic of industrial debates in the United States. Those who vilified cartels expressed peculiarly American sentiments, for in other countries railway industry concentration was taken for granted. As B.H. Meyer remarked in 1903: "In England, Germany, France, and Austria, the limitations of competition were recognized in the deliberations accompanying the granting of the first [railway] charters" (p. 21). Hence, most European governments prohibited the construction of railroads that would compete with existing lines, and most used public powers to set railway rates. British legislators recognized that cartelization and amalgamation were a natural course for the railway industry to take, and French legislators actually mandated the concentration of the industry so that the number of railroads declined from thirty-three in 1846 to six in 1859, where it remained. Where other governments sought to directly control the behavior of railroads, Americans insisted that the government should control the behavior of firms indirectly by sustaining competition in the industry.

Shippers and grangers, who had proposed federal regulation in the first place, argued against pooling because it undermined price competition. In their minds, pooling was tantamount to monopolization. In a letter to the House Committee on Commerce Josiah White, representing New York merchants, presents both sides of the pooling debate. In places he quotes a letter to the committee from Albert Fink, who had organized the trunk line pool among the huge railways in 1877:

> Too many 'commercial' men have felt the want of 'competition' during the *regime* of the 'pool' to agree with the averment that competition is 'kept alive by it' and 'that it is the best protection against consolidated monopoly,' on the contrary, their experience and belief is that 'pooling' is a potent instrument to abet 'consolidated monopoly.' As to whether pooling is a preventative of 'unjust discrimination,'

experience of the 'commercial man' is that it has not been a preventative. Last year, I take it, was the most successful year of the 'pool.' Ask the members of the produce exchange, who have dealings upon its floors, whether there were any discriminations in favor of individuals or cliques, and if they will divulge their knowledge they will testify to discriminations in the shape of rebates, &c., which the general public would call unjust. (U.S. House 1884, p. 154)

Representative John Reagan of Texas, who was Congress's most active proponent of regulation, argued that pooling threatened the very foundation of democracy:

The railroad managers recommend a universal pool, or federation of all the railroads in the country, and its recognition and the enforcement of its provisions by law. This [the] Congress has no power to do under the Constitution. If this could be done it would be the creation of one vast and overpowering monopoly out of the many which now exist; and such a course would enable it to control the transportation and commerce of the country, and soon perhaps to control the legislation of the country, and to become the masters of the people and of their liberties. (U.S. Congressional Record, Session 49, 1886, p. 7282)

Fink and his fellow railwaymen disagreed. They suggested that the only way to protect small firms, and prevent monopolization, was to *enforce* pooling. Trunk line rate competition had been extremely costly to large firms, which now backed efforts to fix rates that would assure them handsome returns. They argued, before Congress, that pooling protected small firms. Railway baron William Vanderbilt argued that pooling could protect against monopolization by preventing large firms from swallowing up their smaller competitors (Gilligan, Marshal, and Weingast 1986). By enforcing pooling, Congress would end the reckless rate discounting that was decimating the ranks of small railway firms. Vanderbilt's argument was not unfounded. Large railway firms had made a practice of discounting rates on the routes where they faced small competitors who only controlled a single stretch of track. By absorbing a loss for a short period of time, big railroads could bankrupt their smaller competitors, one by one, and extinguish competition. They often bought out their competitors when the price was right.

Railway interests wanted to see government enforcement of pooling because their privately organized pools had broken down. Countless pooling arrangements were attempted in the 1870s, only to disintegrate when one railway discounted rates (Kolko 1965, p. 17). The railroads also wanted Congress to outlaw a number of other practices, such as rebating, that undermined pools. But Reagan's argument eventually won Congress over – an anti-pooling clause was included in the final regulatory bill. The paradox of anti-cartel policy was soon recognized: "While cartels were illegal, . . . mergers that created monopolies or near monopolies . . . were not illegal, even if they were intended to restrain trade" (Fligstein 1990, p. 35). In the end, the act encouraged the creation of large integrated firms in the railway sector just as the Sherman Antitrust Act did in other sectors of the economy (Hollingsworth 1991, p. 41).

In sum, congressional debates over railway regulation demonstrate a tension between two American ideals with the same source. Proponents of regulation, from the Anti-Monopoly League of New York to the farflung Grange chapters, attacked the concentration of economic power and control that surfaced in naturally monopolistic railway companies. They saw that concentration as evil and corrupting. Opponents of regulation argued against the concentration of administrative power in the state itself, and cited the anti-statist ideals of the writers of the Constitution as well as the corruption that characterized state and federal railway promotion.

In the debates over railway regulation, a new, positive, industrial policy paradigm began to emerge to fill the void left by the demise of the paradigm of active localism. Government policies that would locate control over industry in market mechanisms, and thereby deny it to public administrators and dominant firms alike, could actually create economic growth. Policies that would shield the natural private economy from external manipulation were increasingly spoken of as part of a positive secular theory of rationality. The report of the first Committee on Commerce, submitted 12 June 1882, concludes:

> The machinery which carries on the great transportation of this land is so complicated that any disturbing element from an outside source may work great harm to the business and producing interests as well as to the transportation interests. (quoted in U.S. House 1884, p. 5)

Here, federal action was posed as a threat to the natural balance of freely operating economic forces that produced economic efficiency. These words hardly depict a transportation system that was financed largely by state and local governments that had every intention of influencing the course of railway development to their own advantage.

The Interstate Commerce Commission and the Court. The Act to Regulate Interstate Commerce of 1887 established the Interstate Commerce Commission (ICC) to oversee several new restrictions on railway practices and to adjudicate conflict in the industry. The final version of the bill represented a compromise that satisfied no one completely. It prohibited pooling in no uncertain terms, but it included a weak prohibition against short haul rate discrimination. It required that railways charge "reasonable" rates, without establishing criteria for determining reasonableness. And it required that railroads post their rates and give ten days' notice of rate changes. The commission was to be composed of five presidential appointees with staggered six-year terms who could not have an interest in carriers subject to the act, and could not participate in proceedings involving any firm they did have an interest in. The ICC was modeled loosely on the adjudicative commissions of Massachusetts and Illinois. Some proponents of regulation had proposed to leave enforcement to the courts; however, the idea of an independent commission that would be able to instigate investigations and proceedings against railroads, as well as respond to grievances, won favor. One of the principal concerns of the pro-commission legislators was that a system of enforcement that depended on the courts would make the smallest rural shipper a co-equal litigant with the largest railroad network. Such a system would poorly protect the rights of rural farmers, minor shippers, and small manufacturers against the railroads. As Senator Shelby Cullom, Republican from Illinois, argued:

> Leaving out of consideration the natural disinclination of the average shipper to engage in litigation with a corporation which may have the power to determine his success or failure in business, and to enter the lists against an adversary with ample resources and the best legal talent at its command and able to wear out an opponent by the tedious delays of the law, it is plain that the average shipper is still at a great disadvantage in seeking redress for grievances under the common law, which places upon the complainant the burden of proof and requires him to affirmatively establish the unreasonableness of a given rate or the fact of an alleged discrimination. (quoted in Skowronek 1982, p. 146)

A commission could, Cullom reasoned, investigate grievances and thereby remove the onus of proof from the complainant. In addition, a commission might undertake investigations on its own initiative to ensure that abuses were not concealed by the reluctance of small shippers to file grievances in the first place. An independent commission would be the common person's ally in government against powerful railroads with influence over the courts and legislatures.

The courts were not entirely excluded from the task of railroad regulation, however. The bill called for the commission to employ the courts to enforce its decisions in cases of noncompliance. Court enforcement was perhaps inevitable because the Constitution afforded citizens avenues for judicial review of administrative decisions. As a result of the clause calling for judicial enforcement, virtually all of the commission's controversial decisions were appealed through the courts, and for nearly two decades the Supreme Court routinely came down on the side of railroads, with the effect of declawing the commission. Between 1887 and 1905, the Supreme Court found against the commission in fifteen of the sixteen rate cases that reached it (Stover 1970, p. 113).

Early scholarship suggested that the ICC suffered a prolonged failure because the Court had been captured by railroad interests, but recent scholarship has converged, in a sense, on an explanation that finds less fault with the judiciary and lays more blame on American state structure. Gabriel Kolko points to a long history of conservative Court interpretations of executive powers, and contends that in this case the Court did not uniformly favor the railroads. Rather, "the Court believed in laissez-faire and judicial supremacy, and took a *literalist* view of its application" (1965, p. 81; see also Hurst 1956, ch. 1; Gold 1983). The Court often ruled against the railroads, but it repeatedly supported judicial supremacy over executive authority. In a similar, if more institutional, vein, Stephen Skowronek suggests that traditional interest group perspectives do not account for the fact that the effort to regulate railroads "lay in complete collapse by 1900" (1982, p. 131). For Skowronek, American state structure afforded too little autonomy to the executive branch. The Supreme Court had the power to assert its own authority over the matters that concerned the ICC, and that is just what it did.

Accordingly, in the *Alabama Midland Ry* decision of 1897 the Court found that railroads did not have to obtain the commission's permission to ignore Section 4 of the act, which prohibited long haul-short haul discrimination. The decision left it to injured parties to seek adherence through litigation. Furthermore, because the act had been vague as to the powers of the new Interstate Commerce Commission, when the Court decided that the ICC did not have the power to set maximum rates or proscribe individual rates in the *Maximum Rate* (1896) and *Social Circle* (1897) cases, it was not gutting the legislation so much as offering a conservative interpretation of an act that was unclear to begin with (Kolko 1965, p. 83).

Support for the expansion of the commission's powers was galvanized around the turn of the century in response to the rapid consolidation of the industry. Between July 1899 and November 1900, 10 percent of the mileage of American railway firms was absorbed by other firms (Kolko 1965, p. 87). By 1906, seven railroads owned 62 percent of the United States' 193,000 miles of line (Stover 1970, p. 93; Chalmers 1976, p. 1). As Robert La Follette, the Republican senator from Wisconsin, would argue:

> I believe that the Government of the United States is bound to exercise all the power of a sovereign nation to the end that the regulation and control of its commerce shall be just and equitable, not only to shippers, but to the whole public. It is bound to see to it that the country is not handed over to a monopoly and to selfish interests. (quoted in Chalmers 1976, p. 14)

Teddy Roosevelt spearheaded new legislation that would broaden the powers of the commission. In a series of bills passed between 1903 and 1913, the commission gained the sort of control over railway rates its original architects had hoped for (Bernstein 1955; Kolko 1965; Chalmers 1976).

Although recent scholarship suggests that the ICC's long struggle for power is a textbook case of weak administrative capacities, because the executive branch held narrow powers and the architects of the Interstate Commerce Act had done little to fortify them, it has a harder time explaining the reinforcement of the commission after the turn of the century. In this case, administrative incapacities did not lead to permanent failure because the dramatic concentration of the railway industry revived the specter of illicit domination in the minds of Americans. The United States' institutionalized antipathy toward concentrated authority won out over her perennially weak state structure.

In short, in the realm of railway pricing and competition, Americans perceived problems where they saw powerful actors abridging the economic liberties of weaker counterparts, and they conceived solutions that permitted the government to establish and enforce ground rules for competition. Only in the United States did the state insist on enforcing competition in an industry that was, by the accounts of all experts, a natural monopoly. Only in America did the state pursue an anti-pooling policy that was "demonstrably irrational" for three decades, up to the Great War (Skowronek 1982, p. 130). France perceived pricing and competition through different lenses. The French took the railway industry to be naturally monopolistic from the 1830s. They saw this as potentially problematic, and as remedies conceived publicly brokered regional mergers, public rate-setting, and governmental controls over management. Their solutions were the furthest thing imaginable from the United States' solution of enforcing market competition. The British perceived predatory behavior on the part of large railroads to be the principal problem in the realms of price-setting and competition. The solutions they conceived – prohibiting mergers and encouraging cartelization in order to prevent predatory price slashing on competitive routes – were designed to harbor independent railroads against the destructive practices of their larger competitors. British solutions protected independent railroads, at the cost of undermining market competition. Indeed, nowhere were private trusts and cartels perceived as a threat to economic liberty as they were in the United States – at the turn of the century most European courts were still enforcing cartels (Cornish 1979).

Conclusion

The railway industry was one of many American settings where industrial governance was transformed during the nineteenth century. Across a wide range of industries, local activism in industrial promotion gave way to state and federal regulation. Gradually, those policies became part of the industrial structure. They soon gained gredit for prosperity. The United States developed an industrial culture based on competition in open markets that was not quite like that of any other nation. Britain's was probably closest, but British industrial culture exalted the entrepreneur rather than the market as the source of industrial dynamism, and the industrial policy paradigm aimed to guard entrepreneurs at the expense of market mechanisms. The United States' industrial policy paradigm fortified markets at the expense of small entrepreneurial firms. Ultimate authority over the economy rested in market selection mechanisms. As Andrew Shonfield would later argue, in the United States "if public authority has a choice, it generally opts for the role of referee rather than that of manager" (1965, p. 330). What this has meant is a series of policies designed to support market mechanisms and an industrial policy paradigm in which those supports represent not state intervention, but efforts to sustain the economic state of nature. By contrast, the sort of positive government role in the promotion of particular firms and industries that characterized the earliest railway policies came to represent irrational, unnatural meddling. Chalmers Johnson dubs this a market-rational state. As opposed to plan-rational states, "a regulatory, or market-rational, state concerns itself with the forms and procedures – the rules, if you will – of economic competition, but does not concern itself with substantive matters" (1982, p. 19). Thus, the United States' modern industrial policy paradigm came to follow Henry Carter Adams' (1954 [1886]) prescription of raising the "plane of competitive action" by setting the ground rules for business competition. And it came to rely on Charles Francis Adams' (1893) administrative prescription of using adjudicative procedures to carry out this strategy.

The particular problems Americans perceived in the four major functional areas, and the solutions they conceived, contributed to the change from local activism to federal market enforcement in American industrial policy. The idea that economic life should be organized by subnational governments seeking to promote regional economic development in collaboration with business interests gave way to the idea that the economy should operate as a free market under a state that established ground rules for competition.

American political culture led citizens to perceive a unique series of problems in the railway industry. They saw railway planning as something that demanded the input of subnational governments, who could represent the community interest by influencing the route decisions of private railroads. They saw finance as the natural province of state and local governments, but saw public financial control over private railroads as problematic. Later they perceived a special kind of evil in the corruption of railway aid schemes, and took corruption as evidence that government participation in economic life is destabilizing and inefficient. Americans believed that technical and managerial coordination should be left to the railroads, and that public opinion would operate to ensure that railroads served the public interest. Americans later perceived a problem when public-spirited railroads that adopted safety devices were disadvantaged relative to self-interested railroads that refused to undertake the expense, and government came to require the use of safety devices. The issues of competition and pricing produced perhaps the industry's greatest problems in the American mind. When they saw railroads behaving monopolistically to restrain the trade of their competitors, or their clients, Americans discerned foul play.

American governments conceived two general sorts of solutions to these problems. In the first stage of railway development, they solved the problems of planning and financing by using positive public action to stimulate the development of private-sector enterprises. They never sought to create public enterprises, but neither did they recoil from using public authority to achieve collective economic aims. These first policies brought the principle of community self-rule to the realm of economic life. In the second stage of railway development they solved problems of pricing and competition by introducing adjudicative mechanisms that made the state into an umpire enforcing the ground rules of competition. This second type of solution brought the principle of federal government as neutral arbiter in political life to the economic realm.

The market-enforcing policy paradigm that was outlined in the Act to Regulate Interstate Commerce was also to be found in the contemporaneous Sherman Antitrust Act. That paradigm came to prevail in the twentieth century. The ICC's regulatory framework was soon extended to other sectors of the economy through the Federal Reserve Board (1913), Federal Trade Commission (1914), Federal Radio Commission (1927), Federal Power Commission (1930), Securities and Exchange Commission (1934), Federal Communications Commission (1934), and National Labor Relations Board (1935). And the Sherman Act's antitrust paradigm for controlling restraints of trade throughout the economy was elaborated in a series of subsequent laws. The paradigm for protecting economic liberties and promoting growth that was embodied by industry regulation and antitrust has become so entrenched that in recent decades Washington's knee-jerk reaction to industrial problems of all varieties has been to enforce market competition. This is true even for sectors that other nations consider to be naturally monopolistic, such as telecommunications, where the Justice Department (U.S. v. Western Electric Company, Inc. et al. 1987) broke up a long distance monopoly, and air transport, where the administration ended price regulation to reinvigorate competition. The market enforcement paradigm has been sustained even for sectors, such as electronics, where the experiences of such nations as Japan and France have vindicated industrial cooperation.

Finally, important elements of the local activism paradigm have survived into the twentieth century, even if the early practice of direct public investment in private enterprises was discredited. As Leon Lindberg and John Campbell (1991, p. 357) argue, state and local governments have been "continuously involved in the constitution of sectors and industries since the colonial period." Yet in the twentieth century, states and localities have avoided direct public investment in favor of tax abatements, construction incentives, "enterprise zones," and other indirect stimuli (Graham 1991). Thus a remnant of rivalistic state mercantilism can still be found at the local and state levels of American government, operating in tandem with federal and state policies designed to effect growth by enforcing the rules of an idealized free market.

3. France

Introduction

Scholarship on nineteenth-century France is characterized by a peculiar sort of schizophrenia. On one side stand those, from Alexis de Tocqueville (1955) to Simon Schama (1989), who see surprising continuity in French political traditions despite the remarkable transformations of that century. France began and ended the century with a centralized, professionalized, state bureaucracy dedicated to orchestrating the nation's military, political, and economic life from Paris. On the other side stand those, from George Lefebvre (1947) to Eric Hobsbawm (1962), who see a radical transformation of the nation's political ideals and very *raison d'être*. France began the century as a nation of subjects oriented to serving the wealth and power of their ruler and ended the century as a nation of citizens oriented to the practice of democracy.

What was most remarkable about French railway policy during this age of revolution was its constancy. During the infancy of the railway industry France was in one moment a monarchy, in the next a republic, and in the next an empire. Nonetheless, France pursued a coherent strategy for promoting and controlling the railways that launched the transition from the Colbertian tradition of mercantilism to a modern industrial policy paradigm based on state concertation. Soon after railway technology appeared in France, the state had made the key strategic decisions about how to govern the industry that would guide policy through the twentieth century. How could France's industrial policy paradigm demonstrate such constancy when the political order was in such flux?

The unique contribution of the American case was to illustrate that national industrial cultures and policy paradigms are not static; the United States' policy paradigm changed dramatically from active localism to market enforcement. The unique contribution of the French case is to illustrate that political culture, as I have been using it to encompass the institutionalized means to political order, is not simply a reflection of political ideals. The *purpose* of France's political structure varied as widely as was imaginable during the nineteenth century. At one point, the purpose of the political structure was to serve an emperor, and at another it was to execute the republican social contract. However, the institutionalized *means* employed to achieve public purposes varied little: Social order and collective goals were to be achieved through the concentration of political control in a central state bureaucracy that could effect the will of a single ruler, and alternately the will of the public. What was constant about the nineteenth-century French state was the institutionalized means emplpyed to achieve political purposes. Just as decentralized institutions had served both colonial and democratic rule in the United States, centralized institutions served both monarchical and republican rule in France. Core characteristics of political culture and state structure survived revolutionary changes in state purposes.

In France, as in the United States, the logic of the political order was projected onto the emergent industrial order during the nineteenth century. Absolutism had been vital to the unification of France, and to its survival as an independent sovereign power, because absolutism enabled the crown to orchestrate the military might of farflung lords who might otherwise have pursued their own interests, to the detriment of the Crown. Absolutism carried the idea that central state concertation of society held the nation together, and the idea that the military escapades of independent seigneurs menaced the nation. This same logic of state coordination of private activity infused policies to promote the railways. Private interests might well provide the impetus for railway development, but the state must orchestrate and plan the endeavor or risk seeing the nation's capital and talents squandered by self-interested entrepreneurs. France's unique policy paradigm of state concertation of private activity would survive into the twentieth century to color subsequent efforts to promote growth. At the core was the notion that state experts can best mobilize private interests in the service of the nation's collective ambitions (Hayward 1986, p. 19).

Before the advent of railways, the French state had played a greater role in the economy than either the American or British states, in part because absolutism had elevated the powers of the king at the expense of those of local lords. Absolutism increased the king's direct interest in agricultural outputs, and thus the Crown came to promote farming innovations with the aim of raising revenues. Meanwhile, Jean-Baptiste Colbert, the architect of Louis XIV's mercantilism, had designed public policies to maximize public revenues for military endeavors. To promote commerce and production, the Crown had subsidized major infrastructural projects by providing public capital and by guaranteeing the return on private capital. Thus, even before the railway age the state had played a leading role in promoting economic growth and in developing large-scale endeavors that would benefit the nation as a whole. This set the stage for railway development.

French state structure

French state centralization has been traced to the requisites of unifying and holding together a culturally diverse territory without natural geographic boundaries to the east and south. Absolutism had entailed central political control in the form of a pyramidal bureaucracy, centrally appointed provincial administrators, a standing army under the control of the crown, national taxation, and codified law in the Roman tradition (Anderson 1974, p. 17). During the nineteenth century, political turmoil was not accompanied by revolutionary changes in the structure of the French state. Instead, the basic structure of government survived the political chaos to leave the indelible imprint of the *ancien régime* on modern industrial culture. As Tocqueville put it, governmental centralization was

> a glorious achievement, . . . but I do deny that it was an achievement of the Revolution. On the contrary, it was a legacy from the old regime and, I may add, the only part of the political constitution of that regime which survived the Revolution – for the good reason that it alone could be adapted to the new social system sponsored by the Revolution. (1955, p. 32)

Although some credit Napoleon rather than *ancien régime* rulers with the structure of the modern state (Suleiman 1974), there is little doubt that *ancien régime* institutions had set the foundation of, and provided raw material for, the nineteenth-century state.

The locus of political authority. The *ancien régime* gradually ended the principle of local seigneurial autonomy – *chaque seigneur souverain dans sa seigneurie* – by posting *maîtres de requêtes* (later, intendants) to assume the political duties that had been carried out by local seigneurs (Machin 1977). The intendant in turn exercised control at the level of the canton through his appointed subdelegates. To maximize the allegiance of intendants to the Crown, and thereby preclude the rise of local strongholds, kings followed despotism's customs of choosing men of humble origins, posting them to alien regions, and regularly rotating their assignments (Tocqueville 1955, pp. 35–38). Although venality came to pervade the system of allocating positions, the Crown retained the right to name office-holders to prevent the rise of local strongholds (Fischer and Lundgreen 1975, p. 499).

Political control was amassed under a pyramidal bureaucracy in which the king's *conseils* carried his will to the nation by directing the activities of the intendants. In consequence, as Tocqueville would write during the railway age, under the *ancien régime* "there was no city, town, village or small hamlet in France . . . which could exercise its independent will in its own affairs, or administer its own goods. Then as today, the administration held all Frenchmen in tutelage" (Tocqueville 1955, p. 122). One result of political centralization was the relative lack of political inputs from outside of the state. The consolidation of power minimized the points of contact between the central state and sectoral or regional representatives (Hall 1986, p. 165). And if the relative weakness of independent interest groups had facilitated the rise of centralized political authority (Hoffmann 1963), the absence of openings for political participation in turn stunted the growth of labor, agricultural, manufacturing, and commercial organizations to mediate between citizen and state (Crozier 1973, p. 79). In consequence, lines of communication between the center and periphery tended to be one-directional.

The concentration of powers. Under the old regime, political powers were highly concentrated in the central state. As Stanley Hoffmann argues, "The need for authority had been inculcated by the Old Regime, whose patient destruction of autonomous sources of power had tended to make all groups dependent on the state" (1963, p. 10). The regime changes between 1789 and 1870 did nothing to alter this; instead, they replaced the king with a premier in one moment and an emperor in the next. One corollary of concentrated political authority was that the actions of the administration were not subject to judicial or legislative challenge, as they were in the United States. Another was that France had a stable bureaucracy that could weather regime shifts without disintegrating. As Tocqueville (1955, p. 202) argues, revolutions and coups toppled the small cadre at the top of the government pyramid but left the foundation intact.

The legal system. Napoleon revived the principles of the Roman *jus publicum*, which extended back to the fifth century B.C. but which had disappeared under the Merovingians and Carolingians (Birnbaum 1979). Roman law depended on a civil code that was written by the state *de novo*, rather than on the legal traditions of the *jus commune*. This system of civil law implied rational canons of evidence, absolute notions of property rights, and a professional judiciary (Anderson 1974, p. 26). Most important, the civil law tradition dictated that the formal legal code served as the ultimate arbiter of the law, whereas in common law countries, laws were subject to judicial review because the law itself was subordinated to legal tradition. Thus the judgments of policymakers in France were immune to interference from the courts (Merryman 1969, p. 3). The pinnacle of the judicial hierarchy under the *ancien régime* was the regional *parlement*. The *parlement* of Paris disputed royal interference with its edicts, and claimed the right to veto new laws by insisting that new legislation concord with existing law (Fischer and Lundgreen 1975, p. 494). The Crown had responded by establishing royal tribunals that the king could dominate. At the end of the fifteenth century, the Crown established the Grand Conseil to rule in the last instance, and later when the Grand Conseil asserted too much independence, the Conseil Privé under the Chancelier. These extra-judiciary conseils further insulated the king from judicial interference and consolidated political power (Tocqueville 1955, p. 52).

In the civil law tradition, post-1789 regimes maintained ultimate authority over the law and its interpretation. In the revolutionary spirit of the times, the masterful Code Napoléon of 1804 had offered a comprehensive and modern system of rational laws. The Code was designed to offer unambiguous rules so as to preclude the need for judicial interpretation, and was to be comprehensible to the common man: "As in many Utopias, one of the objectives of the Revolution was to make lawyers unnecessary" (Merryman 1969, p. 29). The idea was that the state was to promulgate rules with unambiguous meaning, and that policymakers, rather than courts, should be the source of clarification.

Office-holding and public expertise. In the process of expanding the central state, French monarchs developed a modern civil service that was unparalleled elsewhere in Europe. The regimes of the nineteenth century sustained the civil service and maintained state centralization, which enabled them to consolidate political power and undermine the threat of revolt at the periphery. One element of the professionalized civil service was public engineering *corps* and *écoles*. France's early standing army had spawned a cadre of military engineers (Corps du Génie) under Louis XIV in 1697, to which entrance was regulated by examination. During Colbert's heyday, the king had appointed military engineers to oversee public works projects, but in 1716 the king constituted an independent Corps des Ponts et Chaussées for bridges and highways that stationed engineers in the regions. An École for bridge and highway engineers was founded around 1747, at the time of the founding of the school for military engineers, but the École des Ponts et Chaussées only became a fullfledged engineering school in 1775 (Weiss 1982, p. 11). Finally, in 1795, France established the École Polytechnique, which became the primary training ground for state technicians (Fischer and Lundgreen 1975). The École des Ponts et Chaussées was soon accepting the best graduates of the École Polytechnique and introducing them to the methods of bridge, tunnel, aqueduct, highway, and canal construction (Smith 1990). By the dawn of the railway age, state engineers had planned some 18,000 kilometers of royal and departmental roads, as well as a vast system of canals and waterways that was far from complete (Audiganne 1858, p. 263). Not all of France's engineers were trained and employed by the state – the private École Centrale des Arts et Manufactures, founded in 1829, trained engineers for many industrial purposes – but most transport engineers were associated with the state (Weiss 1982, p. 3).

State fiscal capacities.   The French state had long played a more active role in the economy than its American and British counterparts, in part because its military exploits demanded huge sums of money. By some accounts, as early as the 1600s, France was collecting four times as much in taxes as Britain (Birnbaum 1979, p. 63; but see Tilly 1986). Late in the seventeenth century, Louis XIV's comptroller general of finance, Jean-Baptiste Colbert, concocted a set of economic policies that included protectionist tariffs, manufacturing incentives, promotion of agricultural innovations, and public capitalization of transport with the dual aims of stimulating growth and expanding public revenues (Zeldin 1977, p. 1044; Kesselman 1977; Tocqueville 1955, p. 41;

Shonfield 1965, p. 77). Colbert and Louis XIV labored under the notion that France's military and economic accomplishments glorified the monarchy in the process of enriching the monarch. The *ancien régime* state had not only been identified with the king ("L'État c'est moi"); the entire kingdom had come to be viewed as the domain of the king ("L'État c'est à moi") and hence as his responsibility (Rowen 1961). The end result was a system of capital allocation that was, in contrast to that found in the United States, centralized and dominated by the public sphere.

Integral to this system of public orchestration of economic life was the practice of state construction and operation of canals and turnpikes to stimulate commerce and provide military transport. In 1666, Colbert convinced the king to back the construction of what would become the Canal du Midi, and thereafter the state took the lead in building the nation's canals (Pilkington 1973). Louis also built "royal roads" from Paris to the far reaches of the kingdom with *corvée* (forced) labor at a time when other nations left road construction to localities and private interests – nearly two centuries after Colbert's heyday American turnpikes were still being built and operated by private parties.

Colbertism marked a high point of developmental statism, but the central tenets of the system survived into the nineteenth century. As Legendre concludes of that century: "Our economic administration was not merely Napoleonic; it was properly speaking that of Louis XIV" (1968, p. 385). Colbertism had a particular influence on the finance sector in France. Government orchestration of finance during the eighteenth century contributed to the relative underdevelopment of private finance. By undertaking major infrastructural projects such as turnpikes and canals, nationalizing significant sectors such as tobacco, and guaranteeing the return on private capital in certain vital industries, France had used public capital and undertaken public risk where other countries left matters to private finance (Lévy-Leboyer 1964, p. 417). In consequence French banks were relatively underdeveloped, and bankers were unusually cautious (Ratcliffe 1972, p. 208). One private-sector corollary of state initiative was a bourgeois investment ethic that favored stability over risk – French bankers were known for their inclination to sacrifice the opportunity for great economic return when it was accompanied by high risk (Hoffmann 1963, p. 6).

French political culture. Again, by political culture I mean the means to political purposes, and to social order, that are institutionalized in state structures rather than the political purposes themselves. There is no one-to-one correspondence between political culture and political ideology. Thus, in France a traditional political culture that placed sovereignty over the polity in the hands of the central state could be consistent with monarchical ideals in one age and with republican ideals in the next. France's enduring government institutions produced a vision of social order in which the state remained aloof from individual interests in order to direct the disarticulated actions of self-interested citizens toward public goals. That vision was variously characterized by Descartes, Rousseau, and Saint-Simon but it was clearly rooted in French experience. In France, absolutism had served to shore up the extremities of the kingdom and to quell internal feuding. The age of revolution merely reinforced absolutist notions of political order. To monarchists, excessive private political power threatened to result in revolution from below. To republicans, excessive privatism threatened to result in the domination of France by elites. Thus, groups with divergent political ideologies embraced a common prescription for political order: "The Napoleonic theory of the supremacy of the state was found to be perfectly compatible with the theory of democracy. The state was supreme because it was the representative of the people" (Suleiman 1974, p. 22). Rousseau depicted a democratic state governed under a social contract, in which individuals alienated their rightful sovereignty to a higher authority.

If political sovereignty was located in the separate communities in the United States, it was symbolically and materially located in the central state in France. From before the revolution of 1789, the French located economic sovereignty as well in the state in the belief that "the effective conduct of a nation's economic life must depend on the concentration of power in the hands of a small number of exceptionally able people, exercising foresight and judgment." The economic paradigm associated with this view presumes that growth depends on "The long view and the wide experience, systematically analyzed by persons of authority" (Shonfield 1965, p. 72). That view brought together several traditional lines of thought, as Peter Hall has argued. First was the notion that the public interest could be achieved only by a central power that could direct self-interested action toward collective goals – an idea that descended directly from the character of feudalism on the continent and the very real need to centralize national military control.

Second was the "longstanding French view, traceable to the enlightenment equation of freedom with rule by law, that legitimate state action must be based on rules" (Hall 1986, p. 177). It followed, in short, that in a setting where absolutism had been a military necessity, freedom could not come from protections for individuals, as in Britain, but had to derive from rules that limited the discretionary powers of the state. Third was the emergent notion of rule by expert technocrats. The state could maximize both justice and rationality by governing through highly trained officials whose status as civil servants and whose expertise could ensure that public policies would be technically efficacious and politically neutral. Expertise and isolation from the political system guaranteed that state bureaucrats would concoct public policies that were both just and rational (Hall 1986, p. 177).

In the railway industry, the logic of French political culture was translated into a principle of modern industrial organization. By the late eighteenth century, public policy had been organized around the idea that the state's neutrality in economic matters assured its ability to act rationally (Hall 1986, p. 176). During the nineteenth century, France consolidated a vision of economic life in which the capitalist state sits above society in order to transcend the interests of particular groups of capitalists in the pursuit of the long-term vitality of capitalism as a whole. The railway age saw concertation generalized from a theory of political harmony and order to a secular theory of industrial rationality.

French railway policy

The United States saw a radical transformation of industrial culture, and the state's industrial policy paradigm, during the nineteenth century. France saw the emergence, elaboration, and evolution of a single industrial culture and a single industrial policy paradigm over the course of the century. The seamless evolution of French industrial policy from the time of Colbertian mercantilism was possible in part because the old regime's economic goal – of enriching the monarchy by increasing the nation's wealth – was entirely consistent with the emergent project of the modern state – of achieving progress by increasing the nation's wealth. This seamless evolution was also facilitated by the fact that the French state had developed administrative capacities that were equal to the task of coordinating economic life and that would not produce the sort of policy failures that emerged in the United States.

When the French faced the four functional realms of railway development that the United States faced, they perceived substantially different problems of governance and conceived entirely different sorts of solutions to those problems. When it came to railway planning, the French were most concerned to ensure that a coherent and rational rail system would be planned. If individual entrepreneurs and local governments were allowed to establish such lines as they pleased, the French believed, the result would be a disarticulated set of poorly built railroads that would soon fall into disrepair. The only solution they could conceive was government planning to guarantee that private railroaders would build a coherent system of lines that would serve the nation's needs. When it came to finance, the French perceived a problem in the idea of private finance, which would give altogether too much power over this key sector to private parties. How could the state fulfill its natural duty to build the infrastructure for this new form of transport when public coffers were empty? One solution was to attract private capital with in-kind public subventions, which would allow the state to retain control but engage private funds. A second solution was to guarantee the return on private capital invested in railroads; this had the advantage of requiring no public capital up front. The French perceived the control of technical and managerial matters by private parties and markets as a threat to the integrity and quality of the rail system. Thus, government technocrats seized control over all technical and managerial matters, in a way that precluded problems of interfirm coordination.

The French perceived pricing and competition in the industry very differently from the Americans. From the very beginning, the French believed that market competition would not be the source of the industry's dynamism, as did the Americans. Instead, they saw private competition as a force that could potentially disrupt the progress of the industry and destroy France's efforts to provide efficient rail transport. To preclude destabilizing competition for passengers and freight, the state established six huge regional monopolies. To preclude the disarticulation that would result from hordes of self-interested entrepreneurs engaging in unrestricted market entry, the state refused to charter independent lines. To preclude irrational market forces from determining which routes would be served, the state operated trains on routes that lost money and later guaranteed profits on all routes. In each realm, public policy afforded control to state technocrats and denied entrepreneurs and market mechanisms the capacity to shape the course of the industry. Mindless markets could never produce rational decisions about the industry, and self-interested entrepreneurs could not be expected to look out for the nation's interests. Industrial efficiency demanded careful, expert, oversight.

Was the extensive state intervention in the rail industry a rational response to economic backwardness, as Alexander Gerschenkron (1962) is wont to argue? I contend that state intervention in the rail industry, which appeared in about 1825, was the direct legacy of earlier tutelage of transport. The engineering corps that took over control of railroads dates back to the early eighteenth century, and France's activist role in highway and canal development dates to before the reign of Louis XIV. David Landes (1969) takes the technical schools established and expanded in France and elsewhere on the Continent to be instances of the "new institutional instruments" Gerschenkron prophesies. But as John Weiss (1982, pp. 11–12) points out, this argument is plausible only if one is "not too strict about when particular countries began to overcome their 'economic backwardness'" because France's technical schools preceded the country's efforts to follow Britain's path to industrialization. The "economic backwardness" perspective confuses correlation with causation by taking longstanding governing institutions to be responses to nineteenth-century events. Military absolutism had generated strong states on the Continent long before Britain's industrial revolution.

Planning

Early state planning: 1823–1833

From the moment the importance of railroads was appreciated in France, a central question posed by technocrats and private rail interests was, "How could the nation plan a rational and coherent network of rail lines?" From that moment there was little doubt that state engineers would be responsible for setting out the nation's railway routes. No other solution was put forth. The only real question concerned how public-sector engineers would effect their plans. In the 1820s, the state's civil engineers influenced the route decisions of private railway promoters by using their authority to grant charters. Thereafter, the corps' engineers won the exclusive right to plan the nation's private railroads.

Before the importance of the railroads was understood in France, private entrepreneurs were allowed to plan their own railed roads to transport coal in horse-drawn carriages. The first recorded railway in France was a horse-drawn line opened by 1782 to carry coal from Mont Cenis to Le Creusot. Over the next decades, a number of groups built lines that, like the Mont Cenis line, operated without the benefit of public charters (Lefranc 1930, p. 301). The first railway charter was granted in 1823 to a group needing the state's powers of expropriation to build a coal-carrying line connecting Andrézieux with St. Étienne. During the 1820s, the corps gave less attention to railroads than they did to canals, and this was largely because they saw more promise in canals. Louis Becquey, director of the Ponts et Chaussées in the 1820s, had believed that canals would form the backbone of the transport system, and hence railroads should not dominate the corps' attention. At first, Becquey did not envision a major government role in the railways because, unlike a highway or canal, "a railroad is a veritable machine, best left to private enterprise" (quoted in Smith 1990, p. 666). Becquey and his colleagues may have been slow to recognize the importance of these "dry canals" in part because the state had committed to a hugely ambitious system of canals in the 1820s, and they were reluctant to concede that a technology that might well supplant water transport had appeared. Even well into the 1830s, some deputies argued that railroads were little more than "de luxe roads" for the wealthy that could never fulfill the nation's basic transport needs (quoted in Adam 1972, p. 40), and as late as 1880 the Ponts et Chaussées took on the construction of an ambitious new project to expand water transport.

Nonetheless, the engineers at the Ponts et Chaussées claimed the right to determine the course of development even for this ancillary form of transport. In the early years, the corps pursued two strategies for influencing the route decisions of private entrepreneurs to guarantee that the rail network would be well integrated with water transportation. First, they sketched plans for the half-dozen routes they deemed most vital, and advertised competitions to attract private parties to bring those routes to fruition. The group that guaranteed the lowest rates would win an exclusive concession for the route, providing they promised to fulfill certain technical requirements. Lines from St. Étienne to Lyon and from Andrézieux to Roanne were conceded after such competitions, and a line from Toulouse to Montauban was conceded to the sole interested party following a competition that failed to elicit proposals. Two other competitions – for lines from Paris to Pontoise and from Paris to Orléans – elicited no interest whatever. The Ponts et Chaussées hoped, with these competitions, to ensure that the lines it deemed essential were provided to the nation at no cost to the state.

The corps' second strategy to encourage private parties to build the lines *it* deemed essential, and discourage them from wasting their energies on lines it deemed unimportant, was to deny virtually every unsolicited application. In the decade that began in 1823 it refused over thirty such applications on the grounds of public interest (Villedeuil 1903). In response to an application for a line from Roanne to Digoin, it argued: "Where there is already a national road, when there will shortly be a second artificial water route . . . it is impossible to recognize . . . the public utility of a third rival route" (quoted in Lefranc 1930, p. 212). The Ponts et Chaussées sought to ensure that the nation's private resources would be put to good use, and because it had already chosen the routes that were, in its mind, most urgently needed, all proposals for other lines failed to meet this test. Of course, even lines that were needed by the nation would fail to serve the public interest if they were poorly built. Thus the corps began by scrutinizing plans' technical particulars. It required detailed blueprints that included cross-sections of all grades and specifications for culverts and embankments, and it summarily rejected proposals that lacked such details. In response to a proposal for a line from Paris to Rouen, it argued: "In the final analysis, the draft presented of this project amounts to no more than a few lines drawn on the map of Cassini . . . Not on the basis of such vague documents can the state delegate to a company the right of compulsory expropriation" (quoted in Lefranc 1930, p. 313). Private promoters who had their own routes in mind thus faced an impossible situation in these early years.

Two contrasts with early American chartering stand out. First, in France charter granting was undertaken by an administrative subunit that had no special legislative mandate to award charters. In the United States, state legislatures alone could grant charters to railroads, and no state agency could intervene to prevent a rail promoter from putting his charter application before lawmakers. Second, calculations about public utility followed completely different principles in the two countries. In the United States, the financial viability of a line was taken to be proof of its public utility, and the existence of willing investors was taken to indicate its financial viability. In France, public officials took a much wider view of the matter and asked whether the line in question would make optimal use of the nation's resources. In doing so, they contended that the economy demanded close government scrutiny and orchestration lest individuals pursue goals that conflicted with the nation's collective interest.

The maturation of public planning

The year 1833 brought a change in route planning, when the unsuccessful applicants for a route between Montrond and Montbrison, which the corps had rejected on a technicality, complained to the legislature. Parliament overruled the corps to grant the concession on 7 July 1833, but the complaint opened a Pandora's box for rail promoters because it stimulated the legislature to reconsider how the nation's railroads should be planned. The government had indicated a willingness to turn over full control of railway planning to state engineers in September of 1832, when it appointed a commission to outline how the state might undertake the engineering studies needed to plan rail connections between Paris and Belgium, Strasbourg, Marseille, Bordeaux, and Nantes (France, Moniteur Universel 1832). The Montbrison debate brought out a number of private parties who promised to provide the nation with railroads at virtually no cost to the state. However, the strongest voice came from the Minister of Commerce and Public Works, Adolphe Thiers.

Arguments in favor of public rail planning were couched in terms of both efficiency and political order. Efficiency arguments centered around the ministry's capacity to see beyond the petty interests of individual entrepreneurs and self-promoting localities. Thiers argued that the corps was best suited to plan the national routes; whereas private rail promoters would choose routes that served only their needs, the corps would sketch out routes with the nation's larger interests in mind. Thiers captured the sentiments of a majority of deputies and journalists when he argued that if capitalists were left to their own devices, France would find itself with a mess of disjointed, poorly constructed stretches of track that would ill serve the nation. Capitalists would squander the nation's resources on local projects without a view to constructing a national network. In asking for funds to plan a national rail network, Thiers argued:

> A crowd of capitalists directs their investments sometimes in one direction, sometimes in another, without any master plan. In this way, no coherent rail system would be developed that could serve the country in the main directions. We want to help you to remedy this situation . . . the Government, which employs a corps of competent engineers, could itself prepare preliminary studies. It could study the routes, estimate the expenses and revenues, do preliminary surveys; with a national plan in mind it could direct the efforts of capitalists in order to prepare continuous and dependable transportation for the nation. (France, Moniteur Universel 1833, v. 86, n. 120, p. 1206)

In turn, Thiers argued, the well-conceived plans drawn up by the Corps would attract entrepreneurs who would build the nation's railroads without public funds: "We would hope that, once the studies are achieved, we would receive many applications for each line" (France, Moniteur Universel 1833, v. 86, n. 120, p. 1206).

Centralized planning by the corps could also preclude the irrationalities of redundancy and overcapacity. Local participation in planning, the corps believed, would undermine the coherence of the national plan and thus it had already taken steps to subdue private planning efforts. It had, in effect, refused to consider unsolicited charter applications. Moreover, its extensive review process discouraged all but the most dedicated, and stubborn, applicants for the lines the corps advocated. When Émile Periere requested a charter in September of 1832 for a corps-planned line from Paris to St. Germain, the corps spent three years making fourteen separate inquiries and investigations before recommending that the Chamber grant the charter. In 1833, to quash local planning and execution of lines, the Chamber dictated, as Inspector General Picard's 3500-page official rail history reports:

> Railways undertaken by the state or by private firms, with or without tolls, with or without subsidization by the Treasury, with or without the expropriation of public lands, may not be executed except by virtue of a legal charter, which may only be passed after an administrative inquiry. (Picard 1887, v. II, p. 25)

Thereafter local and regional governments could not plan or charter lines of any sort – even private lines that were to be built on private soil – without the blessing of the ministry and the Chamber.

The corps' belief that local participation could only disrupt the rational planning of railways extended to localities' efforts to lobby the state's route planners. The engineers steadfastly refused to pay attention to cities that pleaded for rail depots. Hence the efforts of the inhabitants of Versailles to gain a depot on the Paris-Orléans line failed, for although the Ponts et Chaussées admitted that a Versailles depot would double the line's traffic, they preferred a direct route that would save 16 kilometers (Dunham 1941, p. 17). In the belief that the railways' primary advantage was speed, the Ponts et Chaussées also disregarded Rouen's petitions in planning a line from Paris to the sea: "It is necessary in principle that [railroads] follow so far as possible the shortest line between the extreme points", but the *Courrier Francais* responded that the ministry's lines went "a little too much as the crow flies" and ignored the potential for increased traffic that intermediate depots provided (quoted in Lefranc 1930, p. 327). The Chamber also treated local involvement as suspect, indeed the efforts of Gironde and Loiret deputies to win state-planned lines stimulated action on a bill to allocate complete authority over route decisions to the Ponts et Chaussées in order to prevent political meddling from interfering with the corps' far-sighted, rational plans (Lefranc 1930, p. 321).

Beyond these arguments that private promoters and local governments would pursue their petty self-interests without a view to France's longterm needs, technocrats and deputies also frequently argued that state engineers were singularly capable of engineering railroads. The fact that the corps had already undertaken the planning and development of some 29,000 kilometers of royal roads and 24,000 of departmental roads, and was in the midst of executing an extensive system of canals, certainly contributed to the belief that the corps was best suited to designing the nation's rail system (Price 1983, p. 37; Pilkington 1973; Price 1983, p. 31; Caron 1979, p. 69). It was widely believed that the French state employed the nation's most able engineers. As a German observer noted at the end of the century:

> To establish railways no country was better prepared because of its administrative organization [than France] . . . Thanks to the competence of their engineers who, in Grands Écoles infused with military discipline, have received an education at once scientific and administrative, and who subsequently acquired considerable practical experience in the execution of impressive public works – canals, dams, ports, and national highways. (Kaufmann 1900, p. 6)

This view was widely held by French observers in the 1830s, and the corps frequently underscored its own expertise when it deplored the quality of the route plans it received from private parties. Thiers argued before the Chamber that private plans were often so inadequate that "the Ponts et Chaussées is obliged to have the plans redrawn" from scratch (France, Moniteur Universel 1833, v. 86, n. 120, p. 1206).

In addition to the various arguments concerning efficiency, a second argument emerged from the corps that linked state planning to France's history of achieving political order and domestic peace through deliberate efforts at military, social, and cultural integration. A state-planned network that linked the provinces with Paris represented a unique political opportunity to further unify France's diverse linguistic and cultural traditions by erasing the distances between regions. Many of those who lived on French territory still held stronger allegiances to their regions than to the nation. This state, which had grown up to tie together the nation's disparate regions, could complete its task of unification by taking command of the new technology. As Inspector General de Berigny of the Ponts et Chaussées argued:

> The importance of the railways is uncontestable, especially if they are constructed properly because considerable distances will disappear, so to speak. The unity of France, which foreigners admire and which gives us our strength, will be fortified; travel will multiply, our knowledge will expand, prejudices will be erased; the populations of our oldest provinces, as business relations grow among us, will extend their affections outside of the lands where they were born and soon we will be but one country. (quoted in Kaufmann 1900, p. 5)

A decade later, Deputy Dufaure, who headed the Chamber's railway committee in 1837, reiterated de Berigny's plea for the state to plan a network that would help to unite France's periphery with Paris:

> The borders of the ancient provinces have disappeared; vestiges of their old idioms are being erased; the era when they were consolidated will soon be forgotten history . . . Brought together in military camps, in schools, under the same masters and under the same flag, the French of the North will become the brothers of those of the South – everything that can strengthen national unity should have the highest priority. (quoted in Picard 1887, v. I, p. 123)

As early as the 1830s, then, the French made a link between their design for political order and their design for industrial efficiency that contrasted sharply with what we saw in the United States. American discussions of planning and charters had posed active localism as the foundation of democratic political order, and as a rational strategy for growth. France's discussion posed central state orchestration as a strategy for furthering political order, and as a rational strategy for growth.

Thiers and his supporters prevailed, and on 27 June 1833 the Chamber allocated 500,000 francs to the Ministry of Commerce and Public Works for the preparation of a national plan for railway development. By 1835 the Ponts et Chaussées had, under the auspices of the 1832 commission, completed a plan for five major routes consisting of 3,600 kilometers of track. In the meantime, the Ponts et Chaussées held a moratorium on railway concessions to prevent the establishment of lines that would not be vital to the nation's network. To an application for a line from Paris to Roissy, it responded: "The Administration cannot permit the avenues to the Capital to be seized with a view to private speculation in such a manner as to impede the general interests of the country" (quoted in Lefranc 1930, p. 323).

The original plan was the brainchild of Émile Legrand who began a 15-year term as director of the Ponts et Chaussées in June 1832. *Efficacité* was the codeword of the plan. France's radiating system was organized around three unusual ideas about efficiency in railway planning. First, Legrand and his corps planned routes that would connect secondary cities with Paris as directly as possible. An efficient system, they believed, would bring passengers and traffic from the minor cities directly to Paris. Thus, instead of designing lines that snaked through the countryside to encounter as many cities as possible, the engineers designed unswerving trunk lines that connected Paris with provincial centers, with tributary lines branching off to smaller towns. Second, lateral connections between peripheral population centers were of little concern to the corps because the main idea was to unite the nation's extremities with Paris. Thus the original plans drawn up by Inspector General de Berigny in 1832 were modified to eliminate two proposed inter-provincial routes "faithful to the Napoleonic spirit of centralization and already prejudiced in favor of a radiating system, [the corps] set aside such of these lines as did not go through Paris" (Lefranc 1930, p. 325). In particular, it abandoned a planned east-west trunk line that would traverse the south of France from Bordeaux to Marseille, and another north-south line in the east connecting Strasbourg with Lyon. Third, because the goal was to connect the provinces with Paris, the planners did not think to facilitate interregional connections *through* Paris. Each of the trunk lines terminated at its own station at the perimeter of Paris, so that interprovincial traffic – both passenger and freight – had to be carted across Paris by road to get from one trunk line to another. This system bore striking parallels to the structure of political authority in France, where sovereignty resided in Paris and lines of political authority ran directly from Paris to the provinces. French political centralization had spawned a plan for the most centralized rail network in the world.

The political turmoil of the 1830s delayed the Chamber's passage of legislation that would give the national plan the force of law. In those years, each government managed to appoint a committee of deputies to review the ministry's proposal, but each fell before it could pass comprehensive legislation (Dunham 1941, p. 22). Nonetheless, in 1835 the Ponts et Chaussées began to lay the groundwork of the system it had designed by recommending that the Chamber approve charters for segments of the network. In 1842, the Chamber finally passed into law the national plan that had been revised under Deputy Dufaure's railway committee in 1837. The act established a network of eight major lines fanning out across the country from Paris with a total trackage of 3600 kilometers (Dunham 1941). The Bordeaux-Marseille line had been revived, but as a way to connect Marseille with Paris given that a more direct route was impracticable. Over the next decade the Ponts et Chaussées granted dozens of concessions to private companies to build segments of this system.

Railways of local interest. In the light of what was occurring in the United States, where state and local governments were involved in the planning of virtually every railway, France's continuing efforts to exclude subcentral governments from railway planning were quite remarkable. Yet the French state did make arrangements for the construction of tramways and short lines "of local interest," including lines of less than 20 kilometers in length that were exempted from Chamber approval under the 1833 legislation. The Chamber first granted the right to build three railways "of local interest" to Alsace in 1836. Over the next decades, applications for local-interest feeder lines were rare because the trunk lines were still incomplete, but in 1865, in response to renewed interest, the Chamber gave control over local lines to the centrally appointed préfets. Départements, communes, and individuals were forbidden to construct even private coal-carrying lines on private property without the acquiescence of the General Council of the Préfecture. Moreover, the right to expropriate land, which was almost always needed, could only be extended after the national Conseil d'État pronounced a declaration of public utility for the project (Kaufmann 1900, p. 110; Picard 1918, p. 23). Supervision of tariffs and general operations was given to the local préfet. Thus, regional governments could only plan even the most minor of tributary lines under the close supervision of the appointed préfet and only with the accord of the Conseil d'État (Kaufmann 1900, p. 109; Doukas 1945, p. 109).

Refinements and extensions of the national plan.   After the national rail plan was accepted by the Chamber in 1842, major refinements and additions were adopted in 1852, 1859, and 1883 when the railways were reorganized. The new blueprints did nothing to alter the corps' control over planning, and did little to alter the main directions of service. In 1852 the regime of Napoleon III reverted to a plan from the early 1830s that would establish six trunk lines extending out from Paris. The plan created six regional monopolies, discussed in more detail later, that were to serve separate geographic areas. Each was to assume control of existing secondary lines in the region and to construct such additional lines as the corps directed. Five of the lines extended in different directions from Paris, and the sixth was formed when the line to the southwest was divided into two operating regions. Between 1852 and 1862, concessions were granted to private firms for the Réseau du Nord, the Réseau de l'Est, the Réseau de l'Ouest, the Réseau de Paris à Orléans, the Paris-Lyon-Méditerannée, and the Midi. The plans of 1859 and 1883 expanded the network by adding secondary and tertiary lines, but did little to alter its principal directions.

In sum, the main problem the French perceived in the realm of railway planning was not, as in the United States, how to ensure that local governments and private parties would undertake planning. Americans believed that the best strategy was to allow state and local governments, with the aid of private railway promoters, to compete to plan and build the lines they hoped would bring them prosperity. The French were concerned to see that a rational and coherent plan for a national network would be developed, and presumed that private entrepreneurs and local governments could only undermine the achievement of an efficient plan. The French perceived willing entrepreneurs who sought to build railways of their own design not as representing the great promise of the future of transport, as did their American counterparts; rather the French saw private promoters as potentially disruptive to efforts to design a coherent network. The British perceived yet another problem in the realm of railway planning. Parliament was particularly concerned to avoid using public powers to expropriate private lands, and thereby abridge property rights, in cases where railway promoters were more interested in speculation than in actually providing rail service. French bureaucrats were not similarly concerned about protecting landowners against undue state expropriation, but they were concerned about the prospect of private railwaymen employing the nation's land, labor, and capital to build lines that would not be of true public utility. Perrhaps what most sets French policymakers apart from their American and British counterparts is that at no time in the century did the French view the railroads as properly private undertakings.

The French conceived a single solution to the problem of designing a railway network. From the moment they recognized the importance of the railways, the French thought only of state planning. It literally did not occur to the French to have the major rail routes planned by private firms. As the Saint-Simonien Henri Fournel argued in 1838:

> Noteworthy fact! The day when the idea of setting up a railroad system in France was sufficiently mature for preliminary steps to be taken for its execution, not only did no one question the intervention of the Government which had the honor of the initiative but no one proposed that one or several companies should undertake the studies: by unanimous consent it pertained to the state alone to stand aloof from local preferences to consider solely the general interest. (quoted in Lefranc 1930, p. 321)

In the earliest debates, the French articulated a vision of rail policy in the mold of military absolutism – the central state alone had the perspective to subdue petty private interests in the name of the nation's collective goals. Rousseau's political philosophy echoed this theory of government by suggesting that political order resulted when individuals gave over their natural sovereignty to a central state that could act in the collective interest. Nothing remotely resembling America's rivalistic state mercantilism was considered in France. The French state gave the regions only the most perfunctory of roles in railway planning. Localities had neither the right to grant concessions independently nor the power to influence decision-making surrounding concessions. Thus, the ordinance chartering the St. Étienne line reported dutifully that the government had acted upon the advice of the local Consulting Chamber of Arts and Manufactures, but failed to mention that the Chamber had voiced the opposition of local stage coach and barge owners who were threatened by the railroad (France, Bulletin des Lois 1823, 7th ser., v. 16, n. 591, p. 193; Lefranc 1930, p. 305).

Finally, even a cursory comparison makes it clear that early French transport policy helped to shape the key interest groups involved in railway planning debates. In the United States, federalism had produced regional, rather than sectoral, interest groups comprising manufacturers, merchants, and farmers who were great boosters of canals and railroads. In Britain, easy access to public transport charters had produced a powerful anti-rail lobby comprising large canal owners. In France, government-built canals and turnpikes contributed to the rise of a public corps of transport engineers who made up an interest group in their own right, and who were disposed to favor rail expansion for the very reasons they had favored canal expansion. Thus, public policy had produced regional pro-rail interest groups in the United States, a sectoral anti-rail interest group in Britain, and a technocratic pro-rail interest group in France. These groups turned out to be the most important players in the initial railway debates, with the possible exception of private rail entrepreneurs themselves.

Finance

The American debates over how to finance the railway0 revolved around the proper locus of control over the economy. Because political authority was symbolically located in the individual and his local community, Americans concluded that economic order would result from the exercise of individual and community self-determination. They believed that the federal government should leave it to private parties and subnational governments to take the lead in railway development and finance. The French state symbolized political order very differently, and as a result French debates over railway finance had a very different character. Because sovereignty was institutionally situated in the central state, the French asked whether it was right for the state to alienate its responsibility for transport facilities to private economic actors. In the United States, federal financial incentives were depicted as a threat to the integrity of the polity. In France, *private* domination of the railways was depicted as a threat to the polity. In brief, the problem the French perceived in railway finance concerned how the state could orchestrate the growth of the industry without footing the entire bill; the problem the Americans perceived concerned how the state could stimulate development without usurping private control.

The source of the French view of railway finance was the state's history of pursuing public goals by transcending the interests of private actors. The public interest was associated with the state's imposition of order on individuals. By contrast, in both the United States and Britain the public interest was identified with the sum of private interests, so that collective goals were achieved when each individual pursued his own ends.

The policy options the French conceived to the problem of imposing order on private actors ranged from public construction and operation of the railroads to joint public-private construction with private operation. Because the French polity was composed of independent, self-interested, private actors who were constrained and guided by the state, French citizens came to believe that their economy should likewise be composed of independent actors under the tutelage of the state. In the policy paradigm that was being worked out, private initiative and public orchestration were both key ingredients of industrial rationality.

French political traditions called for the state to guard against the rise of intermediate, private, powers that could come to dominate subjects. Likewise, protections against the rise of powerful, independent *economic* parties soon came to be integral to French republican ideology, and to economic thought. Just as in the United States the political ideal of economic liberty became intertwined with an industrial policy paradigm oriented to precluding the "restraint of trade" by enforcing market competition, in France the political ideal of a direct link between citizen and state, free from private intermediation, became intertwined with an industrial policy paradigm oriented to preventing strong economic actors from interfering with state tutelage of private enterprise.

The debate: Should the railways be public or private?

The debates of the 1837 and 1839 parliamentary commissions studying the railways encapsulate French thinking about public and private roles in the rail industry. By the late 1830s there was wide agreement that only the state had the vision, collective purpose, and technical proficiency to design a coherent, rational, rail network. Thus the real debate over the nature of the industry concerned who would build and operate the routes planned by state engineers. The players in these debates looked quite different from the hodge-podge of promoters and local officials who debated railway finance in the United States' town halls and state houses. State-building in France had generated a powerful group of government technocrats, with roots in the traditions of military engineering. Railroad entrepreneurs employed private engineers to make counterarguments; thus in France the criteria for participation in the debate over rail finance was technical expertise rather than political clout. But even before the debates of the 1830s, the eventual fate of the French railroads was sealed. Since the Montrond-Montbrison charter of 1833, charters had stipulated that concessions were temporary, and that the rail lines would revert to the state after 99 years.

The arguments for public railroads.   As the preeminent analyst of early rail debates in France describes the principal argument for public railroads, "The construction of all major means of transport was analyzed as a right of sovereignty of the state, which had, on the other hand, a duty to assure the profit of the collectivity" (Adam 1972, p. 29). In the early debates, deputies linked France's greatness with its zealous statism. What set France apart was its activist state, they argued, and France's continued strength depended on public coordination of private activity. For the proponents of statism, France had been run on clear principles that suggested it was the responsibility of the state to assume control of this new technology. As one member of the first railway commission argued:

> My opinion . . . is based on the fundamental principle underlying the great success of France . . . We regard (great transportation lines) as inalienable public property of the State. And in France the State is charged with making the routes that unite the extremities of the kingdom. (quoted in Adam 1972, p. 29)

These deputies maintained that the state could not in good conscience alienate control over transport to private parties. One deputy argued: "The State has the right and duty to execute all of the major railway lines, just as it executed the royal roads, and I don't think it can delegate this right of sovereignty" simply because the Treasury faces a fiscal crisis (quoted in Adam 1972, p. 31).

In addition to the sentiment that it was the state's duty to provide the transport infrastructure, proponents of public railroads argued that the state alone was motivated by the public interest, and thus the state alone could build and operate an efficient rail system to serve the nation. This sentiment dated back at least to Louis XIV and Colbert's stress on quality in goods and services, which contrasted sharply with the British stress on productivity. In Colbertian thought, quality was always the "decisive factor," and where guaranteeing high quality is valued over reducing cost, a strong argument can be made for state regulation of production (Shonfield 1965, pp. 78–79). In the case of the railways, state engineers wanted France to build the best lines in the world, and that meant doing the job themselves to ensure that it was done right. French engineers believed that without constant oversight of both construction and management of the railroads, France would find itself with a poorly built and badly managed rail system. Should cost be the primary consideration when a transport system that would serve the nation's military and commercial needs was at stake?

By permitting profit-driven entrepreneurs to take charge of the railroads, the state would place the rail system at risk. One deputy argued that the state "can and must *make sacrifices which Companies recoil from* which have neither the aim nor the motive" to build lines that would benefit the nation regardless of cost (quoted in Adam 1972, p. 30). The state must spare no reasonable expense in building railroads. Deputies characterized private groups who wanted to build railroads as "squanderers of the citizens' wealth who speculate with the nation's purse, and frauds of all types" and insisted that the state must take charge of building lines to ensure their success (quoted in Adam 1972, p. 40).

Deputies contended that private construction would result in cheaply built roads that would waste the nation's resources. They characterized the national economy as a zero-sum game, reasoning that the French would pay for the railways whether through the Treasury or the stock market. Thus it was foolhardy to turn construction over to private firms that would scrimp on construction and try to extract as much as possible in profits. One deputy argued, "The concession is, by nature, a precarious tactic which, whether it succeeds or not, is inadvisable for a nation that is willing to bear the cost [of railways] but wants to pay no more than it must" (quoted in Adam, 1972, p. 32). In the end, they reasoned, the nation would pay more than it should for private railroads because bidding for concessions would drive down the quality of the roads, private construction would drive up the cost, and private builders would bastardize the corps' efficient route plans to save money. As Thiers argued, "Thinking of nothing but immediate profit, they would sacrifice the proper routing of a line to avoid an expense or go out of the way to meet with great profit" (quoted in Smith 1990, p. 670).

Legrand argued, in a debate over public versus private construction of a line from Bayonne to Bordeaux, that private sponsors would only build a sturdy line if the state underwrote the cost. Thus the state might as well build the line itself:

> The engineers would much prefer direct execution out of Treasury funds . . . the state will indirectly derive from the opening of a railroad across the *landes* of Gascony many advantages . . . A large subvention would be indispensable if concessionaires were to be forced to execute solid and durable work; and in that case the concession method loses its principal advantage, which is to relieve the state of the whole or at least of a very large part of the expense. (quoted in Lefranc 1930, p. 323)

Why permit private parties to build railroads when the state was better equipped to build them and when the state would end up paying the cost in one way or another – either by providing subventions in the first place or by paying the later cost of replacing poorly built lines?

Arguments for private railroads.   The most compelling argument for making the railroads private was simply that the state could not afford to finance rail construction in the foreseeable future. In 1840, Council-president Thiers argued:

> There is an invincible argument against state construction . . . today when our most essential public works projects are incomplete and moreover our military projects have not been started, I say it is impossible to demand 5 or 600 million from the legislature for other public works. (quoted in Peyret 1949, p. 203)

In addition to the pragmatists who preferred to see the railways built quickly than to wait for the condition of the Treasury to permit public construction, some analysts contended that private construction and operation under strict state controls would cost the nation less than a public rail system. They argued that private initiative was more cost-effective than public enterprise. The profit motive led private entrepreneurs to seek the least expensive solutions to engineering, construction, and operating problems; by contrast, the state's engineers had shown themselves to be callous to issues of cost. Although the Ponts et Chaussées would build exemplary railways, their exacting construction standards would cause costs to skyrocket. Deputy Jaubert argued, "While the [Ponts et Chaussées's] engineers have technical expertise, they do not have business sense. When they undertake large construction projects, it is always in the most expensive manner" (quoted in Adam 1972, p. 31). Backers of private railways argued that entrepreneurialism had succeeded in Britain, and that self-interest ensured that railways would be efficiently constructed and operated by private concerns. In 1838, Deputy Legentil put the rhetorical question to his committee members: Would "the private companies not execute the lines more quickly and for a better price than the state?" The same opinion was expressed by Deputy Billault, who argued: "As builder, the state would neither be faster, better, nor cheaper than the companies" (quoted in Adam 1972, p. 39). In those years, the committees put some stock in arguments that private firms could build the lines most economically, and of course the companies themselves touted their own strengths. In its *Memoire addressé à Monsieur Le Ministre des Travaux Publics* of 1839, the Paris à Rouen company argued:

> Private industry avidly supports progress, because progress is the foundation of its success. It proceeds without rest with investigations and reports. There are no methods that it does not investigate and attempt to incorporate in its own works that might increase economy and speed. (quoted in Leclercq 1987, p. 163)

Yet this view was not necessarily incompatible with state tutelage of industry. The very same document goes on to extol the virtues of state orchestration of private enterprise: "To succeed private industry needs to be constantly directed" by the state (quoted in Leclercq 1987, p. 163). On the whole, the supporters of private construction believed that the state should give the industry direction, but insisted that private parties were better suited and motivated to operate lines profitably and efficiently. In 1842, another proponent of privatism insisted that private companies should be allowed to decide when and in which order to build the state-planned lines on economic grounds: "Leave it to the instincts of capitalists to research the most profitable routes" and build them first (quoted in Leclercq 1987, p. 162).

In France, the idea that entrepreneurs could play an integral role in rationalizing economic life was quite new during these years. The notion that profitability, rather than quality in goods or dependability in services, was the best measure of *efficacité* did not gain hold among Polytechniciens until the middle of the century. And what William

Reddy (1984) calls market culture was still emerging. The French worldview would never, in the nineteenth century, give to markets, entrepreneurs, and price competition the major roles in producing economic growth that the British worldview gave them. Even in British thinking, the term laissez faire and the associated notion of the importance of entrepreneurial drive did not really gain currency until the 1830s, though this way of thinking had certainly been articulated by Adam Smith. Thus, in the years when France was debating how to finance railroads, it is not surprising that a fully formed rhetoric of private initiative did not appear.

The debate over the efficiency of private financing and construction of the railroads was joined in 1838 by engineers from France's private engineering academy, the École Centrale. In France, and throughout the West, the engineering community was then debating the merits of two competing design strategies. One strategy, which was favored in Prussia and the United States, was to adapt the track to the terrain by climbing and descending hills and valleys, circumnavigating mountains, and making every effort to avoid crossing water. The other, favored by the corps, was to adapt the terrain to allow for the track to be straight and level by cutting hills, filling valleys, tunneling through mountains, and bridging rivers and lakes. Legrand and the corps insisted that although initial costs for this second strategy would be high, in the long run it would pay off by increasing speed and reducing fuel costs. In 1838, École Centrale engineers, supported by private railwaymen, helped to defeat Legrand's proposal for public railroads by arguing that the corps' construction strategy would cost double the projected 1 billion francs, and thus was prohibitively expensive (Smith 1990, p. 671). Again, in 1842, when Legrand proposed his star-shaped network, the École Centrale provided opposition, in the person of Auguste Perdonnet who compiled British and Belgian data to show that the corps' extravagant construction standards would do little to reduce operating costs. Perdonnet had offered the first course on railway engineering in the world in 1837, and as engineer-in-chief for the Paris Versailles railroad he was well versed in practical engineering matters (Weiss 1982, p. 141). Double track, gentle gradients, and wide curves would cause initial costs to skyrocket. Moreover, the meager savings in delays, reduced fuel consumption, and increased speed would not permit the companies to recover these costs. Thus, Perdonnet argued that the state should allow the companies, who would naturally choose the most cost-effective method, to establish their own technical standards as other countries had done (Smith 1990, p. 674). Again, in 1848, under the banner of Second Republic liberalism, École Central engineers called for state engineers to adopt more lax construction standards in order to reduce the cost of building railways. This time the private engineers did not challenge the corps' right to govern technical decisions, but argued that they set impossibly high standards. While private-sector engineers lost this round as well, the idea that private firms would build railroads more economically did not disappear from public discourse after 1842.

Note that in France alone, the debate over how to finance railway construction was dominated by engineers. The corps had become an interest group in its own right as a result of public policies that built up its numbers and powers in the process of creating a system of public highways and canals. Private railroaders responded to the corps' technical arguments in kind by engaging private-sector engineers to fight for their cause. Again, in the United States it was politicians, merchants, farmers, manufacturers, railway promoters – indeed everyone but engineers – who argued over the merits of public versus private financing.

The first state subventions. Even before the Chamber settled on how to finance railway construction, the state had provided two kinds of construction aid on an interim basis. First, in response to the depression of 1837–1839, the state made loans to four companies to prevent the cessation of construction. Second, a law of 7 July 1838 had authorized the construction of a line from Paris to Orléans, but when the same economic downturn caused private subscribers to default on their capital obligations, the government passed a law that would draw new capital by guaranteeing 4 percent interest for 40 years on the initial capitalization of 40 million francs (Leclercq 1987, pp. 182–184). In both cases, public administrators argued that the ministry's plans, which promoted the nation's interest, must not falter as a result of the vacillation of the economy.

The compromise: Mixed construction and private operation

Most proponents of state railroads, including some key public-sector engineers, came to believe that because the state's fiscal situation precluded public construction in the short term, Paris should employ private capital and exercise strict controls over the industry. The commission established to review the problem wrote that in light of the fiscal realities of the day, the state could delegate responsibility for railway construction to well-supervised private companies:

> The commission thinks that railway lines of political and commercial importance should be reserved for State construction; yet if the Companies offer all the necessary guarantees, the State may concede the routes for execution. (quoted in Adam 1972, p. 40)

Even Inspector Legrand, who was one of France's most vocal advocates of public railways, had come to accept that a compromise might be necessary if the railways were to be built forthwith. He argued that as long as the state controlled the industry with the aim of eventual nationalization, private capital could be employed:

> The great railway lines . . . are among the great reins of government; the state must be able to keep them in its hands; and if we are to concede these works to private industry, it will have to be in the form of a franchise, including a decree, in writing, that one day the government will be able to retrieve into its full possession this great means of transport, if the interest of the nation requires it. (quoted in Audiganne 1858, p. 461)

Joint public-private construction did not necessarily mean the state had to recuse itself, Legrand believed. The state could fulfill its duty to the nation by establishing engineering standards, by planning and designing routes, and by carefully scrutinizing construction.

The Law of 11 June 1842 followed the blueprint offered by the 1839 commission to set the ground rules for railway construction and operation for the next century, until the railways were nationalized under the Societé Nationale des Chemins de Fer. Several subsequent reorganizations adjusted the details of construction financing in response to recessions and wars, but those changes did not alter the principles of the 1842 act. Construction was divided up, with the state responsible for infrastructure and the companies responsible for superstructure. The state would plan each railway route, purchase the right-of-way, grade the land, and build bridges and tunnels. Private concessionaires would lay the track, erect terminals and other buildings, and purchase rolling stock. In return, concessionaires would receive operating franchises. The Ponts et Chaussées estimated that the government's share of construction costs would be 150,000 francs per kilometer, and the private share 125,000 francs (Thevenez 1930, V. I, p. 9). This solution resolved the controversy over the two principal design strategies – of adapting the track to the terrain or the terrain to the track, by permitting the corps to select the design but requiring the state to pay for cutting and filling, and for building bridges and tunnels. In the end the state provided over half of the capital used to build French railways. Upon completion of a line, the right-of-way would remain the property of the state, but the privately financed track, buildings, and rolling stock would belong to the company, whom the state would have to indemnify in the case of nationalization. Nationalization was inevitable, in that since 1833 the concessions had called for railroads to revert to the state after a period of 99 years. In the words of railway analyst Kimon Doukas, "The theory seemed to be that a franchise or a 'concession' did not confer on the operators other than a personal right to an undertaking which remained part of the 'inalienable' and unassignable public domain" (1945, p. 28). In his report to the Chamber on the proposed compromise, Deputy Dufaure conceded that it solved the state's fiscal problem without turning authority over to the private sector:

> This system is the most reasonable solution we have the power to adopt, under the circumstances. The expenses that will accompany the creation and exploitation of a railroad will be divided as close to equally as possible between the State and private industry: the State will retain ownership of the road, and the company will be nothing more than an exploiter by virtue of a lease. (quoted in Leclercq 1987, p. 186)

The initial legislation called for localities to provide two-thirds of the public monies, but that clause proved unenforceable for two reasons, and a law of 9 July 1845 rescinded it. First, the Ponts et Chaussées' preference for direct routes between large cities meant that many secondary cities that might have contributed to railway costs never gained depots on the trunk lines. Second, France's fiscally weak local governments had meager resources and few avenues for raising revenues, as Colbert had discovered when he tried to get them to underwrite the cost of the Canal du Midi 150 years earlier. Colbert had been forced to abandon the requirement for local contributions just as his successors were (Pilkington 1973). In the rail industry, one result of the weak fiscal capacities of local and provincial governments was that by 1858 they had provided only 1 percent of the capital invested in French railways, compared with an estimated 30 percent by 1861 in the United States (Kaufmann 1900, p. 68).

The controversies surrounding planning and finance had delayed the progress of the railway industry between 1833 and 1842, but over the following years concessions for a number of trunk lines were granted, and construction was begun on lines from Rouen to Le Havre, Paris via Nancy to Strasbourg, Paris to Lyon, Lyon to Avignon, Orléans to Bordeaux, Bordeaux to Sete, and Paris to Rennes. Each segment was envisioned as a step toward a network that would link Paris to the provinces. Between 1843 and 1847, 1,250 kilometers of track were laid (Doukas 1945).

The loss of local control.   French policy in those years also led to a decline in the role of local, *private,* capital, and by extension to a decline in the role of local groups in route decisions, just when American policy was helping local groups to finance railways and to influence route decisions. French rail capitalization changed between the 1820s, when local interests dominated, and the 1830s, when France's largest banks gained control. A key factor was the state's decision to build the trunk lines first, and delay construction of secondary lines. Whereas early coal-carrying lines had not demanded huge sums of money and thus had been backed by local groups who stood to benefit from them, the trunk lines would require great sums, and this meant that only the nation's largest banks would be able to arrange private financing. The history of the Paris-Orléans line reflects the change in financing that occurred in the 1830s. A charter was originally obtained by Casimir Leconte, who had managed France's largest stage coach company, in August of 1838. Leconte had promises of capital from businessmen who stood to benefit from the line. However, the Parisian *hautes banques* were then becoming involved in the industry, and the bankers on Leconte's board replaced him with a Rothschild crony, François Bartholony, who turned to large banks to collect the remaining capital (Dunham 1941, p. 17; Ratcliffe 1973; Lévy-Leboyer 1964, p. 622). The result of the general trend was that, although the St. Étienne-Andrézieux line had been capitalized in the 1820s by four metal works in need of coal, by the mid-'30s the *haute banques* had come to dominate rail finance and had thwarted the efforts of business groups to influence route decisions and speed the construction of particular lines.

New plans for nationalization: 1848.   The revolution of 1848 led to the establishment of the short-lived Second Republic, whose architects revived plans to nationalize the railway network and proceed with state construction of new lines. As it reorganized the state, the 1848 regime came to see private railway ownership as a major defect – as an aberrant alienation of the public domain. Socialist thinker Pierre Joseph Proudhon argued that the companies, like all forms of private property, were essentially aristocratic and should be swept away along with the government that enfranchised them. He equated the institution of private property with capitalism and monarchism alike. A commission established in 1848 to study the railways concurred with Proudhon that the system of private railway operation established by the 1842 act was distinctly aristocratic in nature. The Minister of Finance, M.E. Duclerc, argued, "the State *alone* has the power and energy to dominate the situation and enforce the rapid dissolution of the old government" and the aristocratic institutions it had created (quoted in Peyret 1949, p. 212). Duclerc contended that private railway financiers, in cahoots with the monarchy, had wrested the railways from the rightful control of the nation:

> In the fact that they are deeply impregnated with aristocratic spirit, financial institutions have necessarily encountered from the monarchy a friendly welcome, while in the general population they met an enlightened and clearly defined opposition. This is what you have seen. After exhausting efforts of all kinds, the monarchy and the companies triumphed together over the resistance of the nation. (quoted in Audiganne 1862, p. 82)

He went on to warn that allowing these powerful organizations to grow and to position themselves betwixt citizen and state was dangerous. The huge railway firms could exert undue influence on individuals by usurping the rightful sovereignty of the state and interfering with individual liberty:

> The companies have considerable personnel. If their reign persists, their personnel will grow. It is a real army that will be in your midst. Don't you foresee a possible danger there? And the multitude of customers who will be submitted to a power independent of the state, isn't this a threat to public security? . . . I admire your confidence in the future, yet it scares me. (quoted in Audiganne 1862, p. 85)

Duclerc's sentiments recalled a state that had earlier suppressed local lords with the aim of guarding the monarchy (cf. Crozier 1964, p. 216).

Notwithstanding France's reluctance to permit the growth of private enterprises with independent powers, many in France continued to believe that private enterprise could bring a form of efficiency to industry that state control could not. In August of 1849, an assembly commission issued a report favoring private concessions. It summarized the principal arguments for concessions:

> Railway concessions are not antithetical to any form of government, so long as the state does not aim to absorb all of its citizens within its exclusive power. The Companies build more economically and better manage the works, with the aim of industrial utility. They generally operate the lines at a better profit for themselves, and for the country in general. They allow the state to become, within a specified period of time, the owner of considerable capital [because the concessions eventually revert to the state] . . . They also protect the government from being put in the difficult situation of competing with private capital. They reduce the Public Works budget and do not consume state funds, which are so precious in times of internal or external crisis. (quoted in Picard 1887, v. I, p. 450)

In short, if there were political arguments to be made in favor of nationalizing the railroads, there were economic arguments to be made in favor of privatism. In the late 1840s, railway observers increasingly argued that because private parties were motivated by self-interest, they would build and operate railways more efficiently than the state could.

This effort to nationalize the companies would ultimately fail, because the Chamber's attention was soon occupied with the June Days civil war in Paris. The next six months were taken up with constitution-writing and the government resisted any radical changes, particularly changes that would drain the Treasury. Yet the new regime's attitude demonstrates how notions of political order can transcend ideological camps. For French republicans, large-scale private enterprises posed a threat to the republic just as for French monarchists they posed a threat to the monarchy. Followers of Saint-Simon made this argument as early as the 1820s when they championed scientific statism, in the place of divine right, as the foundation of government authority. State-led industrialization could overcome the inequities and anti-republican character of the *ancien régime*. In arguing for national railways, the Saint-Simonien S. Charlety implored the throne to "constitute herself as the force charged with putting the feudal and religious regime in the past and establishing an industrial and scientific regime" (quoted in Peyret 1949, p. 194). The Saint-Simoniens saw state construction and operation of the railroads as a means to further the causes of modernization and republicanism.

These arguments were diametrically opposed to those being made by Americans about the nature of democratic government. Just when Americans were characterizing statism as anti-democratic and a strong private sector as the foundation of liberty, the French were characterizing privatism as distinctly aristocratic and a strong state sector as the basis of liberty. In each country, liberal thinkers sketched a form of democracy in the image of their respective colonial and aristocratic regimes. As Tocqueville suggests, traditional state practices had become the building blocks of revolutionary regimes.

The response to corruption. France's response to corruption in the provision of public aid contrasts sharply with the American experience. The 1865 bill that provided public funds for the construction of railways "of local interest" led to a series of abuses that paralleled the United States' history of corruption in local railway aid. However, French political culture led to entirely different interpretations of, and responses to, these incidents. In the United States the corruption of public aid schemes was taken to indicate that the state had become involved in a realm that properly belonged to the private sector, and the response was to scale back public intervention. By contrast in France, corruption was taken to be the result of inadequate state oversight of private-sector activity, and the response was to expand public intervention. Alfred Picard, the longstanding head of the corps and author of France's encyclopedic official history of the railways, explained the weakness of the 1865 legislation after it had been repealed:

> Despite the precautions, in practice the system of direct public construction aid was far from what had been envisioned by the legislature. If it afforded funding for the concessionaires during the period of construction, it was, in retrospect, a most serious mistake not to provide any guarantees for the return of such capital, not to demand for the départements any promises that they would be completed. More than once, the concessionaires simply fed their speculations; more than once they eagerly realized enormous benefits, by means of issuing stock and then making construction agreements at prices that were scandalously over-estimated, then abandoning the enterprises they had initiated, leaving the départements with inextricable difficulties and embarrassments. (Picard 1887, V. II, p. 267)

In 1880, the law of 1865, which offered cash aid to railroad promoters, was replaced by a new bill that offered public interest guarantees on the private capital railway promoters collected. This administrative innovation eliminated the exposure of public capital while maintaining public support, and as a further guarantee the bill subjected the issuance of capital stock and the managerial bylaws of roads to the approval of the Ministry of Public Works, in consultation with the Minister of Finance. The *cahiers des charges* for new railroads were also subjected to review by the Conseil d'Etat. In short, when their schemes to provide direct aid to railroads led to corruption, Americans blamed the expansion of state powers and passed constitutional amendments prohibiting future public funding, and the French blamed inadequate public regulation and expanded state controls.

In this second functional realm of railway development – finance – the French, like the Americans, perceived a problem in the scarcity of capital available for rail construction. However, their articulation of the problem took a somewhat different form. Where the Americans struggled with how government could play a role in financing the railroads without trampling the economic liberties of private parties, the French struggled with how the state could engage private capital without giving up its duty to provide transport facilities for the nation. The French saw it as a right and duty of the state to undertake rail development. In Britain the attitude toward railway capitalization was different still; the British never perceived railway finance as a matter of government concern despite the fact that railroads had difficulty winning bank financing.

Although governments in both the United States and France addressed the problem of railway capitalization, the solutions they conceived were altogether different. Americans saw the railroads as properly private enterprises and devised solutions to ensure that railroads were privately held and operated, even when governments provided virtually all of the financing. Thus American governments refused to exercise their normal shareholder rights on railroad boards, even when they were the majority owners. The French described railroads as public endeavors, placed control over them in public hands, and conceived finance strategies that would cause them to revert to the state, even when private investors provided the bulk of the capital. France's in-kind aid schemes afforded state engineers substantial control over route and construction decisions, and the joint construction agreements retained state ownership of the right of way. In France, then, policymakers never conceived truly private solutions to the problem of finance; rather, the French options were limited, in the words of a German historian, to, "Would the state build rail lines through the Ponts et Chaussées, through a special administrative unit, or through entrepreneurs or contestants working under its surveillance?" (Kaufmann 1900, p. 11).

The alternative that was most often spoken of in France, and that continued to be broached whenever the industry faced a crisis, was nationalization. When railway financing was rethought in 1852, 1859, and 1883, proposals for nationalization were revived. These reorganizations led to significant expansions in public financial involvement, including public interest guarantees for railway capital (discussed later). By contrast, the United States' oft-heard alternative to local sponsorship – full private financing – was virtually never mentioned in France. Only one serious call for making the railroads entirely private was made, and the Government barely paid notice to it. In June of 1871, M. Raudot, the author of a book titled *La Décadence de la France,* proposed that the 99-year private railway concessions be made perpetual and that the state refrain from future involvement in the industry. This would bring to an end all public subventions of the railways, and set France on the course Great Britain had taken. The commission that was then considering the future of railway policy stated, through its secretary, that it did not have the time to consider such a proposal. The committee "judged it impossible to not oversee, to not regulate an industry of such interest to the public at large and which, necessarily, was exempt from the laws of competition" (quoted in Kaufmann 1900, p. 181). No more was heard of removing public influence. When the Ministry of Public Works sent a prominent engineer to the United States to assess the transport system there, Émile Malézieux reported back, with some alarm, that federal and state governments had failed to exercise adequate oversight and as a result had completely lost control of both canals and railroads:

> The federal government, which had . . . attempted the construction of certain roads, of long distance and of national interest, has totally ceased its involvement. . . . The Congress has never intervened in the construction, administration, or the finances of the canals or of the railways. . . . The states, after having attempted by themselves a certain number of canals which they had not been able to bring to successful completion, have abandoned them to private industry. (Malézieux 1875, p. 13)

Malézieux cautioned that France must make every effort to avoid falling into such an unfortunate situation, in which private parties exercised tyrannical control over transport routes that belonged, by all rights, to the nation as a whole.

Technical and managerial coordination

French policymakers saw the private control of technical and managerial decisions as a potential source of irrationality in the rail industry. In the language of the early debates as well as in the initial ordinances, policymakers described government orchestration of the industry as the only means to order. The railway network was one huge complex machine that could only operate effectively through careful coordination. Deputies, ministry officials, engineers, and railroad officials saw private decision-making as problematic because it (1) used cost as the primary consideration in decisions, rather than quality and dependability, (2) was oriented to current consumer demand, rather than to the nation's longterm goals, and (3) depended on the unproven technical abilities of private engineers and administrators rather than the proven expertise of state technocrats.

The solution the French adopted was to give state technocrats a free hand in establishing technical standards and managerial guidelines. Railway entrepreneurs exercised surprisingly little control over their own enterprises. They sometimes complained of this, but just as often they hailed the good sense of the state engineers who made key decisions for the industry. As a result of this proactive approach to technical and managerial matters, which involved public engineers in the ongoing management of the industry, most of the issues of interfirm coordination that the United States faced never appeared in France. Public management preempted most matters of interfirm coordination by effecting standardization.

The early franchises

On 26 February 1823 a royal ordinance was issued authorizing Messrs. de Lur Saluces, Boigues, Milleret, Hochet, Bricogne, and Beaunier to establish a road to carry coal from the mines in St. Étienne to the Loire river at Andrézieux. This was the first such line to require a royal ordinance because it was the first to require public expropriation. Lur

Saluces and his associates argued that a few reluctant landowners should not be able to stand in the way of a project of national importance. In England, they recalled, some

> [rail] roads, properly considered to constitute a public utility, were constructed by virtue of concessions authorizing legal expropriation, the owners to be suitably indemnified. . . . It is necessary immediately to settle the case where the refusal of a single owner to cede the land included in plans would make impossible the work in question, a work which is actually very really a matter of the highest public utility. (quoted in Lefranc 1930, p. 299)

The applicants contended that railroads might serve the public in much the same way that canals had. The Ponts et Chaussées concurred. The state's engineers drafted a charter that was revised and signed into law by interior minister Corbière in the name of King Louis XVIII. At the turn of the century, Richard von Kaufmann said of this, France's first railway charter, "This first official document contained the outline of future railroad regulation in France" (Kaufmann 1900, p. 2). The charter gave the state control over every aspect of railway construction, charges, and operations. It called for more extensive state controls over the road than the United States or Britain exercised over any railroad during the nineteenth century. More generally, state engineers drafted France's railway charters, and this enabled them to include whatever technical and operational requirements they chose to. By contrast, American and British railroads wrote their own charters and thereby set their own terms, subject to legislative approval.

To afford the Ponts et Chaussées control over the exact route to be followed by the railroad, and the design of the road, the St. Étienne ordinance stipulated that "the final plan for the route and construction of the line will be given to the préfet of the département, who will transmit it to the Director of the Ponts et Chaussées with his recommendation. The plan will be submitted for our approval by the Minister of the Interior" (France, Bulletin des Lois 1823, 7th ser., v. 16, n. 591, p. 194). The final plan, accepted in an ordinance of 30 June 1824, specified the route, rail gauge, location of stations, radius of curves, and grade of inclines (Lefranc 1930, p. 307). To ensure that the Ponts et Chaussées would retain authority over highway and waterway crossings, the ordinance stipulated that in the event of a dispute between the company and the state's engineers, crossings "will be constructed under the direction of the Ponts et Chaussées' engineers" at the expense of the company (France, Bulletin des Lois 1823, 7th ser., v. 16, n. 591, p. 195). To guarantee state control of rates, the ordinance set transport charges for the line in perpetuity at .0186 francs per 100 liters of coal, or per 50 kilograms of other goods, for each kilometer. Article 11 compelled the company to affix a copy of the ordinance to the doors of all stations and offices to make that price known to the public. Finally, to guarantee state control over the management of the line, the ordinance decreed that on completion of the line the Loire préfet must submit to the Minister of the Interior for approval, "a plan of rules that will establish the procedures for loading, transport, and unloading of merchandise" (France, Bulletin des Lois 1823, 7th ser., v. 16, n. 591, p. 197).

In the decade after the St. Étienne-Andrézieux concession was made, other concessions were granted for lines from St. Étienne to Lyon, Andrézieux to Roanne, Epinac to the Canal de Bourgogne, and Toulouse to Mountauban. The royal ordinances conceding those lines roughly duplicated that for the St. Étienne-Andrézieux line. Charters were granted exclusively by the central government, and they included construction, rate, and operating specifications. The Ponts et Chaussées drafted the ordinances so that it would retain final say over all details. What explains the French state's inclination to assume control over railway operations? The language of the earliest ordinances depicts transport as a natural duty of the state. The St. Étienne charter suggested that the concessionaires were performing a service for the state. In explaining why they should be allowed to charge public carriers for the use of the line, the charter suggested that just as public canals and highways had charged tolls to public carriers, M. Lur Saluces and associates should be permitted to charge tolls to remunerate them for the service they provided:

> In order to indemnify them for the expense of construction and maintenance of the road, the expense of maintaining their cars, and all other [outlays] they will be forced to make for the transport of coal and merchandise which they will be responsible for. (France, Bulletin des Lois 1827, 7th ser., v. 16, n. 591, p. 196)

The Ponts et Chaussées' view that the railways were part of the public domain is also found in the language that describes charges as tolls (*droits*) rather than as rates, as if railroads were public routes. Moreover in 1827, in response to the question of whether disputes involving the railways would be adjudicated through the channels used for public agencies or those used for private firms, the Ponts et Chaussées held that the railways were part of the public domain (Lefranc 1930, p. 310).

In addition to the powers the Ministry of Public Works was granted in individual charters, the ministry's general powers over technical and operational matters were extensive. The ministry took upon itself the task of investigating new railway technology, beginning in 1823 when the minister testified before the Chamber that these railroads with self-propelled carriages that had generated so much discussion in Britain were impracticable because the wheels of heavy locomotives would simply spin in place on smooth iron track (Kaufmann 1900, p. 5). The state's engineers believed that trains might slide uncontrollably downhill on their tracks, topple off their tracks on curves, and break apart during acceleration. Hence, in the 1820s and '30s the corps carried out dozens of studies examining gauge, the circumference of curves, locomotive design, the traction of metal wheels on iron tack, and train movement on steep inclines (France, Corps Royaux 1843). The corps undertook these studies on its own authority, and with the aim of improving its decisions about transport technology. Nothing like this agency, with independent power to examine a new transport technology, existed in the United States or Britain. In those countries, equipment manufacturers undertook the key studies, supplemented by an occasional state-sponsored competition to test locomotives or brakes.

The expansion of state controls

After the 1830s, the ministry won expanded powers to govern the internal technical and managerial decisions of railways. In July of 1845 the Chamber gave the minister wide discretion in policing the operation of railways in response to a gruesome accident on the Paris-Versailles line. In the same month the Chamber standardized rules governing the constitution and capitalization of railways, with the aim of preventing rampant speculation (Guillamot 1899, p. 15). The ordinance of 15 November 1846 reaffirmed the ministry's authority by empowering it to set carriage and locomotive standards and by requiring companies to submit operating procedures for the ministry's approval (Picard 1887, v. III, p. 334). In practice this meant that the Ponts et Chaussées worked closely with the railways in the development of new carriage designs and operating procedures. Then when the industry was reorganized in the 1850s under Louis Napoleon III, the state dictated what the railways' internal administrative structure would look like and claimed the right to veto proposed directors (Doukas 1945, p. 31). In 1857 the administration adopted seventy standard articles to be included in the *cahiers des charges*, the special stipulations appended to each charter that covered everything from rates to gauge to locomotive specifications (Kaufmann 1900, p. 407). In short, when it came to gauge; rolling stock specifications; engineering specifications for routes, bridges, and tunnels; safety specifications; operating procedures; and loading procedures the state's engineers asserted control when each railway was first chartered. Over the course of the century, the authority of the Ponts et Chaussées was regularly expanded by the Chamber.

Railway investors sometimes contested state intervention by arguing that the state fettered free enterprise with its controls and regulations. J. Milleret, a former deputy who had become a rail investor, argued in a treatise in 1839: "The administration of the Ponts et Chaussées is a sort of power of its own, an oligarchy . . . which, with its forms, its rules, its habits, and its pretentions, can do little but create an obstacle to the march of industry and to new discoveries." In 1841 a former préfet echoed these sentiments: "The engineers in France aren't only agents of execution, they are also the directors or judges of execution . . . they present themselves as intermediaries between the state and true capitalists . . . [who must] submit themselves with difficulty to the role of passive cashiers" in the pursuit of the engineers' plans (quoted in Leclercq 1987, pp. 70–71). The state's engineers so narrowly controlled the railway industry that private entrepreneurs were left little room for innovation and little room for discretion of any sort. Rail investors charged that the state was merely using them as a source of capital, without letting them control their own enterprises. Did this mean that the railroads were in practice run by the state? Far from it. Although the Ponts et Chaussées retained the authority to make technical and managerial decisions, in practice railroads exercised autonomy in daily operations. Of course, the Ponts et Chaussées exercised indirect control over private railroads by placing their own engineers in important positions. For instance, Louis Martin attained the rank of *conducteur des ponts et chaussées* in 1844 and joined the team planning the Paris-Strasbourg line, but in 1849 he made a typical career move to section head at the Compagnie de l'Est (Day 1987, p. 220).

How did France control the particular technical and managerial matters that troubled policymakers in the United States and Britain? I discuss this next in an examination of gauge and safety standards.

Gauge. The issue of gauge virtually never came up in political debates in the United States, where each railroad built in the gauge it preferred and where gauge standardization was eventually carried out by private railroads on their own initiative. In Britain the state eventually recommended a standard gauge but did not impose it on firms. In France the issue of gauge seldom came up because state engineers established a standard gauge of 1.44 meters at the beginning of the railway era and dictated that all railroads would be built in that gauge. French engineers had argued that without gauge standardization the railroads would not form a true network, because gauge incongruity would prevent continuous transport between lines. Early railway entrepreneurs did not object to the government's standard; however, in the 1850s some provincial and local governments sought permission to build narrow-gauge secondary lines. In cities, narrow-gauge lines could often be squeezed in between buildings where standard-gauge lines would not fit. In 1861 a commission was formed by the Ministry of Public Works to explore whether to allow narrow gauge lines to be built on routes "of local interest." The Ponts et Chaussées had long since identified two classes of railways – those of local interest and those of general, or national, interest. The latter enjoyed favored status because they were integral to the system of lines that fed Paris. The commission concluded that railway gauge should be allowed to vary on local interest lines, and in a 1865 law the government stipulated that the standard gauge was not an absolute. Yet by 1881 there were only six narrow-gauge rail lines in all of France; whereas in the United States by that date 6 percent of total mileage was in narrow gauge (Picard 1887, v. II, p. 706). Narrow-gauge lines remained rare in France because from 1865 Paris offered reduced construction aid for them on the principle that they could never be integrated into the national network. Thus, for regional governments the cost differential between narrow and standard gauge lines was inverted when state subsidies were taken into account; hence they only built in the narrow gauge when engineering factors prevented standard-gauge construction (Picard 1887, v. II,

p. 704). In short, the corps and ministry succeeded in standardizing gauge by stipulating a common gauge in all concessions, and by providing financial disincentives to the construction of non-standard lines. In France, no one argued that private railroads should have the liberty to build lines in the gauge they preferred.

Safety.   From the time of the very first railway charter the Ponts et Chaussées preempted the railways in the establishment of safety standards. Safety concerns centered around braking and signaling systems. The Ministry of Public Works took up the issue of brakes in 1846 – decades before reliable hydraulic brakes were invented – and on 15 November issued an ordinance requiring every passenger train to carry a brake on at least one axle in one of the rear cars. The edict also required railways to submit brake proposals for each passenger train to the ministry, and left it to the ministry to decide how many axles would have to be equipped with brakes on each train. The number of axles with brakes was to be a function of the incline of the route and the number of carriages (Picard 1887, v. III, pp. 321–322). The 1870s saw the perfection of the Westinghouse hydraulic brake, which enabled the train driver to apply braking pressure to all axles simultaneously. In 1879 the Ministry of Public Works appointed a commission to test the several brakes available, and within a matter of months the Ministry ordered that all express trains be equipped with continuous hydraulic brakes (Picard 1887, v. III, p. 332). Did the ministry need to claim special authority to demand the installation of brakes? The Conseil d'État argued that the ministry had since 1846 held full authority to dictate safety specifications to the railroads: "Because it is undeniably the role of the administration to coordinate the goals and undertakings of companies and to take, when necessary, measures of unification that would be simultaneously exacting and prudent, the minister has already in its power the ability to" (1) dictate equipment requirements to ensure the security of travellers, under the ordinance of 15 November 1846, (2) approve and revise companies' operating rules, under the same ordinance, and (3) control the operating procedures and technical specifications of all rolling stock under article 32 of the *cahiers des charges* (quoted in Picard, 1887, v. III, p. 334).

The Conseil was of the opinion that the ministry already had full authority over technical specifications, and needed no special legislation. If the ministry already had full power over matters affecting safety, should it choose the brand of brakes that railways would be required to install? The Railway Committee of 1879 came to the conclusion that the ministry would do best to permit railroads some leeway in choosing their own brake designs. By 1886 the ministry had expanded the 1879 order to require brakes on all trains that traveled at speeds over 60 kilometers per hour, but allowed the railroads to employ any approved brand of brake.

The French state waited until 1885 to impose signaling standards, yet from the birth of the industry the Ministry held authority over signaling practices because it held the power to approve railroads' operating procedures. Although early *cahiers* did not set out signaling standards, the Commission of 1857 recommended that railways adopt "a sort of universal language, of identical signals that will mean the same thing to all eyes and that, by being quickly understood even by persons unfamiliar with railroads, will prevent numerous accidents" (quoted in Picard 1887, v. III, p. 263). But the ministry did not consider signaling standardization between the six networks to be imperative, because each network, for all intents and purposes, operated as a self-contained system. As long as signaling was standardized within networks, standardization among them seemed unnecessary. No action was taken on the 1857 commission's suggestion.

In 1884 the Conseil d'État, in response to suggestions from a ministerial committee, pronounced that "it would be useful to make uniform rules relative to the meaning of the signals, for this has been left to the discretion of the companies" (quoted in Picard 1887, v. III, p. 263). Soon the minister began to work out a *Code des signaux* that would "unify the language of the optical signals and acoustical exchanges between agents on the trains and agents on the ground or in the stations" (quoted in Picard, v. III, p. 265). On 15 November 1885 a code, comprising thirty-four articles, was adopted by the ministry. Thereafter, signaling was standardized. Meanwhile, in the United States, signaling standardization had been considered a problem of private industrial management. Some states had recommended signaling standards but state governments did nothing to coordinate signaling for interstate traffic, and in 1884 the private General Time Convention adopted signaling standards.

In 1889 the Assembly extended state control over safety again, with legislation that restricted working hours and established a retirement age to ensure that train personnel would not be compromised by fatigue or infirmity. The legislation also reiterated signaling guidelines and called for the installation of communication systems that would allow passengers and employees to convey the presence of emergencies to the train driver (Picard 1918, p. 147).

In sum, the French saw a problem with allowing private parties and market mechanisms to make key technical and managerial decisions for the railway industry. Private control over gauge decisions would lead to a system of disarticulated lines. Private control over safety matters could never guarantee passenger security, because railroads would sacrifice safety to economy. The French favored public control over these matters, and saw private and market control as inefficient largely because state ministries had monopolized transport administration since before Louis XIV and the corps had all but monopolized transport engineering since 1716. In the process of providing turnpike and canal facilities, the French state had contributed to the construction of public-sector efficiency. As a consequence, with the emergence of rail technology, policymakers, coal companies, bankers, and rail promoters presumed that the state was best suited to rule the industry. In turn, the state's dominance of technical and managerial matters in the rail industry contributed to French notions of the efficiency of state concertation of industry, and to notions of the incapacity of private actors to reach efficient solutions on their own.

By contrast, American policymakers perceived government intervention in the internal operations of railroads to be tyrannical. They adopted policies that would guarantee railroads authority over technical and operational decisions. Railway charters, drafted by rail promoters, gave railways full control over gauge, rolling stock, operating procedures, and safety standards. When problems of coordination arose – as they did frequently because the state had not taken preemptory action to standardize technology and management – the railroads met among themselves to solve them. In the United States, the solution was to locate decision authority in private hands. The American solution gave rise to a profusion of diverse technical and managerial standards that made modern industry appear to be far beyond the control of state managers, whereas the French solution precluded technical and managerial diversity, and this made modern industry appear highly manageable.

In Britain, policymakers similarly perceived public intervention in firms' internal decisions to be tyrannical and inefficient. Parliament rejected all proposals that would have involved government appointees in railway management. We will see that the ideals of noblesse oblige and individualism combined to cause the state to demand fundamental safety devices, such as walls and roofs, on third class "carriages." However, for most technical and managerial matters, including safety, Parliament conceived solutions that would merely keep the populace informed of the behavior of railroads so that public opinion could do its job of constraining them to act in the public interest. Britain, then, perceived technical and managerial problems much as the United States did, but policymakers conceived a distinct sort of solution to these problems. The French neither believed that public opinion would compel railways to provide safe passage, nor that groups of private actors might through private action come to effective decisions about how to organize the industry technically.

Finally, in France the state's legitimate authority to dictate to private firms was so widely accepted that railroads offered little challenge to the ministry's decisions. In the United States, railways successfully undermined state regulatory commissions and, for a period of two decades, the Interstate Commerce Commission as well. In Britain, railways put the Railway Board out of business with the argument that it had assumed duties that were beyond the authority of any government board. In those countries, railways successfully argued against the authority of the state to interfere with their internal operations. In republican France, however, when railroads were displeased with the dictates of the ministry they made substantive appeals, but never questioned the rightful authority of the ministry to govern them.

Pricing and competition

In planning, finance, and coordination, French railway policy was oriented to state control, but only with the development of pricing and competition policies was the French logic of efficiency fully articulated. Competent technical decision-making, experienced management, and far-sighted concertation by government planners were the three legs on which efficiency stood. French policymakers did not see unhindered privatism, in the form of freedom to enter the market or freedom to set rates, as integral to economic liberty or efficiency. Nor did they see market mechanisms – in the form of market-driven decisions about where to build lines, where to terminate service, or how much to charge – as a source of rationality or efficiency. Throughout the century we find arguments that public officials, motivated by the public interest, can best orchestrate the actions of private entrepreneurs toward the nation's goals. How could unthinking markets decide that one rail route or another was vital to the nation's longterm prosperity? How could self-concerned entrepreneurs be permitted to decide how much to charge for rail services?

Early rate-setting

The earliest *cahiers des charges* had set rates in perpetuity. The Montbrison-Montrond railroad, for instance, could not charge more than "15 centimes per thousand kilograms of merchandise, and per thousand meters of distance" (France, Moniteur Universel 1833, v. 86, n. 51, p. 255). Yet by 1836 the ministry recognized the fallibility of perpetual rates and stipulated in new *cahiers* that the state would periodically review rates. The *cahier des charges* attached to the law of 9 July 1836, authorizing a line from Montpellier to Cette, stated, "If it is the case, after a period of fifty years, that the average dividend in the preceding five years has exceeded ten percent on capital invested" the tariffs will be reduced accordingly (quoted in Picard 1887, V. IV, p. 64). Subsequent *cahiers des charges* stated, similarly, that after a specified period the state would revise rates downward if the rate of return exceeded a certain level (Picard 1887, v. IV, p. 64). Because the corps drafted railway legislation, subject to the revisions of the ministry, the state retained complete control over rates from the time of the very first charter. Early rate-setting was designed to guard the public interest, and to ensure that railroads would charge the same rates to friends and foe.

After the passage of the 1842 legislation establishing the nation's principal railway routes, the ministry began trying to standardize the rates set out in the *cahiers des charges*. In these years, rate-setting was designed to achieve uniformity across regions, and low prices for consumers. Railways soon appealed to the Chamber to decide whether uniformity was paramount, which would mean that state-established rates would be treated as fixed, or whether low prices were paramount, which would mean that established rates would be treated as upper limits. Messrs. Legrand and Dufaure argued that it was in the public interest to allow railways to charge *lower* rates when they chose to. All sorts of circumstances might combine to allow a railroad to lower rates – for instance, a railroad that could be certain of full freight cars on the return journey might charge less than a railroad that could be certain of empty cars. As Legrand put it, any reduced rates that are established, "within the limits of the tariffs, under the authority and supervision of the administration, are most legal. They benefit equally the public and the company. To prevent the use of differential prices is to work against the interest of the company that has the concession. It is also to deprive society of all the tariff reductions that the companies could concede" (quoted in Kaufmann 1900, p. 35). The ministry took charge of rate-setting to ensure that railroads, which held transport monopolies, would not abuse those monopolies by charging excessive rates. As long as a railroad could remain financially viable by charging less than the maximum rates, the nation would benefit. Needless to say, the idea that the state should establish maximum rates to promote the public interest was quite at odds with contemporary American and British thinking.

During the 1840s, the engineers at the Ponts et Chaussées articulated a view of railway economics that contrasted starkly with the view then being taken in the United States and Britain. Their perspective had implications for both capitalization and rates. In the United States and Britain alike, railways were expected to produce revenues sufficient to allow them to pay for themselves. The evaluation of whether a railroad was worth building, and maintaining, was made on the basis of the *primary* returns it would produce. Those primary returns might be calculated on the basis of new demand generated by a railroad, but all parties believed that railroads should make money. Railroads that could not be expected to turn a profit should not be built in the first place, and those that regularly lost money should be abandoned. Inspector-general Dupuit of the Ponts et Chaussées published two influential treatises in the *Annales des Ponts et Chaussées* in the 1840s that set out the ministry's position. Alfred Picard later paraphrased these "well-known, classical" treatises on railway economics, arguing that Dupuit drew from his analyses and observations "a reason to favor state exploitation because, contrary to what private concessionaires would do, it would apply the lowest tariff, if this tariff is high enough to cover charges, and the state could even consent to a certain loss, as long as it finds compensation of another type" (Picard 1918, p. 281). Dupuit argued, in essence, that in contrast to private concessionaires who must always look for a profit, the state had the nation's wider interest in mind and thus recognized that *primary* revenues were not the only important consideration. It was the state's role to take account of the *secondary* economic benefits railways promised, in the form of the expansion of commerce and manufacturing, and supplement railway income where the secondary benefits would make supplements worthwhile.

This thinking provided a foundation for the decision to establish uniform rates throughout the country, regardless of customers' ability to pay or of demand, as a stimulus to economic expansion. Thus, when the *cahiers des charges* were standardized in 1857, uniform passenger and freight rates, based on distance, were included (Doukas 1945, p. 23). The rate-making formula that evolved became more complex over time but it was based on the principles of uniformity and coherence rather than on the cost principle, as with cost-plus rate-setting, which guaranteed a certain rate of return, or on the demand principle, as with demand-based rate-making. It also provided a foundation for the decision to provide public construction aid for all railroads, and for future decisions to invest public monies in the expansion, and sustenance, of the industry.

Whereas a French ministry had dictated railway rates from the time of the very first charter, in the United States we saw that the few, poorly administered efforts of states to set rail rates failed completely when the railroads ignored Granger commission edicts and continued to charge what they pleased. In Britain, as we will see, the railways wrote their own charters and stipulated extravagant rates that greatly exceeded what the traffic would bear in order to preempt government efforts to control rates. The British government set rates only for the poorest class of passengers, and they did so in the name of public welfare rather than in the name of efficiency or profitability.

Industry structure and competition

The political upheaval of 1848 was followed by a severe depression in 1851 and on 2 December by a coup d'état that marked the beginning of the Second Napoleonic Empire. Louis Napoleon made three major changes in railway policy: He reorganized the nation's lines into a handful of wedge-shaped territorial monopolies; he passed a "repurchase" option that would allow the state to buy out concessionaires in the future and made it certain that the railways would eventually "revert" to the state; and he took over the operation of nearly 400 kilometers of abandoned trackage (Caron 1973, p. 75). Those changes signaled the state's attitude toward competition, privatism, and market mechanisms. The establishment of huge regional monopolies, which would survive until nationalization in 1937, suggested that free market entry and operation were not integral to the French understanding of industrial efficiency. The "repurchase option" made it clear that Louis would endure private concessions only until the condition of the Treasury would permit nationalization. The state takeover of failing lines sent the message that market forces would not be permitted to influence service decisions; the nation's state-planned railways must continue to operate.

The regional monopolies.   Louis Napoleon favored nationalization of the railways; however, France's fiscal situation precluded an immediate state takeover. His first endeavor was to commission a new route study, undertaken by Ernest de Franqueville of the corps, which led to the repeal of the 1842 act that called for eight trunk lines. The government returned to the Ponts et Chaussées's original plan calling for six trunk lines radiating from Paris. But under Napoleon's direction, Franqueville went one step further by consolidating twenty-eight independent railroads into the six regional monopolies. Under the new system, when the profits of the new Grandes Compagnies exceeded a certain minimum they were to use the excess to help build the tributary lines planned by the corps. This new scheme allowed Louis Napoleon to achieve administrative centralization and coherence without nationalizing the railways, and to expand the network. Because there were no interregional routes in this plan, each regional network would operate as an autonomous rail system. Yet from the perspective of American observers, this policy change abridged the economic liberties of independent railway operators, by forcing them to merge, and trampled on fundamental economic rights, by ruling out future market entry. After 1852, the Chamber would not charter a single new independent railroad. The reorganization had a marked effect on the capacity of the Ponts et Chaussées to control railroads, because it folded various and sundry rail companies into six major companies with offices in Paris. The state's engineers increasingly insinuated themselves into the day-to-day operations of the railways, so that by the mid-1870s the railway section had grown to occupy 356 of the corps' engineers (Smith 1990, p. 677).

The repurchase clause.   The new legislation gave the government the right to "repurchase" the concessions after fifteen years of opera-tion, and dictated that the lines would automatically "revert" to the state after ninety-nine years. The legislation would enable the state to rescind the franchises and nationalize the lines whenever the condition of the Treasury permitted. The law stated that in the event of nation-alization the Treasury would assume companies' financial liabilities, pur-chase rolling stock, and reimburse companies for the track and buildings at a price based on net income. Since 1833, when the Montbrison-Montrond charter first stipulated that the "concession will not exceed ninety-nine years," all charters had called for roads to revert to the state eventually. However, the repurchase clause of 1852 guaranteed the state's prerogative to take over a railroad at its discre-tion (France, Moniteur Universel 1833, v. 86, n. 51, p. 255; Peyret 1949). These repurchase clauses were designed to be used as soon as the state had the capital to take over the railroads, unlike the British repurchase clauses, which were initiated later with the express purpose of giving Parliament regulatory leverage, in the form of the threat of nationalization, over railroads that violated the public trust. Parlia-ment, as we will see, adopted repurchase clauses without the slightest intention of nationalizing railroads.

State operation of abandoned lines.   Louis Napoleon took two steps to ensure the continuation of service on lines that had been devas-tated by the depression. The Chamber voted 579 million francs in treasury loans to existing companies to cover operating expenses, in order to forestall bankruptcies, and the Ministry of Public Works as-sumed control of 383 kilometers of track upon which service had been abandoned (Kaufmann 1900). Insolvency was not taken, by the French, as evidence that a line was superfluous or inefficient. To aban-don service on part of the national rail system would be to abandon the coherence of the Ponts et Chaussées' grand scheme. As Charles Collig-non put it in a pamphlet on railways in 1845, France was "quite far from the principle of Adam Smith that no transport lines should be built except those that can pay for themselves with their direct reve-nues" (quoted in Smith 1990, p. 676). The lines planned by the corps served the long-term interests of the nation even when short term prof-itability was problematic. It was the state "looking perforce to the future from the height from which it looks down upon the narrower combinations of private interests" that would guard the public interest (Collignon quoted in Smith 1990, p. 676). Markets could not possibly exercise foresight and planning, and therefore they could not be permitted to put a line that had been built with a clear public purpose out of business.

How did the French railways feel about the curtailment of their economic liberties in this new plan? Some railroads objected to being folded in to large networks, but on the whole the railways acquiesced and attributed the industry's success to date to state tutelage. In 1858, a report of the Compagnie de l'Ouest applauded the government's 1852 scheme, and argued that those who would deny the companies the benefit of state coordination had no interest in progress:

> The government we are speaking about is the one which, in 1852, gave such a strong impulse to our industry; it is the [government] which, taking the broadest perspective of the general interest, has rejected the narrow and jealous state of mind which would prefer to dry up the source of public prosperity than to see public intervention. This government has been strongly applauded because of admirable growth in national wealth; it has been too widely praised for the push it has given to great enterprises for us not to follow its initial lead. Consequently we must give [the state] our confidence. (quoted in Audiganne 1862, p. 143)

Over the next decades the core elements of the 1852 scheme were sustained. Little changed before the nationalization of the railways in the midst of the Great Depression. Insolvency was never permitted to put a railway out of business, although the policies used to continue service on failing lines varied over time. The nationalization of the industry was treated as inevitable, and at each crisis some in the corps and the Ministry of Public Works called for immediate nationalization. Although the main lines of policy remained unchanged, vacillations in the economy brought about policy shifts that caused the relationship between public orchestration and private entrepreneurialism to evolve.

The maturation of pricing and competition policy

The 1859 dividend guarantees. The Crimean War of 1854–56 sparked an economic crisis in France that curbed railway revenues and brought new construction to a standstill. The Emperor was concerned to ensure that companies would continue with construction, and would not terminate service on lines that were losing money. When the railways asked for aid, the government responded with the Act of 11 June 1859, which took state participation one step further. In better times, the state might have responded by assuming full responsibility for construction costs. But lacking the resources to do that, the government chose to guarantee a generous rate of return on the capital invested in railroads. In so doing, it attracted new capital to build planned lines and simultaneously prevented the companies from abandoning service on unprofitable routes. The legislation divided each of the grand companies into an old network of lines that were operating, or under construction, by 1857 (7774 km.), and a new network of lines that were planned, but not yet under construction (8578 km.). Capital invested in the old networks was guaranteed a return of 5.75 percent, and capital invested in the new lines was guaranteed a return of 4.65 percent. In the event that companies could not return these rates to investors, the state was to supply the difference in the form of treasury loans, which could be repaid when the companies did make a profit. When profits on a concession's old network exceeded 5.75 percent, the next 1.1 percent was to be applied to construction of the new network. Excess profits could be distributed to shareholders, with the provision that after 1872 the state would share half of the profits above 6 percent for the old network and above 8 percent for the new network (Picard 1918, p. 19; Doukas 1945, p. 35). The state had promoted itself from partner in construction to partner in operation, but this policy was hardly without precedent in France. The state had insured investments in a wide range of projects of public interest, including the Paris-Orléans railway in 1840, and in the process had spoiled investors who came to expect state guarantees for risky ventures that were in the public interest (Lévy-Leboyer 1964).

The government network.   The next extension of state responsibility for railways came as a result of the failure of a series of small rail lines. Many of the secondary lines designed by the corps to feed trunk lines were unprofitable, and this was a particular problem in the sparsely-populated Southwest region of France. Ten lines "of local interest" appealed to Paris for aid in 1875. Some of those lines were on the point of declaring bankruptcy, and in response to their appeal the ministry reiterated that it could not allow lines planned with the nation's future in mind to be destroyed by market forces; this would subvert the coherence of the corps' grand scheme (Peyret 1949, p. 243). In March of 1877 the Chamber approved an agreement that was signed by the companies and ratified 18 May 1878 calling for the state to "repurchase" the concessions for the price of the original private investments. The result was a seventh regional monopoly in the southwest operating under the Ministry of Public Works (Peyret 1949, p. 245).

New financial guarantees: The Freycinet plan. In the late 1870s the long European depression threatened railway construction and operation. A broad-based nonpartisan plan for recovery was popularized in 1877. It called for massive public works expenditures to increase employment and simultaneously expand the transport infrastructure. Charles de Freycinet became Minister of Public Works in the midst of this commotion, and under his leadership the ministry gave form to these proposals. The new plan called for close to a billion francs for waterway improvement, at a time when farsighted men and women realized that water transport was in decline, and for an additional 5,000 kilometers of rail lines to be built.

The ministry never contended that the proposed extensions, which would mostly provide spurs to secondary cities, could pay for themselves at a time when the trunk lines were having difficulty turning a profit. In a Senate debate in which critics espoused the primary-returns doctrine that prevailed in the United States and Britain – that a rail line should not be built unless its projected receipts would be sufficient to repay the initial capital with interest – Freycinet countered:

> Such reasoning is a private reasoning, a commercial reasoning, or the reasoning of a merchant, but it is not the reasoning of a man of the State . . . In the railroads . . . [you have to consider the direct relationship] between the money you put in and the income the railroads are likely to generate. Here you have the perspective that must be taken by the industrial entrepreneur, the merchant, or the financial partnership that wants to invest in a railroad. But there is also that which we don't see as plainly, and which does not touch the entrepreneur, the merchant, or the financial society but which must be of importance from the perspective of the state. There is an enormous savings realized by the public in these transportation projects. There is also massive public income in the form of taxes, as the president of the Compagnie du Nord has recently pointed out. The state's income from the Nord, according to Mr. Rothschild himself, nearly equals the income of the shareholders, and taxes are not the only benefits. (quoted in Picard, 1918, p. 287)

Another undeniable benefit, argued Freycinet, is the stimulus railroads give to manufacturing and commerce, the growth of which benefits the nation and the state. In short, the direct returns of railway investment are belittled by the many indirect returns, in the form of economic growth, that result from the establishment of railroads. Freycinet insisted that these secondary returns must be taken into account by state policymakers. What mattered was whether the total benefits to the nation outweighed the cost of construction.

Although some deputies had opposed state construction aid, others trotted out the old standby, nationalization, to solve the current crisis. In 1879, Jean David, a deputy from Gens, proposed that the state repurchase the nation's railways and break down management into several operating groups under the Ministry of Agriculture and Commerce. Construction of new lines would be delegated to the Ministry of Public Works, and rates would be set by the legislature. This proposal spurred the nomination of a thirty-three-member commission whose 1880 report favored the plan. However, the Treasury was in worse shape than usual and the government decided that nationalization would have to wait (Peyret 1949, p. 257). Under the spell of Freycinet's arguments that railway investment provided important indirect returns in the form of economic expansion, the Chamber approved an expanded version of the ministry's plan that called for not 5,000 but 8,000 kilometers of new lines to be built, in 180 separate extensions (Smith 1990, p. 683). At the same time, the state took over another 1,800 kilometers of unprofitable private lines, to be operated under the ministry's "seventh" rail network.

The economic panic of 1882 decimated rail profits and caused railways to terminate service on secondary routes. The panic catalyzed the Government to announce negotiations with the Grandes Compagnies on 22 February 1883 which aimed to "facilitate the execution of the major public works without any further charges against the state's credit" (Jules Ferry quoted in Picard 1918, p. 55). One problem was that many of the newer lines planned by the Ponts et Chaussées were tertiary lines that provided little business, and as a result the companies were reluctant to build them and were inclined to terminate service when they proved unprofitable. With Freycinet's secondary-returns logic in mind, and in the hope of providing employment during the economic dip, the framers of the 1883 agreements markedly improved the state's long-term guarantees to the companies, while reducing the state's short-term obligations. The six companies agreed to (a) take over state-operated lines in their regions to relieve the Treasury, (b) continue with construction on lines planned by Freycinet, and (c) resume operation on all lines.

In return, the state abolished the distinction it made between old and new lines, and guaranteed a return of 5.75 percent on all lines. As compensation for these new guarantees, the state's concessionary fee was raised from one-half of excess profits to two-thirds. For the four companies that still owed the state money for earlier interest subventions, the remaining debt would bear no interest and payments would be reinvested in the companies as part of the government's contribution for new construction. The agreements also increased the Treasury's contribution toward new construction. The state would pay for the construction of infrastructure *and* superstructure, so that in addition to paying for a prepared roadbed and all bridges and tunnels, the state would now also pay for the laying of the track. The companies were responsible for part of the costs associated with erecting buildings and purchasing rolling stock, and they were to contribute 5–10 percent of the estimated construction costs of 250,000 francs per kilometer. The companies were to arrange for construction by floating loans on behalf of the Treasury for the necessary capital, which obviated the immediate need for public capital (Doukas 1945, p. 45). By guaranteeing the interest on private capital, the Chamber had essentially transformed railroad holdings into public bonds. By assuming virtually the whole cost of building future lines, the state was able to guarantee that the lines it desired would indeed be built.

The year 1883 marked the last major change in French railway financing to appear in the nineteenth century, but the next century would bring long-anticipated shifts. The Compagnie de l'Ouest suffered financial losses that led the state to nationalize it in 1911. In 1923, the state established a Conseil Supérieur des Chemins de Fer to unify the policies of the Grandes Compagnies and divide up operating losses. These measures extended the logic of early rail policies, which had transformed independent railroads into part of a public service (Zeldin 1977, p. 1050). Finally, in 1937, pressed between the economic exigencies of the depression and the impending threat of war with Germany, France nationalized the railways under the Societé Nationale des Chemins de Fer (SNCF). The new legislation gave the state a majority interest in the national railroad, and provided for it to gradually assume full ownership. Of course, because the ninety-nine year charters called for the railways to begin to revert to the state in another two decades, the 1937 legislation merely hastened the arrival of the inevitable.

What problems did the French perceive in the realm of pricing and competition? Again, the French perceived private decision-making and market control as destabilizing and destructive, and sought to impose state control over these realms. The French never perceived a problem in the disappearance of competition. In fact, state rate-setting had prevented price competition from emerging in the first place, and the establishment of regional monopolies put an end to any possibility of competition. Throughout the century, the Chamber acted to ensure that market forces would not undermine the corps' plans for the industry. The Americans had asked how they could sustain price competition in an industry that seemed to invite collusion, how they could sustain competitive price structures even on monopolistic routes, and how they could ensure that competition, rather than restraints of trade, would decide which railways failed and which survived. The French asked how they could ensure that construction would continue even when profits lagged; how lines that did not achieve profitability could be kept open; and how the state could eventually attain its rightful possession of the industry. The British, as we will see, were most concerned to sustain multitudes of entrepreneurial firms even when that meant sacrificing market competition.

France thus conceived unique solutions to problems of pricing and competition. American and British governments protected the right of market entry under the banner of economic liberty, whereas in France the Ministry of Public Works issued monopolistic charters that guaranteed that competing lines would not be chartered. The Chamber later created huge regional monopolies and forbade the founding of independent firms. Such charter monopolies had frequently been sold to enterprises in other industries by the *ancien régime* (Shonfield 1965, p. 82). In the French view it would have been irrational to allow markets and competition to take care of railway planning, and it would have been equally irrational to permit markets to disrupt service merely because a line that had been designed with public goals in mind was not immediately profitable. Markets had no capacity to take the wider view and to take into account the indirect economic contribution of a rail line. In 1955, Herbert Luthy summed up the traditional French perspective, which carries

> an ingrained mistrust of the natural play of forces of a free economy, and a profound conviction that it is better to produce synthetically, as in a laboratory, the theoretical conditions of a competitive market than to risk the shocks and hazards of real competition . . . In the last

resort, however, this synthetic capitalism with which it is desired to endow France is completely in the tradition of the French mercantilism which was inherited from the *ancien régime* and consists of protectionism and enlightened state intervention. (p. 455)

The French had exercised excessive care to ensure that market forces did not determine the course of the railway industry, and to ensure that private actors could not pursue their own petty goals to the detriment of the country's greater purposes. Markets, competition, and entrepreneurialism were prevented from governing key decisions at every stage of the industry's evolution.

Finally, did the railroads in France battle against state controls over rates, over the service they would provide, or over their financing arrangements? Did they fight, like their American counterparts, every government effort to dictate to them? As with technical and managerial matters, the French railroads sometimes bemoaned the lack of control they had over their own rates or service, but they offered few challenges to the *authority* of the state to dictate to them. Thus, whereas American railroads challenged the constitutional authority of the Interstate Commerce Commission to investigate rate inequities from 1887 when the commission was formed, French railroads had conceded the state's right to set rates as early as 1823. When French railroads disagreed with the ministry's edicts, they lobbied and cajoled the state's engineers to get their way rather than challenging the state's right to control the industry.

Conclusion

That France experienced earth-shattering political changes during the nineteenth century there is no question. Nonetheless, French railway policy developed along a linear and seamless trajectory. Revolutions and regime changes did surprisingly little to disrupt rail development. This continuity had something to do with the insulation of the public bureaucracy from the political process. State technocrats went about their business relatively unaffected by the political trials and tribulations of the day. Continuity also had something to do with the state's longstanding commitment to the expansion of national income through economic concertation, which meant that in public policy generally and in transport policy in particular the state had already begun to work out a modern role. The French state had long considered the enrichment of the monarchy through internal development to be one of its principal tasks, and this attitude coincided perfectly with the emergent project of the modern state.

In the course of developing rail policies, the French worked out a vision of how the modern economy would operate, and particularly of the roles of public and private actors in the economy. They perceived unique problems in the rail industry and conceived unique solutions to those problems. In the process, they fashioned an industrial policy paradigm that allocated a vital role to private initiative, while guarding the state's task of orchestrating economic activity. French policy gave the state the same role in the nation's industrial life that it had assumed in military and political life – that of guiding the actions of self-interested individuals toward the achievement of the nation's goals. Political culture had sought to preclude disarticulated private activity from creating military and political chaos, and similarly the industrial policy paradigm that emerged sought to preclude self-interested private action from creating industrial chaos.

In the rail industry, the French perceived industrial practices that afforded control to private entrepreneurs and to market mechanisms to be problematic. In each of the four functional realms, they sought policy solutions when they saw such practices. They perceived a problem in planning by private parties and local governments. They perceived a problem in private financial control of the industry. They perceived problems in private control of technical and managerial matters. And they perceived problems when market forces and private profit-seeking seemed to be influencing rates, service decisions, and industry structure.

The solutions the French conceived to these problems permitted the state to engage private entrepreneurial spirit in the rail industry without relinquishing public control over important decisions. In planning, the only solution heard in France was for the state's technocrats to set out the routes from Paris to the nation's extremities. In finance, policymakers debated whether the state should give private enterprise any role in the industry, but in the end the proposals ranged from fully public railroads to joint construction and private operation under temporary concessions that would eventually revert to the state. Policymakers argued that the profit motive would reduce the costs of construction and operation, and thus that this solution would combine the benefits of public vision and private economy. When it came to technical and managerial coordination, French policymakers' knee-jerk reaction precluded full consideration of the options. The corps closely regulated every aspect of the industry from the time of the very first charter. Close state supervision prevented the problems of inter-firm coordination – such as gauge incompatibility and signaling diversity – that the United States and Britain faced. When it came to competition, the state considered, and enacted, a variety of proposals to prevent market mechanisms from interfering with its plans for the industry. Thus it created six huge regional monopolies that would enhance coordination and preclude price competition, took over finan-cially failing routes to prevent market mechanisms from causing the suspension of service; and guaranteed the interest on private rail invest-ments so that market pressures would not terminate service or stall construction. These policies contributed to the rise of an industrial culture in which market mechanisms could only disrupt rational public planning of growth by expert technocrats.

In the railway age, France's industrial dilemma was how to fashion a system of economic organization that would not subordinate tradition-al economic and social customs to market forces, because such a system would not have been consonant with cultural traditions, yet which would stimulate growth rather than merely sustain traditional econom-ic life. Indeed, analysts would later attribute France's developmental delay to its adherence to tradition and reluctance to submit social life to market forces (Crozier 1973).

During the early railway era, the French worked out a unique solu-tion to this dilemma. Ministers and governments sought to harness entrepreneurialism in the service of public goals without surrendering the state's prerogative to choose the course of the nation's future. I have traced these policies to the legacy of a top-down account of political order that allocated sovereignty unambiguously to the central state. Richard de Kaufmann characterizes the logic of concertation that drove policy decisions:

> In France, the idea that has always prevailed, which the heads of State of the country have proclaimed . . . is that the State is the absolute proprietor of the railways: it gives the momentum, the direction nec-essary to the development of the networks; the state constantly over-sees the railroads, exercising strict control; but at the same time it delegates, under temporary charters, the establishment and operation of the networks to individual energy and private interests – the two great promoters of human action – to which we owe railways, this

> great tool of economic development. If particular interests express
> themselves too strongly, the state imposes limits on them; if, on the
> contrary, private initiative does not succeed in reaching the goals the
> state proposes, the State goes to their aid. Private parties must always
> submit themselves to the general interest and contribute to serving it.
> (Kaufmann 1900, p. vii)

French governments thus worked out a strategy for railway promotion
that did not cede this key industry to the private sector so much as
utilize private initiative for collective ends. This solved the problem of
how to reconcile political culture, which assigned responsibility for and
sovereignty over the nation's economy to the state, with the economic
realities of capitalist industrialization.

The industrial policy paradigm that emerged in the rail industry did
not represent a sharp break with the past. Its roots can be found in
earlier approaches to canals, turnpikes, munitions, and an array of
manufacturing sectors. For instance, the state had combined public
orchestration with private initiative in the turnpike and canal industries by designing and building infrastructure, and then charging public
carriers with providing competitive service. In turn, the policy paradigm that was developed for the railways influenced the policies that
would be adopted for subsequent industries. In 1889, the state established a public telecommunications monopoly. To ensure that vital
industries were not threatened by market vacillations or entrepreneurial folly, France assumed control of significant segments of munitions, construction, gunpowder, banking, airplanes, horse-breeding,
insurance, forestry, map-making, and publishing by early in the twentieth century (Zeldin 1977, p. 1044). During the Great War, France
organized a virtual command economy under the state's close control,
and in the 1920s the state expanded tutelage over such key industries as
mining, shipbuilding, electricity generation, oil, and air transport
through mixed enterprise experiments and public takeovers (Kuisel
1967, pp. 8–44; Zeldin 1977, ch. 21; Sauvy 1967, V. 1). And in the
1930s, of course, the state nationalized the rail system and expanded
the public role in munitions. After World War II, the state undertook a
series of nationalizations, and turned from a strategy based on the
coordination of individual industries to "indicative planning" through
five-year plans designed to orchestrate the growth of every sector of the
economy under a single, integrated, plan (Cohen 1977).

In short, the forms of industrial governance worked out in the railway industry and elsewhere in the nineteenth century would carry on into the twentieth century when, in the words of Jack Hayward, "The normative weight of national tradition was tilted in favor of state force rather than market forces and it was taken for granted that governments could decide what they wanted to happen and were able to make it happen provided they had the will" (1986, p. xiii). Did this mean that *every* industry would be subject to the sort of state concertation that the railway industry saw? No. Even under the comprehensive system of indicative planning that emerged in the 1950s, the French made a distinction between the vital manufacturing and infrastructural sectors whose fate could not be left up to entrepreneurs and market mechanisms, and the less vital industries that could be risked to entrepreneurs. Nonetheless, the idea that state technocrats could efficiently orchestrate the development of the private economy became embedded in public policy during the railway age.

4. Britain

Introduction

Because Britain was the first nation to undergo an industrial revolution, the British soon became convinced that their peculiarly noninterventionist state traditions deserved much of the credit. There was no evidence in the experiences of other nations to refute this idea. By the beginning of the nineteenth century, Adam Smith had articulated a positive theory of economic growth based on English political traditions. By the 1830s, the term laissez faire was being used to describe an industrial culture in which unfettered individual initiative produced economic dynamism and growth. Laissez faire referred to the state's role, which was to refrain from interference with the private economy for fear of disrupting the internal dynamic of growth. In the railway industry, laissez faire translated into policies that gave the state no role in the planning, construction, or operation of railroads. However, over the course of the century the principle was altered as the state began to intervene to protect citizens' rights. Parliament scrutinized railway charters to protect landowners from unnecessary expropriation, oversaw railway operations to protect citizens against the untold perils of railway travel, and regulated third-class rates to guard the poor from the excesses of greedy entrepreneurs. These early interventions helped to open the door for positive industrial policies, which came in the form of protections for the small firms that the British had come to see as the mainspring of economic growth. By the end of the nineteenth century, a new industrial policy paradigm had emerged in the railway industry. Pure laissez faire had given way to policies designed to shield entrepreneurial firms against harm from politics and markets. Thus, in Britain, a traditional political culture organized around the sovereignty of individuals at first spawned an industrial policy paradigm that was explicitly laissez-faire, and later spawned an industrial policy paradigm based on active protections for entrepreneurial firms.

English political traditions gave sovereignty to elite individuals rather than to autonomous communities, as in the United States, or to the central state, as in France. Over the course of the nineteenth century, English political individualism was gradually extended to the masses as the polity became democratized. During this same period, the principle of atomized sovereignty was extended to the industrial realm. Under feudalism, members of the landed class had been protected from the Crown and from their neighbors, and over the course of the nineteenth century public policy guaranteed similar protections to industrialists. It was thus that core features of political culture came to be mirrored in Britain's industrial culture. In effect, Britain had translated the political imperative to guard the prerogatives of sovereign citizens into an industrial imperative to guard sovereign firms. Britain heralded individual initiative as the dynamic force behind growth and devised policies to foster the multiplication of independent firms. And, as Alfred Chandler has argued, small-scale entrepreneurial capitalism continued to rule in Britain even as a more bureaucratic, managerial, form had begun to rise in the United States: "What differentiated British . . . enterprises from those of the United States or Germany was that the entrepreneurs assembled smaller management teams, and . . . they and their heirs continued to play a larger role in the making of middle- and top-management decisions" (1990, p. 240). Whereas the entrepreneurial spirit was believed to be integral to the process of economic growth in the United States and France as well, only in Britain did public policy come to support entrepreneurial liberty by subduing market forces and political control. In Britain, small-scale entrepreneurialism was not merely a source of economic initiative, to be shaped toward collective economic ends by markets or technocrats. In British thought, masses of economic actors freely pursuing their interests were all that was needed to achieve growth.

The British state came to guard economic liberties by ensuring that firms did not fall prey to their overzealous competitors or to the vicissitudes of the market. The version of laissez faire that emerged was significantly different from the market-centered laissez faire being pursued across the Atlantic. Both the United States and Britain saw what they were doing as nonintervention because both designed policies to locate authority over industry outside of the state. But whereas the Americans came to nurture and shield market mechanisms as a rationalizing force, the British protected the vitality and independence of individual firms as the source of industrial efficiency. The logic of British policy was that rationality ensued when scores of small entrepreneurs competed freely without interference from politics or from larger, dominant, firms. The essential difference is exemplified by the two countries' approaches to cartels. The United States outlawed cartels to guard economic liberties and protect market mechanisms, which would produce natural selection effects that favored the best-run firms. Britain fostered cartelization as a way to protect small firms from predatory pricing practices and sustain multitudes of small-scale economic actors. The British understood competition to be essential to economic growth, yet they came to see price competition as a potential hazard to the vitality of the firms that were necessary to growth.

One important contribution of the British case is its unique industrial culture, emphasizing entrepreneurial autonomy rather than market mechanisms or state orchestration. With this third case, it becomes clear that industrial cultures do not line up on a market-state continuum, but that (1) nations may attribute macro-industrial efficiency to any number of different rationalized processes, and (2) strategies that are rhetorically similar, such as those of the United States and Britain, may be based on radically different precepts. Recent studies suggest that other countries, such as Japan and Germany, have industrial cultures that locate rationality in still other processes (Johnson 1982; Zysman 1983; Cornish 1979).

British state structure

Whereas France had struggled to unify a kingdom with unstable borders by installing absolutism, England had the advantage of a natural moat that discouraged aggressors and obviated the need for military centralization. The endurance of a decentralized form of feudalism in England made for substantially different political institutions than those found on the Continent (Hintze 1975). In contrast to France, where the Crown's bureaucracy came to dominate the landed elite, in England the system of "parcelized sovereignties" sustained the power of the landed class (Anderson 1974, p. 19). Independent elites checked the strength of the English state from the signing of the Magna Carta in 1215, and it was the weakness, not the strength, of the center that preserved the allegiance of the landed class. Under British feudalism, each lord reigned supreme on his own turf, and in the seventeenth century this system was reinforced when the gentry won greater independence and tipped the balance of power toward the representative Parliament (Stone 1965).

The locus of political authority.   English political sovereignty was unusually atomized. Individuals retained independence from the Crown, and expressed their political will through their representatives in the two houses of Parliament. At the core of the polity was a weak Crown surrounded by a strong "committee of landlords" who made up the legislature (Moore 1966). Over the course of the nineteenth century, the expansion of suffrage democratized the idea that each lord reigns supreme in his own realm. Sovereignty was not centralized in the way that it was in France, where it accrued to a single ruler and his pyramidal bureaucracy, in large measure because the Crown did not dominate Parliament and the administration. Substantial authority was located in individuals and their representatives.

The concentration of powers.   In England, government powers were concentrated in Parliament, rather than divided among different branches and levels of government. Under parliamentary rule, the executive and legislative functions were effectively fused and the judiciary's powers were narrowly circumscribed (Bagehot 1928 [1867], p. 9). By contrast to the United States, the British state was not impaired by fragmentation. By contrast to France, the legislature dominated the bureaucracy rather than vice versa. Yet the powers concentrated in Parliament and the ministries were relatively weak. To enforce the law, England had neither public prosecutors, as did the United States, nor a proactive public bureaucracy, as did France. England's lack of basic mechanisms for administrative or judicial oversight of private activity reinforced the principle of individualism. The traditional view was that the law would enforce itself as self-interested individuals used grand juries and common informers to protect their rights (Parris 1969, p. 164; Chester 1981, p. 57). Between the 1830s and the 1850s, a new "inspectorate" model of governance, promoted by Jeremy Bentham, was adopted in more than a dozen government realms. Inspectorates documented noncompliance with the law and provided grounds for private legal action, but because they were prohibited from imposing sanctions, private legal action remained the means to enforcement.

The legal system.   England did not have the system of public prosecutors found in the United States, but like the United States, England's common law doctrine located ultimate authority over the content of the law in tradition. Common law afforded the state only weak control over the corpus of legal doctrine, because it gave tradition precedence over Parliament's whims. Practically, English common law precluded the rise of the kind of statism found in France because it did not give the state the authority to determine its own scope of power. Moreover, England had nothing like the highly professionalized legal system found in France (Anderson 1974). The courts were presided over by volunteers from the gentry and cases were decided by juries made up of citizens. Yet Britain's unwritten constitution did not contain the deliberate separation of powers found in the United States, and thus court authority to interpret and disable legislation was highly circumscribed.

Office-holding and public expertise.   Traditionally, English government posts were staffed by the landed gentry rather than by members of a professional administrative corps. This was just as true of local administrative posts as of ministerial positions. One corollary of the amateur nature of public service in England, and of the private nature of the nation's canals and turnpikes, was that expertise in transport design, construction, and administration was located in the private sector rather than in the state (Francis 1851, v. 1, p. 35). Another corollary was that local parish officers were recruited from among local citizens who held the franchise rather than being appointed by the central government, as in France (Shefter 1977). This meant that local governments were locally run, as in the United States, but they lacked the independence of American localities because local posts were established by Parliament and officials carried out parliamentary policy (Chester 1981, pp. 52–58).

State fiscal capacities.   English state traditions had situated decisions over capital allocation in the private sector. At the turn of the nineteenth century, London was the world's financial capital, but banks had not developed long-term industrial lending practices because England's incremental industrialization had relied on direct capital investment and reinvestment by entrepreneurs (Gerschenkron 1962, p. 12). And because of the practice of self-capitalization, industry and finance had not developed close operational ties (Zysman 1983, p. 190). As a result of the practice *of private* capitalization, government and finance had not developed close ties and the London banks operated virtually free from public oversight (Hall 1986). Britain's lack of government participation in finance was striking in light of French activism, but it was not a direct result of Britain's early industrialization as Alexander Gerschenkron (1962) has argued. French state financing of major infrastructural and industrial projects extends back beyond the time of Colbert, who used public moneys to build canals for his king. British state abstention extends back equally far.

In sum, British state institutional capacities looked very different from those in the United States or France at the dawn of the railway age. On the one hand, the British state did not face the fragmentation that characterized the American state, where decision authority was dispersed across three levels of government and three branches at each level. In Britain, the legislative and executive functions were fused, and the courts were subordinated to Parliament. In consequence, the British state had a greater ability to effect its policies than did America's federal state. On the other hand, the British bureaucracy was underdeveloped by contrast to the French bureaucracy. Britain lacked a cadre of publicly educated engineers and managers bent on controlling the course of economic development, and regimes did not have full discretion to alter the legal code. If the British state had no built-in administrative weaknesses akin to the divided powers found in the United States, neither did it have a talented and powerful internal constituency that would try to take control of railway development and shape future industrial policies.

British political culture. British state institutions produced a polity much different from the polities of the United States and France. In Britain, political order emanated neither from self-governing communities acting on their own nor from central state orchestration of civil society. British institutions afforded sovereignty to individuals, and made them the foundation of the polity. Parliament was the core of government – not the Crown, the bureaucracy, or the town council – and by vesting authority in this representative body, British political institutions exalted individualism. Since the conflicts of the seventeenth century, England had been governed on the principle that individuals collectively held sovereignty even over the king. The legislature had been the forum in which men of substance who ruled the nation's "parcelized sovereignties" decided their common fate. Parliamentary sovereignty was thus identified with noble individualism, and the nobility never gained the kind of collective, corporate status their French counterparts attained in the Estates General. Moreover, whereas French absolutism had subjugated aristocrats by undermining their local sovereignty and bringing them to the level of vassals, the gradual extension of citizenship rights under British parliamentary rule had the opposite effect of extending the notion of noble sovereignty to all citizens.

By the beginning of the nineteenth century, the British had articulated a principle of economic order, parallel to that of the political order, in which economic sovereignty was diffused among masses of individual economic actors. This occurred in part because Britain's early industrial takeoff convinced the nation that government nonintervention was key to economic growth. "Classical economics, which was largely a British invention, converted the British experience – or rather what the British hoped would eventually emerge from the trend which they had detected in their own story – into something very like the Platonic idea of capitalism" (Shonfield 1965, p. 71). David Ricardo depicted a perfect market with innumerable buyers and sellers – none of them strong enough to impose his will on the others. And with no public authority strong enough to meddle in the affairs of these actors. The "great glory" of this system was that no firm could impose a direction on economic activity from within the market, and no political authority could impose a direction from without. The logic was that growth would ensue if economic actors were shielded from interference by more powerful, private or public, actors. This logic perfectly paralleled the logic of the traditional political culture, which guarded the prerogatives of (elite) individuals against incursions from neighboring elites and from the Crown. Moreover, this economic logic was soon inextricably intertwined with Britain's rhetoric of political liberty, as the ideas of the market, the small trader, and laissez-faire government were associated with freedom and democracy (Shonfield 1965, p. 71). Thus, where American liberty had become associated with the notion of community economic self-determination, and French liberty had become associated with the notion of a sovereign state that could preclude aristocratic dominance of economic life, British liberty had become associated with the notion of individual economic actors free from public or private interference.

What had begun as a political precept – the preeminence of individual actors and individual rights – came to be a precept of economic life. Britain's industrial class had come to champion nonintervention in part because public policy had traditionally been used to protect the economic interests of landowners. In Eric Hobsbawm's (1968) view, long before the railway age, men of commerce and industry had signaled their antipathy toward traditional state intervention by opposing policies that interfered with the free employment of private property, the free movement of labor, and free trade. The enclosure movement of the eighteenth century broke traditional claims of cultivators to private lands, and allowed landowners to use their property as they saw fit (Moore 1966). The new Poor Law of 1834 effectively ended public supports for farm laborers and encouraged them to seek industrial employment. And the repeal of the Corn Laws in 1846 ended tariffs on imported grain and introduced a market-based pricing system. As Karl Polanyi (1944, p. 140) argues, the free markets that emerged in Britain were linked to a policy paradigm dubbed laissez faire that, in reality, involved a wide range of positive policy interventions to create free trade in labor and goods. Free markets were not marked by the *absence* of policy instruments, but by the introduction of a new set of policy instruments. Nonetheless Britain's growing commercial and industrial class saw these shifts, and an array of other policy shifts, as part of an effort to eradicate traditional supports for agriculture and support industry. The putatively laissez-faire policies Britain embraced in the early nineteenth century involved calculated interventions to create, and sustain, a particular set of economic practices that were then associated with the "free market." In the railway industry, as in other sectors, the policy instruments associated with laissez faire would evolve as the industry matured.

Railway policy

Over the course of the nineteenth century, Britain struggled with an inherent contradiction in the principles of economic individualism and laissez faire. The dangers inherent in the industrial economy led to calls for the state to guard weak citizens and firms, yet how could the state do so without expanding public powers to the point of tyranny? A similar tension had characterized American policy, where the evil of concentrated federal power was finally reconciled with the evil of concentrated economic power in policies that regulated monopolies.

By the end of the nineteenth century, this tension had been resolved in an industrial policy paradigm that provided protection for individual firms. The state had a duty to guard the weak economic actors that comprised the economy, just as it had a duty to guard the weak political actors that comprised the polity. In the emergent vision of industrial rationality, multitudes of small manufacturing and service establishments competed on quality and price, and the state sustained that competition by guarding them from their predatory peers.

The British perceived fundamentally different problems of railway governance than their American and French peers. With state structures that shielded individual prerogative against powerful private parties and public officials, the British questioned whether the state should nullify the rights of landowners to satisfy rail promoters, asked whether the state was not obliged to protect passengers from railways callous to their security, and wondered whether Parliament might outlaw mergers to prevent large predatory firms from devouring their competitors. These issues centered around the sovereignty of individuals, and the state's duty to protect them from external influence. The policies Britain conceived were dramatically different from those of the United States, and they contributed to a unique vision of industrial efficiency. Britain's strategy was not to turn the state into the referee of a free market, as in the United States, or the conductor of an industrial orchestra, as in France. For much of the nineteenth century, British policymakers sought to mobilize public opinion to make entrepreneurs realize that their interest coincided with the public interest. When that failed, they made the state the guardian of weak passengers, employees, and firms.

Planning

As with the canals, the British believed that private parties would plan and build the rail routes that showed the greatest promise of turning a profit and serving the nation. In their discussions of railway planning, the British identified the public interest with the aggregation of private interests. They did not perceive the problem that the Americans perceived – how to use government resources to stimulate private planning. And they did not perceive the problem that the French perceived – how to retain public control over planning. Parliament reviewed France's decision to allocate planning to government engineers and Belgium's early decision to build a public rail system, but politicians never argued for either model. The only mention of government planning came from the Duke of Wellington, who twice recommended that the government might have surveys drawn up to help private entrepreneurs make route decisions. The Duke was concerned that without any coordination whatsoever, private parties might build lines that would not intersect where they ought to, and that this would hinder through traffic. In 1838, his argument before Parliament, as transcribed in the third person, was that

> in Ireland the Government had taken the precaution of instituting a general survey, that the railways might be constructed with some reference to one another; and he thought that it was extremely unfortunate that something of this kind had not been done in this country . . . In the construction of railways it was important that they should be made to communicate easily with one another (Great Britain, Parliamentary Debates 1838, c. 805)

But Parliament declined to discuss the matter. Beyond this, the state gave no consideration to the idea of positive public involvement in planning.

The battle over expropriation

The main problem the British perceived when it came to railway planning concerned public powers of expropriation. Should the state use its powers of eminent domain to facilitate free private planning and construction of railroads, even when to do so meant forcibly taking the lands of people who wanted no part of railways? Parliament now faced a quandary, because they could only allow full freedom to railroad promoters by trespassing upon the rights of property owners. Landowners and canal operators argued that some railwaymen sought charters solely for the purpose of speculation, and that others proposed railroads that would duplicate existing transport routes without offering any new advantages to the public. Parliament was asked to scrutinize the plans presented by transport entrepreneurs to evaluate two concerns. First, because some applicants were interested only in speculation, Parliament asked whether applicants sought charters for the purpose of selling them to the highest bidder. Second, Parliament asked whether the proposed lines would only enrich the rail promoters, at the expense of canals, turnpikes, and landowners, without offering advantages to the public.

The demand for Parliamentary approval of charters reflected Britain's changing political economy. The principle of laissez faire, which was just gaining currency, suggested that the state should refrain from meddling in private economic affairs. But as the economy became more interdependent and complex, the state was called upon with increasing frequency to settle competing claims by groups wishing to exercise their economic liberties.

The Liverpool-Manchester concession.   The earliest railed roads in Britain did not generate public debate because they did not necessitate public powers of expropriation. The first British railways date to the beginning of the seventeenth century, when tracks were laid to carry coal from pits to nearby rivers for further transport. Horse-drawn carriages were operated on such lines between Nottingham and the Trent River, Brosley and the Severn, and Northumberland and the River Blyth (Parris 1965, p. 1). By the beginning of the nineteenth century, these railed wagon-ways were widespread. In the first quarter of the century, twenty-nine of these lines, ranging from 4 to 34 miles in length, were constructed to cart coal, lumber, or stone (Francis 1851).

This changed in the 1820s, when entrepreneurs recognized that railroads could transport passengers and freight and began submitting "private" bills to Parliament, like those used to expropriate lands for canals and turnpikes. The charter debate over the Liverpool and Manchester Railway, which opened for service 15 September 1830, is illustrative. In 1822, Thomas Gray envisioned a public railway from Liverpool to Manchester, and soon engaged George Stephenson, the noted locomotive engineer, and his brother Robert to survey the route and prepare a prospectus (Francis 1851, v. 1, p. 129). Three years later, Gray's charter proposal came before an ad hoc parliamentary committee composed of members of both houses. On 21 March 1825, the committee began its proceedings with 150 petitions from opponents of the bill in hand. The committee's published proceedings fill some 800 pages (Great Britain, Parliament 1825). The three canal companies that serviced the Liverpool and Manchester route joined with landowners to question the public utility of the proposed railroad. They contended that the expropriation of private lands constituted a serious infringement of private property rights. A Mr. Harrison, representing three landowners, argued "I think that one of the first and greatest principles of our Constitution is that old common principle, 'That every man's house is his castle' and that property is not to be invaded at the suggestion of any joint stock company of speculators." Harrison went on to argue that private property had long been considered sacrosanct in Britain: "When these private rights of property lose the protection which is given by the Law and the Constitution . . . the strongest safeguard of our public liberty, in the regard which is paid to the protection of the property of the meanest individual, will be abandoned" (Great Britain, Parliament 1825, p. 322). Landowners feared that this rail line would, in addition to bisecting their properties, sully everything in its vicinity. It would scare away pheasants and foxes, drive horses mad, and destroy market crops and flowers with its smoke (Chester 1981). Landowners, abetted by the representatives of canal companies, demanded the right to employ their lands as they saw fit and contended that the proposed parliamentary interference would abrogate the traditional public protections for private property that the British guarded so closely as the foundation of political order (Carlson 1969, p. 125).

The landowners and canal companies granted that the state might expropriate lands in cases of clear and unquestioned public utility, but contended that this was not such a case because the three canals already serving Liverpool and Manchester provided adequate transport and a fourth rail route would not provide any additional benefits. Furthermore, they argued, the line was so poorly designed that it might never be opened for transport, and if it were opened it would soon fall into disrepair and disuse. One opponent argued that George Stephenson never produced a full engineering plan for the route:

> I say he never had a plan: I do not believe he is capable of making one ... he neither knows whether he is to make bridges over roads or rivers; or of one size or another; or to make embankments, or cuttings, or inclined planes, or in what way the thing is to be carried into effect. (quoted in Francis 1851, v. 1, p. 109)

Stephenson's detractors argued that he had not given careful consideration to whether the proposed line was practicable. If Parliament awarded charters on the basis of such shoddy plans, they warned, Britain would soon be crisscrossed by strips of fallow land owned by defunct rail companies (Parris 1965). This was not an outcome that could justify the expropriation of private lands.

Proponents of the line also emphasized the issue of public utility. They argued that the existing water routes failed to serve the public because they did not meet demand. Service was inadequate on the Liverpool-Manchester route in part because demand was great, and in part because competition had broken down. Competition to provide fast and reliable service had disappeared altogether. As Mr. Adams argued in his opening speech, "goods have taken twenty-one days in coming from America to Liverpool, and . . . they have [then] staid upon the wharfs before they could get the means of conveyance to Manchester for more than six weeks" (Great Britain, Parliament 1825, p. 5). Price competition had also disappeared. Rivalry had been wiped out on the route, the rail promoters argued, because the two most direct canals, the Duke of Bridgewater's canal and the Old Quay Company's canal, had routinely fixed prices. Moreover, despite the fact that they were required to allow public carriers to use the canals in return for paying a toll, they had driven independent competitors out of business by colluding to depress their own rates until independents disappeared. Mr. Sergeant Spankie, in summing up the case for the railroads, argued that the two companies possessed "an entire monopoly – that they have an opportunity for dictating the charge for carriage; and that [they] published advertisements in precisely the same words and figures, only changing the names, setting the rate at which they would carry." They had used their duopoly to "lower their terms for a year or two, so that no private carrier can think in terms of coming into competition with them" and then increase prices to take advantage of the public's dependence on their services. They had also used their control of warehouses and surrounding acreage to preclude the rise of competing barge services by refusing public carriers access to storage (Great Britain, Parliament 1825, pp. 306–7). A competing rail route could restore the advantages of competition to the route, and could ensure that demand would be promptly filled.

The promoters also tried to demonstrate that, on average, landowner wishes would be served by the concession. They surveyed the owners along the route and counted only 86 who opposed the railroad, but 152 who approved of it and 97 who were neutral (Carlson 1969, p. 115). However, the ad hoc committee was not taking a vote. It reasoned that because the promoters had not demonstrated that the railroad would serve the public interest, it would be wrong for the state to void the property rights of even one reluctant landowner. The bill died in committee. George Stephenson returned to the drawing board to produce a more detailed engineering plan that would convince a second parliamentary committee to approve the railroad, but this debate was characteristic of the early battles over expropriation.

By 1840, Parliament had come around to the argument that railroads were virtually always in the public interest because they offered advantages in speed, price, and dependability in inclement weather. Thereafter, they granted charters to nearly all applicants who came with detailed technical plans, and railway promoters had learned to produce plans that could not be challenged on technical grounds. The principle of public utility had won out over the rights of individual landowners.

Note that the two interests involved in these controversies were constituted in the first place by British transport policy. The early decision to leave transport development to private parties had given rise to a group of financially powerful canal and turnpike operators, and it spawned a group of private railway entrepreneurs in the 1820s with opposing interests. In France, by contrast, the early decision to build turnpikes and canals publicly gave rise to an interest group composed of public transport technocrats who tended to favor transport development of all sorts.

The railway mania and the Railway Board. In the 1840s, the British perceived two pressing problems with the system of chartering railroads. First, the charters bestowed unique powers on railroads that enabled them to disregard the public interest. Charters typically granted transport monopolies, which meant that competition did not check the railroads' behavior. Even when charters contained provisions to protect the public from the abuse of those monopolies, they did not stipulate enforcement mechanisms. For instance, the Liverpool and Manchester ignored with impunity a provision that called for them to reduce rates when dividends exceeded 10 percent (Parris 1965, p. 23). The problem boiled down to the fact that Britain had neither public prosecutors nor an independent transport administration to enforce charter provisions. In the 1830s, legislators had called for a regulatory body to oversee the railroads and enforce charters, yet Parliament initially rejected the idea as tyrannical. By 1840, however, the public believed that railway companies regularly abused their powers and wanted them called to account in court: "But who was to do it? English law had no place for a Public Prosecutor" (Parris 1965, p. 13). In response to such calls, Joseph Hume argued before Parliament: "The Government ought not to interfere. The very best check against the danger to be apprehended from [railroads] is each individual's own interest," expressed in private legal action (Great Britain, Parliamentary Debates 1836, c. 684–5). Nonetheless, in 1840, Parliament established a Railway Department within the Board of Trade and charged it with inspecting new rail lines to ensure they had abided by the construction provisions of their charters. The department had no powers of sanction, and it was not to meddle in Parliament's work of granting concessions.

Second was the old problem of unwarranted public expropriation of private lands. By 1844, Parliament was receiving many more concession applications than it could scrutinize with care, and members became concerned that they might abridge landowners rights by unwittingly sanctioning expropriations that served no public purpose. In the Railway Mania that peaked in the mid-1840s, Parliament was inundated with private railway bills. Between 1845 and 1847, over 900 railway bills were submitted (Simmons 1978, p. 40). In 1845 alone, Parliament approved nearly as many miles of track (2,700) as had been approved in all previous years combined (3,000). Some members argued for an independent railway department that could scrutinize applications to protect landowners and prospective investors alike. They argued that the existence of willing investors did not prove the public utility of a line:

> [The] willingness of parties to expend capital in making a new Railway is not to be at once taken as a sufficient ground for granting the necessary powers [of expropriation], since proprietary rights are not to be set aside except for adequate and great public advantage . . . since there may sometimes be indirect purposes in the proposal to construct new Line. (Great Britain, Parliamentary Papers. 1844, p. xi)

These "indirect purposes" included speculation in railway securities and the misuse of private investors' money. A House of Lords committee later argued that it had become difficult to sort out railway speculators from earnest promoters: "Schemes have been frequently got up and Acts obtained by Parties, for the mere purpose of speculation, without any definite object beyond that of selling them to the companies with which they may compete" (quoted in Jagtiani 1924, p. 20). These concerns led to the establishment of the 1844 Select Committee on Railway Acts Enactments, known as Gladstone's committee, which called for a department to examine the public utility of proposed lines and the integrity of their promoters. The root of the problem was that the British state depended on private parties to examine charters because it had no provision for administrative review of "private" bills and thus, the committee concluded, only the bills challenged by landowners were investigated: "The demands of companies have not been and could not have been scrutinized unless there were opposing parties in the field." It found that there had been many applications that "were not resisted by any particular interests which nevertheless it would have been important to sift and investigate in the interests of the public" (Great Britain, Parliamentary Papers. 1844, p. vii). The board proposed by Gladstone's committee might dampen speculation and at the same time protect property owners from undue expropriations (Cleveland-Stevens 1915, p. 133). A resolution in the House of Commons installed the Railway Board.

But the board was doomed by the appearance that it had assumed powers over private firms that duly belonged to Parliament. As a representative body composed of individuals, Parliament could exercise power over citizens without appearing to undermine individualism. However, when an administrative office exercised the same power, the British saw tyranny. At issue was the board's capacity to quash railway proposals without a full hearing before Parliament. The Board recommended action on each railway proposal, and because Parliament went along with these recommendations in nine out of ten cases railway promoters saw despotism and arbitrariness in everything the board did. First, railway directors questioned the secret nature of the board's proceedings. Robert Stephenson, representing the Liverpool and Manchester Railway, later contended, "the whole cause of the failure of the Board was, I believe, owing to their receiving evidence in the closet" (quoted in Jagtiani 1924, p. 20). Second, they argued that the board's judgments were arbitrary and capricious because the board announced its recommendations without explanation, and only later published full reports (Parris 1965, p. 74). Third, because the board's decision process was unclear, critics speculated that the junior members dominated. An outsider characterized the board as "a cumbrous and inconvenient mode of proceeding [which] raised subordinate members of the Board of Trade to a parity with the President or Vice-President" of the board (quoted in Parris 1965, p. 69). Fourth, backers of lines that received negative reports, such as the London-York line, cited damaging inaccuracies in board reports (Parris 1965, p. 80). Fifth, railway promoters argued that reports were prepared too hastily, which was no doubt often true given the volume of work to be done. Finally, opponents charged that the board was corrupt because some of its decisions were leaked to speculators before they appeared in the London Gazette (Parris 1965, p. 81). In brief, discouraged charter applicants charged that the board was now making railway policy and hence had usurped Parliamentary authority (Parris 1965, p. 84).

Conflict over the board came to a head in mid-1845. Lord Dalhousie, the Railway Board's president and second in command at the Board of Trade, believed that the Railway Board's reports constituted the position of the Government. Prime Minister Sir Robert Peel disagreed vigorously:

> It was never the intention of the government to fetter the House by any opinions of reports presented by [the board] . . . [Parliament did not have] the most distant intention of compromising the neutrality of the government upon such questions. (Great Britain, Parliamentary Debates 1845, c. 174–5)

When Peel later disagreed with the board's decision to reject the Great Western Railway Bill, and set aside the board's report, Dalhousie responded:

> I have the mortification of finding that you have departed, as you stated, from the ordinary practice which leads the ministers of the Crown to stand neutral and abstain from interfering in private business at all; . . . You had gone out of your way to oppose your Board. . . . the practical effect of the step you have taken is to overturn the authority . . . of the [board] and to throw discredit on the officer who conducts it. (quoted in Parris 1965, p. 85)

However, Peel stood firm in denying the board the power to dictate the government's position on railway bills, and when the board's members resigned in protest they were not replaced. Although this initial experiment with rail administration was doomed by the fact that the board appeared to be making public policy, across the Channel French public administrators had been deciding which concession applications to forward to the legislature from the birth of the industry – without any special legislative mandate to do so.

In sum, the British perceived entirely different problems in the realm of railway planning than their American and French counterparts perceived. Britain perceived a problem in the conflicting economic rights of citizens. Property rights were at the very core of British possessive individualism (McPherson 1962), and thus the state was reluctant to expropriate private property where there was any question about the merit of the project. The contradiction between the state's efforts to guard the property rights of landowners and to guard the economic liberties of prospective railwaymen was at the heart of the matter. In planning, American governments became preoccupied with the problem of stimulating private parties to design and build railroads, rather than with the problem of balancing the rights of railroaders and land-owners, and the French were most concerned to ensure that a coherent national network of rail lines would be planned and not a hodgepodge of disarticulated lines.

The solution the British conceived was to deny charters when there was any question of public utility. This contradicted the American strategy for stimulating planning, which at first centered around un-restrained charter-granting and later centered around general railway incorporation laws that allowed any thirteen citizens to receive a char-ter without going through the legislature. On the face of it, Britain shared France's concern with public utility; however, their concerns were motivated by radically different ideas about public utility. Both countries denied early charters on grounds of public utility, but the British were concerned to protect landowners against unnecessary ex-propriation, whereas the French were concerned to ensure that the nation's resources were used to their fullest effect. French technocrats believed that the lines they planned would make the best use of the nation's land, capital, and engineering talents, yet private planning would lead to suboptimal utilization of these assets. Whereas French officials felt a duty to orchestrate the use of the nation's resources, British officials merely felt a duty to guarantee that private parties could employ their own resources as they saw fit.

Finance

British politicians did not perceive the capitalization of railways as a matter for government concern. For the British, railways were a prop-erly private undertaking, and the state could best promote the industry by allowing private capital to divine, and support, the most promising projects. Not only did Parliament fail to offer capital to the railways, for the most part it refused to interfere with the application of private capital.

Britain's decision not to provide public construction aid for the rail-ways singled it out from the rest of the world: "The United Kingdom is the only important country whose railways have been developed prac-tically without public aid" (Dunn 1913, p. 17). And as H.M. Jagtiani remarked in 1924:

> England may be very aptly described as the classic instance of the achievements of private enterprise in railways. The State has offered

no aid beyond what is implied in the mere granting of a concession
and a right to expropriate the owners of the land through which a line
may run. (p. 14)

The British government did not even purchase rights-of-way for railroads, as did governments in both the United States and France. Parliament's only discussion of public funding came when it patted itself on
the back for not being as foolish as the Belgians. In 1844, members of
Parliament reviewed the Belgian experiment with public capitalization
to their great satisfaction. They recalled that in 1834, Belgium, in the
bloom of its newfound independence, had decided to build a rail network with public funds. Despite its enthusiasm, the government had
made a number of serious blunders, such as taking over the tasks of
shippers by providing door-to-door service. As a result, the experiment
had proven a resounding failure, as evidenced by the paltry 2.5 percent
rate of return earned on the government's investment (Parris 1965, p.
12). To Parliament the Belgian example proved the superiority of the
British course of action. In 1865, a royal commission examined the
whole issue of railway ownership again, concluding that Britain had
followed the optimal course and would be ill-served by a change in
policy: "It is inexpedient at present to subvert the policy which has
hitherto been adopted of leaving the construction and management of
railways to free enterprise of the people" (quoted in Bagwell and
Mingay 1970, p. 35).

Britain's local governments also refrained from capitalizing railroads. Local groups tried to influence route planning with financial
incentives, just as their American and French counterparts did, but in
Britain these efforts were carried out privately. For instance, Quakers
in the region provided most of the capital for the early Stockton and
Darlington line (est. 1825). Liverpool merchants who were dissatisfied
with canal transport helped to finance the Liverpool and Manchester
(Bagwell and Mingay 1970, p. 28). In the 1820s and '30s, local groups
often backed railroads because London banks did not make longterm
industrial loans, and in the '30s and '40s railroad enthusiasts helped to
establish regional stock exchanges to mobilize capital in Liverpool,
Manchester, Leeds, Glasgow, Edinburgh, and elsewhere. They solicited
stock subscriptions through advertisements and public meetings
(Gourvish 1980, p. 17), but did not engage the offices of local governments in their efforts. In comparative perspective, the absence of a
source of longterm loans in Britain and the need to establish new
institutions to draw capital tends to undermine the received wisdom

that British railways were financed privately principally because capital was so readily available there.

The only exception to Parliament's hands-off rule for railway capitalization came when members of Parliament proposed a sort of countercyclical solution to Ireland's disastrous economic conditions in the 1840s. With half a million Irish living on poor relief in 1846, the new president of the Commissioners of Railways argued that "capital immediately laid out on railways would cause trade to spring up at once, and give employment to many of the starving inhabitants" (quoted in Lewin 1936, p. 291). He proposed that the government lend Irish railroads two-thirds of the capital they would require to build new lines, to match one-third collected privately. Parliament rejected the proposal, but the Government later substituted a less ambitious bill that granted 600,000 pounds to three Irish railroads, and in 1849 it loaned the Midland Great Western Company another 500,000 pounds (Lewin 1936, p. 421).

The one thing that did get Parliament to intervene in private rail finance was the recurrent issue of unnecessary expropriations. In the late 1830s, the problem of insincere charter applications came, again, to the attention of Parliament. In the case of most early applications, like that for the Liverpool and Manchester, it had seemed clear that the promoters actually wanted to build. However, by the end of the 1830s, Parliament had granted charters to a number of groups whose purposes, it turned out, were entirely speculative. Parliament came to believe that charter applicants often sought to seize the right to build a particular line in order to sell that right to the highest bidder. This kind of speculation would lead to unnecessary expropriation. To make matters worse, parties that acted deceitfully would profit from the sale of lands to which they had no genuine claim, to the detriment of the original landowners, who would not receive full value, and of the public, who would wind up paying inflated transport rates. To put an end to this practice, Parliament in 1840 required that railroad charter applicants deposit an amount equal to one-tenth of their estimated construction costs with the Exchequer before they could receive a charter (Great Britain, Parliamentary Debates 1840). This was Parliament's sole intrusion into railway finance.

The decision to allot responsibility for financing railroads to the private sector had much to do with enduring characteristics of political culture. The British had already seen their political culture boiled down to a positive theory of political economy by Adam Smith. By the 1830s, the rhetoric of laissez faire was becoming integral to Britain's notion of industrial rationality. The idea of leaving matters up to private parties had become the foundation of a positive industrial policy paradigm. As Samuel Dunn wrote in 1913: "This was the *laissez-faire* era in England. Government and people thought that all that was needed to cause the railways to furnish good service at reasonable rates was to maintain competition" (p. 18). In financing as in planning, industry would take care of itself as long as the state guarded economic liberties and prevented politicians and private parties from exerting unwanted influence over free entrepreneurs.

In sum, in railway finance the British perceived the protection of the rights of landowners and investors as a problem that merited public attention, but otherwise believed that railway finance should remain in private hands. There were virtually no exceptions to this rule. Over the course of three-quarters of a century, not once did a politician, officeholder, or entrepreneur advocate government financing for the railroads. Americans perceived railway promotion, and industrial development generally, to be a duty of state and local government, and as a result they developed all sorts of schemes for public capitalization of rail lines, though they came to repudiate those schemes by the turn of the century. The French perceived railway capitalization to be a duty of the central state, and fiscal constraints alone stopped them from building the entire network with public funds. Economic historians suggest that the British government did not get involved in railway finance because private capital was plentiful there, whereas it was scarce in other countries. We have seen, however, that because London banks did not make longterm industrial loans, railroads did not have ready access to capital, and instead their promoters had to form new institutions to amass capital, in the form of regional stock markets. Local groups in Britain faced the same problem of capital scarcity that local groups in the United States faced, though they went about remedying that problem privately rather than publicly because Britain's political culture gave government no positive role in the economy.

Technical and managerial coordination

In the realms of technical and managerial coordination, the British perceived only one problem that demanded public attention: safety. Parliament assumed responsibility for protecting sovereign individuals from the dangers associated with the new industrial economy. The large-scale profit-oriented enterprises that fueled industrial growth frequently endangered employees and customers. The railways were a prime example, but Parliament's first industrial interventions in many sectors were oriented to guarding groups such as factory workers, seamen, coal miners, and rail passengers. By contrast to their American and French counterparts, British policymakers did not see broader problems of coordination that affected only efficiency as government concerns. Parliament made some belated, half-hearted, efforts to promote technical standardization, but the belief that private initiative could best effect coordination persisted. Parliament's only passion for intervention came with issues such as carriage roofs for third-class carriages.

When the British thought about governmental solutions to the problem of safety, they were perplexed by two corollaries of British individualism that seemed to be at odds. One held that state expansion was antithetical to individual freedom; the other held that the state had a responsibility to guard its sovereign citizens from other powerful private parties. How could the state protect citizens from the tyranny of large enterprises without, in the process, threatening them with the tyranny of big government? Over the course of the century, the British experimented with a series of solutions that would reconcile these two principles. Britain's initial policy strategy was to allow public opinion to take care of safety matters, with the logic that the interests of the railways and the public coincided. This logic was part of the foundation of laissez faire: The nation's interest will be served by individuals pursuing their own interests free from government interference. Public opinion would cause railways to pursue strategies that benefitted the nation, because railways that failed to do so would fail themselves. Britain's second strategy was to use a government inspectorate to inform public opinion, and thereby make railways cognizant that they served themselves when they served the nation. The early policy strategies, in which the government employed public opinion and market mechanisms to achieve public ends, were judged ineffective by the end of the 1880s because many railroads had not installed even rudimentary safety devices. In 1889, the policy paradigm changed when Parliament required railroads to install signaling systems on their routes and brakes on their trains. Although Britain's policy stance on safety had changed markedly, Parliament continued to espouse laissez faire in most matters of efficiency. Coordination of technical standards and managerial practices that affected only efficacy was left to railroads.

Safety

Construction standards. During the 1830s, railway observers noted that firms were under no compulsion to comply with the terms of their charters, and Parliament became particularly concerned that railroads could cut corners on bridge and tunnel construction. There was nothing to stop railroads that had presented exemplary construction plans in their charter applications from turning around and building shoddy roads that would imperil passengers. We saw that in France public controls were predicated on the notion that the interests of capitalists and those of the nation were frequently at odds, and that national goals could best be achieved through the public coordination and oversight of private initiative. In Parliament's debates over how to hold railways to their charters, there appears the very different idea that the interests of private capital and those of the public naturally coincide. In the 1840 parliamentary debates over regulation, a Mr. Easthope argued that

> the individuals to whose direction the railways throughout this country were confided, fully felt and understood that their own true interests, and the interests of the proprietors of these public undertakings, were identical with the interests of the public . . . railway directors were anxious to adopt those plans that were the best calculated to promote economy and utility; . . . the best plan was to let them proceed in that course without dangerous meddling. (Great Britain, Parliamentary Debates 1840, c. 907)

To British observers, the beauty of the modern economy was that public goals were naturally achieved by private initiative. As Mr. Turner argued in the same debate: "the interests of the public and of the company [are] in exact concurrence," hence governmental regulation is unnecessary (Great Britain, Parliamentary Debates 1840, c. 930).

Just how little public oversight there was in the railway industry became clear in the early 1840s in a parliamentary investigation into the administration of charters. It was discovered that the general articles included in the Liverpool and Manchester charter had been lifted directly from a canal charter, and that they were in turn copied into virtually every subsequent railroad bill (Cleveland-Stevens 1915, p. 11). Many of the clauses were nonsensical when applied to railroads, but it had taken nearly two decades for this to come to the attention of Parliament because the government had no office responsible for overseeing the administration of bills. An 1842 investigation of a dispute between the Grand Junction and the Manchester and Burlington companies found

> that a clause requiring that no carriage should be used upon the railway whose weight, *inclusive of its load*, should exceed four tons, had been copied from the original Act of the Liverpool and Manchester Railway into almost all subsequent railway Acts, but that this clause has been completely disregarded in practice. (Great Britain, Parliamentary Debates 1843, c. 19)

Parliament retroactively expunged the clause from all railway acts, but cases like this helped to convince members that their inattention to construction and operating standards threatened public safety by encouraging railways to build lines on the cheap, in contravention of their charters. But how could Parliament remedy the problem?

In the 1830s, Parliament became concerned with safety in a number of industrial realms, and experimented with inspectorates that might resolve safety problems. The idea of a national commission with responsibility for inspection can be traced to excise inspection of spirits, glass, and paper factories (Lubenow 1971; MacDonagh 1958). Jeremy Bentham's *Civil Code* formalized the model and offered it as a solution to the problem of governing industry with a spineless state bureaucracy. The inspectorate represented a revolutionary break with British tradition, but it made a kind of sense to the utilitarians (MacDonagh 1958). In most affairs, utility was achieved by adherence to laissez faire, they believed, yet there were instances where laissez faire failed to serve the public interest. This was especially the case in sectors dominated by large enterprises, where there were not multitudes of competing producers:

> When it was asked 'Since free competition does not work in the field of railway enterprise, would public regulation tend to the greatest happiness of the greater number?' the answer (in 1840) was 'Yes'. The question was then, as indeed it is today, not *laissez faire or* state intervention, but where, in the light of constantly changing circumstances, the line between them should be drawn. (Parris 1960, pp. 36–37)

The inspectorate was not designed to impose the government's will on enterprises, but to inform public opinion and thereby bring it to bear on industry. It was believed that consumers of factory goods, buyers of coal, and railway passengers would eschew companies that had been negatively evaluated by government inspectors. Likewise, local government agencies would fall into line if their illicit activities were publicized. The Factory Act of 1833 established the first modern inspectorate to oversee working conditions in new industries. Between 1834 and 1850, Parliament established the Poor Law Commission, the Prison Inspectorate, the Education Committee, the Railway Department, the Mining Inspectorate, the Lunacy Commission, the General Board of Health, the Merchant Marine Department, the Charity Commission, and the Department of Science and Art (Roberts 1960, p. 195). Each was oriented to the new policy logic, in which the state could effect the public will by inspecting local establishments and reporting their findings to the public. The invisible hand of the market would then take over and compel firms to act in the public interest (Roberts 1959, p. 106).

In 1840, Parliament established a Railway Department in the Board of Trade to inspect new lines before they were opened and to review the bylaws of railway companies, with the aim of ensuring that railways followed the construction specifications sketched out in their charters (Hodges 1889, pp. 12–15). The department was to publish the violations it found, but was not to interfere with the opening or operation of railways. Parliament had debated the powers to be conferred on the new inspectorate with a keen eye to protecting the economic liberties of railway entrepreneurs. One disputed clause required railways to give the board a month's notice before opening a new line so that the board could conduct a safety inspection. The legislation did not permit the government to delay the opening of a line, and provided no "penalty for opening railroads declared unfit," argued Mr. Finch, and thus the board could have no reason to demand a month's notice (Great Britain, Parliamentary Debates 1840, c. 910). Finch agreed with the authors of the bill that no government department *should* have the authority to penalize railroads by delaying their opening, but concluded that as a result the notification clause served no purpose. Lord Seymour, in advocating the bill, argued that it intentionally lacked penalties, for

> if the Board of Trade should remonstrate against the road as unfit to be opened, or as endangering the public, it was so much the interest of the railways to attend to the remonstrance, that it was not necessary to give the Board of Trade the absolute power of saying whether it

should be opened or not. (Great Britain, Parliamentary Debates 1840, c. 910)

Mr. Easthope noted that the railway companies could not object to a clause designed to notify the public of safety violations, because they were already subject to lawsuits when their disregard for safety resulted in injury:

> The responsibility with regard to the opening of railways now rested upon the directors, under the guidance of their engineers. If they threw open the works before they were in a condition to be employed with safety to the public, and if the public were injured thereby, he was confident that he should be told by the hon. and learned Attorney-general, that if such a case were brought into a court of justice, it would bring upon them damages proportioned to their offense. (Great Britain, Parliamentary Debates 1840, c. 914)

It was in the interest of railways to comply with the construction standards they had written into their charters to ensure public safety. If they did not do so, they would face material sanctions in the forms of lost business and litigation. Mr. Labouchere thought "that it was decidedly best not to encourage the interference of the Government, but to limit it to the smallest possible degree." The purpose here was to allow the board to

> give a warning to the railway company of the neglect of which they had been guilty . . . without the authority of the Board of Trade being pushed too far . . . it would be going very far to allow a Government board . . . to stop the progress of any public work merely upon their own declaration. (Great Britain, Parliamentary Debates 1840, c. 917)

Viscount Sandon agreed that a public remonstrance would have the desired effect: "No one would travel on the line after such a remonstrance had been given" (Great Britain, Parliamentary Debates 1840, c. 911). But the Viscount went on to argue that even this bill placed a dangerous "power of condemnation" in the hands of the administration. What if a line was inspected a month prior to opening and it was indeed not yet prepared, but in the subsequent weeks it was completed? By issuing a remonstrance, the state "would injure materially the whole property of the proprietors, and would not promote the interests of the public" (Great Britain, Parliamentary Debates 1840, c. 911). He thus opposed affording even the power of inspection to the proposed board. Mr. Muntz chimed in that he "looked with very great jealousy upon any government interference in these matters, and unless very ample grounds were shown to warrant it, he considered that it would be quite unnecessary," while Mr. Ewart was of the opinion "that all government interference was highly impolitic" (Great Britain, Parliamentary Debates 1840, c. 917). In the end, the bill passed without the clause giving the board the power to demand a month's notice before a railway could open. In 1842, Parliament amended the bill to afford that power to the board.

A second clause included in the original draft of the bill required railway companies to maintain such accounting records as the Board of Trade required, for the latter's inspection. Captain Boldero responded that he could "not but feel surprised that a clause so obnoxious and tyrannical should have been introduced" (Great Britain, Parliamentary Debates 1840, c. 922). Boldero suggested that such intrusions into the accounts of a private company could never be justified, and reported that he would vote against the bill unless "so monstrous" a clause was purged. This second clause was struck from the bill.

Parliament insisted on minimizing state power over railways and enforcing compliance through private litigation and public opinion. These debates are particularly remarkable when contrasted with the situation in France where the Corps des Ponts et Chaussées took it upon themselves to dictate how railroads would be built, oversee construction, and demand the accounts of railroads. The corps not only assumed the power to delay the opening of lines and suspend service on operating lines, it established engineering and technical specifications for each line in the first place. The very tasks that Parliament believed to be beyond the scope of state power had in France been appropriated by an administrative subunit without the express consent of the Chamber and without substantial challenge from railways. And in France those powers were sustained by republican regimes bent on creating democratic institutions, because they were not perceived to be inimical to liberty.

Third-class carriages.   The second problem of safety to come to the attention of Parliament concerned third-class trains. The safety of the poorer classes came to be a central concern of Parliament from the 1840s, and in the railway industry, as elsewhere, Parliament believed it had a duty to prevent powerful private actors from injuring Britain's weaker residents. Here, again, individualism and excessive private power were at stake. In 1846, Lord Campbell's act made British firms legally liable for accidental injuries (Schivelbusch 1986, p. 134). In the

same era, the Mercantile Marine Acts (1850, 1854) created comprehensive protections for seamen; the Adulteration of Food Act
(1860) protected consumers from tainted food; acts of 1848, 1867, and
1869 gave the Privy Council control over diseased livestock. Later such
legislation as the Ship Hours Acts (1892, 1895) and the Seats for Shop
Assistants Act (1899) regulated working conditions (Grove 1962). In
the case of railways, Parliament rightly became alarmed at the conditions of third-class travel. Some companies did not offer third-class
transport, or offered it infrequently. Mr. Wallace reported to Parliament on 5 February 1840 that the line between Lancaster and London
often offered neither second- nor third-class carriages, and he had witnessed "poor fellows, honest, sober, steady cotton-jackets" forced to
pay first class fares – "now this was a monstrous case." Furthermore,
third-class passengers were often carried on open flat bed cars without
roofs or seats: "Take the question of the third-class passengers who
were going to Bath. They could not go by day, and when they proceeded at night, they had to stand all the way" (Great Britain, Parliamentary Debates 1844, c. 249). Wallace insisted that it was
Parliament's duty to intervene to protect the less fortunate classes.

The dangers of open third-class carriages were chronicled by John
Francis in a treatise published a few years later:

> Delicate women – delicate though poor, and valuable members of
> society, though belonging to the working class – half clothed and half
> fed, are unable to contend with an inclement season, and often receive
> into their frames the seeds of indispositions which shorten their lives.
> The skilled artisan, too, enervated by the confined character of his
> labour, to whom many look for support, and on whom many hopes
> depend, is liable to cold, catarrh, and consumption. It is a class to
> which England owes much, and over the comfort of which she should
> watch. But railway proprietors are not social economists and railway
> directors are [only] men. (1851 v. 2, p. 104)

For Francis, Britain's less fortunate citizens were the bedrock of the
nation, and the country owed them protection from powerful private
railroads interested only in profits. In the early 1840s, the Railway
Department had taken a stand on open carriages. It "recommended"
that third-class carriages be equipped with sides of at least four feet in
height in the wake of an accident on Christmas Eve, 1841 when a Great
Western train ran into a slip of earth in Sonning Culting and all of the
passengers in the two, flatbed, third-class carriages were thrown from
the train. Eight died and seventeen were injured (Parris 1965, p. 45).

The essence of the problem was that British railways did not take the comfort or safety of third-class passengers into account, because "they were regarded not as recipients of passenger service but as freight goods" (Schivelbusch 1986, p. 72).

The "cheap train provision" of the 1844 bill addressed monopolistic pricing practices and lax safety standards by requiring that future railways offer third-class service on every route, at least once a day, in covered carriages with seats at a cost of a penny a mile. The bill charged the Board of Trade with administering the clause, which meant that the Railway Department was to survey passenger lines to ensure that they offered such service.

The authors of the bill were concerned that the state had been unable to enforce the stipulations contained in railway charters, and they devised a new enforcement strategy in the form of a threat. The bill gave the state the right to purchase any railway company subsequently built after twenty-one years of operation: "It shall be lawful for the said Lords Commissioners, . . . at any time after the expiration of the said term of twenty-one years, to purchase any such railway" (quoted in Hodges 1889, p. 26). This resembles the "repurchase" provisions of French railway law, but it was proposed because railroads had argued that Parliament had no right to pass blanket legislation that would annul clauses in their charters. The repurchase clause would give Parliament leverage against firms that opposed blanket legislation. As W.E. Gladstone, President of the Board of Trade, described the state purchase option: "The whole effect . . . is, that instead of Parliament having its hands tied and fettered as they are now, they shall be free to deal with these matters for the public good" (quoted in Lubenow 1971, p. 115).

As noted in the section on planning, the board set up in 1844 was dismantled in short order because it appeared to be usurping the representative powers of Parliament. In 1846, the Whigs set up the Commissioners of Railways, with greater powers and resources than the Railway Board and with autonomy from the Board of Trade. The Whigs planned to make the commissioners responsible for reporting on railway bills, as the board had been, but opposition to expanding state powers thwarted that goal. The railway mania soon subsided, and the commissioners were folded back into the Board of Trade as a reconstituted Railway Department (Parris 1965, p. 104; Bagwell 1974, p. 163).

Safety devices. Over the next decades, the inspectorate struggled to achieve desired safety outcomes by informing the public of dangers, but in 1889 Parliament became frustrated with the pace of progress and expanded public controls once again. The laissez-faire strategy (1825–1840) and the inspectorate strategy (1840–1889) had failed. Although the inspectorate carried on, new public legislation required railroads to install safety devices. From its inception, Britain's railway inspectorate, in its various incarnations, had called for Parliament to regulate safety procedures and to mandate the use of safety devices, but Parliament stubbornly refused to limit the liberties of railwaymen. As early as 1840 a department accident investigation revealed that passengers were often injured when an engine driver, on approaching a station, detached the locomotive and let the carriages coast to a stop. The carriages frequently crashed into terminal walls when drivers miscalculated speed and distance. The department recommended that Parliament prohibit this practice and require that carriages carry brakes. The report concludes: "It is evident that if the Board of Trade had the power of enforcing these recommendations, accidents of such a nature as that last described could not by possibility occur" (Great Britain, Railway Department 1841 [Jan.], p. 4). Later that year, after two passengers were killed when a luggage train plowed into a passenger train that was behind schedule departing from Taylor's Junction, Sir Frederick Smith of the department suggested "the necessity of empowering the Government to make general regulations in such cases, in order to insure the punctuality which is essential for the safety as well as the convenience of passengers" (Great Britain, Railway Department 1841 [Jan.], p. 9). Punctuality was essential because most trains had no brakes, and even those with brakes could not stop rapidly. By the time a driver could see a stalled or tardy train on the track, it was too late to avoid an accident. However, Parliament refused to give the department the power to demand operating procedures that would minimize this risk, or to demand the installation of brakes. Legislators had confidence that for most purposes public opinion would compel railways to practice safety precautions.

Soon after its establishment in 1840, the inspectorate found most of its time taken up by accident inquiries. The department's duties expanded with the growth of the railways, as reported accidents rose from 35 for the last half of 1840 to 372 for the year of 1875 (Great Britain, Railway Department 1840 [Jan.], pp. 2–3; 1876 [Jan.], p. 18).

Although railroads had adamantly opposed the imposition of safety standards, they went along with these investigations in the belief that the state had a right to inform the public about accidents. Beyond this, the investigations often exonerated railway operators. For instance, when a coroner's jury concluded from the driver's testimony that poor engine design had led to a fatal accident in 1841 on the London-Brighton line, the company removed all similar engines from service. The department's subsequent inquiry threw blame back on the driver, which enabled the railway to reinstate the engines and terminate the driver (Parris 1965, p. 43). In the six months between 1 August 1840 and 30 January 1841 the department cited employee misconduct as a principal cause in nineteen of the twenty-eight accidents for which they identified a cause (Great Britain, Railway Department, 1841 [Jan.], pp. 2–3). In these cases, railways commonly fired the employee whose conduct had been impugned, and carried on as usual. Companies had little to lose from an investigation that laid blame on management, because the inspectorate had no powers to sanction railroads and because, in the absence of a report that laid blame elsewhere, the public generally blamed railways anyway.

In 1846, Parliament encouraged railway safety by making lines legally liable for death and injury to customers, but not to employees. Lord Campbell's act, it was hoped, would cause railways to do what they could to minimize the risk of accident. A central selling point was that the act would not involve Parliament in the internal affairs of firms (Bagwell 1974, p. 178). Here again, Parliament hoped that it could convince railways to act in the public interest by mobilizing public opinion and market mechanisms. By 1853, the Lancashire and Yorkshire Railway was held liable for as much as 3,000 pounds sterling in the death of a single passenger, although as late as 1870 it commonly paid no more than ten pounds to *employees'* survivors. The success of the act may be seen in the fact that only 155 *passengers* were killed between 1872 and 1875, inclusive, whereas nearly 3,000 *employees* were killed (Bagwell 1974, p. 182).

Safety concerns persisted, however, and in 1874 a royal commission was appointed to inquire "into the causes of accidents on railways, and into the possibility of removing any such causes by further legislation" (quoted in Fowler 1877, p. 661). The commission's report recommended expanding public powers to enable the state to require brakes, blocking, and other safety measures. The report did not lead to legislation, but the fact that 336 witnesses appeared to testify as to the advisability of trying to legislate safety measures suggests that the issue of intervention was highly salient.

In 1871, the Regulation of Railways Act had reiterated that the Board of Trade's powers were restricted to inspection of new lines and accident investigations and that no member of the board "shall exercise any power of interference in the affairs of any company" (Fowler 1377, p. 661). Should the board be empowered to compel the installation of brakes or the adoption of other safety measures? There was great disagreement even within the Board of Trade over this; unlike their French counterparts, members of the board did not uniformly favor expanded public powers. The board's Secretary, Mr. Farrar, argued: "I think that the disadvantage which would result from carrying the power of the Board of Trade inspector further than it is now carried, would much more than counterbalance any advantage which would be derived from the additional power." He went on to argue that it would be in the companies' interests to pursue the public good: "My own opinion is, that the railway companies would generally do for their own interest what the inspector requires" (quoted in Fowler 1877, p. 652). In his testimony Captain Tyler, a railway inspector with twenty years' experience, concurred:

> While I see, on the one hand, very great advantages which might arise from the Board of Trade having a little more power in directing railway companies to do certain things . . . I always see so many evils in the way of any detailed interference in railway management . . . that you would do a great deal more harm than good by conferring additional powers upon the Board of Trade, with a view to their undertaking, so to speak, the management of the railways. (quoted in Fowler 1877, p. 653)

Proposals to allow the board to mandate safety measures were widely regarded as threats to company authority. On the one hand, it was argued, such a change would appear to transfer the responsibility for safety from the company to the state. If the state took control of safety standards, would the state then be liable in the case of accidents? Captain Tyler maintained that "where you attempt to interfere you will tend to relieve the railway company of the responsibility and put it upon the Board of Trade" (quoted in Fowler 1877, p. 657). In the same vein, the general manager of the London and North Western, a Mr. Findley, argued that such a change would amount to a public takeover of the finances of private railroads:

> If an inspecting officer of the Board of Trade has the power to go upon an old line and order new works to be done, . . . the officer would then not only be responsible for the safety of the line, but he must be responsible to the shareholders for the commercial success of the undertaking. (quoted in Fowler 1877, p. 657)

The Board of Trade's Mr. Farrar concurred by stating that new expenditures on the part of the railroads "could not be prescribed by Government without taking the management of the concern, financial and otherwise, out of the hands of the company" (quoted in Fowler 1877, p. 657).

Although the divided Royal Commission forwarded a report that called for the board to be empowered to require brakes, absolute blocking, and such additional specific safety measures as it deemed necessary, Parliament did not approve the recommendations. The contrast with France, where the corps mandated the installation of various safety devices and procedures as early as the 1820s without any special legislative dispensation to do so, is striking.

As a result of Parliament's reluctance to require safety measures, for most of the nineteenth century Britain depended upon accident inspections to encourage railway safety. When it came to brakes and signaling systems, Parliament encouraged adoption by asking the department for annual reports on the progress each railway had made. Only after the policy paradigm that employed inspection and informed public opinion to ensure safety had been given half a century's trial, and had still failed to make brakes universal, did Parliament proclaim the strategy a failure and expand public powers.

Brakes.   Braking was probably the worst railway safety problem. Early trains had no brakes at all, or at best rudimentary brakes made of wooden blocks on one or two axles. From the beginning the department had argued that railways should install brakes on passenger trains: "The last carriage, and at least every fourth carriage, in trains by which passengers are conveyed, [ought] to be provided with a proper break (sic)" (Great Britain, Railway Department 1841 [Jan.], p. 13). Parliament concurred, and hoped that public opinion would effect the department's wishes. In the middle of the 1850s the department again bemoaned the lack of continuous brakes, operating on all axles simultaneously:

> A large number of [accidents], the very lamentable one at Bullhouse being included, by which so many passengers were killed and injured, might, according to the statements in the reports of inquiries, have been either entirely prevented or to their effects mitigated had the trains been fitted with quick-acting, continuous automatic brakes. (Great Britain, Railway Department 1855a, p. 25)

Again, this call had no effect. Before 1852, braking technology was very rudimentary, yet by 1860 several braking systems had proven reasonably dependable, and Board of Trade inspectors began to encourage companies to follow the lead of the Lancashire and Yorkshire Company by installing brakes on all trains. In 1874, the department conducted extensive tests of available braking systems, and in 1881 Parliament asked the department to add to its annual report data on the proportion of each company's rolling stock furnished with brakes, and data on accidents involving cars without continuous brakes. Parliament had hoped with this measure to engage public opinion to convince the railways to install brakes, but railways resisted for reasons of cost, and by 1885 only 37 percent of the 50,512 locomotives and cars used in British passenger trains carried approved braking systems (Simmons 1978).

Signaling systems. The second longstanding safety problem that the department sought to remedy involved collisions. Beginning in the 1840s, the companies adopted various systems to prevent collisions of trains operating on the same track. The only reliable solution was absolute blocking, in which each line was divided into sections and trains were prevented from entering a section until they received the "all clear" signal from the other end (Simmons 1978, p. 217). Under absolute blocking, no two trains could operate in the same section simultaneously. Although blocking was effective, mechanical blocking systems were expensive and railways were reluctant to install them. By 1873, 49 percent of British railway mileage was operated with absolute blocking, and to encourage railways to make the system universal, Parliament asked the department to report annually on the proportion of each company's trackage that had been converted to absolute blocking. Again it hoped that informed public opinion would elicit change. In seven years' time, 81 percent of the nation's mileage was being worked on the block system, but thereafter adoption stagnated.

Finally, in 1889 an accident on the Great Northern that killed 78 and seriously injured 260 spurred Parliament to acknowledge that informed public opinion was not having the desired effect. Parliament's first effort at mandating safety mechanisms had come in 1868, when it required bell-and-cord mechanisms that would enable passengers to notify train drivers of emergencies, but the Board of Trade soon judged that the mechanisms were not dependable and withdrew the requirement. In 1873, Parliament heard a proposal to require continuous braking systems and mechanical blocking systems, but rejected the proposals as excessive meddling. Within a week of the 1889 accident, new legislation compelled the railways to install continuous brakes and blocking systems (Bagwell 1974, p. 181). This act constituted an admission that informed public opinion and the invisible hand had failed, and a reluctant acceptance of positive governmental intervention.

As Jack Simmons has argued, railwaymen still adamantly opposed the idea of the government dictating the use of particular technologies: "It was not the Board of Trade's business to impose one system. Had it attempted to do anything of the kind, it would have met with howls of protest from the companies" (Simmons 1978, pp. 219–225). To pacify them, proponents of regulation wrote a bill that allowed railways to install any braking or blocking system that met with the department's approval.

Administrative weaknesses did not delay government safety standards in Britain, as recent institutional/statist theorists might argue. On the contrary, the department was able to enforce safety standards where Parliament decreed that it should, as in the case of standards for third-class passengers. The department was well prepared to discern which firms lacked particular safety devices because it published regular, comprehensive, reports on the use of those devices. The department was also perfectly capable of seeing to enforcement by advising the law officers of the Board of Trade of infractions, as it did to enforce third-class safety standards. It was Britain's political culture, which treated public dictates to private actors as illicit, that delayed the imposition of safety standards.

Operations, gauge, scheduling, and time

Other matters of technical and managerial coordination were largely left up to the private sector. Parliament tried to effect some standardization by revising the private bill system, but its aim was as much to reduce the work of the government in dealing with myriad clauses in non-standard railway bills as it was to facilitate coordination in the industry. In the end, these efforts had little effect on the railways. Parliament never sought to rationalize the industry by imposing standards or establishing regulations.

The private bill system was a cumbersome way to charter railroads because it did not allow Parliament to standardize, and thereby simplify, charters. However, the British believed that charter standardization amounted to public regulation because it meant that the state would be meddling in the internal affairs of private concerns. Those who wanted to revise the private bill system in order to standardize technology, particularly gauge width, and operating procedures thus faced opposition from railway promoters who argued that standardization would interfere with the freedoms of private railroads.

Operations and construction specifications. Under the private bill system, promoters wrote their own bills and thus could build and operate lines on their own terms. Several problems arose from the absence of standardization in construction and operations. First, the private bill system increased the work of the ad hoc committees that reviewed bills, which in principle had the task of examining each unique clause. Second, the private bill system complicated the duties of the Railway Department, which in principle had to check each unique construction clause when they inspected new lines. Third, in practice neither railroads nor the government paid attention to the clauses included in railway charters which meant that, as we have seen, railways routinely operated in violation of the law. In 1845 Parliament reconsidered the notion that railroads should be able to write their own charters exactly as they saw fit. The Railway Clauses Consolidation Act, passed 8 May 1845, contained 165 standard clauses to be appended to all new railway bills (Lewin 1925, p. 106). The act begins,

> Whereas it is expedient to comprise in one general act sundry provisions relating to the constitution and management of joint-stock companies, . . . May it therefore please your Majesty . . . that this act shall apply to every joint-stock company which shall by any act which shall hereafter be passed be incorporated. (quoted in Hodges 1889, v. 1, p. 33)

Parliament stopped short of decreeing that railways must abide by the 165 clauses. It maintained railways' authority to draft charters and gave railways the power to void and replace any of the standard clauses they objected to.

Gauge.   The reluctance to interfere with the operation of private railroads had also prevented Parliament from setting, or recommending, a standard gauge for early railroads. In 1837, a Mr. Pease asked Parliament to confer on the administration the power to set a standard gauge. Poulett Thomson argued against the idea of Parliament interfering with the application of private capital by dictating gauge width, and reminded Mr. Pease that a parliamentary committee on railways had supported this view. In Thomson's words, as recorded in the third person:

> The committee had recommended to leave railways, like every other speculation, to the discretion of those who embarked their capital in them, subject only to a severe scrutiny from Parliament. In that recommendation he most cordially concurred, and he hoped the House would set the seal of its approbation to the report of their own committee. He did not deny that capital had been thrown away upon these speculations, but then they would find it impossible to regulate the expenditure of capital by any Act of Parliament, *it was by the government not meddling with capital that this country has been able to obtain a superiority over every other country.* (Great Britain, Parliamentary Debates 1837, c. 1162) (emphasis added)

Thomson prevailed and Pease's proposal was rejected, but the issue was revived as the railway network grew more dense. By the middle of 1845 there were 1901 miles of narrow-gauge track (4 feet 8½ inches) being operated in England as well as 274 miles of broad-gauge (seven foot) track (Lewin 1925, p. 108). In June of 1845, a royal commission was appointed to study the possibility of adopting a uniform gauge and "enquire whether any other mode of obviating or mitigating the serious impediments to the internal traffic of the country . . . could be adopted" (quoted in Lewin 1925, p. 108). The commission found that alternative solutions, such as installing telescoping carriage axles or laying three rails to accommodate both carriage widths, caused more problems than they solved (Lewin 1925, p. 125). The commission recommended that all new lines be built in the narrow gauge and that existing lines be adapted to it. The Board of Trade then produced a watered down version of the bill, which the Lords Select Committee on Railways diluted again. The final version decreed that new railways should be constructed in the 4 foot 8½ inch gauge but made no provision for changing the gauge of existing lines. As a result, some lines did not convert to the standard gauge until the 1890s (Bagwell and Mingay 1970, p. 26). In addition, a clause was included that exempted "any railway constructed or to be constructed under the provisions of any present or future Act containing a special enactment defining the gauge or gauges of such railway, or any part thereof" (quoted in Hodges 1889, v. 1., p. 141). This second clause effectively repealed the first by permitting railroaders to build in any gauge, so long as they specified that gauge in their charters.

Scheduling and time zones.   In the end, railways standardized operating procedures, such as the signaling practices of flagmen, and technical specifications, such as rail gauge, through private agreements. In 1842, the problem of coordinating the schedules of different railroads to facilitate through traffic gave rise to a private railway organization along the lines of the United States' General Time Convention. The Railway Clearing House was initially established to coordinate connection scheduling, joint rates, and the transfer of goods between lines. Its efforts greatly improved through-communications between adjacent lines (Bagwell and Mingay 1970, p. 26). In the 1840s, the clearing house also convinced the railroads to operate on Greenwich time, but it was not until 1880 that "railroad time" became standard outside of the industry (Schivelbusch 1986, pp. 29–43).

In sum, the only technical and managerial problems the British saw that demanded public attention had to do with safety. They were intensely concerned about the capacity of large railroads to place passengers and employees in physical danger. The reason for this concern may be traced to Britain's noblesse oblige tradition, and to the tradition of protecting individualism by guarding citizens against stronger private parties. Throughout the controversy over public safety controls, countervailing pressure against regulation appeared in the rhetoric of laissez faire. In Britain, nonintervention had been articulated as a tenet of political liberty and simultaneously as a tenet of economic efficiency and growth from the very first days of the railway industry. In the United States, by contrast, the idea that the state should prevent restraints of trade to promote political liberty dominated policymaking in the fourth quarter of the century, but the link between these policies and economic efficiency only became fully formed toward the end of the century.

By contrast to the British, Americans perceived virtually no technical or managerial problems that demanded state action. But like the British, their main concern was to prevent the growth of state powers. The French, on the other hand, perceived a danger in leaving technical and managerial matters up to entrepreneurs and markets. For the French, only public coordination could produce efficiency in the industry, whereas Parliament in Britain never once suggested that government could play a positive role in the pursuit of efficiency.

The solutions the British conceived to problems of safety looked quite different from the solutions the French conceived to problems of coordination. In France, technocrats took charge of the industry and acted as surrogate managers. In Britain, policy went through three phases. At first, Parliament believed that public opinion and market mechanisms would ensure safety (1825–1840). After 1840 it developed the "inspectorate" model by which the state would inform public opinion to stimulate the operation of natural market controls. After 1889, Parliament reluctantly mandated the use of safety devices. The first two strategies sought to locate authority in the private sector and make railroads see that their interests coincided with the public interest. The inspectorate model reinforced the logic of laissez-faire government, in which multitudes of producers competed for market share and the public frequented those who offered the best goods and services, but the inspectorate was designed to bring public opinion to bear even in an industry such as the railways where competition was frequently absent. The conspicuous failure of this policy strategy contributed to the idea that laissez faire would not always promote the public interest.

Pricing and competition

Like the Americans, the British heralded free competition as the source of the nation's prosperity. However, British thinking was fundamentally different from American. The British were concerned to prevent powerful private actors from dominating economic life and adversely affecting others, rather than to maintain price competition per se. In the realm of rates, the British perceived a problem in the fact that railroads held monopolies that allowed them to charge exorbitant rates. The first solution they conceived was to use the threat of competition against railroads. However, they soon saw that this was an empty threat, and developed the more activist solution of setting rates for third-class passengers to protect Britain's weakest citizens – the poor – from its strongest – capitalists.

When it came to issues surrounding competition and industry structure – amalgamations, cartelization, and rate discrimination – British policymakers perceived two problems: (1) Large predatory railways forced unwanted mergers on their smaller competitors, and (2) railways used unfair pricing strategies to hurt certain customers and competitors. To solve these problems they refused to permit predatory acquisitions, forbade the rate discrimination that had allowed firms to bankrupt their competitors, and encouraged cartelization to end cutthroat price competition. The effect of pro-cartel policies was to put a halt to price competition in order to guard the income of small railroads and prevent bankruptcies.

The early policy paradigm that went by the name of laissez faire in Britain consisted of a series of positive state interventions to create idealized conditions of free economic exchange (Polanyi 1944). Over the course of the nineteenth century, the attendant belief in an economy made up of multitudes of small producers spawned a series of interventionist policies to protect small firms against large combines. The new policies determined whether firms could freely merge, whether they could charge competitive rates, and whether they could try to expand their market share and put their competitors out of business. There is a curious parallel between Britain's safety policies and its competition policies. In both realms, policy was designed to protect the weak from the strong. In essence, Parliament had generalized the principle that political order could be effected by bolstering parcelized, feudal, sovereignties to the modern industrial realm; economic order would be achieved by bolstering sovereign economic entities. Thus, despite Britain's rhetorical commitment to laissez faire, the British came to believe that unchecked competition could destroy small-scale economic actors and thereby produce economic irrationalities.

Rates

Early British rail charters specified rates in detail, much like early French charters. In Britain, the companies themselves wrote rate schedules into their charters in order to preclude government price-setting, whereas in France the state had insisted on defining rates in charters in order to preclude price gouging. The Liverpool-Manchester Act of 5 May 1826 is illustrative. It carried detailed freight rates that were substantially higher than actual charges, to guard the company's prerogative to raise rates in the future. Specific rates were set for everything from dung, coal, lime, clay, and sand to wine, spirits, vitriol, and glass. The act reserved the company's right to charge whatever it pleased for passengers and animals, and specified that horses, oxen, and asses would be transported at one rate, and calves, sheep, lambs, and pigs would be carried at another. In brief, French charters established the state's prerogative to set rates whereas British charters established railways' prerogative (Chester 1981, pp. 177–179).

Parliament soon recognized that because most railroads held service monopolies that exempted them from competitive pressures, there was little to prevent them from offering poor service at high prices. In the 1840s, Parliament became particularly concerned that monopolistic rate-setting injured the poor, and this inspired the 1844 legislation regulating third- class rates. Some argued that the state should regulate first- and second-class rates as well, but opponents claimed that although railways' state-proffered monopolies tended to exempt them from competition in the short run, the state could encourage public-mindedness in the long run by threatening to charter competing lines. High rates and poor service would put a line out of business in the face of healthy competition. In the discussions surrounding the establishment of the Select Committee on Railways of 1844, Mr. Wallace argued that the state should not establish rates or even demand accounting returns. In his opinion,

> the natural control over these companies [is] not by minute interference with their gains, or their management, but by holding out to them the menace of competition. . . . the House might say this to a railway company. We find your profits oppressive to the public pocket; we find your means of communication wilfully inadequate to the public accommodation, we shall, ere long, think ourselves justified in encouraging a new company, to supply the advantages you withhold. (Great Britain, Parliamentary Debates 1844, cc. 250–251)

The director of the Board of Trade countered that railways would never operate under truly competitive conditions, and championed a select committee to consider "whether any and what sort of jurisdiction should exist with respect to railroad bills" (Great Britain, Parliamentary Debates 1844, c. 236). Parliament could not depend on [competition between rival lines] keeping down prices in the same sense and with the assured results which they could in other matters . . . the circumstance, that the parties . . . were limited in number, made arrangements between rival lines easy of accomplishment. (Great Britain, Parliamentary Debates 1844, c. 236)

Gladstone maintained that the threat of competition held prices in check only where barriers to market entry were low, and that the immense cost of establishing a railroad discouraged market entry and encouraged price-fixing among existing competitors.

Parliament ultimately concluded that it was better to risk unfair rates than to risk expanding public authority. The 1844 bill established third-class rates, but for first- and second-class passage and for freight it merely gave Parliament the power to revise the rates specified in charters and to rescind railway charters in extreme circumstances. These clauses served notice that the state would not tolerate excessive rates. However, the fact that the state never put them to use mitigated that notice.

The strategy of using the threat of competing charters to encourage reasonable rates underwent an important change later in the century. As the industry matured, the British were forced to choose between trying to foster price competition and trying to foster stability by allowing price-fixing. Parliament chose the latter. In the process it helped to designate small-scale entrepreneurial capitalism involving multitudes of firms, rather than price competition per se, as the key to economic efficiency and growth.

Competition

The industry's monopolistic tendency quickly became evident to Parliament. As the third report from the Select Committee on Railway Communications found in 1840, Parliament's original error in thinking that railways would operate like canals, with competing public carriers providing service on publicly accessible routes

consisted in a total misapprehension of the best means of providing locomotive power on railways: Parliament at first considered that this might be safely left to be supplied by public competition; . . . The general impression of Parliament appears to have been, that there existed a close analogy between the principles which govern the means of conveyance by Railway and by Canal, and this indeed appears to have been the opinion of the Railway Proprietors themselves

> . . . The Legislature, in its anxiety to prevent a monopoly which was
> not sought even by the promoters of the Bills, enacted that any person
> might place and run his own engines, carriages, and waggons (sic) on
> a Railway. (Great Britain, Parliamentary Papers 1840, p. 3)

By 1840, Parliament recognized that railway technology made free public access to the rails impracticable and that rail companies would operate monopolies on their own routes, while facing competition from the owners of alternate routes. The industry soon devised an array of strategies for dampening price competition among railroads to mitigate the effects of asset-specificity, high entry costs, and a high ratio of fixed to variable costs. Which of these strategies would the British perceive to be problematic?

British policy diverged quite fundamentally from American policy on the issues of mergers, cartels, and rate discrimination. Like the Americans the British came to believe that competition and entrepreneurialism were key to economic efficiency and progress, yet in Britain competition was not supposed to kill off weak firms. British competition policies fall into place once that is understood. Parliament permitted cartels in order to protect small firms from predatory competitors, despite the knowledge that this would eliminate price competition. Parliament's merger policy was uneven because it vacillated between forbidding mergers to protect firms from predators and permitting them on the principle that firms should be free to act as they pleased. Parliament had no difficulty agreeing to forbid certain forms of rate discrimination that were anti-competitive *and* damaged small firms.

Amalgamations.   Mergers were associated with two evils in the minds of the British. The first was the shotgun wedding between a big railway and its smaller competitor. Large railways that owned vast networks could ruin their competitors by charging below-cost rates, and then acquire those competitors at fire-sale prices. The second problem was the acquisition of public charters for the purpose of speculation. Entrepreneurs had often won charters for routes that would extend existing railways, or compete with existing railways, for the sole purpose of selling the charters to those very railways at inflated prices. By prohibiting mergers, Parliament hoped to resolve the first problem by guarding small firms against acquisition, and the second by making it impossible for existing railroads to purchase unfulfilled charters or completed lines.

The British were uniquely troubled by the fact that mergers put small firms out of business and reduced the number of railway companies. In the early years, Parliament had actively encouraged the multiplication of railway firms by chartering competing lines for a number of routes. Competition was expected to achieve the goals the French state achieved through proactive regulation, in the realms of safety, service, and especially rates. As Mr. Turner argued of railroads in the 1840 debates over regulation: "Their monopoly was complete; but the House had this check upon them – they might establish rival companies" (Great Britain, Parliamentary Debates 1840, c. 930). However, that threat did not always check the behavior of railway operators. Because entry costs were high and because the construction of parallel routes often generated overcapacity, rivals were sometimes slow to appear and when they did appear they often colluded to fix prices. Moreover, technical and managerial considerations often caused adjacent or competing railroads to merge.

In response to alarm about proposals that threatened to eliminate competition on important routes, Parliament instituted select committees on railway amalgamations in 1846, 1852, and 1872. Each of the committees considered the possibility of outlawing all mergers, but in each case Parliament decided that such blanket legislation would interfere with the liberties of firms that wished to merge for good reasons. In the end, each committee called for a permanent tribunal to review proposed mergers.

The 1846 committee reviewed 161 bills involving amalgamation, but was unable to recommend a universal policy outlawing mergers. The 1852 committee, known as Cardwell's committee, was set up to examine major amalgamation proposals between (a) the London and South Western and the London, Brighton, and South Coast, and (b) the London and North Western and the Midland. The latter promised to create a single company that would command nearly a quarter of the nation's rail revenues and control fully a sixth of Britain's trackage (Bagwell 1974, p. 164). The committee convinced Parliament to deny these proposals (Cleveland-Stevens 1915, pp. 59–60), and in tackling the more general issue recognized that the railway industry was not naturally competitive:

> It is natural for traders to compete where the opportunity is unlimited for new rivals to enter the field from time to time; it is quite as natural

for traders to combine as soon as . . . the whole number of possible competitors may be ascertained and limited. (Great Britain, Parliamentary Papers. 1853, p. 4)

Cardwell's committee was of the opinion that the industry's natural inclination to combine could, and should, be discouraged by public policy. Parliament should "refuse to sanction amalgamations except for working arrangements made for limited periods of time" (quoted in Bagwell and Mingay 1970, p. 36).

The committee's Report led to the 1854 Railway and Canal Traffic Act, known as Cardwell's act. The committee had suggested a bill to outlaw mergers and rate discrimination that would facilitate cartelization to relieve the pressure to merge. However, the final version of the bill merely outlawed discrimination. After Cardwell's committee prevented two large mergers in 1853, Parliament allowed several mergers in 1854. Policy reversals on amalgamations continued over the next decades, as Parliament found it impossible to decide between the argument that entrepreneurial firms should retain their independence from predatory competitors, and the argument that free firms should be able to choose their own destinies and merge as they desire.

The 1872 select committee was convened to consider a merger between the 1,500-mile London and North Western and the 427-mile Lancashire and Yorkshire, and more generally to review amalgamation policy in light of the fact that bills had been submitted that would have affected every important line in England and most important lines in Scotland (Bagwell 1974, p. 166). Like the 1846 and 1852 committees, the 1872 panel recommended the establishment of a tribunal to examine future amalgamation proposals. Some factions in Parliament wanted a consistent national policy governing mergers and the committee hoped that railway amalgamation might

follow certain fixed lines or principles, instead of leaving the matter as heretofore, to the chance medley of struggles between rival companies and the inconsistent decisions of successive Parliamentary Committees. (Great Britain, Parliamentary Papers. 1872, xi)

In 1872, Parliament established the Committee on Amalgamations to review proposals, as well as the Railway Commission to adjudicate cases of rate discrimination. However, when the committee killed the existing proposals for mergers in 1873 it generated widespread discontent among railway owners, and Parliament failed to renew it in the following year (Cleveland-Stevens 1915, p. 275). The Railway Commission, by contrast, survived to administer the rate discrimination clause of Cardwell's act by adjudicating disputes among companies.

Parliament did not succeed in halting consolidation. Britain's railways had been built in short stretches by independent companies, and as Edward Cleveland-Stevens wrote in 1915, consolidation was "a large part of the history of the English railways" (p. iv). Nonetheless, the long-term effect of Britain's vacillating merger policy was to discourage firms from attempting mergers when they could pursue cartelization instead. Thus, the threat of Parliamentary disapproval, in the wake of the denial of the merger applications of the early 1870s, "appears to have effectively removed the option of growth through large-scale amalgamations and was therefore a major influence on the relatively stable level of concentration until 1921," when the state merged the nation's railways into four regional systems (Channon 1983, p. 59). British railroads faced many of the same competitive pressures that their American counterparts faced, but Parliament's anti-merger stance, coupled with supports for cartelization, led them to pursue price fixing and pooling arrangements in the last quarter of the century in lieu of formal mergers (Channon 1983). Where anti-cartel policies nudged American firms in the direction of formal consolidation, merger prohibitions nudged British firms toward cartelization.

Rate discrimination. Although Parliament's commitment to laissez faire prevented it from outlawing acquisitions outright, it could dampen mergers by outlawing two forms of rate discrimination. Large railroads had destroyed their smaller competitors by charging discriminatory rates for through-goods transferred from them. They had also monopolized the business of large shippers by offering special rates to those that promised to eschew other rail companies, and they sometimes refused to carry the goods of shippers that used competing railroads. Parliament had been aware of these practices, but was at first reluctant to require railroads to treat all customers equally. In 1839, for instance, 180 petitioners brought complaints against the London and Birmingham Railway for flatly refusing to carry goods for some customers. Upon applying to the Court of the Queen's Bench for a *mandamus* that would compel the company to serve everyone who presented goods for transport, they were told that the court had no authority in the matter because the railway's charter did not afford the courts any powers of compulsion. Parliament concurred that separate legislation would have to be enacted before railways could be compelled to carry goods for all comers, but was reticent to expand public powers in such a way (Great Britain, Parliamentary Debates 1839, c. 1221).

Rate discrimination was commonly used to injure competing railroads, but it sometimes harmed domestic producers, and that particularly disturbed legislators (Cleveland-Stevens 1915, pp. 189–200). When railways used discrimination to take foreign produce contracts away from ship owners, Britain's wheat, livestock, and dairy farmers suffered losses. Continental farmers chose between maximizing the rail portion of transport, by shipping goods to British ports close to the Continent and then transporting them long distances by rail to the point of sale, or the sea portion of the journey, by shipping goods to a port close to the point of sale and then finishing the trip by rail. To encourage the former, railroads offered special rates for produce carried from ports near the Continent while charging full price for internal produce transport (Bagwell 1974, p. 173). As a result, some Continental farmers could move their goods to British markets more cheaply than British farmers.

The three-member Railway Commission established in 1873 adjudicated rate discrimination disputes generated by Cardwell's act. Thenceforth, the Railway Department could bring contested discrimination cases before the tribunal, and complainants could appeal directly to the tribunal. Like the earlier Railway Board, the Railway Commission, which was renamed the Railway and Canal Commission in 1888 and given authority over canals as well, faced charges that it arrogated powers that rightly belonged to Parliament. Opponents of the bill that established the commission, particularly railwaymen who had benefited from the state's inability to enforce the rate discrimination clause, argued that an extra-parliamentary body such as this had no right to set aside the rate-setting powers guaranteed to railways in their charters. Mr. Pease

> very much doubted how far Parliament could sanction the powers which this Bill gave to revise every special Act and special toll, and to treat as waste paper, agreements between existing companies which had been sanctioned . . . by the House . . . [the bill] proposed to transfer the whole railway power of the kingdom to three Commissioners. (Great Britain, Parliamentary Debates 1873, c. 1046)

Members of Parliament were reluctant to alienate their authority to a ministerial unit, worrying that the commission would abridge individuals' economic rights. They settled this concern by allowing disputants to appeal commission decisions via "motions for a prohibition where it was alleged that the commissioners were exercising powers in excess of their jurisdiction" to the House itself (Great Britain, Parliamentary Papers 1880, c. 2504). The commission survived, but from 1877 most important cases were appealed to Parliament.

To prevent injurious rate discrimination, the Railway and Canal Traffic Act of 1888 authorized the commission to forge a national rate agreement among railways – just a year after the United States passed legislation that made price-fixing illegal. The commission charged the companies with deciding on common prices, and the companies drew directly on the experience of the Railway Clearing House, which had negotiated joint rate agreements since the 1840s for traffic that had to be transported on more than one railroad to reach its destination. January 1, 1893 marked the inauguration of the new common rate schedules. The rate agreements were relatively effective compared with the American cartel agreements of the 1870s and '80s, which fell apart when participants undercut common prices to expand their market share. However, because English railroads sometimes diverged from the national agreements, regional cartels still played a role in stabilizing prices. The relative success of price fixing in Britain was linked to Parliament's anti-acquisition stance, which made it impossible to acquire the assets of a competing firm after destroying it through predatory pricing.

Cartelization. In the late nineteenth century, cartelization became widespread in British industry, as Parliament encouraged sectors to dampen domestic competition through price-fixing. Parliament's rationale was that British industry needed to regroup to compete with such rapidly industrializing countries as Germany and the United States. From as early as 1873 the state supported cartels in such industries as cotton spinning, cement, wallpaper, tobacco, and calico printing (Grove 1962). Policymakers recognized this as a change of direction, but argued that it was illogical to allow domestic competition to threaten British firms when their real industrial foes were overseas. The new policy paradigm of "laissez-collectives-faire" would enable firms to act in concert against their foreign competitors (Grove 1962, p. 28). The received wisdom about the period is that the entire cartelization movement was designed to mitigate the effects of international competition.

State supervision of railway cartels and pools had first been proposed in the initial draft of Cardwell's act, although the idea collapsed under opposition to the new public powers it would require. One clause of Cardwell's act, later expunged, would have permitted competing companies to join together, share track and rolling stock, and apportion traffic and income as they saw fit. Parliament did not object to the substance of the clause, but to the fact that these agreements would be "subject to the approval of the Board of Trade" and would thereby confer the right of approval on the board (Cleveland-Stevens 1915, p. 196). This clause fell prey to the same sentiments that killed the Railway Board – members of Parliament saw it as a threat to their sovereignty and hence to individual rights.

English law did, however, allow companies to submit private bills to Parliament that would sanction interfirm pricing and traffic agreements. For instance, the Octuple Agreement, reached in 1850, controlled prices and apportioned traffic for the eight lines that served London, Edinburgh, and Glasgow (Bagwell 1974, p. 165). Parliament withheld approval of such bills only when affected parties objected to the agreements. In 1858, for instance, the North Western, the Sheffield, and the Great Northern entered into an agreement called "The Three Companies' Agreement" that eliminated competition among them and committed them to fending off upstarts by refusing to carry goods transferred from other lines. Parliament refused to sanction the bill when the Midland Company, an excluded competitor, argued that it would abridge the Midland's right to compete freely. The failure of the bill meant that the three companies could not use public powers to compel one another to abide by rate agreements, but nothing stopped them from voluntarily doing so – and so they did, to the chagrin of the Midland (Williams 1886, pp. 115–116). By 1860, railways convened regular conferences to set prices and apportion traffic (Armitage 1969, p. 47). Most of the private pooling and cartel agreements submitted to Parliament went unopposed. For instance, the South Eastern reached an agreement in 1865 with the new Chatham railroad stipulating that the latter would not practice price competition and, in return, would receive 40,000 pounds annually for traffic it did not carry. The two companies formally merged in 1899 (Cleveland-Stevens 1915, p. 306).

By 1885, British railways were using an array of mechanisms, in addition to these cartel agreements, to escape competition without merging. First, they engaged in pools in which two or more lines operated jointly and apportioned profits among themselves at a set ratio. This was the case for the 29-mile Ashby-Nuneaton route, which was operated by the L & NWR and the Midland. Second, one operator might lease his route to a competitor under terms that called for a fixed annual payment or for a payment based on revenues collected. For instance, the Furniss company operated the 9 miles of track owned by the Midland between Carnforth and Wennington. Third, in some cases a committee representing the various owners managed companies that operated in combination. The Cheshire lines, which totalled 104 miles, were owned by three companies, the Great Northern, the Midland, and the MS & L, and operated by a separate committee appointed by the three (Williams 1885, p. 453).

Then, in 1888, the Railway Commission was given a formal role in effecting national pricing agreements. By 1908, Emil Davies wrote that third-class passage from London to Liverpool was set at 16 shillings six pence and passengers would pay that amount whether they traveled by the North-Western, the Midland, the Great Northern, the Great Central, or the Great Western (1924, p. 35).

In permitting, and later organizing, rail cartels, Parliament seemed to be applying the principle of "laissez-collectives-faire" to the domestic railway industry. This experience, and the experiences of other industries that faced no rivals from abroad such as building trades, tends to undermine the argument that Parliament condoned cartels to mitigate the effects of foreign competition. In these cases, cartelization was designed to protect small enterprises from extinction at the hands of *domestic* market forces. I mean to suggest that Parliament was extending the feudal mandate to protect the sovereignty of individual lords, which had become institutionalized in modern political life, to the industrial economy by shielding individual firms.

In sum, the problems British policymakers perceived to be of pressing importance in the realms of pricing and competition changed as the industry matured. As a result, Britain's industrial policy paradigm and industrial culture changed. British policymakers, like their American counterparts, saw economic concentration as a problem because they believed that it threatened economic liberty. At first they encouraged market entry in the industry to spawn new enterprises and to protect the liberties of customers by creating price competition. The main drawback of economic concentration – that it enabled powerful firms to harm their smaller competitors and customers – was solved by the creation of competing enterprises. Parliament also undermined efforts by strong firms to damage weak ones by outlawing rate discrimination aimed at denying traffic to other roads.

These early policies produced price competition. However, over time Parliament perceived a problem in the fact that competition often put small firms out of business. Parliament soon had to choose between promoting price competition and supporting small firms. In the decision to enforce private cartels and pools, and to actively organize rate conferences from 1888, Parliament signaled that protecting small firms was most important. By contrast, American legislators saw the disappearance of price competition as a greater evil, and hence outlawed pools and cartels. The French, of course, perceived competition in the industry to be potentially destabilizing and irrational, and at an early time the state forced railways to merge into huge, noncompetitive, regional monopolies.

Britain had adopted pro-cartel policies with the aim of shielding political and economic liberties, but those policies were soon taken to be part of a rationalized strategy for growth. Public policy symbolized the presence of multitudes of small entrepreneurial firms as the driving force of progress, and market selection mechanisms that depended on strong firms destroying weak ones as potentially irrational. In the emergent British view of economic rationality, small firms should compete with one another to provide the best service, but they should not try to put one another out of business because that would undercut entrepreneurialism.

Conclusion

Over the course of the nineteenth century, Britain's industrial policy paradigm changed markedly. In the first decades of the century, Parliament pursued policies that would create idealized free-market conditions and eradicate supports for agricultural traditions. By the 1830s, laissez faire was popularized as a positive prescription for economic growth. That approach gradually changed, and by the end of the century Britain was following railway policies designed to prop up existing firms by guarding them from political interference and from market competition. Britain's particular free market industrial culture and non-interventionist public policy paradigm came to emphasize masses of small producers rather than price competition. Policy came to focus on sustaining entrepreneurs rather than on sustaining market mechanisms.

In each of the four functional realms, the British perceived problems that were radically different from those perceived by the Americans and the French. The problems they perceived and addressed, in turn, helped to shape the emergent industrial policy paradigm. For the British, railway planning and finance belonged entirely to the private sector. Private actors would achieve both ends if left to their own devices. The only problem Parliament perceived concerned the expropriation of private lands for projects that were of no public merit or for projects with crooked promoters whose aims were entirely speculative. Could the state take the title to private lands by force if Parliament was unsure that the public would be served? When it came to technical and managerial decisions, Parliament believed that all problems associated with efficiency would be best solved in the private realm. From 1840, Parliament did give consistent attention to the problem of safety in order to guard the exalted, sovereign, individuals who made up the polity from powerful, profit-oriented, railroads. But for most of the century it denied its own Board of Trade the power to meddle in the affairs of private railroads by setting safety standards. When it came to pricing and competition, Parliament first perceived problems where powerful railroads used their monopolies to harm their poorest customers. Its conception of competition led to policies that set the nation on a very different course from the United States. The British saw that price-fixing quelled competition, but came to support it as a way to prop up small railroads by stabilizing profits. In the end, Parliament prevented mergers and encouraged cartelization. Ultimately the problems the British perceived in railway competition can be traced to a political culture oriented to guarding the sovereignty of each landowner. Parliament could no more stand by and watch new industrial "parcelized sovereignties" be acquired than it could stand by and watch landowners be routed by their neighbors.

The policy strategies the British conceived evolved as Britain's idea of how to effect public goals developed. Parliament had eschewed participation in railway planning and financing in the belief that public goals would be achieved if private parties were left to pursue their own interests. The public interest was synonymous with the aggregation of private interests. A key to this way of thinking was the idea that public opinion would favor the firms that provided the best services and goods. Hordes of small producers doing their best to win the public's business would serve the nation best. In the railway industry, as in a number of other sectors, this approach was called into question because firms held monopolies. After 1840, the inspectorate was to *inform* the public about the activities of railways, and although dissatisfied customers could not often choose another railway for service between two points, *informed* public opinion would bring pressure to bear even on railroads that held monopolies. In this way, Parliament hoped to make railwaymen aware that their interests coincided with the public interest. This policy paradigm clearly failed in matters of public safety, and Parliament reluctantly adopted a new paradigm in 1889 when it imposed safety standards on railroads. The seeds of that paradigm can be traced to the 1840s, when Parliament established safety standards for third-class trains. This final step in the evolution of public enforcement reflected resignation to the fact that the state would sometimes be called upon to dictate to private firms, for public opinion could not effect all desired ends.

Britain's strategy for achieving economic growth also evolved over time. At the dawn of the railway age, the laissez-faire paradigm called for the state to stand back and allow private parties to pursue their interests. But later, by deciding to outlaw rate discrimination, prevent mergers, and enforce cartel agreements, Parliament created policies that involved the state in the internal operations of private firms. By telling firms what they could charge and whom they could merge with, Britain had moved away from laissez faire. The term laissez faire was still bandied about in Britain, but public policy had moved away from simply establishing the conditions for free exchange and toward interventionist attempts to sustain the autonomy of individual firms.

The policy strategies employed in the railway industry paralleled those being used elsewhere in the British economy. The inspectorate model of industrial governance was adopted in a number of sectors in the 1830s and 1840s. Later, the pro-cartel policies we saw in the railway industry were used in all sorts of sectors – export oriented and purely domestic. The new policy paradigm that prevailed at century's end, in which policy helped to sustain competition by checking consolidation and bolstering entrepreneurial autonomy, shaped what was to come in Britain. Parliament responded to the Great War by maximizing the liberties of firms throughout the economy – especially armaments producers – on the principle that "the greater the freedom allowed the private contractor, the greater would be the increase in the supply" (Lloyd 1978, p. 23). During the 1920s, Britain responded to economic malaise by encouraging cartelization and by subsidizing imperiled firms to ensure the survival of entrepreneurialism. At the height of the Great Depression, Britain briefly experimented with "rationalisation" schemes to regroup small firms into large enterprises that could achieve economies of scale on the principle that only a reversal of traditional policies could reverse the economic decline, but policy returned to normal by the end of the 1930s (Dobbin 1993). During World War II, private contracting was again used to stimulate production, and firms that were adversely affected by the war were given temporary supports. In the postwar period, policies designed to guard firms against dissolution at the hands of market forces, and against irrational political meddling, continued to prevail. Nationalized firms were given autonomous management teams that were free from government interference. Financial bailouts for failing firms became commonplace as a means to shield individual firms from devastation at the hands of markets. British industrial policies have taken a number of forms over the years, but at their core is a commitment to sustain the autonomy of the firm, rather than to maintain market mechanisms as in the United States and Germany, to promote the national interest as in France, or to sustain the productivity of the firm as in Japan (Wilks 1983, p. 139). Britain's protection of firms from market pressures through subsidies, production quotas, protectionism, and price fixing schemes has often been cited as a cause of industry's failure to rationalize and, in turn, of Britain's longterm economic decline (Hall 1986, p. 56).

Throughout this period, British industrial policy has been oriented to guarding citizens against harm as much as to promoting economic growth. Thus, Britain's proactive industrial policies have for decades been dominated by programs that offer inducements to firms to locate in high-unemployment regions, to protect workers from the hardship of being forced to move to find work. Guarding workers' rights has taken precedence over promoting overall efficiency. Bailouts for inefficient industrial giants have also been based on arguments about the displacement of workers, rather than on arguments about longterm growth and efficiency. British energy policy, particularly vis-à-vis coal, has likewise been oriented to protecting a particular segment of the labor market. And British policies governing work and technology have continued to focus on issues of working conditions and safety rather than on issues of efficiency or effectiveness. Although Britain has developed a clear and interventionist, albeit piecemeal, policy paradigm oriented to creating efficiency, the issue of protecting the sovereign individuals who comprise the polity continues to loom large in industrial policy debates.

5. Conclusion

Introduction

My point of departure was the observation that by the beginning of the twentieth century the United States, France, and Britain had developed dramatically different strategies for promoting industrial growth that have since survived tremendous political changes. The parallels between these nations' modern industrial policy paradigms and their traditional paradigms of political order are striking. Most analysts have taken parallels between nations' political and economic systems for granted by using sweeping terms such as laissez-faire, liberalism, statism, and authoritarianism to characterize both systems at once. My aim has been to problematize these parallels and to suggest that comprehending them is the key to grasping why cross-national policy differences persist. I have tried to discover how industrial cultures came to resemble political cultures by studying how early nineteenth-century state institutions influenced the subsequent development of railway policy. I do not suggest that the industrial policy paradigms that emerged in these countries were overdetermined by political culture – indeed, the United States' earliest industrial policy paradigm was rejected and replaced during the nineteenth century. Rather, I have argued that by designating certain social processes as constitutive of order and others as destructive of order, institutionalized political culture shaped the kinds of industrial practices nations would try to create, and the kinds they would try to prevent. That is, by symbolizing certain means-ends relationships in social life, political culture shaped the means nations would conceive to the ends of industrial organization and growth.

In lieu of a reprise of the cross-national comparisons that are made in Chapters 2 through 4, in this final chapter I focus on the theoretical implications of the findings. The evidence suggests that a social constructionist view of modernity, which sets aside the depictions of poli-

213

cymaking offered by the modern worldview, leads to an unconventional understanding of policymaking. This understanding departs significantly from prevailing social science paradigms, and it cannot possibly be defended in the space of one short book. Thus my goal has not been to systematically refute existing theories, but to offer some evidence to support an alternative view of the roles of culture, politics, economics, and institutions in policymaking among modern, rationalized, nation-states. Before turning to the role of rationalized meaning in each of these realms, I discuss the historical implications of the argument.

The rise of industrial policy paradigms

Political culture had an unmistakable effect on how these nations came to understand, and institutionalize, economic rationality. In each country, traditional state institutions had supported certain social practices and subdued others, with the effect of constructing certain practices as constitutive of order and others as inimical to order. When faced with rapid change in the economy, policymakers applied these principles of political order to the industrial realm. Thus the logic of political organization became the logic of industrial organization. Broadly speaking, states had achieved political order by locating sovereignty in the local community, the central state, or the individual. In each case, political institutions had symbolized control by other realms as threatening to order.

American political culture symbolized community sovereignty as the means to political order, and early rail policies made community control over planning and finance the key to economic order. These early policies were designed to deny control over industry to powerful private actors and to central political authorities, but when they instead bolstered the illicit powers of firms and governments, Americans embraced a new policy paradigm. The new paradigm transformed the central state into a market referee, with the effect of locating authority once again in civil society, but this time in market forces rather than in town meetings. By the end of the century, the United States had developed a distinctly market-oriented conception of economic rationality.

French political culture constructed state sovereignty as the key to political order, and rail policies made state control over planning, finance, coordination, and competition the key to economic order and efficiency. In French political life, intermediate private actors who might interfere with the direct relationship of sovereignty between state and citizen posed a threat to the polity, hence private parties, corporations, and local governments were denied roles in political decisions. In turn French rail policies designed to wrest control of the industry from autonomous private actors, and from unthinking market mechanisms, became integral to the conception of economic rationality. The driving idea behind military absolutism – that the state must regulate privatism to achieve order – thus came to shape industrial institutions. By 1900, the French had articulated a vision of economic rationality in which government concertation of private, self-interested, action was indispensable to growth.

British political culture symbolized inalienable, individual sovereignty as the key to political order, and rail policies made entrepreneurial control over planning, finance, coordination, and competition the key to economic order and rationality. Britain's political institutions had denied authority to powerful individuals, to the Crown, and to the administration by empowering individuals and their representatives in Parliament. Rail policy was likewise designed to wrest control from dominant railways, by constraining their activities and limiting their ability to expand; from state officials, by denying them the power to dictate to railroads; and from market forces, by shielding firms against devastating competition. Between the time of Adam Smith and the close of the 1900s, Britain's institutional depiction of rationality was little changed – the key was the free pursuit of economic self-interest by masses of entrepreneurial firms. The conception of the state's role had changed, though, as laissez faire gave way to the notion that the state would have to actively defend entrepreneurs.

Each case provides unique insights into the institutionalization of rationalized meaning in public policy. America's rail history demonstrates how a constructionist approach to rationality can account for change. Its initial industrial policy paradigm of active, rivalistic, localism was replaced by a paradigm of passive enforcement of market mechanisms. Why? Americans saw nothing wrong with active localism per se, but localism produced abuses of concentrated authority, such as monopolistic pricing and corruption. Because their political institutions had portrayed concentrated authority as inimical to political order, Americans saw these practices as particularly heinous, and sought to bring them to an end. Hence, the United States' initial policy paradigm changed because it generated unanticipated practices. Paradigms can change for a variety of other reasons as well. On the one hand, policy paradigms undergo frequent incremental adjustments, much like scientific paradigms, when secondary hypotheses are tested. For instance, for the past two decades American policymakers have tested the idea that market mechanisms generate efficiency even in oligopolistic sectors with high fixed costs, such as air transport and telecommunications. On the other hand, like scientific paradigms, policy paradigms are especially prone to dramatic changes when the cause-effect relationships they embody are falsified. For instance, at the beginning of the Great Depression, nations briefly embraced new industrial strategies in the belief that their traditional paradigms had backfired (Dobbin 1993).

The French case illustrates Tocqueville's point that *political culture,* in the narrow sense of the institutionalized logic of order, is not determined by *political ideology* alone. For one thing, a particular set of political practices and meanings may be compatible with several different ideologies. In France, the traditional political culture survived a series of revolutions and regime changes that brought groups with widely different ideologies to power. The institutions of centralized, technocratic, governance proved workable when France was an empire, a monarchy, and a republic. Conversely, a particular ideology may be compatible with several different sets of practices and meanings. Democratic ideology was compatible with the decentralized, federal structure of the United States as well as with the centralized state structure of France. Not only were diverse political cultures compatible with democracy, but in each country, democratic theorists argued that their political traditions were *indispensable to* democracy. Institutional models of political order thus transcended the break from colonial to democratic rule in the United States, from monarchy to Victorian democracy in Britain, and from absolutism to republicanism in France. If ideas about the causal mechanisms underlying social and economic order can be autonomous from ideology, then it is not difficult to understand how political camps with very different ideologies can embrace common understandings of how political order and industrial rationality are achieved. Thus, American leftists and rightists may share a belief in the efficacy of market mechanisms, while their French counterparts may share a belief in the efficacy of state concertation.

Britain demonstrates two important points. First, the Britain-U.S. contrast shows that a state-market continuum poorly captures differences among nations. Although these two "laissez-faire" nations similarly located industrial control outside of the state, they located control in very different realms and constituted industrial rationality in very different ways. American policies enforced market mechanisms at the cost of destroying many small firms; British policies reinforced small firms via cartels at the cost of destroying market mechanisms. However, my aim has not been to replace the state-market dichotomy with a state-market-firm trichotomy, but rather to suggest that this kind of schema may not be well suited to explaining cross-national policy differences. In its place, I have offered a method for studying policy paradigms. Second, the contrast between Britain and France underscores that nineteenth-century rail policies were direct extensions of pre-industrial canal and turnpike policies rather than rational responses to the industry's special economic characteristics, as economic historians have been prone to argue. The fact that rail policies differed sharply among nations, but were virtually identical with canal policies within nations, tends to undermine economic determinist arguments. Moreover, all three countries continued to use the policy paradigms seen here for all sorts of new industries, most notably industries that share none of the railway industry's economic characteristics of high fixed costs, asset specificity, and small numbers of direct competitors. In the postwar electronics industry, for instance, the United States imposed price competition, France consolidated the sector and orchestrated expansion, and Britain propped up existing firms (Dobbin 1992b). Industrial policies appear to be oriented more to past practices than to the special economic needs of industries.

The elaboration of these cultural models of policy operates somewhat differently today than it did in the nineteenth century. In the early railway age, industrial policy was unknown and policymakers had to apply principles of causation from social life generally. Today's policymakers still copy strategies, but they can draw from entrenched industry policy paradigms that have been experimented with and refined for over a century. The strategy of applying constructed principles of causation is still the same, but the search process is much simplified.

Next, I turn to more general theoretical implications of the findings, as they highlight the role of rationality in modern culture, politics, economics, and institutions.

Culture and rationality

Rationalized cultural meaning, as embodied in the public policy institutions of these three nations, proved to be more *collective and structural* than "national character" and other prevailing cultural approaches would suggest. Those theories locate culture and cultural continuity largely in individual cognitive frameworks. In the history of railway policy, cultural meaning appears to be located squarely in tangible social practices. Meaning proved to be more *institutional* than Hegelian ideas about collective political sensibility suggest with terms like *geist* and *weltanschauung*. There was nothing at all etherial about the principles of industrial efficiency that became institutionalized in each of these countries, although in each actors believed that transcendental, *geist*-like, laws of economic rationality were reflected in modern institutions. Meaning proved to be *actively constructed* to a greater extent than reflection theories of culture, which make culture nothing more than a mirror of social reality, would suggest. We saw people actively trying to make sense of political structures in order to extract principles with which to organize industrial life. As part of that effort, people reinterpreted history teleologically so that it produced idealized, perfectly rational, social and economic institutions. Meaning proved to be more *variable and contingent* than most social science treatments of economic culture suggest. The central principles of economic rationality varied dramatically across these three countries. Most treatments of economic culture suggest that economic practices are influenced at the margins by cultural practices or social networks. Here they seemed to be influenced at the very core by cultural practice, which suggests that the central rules of economic rationality that neoclassical theory posits may simply be abstractions from a single strong case. Parallel sets of abstractions from other, equally efficient, social systems may be possible as well. In short, these findings inform current debates about culture and meaning, but they provide perhaps the greatest challenge to current thinking about rationality. They suggest that rationality has a *semiotic* dimension that social scientists have neglected because they have presumed rationality to be transparent and self-evident rather than meaningful.

Politics and rationality

Political realist approaches to policy-making begin with the premise that policy choices reflect the will of competing social groups with divergent material interests. The approach depends on the ideas that political collectivities form around naturally occurring economic groups, that these groups express and pursue objective material interests, and that policy choices reflect the relative political clout of competing groups. The evidence from railway history has suggested somewhat different understandings of the political processes these analysts explore.

Are interest groups primordial or constructed?

Where do interest groups come from? For most political analysts they reflect naturally occurring economic factions that emerge as capitalism progresses. Capitalism is thought to evolve according to its own internal dynamic; thus, interest groups are produced by forces exogenous to the state. The evidence presented in these pages suggests, instead, that interest groups are constituted by characteristics of states – this was true even of those groups involved in the earliest charter debates. The United States' interstate rivalries brought together merchants, manufacturers, and farmers in regional groups to promote canals and railways alike. France's early public transport policies generated a potent lobby of state engineers who backed rail development just as they backed all transport development. Britain's laissez-faire transport policy produced a strong group of private canal owners who opposed the granting of railway charters. Policy outcomes were then shaped by the goals of these groups. In reaction to transport boosterism from regional elites, American states underwrote railroads and granted charters to all comers; in response to state technocrats who coveted control over railroads, France granted only charters for lines planned by state engineers; in reaction to challenges from canal operators, Britain demanded exacting engineering studies from prospective railroads. Interest groups certainly played important roles in policymaking, but groups themselves were largely the products of policy institutions (DiMaggio 1988; Dobbin 1992).

Are interests objective or subjective?

The idea that naturally occurring interest groups are driven by *objective* material interests has been demonstrated by rational choice theorists and other interest-centered analysts, with evidence that people pursue predictable material preferences via predictable strategies. Critics have chipped away at the edges of economic interest theories by arguing that not all goals are economic (for example, love) or that not all behavior is self-interested (for example, altruism), but they have not challenged the core ideas about interests and rationality. I have tried to show that even in the case of economic utility maximization, "objective" interests are conditioned by local social constructions of efficiency; thus, "objective" interests are highly subjective because they are influenced by nations' cultural representations of rationality and self-interest. In other words, national institutions embody very different ideas about how economic rationality operates, and those ideas color how people think about their interests. The most compelling cross-national evidence against the notion that "objective" interests drive policy preferences is simply that railroads in different countries advocated widely different policies in each of the four policy arenas. Take the issue of finance. It would seem to have been in the interest of every railroad to favor all varieties of public aid. However, because Americans believed that competition between localities would spur growth and that federal action would merely spawn graft, most American railroads backed state and local government financing but not federal financing. Because the French believed that growth must be orchestrated by the central state, French railroads backed central state financing but eschewed provincial and local financing as irrational. Because the British believed that all government meddling was inefficient, British railroads opposed government financing of all kinds. These and other ideas about self-interest were clearly conditioned by national context.

To suggest that railroads should have predictable, universal, policy preferences is to caricature interest group approaches. But if national context is needed to predict how "objective" material interests will be perceived and pursued, then national context may deserve pride of place in theories of interest. At most points in railway history, in fact, we could have predicted a person's policy preferences much better by knowing his nationality than by knowing his relationship to the means of production.

Does the strongest group always win?

Interest-group analysts take it as an article of faith that policy choices reflect the will of the most powerful interest group or coalition, and this leads to the unfortunate tautology that the group that appears to get its way must wield the most power. To bolster their theory, interest-group theorists analyze cases where powerful groups *seem to* lose important battles and demonstrate that (1) some other group was actually more powerful, or (2) the policy chosen was actually favored by the powerful group. The debate over the Act to Regulate Interstate Commerce, which was opposed by powerful railroads, is a case in point. A veritable army of analysts sought to show, following strategy (1), that farmers, merchants, oilmen, or some combination thereof actually held more political clout than the railways, and thereby won the battle over railway regulation. Gabriel Kolko (1965) then sought to resolve the dilemma with strategy (2) by arguing that railways had come to favor regulation by the time the act passed. I have suggested, by contrast, that the major railroads indeed had tremendous political clout, and that they indeed lost a battle they deemed important when the act was passed. The act outlawed price fixing, whereas railroads wanted it legalized. They lost because their opponents had an invincible rhetorical weapon in a central precept of political culture. American state institutions had depicted concentrated authority as hazardous to political order by guarding against it so doggedly. Proponents of regulation made the compelling argument that the state must guard against concentration in the industrial realm just as it did in the political realm.

It is perhaps an obvious point, but it may be one worth making given how pervasive interest-group thinking is in the social sciences. Strong interest groups lose political battles all the time, and it is often because political culture offers their opponents compelling arguments and offers them little in the way of rebuttal. This is the case because institutionalized political culture carries not only clear *prescriptions* for how to achieve social ends, but also clear *admonitions* about the sorts of social practices that are disruptive and inefficient. These prescriptions and admonitions are the building blocks of rhetorical strategies, which are often highly institutionalized themselves. Diverse rhetorical resources enabled American railway customers to oppose cartels by arguing that they created a tyrannical concentration of authority, British railways to promote cartels by arguing that they would shield vital entrepreneurial railroads from predatory price competition, and French technocrats to back state-brokered monopolies by arguing that centralized management would produce efficiency. Today, the United States' distinct ideas about rationality, and the attendant rhetorical resources, make it difficult to imagine an American industry, no matter how politically powerful, winning federal policies that would foster the creation of a single, monopolistic, "national champion," yet the French do this routinely. This is partly because American ideas about rationality depict such policies as irrational, but it is also partly because it is difficult to believe an industry could construct a compelling argument for the approach.

Economics and rationality

Many policy analysts begin with the assumption that transcendental economic laws govern the universe, and take policy to be responsive to those laws. In the first chapter I argued that the belief in exogenous economic laws is an artifact of the modern, rationalized, meaning system, which depicts social reality as governed by the kind of general theory that physicists subscribe to. Two kinds of evidence undermine such economic determinist arguments. First, I review evidence that policies organized around widely different economic principles produced similar outcomes in terms of industry growth and prosperity. Second, I review evidence that the economic laws these nations discovered reflect local institutional history rather than exogenous, transhistorical, laws.

Economics as a natural science

Economic determinist approaches suggest that policy outcomes reflect the rational application of natural economic principles by policymakers, or alternatively that natural laws select out optimal policies for survival. The emergence of three very different policy strategies, and attendant notions of economic rationality, in these three countries tends to undermine this way of thinking. In each nation, policymakers believed beyond all reason in the efficacy of their own idiosyncratic national policy strategy. They were certain that they understood the economic laws that ruled the railways and that only strict adherence to those laws would result in progress. However, when nations broke each other's core economic rules their railway industries did not fall apart. Thus, although the French were certain that if they allowed private parties to plan railroads the result would be a disarticulated, incoherent, and ineffectual rail system, that strategy proved workable in both the United States and Britain.

The most compelling evidence that economic laws do not narrowly circumscribe what is efficient is simply that the radically different strategies of the United States, France, and Britain produced rapid, dependable, and cost-effective transport systems in relatively short order. There were important differences in these rail systems, to be sure. By encouraging market entry, British policy caused the railways to be built quickly, and by carefully planning routes France avoided overcapacity and redundancy. Yet no strategy failed in any important sense. More generally, evidence has mounted in recent years that widely different industrial policy paradigms can produce similar rates of growth. In the early decades of this century, the United States' strategy of enforcing price competition coincided with tremendous growth, but then so did Germany's strategy of supporting cartels (Chandler 1990). In the years after World War II, government industrial planning in France appears to have been a resounding success, but then so does Japan's policy of export-orientated interfirm collaboration (Shonfield 1965; Johnson 1982). Japan's experience led Western analysts to champion a new Southeast Asian policy paradigm for competitiveness, until Singapore, Hong Kong, Taiwan, and South Korea achieved similar feats with entirely different policy strategies (Deyo 1987; Hamilton and Biggart 1988; Chiu 1992). Every time analysts think they have found the "one best way" to generate growth, history seems to generate an array of counterexamples. The obvious lesson is not that *all* roads lead to Rome, but that *many* do. What is somewhat surprising, given the overwhelming evidence that growth can be produced by a wide array of economic systems, is that economic theorists continue to hold that there is one best way, and continue to embrace Adam Smith's view of it. Equally surprising is that Latin America and Eastern Europe follow the dictates of Milton Friedman and Jeffrey Sachs, whose ideas appear to be contradicted by virtually all recent success cases.

Paradoxically, British and American rail history suggests not only that the countries that provide the case material for neoclassical economics pursued *interventionist* policies, as Karl Polanyi and James Q. Wilson have pointed out, but that they pursued *completely different* policies. In the first three-quarters of the nineteenth century, Parliament carefully avoided directing the course of economic growth, while American states were actively investing in canals, turnpikes, banks, railroads, and factories. Since the last quarter of the nineteenth century, Britain has guarded small firms against destructive price competition, while American state and federal governments have enforced price competition. Both countries claimed the legacy of Adam Smith, and although both developed industrial policy paradigms that situated sovereignty over economic life outside of the state, those paradigms actually aimed to produce progress in very different ways. The United States pursued growth with market selection mechanisms that killed off weak firms, whereas Britain pursued growth with supports for small entrepreneurs that destroyed market competition.

Economic determinists are not oblivious to evidence that nations industrialized under very different policy regimes. They reconcile this evidence with their metatheoretical commitment to a general economic theory by arguing (1) that optimal policy strategies vary by level of development, or (2) that optimal strategies vary by sequence of development – late developers differ from early developers in that they need more extensive state intervention. The level-of-development thesis falls apart in the light of evidence that over the course of railway history the policies of the United States, France, and Britain followed no discernable developmental pattern. The sequencing or late-development thesis is contradicted in two ways. First, the theory suggests that the United States, as the laggard of the three, should have pursued more active intervention in the economy than did France. That was not the case. Second, one implication of Gerschenkron's argument is that during industrialization, nations choose different levels of state intervention to suit their developmental needs. However, British and French rail policies descended directly from turnpike and canal policies that dated from the seventeenth century. French technocrats had taken charge of turnpike and canal development to ensure military transport, and the state later took charge of railways by habit more than by design. More generally, interventionism among Britain's late-developing Continental neighbors is key to Gerschenkron's argument. However, in France and elsewhere on the Continent, the legacy of absolutist states that fielded standing armies to guard fragile borders seems to better explain the rise of industrial interventionism than the imperatives of late development.

The social origins of economic principles

Where, then, do nations' distinct ideas about the nature of industrial rationality come from if not from transcendental economic laws? The evidence points to three processes. First, these three nations imputed purpose to existing social institutions during the nineteenth century. They imputed the contemporary purpose of economic growth to institutions that emerged, by all accounts, to achieve military domination (France's absolutist administrative system), political harmony among rival agricultural elites (England's participating parliamentary system), or political array in a set of expanding colonies (the United States' local self-rule). Each country reinterpreted its state institutions in a way that made them integral to a positive, rationalized, theory of economic growth. By the beginning of the railway age, Jean-Baptiste Colbert and Henri de Saint-Simon had articulated state concertation as a prescription for growth in France, Adam Smith and David Ricardo had articulated the protection of economic liberties as a tactic for expansion in England, and Thomas Jefferson and Andrew Jackson had articulated decentralized rule and community self-determination as a strategy for progress in the United States. The lesson of these experiences is, in part, that in the modern world we presume that institutions have purposes and we tend to believe that those institutions that have survived the test of time must serve present purposes. In the absence of evidence that social institutions are dysfunctional, we take them to be functional for present goals and construct theories about how they operate.

Second, turn-of-the-century industrial policy paradigms have shown remarkable resilience, and I have suggested that this is partly because in developing those paradigms nations interpreted policies that upheld political order and liberty to be integral to growth. Each nation developed an industrial ideology that was isomorphic with its political culture, as the policies it adopted to guard political rights became associated in the public mind with economic growth. In the United States, restraints of trade were associated with political tyranny, and policies adopted to guard liberty by precluding restraints of trade were soon cast as positive measures to promote growth. In France, railway policies designed to prevent powerful private enterprises from interfering with the relationship of political sovereignty between state and citizen were soon depicted as essential to the industry's coherence and effectiveness. State tutelage thus became a positive prescription for industrial rationality. In Britain, policies designed to protect the political liberties of citizen-entrepreneurs by declawing their predatory competitors were in short order described as integral to an economic system that depended for its vitality on the existence of multitudes of small firms. Thus, in the United States political liberty became linked with free market competition; in France efforts to give pride of place to the nation's interest over private interests became linked with rationalizing industrial concertation; and in Britain the reinforcement of citizenship rights became tied to supports for dynamic, small-scale, entrepreneurialism. Because industrial policy paradigms became associated with policies designed to sustain political order and liberty, they became resistant to change. Changing the industrial policy paradigm would now require a new articulation of political order. In the United States, Roosevelt discovered this during the Great Depression when he tried to replace antitrust and railway regulation with policies that would create cartels, and found that he had to articulate a new, collaborative, and collectivist rhetoric of democracy (Dobbin 1993).

Not all policy paradigms are so intimately tied up with the sustenance of the polity. For instance, most countries decoupled macroeconomic policy from political culture, and this enabled them to treat fiscal and monetary theory as a set of transnational, falsifiable, hypotheses. One result was that it was relatively easy for nations to reject orthodox macroeconomic policy and replace it with Keynesianism after the Great Depression (Hall 1989; Gourevitch 1986).

A third type of evidence of the social origins of economic principles is that in addition to interpreting policies that had been adopted with political ends in mind to be economically efficacious, these nations adapted the causal designations they found in political institutions to the end of economic growth. In the United States, local sovereignty under a neutral federal superstructure was the source of political order. Americans first generalized the principle of local sovereignty to industry, with interventionist policies, and later generalized the principle of neutral federal oversight to industry, with policies that turned the government into the neutral referee of a free market. In France, central state orchestration of military and political life was the source of order. The French generalized this principle to the industrial realm, and elaborated it over the course of the nineteenth century to devise a policy strategy that combined public concertation and private initiative. In Britain, a weak central state that guarded the political liberties of individuals was the source of political order. The British generalized this principle by designing self-consciously noninterventionist industrial policies that would guard individual liberty to promote economic order and growth.

Finally, international diffusion played a surprisingly small role in the creation of railway policies, given the central role it has played in other sectors. Recent studies have shown that many policy strategies diffuse cross-nationally in a process akin to contagion (Strang and Meyer forthcoming). Keynesianism (Hall 1989), privatization (Suleiman and Waterbury 1990), mass education (Meyer, Ramirez, and Soysal 1992), and particular citizenship rights (Boli 1987) have all been found to diffuse internationally so that across nations, policies show striking isomorphism. This was not the case with railway policies. Certain technical ideas diffused. For instance, once Britain judged it impracticable to allow competing public carriers to operate trains on the same track, the United States and France soon altered their charter stipulations in accordance. Yet there is little evidence of cross-fertilization among the broad industrial policy paradigms these nations developed. I have already suggested that industrial policy paradigms tended to retain their uniqueness in these countries, rather than conform to international fashions, because they were entangled with political culture. These particular policy paradigms also survived, in part, because the cases were selected to control for successful industrialization. We know that countries that have undergone significant reversals on the path to industrialization, such as Brazil (Schneider 1991), are more likely to abandon their policy paradigms in favor of the latest fashion. Economic growth is the arbiter of industrial policy success in the modern world, and the three countries discussed here received, for the most part, evidence that confirmed the paths they chose.

Accordingly, bad economic times often lead even successful nations to cast about for new industrial strategies. In the 1960s Britain experimented with several state-planning models that were all the rage among industrial policy experts, but when the economy did not revive they reverted to their traditional failed policies rather than sticking by these new failed policies. In France, political groups from the right and the left have been extolling the virtues of privatization since the early 1980s. Perhaps privatization will have a greater longterm impact on France than planning had on Britain, but history suggests that these international trends have little permanent effect on industrial policy paradigms in advanced capitalist nations.

Institutions and rationality

How does path-dependence operate? That is, how is it that nations' policy choices at time t shape their policy choices at time $t+1$? The new institutional/statist approach to comparative policy suggests that old policies produce isomorphic new policies by generating particular *organizational avenues* for problem-solving. I have tried to argue that this approach neglects the ways in which extant policies shape what is *culturally conceivable*. Institutionalized policy strategies influence how we think about causes and effects, and this has proven to be at least as important as the fact that they also provide organizational avenues for action. The difficulty of sorting out the effects of organizational capacities and cultural prescriptions has been manifest in this book, and it is linked to the very nature of social structure and meaning. Social practices become institutionalized only insofar as they achieve collective meaning – that is, actors reproduce practices only when they apprehend the purposes of those practices. Hence, all structure, or regularized social practice, has meaning. Empirically these things are difficult to sort out because they are of a piece, and hence run in the same direction in any country. Thus, there are no countries that have the market-oriented *culture* of the United States – and also the state-oriented *structure* of France – that we can study to assess which factor is causal. Although it doesn't make a great deal of sense to treat structure and culture as separate dimensions (cf. Sewell 1992), at some points in the analysis I have tried to disentangle the two analytically to counter anti-cultural arguments.

The typical chronology of policy development that we saw in the rail industry underscores the role of cultural notions of causation. Broadly, nations exclude alien policy solutions and reproduce familiar ones at the stage of *conception,* which is guided by ideas about causation, rather than at the stage of *implementation,* which is to a greater extent guided by structural constraints and opportunities. We found that in matters of planning, finance, coordination, and competition, these countries conceived mutually exclusive sets of policy options to choose from.

Cross-case comparisons challenge strict structural approaches to institutions. First, the "administrative capacities" approach commonly links policy continuity to negative selection that results from administrative *in*capacities; new policies that overtax existing administrative structures fail and are terminated. The evidence we have seen suggests that weak administrative capacities are not irreversible. On the one hand, although administrative capacities sometimes undermined policies, governments routinely expanded capacities when their policy prescriptions called for it. On the issue of public construction aid, the American case would seem to support the "capacities" thesis because when weakly regulated aid spawned corruption, policymakers abandoned aid. Yet in France, policymakers responded to the same situation – of corruption brought on by weak regulation – by fortifying regulation and sustaining aid because they were committed to public control. When policies failed for structural reasons, here and in a number of other cases, governments chose between building stronger structures and abandoning the policies. The outcome depended more on their ideas about the appropriate role of government than on the initial episode of failure. On the other hand, incapacity was seldom a problem outside of the United States, where the Revolution had left governments with prominent symbolic roles but weak administrative powers. British rail policy failures more often resulted when new administrative structures overstepped the symbolic boundaries of laissez faire, as when the Railway Board was closed down because opponents claimed it had usurped Parliament's rightful authority over railway bills. Outside of the United States, policymakers almost always chose policies that underutilized public administrative capacities. If policymakers can expand state capacities when they have a compelling argument for doing so, and if they normally choose policies that are workable within existing state capacities, then administrative failure may not play a central role in the policy process.

Other institutionalists hypothesize that when nations face new problems they are more likely to expand existing institutions than to design new institutions, and institutional structures thereby influence policy choices (Weir and Skocpol 1985). There is some evidence for this in the French case, in that France turned over rail governance to the Ponts et Chaussées, which had governed canals and turnpikes. But this evidence can also be seen as a special case of the rule that policymakers replicate the *logic* embedded in existing policies when they address new problems. They may replicate that logic by using existing institutional frameworks, but where that is not possible they will establish new institutions. In the United States, state governments built new agencies to govern railroads by copying the regulatory logic of state banking commissions. In Britain, Parliament built a new agency to govern railroads by copying the logic of the early factory inspectorate. One result of this logic-copying was that industrial institutions gained a sort of causal coherence within nations. The railway policy strategies that were modified from other industries, and that met with apparent success in the railroads, were subsequently copied for various other sectors. The railways, like a number of other early industries, served as a proving ground for modern industrial policies; those dubbed successful were widely adopted by the architects of twentieth-century strategies.

John Zysman (1983) makes the pertinent argument that national financial systems, comprising both public and private organizations, delimit the industrial strategies nations have at their disposal. For instance, countries without national banks cannot realistically consider nationalization as an industrial strategy. Zysman expects that there will be little innovation in industrial strategy at the national level as a result of such constraints. Yet, in the early rail industry, before modern financial systems gelled, we saw a great deal of innovation. American states responded to the birth of the railroads by devising a system of public bond guarantees to attract capital. The French government devised a system of mixed public-private capitalization and temporary private concessions that was equally novel, and that was clearly responsive to contemporaneous fiscal pressures. In Britain, the railways played a major role in the emergence of regional stock exchanges that could assemble local capital for the construction of local-interest lines. It may well be that financial systems constrain public policy choices in today's world, but in the nineteenth century it appears that nations were not narrowly constrained by existing institutional arrangements.

I have argued for a more anthropological approach to modern state institutions, which treats the organizational avenues for action they offer and the cultural prescriptions they offer as two dimensions of one thing. This approach renders the distinctions we make between structure and meaning, and between the instrumental and the meaning-laden, nonsensical. In the railway industry, organizational avenues and cultural prescriptions influenced the course of policy by determining the kinds of policy solutions that were organizationally possible and culturally imaginable. Although it is difficult to disentangle the organizational and cultural aspects of social customs to evaluate their relative importance, I have tried to show that culture shapes the sorts of means people can envision when they first think about solving a problem.

Conclusion

One theme of my argument has been that prevailing explanations of policy are asociological in that they take the socially constructed categories and tenets of modern societies at face value and then turn around and analyze social action through those categories and tenets. The modern worldview depicts policy choices as resulting from competition among primordial interest groups – operating within narrow political-institutional constraints – that seek policies that will be to their advantage according to the tenets of universal economic laws that all actors comprehend. This worldview also depicts overarching economic rules that contribute to the selection of efficient policy outcomes. But it should be clear that the commonsense categories and tenets implied by these depictions are social constructs, just as are the categories and tenets found in societies with nonrational meaning systems. When anthropologists visit nonrational societies they view local meaning systems with great skepticism, assuming that the causal relationships and social categories embodied by social customs are cultural phenomena that merit examination. My aim has been to treat notions of industrial rationality skeptically by looking for their origins in social practices and history, rather than in a set of exogenous, rationalized principles that govern the universe.

Bibliography

Acworth, William M. 1908. *The Relation of Railroads to the State*. Philadelphia: Allen, Lane, and Scott.

Acworth, William M. 1917. *Historical Sketch of Government Ownership of Railroads in Foreign Countries*. Washington: "Presented to the Joint Committee of Congress on Interstate Commerce."

Acworth, William M. 1920. *Historical Sketch of State Railway Ownership*. London: John Murray.

Adam, Jean-Paul. 1972. *Instauration de la Politique des Chemins de Fer en France*. Paris: Presses Universitaires de France.

Adams, Charles Francis, Jr. 1887. *Railroads: Their Origins and Problems*. New York: Putnam.

Adams, Charles Francis, Jr. 1893. *Railroads: Their Origins and Problems*. Revised Edition. New York: Putnam.

Adams, Henry Carter. 1954 [1886]. "The Relation of the State to Industrial Action." Reprinted in *Two Essays by Henry Carter Adams*. Edited by Joseph Dorfman. New York: Columbia University Press.

Adams, James Truslow. 1927. *Provincial Society*. New York: Macmillan.

Adams, R.J.Q. 1978. *Arms and the Wizard: Lloyd George and the Ministry of Munitions 1915–1916*. College Station, TX: Texas A&M University Press.

Almond, Gabriel, and Sidney Verba. 1963. *The Civic Culture: Political Attitudes and Democracy in Five Nations*. Princeton: Princeton University Press.

Andersen, Svein S. "The Power of Policy Paradigms." Working Paper: Norwegian School of Management. Oslo.

Anderson, Benedict. 1983. *Imagined Communities: Reflections on the Origin and Spread of Nationalism*. London: Verso.

Anderson, Perry. 1974. *Lineages of the Absolutist State*. London: New Left Books.

Armitage, Susan. 1969. *The Politics of Decontrol of Industry: Britain and the United States*. London, Weidenfeld and Nicolson.

Ashcraft, Richard. 1986. *Revolutionary Politics and Locke's Two Treatises of Government*. Princeton: Princeton University Press.

Ashford, Douglas E. 1986. *The Emergence of the Welfare States*. Oxford: Basil Blackwell.

Ashford, Douglas E. 1977. "Political Science and Policy Studies: Toward a Structural Solution." *Policy Studies Journal* 5: 570–583.

Ashford, Douglas E. 1978. "The Structural Analysis of Policy or Institutions Really Do Matter." Pp. 81–99 in *Comparing Public Policies: New Concepts and Methods*. Douglas E. Ashford (editor). Sage: Beverly Hills.

Audiganne, Armand. 1858. *Les Chemins de Fer Aujourd'hui et dans Cent Ans*, Volume I. Paris: Capelle-Librairie.

233

Audiganne, Armand. 1862. *Les Chemins de Fer Aujourd'hui et dans Cent Ans,* Volume II. Paris: Capelle-Librairie.

Bachrach, Peter and Morton S. Baratz. 1963. "Decisions and Nondecisions: An Analytic Framework." *American Political Science Review* 57: 632–642.

Bagehot, Walter. 1928 (1867). *The English Constitution.* Oxford: Oxford University Press.

Bagwell, Philip S., and G.E. Mingay. 1970. *Britain and America: A Study of Economic Change, 1850–1939.* London: Routledge and Kegan Paul.

Bagwell, Philip S. 1974. *The Transport Revolution.* London: Routledge.

Barker, Richard J., 1969 "The Conseil General des Manufactures under Napoleon (1810–1814)." *French Historical Studies* 6:185–213.

Beer, Samuel. 1965. *British Politics in the Collectivist Age.* New York:Knopf.

Behrman, Jack N. 1984. "Industrial Policy in The United States." Pp. 215–228 in *National Industrial Policies.* Robert E. Driscoll and Jack N. Behrman (editors). Cambridge, MA: Oelgeschlager, Gunn and Hain.

Benson, Lee. 1955. *Merchants, Farmers, and Railroads: Railroad Regulation and New York Politics, 1850–1887.* Cambridge, MA: Harvard University Press.

Berger, Peter, and Thomas Luckmann. 1966. *The Social Construction of Reality: A Treatise on the Sociology of Knowledge.* Garden City: Doubleday.

Bernstein, Marver H. 1955. *Regulating Business by Independent Commission.* Princeton: Princeton University Press.

Birnbaum, Pierre. 1979. "State, Centre, and Bureaucracy." Paper presented at the International Political Science Association Meetings, Moscow.

Bishop, Avard Longley. 1907. "The State Works of Pennsylvania." *Transactions* 8:147–297.

Bloch, Marc. *Feudal Society, Volume 1 - The Growth of Ties of Dependence.* Chicago: University of Chicago Press.

Bloor, David. 1976. *Knowledge and Social Imagery.* London: Routledge.

Boli, John. 1987. "Human Rights or State Expansion? Cross-national Definitions of Constitutional Rights." Pp. 133–149 in *Institutional Structure: Constituting State, Society, and the Individual.* Edited by George M. Thomas, John W. Meyer, Francisco O. Ramirez, and John Boli. Beverly Hills: Sage.

Bourdieu, Pierre. 1977. *Outline of a Theory of Practice.* Cambridge; Cambridge University Press.

Bowles, Samuel, and Hergert Gintis. 1986. *Democracy and Capitalism: Property, Community, and the Contradictions of Modern Social Thought.* New York: Basic.

Brame, Edouard. 1854. *Chemin de Fer de Jonction Des Halles Centrales avec le Chemin de Ceinture.* Paris: Bureau de la Revue Municipale.

Brandes, Stuart D. 1976. *American Welfare Capitalism, 1880–1940.* Chicago: University of Chicago Press.

Broadbridge, Seymour. 1970. *Studies in Railway Expansion and the Capital Market in England: 1825–73.* London: Cass.

Broadway, Frank. 1970. *State Intervention in British Industry.* Madison WI: Fairleigh Dickinson University Press.

Bruchey, Stuart. 1990. *Enterprise: The Dynamic Economy of a Free People.* Cambridge: Harvard University Press.

Buck, Solon. 1913. *The Granger Movement.* Cambridge, MA: Harvard University Press.

Callender. G.S. 1902. "The Early Transportation and Banking Enterprises of the States in Relation to the Growth of Corporations." *Quarterly Journal of Economics* 17:111–162.

Carlson, Robert E. 1969. *The Liverpool and Manchester Railway Project, 1821–1831.* Newton Abbot: David & Charles.

Caron, François. 1970. "French Railroad Investment, 1850–1914." Pp. 315–340 in *Essays in French Economic History.* Rondo Cameron (editor). Homewood, IL: Irwin.

Caron, François. 1973. *Histoire de l'Exploitation d'un Grand Réseau: La Compagnie du Chemin de Fer du Nord, 1846–1937.* Paris: Mouton.

Caron, François. 1979. *An Economic History of Modern France.* New York: Columbia University Press.

Caron, François. 1981. *Histoire Economique de la France XIXe-XXe Siecles.* Paris: Armand Colin.

Carter, Huntly. 1919. *The Limits of State Industrial Control: A Symposium on the Present Situation and How to Meet it.* London: Unwin.

Chalmers, David M. 1976. *Neither Socialism Nor Monopoly: Theodore Roosevelt and the Decision to Regulate the Railroads.* Philadelphia: Lippincott.

Chandler, Alfred D., Jr. 1956. *Henry Varnum Poor: Business Editor, Analyst, and Reformer.* Cambridge, MA: Harvard University Press.

Chandler, Alfred D., Jr. ed. 1965. *Railroads: The Nation's First Big Business.* New York: Harcourt, Brace, and World.

Chandler, Alfred D., Jr. 1977. *The Visible Hand: The Managerial Revolution in American Business.* Cambridge, MA: Harvard University Press.

Chandler, Alfred D., Jr. 1990. *Scale and Scope.* Cambridge, MA: Harvard University Press.

Channon, Geoffrey. 1983. "A.D. Chandler's 'Visible Hand' in Transport History." *The Journal of Transport History.* Third Series 2: 53–64.

Chester, Daniel. 1981. *The English Administrative System, 1780–1870.* Oxford: Clarendon.

Chevalier, Michael. 1839. *Society, Manners and Politics in the United States: Being a Series of Letters on North America.* Boston: Weeks, Jordan and Company.

Chiu, Stephen. 1992. "The State and Industrial Development in the East Asian Newly Industrializing Countries." Ph.D. Dissertation. Princeton University, Department of Sociology.

Clarke, Jeffrey J. 1977. "The Nationalization of War Industries in France, 1936–1937: A Case Study." *Journal of Modern History* 49:411–430.

Cleveland, Frederick, and Fred Powell. 1909. *Railroad Promotion and Capitalization in the United States.* New York: Longmans, Green, and Co.

Cleveland, Frederick, and Fred Powell. 1965. "Financing Construction." Pp. 48–58 in *Railroads: The Nation's First Big Business.* Edited by Alfred D. Chandler Jr. New York: Harcourt Brace, and World.

Cleveland-Stevens, Edward. 1915. *English Railways: Their Development and Their Relation to the State.* London: George Routledge and Sons.

Cochran, Thomas. 1972. *Business in American Life: A History.* New York: McGraw-Hill.

Cohen, Stephen S. 1977. *Modern Capitalist Planning: The French Model* Second Edition. Berkeley, CA: Campus.

Commons, John R. 1934. *Institutional Economics: Its Place in Political Economy.* New York: Macmillan.

Conde, Georges F.E. 1846 *Projets de Chemins de Fer: Report a le Ministre des Travaux Publiques.* Paris: A. Henry.

Cornish, William R. 1979. "Legal Control Over Cartels and Monopolization, 1880–

1914: A Comparison." In Norbert Horn and Jürgen Kocka, editors, *Law and the Formation of the Big Enterprises in the Nineteenth and Early Twentieth Centuries: Studies in the History of Industrialization in Germany, France, Great Britain, and the United States*. Göttingen: Vandenhoeck and Ruprecht.

Cottrell, P.L. and G. Ottley. 1972. "The Beginnings of the Stockton and Darlington Railway." *The Journal of Transport History*. New Series 3:86–93.

Crafts, N.F.R. 1982. "British Economic Growth 1700–1831: A Review of the Evidence." Paper presented to the New Economic History Workshop, Oxford University.

Crawford, Jay Boyd. 1880. *The Credit Mobilier of America*. Boston: C.W. Calkins.

Creighton, Andrew. 1989. "The Emergence of Incorporation: Standardization and Growth in the Nineteenth Century." Ph.D. Dissertation. Stanford University Department of Sociology.

Croce, Benedetto. 1933. *History of Europe in the Nineteenth Century*. New York: Harcourt, Brace, and World.

Crozier, Michel. 1964. *The Bureaucratic Phenomenon*. Chicago: University of Chicago Press.

Crozier, Michel, 1973. *The Stalled Society*. New York: Viking.

Curzon Price, Victoria. 1981. *Industrial Policies in the European Community*. London, Macmillan.

Dalzell, Robert F. 1987. *Enterprising Elite: The Boston Associates and the World They Made*. Cambridge: Harvard University Press.

Davenport, Michael. 1983. "Industrial Policy in the United Kingdom." Pp. 331–354 in *Industrial Policies for Growth and Competitiveness*. Gerard Adams and Lawrence R. Klein (editors). Lexington, MA: Lexington Books.

Davies, A. Emil. 1924. *British Railways, 1825–1924. Why Nationalisation is Inevitable*. London, Railway Nationalisation Society.

Davis, Natalie Zemon. 1965. *Society and Culture in Early Modern France*. Stanford, CA: Stanford University Press.

Day, Charles R. 1987. *Education for the Industrial World: The Ecoles d'Arts et Métiers and the Rise of French Industrial Engineering*. Cambridge: MIT Press.

Decker, Leslie. 1960. "The Railroads and the Land Office: Administrative Policy and the Land Patent Controversy, 1864–1896." *Mississippi Valley Historical Review* XLVI: 679–699.

Deniel, Pierre. 1845. *De La Construction et de l'Exploitation des Chemins de Fer en France*. Paris: Hopkins.

Derfler, Leslie. 1966. *The Third French Republic, 1870–1940*. Princeton: D. Van Nostrand.

Detoeuf, Auguste. 1936. "La Fin du Liberalisme." *Bulletin du Centre Polytechnicien d'Etudes Economique* 31: 37–57.

DeWitt, François. 1983. "French Industrial Policy from 1945–1981: An Assessment." Pp. 221–246 in *Industrial Policies for Growth and Competitiveness*. Gerard Adams and Lawrence R. Klein (editors). Lexington, MA: Lexington Books.

Deyo, Frederic. Editor. 1987. *The Political Economy of the New Asian Industrialism*. Ithaca: Cornell University Press.

Diebold, William, Jr. 1982. "Past and Future Industrial Policy in the United States." Pp. 159–205 in *National Industrial Strategies and the World Economy*. John Pinder (editor). London, Croom Helm.

DiMaggio, Paul. 1988. "Interest and Agency in Institutional Theory." Pp. 3–22 in *Institutional Patterns and Organizations: Culture and Environment*. Cambridge: Ballinger.

DiMaggio, Paul J., and Walter W. Powell. 1983. "The Iron Cage Revisited: Institutionalized Isomorphism and Collective Rationality in Organizational Fields." *American
Sociological Review* 48: 147–160.

DiMaggio, Paul J., and Walter W. Powell. 1991. "Introduction." Pp. 1–40 in *The New
Institutionalism in Organizational Analysis*. Edited by Walter W. Powell and Paul J.
DiMaggio. Chicago: University of Chicago Press.

Dobbin, Frank. Forthcoming. "What do Markets have in Common? Toward a Fast Train
Policy in the European Community." In *Policy Development in an Emerging European State*. Edited by Kjell Eliassen and Svein Andersen. London: Sage.

Dobbin, Frank. In press. "Public Policy and the Development of High Speed Trains in
France and the United States." In *High Speed Trains: Entrepreneurship and Society*.
Edited by Staffan Hultén and Torbjörn Flink. London: Leading Edge.

Dobbin, Frank. 1992a. "The Origins of Private Social Insurance: Public Policy and
Fringe Benefits in America, 1920–1950." *American Journal of Sociology* 97: 1416–
1450.

Dobbin, Frank. 1992b. "Metaphors for Industrial Rationality: The Social Construction
of Electronics Policy in the United States and France." Pp. 185–206 in *Vocabularies
of Public Life: Empirical Essays in Symbolic Structure*. Edited by Robert Wuthnow.
London: Routledge.

Dobbin, Frank. 1993. "The Social Construction of the Great Depression: Industrial
Policy During the 1930s in the United States, Britain, and France." *Theory and
Society.*

Dorsey, Edward Bates. 1887. *English and American Railroads Compared*, Second Edition. New York: Wiley.

Dosi, Giovanni. 1981. "Institutions and Markets in High Technology: Government
Support for Micro-electronics in Europe." Pp. 182–201 in *Industrial Policy and
Innovation*. Charles Carter (editor). London, Heinemann.

Douglas, Mary. 1986. *How Institutions Think*. Syracuse, NY: Syracuse University Press.

Doukas, Kimon A. 1945. *The French Railroads and the State*. New York: Columbia
University Press.

Duby, Georges, and Robert Mandrou. 1976. *Histoire de la Civilisation Française,
XVIIe-XXe Siecle*. Paris: Armand Colin.

Dunham, Arthur L. 1941. "How the First French Railways Were Planned." *Journal of
Economic History* 14: 12–25.

Dunlavy, Colleen. 1991. "Mirror Images: Political Structure and Early Railroad Policy in
the United States and Prussia." *Studies in American Political Development* 5:1–35.

Dunlavy, Colleen. Forthcoming. *Politics and Industrialization: Early Railroads in the
United States and Prussia*. Princeton: Princeton University Press.

Dunn, Samuel O. 1913. *Government Ownership of Railways*. New York: Appleton.

Dunn, Samuel O. 1915. "What is the Matter with Railway Regulation." *North American Review* 736–748.

Dunn, Samuel O. 1918. *Regulation of Railways*. New York: Appleton.

Durkheim, Emile. 1933. *The Division of Labor in Society*, George Simpson (trans.). New
York: Free Press.

Dyson, Kenneth. 1983. "The Cultural, Ideological and Structural Context." Pp. 26–66
in *Industrial Crisis: A Comparative Study of the State and Industry*. Kenneth Dyson
and Stephen Wilks (editors). Oxford: Martin Robinson.

Edelman, Murray. 1964. *The Symbolic Uses of Politics*. Urbana: University of Illinois
Press.

Edmonds, Martin. 1983. "Market Ideology and Corporate Power: The United States."

Pp. 67–101 in *Industrial Crisis: A Comparative Study of the State and Industry.* Kenneth Dyson and Stephen Wilks (editors). Oxford: Martin Robinson.

Ehrmann, Henry W. 1957. *Organized Business in France.* Princeton: Princeton University Press.

Eisenstadt, S.N., M. Abitbol, and N. Chazan. 1987. "Cultural Premises, Political Structures and Dynamics." *International Political Science Review* 8:291–306.

Ellis, David M. 1946. "The Forfeiture of Railroad Land Grants, 1867–1894." *Mississippi Valley Historical Review* XXVIII: 25–47.

Elster, Jon. 1989. *The Cement of Society: A Study of Social Order.* New York: Cambridge University Press.

Engineering News Publishing Company. 1889. *Atlas of Railway Progress 1888–1889.* New York: Engineering News.

Estrin, Saul and Peter Holmes. 1983. *French Planning in Theory and Practice.* London: Allen and Unwin.

Far, André de la. 1972. *Les Chemins de Fer.* Paris: André Bonne.

Feraud-Giraud, L.-J.-D. 1853. *Legislation des Chemins de Fer Par Rapport aux Proprietes Riveraines.* Paris: Aubin.

Firth, Raymond. 1983 [1936]. *We, the Tikopia: A Sociological Study of Kinship in Primitive Polynesia.* Stanford: Stanford University Press.

Fischer, Wolfram and Peter Lundgreen. 1975. "The Recruitment and Training of Administrative Personnel." Pp. 456–561 in *The Formation of National States in Western Europe.* Edited by Charles Tilly. Princeton, NJ: Princeton University Press.

Fisher, Charles E. 1947. *Whistler's Railroad: The Western Railroad of Massachusetts.* Bulletin No. 69. Boston: The Railway and Locomotive Historical Society.

Fishlow, Albert. 1965. *American Railroads and the Transformation of the Ante-Bellum Economy.* Cambridge, MA: Harvard University Press.

Fleming M., and G. Merkel. 1909. *Grosse Atlas der Eisenbahnen von Mittel-Europa.* Berlin: Grosse.

Fligstein, Neil. 1990. *The Transformation of Corporate Control.* Cambridge, MA: Harvard University Press.

Florence, P. Sargent. 1953. *The Logic of British and American Industry: A Realistic Analysis of Economic Structure and Government.* London, Routledge and Kegan Paul.

Fogel, Robert O. 1960. *The Union Pacific Railroad: A Case in Premature Enterprise.* Baltimore: The Johns Hopkins Press.

Fogel, Robert O. 1964. *Railroads and American Economic Growth: Essays in Econometric History.* Baltimore: The Johns Hopkins Press.

Fowler, John. 1877. "Railway Accidents." *The Nineteenth Century* 1: 646–664.

France, Bulletin des Lois [Chambres]. Various Years. *Bulletin des Lois.* Paris: Imprimerie Royale.

France, Direction Generale Des Chemins de Fer. 1855. *Repertoire de la Legislation Des Chemins de Fer.* Paris: Napoleon Chaix.

France, Corps Royaux [des Ponts et Chausées et des Mines]. 1843. *Annales des Ponts et Chausées.* Premier Serie; 1831–1840. Paris: Carilian-Goeury et V. Dalmont.

France, Moniteur Universel. Various Years. *Moniteur Universel.* Paris.

Francis, John. 1851. *A History of the English Railway; Its Social Relations and Revelations* Two Volumes. London: Longman, Brown, Green and Longman.

Franko, Lawrence G. and Jack N. Behrman. 1984. "Industrial Policy in France." Pp. 57–71 in *National Industrial Policies.* Robert E. Driscoll and Jack N. Behrman (editors). Cambridge, MA: Oelgeschlager, Gunn, and Hain.

Freitag, Peter. 1985. "Class Conflict and the Rise of Government Regulation." *Insurgent Sociologist* 12: 55–66.

Fry, Geoffrey K. 1979. *The Growth of Government: The Development of Ideas about the Role of the State and Machinery and Functions of Government in Britain Since 1780.* London: Frank Cass.

Gabwell, Philip S. 1963. *The Railwaymen.* London: George Allen and Unwin.

Galbraith, John Kenneth. 1952. *American Capitalism: The Concept of Countervailing Power.* White Plains, NY: M.E. Sharpe.

Galbraith, John Kenneth. 1978. *The New Industrial State* Third Edition. Boston: Houghton Mifflin.

Galt, William. 1864. *Railway Reform.* London: Woodfall and Kinder.

Geertz, Clifford. 1980. *Negara: The Theatre-State in Nineteenth Century Bali.* Princeton: Princeton University Press.

Geertz, Clifford. 1983. *Local Knowledge: Further Essays in Interpretive Anthropology.* New York: Basic.

Gerschenkron, Alexander. 1962. *Economic Backwardness in Historical Perspective.* Cambridge: Harvard University Press.

Gilbert, James. 1972. *Designing the Industrial State: The Intellectual Pursuit of Collectivism in America, 1880–1940.* Chicago: Quadrangle.

Gille, Bertrand. 1961. *Repertoire Numerique Des Archives de la Compagnie du Chemin de Fer au Nord Conservee aux Archives Nationales (48 AQ).* Paris: Imprimerie Nationale.

Gilligan, Thomas W., William J. Marshal, and Barry R. Weingast. 1986. *A Reconsideration of the Railroad Problem: the Economics and Politics of the Interstate Commerce Act.* Stanford, CA: Hoover Institution Working Papers in Political Science.

Gilpin, Robert. 1968. *France in the Age of the Scientific State.* Princeton: Princeton University Press.

Gisclard, Auguste. 1882. *Code des Chemins de Fer D'Interet Local.* Paris: Pedone-Lauriel.

Godet, Adrien. 1903. *Recueil de la Legislation des Chemins de Fer D'Interet General.* Paris: Librairie Nouvelle de Droit et de Jurisprudence.

Gold, David M. 1983. "Redfield, Railroads, and the Roots of 'Laissez-Faire Constitutionalism'." *The American Journal of Legal History* 27: 254–268.

Goodrich, Carter. 1949. "The Virginia System of Mixed Enterprise: A Study of State Planning of Internal Improvements." *Political Science Quarterly* 64: 355–387.

Goodrich, Carter. 1960. *Government Promotion of American Canals and Railroads 1800–1890.* New York: Columbia University Press.

Goodrich, Carter. 1968. "State In, State Out – A Pattern of Development Policy." *Journal of Economic Issues* 30: 365–383.

Goodrich, Carter, and Harvey S. Segal. 1953. "Baltimore's Aid to Railroads: A Study in the Municipal Planning of Internal Improvements." *Journal of Economic History* 8:2–35.

Gourevitch, Peter, 1984. "Breaking with Orthodoxy: The Politics of Economic Policy Responses to the Depression of the 1930s." *Industrial Organization* 38: 95–129.

Gourevitch, Peter. 1986. *Politics in Hard Times: Comparative Responses to International Economic Crises.* Ithaca, NY: Cornell University Press.

Gournerie, Jules de la. 1880. *Etudes Economiques sur L'Exploitation des Chemins de Fer.* Paris: Gauthier-Villars.

Gourvish, T.R. 1980. *Railways in the British Economy: 1813–1914.* London: Macmillan.

Graham, Otis L., Jr. 1991. *Losing Time: The Industrial Policy Debate.* Cambridge: Harvard University Press.

Gramsci, Antonio. 1971. *Selections from the Prison Notebooks.* New York: International.

Granovetter, Mark. 1985. "Economic Action and Social Structure: The Problem of Embeddedness." *American Journal of Sociology* 91: 481–510.

Grant, Wyn. 1982. *The Political Economy of Industrial Policy.* London, Butterworths.

Great Britain, Board of Trade. 1845. *Report of the Railway Department on Various Schemes and Projects.* London: HMSO.

Great Britain, Parliament. 1825. *Proceedings of the Committee on the Liverpool and Manchester Railroad Bill.* London: Thomas Davison.

Great Britain, Parliament. 1841. *Report of the Officers of the Railway Department.* London: HMSO.

Great Britain, Parliament. 1844. *General Railway Legislation: General Railway Acts and Minute (sic) of the Board of Trade, etc.* London: HMSO.

Great Britain, Parliament. 1863. *Report from the Select Committee on Private Bill Legislation.* London: HMSO.

Great Britain, Parliament. 1880s. *Returns of Accidents and Casualties, Railways,* Series. London: HMSO.

Great Britain, Parliament. 1883. *Supplement to the Thirteenth Edition of the General Railway Acts.* James Bigg (editor). London: HMSO.

Great Britain, Parliamentary Debates. Various Years. *Parliamentary Debates.* London: T.C. Hansard.

Great Britain, Parliamentary Papers. 1840. *Report of the Select Committee on Railway Communications.* Shannon: Irish University Press.

Great Britain, Parliamentary Papers. 1844. *Fifth Report of the Select Committee on Railways.* Shannon: Irish University Press.

Great Britain, Parliamentary Papers. 1844a. *Third Report of the Select Committee on Railways.* Shannon: Irish University Press.

Great Britain, Parliamentary Papers. 1853. *Fourth report of the Select Committee on Railway and Canal Bills.* Shannon: Irish University Press.

Great Britain, Parliamentary Papers. 1872. *Report of the Select Committee on Railway Companies Amalgamations.* Shannon: Irish University Press.

Great Britain, Parliamentary Papers. 1880. *Sixth Annual Report of the Railway Commissioners.* Shannon: Irish University Press.

Great Britain, Railway Department. 1840–1890. *General Report to the Board of Trade upon the Accidents which have occurred on the Railways of the United Kingdom.* London: Eyre and Spottiswood.

Great Britain, Railway Department. 1840–1890a. *Report of the Officers of the Railway Department.* London, HMSO.

Grove, J.W. 1962. *Government and Industry in Britain.* London: Longmans.

Guillamot, Georges. 1899. *L'Organisation des Chemins de Fer en France.* Paris: Arthur Rousseau.

Gusfield, Joseph R., and Jerzy Michalowicz. 1984. "Secular Symbolism: Studies of Ritual, Ceremony, and the Symbolic Order in Modern Life." Pp. 417–435 in *Annual Review of Sociology.* Ralph Turner (editor). New York: Annual Review Press.

Habermas, Jürgen. 1984. *The Theory of Communicative Action. Volume One. Reason and the Rationalization of Society.* Boston: Beacon.

Hall, Peter A. 1986. *Governing the Economy: The Politics of State Intervention in Britain and France.* New York: Oxford University Press.

Hall, Peter A. 1989. *The Political Power of Economic Ideas: Keynesianism Across Nations.* Princeton, NJ: Princeton University Press.

Hall, Peter A. 1992. "The Movement From Keynesianism to Monetarism: Institutional Analysis and British Economic Policy in the 1970s." Pp. 90–113 in *Historical Institutionalism in Comparative Politics: State, Society, and Economy.* Edited by Svein Steinmo, Kathleen Thelen, and Frank Longstreth. New York: Cambridge University Press.

Hall, Peter A. Forthcoming. "Policy Paradigms, Social Learning and the State: The Case of Economic Policy-making in Britain." *Comparative Politics.*

Hamilton, Alexander. 1968 (reprint). "Report on Manufactures." Pp. 111–122 in *Private Life and Public Order: The Context of Modern Public Policy.* Theodore J. Lowi (editor). New York: Norton.

Hamilton, Gary G. and Nicole Woolsey Biggart. 1988. "Market, Culture, and Authority: A Comparative Analysis of Management and Organization in the Far East." *American Journal of Sociology* 94: S52-S94.

Hamilton, Walton H. 1974. *Industrial Policy and Institutionalism,* Reprints of Economic Classics Series. Clifton, NJ: Clifton.

Handlin, Oscar and Mary F. Handlin. 1945. "Origins of the American Business Corporation." *Journal of Economic History* 5: 1–24.

Handlin, Oscar and Mary F. Handlin. 1947. *Commonwealth: A Study of the Role of Government in the American Economy: Massachusetts, 1774–1861.* Cambridge, MA: Harvard University Press.

Haney, Lewis Henry. 1908. *A Congressional History of Railways in the United States to 1850,* University of Wisconsin Bulletin 211. Madison: University of Wisconsin Press.

Haney, Lewis Henry. 1910. *A Congressional History of Railways in the United States 1850 to 1887,* University of Wisconsin Bulletin 342. Madison: University of Wisconsin Press.

Hannah, Leslie. 1980. "Government and Business in Britain: The Evolution of the Modern Relationship." Pp. 107–124 in *Government and Business.* Keiichiro Nakagawa (editor). Tokyo, University of Tokyo Press.

Hartz, Louis. 1943. "Laissez-Faire Thought in Pennsylvania, 1776–1860." *The Journal of Economic History* III (supplement): 66–77.

Hartz, Louis. 1948. *Economic Policy and Democratic Thought: Pennsylvania, 1776–1860.* Cambridge: Harvard University Press.

Hartz, Louis. 1955. *The Liberal Tradition in America.* New York: Harcourt Brace.

Hayward, Jack. 1974. *The One and Indivisible French Republic.* New York: Norton.

Hayward, Jack. 1982. "Mobilising Private Interests in the Service of Public Ambitions: The Salient Element in the Dual French Policy Style?" Pp. 111–140 in *Policy Styles in Western Europe,* edited by Jeremy Richardson. London: Allen and Unwin.

Hayward, Jack. 1986. *The State and the Market Economy: Industrial Patriotism and Economic Intervention in France.* New York: New York University Press.

Heclo, Hugh. 1974. *Modern Social Politics in Britain and Sweden.* New Haven, CT: Yale University Press.

Heclo, Hugh, and Aaron Wildavsky. 1974. *The Private Government of Public Money.* Berkeley: University of California Press.

Henry, Robert S. 1945. "The American Land Grant Legend in American History Texts." *Mississippi Valley Historical Review,* 32: 171–194.

Hercules (pseudonym). 1885. *British Railways and Canals in Relation to British Trade and Government Control.* London: Field and Tuer.

Heydinger, Earl L. 1954. "The English Influence on American Railroads." *Railway and Locomotive History Bulletin* 91: 7–45.

Hill, Christopher. 1980. *The Century of Revolution, 1603–1714.* Second Edition. Walton-on-Thames: Nelson.

Hintze, Otto. 1975 (reprints). *The Historical Essays of Otto Hintze.* Felix Gilbert (editor). New York: Oxford University Press.

Hirschman, Albert O. 1977. *The Passions and the Interests: Political Arguments for Capitalism before its Triumph.* Princeton: Princeton University Press.

Hobsbawm, Eric J. 1962. *The Age of Revolution, 1789–1848.* New York: World.

Hobsbawm, Eric. 1968. *Industry and Empire.* New York: Pantheon.

Hodges, Sir William, and John M. Lely. 1889. *A Treatise on the Law of Railways, Railway Companies, and Railway Investments,* Seventh Edition. London: Sweet and Maxwell.

Hoffmann, Stanley (ed). 1963. *In Search of France.* Cambridge: Harvard University Press.

Hofstadter, Richard. 1955. *The Age of Reform.* New York: Vintage.

Holbrook, Stewart. 1981. *The Story of American Railroads.* New York: Crown.

Hollingsworth, J. Rogers. 1991. "The Logic of Coordinating American Manufacturing Sectors." Pp. 35–74 in *Governance of the American Economy.* Edited by John L. Campbell, J. Rogers Hollingsworth, and Leon N. Lindberg. New York: Cambridge University Press.

Hoogenboom, Ari, and Olive Hoogenboom. 1976. *A History of the Interstate Commerce Commission: From Panacea to Palliative.* New York: Norton.

Horwitz, Morton. 1975. "The Rise of Legal Formalism." *American Journal of Legal History* 18: 251–264.

Hungerford, Edward. 1928. *The Story of the B. & O. Railroad,* Two Volumes. New York: Putnam.

Huntington, Samuel P. 1982. "American Ideals Versus American Institutions." *Political Science Quarterly* 97: 1–37.

Hurst, James Willard. 1956. *Law and the Conditions of Freedom in the Nineteenth-Century United States.* Madison, WI: University of Wisconsin Press.

Ikenberry, G. John. 1988. *Reasons of State: Oil Politics and the Capacities of American Government.* Ithaca: Cornell University Press.

Irving, R.J. 1984. "The Capitalisation of Britain's Railways, 1830–1914." *Journal of Transport History.* Third Series 5: 1–24.

Jagtiani, H.M. 1924. *The Role of the State in the Provision of Railways.* London: P.S. King and Son.

Jepperson, Ronald. 1991. "Institutions, Institutional Effects, and Institutionalism." Pp. 143–163 in *The New Institutionalism in Organizational Analysis.* Edited by Walter Powell and Paul DiMaggio. Chicago: University of Chicago Press.

Joby, R.S. 1983. *The Railway Builders.* Newton Abbot: David & Charles.

Johnson, Chalmers. 1982. *MITI and the Japanese Miracle.* Stanford, CA: Stanford University Press.

Jones, Elliot, and Homer B. Vanderblue (editors). 1925. *Railroads: Cases and Selections.* New York: Macmillan.

Kahn, Alfred E. 1946. *Great Britain in the World Economy.* New York: Columbia University Press.

Kariel, Henry S. 1961. *The Decline of American Pluralism.* Stanford: Stanford University Press.

Kasson, John F. 1976. *Civilizing the Machine: Technology and Republican Values in America, 1776–1900.* New York: Penguin.

Katzenstein, Peter J. (editor). 1978. *Between Power and Plenty: Foreign Economic Policies of Advanced Industrial States.* Madison: University of Wisconsin Press.

Katzenstein, Peter J. 1984. *Corporatism and Change: Switzerland, Austria, and the Politics of Industry.* Ithaca, NY: Cornell University Press.

Kaufmann, Richard de. 1900. *La Politique Française en Matiere de Chemins de Fer.* Paris: Librarie Polytechnique.

Keeler, Theodore E. 1983. *Railroads, Freight, and Public Policy.* Washington: Brookings.

Kemp, Tom. 1972. *The French Economy 1913–1939: The History of a Decline.* London: Longmans.

Kenna, Edward Dudley. 1914. *Railway Misrule.* New York: Duffield.

Kennedy, Charles J. 1961. "The Influence of Government Regulation on the Management Decisions of Forty-Five New England Railroads, 1830–1900." *The Railway and Local Historical Society Bulletin* 105: 6–22.

Kennedy, Robert Dawson, Jr. 1991. "The Statist Evolution of Rail Governance in the United States, 1830–1986." Pp. 138–181 in *Governance of the American Economy.* Edited by John L. Campbell, J. Rogers Hollingsworth, and Leon N. Lindberg. New York: Cambridge University Press.

Kesselman, Mark. 1977. *The Ambiguous Consensus: A Study of Local Government in France.* New York: Knopf.

Kidd, Howard C. 1929. *A New Era for British Railways: A Study of the Railways Act, 1921, from an American Standpoint, with Special Reference to Amalgamation.* London: Bouverie House.

Kirkland, Edward C. 1948. *Men, Cities, and Transportation: A Study in New England History 1820–1900,* Two Volumes. Cambridge, MA: Harvard University Press.

Knorst, William J. 1953. *Interstate Commerce Law and Practice,* Volume One. Chicago: College of Advanced Traffic.

Kolko, Gabriel. 1965. *Railroads and Regulation 1877–1916.* Princeton: Princeton University Press.

Krasner, Stephen D. 1978. *Defending the National Interest: Raw Materials Investments and U.S. Foreign Policy.* Princeton: Princeton University Press.

Krasner, Stephen D. (editor). 1983. *International Regimes.* Ithaca: Cornell University Press.

Krasner, Stephen D. 1984. "Approaches to the State: Alternative Conceptions and Historical Dynamics." *Comparative Politics* 17: 223–246.

Krasner, Stephen D. Forthcoming. "Westphalia." In *Ideas and Foreign Policy.* Edited by J. Goldstein and R. Keohane. Ithaca: Cornell University Press.

Kuisel, Richard F. 1967. *Ernest Mercier: French Technocrat.* Berkeley, CA: University of California Press.

Kuisel, Richard F. 1981. *Capitalism and the State in Modern France: Renovation and Economic Management in the Twentieth Century.* Cambridge: Cambridge University Press.

Lamont, Michèle. 1987. "How to Become a Dominant French Philosopher: The Case of Jacques Derrida." *American Journal of Sociology* 93: 584–622.

Lamont, Michèle. 1992. *Money, Morals, and Manners: The Culture of the French and American Upper-middle Class.* Chicago: University of Chicago Press.

Landes, David S. 1969. *The Unbound Prometheus: Technological Change and Industrial Development in Western Europe from 1750 to the Present.* Cambridge: Cambridge University Press.

Lapierre, Suzanne. 1940. *La SNCF et la Politique Française de Coordination, du Rail et de la Route.* Paris: Presses Universitaires.

LaPolombara, Joseph. 1964. *Interest Groups in Italian Politics*. Princeton: Princeton University Press.

Larson, John Lauritz. 1984. *Bonds of Enterprise: John Murray Forbes and Western Development in America's Railway Age*. Cambridge, MA: Harvard University Press.

Lartilleux, Henri. 1948. *Le Reseau National Des Chemins de Fer Français*. Paris: Editions P.P.C..

Latour, Bruno. 1987. *Science in Action*. Cambridge, MA: Harvard University Press.

Latour, Bruno. 1992. "One More Turn After the Social Turn." Mimeo. CSI-Ecole des Mines, Paris.

Lazerges, Pierre. 1882. *Chemins de Fer Executes Par L'Etat: Guide Pratique Des Expropriations des Terrains*. Paris: Dunod.

Leclercq, Yves. 1987. *Le Réseau Impossible: La Résistance au Système des Grandes Compagnies Ferrovaires et la Politique Économique en France, 1820–1852*. Geneva: Librairie Droz.

Lefebvre, Georges. 1947. *The Coming of the French Revolution*. R.R. Palmer (trans.). New York: Vintage.

Lefranc, Georges. 1930. "The French Railroads, 1823–1842." *Journal of Economic and Business History* 299–331.

Legendre, Pierre. 1968. *Histoire de l'administration de 1750 a nos jours*. Paris: Presses Universitaires de France.

Lévy-Leboyer, Maurice. 1964. *Les Banques Européenes et l'Industrialisation Internationale*. Paris: Presses Universitaires de France.

Lewin, Henry Grote. 1925. *Early British Railways: A Short History of Their Origin and Development 1801–1844*. London: The Locomotive Publishing Company.

Lewin, Henry Grote. 1936. *The Railway Mania and its Aftermath: 1845–1852*. New York: Kelley.

Liggins, David. 1975. *National Economic Planning in France*. Lexington, MA: Lexington Books.

Lightner, David. 1983. "Railroads and the American Economy: The Fogel Thesis in Retrospect." *The Journal of Transport History*. Third Series 4: 20–34.

Lindberg, Leon and John L. Campbell. 1991. "The State and the Organization of Economic Activity." Pp. 356–95 in *Governance of the American Economy*. Edited by John L. Campbell, J. Rogers Hollingsworth, and Leon N. Lindberg. New York: Cambridge University Press.

Lindblom, Charles E. 1977. *Politics and Markets: The World's Political-Economic Systems*. New York: Basic.

Lipset, Seymour Martin. 1963. *The First New Nation: The United States in Historical and Comparative Perspective*. New York: Norton.

Lipset, Seymour Martin, and Stein Rokkan, eds. 1967. *Party Systems and Voter Alignments: Cross-National Perspectives*. New York: Free Press.

Lively, Robert A. 1955. "The American System: A Review Article." *The Business History Review* 29.

Lopata, Edwin L. 1937. *Local Aid to Railroads in Missouri*. Ph.D. Thesis, Columbia University.

Locklin, David. 1954. *Economics of Transportation*, Fourth Edition. Homewood IL: Irwin.

Lowi, Theodore J. 1969. *The End of Liberalism: Ideology, Policy and the Crisis of Public Authority*. New York: Norton.

Lubenow, William C. 1971. *The Politics of Government Growth: Early Victorian Attitudes Toward State Intervention, 1833–1848*. Hamden, CT: Archon Books.

Lucas, Arthur Fletcher. 1937. *Industrial Reconstruction and the Control of Competition: The British Experiments*. London: Longmans Green.

Lukes, Steven. 1974. *Power: A Radical View*. London: Oxford University Press.

Luthy, Herbert. 1955. *The State in France*. New York.

MacDonagh, Oliver. 1958. "The Nineteenth-Century Revolution in Government: A Reappraisal." *The Historical Journal* 1: 52–67.

Machin, Howard. 1977. *The Préfect in French Public Administration*. London: Croom Helm.

Magaziner, Ira C., and Robert B. Reich. 1982. *Minding America's Business: The Decline and Rise of the American Economy*. New York: Harcourt Brace Jovanovitch.

Maillet, Pierre. 1984. *La Politique Industrielle*. Paris: Presses Universitaires de France.

Malezieux, M. Émile. 1874. *Les Chemins de Fer Anglais en 1873*. Paris: Dunod.

Malézieux, M. Émile. 1875. *Travaux Publics des États-unis d'Amérique en 1870*. Paris: Librarie des Corps des Points et Chausées ets des Mines.

Mann, Horace. 1869. "On the Cost and Organization of the Civil Service." *Journal of the Royal Statistical Society* 32: 38–60.

March, James G. and Johan P. Olsen. 1984. "The New Institutionalism: Organizational Factors in Political Life." *American Political Science Review* 78:734–749.

Marchal, P.E. and Laurent Seguin. 1957. *Marc Seguin 1786–1875: La Naissance du Premier Chemin de Fer Français*. Paris: J. Cuzin.

Martin, Albro. 1981. *Enterprise Denied: Origins of the Decline of American Railroads, 1897–1917*. New York: Columbia University Press.

Marx, Karl. 1963 (reprint). *The Eighteenth Brumaire of Louis Bonaparte*. New York: International Publishers.

Massachusetts Board of Railroad Commissioners. 1869–1922. *Annual Report of the Railroad Commissioners*. Boston: Commonwealth of Massachusetts.

Massachusetts Committee on Railways and Canals. 1838–1856. *Annual Report of the Railroad Corporations of Massachusetts*. Boston: Commonwealth of Massachusetts.

Massachusetts, General Court of. 1825–1922. *Acts and Resolves of the General Court of Massachusetts*. Boston: State Printers.

McArthur, John H. and Bruce R. Scott. 1969. *Industrial Planning in France*. Boston: Little Brown.

McCabe, James Dabney. 1873. *Behind the Scenes in Washington*. New York: Continental.

McCraw, Thomas K. 1984. *Prophets of Regulation*. Cambridge, MA: Harvard University Press.

McCraw, Thomas K. 1975. "Regulation in America: A Review Article." *Business History Review* 49.

McCraw, Thomas K. 1980. "Regulatory Agencies in American History, 1869–1977." Pp. 187–208 in *Government and Business: Proceedings of the Fifth Fuji Conference*. Keiichiro Nakagawa (editor). Tokyo: University of Tokyo Press.

McFadyean, Sir Andrew. 1935. *Government Intervention in Industry*. London: Lovat Dickson.

McGuire, Patrick, Mark Granovetter, and Michael Schwartz. Forthcoming. *The Social Construction of Industry: Human Agency in the Development, Diffusion, and Institutionalization of the Electric Utility Industry*. New York: Cambridge University Press.

McKie, James W. 1979. "Government Intervention in the Economy of the United States," Pp. 72–100 in *Government Intervention in the Developed Economy*. Peter Maunder (editor). New York: Praeger.

McPherson, Crawford B. 1962. *The Political Theory of Possessive Individualism: Hobbes to Locke.* New York: Oxford University Press.

Mercer. Lloyd. 1982. *Railroads and Land Grant Policy.* New York: Academic Press.

Merryman, John. 1969. *The Civil Law Tradition.* Stanford: Stanford University Press.

Meyer, Balthasar Henry. 1903. *Railway Legislation in the United States.* New York: Macmillan.

Meyer, John W. 1988. "Society Without Culture: A Nineteenth Century Legacy." Pp. 193–202 in *Rethinking the Nineteenth Century.* Edited by Francisco Ramirez. New York: Greenwood.

Meyer, John W., John Boli, and George Thomas. 1987. "Ontology and Rationalization in the Western Cultural Account." Pp. 12–37 in *Institutional Structure: Constituting State, Society, and the Individual.* Edited by George M. Thomas, John W. Meyer, Francisco O. Ramirez, and John Boli. Beverly Hills: Sage.

Meyer, John W., Francisco Ramirez, and Yasemin Soysal. 1992. "World Expansion of Mass Education, 1870–1980." *Sociology of Education* 63: 128–149.

Meyer, John W., and Brian Rowan. 1977. "Institutionalized Organizations: Formal Structure as Myth and Ceremony." *American Journal of Sociology* 83: 340–363.

Meyer, John W., and W. Richard Scott. 1983. "Centralization and the Legitimacy Problems of Local Government." Pp. 199–217 in *Organizational Environments: Ritual and Rationality.* John W. Meyer and W. Richard Scott (editors) Beverly Hills: Sage.

Miliband, Ralph. 1969. *The State in Capitalist Society.* London: Weidenfeld and Nicolson.

Miller, John C. 1959. *Origins of the American Revolution.* Revised Edition. Stanford, CA: Stanford University Press.

Mills, C. Wright. 1956. *The Power Elite.* New York: Oxford University Press.

Monkswell, Lord. 1911. *French Railways.* London: Smith Elder.

Moody, Linwood W. 1938. "The Muddle of the Gauges." *Railway and Locomotive Historical Society Bulletin* 47: 59–66.

Moore, Arthur. 1859. *A Handbook of Railway Law, 1838–1858.* London: W.H. Smith and Son.

Moore, Barrington, Jr. 1966. *The Social Origins of Dictatorship and Democracy.* Boston: Beacon.

Mountfield, David. 1979. *The Railway Barons.* New York: Norton.

Mulhall, Michael G. 1969 [1899]. *The Dictionary of Statistics.* London: Routledge.

Nash, Gerald D. 1957. "Origins of the International Commerce Act of 1887." *Pennsylvania History* 24: 181–190.

Nef, John U. 1957 (1940). *Industry and Government in France and England, 1540–1640.* Ithaca: Cornell University Press.

Nock, O.S. 1977. *Railways of Western Europe.* London: Adam and Charles Black.

Nock, O.S. 1979. *Railways of the U.S.A.* London: Adam and Charles Black.

North, Douglass. 1981. *Structure and Change in Economic History.* New York: Norton.

North, Douglass. 1990. *Institutions, Institutional Change and Economic Performance.* New York: Cambridge University Press.

O'Brien, Patrick. 1977. *The New Economic History of the Railways.* London: Croom Helm.

O'Brien, Patrick. 1983. *Railways and the Economic Development of Western Europe: 1830–1914.* New York: St. Martin's.

OECD. 1970. *United States Industrial Policies.* Paris: OECD.

OECD. 1971. *Industrial Policies of Fourteen Member Countries.* Paris: OECD.

Orloff, Ann, and Theda Skocpol. 1985. "Why Not Equal Protection? Explaining the

Politics of Public Social Spending in Britain, 1900–1911, and the United States, 1880s–1920." *American Sociological Review* 49: 726–751.

Palaa, J.-G. 1894. *Dictionnaire Legislatif et Reglementaire Des Chemins de Fer: Supplement General de la 3e Edition.* Paris: Marchal et Billard.

Papon, Pierre. 1975. "The State and Technological Competition in France or Colbertism in the Twentieth Century." *Research Policy* 4: 214–244.

Papon, Pierre. 1979. *Le Pouvoir et la Science en France.* Paris: Centurion.

Parks, Robert J. 1972. *Democracy's Railroads: Public Enterprise in Jacksonian Michigan.* Port Washington, NY: National University Publications.

Parris, Henry. 1960. "The Nineteenth-Century Revolution in Government: A Reappraisal Reappraised." *The Historical Journal* 3: 17–37.

Parris, Henry. 1965. *Government and the Railways in Nineteenth Century Britain.* London: Royal Institute of Public Administration.

Parris, Henry. 1969. *Constitutional Bureaucracy: The Development of the British Central Administration Since the Eighteenth Century.* London: George Allen and Unwin.

Parsons, Talcott. 1951. *The Social System.* Glencoe, Ill.: Free Press.

Parsons, Talcott. 1971. *The System of Modern Societies.* Englewood Cliffs, N.J.: Prentice Hall.

Peyret, Henry. 1949. *Histoire des Chemins de Fer en France et Dans le Monde.* Paris: Societe d'Editions Françaises et Internationales.

Picard, Alfred. 1887. *Les Chemins De Fer Français,* Four Volumes. Paris: Ministere des Travaux Publics.

Picard, Alfred. 1918. *Les Chemins de Fer: Apercu Historique.* Paris: Dunod et Pinat.

Pierce, Harry H. 1953. *Railroads of New York: A Study of Government Aid 1826–1875.* Cambridge, MA: Harvard University Press.

Pilkington, Roger. 1973. "Pierre-Paul Riquet and the Canal du Midi." *History Today* 23: 170–176.

Pinder, John, Takashi Hosomi, and William Diebold. 1979. *Industrial Policy and the International Economy.* New York: Trilateral Commission.

Piore, Michael J., and Charles F. Sabel. 1984. *The Second Industrial Divide: Possibilities for Prosperity.* New York: Basic.

Poggi, Gianfranco. 1978. *The Development of the Modern State.* Stanford: Stanford University Press.

Pollack, Andrew. 1989. "America's Answer to Japan's Miti." *New York Times* March 5.

Polanyi, Karl. 1944. *The Great Transformation: The Political and Economic Origins of our Time.* New York: Rinehart.

Poor, Henry V. 1860. *History of the Railroads and Canals of the United States of America, Exhibiting their Progress, Cost, Revenues, Expenditures and Present Condition.* Volume 1 of 11. New York: John H Schultz.

Poor, Henry V. Annual from 1869. *Manual of the Railroads of the United States.* New York: H.V. and H.W. Poor.

Poor, Henry V. 1871. *Manual of the Railroads of the United States for 1871–1872.* New York: Poor.

Poor's Railroad Company. Annual from 1884. *Poor's Directory of Railroad Officials.* New York: H.V. and H.W. Poor.

Price, Roger. 1981. *The Economic History of Modern France, 1730–1914.* London: Macmillan.

Price, Roger. 1983. *The Modernization of Rural France: Communications Networks and Agricultural Market Structure in Nineteenth-Century France.* New York: St. Martin's.

Primm, James Neal. 1954. *Economic Policy in the Development of a Western State: Missouri, 1820–1960.* Cambridge, MA: Harvard University Press.

Ratcliffe, Barrie M. 1972. "The Origins of the Paris-Saint-Germain Railway." *The Journal of Transport History.* New Series 1: 197–219.

Ratcliffe, Barrie M. 1973. "The Building of the Paris-Saint-Germain Railway." *The Journal of Transport History.* New Series 6: 20–40.

Reddy, William M. 1984. *The Rise of Market Culture: The Textile Trade and French Society, 1750–1900.* Cambridge: Cambridge University Press.

Reich, Robert. 1983. *The Next American Frontier.* New York: Times Books.

Richardson, James D. ed. 1896–1899. *A Compilation of the Messages and Papers of the Presidents, 1789–1897.* Ten Volumes. Washington, D.C.: U.S. Government Printing Office.

Ripley, William Z. 1912. *Railroads, Rates and Regulation.* New York: Longman's Green.

Ripley, William Z. 1915. *Railroads, Finance and Organization.* New York: Longman's Green.

Roberts, David. 1959. "Jeremy Bentham and the Victorian State." *Victorian Studies* 2: 13–210.

Roberts, David. 1960. *Victorian Origins of the British Welfare State.* New Haven: Yale University Press.

Rostow, Eugene. 1959. *Planning for Freedom.* New Haven; Yale University Press.

Rousseau, Jean-Jacques. 1947 (reprint). *The Social Contract.* New York: Hafner.

Rowen, Herbert H. 1961. "'L'Etat C'est a Moi': Louis XIV and the State." *French Historical Studies* 2: 83–98.

Rubinson, Richard and Joan Sokolovsky. 1988. "Patterns of Industrial Regulation: Railroads in the World Economy." Pp. 3–21 in *Rethinking the Nineteenth Century.* Edited by Francisco Ramirez. New York: Greenwood.

Ruggie, John Gerard. Forthcoming. "Territoriality and Beyond: Problematizing Modernity in International Relations." *International Organization.*

Sachs, Jeffrey. 1989. "My Plan for Poland." *International Economy* 3: 24–29.

Sanborn, John Bell. 1899. *Congressional Grants of Land in Aid of Railways.* Madison: University of Wisconsin Press.

Sanders, M. Elizabeth. 1981. *The Regulation of Natural Gas: Policy and Politics, 1938–1981.* Philadelphia: Temple University Press.

Sauvy, Alfred. 1967. *Histoire Economique de la France Entre les Deux Guerres, 1919–1939.* Two Volumes. Paris: Fayard.

Schama, Simon. 1989. *Citizens: A Chronicle of the French Revolution.* New York: Knopf.

Scheiber, Harry N. 1975. "Instrumentalism and Property Rights." *Wisconsin Law Review* 1: 1–18.

Scheiber, Harry N. 1981. "Regulation, Property Rights, and Definition of 'the Market': Law and the American Economy." *The Journal of Economic History* 41: 103–109.

Schivelbusch, Wolfgang. 1986 [1977]. *The Railway Journey: The Industrialization of Time and Space in the 19th Century.* Berkeley, CA: University of California Press.

Schneider, Ben R. 1991. *Politics Within the State: Elite Bureaucrats and Industrial Policy in Authoritarian Brazil.* Pittsburgh: University of Pittsburgh Press.

Schutz, Alfred, and Thomas Luckman. 1973. *The Structures of the Life-World.* Evanston: Northwestern University Press.

Schwartz, Bernard. 1973. *The Economic Regulation of Business and Industry: A Legislative History of U.S. Regulatory Agencies.* New York: Chelsea.

Scott, W. Richard. 1987. "The Adolescence of Institutional Theory." *Administrative Science Quarterly* 32: 493–511.

Scott, W. Richard. 1992. "Institutions and Organizations: Toward a Theoretical Synthesis." Mimeo. Stanford University, Department of Sociology.

Selznick, Philip. 1949. *TVA and the Grass Roots.* Berkeley: University of California Press.

Sewell, William H., Jr. 1985. "Ideologies and Social Revolutions: Reflections on the French Case." *Journal of Modern History* 57: 57–85.

Sewell, William H., Jr. 1992. "A Theory of Structure: Duality, Agency, and Transformation." *American Journal of Sociology* 98: 1–29.

Shefter, Martin. 1977. "Party and Patronage: Germany, England, and Italy." *Politics and Society* 7:403–451.

Shonfield, Alfred. 1965. *Modern Capitalism.* London: Oxford University Press.

Shonfield, Alfred. 1982. *The Uses of Public Power.* Edited by Zuzanna Shonfield. New York: Oxford University Press.

Sich, Rupert L. 1960. "Current Legislation in the United Kingdom Dealing with Restrictive Business Agreements." Pp. 3–17 in *Proceedings, International Conference on Control of Restrictive Business Practices.* University of Chicago, Graduate School of Business. Glencoe, IL: Free Press.

Silberston, Aubrey. 1981. "Industrial Policies in Britain 1960–1980." Pp. 45–62 in *Industrial Policy and Innovation.* Charles Carter (editor). London, Heinemann.

Simmons, Jack. 1978. *The Railway in England and Wales 1830–1914.* Leicester: Leicester University Press.

Skocpol, Theda. 1979. *States and Social Revolutions: A Comparative Analysis of France, Russia, and China.* New York: Cambridge University Press.

Skocpol, Theda. 1985. "Cultural Idioms and Political Ideologies in the Revolutionary Reconstruction of State Power: A Rejoinder to Sewell." *Journal of Modern History* 57: 86–96.

Skocpol, Theda, and Kenneth Finegold. 1982. "State Capacity and Economic Intervention in the Early New Deal." *Political Science Quarterly* 97: 255–278.

Skowronek, Stephen. 1982. *Building a New American State: The Expansion of National Administrative Capacities: 1877–1920.* New York: Cambridge University Press.

Smith, Cecil O., Jr. 1990. "The Longest Run: Public Engineering and Planning in France." *American Historical Review* 95: 657–692.

Smith, Elmer A. 1944. *The Interstate Commerce Commission: An Independent Tribunal or a Subordinate of the Department of Justice.* Washington: Association of Interstate Commerce Commission Practitioners.

Solo, Robert. 1974. *The Political Authority and the Market System.* Cincinnati: South-Western.

Soltau, Roger. 1959. *French Political Thought in the 19th Century.* New York: Russell and Russell.

Stapleton, Darwin. 1978. "The Origin of American Railroad Technology, 1825–1840." *Railroad History* 139: 22–36.

Stone, Lawrence. 1965. *The Crisis of the Aristocracy 1558–1641.* Oxford: Clarendon.

Stone, Richard D. 1991. *The Interstate Commerce Commission and the Railroad Industry: A History of Regulatory Policy.* New York: Praeger.

Stover, John F. 1970. *The Life and Death of the American Railroad.* New York: Oxford University Press.

Stover, John F. 1987. *History of the Baltimore and Ohio Railroad.* West Lafayette, IN: Purdue University Press.

Strang, David, and John Meyer. Forthcoming. "Institutional Conditions for Diffusion." *Theory and Society.*

Suleiman, Ezra. 1974. *Politics, Power and Bureaucracy in France: The Administrative Elite.* Princeton, NJ: Princeton University Press.

Suleiman, Ezra N. 1975. "Industrial Policy Formulation in France." Pp. 23–42 in *Industrial Policies in Western Europe.* Edited by Steven J. Warnecke and Ezra N. Suleiman. New York: Praeger.

Suleiman, Ezra N. (editor). 1984. *Higher Civil Servants in the Policy Making Process.* London: Holmes and Meier.

Suleiman, Ezra and John Waterbury. Editors. 1990. *The Political Economy of Public Sector Reform and Privatization.* Boulder: Westview.

Summers, Mark W. 1984. *Railroads, Reconstruction, and the Gospel of Prosperity: Aid Under the Radical Republicans 1865–1877.* Princeton: Princeton University P,ess.

Swann, Dennis. 1983. *Competition and Industrial Policy in the European Community.* London: Methuen.

Swidler, Ann. 1986. "Culture in Action: Symbols and Strategies." *American Sociological Review* 51: 273–286.

Talbott, E.H. 1880. *Railway Land Grants in the United States: Their History, Economy and Influence upon the Development and Prosperity of the Country.* Chicago: The Railway Age Publishing Company.

Tarbell, Ida M. 1904. *The History of the Standard Oil Company.* New York: Macmillan.

Taylor, George Rogers. 1951. *The Transportation Revolution, 1815–1860.* New York: Harper.

Teagarden, Ernest M. 1972. "Industrial Railroad Rate Divisions and the Interstate Commerce Commission." *Journal of Transport History* New Series 1: 161–168.

Temin, Peter. 1986. "Capital Formation in American Industrialization." Pp. 13–21 in *The World of the Industrial Revolution.* Edited by Robert Weible. Lowell, MA: Museum of American Textile History.

Thelen, Kathleen, and Sven Steinmo. 1992. "Historical Institutionalism in Comparative Politics." Pp. 1–32 in *Structuring Politics: Historical Institutionalism in Comparative Analysis..* Edited by Sven Steinmo, Kathleen Thelen, and Frank Longstreth. New York: Cambridge University Press.

Thevenez, Rene. 1930. *Legislation des Chemins de Fer,* Two Volumes. Paris: Rousseau.

Thomas, George M., and John W. Meyer. 1984 "The Expansion of the State." *Annual Review of Sociology* 10:461–482.

Thompson, Dennis L. 1981. *Taxation of American Railroads: A Policy Analysis.* Westport CT: Greenwood.

Thompson, Margaret Susan. 1983. "Corruption – or Confusion? Lobbying and Congressional Government in the Early Gilded Age." *Congress and the Presidency* 10: 169–192.

Tilly, Charles, ed. 1975. *The Formation of National States in Western Europe.* Princeton: Princeton University Press.

Tilly, Charles. 1986. *The Contentious French: Four Centuries of Popular Struggle.* Cambridge: Belknap.

Tocqueville, Alexis de. 1945 (reprint). *Democracy in America.* Two Volumes. Henry Reeve and Phillips Bradley (trans.). New York: Vintage.

Tocqueville, Alexis de. 1955 (reprint). *The Old Regime and the French Revolution.* Garden City: Doubleday.

Tolbert, Pamela, and Lynne G. Zucker. 1983. "Institutional Sources of Change in the Formal Structure of Organizations: The Diffusion of Civil Service Reforms, 1880–1935." *Administrative Science Quarterly* 23: 22–39.

Trachtenberg, Marc. 1977. "'A New Economic Order': Étienne Clementel and French Economic Diplomacy During the First World War". *French Historical Studies* 10:315–341.

Trent, Logan Douglas. 1981. *The Credit Mobilier.* New York: Arno.

Truman, David B. 1951. *The Governmental Process: Political Interests and Public Opinion.* New York: Alfred A. Knopf.

Tyson, Laura and John Zysman. 1983. "American Industry in International Competition." Pp. 15–59 in *American Industry in International Competition.* Laura Tyson and John Zysman (editors). Ithaca: Cornell University Press.

United States, Congressional Globe. 1860s. *Congressional Globe.* Washington: USGPO.

United States, Congressional Record. 1880s-1890s. *Congressional Record.* Washington: USGPO.

United States, Department of the Interior. 1890. *Congressional Land Grants in Aid of the Construction of Railroads.* Washington: National Archives Record Group 48, Railroad Package 305.

United States, General Land Office. 1860s. *Railroad Rights-of-Way Files: Union Pacific Railroad, Correspondence.* Washington: National Archives, Record Group 49, Division F.

United States, General Land Office. 1866. *Pacific Railroad Commission, Journal of Proceedings.* Washington: National Archives, Record Group 48, Railroad Package 180.

United States, General Land Office. 1869. *Pacific Railroad Commission, Report.* Washington: National Archives, Record Group 48, Railroad Package 181.

United States, General Land Office. 1870s. *Opinions of the Assistant Attorney General.* Washington: National Archives, Record Group 48, Railroad Package 303.

United States, House [Committee on Commerce]. 1884. *Arguments and Statements Before the Committee on Commerce in Relation to Certain Bills Referred to that Committee Proposing Congressional Regulation of Interstate Commerce.* Washington: USGPO.

United States, Secretary of the Interior. 1869. *Annual Report oʄ ʋɦe Government Directors of the Union Pacific Railroad.* Washington: National Archives, Record Group 48, Railroad Package 320.

United States, Senate Select Committee on Interstate Commerce. 1886. *Report of the Senate Select Committee on Interstate Commerce.* Washington: USGPO.

Villedeuil, Laurent de. 1903. *Bibliographie des Chemins de Fer.* Paris: Villedeuil.

Veblen, Thorstein. 1904. *The Theory of Business Enterprise.* New York: Scribner's.

Vogel, David. 1986. *National Styles of Regulation: Environmental Policy in Great Britain and the United States.* Ithaca: Cornell University Press.

Wallon, Maurice. 1908. *Les Saint-Simoniens et les Chemins de Fer.* Paris: Pedone.

Weber, Eugen. 1976. *Peasants into Frenchmen: The Modernization of Rural France, 1870–1914.* Stanford CA: Stanford University Press.

Weber, Max. 1958. *The Protestant Ethic and the Spirit of Capitalism.* New York: Scribner.

Weber, Max. 1978. *Economy and Society.* Two Volumes. Edited by Guenther Roth and Claus Wittich. Berkeley: University of California Press.

Weir, Margaret, and Theda Skocpol. 1985. "State Structures and the Possibilities for 'Keynesian' Responses to the Great Depression in Sweden, Britain, and the United States." Pp. 107–163 in *Bringing the State Back In.* Edited by Peter Evans, Dietrich Rueschemeyer, and Theda Skocpol. New York: Cambridge University Press.

Weiss, John. 1982. *The Making of Technological Man: The Social Origins of French Engineering Education.* Cambridge: MIT Press.

Wescott, Robert F. 1983. "U.S. Approaches to Industrial Policy." Pp. 87–151 in *Industrial Policies for Growth and CompetitivenesA*. Gerard Adams and Lawrence R. Klein (editors). Lexington, MA: Lexington Books.

Westbay, J.H. 1934. "The Standardization of the Track Gauge on American Railways." *Railway and Local Historical Society Bulletin* 34: 28–35.

Wettenhall, R.L. 1970. *The Iron Road and the State: W.M. Acworth as Scholar, Critic, and Reformer.* Hobart: University of Tasmania.

White, Harrison C. 1981. "Where Do Markets Come From?" *American Journal of Sociology* 87: 517–547.

White, Harrison C. 1988. "Varieties of Markets." Pp. 226–260 in *Social Structures: A Network Approach.* Edited by Barry Wellman and Stephen D. Berkowitz. New York: Cambridge University Press.

Whitney, Simon N. 1958. *Antitrust Policies: American Experience in Twenty Industries,* Volume 1. New York: The Twentieth Century Fund.

Wilcox, Clair. 1960. *Public Policies Toward Business,* Revised Edition. Homewood, IL: Irwin.

Wildavsky, Aaron. 1984. "Squaring the Political Circle: Industrial Policies and the American Dream." Pp. 27–44 in *The Industrial Policy Debate.* Edited by Chalmers Johnson. San Francisco: Institute for Contemporary Studies Press.

Wilks, Stephen. 1983. "Liberal State and Party Competition: Britain." Pp. 128–160 in *Industrial Crisis: A Comparative Study of the State and Industry.* Kenneth Dyson and Stephen Wilks (editors). Oxford: Martin Robinson.

Williams, Frederick S. 1885. *Our Iron Roads: Their History, Construction, and Administration,* Sixth Edition. London, Bemrose and Sons.

Williams, Frederick S. 1886. *The Midland Railway: Its Rise and Progress.* Nottingham: Frederick Williams.

Williams, P.M. 1952. "Public Opinion and the Railway Rates Question in 1886." *English Historical Review* 67.

Williamson, Oliver E. 1975. *Markets and Hierarchies: Analysis and Antitrust Implications.* New York: Free Press.

Williamson, Oliver E. 1985. *The Economic Institutions of Capitalism.* New York: Free Press.

Wilson, James Q., ed. 1980. *The Politics of Regulation.* New York: Basic.

Wuthnow, Robert. 1987. *Meaning and Moral Order: Explorations in Cultural Analysis.* Berkeley: University of California Press.

Wuthnow, Robert. 1989. *Communities of Discourse: Ideology and Social Structure in the Reformation, the Enlightenment, and European Socialism.* Cambridge: Harvard University Press.

Wuthnow, Robert and Marsha Witten. 1990. "New Directions in the Study of Culture." *Annual Review of Sociology,* edited by W. Richard Scott. Palo Alto, CA: Annual Reviews Inc.

Wymond, Mark. 1917. *Government Partnership in Railroads.* Chicago: Wymond and Clark.

Young, Stephen, and Neil Hood. 1984. "Industrial Policy in The United Kingdom." Pp. 197–214 in *National Industrial Policies.* Robert E. Driscoll and Jack N. Behrman (editors). Cambridge, MA: Oelgeschlager, Gunn, and Hain.

Young, Stephen with A.V. Lowe. 1974. *Intervention in the Mixed Economy: The Evolution of British Industrial Policy 1964–1972.* London: Croom Helm.

Zeldin, Theodore. 1977. *France, 1848–1945: Intellect, Taste and Anxiety.* Oxford: Clarendon.

Zeldin, Theodore. 1980. *France, 1848–1945: Taste and Corruption.* New York: Oxford University Press.

Zelizer, Viviana A. 1988. "Beyond the Polemics of the Market: Establishing a Theoretical and Empirical Agenda." *Sociological Forum* 4: 614–634.

Zelizer, Viviana. Forthcoming. "Making Multiple Monies." In *Explorations in Economic Sociology.* Edited by Richard Swedberg. New York: Russell Sage Foundation.

Zucker, Lynne G. 1977. "The Role of Institutionalization in Cultural Persistence." *American Sociological Review* 42: 726–743.

Zysman, John. 1977. *Political Strategies for Industrial Order: State, Market, and Industry in France.* Berkeley, University of California Press.

Zysman, John. 1983. *Governments, Markets, and Growth: Financial Systems and the Politics of Industrial Change.* Ithaca, Cornell University Press.

Index

FEMINISM ON TRIAL

FEMINISM ON TRIAL

The Ginny Foat Case
and the Future of
the Women's Movement

ELLEN HAWKES

William Morrow and Company, Inc.   New York

Library of Congress Cataloging-in-Publication Data

Hawkes, Ellen.
  Feminism on trial

  Includes index.
  1. Foat, Ginny.   2. National Organization for
Women.   3. Feminists—United States—Biography.
4. Feminism—United States.   I. Title.
HQ1413.F63H39   1986   305.4'2'0973   85-31968
ISBN 0-688-04850-1

Printed in the United States of America

First Edition

1 2 3 4 5 6 7 8 9 10

BOOK DESIGN BY JAYE ZIMET

To Peter Manso with love,
To Rhoda and Will Rossmoore with gratitude,
And in memory of my father.

Foreword

WHEN Ginny Foat, president of the California chapter of the
National Organization for Women, was arrested for murder on January 11, 1983, I read the news reports with both dismay and curiosity. Shock was part of it, too, a horror shared by feminists across
the country, since it took no great stretch of the imagination to guess
what the opponents of the women's movement would do with the
story. A leading feminist charged with the tire-iron bludgeoning of
a middle-åged businessman outside New Orleans eighteen years before? The right wing would jump for joy, taking it as confirmation
of its worst suspicions: "You see, those women libbers, they're literally man-killers."

On the other hand, the first articles to come in suggested a story
so bizarre, so incongruous with NOW's respectable image, as to
pique everyone's interest. How Ginny Foat had come to be charged
with the murder was fascinating in itself, a saga of a woman who
reportedly came from the wrong side of the tracks, lived a sordid,
knock-around life on the road with her second of four husbands,
then transformed herself into a successful businesswoman, finding
her true "identity" through feminism and leadership in NOW. Here
alone, the story was filled with dramatic possibilities, a sort of Sister Carrie tale played out in California where everything, including
feminist politics, is somehow brightly lit and seemingly less shaded
by ambiguity and complexities. Further, with so many interwoven
strands of coincidence, there was the possibility that Ginny Foat had
indeed been caught in a web of antifeminist conspiracy. The outraged cries of Foat's supporters had to be taken seriously: Was her
arrest an indication that feminists were now fair game, that with the

conservative trend in the country, law-enforcement agencies were sanctioned to find any excuse to go after leaders of the women's movement?

Soon after my preliminary interviews with Foat's colleagues, friends, and enemies, with lawyers and police, it became apparent that the Foat case was as inextricably connected to the politics of the women's movement as it was to antifeminism. The internal schisms and controversies, factionalism and dissension within NOW's ranks, not only in California but nationally, were crucial to the motivations behind Ginny Foat's arrest. All too familiar with feminist rhetoric, I found myself dissatisfied with the miasma of ideology surrounding just who Ginny Foat was and why she'd prompted such contradictory feelings from her feminist colleagues. Among both her defenders and her accusers there was a pointed desire to keep writers at a distance; no matter how sympathetic or how "qualified" our feminist credentials, we were suspect. There was, of course, legitimate concern that further commentary or coverage might hurt Foat's defense, but there was also the less than justifiable anxiety, seeming to border on paranoia, that further details of the case or Foat's background could have but one result: injury to the women's movement.

The importance of the case thus went beyond Foat's innocence or guilt. *That* would be settled in a courtroom. More crucial was what the Foat affair might tell us about feminism in the eighties, what had happened in the last few years to deplete its energy and render the movement so vulnerable to attacks from the Right. Internal jealousies and power plays, ideological confusion, even plain exhaustion in the era of Reagan, all had to be presumed relevant. By the same token, too, it was inevitable that in whatever measure, feminism would go on trial with Ginny Foat; her courtroom drama could only be a litmus test of the country's attitudes in general. With the symbolic meaning of the case far outrunning the facts of Foat's life, one's focus, necessarily, had to be wider than the narrative of her story.

A word, however, about my early sympathies. While the proffered scenarios of entrapment by the LA police, the FBI, and Louisiana authorities weren't totally to be dismissed, I began without the same kind of sympathy for my subject that Diana Trilling initially felt for Jean Harris. Nor did my feelings bear much resemblance to Shana Alexander's identification with both Harris and her earlier subject, Patty Hearst; in fact I'd often joked that Alexander's Harris book should have been called *Anyone's Mother* as the companion piece to her Hearst effort, *Anyone's Daughter*. In this instance, however, I was even more skeptical of calling the Foat case an "everywoman's" story. The defense committee's line, "You, my dear sisters, stand accused," just didn't have the ring of authenticity. What I learned about Foat's plight prompted pity—her earlier life with her ex-husband and accuser sounded horrendous, and details of her apprenticeship as a barmaid (and according to some reports, a go-go dancer) weren't any better. But I felt no "there but for the grace of God" bonding that often sets writers going. There were too many loose ends, psychic and factual inconsistencies both, and Foat, I sensed, was more than a helpless victim of male oppression.

Still, at the center of my interest lay my concern, my sympathetic identification with feminism. Like other women of my generation, my thinking had evolved from sixties activism in the civil rights and antiwar movements. I was not a NOW member, since in those more radical and frantic days it was commonplace to criticize NOW for its mainstream emphasis and its predominantly white, middle-class, professional membership. But NOW had won legislative triumphs, there was no denying this. Many of us had moved into professional ranks precisely because of the group's efforts, or at least because we'd all profited from the climate of values that NOW, ineluctably, had a hand in creating. We had come to realize that "the personal *is* political," and that political gains, in great part won by NOW's efforts, were basic to what I can only call all women's sanity. In equal opportunities, equal wages, and, yes, certainly not to be overlooked either, freedom of choice in our sexual and reproductive lives, we'd made important gains.

The recognition of NOW's importance was shared by feminists across the country. When NOW presidents Karen DeCrow and Ellie Smeal launched their "out of the mainstream, into the revolution" campaign in the mid-seventies, the so-called revolution had almost dwindled to nothing, yet the slogan betokened a drawing together of our moderate and radical factions. With the campaign for the Equal Rights Amendment there was a new unity, a unity that held even in the face of ERA's defeat. Likewise, NOW had paved the way for the country's first female mainstream vice-presidential candidate. Whatever questions or problems Geraldine Ferraro's candidacy later raised, it was a thrilling moment of promise and possibility, and, indeed, one didn't have to be a George Will or a resident of the Brookings Institution to know that the Democratic party, finding itself in extremis, had seen its salvation (ethical, if not electoral) in a woman.

Even so, within the feminist movement there was a widespread feeling of fatigue, a kind of resignation in the wake of Ferraro's nomination. Many of us who remembered the heady times of change in the sixties and seventies sensed that feminism as a force had gone flat and stale. Why? Because although there were many women who had never felt a part of the movement but had still benefited from it, the right wing now was able to exaggerate this diffidence into hostility. At a time when the economic realities of the poor should have sparked more attention to feminism's campaign for economic justice, why did the movement seem so lifeless that hostile commentators could predict its demise with little argument to the contrary? Had the movement become so inward-looking, so consumed by its own internal battles, as to forget how most women were living their lives, especially women living beyond the glitz of New York, Los Angeles, or San Francisco? Did tirades against pornography, for example, upstage the day-to-day reality of how women outside the movement perceived themselves and their families? At a time when the women's movement was most needed, why had it failed to take a more comprehensive stance, to voice most women's simple needs and wants?

The trouble was not just the "new conservatism," for we feminists had to accept responsibility as well. NOW was struggling through lobbying and legislative action against the Reagan administation's determined assault on gains made over the last twenty years. Nonetheless, it was wide of the mark. Most women didn't care. Many regarded feminism as passé, and the movement itself as stalled in rhetoric, cliché, and ideological bickering. And among so-called committed feminists, those who had "grown up" in the movement, the factionalism was disturbing, more a matter of style than substance, but still wearisome. In some terribly perverse way, once we had achieved a certain measure of success, it was as though our movement had adopted the worst habits of those who had kept us down.

But to bring the argument full circle: As I investigated the Foat case I discovered that the conflicts and controversies behind her arrest seemed to be emblematic of the very difficulties that had sapped and weakened feminism. An artificial construct? A writer's conceit? Hardly. This was no ordinary murder trial, not by a long shot. There was Foat's own "conversion"; her support factions ranging from middle-class feminists to separatist gays; the issues of sisterhood and a "feminist" defense; the media, and, no less, what was presumed to be the retrograde ways of Louisiana, an all-male prosecution team as well as southern attitudes toward women. Then, too, there was John Sidote, ex-husband, alleged wife-beater, self-confessed murderer, and Foat's chief accuser. Was he only out for revenge? And finally, what was one to think of NOW's official statement, which while sympathizing with Foat's "personal tragedy" effectively distanced the organization from her case? Disloyalty or political savvy? This was the issue not only for NOW but something that confronted feminists everywhere.

"Aren't you afraid your book will hurt the women's movement?" I was frequently asked. The implications were obvious. In past years I might have been tempted to back off, adopting the old "it's bad for" hedge against airing dirty linen in public. Now I think not. The women's movement is large enough and strong enough to absorb criticism; if it is not, we have all been misled, most disturbingly by ourselves. The issue isn't political any longer, not if what one means by "political" is the matter of power, who has it and who doesn't. No, because there is something prior, something that takes precedence. Call it housecleaning. Most revolutions or progressive movements become corrupted; only a fool would argue otherwise. But while recognizing this, it becomes a test of our intentions not only when we choose our metaphors but how we address them. Ginny Foat, both the person and figurehead, is precisely such a metaphor.

Over the last three years I have interviewed people directly involved in the Foat case as well as those who watched it from afar, well aware of its effect on feminism and the public perception of the women's movement. It is an understatement to say that I am grateful to all of them for agreeing to talk on the record, not only about the case itself but about the shadowy corners—those perplexing motivations and sometimes disappointing practices that Foat's story brought to light. They did so in good faith, and I trust they share with me a common intention: to consider how feminism can be revitalized by new voices and fresh ideas. The cheap shots that can be taken at the movement as a result of this story were predictable from the beginning; but they can have little effect when we, as feminists, not only explore the problems in our organizations but also commit ourselves to making ourselves better.

Acknowledgments

MY gratitude goes to a number of people without whom this book could not have been written:

First and foremost, to all those who agreed to be interviewed about the Foat case and feminist politics. For the most part, their names appear in these pages, but I must thank as well those who preferred to remain anonymous. It was from these wide-ranging interviews that I constructed my narrative and re-created crucial scenes, and I am especially grateful to those sources who were patient enough to respond to second and third follow-up interviews.

To the colleagues with whom I covered the Foat trial in November 1983, my thanks, not only for the special camaraderie that develops in a courtroom press section but also for their lively minds and lasting friendship: Julia Cass, Paul Galloway, Barbara Grizzuti Harrison, Patt Morrison, Nicole Yorkin, and Richard Boyd, who shared insights and information as well as good food and moments of relaxation. While she did not cover the trial, Janet Plume of UPI in New Orleans was also especially helpful.

During the two weeks of the trial, the staff of Soniat Guest House was extraordinarily attentive, and I'd like to thank them for all the services rendered in a lovely setting during a grueling two weeks.

To my agent, Lois Wallace, my appreciation for her confidence in this book. To Lisa Drew, my editor at Morrow, my esteem for her intelligence, thoroughness, superlative editorial skills, and continued faith in this project. My thanks as well to David Currier, senior editor, and editor Walter Anderson of *Parade* magazine for their suggestions both for my article about the trial and for this book.

One person deserves more thanks than I can ever express: Alice

Ruckert. Without her scrupulous attention, unfailing commitment to getting the job done, and good humor, the preparation and editing of this manuscript would never have gone so well or so quickly.

My thanks also to others who helped in the completion of this manuscript: Amy Germain, Ellen O'Donnell, and the Provincetown Art Association.

The people to whom this book is dedicated have my profound appreciation. Rhoda and Will Rossmoore showed unwavering encouragement, and their patience, cheerfulness, tennis games, and daily swims kept me going during a difficult three months.

To Peter Manso, my partner and best friend, I give my deepest love. As a fellow writer, he understood what it meant to finish this book, and I knew I could count on him for his affection and support as well as for his honest criticism.

And, finally, to the memory of my father, whose pride in my work always reassured me that it was worth doing.

Ellen Hawkes
Provincetown, Massachusetts
December 1985

Contents

The happiest women, like the happiest nations, have no history.
—GEORGE ELIOT, *The Mill on the Floss*

When a girl leaves home at eighteen, she does one of two things. Either she falls into saving hands and becomes better, or she rapidly assumes the cosmopolitan standard of virtue and becomes worse.
—THEODORE DREISER, *Sister Carrie*

Society is afraid of both the feminist and the murderer, for each of them, in her own way, tests society's established boundaries.
—ANN JONES, *Women Who Kill*

ONE

No Clapping,

No Cheering,

No Blowing Kisses

TUESDAY, January 11, 1983, began as an ordinary day for Ginny Foat. As the state coordinator of the California chapter of NOW—the National Organization for Women—she always had a full agenda of speaking engagements, meetings with local Democratic political leaders, plus she had to attend to the administrative details of her statewide organization, the largest NOW chapter in the country, taking the numerous phone calls from local chapters around the state, giving advice, solving problems big or small. She had to do a lot of hand-holding in her job, that was a given, but she was known for her patience. Then, too, there was reading to catch up on for the extension courses she was taking to finish her BA so that she could apply to law school. Still, she was used to this exhausting pace. Since she'd become a full-time women's rights activist, every waking hour was crammed with work for NOW.

But she also felt that NOW had become too tied to mainstream politics, and as part of her effort to change the organization's policies, she was running for a position on NOW's national executive board. Her decision to run had come earlier that fall after having lost her bid for national NOW vice-president. Some NOW members had opposed her candidacy for more personal than political reasons, but even her closest friends felt that since she hadn't yet served at the national level, an executive-board position would give her useful experience. It would also provide an opportunity to try to move NOW away from its emphasis on Washington, D.C., lobbying, and she often quoted Ellen Goodman, the syndicated columnist, who had accused NOW of becoming just an arm of the Democratic party. She had her own way of putting it as well: "National NOW leaders are dying to get into the right cocktail parties instead of worrying about women dying in the streets." Her forceful criticism of NOW policy was one of the reasons why her colleagues in California NOW, like Jan Holden, a television writer, and Jean Conger, a former national executive of NOW, the two friends who had managed her vice-presidential campaign, and her best friend, Kay Tsenin, a lawyer, were all in favor of her running for the national executive board. But now like other Tuesday mornings, she had to concentrate less on such heady issues than on the practical necessity of getting Kay to the airport on time.

Six years her junior (they'd just celebrated Kay's thirty-fifth birthday with a party at a restaurant that weekend), Kay seemed more sophisticated and cosmopolitan than Ginny. She was the daughter of Russian immigrants, had lived in China until she was eight, and then grown up in San Francisco. Attending San Francisco State in the late sixties had put her in the midst of Bay Area protest, and in many respects she was more radical than Ginny, with a wider streak of rebellion and cynicism in her personality. Kay saw her own anarchic tendencies as a complement to Ginny's propensity to take rules too seriously, or as Kay often put it, her tendency to want to please everyone 99 percent of the time.

A personal-injury lawyer who lived in Marin County but practiced in San Francisco, Kay spent Friday through Monday in Los Angeles, then rushed back to her Tuesday appointments. In contrast to Ginny, who often said that her identity was totally entwined with NOW, Kay derived her sense of herself more from her practice as a lawyer than from her position as vice-president for action in California NOW. In the past she'd pulled back from NOW to devote more time to her legal practice and the Marin Abused Women's Shelter, but since Ginny had been elected state coordinator (or, as she was called later, president) she'd returned to NOW more actively and become one of the state's six vice-presidents. She, too, had supported Ginny's candidacy for national vice-president. But beyond their political alliance, a close friendship had developed over the past several years. Her weekly visit to Los Angeles was a given part of her schedule, the smog notwithstanding. Fifteen years before she'd transferred from the Los Angeles campus of Loyola law school to the University of San Francisco because of the befouled air; now she put up with it for the sake of being in touch with the southern California chapters while also having time with Ginny.

Since Kay would go directly to her law office, she wore one of her dress-for-success suits and high-necked blouses, the uniform of so many other NOW executives, the wire-rimmed granny glasses framing her blue eyes the only remnant of her more radical days. Her sandy brown hair was short and brushed away from her round face, giving the impression of being on the run, which she usually was, rushing from one appointment to another.

Ginny wore black pants and a white blouse this morning, but she, too, looked the part of the female executive, a style she had cultivated since becoming a successful businesswoman in the mid-seventies. Both women were slightly overweight, Kay more so than Ginny, and they seemed almost matronly. Ginny's short silver-gray hair especially made her seem older than her forty-one years, despite her unlined face, clear complexion, and dark brown eyes emphasized by carefully applied mascara and eyeliner. Some NOW colleagues had initially been startled by her makeup, long, polished fingernails, jewelry, and high heels. But as she instructed other women in the organization, people seemed more willing to listen to a feminist if she presented a nonthreatening image. And indeed, Ginny's carefully plucked eyebrows, blush-accentuated cheekbones, and full, glossy lips gave her a conventional feminine attractiveness, the only defect, the space between her two front teeth—what Chaucer called "gat tooth" in "The Wife of Bath's Tale." Supposedly a sign of sensuality and good luck, in Ginny's case it seemed also to indicate that braces were too expensive for her working class, Italian Catholic family.

Hurrying out the door and down the steps from Ginny's duplex apartment at 1301½ Lucille, they threw their bags and briefcases into the backseat of Ginny's metallic silver-blue, four-door Chevy. Kay climbed into the passenger seat and Ginny behind the wheel. Ginny didn't fasten her seat belt. Ever since her months in jail in 1977, the constraining pressure of the shoulder harness revived too many memories of chains and handcuffs, just as she still couldn't eat off paper plates without painful images flashing in her mind. The car started immediately, and as Ginny sped down the hill, taking what she knew would be the shortest route to the freeway, neither noticed the car that had been parked down the street and now pulled slowly away from the curb.

The Silver Lake district was quiet and peaceful, and only a few neighbors were out in the early morning. It was a close-knit community, predominantly Hispanic, and showing signs of upward mobility. Pastel houses clinging to the hillsides' narrow streets resembled San Francisco or Sausalito more than Beverly Hills or Westwood, as did its similar Bohemian and left-of-center atmosphere, its free, "artistic" reputation drawing a large gay population as well.

When they reached the freeway, Ginny stepped on it as Kay watched out the back window for police cruisers. They were lucky that morning. No cops were in sight, and since the traffic wasn't bad, they soon arrived at the Burbank airport.

Unlike large eastern airports, Burbank is not a maze of departure and arrival ramps, but one sweeping crescent drive beside the Quonset huts housing the various airlines. Now, as Ginny and Kay drove into the first arc of the main circle, they became aware of a cluster of people and police cars in front of the main terminal. Uniformed men with rifles appeared on the terminal steps and roof, and from above could be heard the clatter of a helicopter. A local TV-news van was parked in front of the terminal, and beside a number of Burbank police cars was a gaggle of TV cameras and reporters.

As Ginny pulled up to the curb, the unmarked car drove up behind them. Two men got out, approached quickly, and identified themselves as Los Angeles Police Department Fugitive Division detectives. With a few quick words, they established Ginny Foat's identity and placed her under arrest for murder.

What Ginny had so often feared had come to pass: The LAPD was holding her on a 1977 Jefferson Parish, Louisiana, fugitive warrant, charging her with the 1965 tire-iron bludgeoning of one Moises Chayo in an isolated area outside New Orleans.

It was 8:15 in the morning when the excitement, ambition, and drive of her new life as a feminist leader came to a screeching halt. Her energy seemed to drain from her as once more her past came back to haunt her, and she replied to the detectives' questions in an uncharacteristic monotone. "I thought we'd been all through that," she said wearily.

As far as the Los Angeles police and the Jefferson Parish sheriff's office were concerned, they hadn't even started, and "Virginia Galluzzo (or Faulk or Fulk or Folke), 5'5", 135 lbs., dark brown hair, olove [sic] complexion" was handcuffed and whisked away to Sybil Brand Institute, Los Angeles County's prison for women.

The news of Ginny's arrest spread quickly among her friends and political associates in the Los Angeles area, as Kay contacted Robert Tuller, Sr., Ginny's lawyer, as well as Jan Holden and Jean Conger. Midge Costanza, the former presidential adviser, had become Ginny's friend since resigning her White House position and moving to southern California. She'd been one of the several women at Kay's birthday party that weekend, and early Tuesday afternoon coincidentally found herself thinking what a great time they'd had just as she returned home from running errands. Both her phones were ringing as she came in the door. She picked up her private line.

"Have you heard?" a friend said. "Ginny was arrested for murder this morning."

"Oh, sure! What's the punch line?" Midge quipped. Then she answered her other phone. That caller gasped, "Oh, Midge," and started to cry. Through the tears Midge heard the news again. Her reaction once more: It must be a joke. It was how she remembered taking the news of President Kennedy's assassination. She'd been in such a good mood, she was sure someone was pulling her leg.

But now, as then, it was no joke. Ginny was sitting in a prison cell, waiting to be arraigned. Midge was one of the few visitors allowed to see her that evening. "I'd never been inside a jail before, and I began to get claustrophobic just picturing myself in there. Ginny was on the other side of the visiting area's window, I had to talk to her by phone, and she looked so lost and sad, I just broke down. I had enough control to realize I shouldn't stand there and sob but I couldn't stop, and she started reassuring me. It was like visiting a terminally ill friend in the hospital and starting to cry, but they say, 'It's gonna be okay.' She was giving me strength, so I stopped and we talked. But after my half hour I sobbed again in the parking lot, it was such a shock seeing her there."

To Kay Tsenin, Jan Holden, and Jean Conger, the closer friends who knew that Ginny had been arrested before in 1977, it was more the shock that this was happening a second time. They assumed that Ginny's hapless ex-husband was behind it again, but the whys and hows they could merely guess, and they suspected the worst—that Louisiana had chosen to revive its charges to go after a prominent feminist. Still, they lined up three other Los Angeles lawyers, Marcia Brewer, Richard Hirsch, and Michael Nasatir to help Bob Tuller fight extradition, and Kay reassured Ginny that they'd already begun to raise money for bail. Ginny's shake of the head stopped her in midsentence. There was no point, Ginny told her. She'd been through this before, and she knew she wouldn't be granted bail while she fought extradition.

"Then I'd better phone the NOW state office, national, too, and tell them you won't be in tomorrow, or for the next few days," said Kay.

Now Ginny laughed. Hadn't Kay seen all the reporters at the airport? Didn't she realize that her arrest would make the TV news and wire services? There was no need for phone calls to various NOW officials. They'd read about it in the newspapers in the morning.

She wasn't wrong. The evening's television news trumpeted the arrest: "Coast NOW Leader Indicted in '65 Slaying."

Like feminists across the country, Karen DeCrow, a lawyer in private practice and a writer who was national NOW president from 1974 to 1977, was taken totally by surprise and utterly dismayed. "I heard about Ginny Foat on the national news that night. John Chancellor or Tom Brokaw or whoever flashed the NOW logo and announced that a woman was arrested at an airport today, 'which isn't really national news except that she's president of California NOW.' I was eating dinner, and my salad flew to the ceiling. Then the phone started ringing, friends as well as local reporters asking me what I knew. The next day they broadcast her photograph, and I recognized her as someone I'd seen at several NOW meetings. My first reaction, seeing the NOW logo, was misery, shock, disbelief. It certainly wasn't, 'Oh, goody, NOW makes national news.' I was very upset, but I knew nothing beyond what was said about her being arrested."

Sensationalism always accompanies bad news about a public figure, male or female, the tabloid quick thrill of fallen heroes or tarnished reputations. But in this case the shock was greater precisely because of Ginny Foat's feminism.

"Of course that's why Ginny Foat's arrest had such an impact," said Midge Costanza. "That was obvious in the first news reports. Tom Brokaw said something like, 'Today in southern California a woman was arrested for murder. What made this special was that she is the state California NOW president.' I was astounded by the blatancy of it. I'm not attacking Tom Brokaw, I'm just saying he reflected the attitudes or was a victim of the same tradition that we all are. In the first place, we don't expect women in public life to be charged with the same crimes as men. But what was even more important was that a feminist was arrested—not a hairdresser, but a feminist."

Equally startling were the first news stories, which provided a bare outline of Foat's past life to explain how the California NOW president had come to be arrested on an eighteen-year-old murder charge. It was hardly the standard biography of a women's rights activist, much less a leader in NOW, the feminist organization considered "mainstream" and "moderate," or as it was sometimes called, more pejoratively than descriptively, "middle class."

Ginny Foat's accuser was John (Jack) Sidote, the second of her four ex-husbands. In 1977 he had confessed to two 1965 robbery-murders, the first of Chayo in New Orleans, the second of a man in Nevada, and implicated his ex-wife in both. He alleged that in 1965 he and the then Virginia Galluzzo had left New Paltz, New York, and gone on the road together. They found work in New Orleans, he as a bouncer, she as a barmaid and go-go dancer, but then, needing money, he alleged, she lured Moises Chayo, an Argentinian businessman, from a Bourbon Street bar into their car and drove to an isolated area outside the city. There Sidote emerged from the trunk and struggled with Chayo until Foat struck the victim with a tire iron. After stealing $1,400, he said, they left the body in a nearby ditch and fled New Orleans, eventually driving to the Reno–Lake Tahoe, Nevada, area, where Foat lured another man from a casino, then shot and robbed him. Extradited first to Nevada, Sidote had pleaded guilty to robbery and manslaughter in exchange for his testimony against his ex-wife. But after he received maximum consecutive sentences totaling twenty-five years, he refused to testify against her and the Nevada charges against her were dropped. When Louisiana did not pursue its case against either of them, she returned to southern California where she had been living with her third husband, Raymond Foat, running a catering business. Before her arrest she'd been a member of NOW, and after her release she rose to positions of leadership, the news accounts mentioning that in 1979 she organized NOW's national convention in California and was elected state vice-president for action; she served as a California Kennedy delegate to the Democratic Convention in 1980, and in 1981 became the state chapter's first paid, full-time coordinator or president. In the fall of 1982, she ran for vice-president of national NOW, but was narrowly defeated. The first news stories also alluded to a brief fourth marriage and no children.

In January 1983, having just been alerted to Foat's whereabouts and learning that Sidote was coincidentally back in a Nevada jail for drunk driving, Louisiana authorities requested Foat's arrest in Los Angeles and convinced Sidote that unless he agreed to testify against his ex-wife, he himself could be prosecuted for the Chayo murder.

Rabid antifeminists were bound to have a field day with the few facts the newspapers had provided: One of those man-hating women was unmasked for what she really was—a woman with a "sordid" past, a killer, too. But even committed feminists couldn't avoid reading between the lines and asking questions. The first accounts hinted at a dramatic story of change: a woman who had lived a seedy life as a cocktail waitress on the road with her boyfriend, moved to the "right" side of the tracks with a third marriage in southern California, and had then become a feminist. Had feminism given her a new identity, just as so many women were discovering new selves based on feminist awakenings? Had she joined NOW out of a feminist commitment or to confirm her respectability in the more moderate and predominantly middle-class women's organization? The few facts provided conveyed the impression of someone embracing feminism late by the standards of those who had come to feminism out of the civil rights and antiwar movements. What had feminism meant to her? even the most sympathetic feminists asked. A refuge? A confirmation of self? A chance to become a new woman, who had left her past behind? An opportunity to "make it" in the women's movement? In the demimonde of southern California politics, among the privileged liberals of Brentwood or Beverly Hills, had personal ambition, visions of power, or allure of class driven her onward and upward in NOW? Or had she joined the women's movement precisely because the difficult and bitter experiences of her past had convinced her of the need for women's equal rights? Was it the not uncommon translation of the personal into the political as her feminist consciousness was raised?

On Tuesday, January 18, a week after Foat's arrest, Sidote testified before the Jefferson Parish grand jury, and it handed down its indictment. In California, Foat was brought into the courtroom amid a demonstration by her friends and political allies. Some wore "Go Foat" T-shirts from her fall NOW campaign, others stood and clapped or blew her kisses or raised their fists in triumphant defiance as she entered the prisoner's dock to hear the indictment against her. As she had predicted, she was denied bail, her lawyer's writ of habeas corpus rejected, and she was returned to jail.

From her cell she issued her first public statement. As if she were well aware of the public shock about her background, she announced: "The only killing in my life was the death of a passive woman named Ginny Foat before the birth of a strong feminist by the same name."

It was a pronouncement that served a dramatic purpose, and to feminists who identified with such significant and rapid changes, it had an appealing ring. Midge Costanza called it Ginny's "metamorphosis" and said hers was a story applicable to all women: "I saw Ginny—without all the complications—as myself."

Nevertheless, the "complications" bothered other women, particularly those who worried that her feminist rebirth was not so immaculate a conception given what one NOW associate was calling "a murky past which hardly foretold the evolution of a strong feminist." Other NOW members were concerned that Foat's forceful statement from jail could not disguise the details of her background that were slowly emerging and that not only shocked many of her NOW colleagues but also tarnished the organization in the eyes of the general public.

Gloria Steinem, however, took up Foat's cause readily. No, she hadn't been shocked by what she heard about Foat's background. It was not that different from what many women had gone through, she thought. She called her statement from jail "very positive and inspiring" and gladly lent her name to Foat's defense-fund committee when Midge Costanza phoned to ask for her support.

Karen DeCrow had a more mixed reaction to Foat's declaration. "My first response, as a feminist, was that I loved it," she said.

"But then I also have to admit that such rhetoric doesn't work for me anymore although it might have in '67. I'm not sure it's because I'm now forty-seven, not thirty, whether I've left my adolescence, or the women's movement, I would hope, has left its adolescence. I still hear that kind of comment when I lecture at colleges from students who are usually both young and new to the movement, and I find their rhetoric either laughable or nauseating, depending on my mood. Or sometimes a woman my age will wander into a NOW meeting, and don't ask me where she's been—in the Peace Corps under a rock in a place where there are no newspapers—but she's heard about feminism yesterday and uses the same kind of language. Then it's *déjà vu,* like looking at a *CBS Reports* program on '68. But as a lawyer, hearing that statement, I would have said to her, 'Please restrain yourself, you're sounding like a crazy person.' On the other hand, if we were going to plead insanity, I'd tell her, 'Keep going.' "

Her lawyers had yet to restrain either Foat or her supporters, and there were loud outcries of political harassment, her arrest an attempt to "get" a leading feminist. Louisiana was a patently antifeminist state, Foat's advocates pointed out, citing Louisiana's unsuccessful suit against NOW for lost revenues when the organization mounted its tourist and convention boycott against states that had failed to pass the ERA. Foat herself saw her arrest in even more general symbolic terms: "I believe with all my heart that a political climate of violence and degradation of women is in a test stage with me as its first victim," she proclaimed.

Feminists of course agreed that there was a climate of antifeminism, given the Reagan administration's persistent attacks on the advances achieved by the women's movement in the last ten years, given that women were predominantly the losers in the budget cutbacks of welfare, food, health, education, and legal programs. "The feminization of poverty" wasn't just an abstraction; there were real victims, as evidenced in the statistics indicating that nearly half of those families living below the poverty line were headed by women. Nevertheless, not all colleagues in the women's movement could readily agree that Foat's arrest was political, nor could they invest it with the same symbolic meaning as Foat had.

Midge Costanza had first proclaimed Foat's arrest as political at her arraignment without really giving it a second thought. "I was interviewed because I had a well-known visible name. At that point

Ginny was not 'an issue' to me. She was a friend, a political colleague, and I was there to support her. The 'issue' came up after that—it just seemed clear to me that she'd been victimized for her feminism, for her position of leadership in the women's movement. After I was quoted extensively, I began to get phone calls. Some people asked me, 'Are you crazy?' and a day later I was told I was 'too controversial' for a job that had been made available to me. But there were also calls from all over the country from people who not only understood my care for her as a human being, my sense of friendship, but also agreed with my feeling that her arrest was 'political,' that Louisiana wouldn't have revived the case if Ginny had just been an anonymous woman."

Others, however, weren't convinced that Louisiana's pursuit of the case signaled political persecution of a feminist. Hesitant to draw that conclusion, Steinem said, "To call her arrest political harassment, you have to define what is meant by political. If by political, it means that some Lousiana official said to himself or even herself, 'I'm going to go after her,' I'm really not sure. But it was political in the feminist or anthropological sense that we live in a patriarchy and uppity women tend to get punished. I also suspect that if Ginny Foat had been playing a traditional female role, there wouldn't have been the same kind of pleasure that people seemed to take in her troubles."

Other NOW leaders in Los Angeles were reluctant to describe the arrest as political even in the "feminist sense." Some argued that since the crime had allegedly been committed in 1965, long before Foat had joined the women's movement, the revival of the warrant was simply a matter of a district attorney pursuing an unsolved case. To buttress this argument they pointed out that when Foat had been arrested in 1977, she hadn't been prominent in the movement, and at the time Louisiana hadn't pursued its case simply because Sidote had refused to testify against her. Further, they were not convinced that her ex-husband's accusations made her case analogous to the political trials of Joan Little or Inez Garcia, whose cases had set precedents for a woman's right to defend herself against attacks. Nor, they said, was it a classic battered woman's case, which NOW and other feminist organizations would consider political, since Foat wasn't accused of killing her abuser but of a robbery-murder.

The question of whether the case was political or not was crucial since in the week following Foat's arrest, NOW national leaders in Washington were meeting to decide what public position the organization would adopt. Ellie Smeal was NOW's president from 1977 to 1982, and then published "The Eleanor Smeal Report," a twice-a-month report on women in politics and feminist issues, as well as heading her own consultant firm and chairing "The Woman's Trust," an independent political action committee. With her offices also in Washington, D.C., she participated in the first meetings about Foat's case at NOW national headquarters and gave her opinion of the political meaning of the case: "Maybe I'm not paranoid enough, but I didn't see her arrest as a sign of antifeminism or an indication that Louisiana was trying to get a noted feminist. My gut reaction was that it wasn't a political case, because it was just too unusual a situation for me to think that. I do think, though, that the way she was arrested at the airport was inordinate and excessive. She was a well-known person, she wasn't going to skip, and the police could have called her up to arrange an arrest that was less publicized, less dramatic, as they often do with people in public positions. So although I didn't agree with Midge Costanza that it was a political trial, I did think she was given all that unnecessary publicity because she was president of California NOW."

One of the original founders of NOW in 1966, Muriel Fox had been executive vice-president of Carl Byoir and Associates, the internationally noted public relations agency, before her semiretirement in 1985. She has held many offices in NOW since its early years, including president of the NOW Legal Defense and Education Fund, and has often handled NOW's public relations. From what she heard and read about the case she did not fully agree with the allegations of political harassment and antifeminism that were leveled so immediately after Foat's arrest: "Whether particular politicians or officials were pursuing the case because of antifeminism is hard to tell. I do think, however, the charges were serious enough in and of themselves to warrant the criminal justice system pursuing them. Perhaps in other situations, Foat might not have been prosecuted as assiduously just on the basis of the testimony of a criminal like her ex-husband. There was also the possibility that some officials liked the publicity and perhaps some lawmakers were chuckling to themselves, delighted that a NOW leader was in such a pickle."

While worrying that such extraordinary press attention could hurt both Foat and NOW, the national leadership had the same gut re-action as Smeal and Fox. Nearly two weeks after Foat's arrest, na-tional NOW President Judy Goldsmith announced the organization's official position: "What we have here is an individual's personal tragedy, for which we have great compassion." "Personal" was the buzz word that alerted fellow feminists. Not only had NOW cut Foat loose, forgoing legal or official financial support, but the em-phasis on Foat's "personal" problem flew directly in the face of all the initial statements from Foat and her defense committee about political persecution.

Lines were being drawn among feminists, and most particularly between Foat and anti-Foat partisans in California NOW. Never-theless, the Foat camp's charge of antifeminism was complicated by a new fact about the case that also came to light in the second week after her arrest. In what seemed the cruelest irony of the still sketchy story, it was revealed that Shelly Mandell, a Los Angeles NOW colleague and once Foat's close friend, had written to Jefferson Par-ish in December 1982, requesting "all criminally related back-ground information regarding Virginia Galluzzo (aka Virginia Foat)." Once again feminists recoiled. It was difficult to mount a convinc-ing argument for an antifeminist conspiracy when a "sister" had in effect dropped the dime on Foat. And no one knew yet why she'd done it.

Still, Foat's supporters continued to accuse the police and legal authorities in both Los Angeles and Louisiana of political harass-ment. When Foat was denied bail on January 18, her defense team pointed to the telegram from Jefferson Parish Sheriff Harry Lee, which stated that his office "had no objection to bail," to prove that Los Angeles authorities were conspiring against a feminist; along with her "staged" arrest at the airport, the refusal of bail was evidence of unfair and discriminatory treatment, they announced. In reply, Los Angeles district attorneys argued that under California extradition law, Foat, like any person charged with murder in another state, was not eligible for bail. To grant bail would have indicated special treatment, not vice versa. Los Angeles police officials were also put on the defensive, and they announced repeatedly that with Foat's arrest they'd simply "gone by the book." Commander William Booth, who was handling press relations on the Foat case, insisted that reporters had been at the airport for her arrest not because they'd been forewarned, but because they routinely listen to police radio bands to find big stories. Then, as if to counterpunch, he added a detail about Foat that began to make its way into reporters' stories. When LAPD officers had been notified of Louisiana's warrant, they'd realized who Foat was, not simply because of her political prominence in the community but because she'd been part of a 1969 investigation of an unsolved murder case: "She was an acquaintance of one Richard Busconi who was shot and killed outside a bar in San Pedro on May 15, 1969. She was questioned at the time, as a witness, not as a suspect."

This information only added to the impression that Foat's earlier years hardly fit the profile one would expect of a NOW leader. A barmaid, a cocktail waitress, on the road with a drunk, hanging around with a small-time hood, four times married. With such publicity swirling around Foat's prolonged fight against extradition and the court's continued refusal to grant bail, Foat's defense committee, and especially Kay Tsenin and Jan Holden, her principal spokespersons, became wary of journalists. Their fund-raising letter and their interviews accused the press of sensationalizing Foat's background. All reporters interested in the Foat case came under close scrutiny, their feminist credentials investigated in an attempt to ensure sympathetic treatment, even though, ironically, most journalists who chose to pursue the story in depth did so from a feminist perspective, sensing that there was indeed a fascinating, perhaps emblematic "woman's" story behind Foat's metamorphosis.

But the defense team wanted to keep reporters away from Foat's past. "We want to stress who she is *today*, not who she was before," Jan Holden said over and over again as she extolled Foat's long-time political commitment. "She even helped organize the 1963 Martin Luther King March on Washington," she would say. But no, she couldn't talk about 1965 when Foat "went south," not to register voters in Mississippi but to hit the road with Jack Sidote. She was willing to discuss Foat's NOW leadership or describe how well she was bearing up under her ordeal, but she would not elaborate on or confirm facts about Foat's "former" life.

At a second hearing on Foat's writ of habeas corpus on February 11, 1983, bail was once again denied; under California law, she could be held in jail for ninety days without bail if she was challenging extradition. After another demonstration—the bailiff's admonition, "No clapping, no cheering, no blowing kisses," notwithstanding—Jan Holden again announced, "Ginny's holding up better than her friends are. After she was arrested we had to give her energy and support. Now she's giving it to us. She was really up yesterday. She got her hair done, and she was very happy that one of the two changes of clothes she's allowed came through in time for today. But what's really wonderful is how terrific she is with the other women prisoners in Sybil Brand. She's a calming influence, and they all identify with her. They see very clearly that this is what happens to any woman who gains power—the male establishment brings her down."

Soon after the February 11 hearing, Foat's defense committee began to temper such remarks about antifeminism and the male establishment. Bob Tuller, her California attorney, and John Reed and Robert Glass, the New Orleans attorneys whom Kay Tsenin had retained for her defense should she go to trial, warned Foat's supporters that such remarks would jeopardize a fair trial in Louisiana. Hence, while Foat waited for California Governor Deukmejian to rule on her petition for an extradition hearing, her supporters muted their accusations of political conspiracy so as not to exacerbate what they still saw as antifeminist prejudice. Privately they said Louisiana had waited until conservative Republican Deukmejian had taken office, since one of his campaign promises was not to block extraditions on political grounds as Governor Jerry Brown had. (This, of course, overlooked the fact that Governor Brown himself had extradited Foat to Nevada in 1977.) Publicly, though, they proclaimed her innocence and their optimism that she would never be extradited.

Foat herself was also obeying her lawyers' orders: no more statements from jail, no interviews with reporters. A virtual media blackout descended, and as the bureaucratic wheels turned slowly, as Foat's California lawyers exhausted all legal measures to block her extradition to Louisiana, the drama of the Foat case was played out behind closed doors.

Nevertheless, for all the charges of antifeminism, antagonism against the NOW leader did not lie exclusively within the domain of the "male establishment." What seemed most perplexing were the actions and motivations of Foat's NOW colleagues both before and after her arrest. Despite concerted attetmpts to keep reporters away from this aspect of the case, initial hints suggested that much of the Foat story was inextricably connected to conflicts within the women's movement. If the personal is political, then certainly the factionalism and political maneuvering behind the Foat case said a great deal about the morality, ethics, and psychological complexity of "sisterhood" in the eighties.

TWO

The Rising Star

STRESSING "who Ginny Foat is today," the Foat defense committee defined her identity exclusively in terms of "the birth of a strong feminist." In a rare allusion to Foat's past, Kay Tsenin said Ginny had felt the first stirrings of a feminist consciousness when she'd worked as a stewardess for Allegheny Airlines after her graduation from high school. But whatever her earlier private speculations about women in society, whatever her personal resentments of constraints against her sex, her spokespersons located her "click" of political awakening in 1974.

In 1971 Ginny had married her third husband, Raymond Foat, an Englishman whom she'd known since 1969 when she worked as a waitress on the *Princess Louise* restaurant, a floating restaurant in San Pedro, California, where he was the manager. In the fall of 1970 she had joined him in Vancouver, and a year after their marriage in May 1971 they had returned to southern California where he managed the restaurant and she was the catering manager in a hotel near Disneyland. Then in 1974, Ginny joined with an old friend, Danny Marcheano, to start a catering business, "Affairs Unlimited."

She was leading a middle-class life, and not yet a feminist, she joined a newly formed Orange County chapter of the Soroptimists, an organization of successful business and career women, the female counterpart of the Optimists. But when a bank refused her a loan for her catering business without her husband's signature, she became interested in the women's movement. She then began to attend meetings of Anaheim NOW, a moderate chapter in Orange County whose members were by and large suburban, middle- or upper-middle-class women. From 1974 to 1977, she was a participant, not yet an organizer or leader, part of what NOW leaders proudly call their "grass-roots" base. She and other local members concentrated on issues they saw as important to their lives, questions of employment discrimination, equal pay, business and career opportunities. It was not a radical brand of feminism, nor were they aware or especially concerned that at this time national NOW was being shaken by internal disputes and dissension.

Founded on October 29, 1966, the National Organization for Women had adopted a moderate and restrained political tone compared to that of the more radical feminist groups that had evolved from the sixties' antiwar and civil rights movements. As Betty Friedan announced in her book *It Changed My Life,* "For the reality of this revolution is that we—the middle-class women who started it—did it for ourselves." As she explained further, "Like most Americans, the women who started the movement would be considered, or considered themselves middle-class, though not all had been to college, not all were white, and their fathers might have worked in a factory or as janitors or started out as peddlers like mine."

But even as the women's movement cut across class lines, and although not all NOW members were white and middle-class, NOW leaders tended to worry that certain issues were too controversial for its predominantly middle-class membership. The emphasis was on a nonthreatening image for the public and political strategies that stressed "working within the system." Moderate feminists like Friedan couched their objections to radical rhetoric and more "outrageous" forms of protest in Madison Avenue-ese—"Would it play in Peoria?"—and argued that radicals would alienate Middle America and suburban women who were just beginning to take notice of the women's movement. In order for NOW to be effective, it had to attract a large number of new members.

While Friedan and other moderates were worried about radicals offending potential converts, NOW was viewed as a radical group by conservative commentators. No matter how carefully NOW leaders watched their language, they were still called bra-burners, man-haters, and lesbians by antifeminists. In 1974 some NOW members were beginning to rebel against the guidelines of what were "appropriate," acceptable issues or forms of political protest. "We're seen as radical anyway," the argument went. "Let's take more risks, let's make a bigger noise, be more confrontational. Perhaps shock has more value than good manners; let's try shaking them up in Peoria rather than worrying whether we've offended them."

Chafing against moderate restraint, this NOW faction argued that feminism's goal was not to achieve a larger piece of the pie for middle-class women but to alter those institutions that affected women of every class. Friedan was worried by their position, however: "I always saw the women's movement as a movement of the mainstream of American society—moving women into and thus changing that mainstream," she wrote in *It Changed My Life*. But her argument overlooked the very real consequence of moving into the mainstream. Too often successful women simply soaked up mainstream values; they were not about to change a system that they'd already bought into, and in some cases, by which they'd already been bought off.

By 1975 more radical NOW members had gained a large enough constituency among the membership for Friedan to say that she was pulling back from the organization to do her own writing since, "The extremists who want to take the women's movement 'out of the mainstream into the revolution' have now taken over NOW." Obliquely, she was referring to the 1975 reelection of Karen De-Crow as national NOW president and Ellie Smeal as board chairperson, which was the culmination of a successful campaign among NOW's seventeen thousand members by the faction calling itself the "Majority Caucus."

Although Karen DeCrow classified herself as "solid upper-middle-class from birth," she had originated the slogan "out of the mainstream into the revolution" after serving her first term as NOW president. "That slogan now sounds gorgeously sixtyish, like having long hair and a miniskirt," she said with a laugh. "Those were heady, 'out of the mainstream' times; in 1985 it seems less contradictory to talk about being both revolutionary and moving women into the mainstream. Still, in '74 there were indeed two philosophies in NOW. Up to that time the organization had been primarily for women who wanted to be lawyers or corporate executives or get into professions. Most were white, well educated, and had money. When I was elected I wanted to broaden the focus of NOW so that it included minorities, blue-collar women, union women. So, for example, I fought to get travel expenses paid for board members to attend meetings so that different people could afford to run for a NOW office. In my second term we had an affirmative action program, and we succeeded in getting I think a third minorities on the board. I also wanted to reexamine and eliminate NOW's somewhat homophobic attitude. Plus, although we had male members of NOW, it seemed single sex and antimale, and I wanted to have the board gender balanced. Of course that always failed by two or three votes. In fact, I think if that had passed, the feminist movement would have taken a different turn. For example, with all of our great campaign for the ERA, the literature never said what the amendment would do for men. In general, though, I wanted to make NOW a more significant organization in American life. But even with our slogan 'into the revolution,' neither Ellie Smeal nor I fit the description of 'crazy radicals.' "

The Majority Caucus had campaigned throughout the country, eliciting support from local chapter members and, having joined the Anaheim NOW chapter the year before, Ginny Foat was a Majority Caucus partisan. "That was the trend when I was first getting involved in NOW," she remembered. "The mainstream leaders had all been opposed to taking on delicate issues, such as the abortion and lesbian questions, but the Majority Caucus felt that NOW needed to move out of just appealing to corporate women in business or white middle-class women. So we were going to bring our organization into the revolution."

The new revolutionary leadership of NOW organized its first action for October 29, 1975, calling it "Alice Doesn't," a general strike by women. "It was my first involvement in a really big way," said Foat. "Although I'd done little actions, this was my first biggie—'Out into the streets.' "

For all Foat's support of the Majority Caucus, her opposition to NOW's middle-class concerns, and talk of "out into the streets," her NOW colleagues of those years were struck by her suburban life-style and "middle-class feminism." Her own non–middle-class background was neither apparent nor discussed. She had moved and joined the San Fernando Valley NOW, and Carol Schmidt, a freelance writer and political activist, met her in 1977 when she'd happened upon the same local chapter. A middle-aged woman with a ready laugh, Schmidt had been recently divorced and, as she put it, she was ready to join any feminist group she could find. San Fernando NOW was close at hand. "It was just having its elections, and I voted for Ginny as treasurer. She didn't affect me a lot then, but I remember she had this great house with Ray Foat from whom she was then in the process of getting divorced. It had a pool and a Jacuzzi and a sunken fireplace, so we had a lot of meetings there, planning meetings and fund-raisers, since in addition to having the house, Ginny ran a catering business and was a terrific cook."

As treasurer of a local chapter Foat would not have been considered a NOW leader. But accepting the "dirty" job with its details of finance, dues, and expenses would be seen as a sign of commitment, and her willingness to put in long hours was the basic prerequisite to becoming a NOW leader. Ginny also organized a task force on self-employed women, an indication of what she then perceived and presented as her central concern. At the time, anyone who thought an issue was neglected formed a NOW task force, and while heading a task force did not necessarily betoken a rise to leadership, it did qualify one as a member of NOW's state board.

Still, in 1977 not many colleagues would have predicted that Foat was destined for leadership. "She didn't impress me that much as someone who would ever get as far as she did in NOW," said Schmidt. "There were a lot of dynamic women in NOW, and we elected Ginny treasurer, not president."

In addition to serving as treasurer and on several committees, including one on violence against women in film, she listed herself in her later NOW campaign literature as a consciousness-raising group leader during those years. Separated from Ray Foat, who was moving to Hawaii (she called hers an "amicable" divorce), she opened her home to other women who were having family problems or going through divorces as well. The house always seemed to be filled with women, yet Ginny was then more a participant in the movement than a rising star.

Suddenly, in May 1977, her middle-class suburban life collapsed when four Los Angeles police detectives arrived at her door with warrants for the arrest of Virginia Galluzzo on charges of murder, one in Nevada, the other in Louisiana. She was led away to be questioned at police headquarters, and after giving the police a twenty-two-page statement, denying her guilt and insisting that her ex-husband and accuser was crazy, she was placed in the Sybil Brand prison, where she remained for ninety-two days while her attorney Bob Tuller unsuccessfully fought her extradition to Nevada.

Carol Schmidt remembered the shock felt by Foat's political colleagues: "One day we woke up and read in the *Los Angeles Times* that our treasurer had been arrested for murder and was in jail waiting to be sent off to Nevada. We quickly checked the treasury, and it was okay. Then we began to investigate, and we learned that it was her ex-husband who was testifying against her."

Kay Tsenin knew her only from NOW conventions, but she wrote her a few letters of support while she was in jail, having heard that her arrest had been prompted by a wife-beater's attempt to exact revenge. When Foat was finally extradited to Nevada and later released on bail, several NOW colleagues visited her there, and Trish Manning wrote a story about her plight for the November 1977 issue of the California *NOW Times.*

The two-column story appeared on the third page of the newsletter following another story about a battered wife who was in jail for having killed her husband. Manning explained that Ginny's plight was a result of her having escaped her abusive husband (the date of his final beating and her flight was given as 1969, not 1970). His accusations against her were the culmination of his threat, she said, to "convince the authorities that she had committed his crimes," and his act of revenge for her having left him. The article, however, didn't present much of Ginny's past except to say that "she has spent a great portion of her life in the fight for equal rights," with her presence "in Washington, D.C., to march with Martin Luther King" and her counseling young women "in self-confidence and leadership" for the Soroptimists cited as examples. But according to Manning, Foat had "kept her fears and the violence she endured in her past to herself."

While the article didn't detail the exact nature of the charges or describe the crimes of which she stood accused, it indicated that of eleven murders to which her ex-husband (he was not mentioned by name) had confessed, he had accused her of committing two, one in Nevada, one in Louisiana. At the time, an arrest on the Louisiana charge seemed a distinct possibility, indeed a likelihood, which made contributions to her defense fund even more imperative: "Ginny will most probably be arrested again if she wins the case in Nevada and extradited to Louisiana. There, it is likely that she will be financially unable to post bail and so will spend her time imprisoned while awaiting trial."

Even though Louisiana chose not to pursue its case once Sidote had refused to testify, anyone with a small knowledge of the law and police work might well have sensed that the Louisiana charge was still unresolved. But since Foat was still low-profile in the organization, no one in NOW paid much attention once Foat was released and had returned to California. Her explanation was accepted at face value, and she returned to her feminist activities. She was another example of a battered woman or, as Manning put it, "of man's brutality to woman," yet she was hardly high on the list of NOW's political priorities. It was International Women's Year, the Houston convention would be held the very month in which the article about Ginny appeared (ironically, Shelly Mandell was named in the same *NOW Times* issue as a California delegate to the convention). Just as important, too, was the ERA extension bill coming before Congress. Little wonder that the details of her case didn't register, and once Ginny was released in Nevada, it would seem that no one gave the Louisiana charge a second thought. And Ginny herself returned to the role in which her NOW sisters had previously known her; as Manning described her, she was "a young, self-determined business woman."

Toni Carabillo had been vaguely acquainted with Ginny Foat because of organizing California support for the Majority Caucus and Ellie Smeal. Prominent in southern California feminist circles, Carabillo was the founder and former president of Los Angeles NOW, and she brought her not inconsiderable business, public relations, and writing skills to building the strength of NOW in California while co-editing and publishing *The National NOW Times* with Judith Meuli at their Los Angeles house. With her short, crisp, gray hair, large owlish glasses, well-tailored suits, and low gravelly voice, she is the epitome of a successful female executive, except that she has devoted her time and energies to NOW since the late sixties. A close friend as well as a political ally of Ellie Smeal, it wasn't surprising that Carabillo, in her leadership position, was only vaguely aware of the arrest of a NOW member in another southern California chapter.

"Ginny wasn't that prominent," said Carabillo, "and I think Jeane Bendorf, who was then state coordinator, first became aware of the arrest. Apparently, she had been under arrest and fighting extradition for a while before the rest of us were informed of it. I read Trish Manning's article, but I don't remember if it mentioned the Louisiana charge. I think after her release, Ginny told people she was okay as long as she didn't set foot in Louisiana, which in hindsight meant the charge wasn't resolved, but I didn't think about it then. I wasn't paying a lot of attention, I wasn't expecting her to become a leader, and I think most of us accepted the image which Trish Manning cultivated—that her ex-husband was a violent criminal and that she was the innocent victim of his desire for revenge because she'd left him. But I don't remember a lot of talk about the battered-wife syndrome."

Foat said she felt embraced as a "sister" on her return, and her story was called a battered woman's worst nightmare. Still, the story in 1977 was fairly sketchy, and like Foat's police statement, it didn't go into detail about her past life as a battered spouse or its connection to Sidote's allegations. While Foat lived with the nightmare of more than three months in jail, her victimization seemed also to give her a new sense of self and feminist zeal, as well as bringing her attention, respect, even a kind of celebrity in California NOW circles. Not only did she feel radicalized by the experience, but having some notoriety among NOW members—her plight compared to the political oppression of all women—her arrest seemed almost a notch in a feminist's belt. Soon after she was released from Nevada, she appeared at an ERA fund-raiser. "It was at one of the members' homes in Granada Hills," recalled Schmidt. "Ginny came in and sort of told us the whole story. It just seemed incredible. She described this guy she'd been married to, but she didn't go into all the details of the battering. She just said, 'Well, he beat me once and tried to kill me.' She believed that since there wasn't enough evidence in Nevada, the Louisiana charges would also be dropped. Maybe she had a little nagging doubt about it, but since Louisiana didn't do anything over the next years, she probably felt that meant it was over."

Ginny Foat's arrest in 1977 was the first time Shelly Mandell had become aware of her as well. Mandell is a short, energetic woman with crisply cut salt-and-pepper hair and a ready grin, and while she is a politico, she retains a Jewish mother's manner with friends, checking over their health and worrying about their welfare. Although she'd worked in a lawyer's office for fifteen years, she saw her life as that of a typical suburban housewife until she rebelled against the traditional female role and joined NOW in the mid-seventies. Soon her time was also devoted to the women's movement as she became more and more involved in both NOW and community politics. She and Ginny Foat had in fact joined NOW at about the same time, and although they were both in the Los Angeles area, Mandell hadn't known her or anything about her until the 1977 arrest.

"The first time I heard about Ginny Foat was when the hat was passed at a Cal NOW meeting to raise money for a NOW woman who had been arrested and was in a big jam," she said. "Then Trish Manning, another NOW member who was a friend of Foat's, called me because she knew I worked for criminal lawyers. She asked me to check on Bob Tuller, the lawyer in Orange County whom Foat had hired. One of my bosses told me he was good, so I called Trish back and told her. That was the last I remembered of her then. I didn't even register her name; I couldn't have said at the time what eventually happened with her case, and I didn't read Trish's article. Then later, while I was planning an abortion rally, a woman volunteered to do some work, and when she brought it back done, I thought, 'I'll have to remember her,' because in NOW you remember those people who are willing to put in the hours. But I don't even know if I put it together that she was the woman who had been arrested. I was too busy, very much into NOW work; it was International Women's Year, I was a delegate, and we were starting the ERA extension campaign. Besides, I'd just gotten my divorce, I was having a great time, and so I was just aware of this woman Ginny who'd surfaced and started to work for NOW. Sometime that year or the next maybe I heard she was involved in the women's prison task force and I wondered why she was working on that. Perhaps then I realized, 'Oh, right, she was the one who was arrested.' Still, my not knowing anything more wasn't so odd, since in NOW you can work with people for years and never know about them or what they do. Like a woman I was with on the NOW board who one day mentioned a husband and six kids. I practically fell off my chair. Basically, the attitude about people's background is, 'Who cares?' "

So the vague awareness of Foat's 1977 arrest and an even vaguer knowledge of her background were not unique. Both in NOW and in the women's movement in general, feminists seemed to leave their pasts behind them as they marched into battle. For practical reasons it made sense: Individuals devoting long hard hours to a political cause will rarely pause to narrate their autobiographies. Further, in predominantly volunteer organizations, there isn't the leisure to "check out" those people who are committed to the cause, a fact that made the FBI's infiltration of such organizations relatively easy in the sixties. But even today, hard work in the present obliterates a concern with someone's past. As NOW President Judy Goldsmith insisted, both in terms of Foat and other NOW members, "Activists all over the country will say that what is most typical and characteristic is that we relate to each other in terms of the organization and the work at hand. It's astonishing but there are people I've known for more than ten years whose personal lives and whose backgrounds I know nothing about. The subject just never comes up, there's never been time."

Doubtless, this tendency was exacerbated in Foat's case by a battered woman's disinclination to talk about her abuse. Although domestic violence is considered a feminist issue, Foat may have felt the lingering guilt common among abused wives: Not only is it supposedly their fault, but such things don't happen in "nice" families. Too, revelations about the past might have underscored the fact that hers had not been a "respectable" or, as she put it, a "conventional convent" background. While referring to her victimization, she may not have wanted to expose that background to the scrutiny of those who had known her as a middle-class career woman in San Fernando Valley. Moreover, psychologically she may have wanted to put those years behind her; once she'd been freed on the Nevada charge, she may have felt she could block out her life with Sidote; perhaps she even came close to believing it had never existed.

Whatever the reasons, after briefly explaining what had brought about her arrest, as her colleagues remember it, she rarely talked about being a battered wife, either in public or to her friends. Even after Kay Tsenin and she had become close, she didn't choose to say much, although Kay herself had been battered and was an active volunteer counselor at the Marin Abused Women's Shelter (MAWS). "We would talk about it in terms of both of us having come from battering relationships," said Kay. "But looking back on it I would talk a lot more about what sort of incidents had happened to me, and Ginny would mostly just listen. She'd acknowledge that she, too, had been in such a relationship, but she never went into any of the graphics."

One significant detail about Foat's past did come to light in court documents from her 1977 pretrial hearing: Her divorce from John Sidote had never been finalized. Although Ray Foat had not proceeded with their divorce during her imprisonment, after her release he quietly filed for an annulment on the grounds of the still existing Sidote marriage. This was not made public at the time, nor did the California NOW newsletter story indicate what court papers revealed: that Sidote had initiated the divorce in 1970, that Foat had made no mention of batterment in her response, that she hadn't appeared in court for the divorce, and that she had failed to take the last legal steps to ensure that the divorce was final.

These details of her story, however, were subsumed by the relief and triumph of her release and the sense that the experience marked a turning point for her. Welcomed home as a "comrade" and a martyred sister by women in NOW, she drew on her recent ordeal to become the co-chair of the NOW task force on women in prison. In 1978 she became highly visible in NOW's ERA campaign and, aligning herself with the California Caucus, the local Ellie Smeal–Majority Caucus supporters (most notably Toni Carabillo and Shelly Mandell in Los Angeles), she was elected a state vice-president.

Like many NOW members she began to make her political life her personal life. To outsiders, her rise to leadership seemed extraordinarily fast, and even some NOW colleagues talked about her as a "political opportunist." A few meant this as a criticism; others argued that all feminists involved in a political arena had to be political opportunists. Those who were more critical thought of her as a "personal opportunist," too, suspecting that she was making a career in the women's movement out of ambitions to get ahead rather than a deep feminist commitment. And there were others who said that Foat could never have become a leader anywhere but in California NOW.

Yet the fact that Foat was soon promoted to positions of leadership wasn't all that unusual. In most volunteer organizations those willing to put in the time generally become the leaders. In addition, she was being pushed onto the public stage, appearing as a NOW spokesperson in the Los Angeles area. Shelly Mandell said that it was she, as president of Los Angeles NOW, who would often send Ginny to events to represent NOW if she herself was too busy. "To this day, I remember telling the press, it's 'boat with an F, Ginny Foat, chair of the Women in Film task force, who's coming.' "

Ellie Smeal insisted that anyone who said Foat's rise in NOW was rapid didn't know the organization very well. In that sense, she said, newspaper accounts of Foat's NOW career were particularly skewed. "Almost every NOW leader could be described that way," she commented. "It's even been said about me. Everything or everybody seems rapid since we've only been in existence for a relatively few years. It's not like AT&T, where it takes you *x* number of years to rise through the levels."

Just as important as her commitment, her long hours, and her "attention to every detail" was her alignment with "the team," which was most powerful in southern California because of its ties to NOW's national leadership. That was often the basis for rising within the state organization, NOW colleagues said, and Toni Carabillo was frequently the one doing the picking.

"You're either 'picked' or 'nonpicked,' " said Carol Schmidt. "When I first joined NOW, I started working on the *NOW Times*, which was then put out from Toni Carabillo and Judith Meuli's home. They're the co-editors, although Toni has the most power since she is such a good friend of Ellie Smeal, then national NOW president. Toni thought I was wonderful until I wrote an article about the stereotype of 'fat dykes.' Toni selectively went through the mailing list and withheld that issue from anyone who might be offended. I was furious about her censorship, and we had a huge fight. But I had broken the rules. We weren't supposed to talk about it or even look like 'fat dykes.' We used to joke about the NOW image. It was okay to be lesbian, but you had to do it in the right way, which meant wearing the right kind of clothes—a blazer and expensive trousers with pleats, 'the blazer dykes,' we called them—and being straitlaced, asexual, and not being comfortable in your body. But after I wrote about 'fat dykes,' I was off the team."

Ginny, however, was acceptable and on the team; she formed a new local chapter in Hollywood, and then achieved more prominence when she was chosen to coordinate NOW's 1979 national convention in Los Angeles, mainly at Carabillo's suggestion and with Shelly Mandell's encouragement.

"If there was any sense of a 'rapid rise' for Foat," said Carabillo, "it was because she was chosen to be the conference coordinator. That was a plum because it's a great jumping-off point and gives you so much national visibility. I suggested her because I knew she was a good hard worker in NOW, plus she was running a catering business. Many of us, including myself, had used her for our parties, and I thought that since a lot of the conference coordinating involved organizing hotel facilities, she'd be a natural with her catering background and her experience as a hotel manager. But that didn't mean she was in charge of the political organizing of the conference."

Shelly Mandell was running the ERA extension campaign and had come to think of Ginny "as a good hard worker," too, enough so that when Shelly, as one of the two NOW national board members from California, was involved in planning the 1979 NOW conference, she agreed that she and Foat should coordinate the conference. Eventually, because of her other NOW activities, Shelly didn't co-coordinate but worked with Ginny on planning.

"That's when I really got to know her," Mandell said, "although at that point we were not yet that close. She was a pretty private person. I wasn't even aware until later that at the time she was living with Jack Meyer, the guy she later married. All I really knew then was that she worked hard, but that she was also a little temperamental. When she got out of hand, people would call me because they knew we were becoming friends. They'd say things like, 'She's impossible, do something.' She liked to get things done her way, and when she didn't, she was a little testy and got to screaming at people. I told her to stop screaming, that it made them crazy, and I gave her one of my kid's stuffed animals, a reindeer, to hold till after the conference. But it was during this time we started to become friends, even though we led very different kinds of lives. She and her friends went out and partied and danced. I didn't, I was a drag in comparison. People would say, 'Ah, Shelly just goes home at night.' Still, I realized that Ginny had run a very good conference, she was very good at what she did, and after the conference, as we became better friends, I also began to teach her about politics."

"She did run a good conference," agreed Carabillo, "but like Shelly, I noticed that when things didn't get done her way, she'd start yelling. I remember, because I made an abortive attempt at roller skating that year, and fell and nearly broke my back so I was attending planning meetings in a lot of pain. I was handling public relations for the conference, and Ginny started pressuring me about things I knew were being taken care of, but just not *her* way. She had similar problems with other people, and she was almost harassing in the way she'd push at them in a nagging way. People would tell her, 'Back off.' Then Ginny fired a staff person because she said she hadn't performed. The woman took it to some fair labor practices committee, and she ended up winning some back pay."

Another characteristic of Ginny Foat became apparent to people who worked with her on the 1979 conference: She suffered from severe migraine headaches. At first it seemed strange that she—an extrovert, friends called her—should have them. But that was presumably a layperson's analysis of migraines. Still, others thought it was related to the part of her that seemed bottled up and tense, the impression they had of her holding herself together when she snapped, "I'm fine, I'm fine," but obviously wasn't. To closer friends she'd admit that a headache was driving her crazy and that she had to take painkillers, go back to bed, and not come into morning meetings until eleven or twelve. During the years when she was the state administrative vice-president, then the state coordinator, other state board members were used to Ginny's late arrivals, her being kind of spacy or, as she put it, "out of it," and not on top of things. While no one really knew when Ginny's headaches had begun, some thought they might be connected to what Ginny had described as some sort of breakdown she'd had in jail in 1977 when she'd been prescribed Thorazine.

This was a side of Ginny Foat few people saw at the 1979 conference, however. It was there that Ginny first came into contact with Jean Conger. Conger worked in NOW's Washington office, having been appointed to a new executive position by Ellie Smeal, who needed more personnel and administrative assistance than her vice-president, Judy Goldsmith, could give her. One of Conger's jobs was to oversee the conference's credentials procedure. "I went out and met Ginny that July," she said. "To be honest, her brand of feminism was not mine—her long, polished fingernails, the spiked heels with blue jeans. I'd never seen that and I guessed it was 'California feminism.' But we worked well together, she respected what I was doing and she cooperated with me one hundred percent on credentialing. I also liked the fact that the people who worked with her had such a good time. Her volunteers seemed almost part of a family even though it was a big group. If there was a meeting at midnight, there would be wine and cheese or a meal for people, and that was all Ginny's doing. She was recognizing people's human needs as well as making sure the job got done."

Others at the 1979 conference were also struck by the way Ginny looked. "We were all running around in our green NOW T-shirts and white pants," said Carol Schmidt, "but she showed up in a skirt and high heels, and her NOW green was a sort of turquoise and a pretty blouse. She seemed a model of traditional attractiveness. She'd finally had her hair cut short in a really good style that pulled everything together. Thin hair had always been a problem, but when she got it cut she looked beautiful. It was as if no one had really paid attention to her before, and suddenly we all said, 'My God, *is* she good-looking!' It was also like she radiated sexuality. Men pick up on it, but I assume Marilyn Monroe was very attractive to women, too. It's a kind of vibrance that a lot of women and men find attractive. Ginny had it, a kind of charisma which certainly helps in politics."

Ginny had blossomed, it seemed. By proving herself at the conference, she guaranteed her place on the team, particularly on Toni Carabillo's. The following year, at NOW's 1980 national convention in San Antonio, Carabillo was a strong supporter of the proposal to change NOW's by-laws to extend Smeal's term of office. The argument for the change was that since the ERA campaign was coming down to the wire, a change in leadership might mean a loss of crucial ground. The proposal provoked vehement debate in the organization. Shelly Mandell, like many others in Los Angeles NOW, joined Carabillo to campaign for the by-laws change and Smeal's term extension.

Foat was at first only lukewarm to the proposal, according to Mandell, and had to be talked into voting for the term extension. "It came down to my being very personal about it. Ginny was being pulled by people—maybe by Kay Tsenin—who said Smeal had been president long enough. I'd voted for the proposal at a national board meeting, even though the extension of Ellie's term meant that I wouldn't run for national vice-president–action, which a number of people wanted me to do. But I decided my own plans weren't as important as the ERA campaign, because I really believed that since Ellie had run the campaign, keeping her on was the only chance we had to win. So finally I went to Ginny and Kay and said, 'Hey, if you won't support it for any other reason, do it for me.' "

Those in California NOW who had criticized Smeal's leadership and campaigned against the term extension called themselves the Loyal Opposition. They argued that the by-laws change undermined NOW's democratic process and granted Smeal and the national office too much power. The split over this issue lasted long after Smeal's reelection, and in California already existing schisms were widened by the dissent among NOW members.

Recalling the 1980 convention, Smeal rued this unforeseen consequence of the by-laws change. The irony, she pointed out, was that she had initially been opposed to the idea. It had been practically foisted on her, she said, and she had to be talked into it: "When Barbara Duke introduced the motion without telling me or anybody else, I was so upset I almost cried. First of all, my husband had gotten a contract to last my original term of office, and my staying on would mess him up. Plus I felt he should have had some say in my decision, not to give his permission but as an equal partner. In the second place, I wanted to step down. I was close to burnout, I was ready to move on, plus my two children were entering their critical teen years. But then I accepted the argument that by staying on I would essentially absorb what we were almost certain would be the defeat of the ERA, so that the new leaders after me would have a fighting chance to move on to something else. I didn't want the future wrapped up in and perhaps strangled by the ERA defeat, so I finally agreed not to change in midstream. That was the positive side, because it eventually did give us an orderly transition, and turned a defeat into a victory. After the 1980 election, we spotted the gender gap, and during the next year and a half we were able to sell it to the press so that we had a launching pad for our political movement phase, and the ERA defeat wasn't a total downer. That phase ultimately became the runway to Ferraro, to our strategy for getting a female vice-presidential candidate.

"The negative side was that people perceived that I stayed on out of personal ambition or an attempt to consolidate my power. Of course, if I *had* been a little dictator, I would have said to the board, 'Don't just extend my term, remove the term limitation entirely.' Still, I think the people who yelled the most about my so-called dictatorship were the ones whose plans were upset by changing the usual term limitation of the presidency. No one thought about that consequence at the time, I didn't realize it until later, but in fairness to my critics, their terms of office or whatever their plans for what they wanted to do in the state or local chapters were thrown off in relation to the NOW presidential term."

NOW elections did, in general, seem to provoke struggles for power, with various factions or teams, the picked and the non-picked, the Majority Caucus and the Loyal Opposition often adopting a tactic of "trashing," as it was known in the feminist trade. In those instances, the political often became personal, and friendships were made or broken over who was supporting whom or which team or which side. Real differences over political issues or strategies were often reduced to personal animosity and feuds. NOW members readily admitted that how one voted in an election or on an issue determined with whom one would have dinner that night or even who spoke to whom the rest of the year.

"In fact I dropped out of NOW from 1977 to 1979, primarily because I couldn't stand the infighting," said Kay Tsenin. "What often happens in NOW—as it did with me—is that if you criticize somebody in power, you're told you're destroying the organization and you're thrown off the team."

Ex-NOW President Karen DeCrow still manages to laugh when she describes NOW factionalism, even though she suspects it's no different from infighting within other large political organizations. But she admits, "Until you've seen a contested NOW election, you haven't seen anything. I had a bodyguard with me when I ran for reelection at the 1975 Philadelphia conference, and I thought, my God, am I going to need armed guards to be head of the sisters! When I left in '77 I felt I would have no trouble being a litigator because I'd been through the NOW wars. I'm frequently in a legal situation where someone will say, 'How can you stay so cool?' I smile sweetly and think back on NOW. If you can live through NOW, you can battle both the *Fortune* 500 and the worst sex-discrimination cases. Of course, I didn't like the need for bodyguards, but I understood why it was necessary. Being president of NOW is one of the best jobs around, and even though it wasn't a paid job when I had it, it was a fabulous opportunity. So it's no wonder why people want it and why the elections are so hotly contested.

"I'm a loyal NOW member but after the '77 convention when my term was up, I didn't go to another convention, so my knowledge of the politicking comes from talking on the phone to friends on various sides of the issues. Yet it does seem that you need a scorecard to keep up with who's good friends with whom in NOW. Sometimes someone will call me and say, 'So-and-so's denouncing so-and-so.' Naïve as I am, I'll say, 'Gosh, I thought they were on the same side.' 'Well, that was yesterday,' they'll reply.

"Eleven years later, when my memory is jogged, I have to admit there was viciousness between the factions. Some people—not all—who opposed my getting elected in 1974 and 1975 were terrible to me, absolutely unbelievable. There was even some talk, for example, that I must be an FBI or CIA agent because how else did I get my money? That's pretty heavy stuff. I didn't have time to practice law, and I earned my money by writing and lecturing. Those kinds of comments hurt. But then some of my friends in Syracuse tried to cheer me up—'Come on, it's great. You'll have terrific credentials—FBI, CIA—if you run for political office in upstate New York.' "

In addition, Ellie Smeal thought the infighting and quarrels in California were worse than in other chapters for a very good reason. "I remember in about '74 Karen DeCrow went out to California to visit. She came back and told me, 'You won't believe it. All the people who weren't talking to each other the last time are now the people who are talking to each other, and vice versa.' There's a lot of argument in any movement, so any person who's been politically active would be aware of it, and it's true of our organization. But the infighting in California has been and still is almost historic, and I would guess that it's because the state's too darned big. It has about ten percent of the national population, but at one time it had about twenty percent of the NOW membership. Yet there were times when California wasn't even represented on the NOW board. With so many people, with twenty, thirty, forty thousand members, the state had a lot of potential leaders. Yet it still could have only one state president, for example, even when it had a disproportionately large number of active, opinionated, and every other kind of person. So you don't have much outlet for leadership there."

Most progressive organizations are prone to factionalism and infighting precisely because their nonhierarchical structures are adopted to try to give everyone a voice. Yet conflicts in NOW also seemed more vicious than in other political organizations since they were often so personalized. What was true of Ginny Foat was true of many other NOW members: They seemed to invest their entire beings, their whole lives in NOW. The women's movement had sanctioned a new sense of self; therefore, what they did in NOW was a personal reflection of themselves. Further, as often as not their involvement in NOW was their introduction to politics, and since they were not active in politics outside the organization, they tended to channel their political ambitions into becoming leaders in NOW. And, of course, given the reality of the world outside their organization, the opportunities for reaching a leadership position in the community or in a political party were severely limited, at least until only the last few years.

Ann Lewis, who is now the national director of Americans for Democratic Action (ADA) but in 1984 was the political director of the Democratic party, has been associated with NOW for several years and agreed that divisions within NOW are more personalized than those in other political organizations. Having grown up in a political family (her brother is Massachusetts congressman Barney Frank), she could speak from the combined perspective of a feminist and an experienced political organizer: "I suspect that there are three basic but overlapping reasons that divisions are so personalized in NOW, especially at the election conventions. First, NOW was formed in the early days of the women's movement when we emphasized consciousness-raising and making the personal political. Many of us learned about ourselves and how we felt about the world in intensely personal sessions, sessions which were often organized by NOW. Since the organization began on that basis, that theme of personal relationship, our sense of the validity of emotion as a way to approach issues, remains central. Second, there are actually very few divisions on issues, on substance. We're not a group that came together to debate priorities or direction—we understand what we have to do, and we're going to do it as hard and as fast as we can. Thus, when you have a choice between two women for office, the major differences between them are personal, and the choice gets played out that way. Third, and finally, the strength of NOW is that so many women feel personally connected and identified with the organization, so that sides on issues or choices of candidates carry with them personal expectations. That's why you'll hear debates couched in terms like, 'I've given x number of years of my life to NOW, this is my organization, so how can you vote that way or for that person?' When someone makes a different decision on an issue or a candidate about which you feel strongly, then it gets interpreted as a personal rebuke or betrayal."

With the 1980 California state convention, Ginny was still on the team, and that year was elected administrative state vice-president with the support of both Carabillo and Mandell. While the two women were not necessarily always on the same side of issues and had had their own political disputes over the years, they agreed that Foat was a good, devoted NOW worker. It was also apparent to Carabillo that Mandell was "tutoring" Ginny in Democratic party politics and wasn't surprised when both women ran as Kennedy delegates to the 1980 Democratic Convention. Foat was elected as an alternate, then appointed as an at-large delegate and floor whip by Kennedy's organization.

"Ginny and I were delegates, and since Karen Peters was California NOW state coordinator, she was appointed, too," Mandell explained. "Elaine Lafferty was an alternate, and we all went to the convention in New York City and spent a lot of time together. That's where I really taught Ginny about the political nitty-gritty. I can count votes that you can bank on, and that's what she learned from me. She also became a very good operative, lobbying, making independent floor decisions, and she made some great ones at that convention, and we became much closer friends."

"Everyone had the impression that Shelly was Ginny's mentor," said Carabillo. "Shelly was clearly more informed politically than Ginny, having been active in the Democratic party for several years. Ginny didn't have that background, and if anyone was teaching her about politics, it must have been Shelly."

Ginny Foat and Kay Tsenin disputed the impression that Shelly had brought Ginny along politically. "Sure, they were very good friends," said Kay. "But they were pretty much on the same level in the organization, and Shelly was never Ginny's mentor."

Nevertheless, it did seem clear that the allegiance of Mandell and Carabillo was crucial to Ginny's higher visibility, from their support of her appointment as 1979 conference coordinator to their high praise for her at national board meetings. More, Ginny's political alliance with Shelly Mandell became a close personal friendship, and after the Democratic Convention, they, along with other mutual friends, rented a houseboat. "We did nothing but eat Ginny's fettuccine," said Mandell. Later they and six or eight others took a mountain cabin together for a vacation. But, Mandell recalled, even as their friendship grew, Foat told her little about her past, and they never discussed her 1977 arrest. "That was probably because we never really had time, we were so busy doing NOW stuff, and beyond that I really didn't go out that much. She probably told others more, people she socialized with, like Trish Manning and Jan Holden in whose duplex she was living in 1979 to 80, and with whom she started Anodos, a feminist fund-raising production company. Maybe Ginny said things to her. Me, I knew zip."

"It was probably a combination of the way we in NOW work and Ginny's personality," Carabillo agreed. "I often work with people whose personal lives I know nothing about because we just tend to get on with business. At some point, if you establish a personal relationship and begin to socialize, then you become closer. In '79–80, I was at least friendly with Ginny, although we never really socialized. Still I don't recall ever learning anything very personal about her, and certainly nothing that gave a hint about her past. I assumed that she was closer in background to other NOW members, say, the usual middle-class upbringing. I'd met her as a businesswoman, those were the messages she was giving, and as is common in NOW anywhere, not just in California, we took her at face value and on the basis of what work she was willing to do. I don't think I was ever aware she hadn't gone to college, we never discussed that, and with the 1977 arrest, I think we all tended to accept what she said, that it had been a terrible error. She was back, nothing had happened, and to be truthful, it just slipped from my and others' minds."

Among Foat's friends was Elaine Lafferty, a younger woman who had recently moved from New York City to Los Angeles. She had worked for Manfred Ohrenstein, the minority leader of the New York State Senate, and had been involved in feminist politics in New York City but not in NOW per se. A thin, intense woman, her large dark eyes seem to confirm her acquaintances' feeling that she is "more an observer than a participant," a characteristic that stood her in good stead as she changed her career from politics and real estate to writing, eventually working for the Herald Community Newspapers, a chain owned by The Hearst Corporation. Her political activity in southern California at first revolved around Americans for Democratic Action, and in 1980 she had contacted Shelly Mandell about a NOW event. Shelly made a lunch date with her and asked Ginny Foat to come along. It was to be a "coalition-building" meeting, and Shelly instructed Foat to "hit her up for the ADA membership list."

"It was something like that," said Elaine, "each of us wanting a favor from the other. I don't think Shelly particularly liked me when we first met, but Ginny and I struck up a friendship, maybe because we are both New Yorkers. My impression was that she was a sharp cookie, very efficient, and that she worked hard and followed through, one of those people in political organizations about whom you'd say, 'Oh, she's a good one.' She struck me as a very warm, friendly, Italian, fun person, but despite all the rumors I've later heard about our relationship, I would not say I ever knew her very well. Part of that was because of the political nature of our friendship and what I noticed seemed especially true of NOW women in California. I've teased them about it, because at least in New York, after working with someone a couple of months, you sit down over a bottle of wine—'Hey, where did you come from?' You start to make contact personally, you need to know about their sensitivities and reactions. But out here in California they just don't seem to do that. NOW people who appear to be dear friends, who've worked together in the ERA campaign, who even have lived together, still know nothing about each other except perhaps what's gone on in the last five years. But with Ginny, it was also the way she presented herself. If I gave it much thought, I realized I didn't really have any idea of who she was. I don't know if I could have pushed closer to her, but I never really had that inclination."

Since her delegate was sick, as an alternate Lafferty was often on the Democratic Convention floor with Foat, Mandell, and Peters. Having had a good deal of experience in New York party politics, she, too, felt that Ginny was learning the ropes at this convention. Watching Shelly and Elaine lobby and work the floor, Foat gave the impression of taking cues from them, and she came away from the experience with newly acquired skills as a party operative.

According to NOW colleagues, by 1980 Foat seemed to have become adept at another political skill, the art of trashing, which a number of NOW members complained was all too common in the organization. Foat participated in a campaign against Jeane Bendorf, who had joined the Loyal Opposition and was running for regional director. At the convention Foat came up with the gimmick of distributing Band-Aids, proclaiming to delegates, "Ask me about my scars." In 1977 Bendorf had brought Ginny's plight to the attention of NOW members, helping to raise defense funds. But now Ginny was referring only to what she perceived as attacks on herself and others who supported Ellie Smeal and Toni Carabillo.

"Ginny certainly knew how to play hardball politics by then," said Shelly Mandell. "Even in 1979 when she coordinated the Los Angeles conference, I'd seen the way she tried to control it, played politics with it, and went over the line a little bit. Every person with power does it, but Ginny went farther than I would. But that's Foat. One of her traits is that she will go over the line a little and then doesn't know when to back off. Maybe it's because she's Italian, but her mentaility is that if you're on her side, you don't even talk to her enemies. If you're in her camp, and you have a drink with someone on the other side, then she seems to take it as an act of betrayal, and you're under suspicion. I remember she was waging war against Jeane Bendorf for regional director. I'd had a lot of fights with Jeane, too, but I still considered her a worthy political adversary, an amusing person, a good feminist, and I'd leave her free tickets for political events and still talk to her. I figure that we as women should have the ability to disagree on a political issue and not take it personally. But with Ginny it's all personal. I once heard her say to someone, 'You do not even speak to my enemies.' If you do, it hurts her because to her it is a breach of loyalty. That's different from the way I think. For example, Toni Carabillo and I waged a big fight over the Los Angeles chapter in 1980, but I considered her a good opponent, and I'd still talk to her and coalesce with her on issues we agreed on."

Carol Schmidt was dismayed by the personal remarks and gossip at the state convention that had women in tears. "I was sickened by the whole thing. I started going click, click, click—this is not the feminism of my ideals. Trashing is so common in NOW—it's happened to me, personally, since I was a leader of the Loyal Opposition. It's happened to a lot of people—and it's what started to turn me against the organization. But Ginny did the same thing back then, too. She and Jan Holden even published a very hurtful story in the NOW newsletter which described me as 'unstable.' "

Foat admitted that she had participated in such campaign tactics and rumormongering. "Much to my discredit, I watched it happen throughout the years to other people and I did not do anything about it."

Realistically, there was probably little she could have done to stop it when she was first rising in the organization. She was on "the winning side" and receiving rewards for her hard work and team loyalty. More, her identity seemed defined by her NOW commitment. As Kay Tsenin, who had returned to NOW work and been elected state action coordinator in 1980, grew closer to Ginny, she became aware of her friend's almost total devotion to the organization. "I have my legal profession, and I probably derive more feelings of who I am from that than from my status in NOW, so I could stay away from NOW for a while. But Ginny didn't have anything else. I think her whole evolution as a human being, to becoming Ginny Foat, came from the women's movement, which for her was NOW. She would always talk about having owed NOW a lot. She saw her birth as a person happen in the women's movement."

Politically, Ginny was recognized for creating liaisons with the Democratic party and unions, such as the AFL-CIO, as well as for her work on the J. P. Stevens boycott for the Amalgamated Clothing and Textiles Union. "The best thing about her was her ability to bring together coalitions and to work with all sorts of people," Kay said. "This, plus her dedication to the movement were important. She would work seventeen, eighteen hours a day, it was her entire life. In addition to my lawyering, I had my work with the Marin Abused Women's Shelter. For me that was very concrete in terms of results and having a sense of accomplishment, in contrast to my feelings that I wasn't getting that much professionally or personally out of NOW. But Ginny remained devoted to NOW and its members. She has incredible patience, which I think comes from her basically being a 'good girl.' That's what was so bizarre about her later being on trial for murder. She's probably the most law-abiding and socialized person I know. I hate rules and regulations, but Ginny functions within the system very well. Part of her success in NOW was that she tried to fulfill everyone's expectations and she did, because she was always putting her desires beneath those of others."

But what were her desires? On one level, of course, she was working for women's rights. But it cannot be overlooked that her political goals must have been coupled with a desire to become a leader of NOW and leave her stamp on it. To do so, she had to fight for her positions and accumulate power and support, and within the organization she came to be seen as politically astute. "She's a scrapper politically and a very good strategist," said Kay. "She has a gut-level feeling for politics, a kind of innate ability to see a situation and turn it around politically either to her advantage or to the side she's working for."

Devoting all her time to NOW, she invested it with the utmost importance. Friends and colleagues noticed it and saw it as one of the primary reasons for her success. "Ginny brought a feeling of importance to NOW," Kay acknowledged. "When I was a NOW officer, I thought, sarcastically, 'Big deal.' But Ginny always has a sense that what she is doing is important and she conveys it to other people. She makes anything she does seem important, from making meatballs to leading California NOW. It was as if she realized that by respecting herself and what she was doing, other people would respect her too. She had vitality and was a good speaker. She's gotten more polished, but in the beginning she had the ability to take a very political speech and in its context put 'homey' little vignettes that were always cute and funny and endearing."

Her background, while not that of the usual middle-class, college-educated woman of NOW, served her well in this respect. While there was no need to spell it out, audiences who might have considered NOW an effete, privileged group seemed to intuit that she was "one of them," that she could speak their language. Certainly there'd been criticism of NOW's middle-class image, and Foat was welcomed as a spokesperson who could contradict the stereotype, someone who was interested in working-class women and identified with grass-roots members. She won support from both more radical and less feminist constituencies.

Priscilla Alexander, a former New Yorker transplanted to San Francisco, is a state NOW leader but also a self-proclaimed radical with a strong streak of healthy cynicism. With her prematurely gray, shoulder-length hair, she knew people invested her with "maturity" and "wisdom." But she also considered herself "street-smart" and saw that as an important part of Ginny's appeal, too. "She was interesting to me because there were contradictions. She would wear all this makeup and nail polish, all those things that didn't fit my image of feminism. Yet she was outspoken, a little bit of a smartass like anybody from New York usually is. She also talked in very real, convincing terms about the issues; she could give a full-blown, highly articulate theoretical analysis of a question, but added a personal point of view, which is an unusual characteristic. She was bright, witty, and driven."

By supporting Smeal and the term extension, however, Foat had also provoked antagonism among NOW members in southern California who identified themselves as the Loyal Opposition. Since trashing was common between the two factions, Ginny's marriage in October 1980 occasioned a great deal of gossip. "We were all doing it," said Carol Schmidt. "I spread the rumors about Ginny's fourth marriage with great glee."

While Ginny was seen as "woman-identified" within the movement, members of the Loyal Opposition took great delight in the news of Foat's fourth marriage to Jack Meyer, a television producer whom she'd met while catering his daughter's wedding. As Schmidt put it, "That little marriage was an embarrassment. I *sure* knew about it, and I have to admit that I helped spread the rumors that she was being married for a giant engagement ring, a sports car, and a three-week trip to Europe. That's what we'd heard, and I remember announcing it as a gossip spreader at a party-type meeting of San Fernando NOW so that everyone was talking about it. I was delighted because it was really considered negative, and when she left the guy after a month or so, that was another wonderful juicy piece of gossip."

Shelly Mandell had been aware of Foat's phone calls to Meyer while they were in New York for the Democratic Convention. She had also learned that her friend had lived with him in 1979, then moved out, then took up with him again. But never did she think that Ginny would marry him: "She was rising in NOW, she was taking aggressive stands, and then she told me she was marrying this guy," said Shelly. "I was sick, but I felt I knew exactly why she was doing it. It was money, it was a midlife crisis. She was almost forty years old, she didn't have an education, she didn't have a way to make money. A good friend of Toni's had just committed suicide, and although Ginny didn't know her well, it freaked her out. I knew what she was doing—I'd been that route: the middle-class, affluent, middle-age Jewish marriage. I'd been in one myself, and my marriage had broken up in '77, '78. It was not a good marriage—thank God I got out of it—but there was a direct correlation to the percentage of my time that was going into the movement. You have to have an extraordinary relationship to survive being in the movement, and I knew Ginny's marriage wasn't going to work. I felt bad because she had so much promise, and I didn't see how she'd sit through those god-awful dinners where no one cares anything about civil rights or women's rights but only where the new great restaurant is or where they're taking their next vacation."

Still, since Shelly was a friend, she was loyal and supportive and was among the ten or so feminists who went to the wedding on October 12. The disparity between Ginny's NOW life and the life she was taking up in her fourth marriage was most apparent, Shelly thought, when some of Meyer's friends sent a stripper telegram with "congratulations" spelled out on the bodies of women dressed in bunny suits. "I thought all the feminists were going to throw up.

It was the most disgusting, sexist thing, and at Ginny's wedding yet! I left soon after that."

Elaine Lafferty attended the wedding as well, but in retrospect she said that Ginny's 1980 marriage hadn't surprised her: "My feeling at that point was, 'Almost nothing she does would surprise me.' I already had the perception that Ginny was a chameleon, which was both her strength and her weakness. She can walk into just about any situation and be comfortable with it, because she's flexible enough to become like them, to talk like them. If everybody has a Boston accent, Ginny will have a Boston accent, and I had already felt that a lot of her feminist rhetoric was part of her chameleon act, that it was pretty much old hat without much substance. As for her marriage, I'd seen her living a different kind of life, and I felt it was another example of her suddenly becoming another person. I think she thought the marriage was a nice idea for financial security, she thought he was somebody she could stand to be around and get a lot of cookies for it. Then after two weeks on another continent, maybe she said, 'I must have been out of my tree, I'm not going to be able to bullshit my way out of this one.' "

With Foat filing for an annulment soon after her return from her honeymoon, the rumor later spread that she no longer found a man sexually attractive, speculation fueled when Jean O'Leary, a leader of the National Gay Task Force, called the marriage "a relapse."

"That was a preposterous remark," said Elaine. "The marriage really had to do with money and security. It's like deciding to take a job because it pays a big salary, but you have to swallow all your other doubts about it. Ginny just discovered she couldn't do it. Besides, if that was the gossip, I'd say that's absolutely not true."

Shelly Mandell also thought that Jean O'Leary's widely printed remark was ridiculous. "Good old Jean. No, the marriage had to do with terror, and it was pretty strictly financial. I'd been annoyed that Ginny was taking her honeymoon right before the 1980 presidential election when we had so much to do. She went to Europe for two weeks, then I was in a shopping center at a rally for Carter and I ran into her, and she told me she was going to get a divorce. I realized that she just couldn't handle the marriage—it had been culture shock. I didn't hear the rumor that she'd realized she didn't want a relationship with a man, or that her marriage was a liability in the movement. No one would have said that to me because they knew we were friends, and I would have turned on them. The real problem was that she'd been used to working eighteen hours a day for the movement, and then suddenly she had to supervise a house and get dinner and sit through all those plastic conversations. She was way beyond that. The marriage had been absolutely calculated, she had it planned that she would stay married a year and a half, but she couldn't stick it out, and so she got a terrible financial settlement. A lot of people who later became pro-Foat were just mortified by her marriage, too. They went around saying, 'How could she do it?' They all thought it was for money, but I had been much more concerned about her personally since I knew how difficult it was going to be for her. That's why, when she told me after her honeymoon that she was going to get a divorce, I was delighted and said, 'Oh, great!' "

But why Ginny left the marriage so quickly was indeed a matter of speculation among NOW members. One rumor was that Ginny did some "paperwork" and discovered that while Meyer was amassing personal accouterments of a lavish life-style, his business was in trouble. Gossip also had it that either she hadn't liked a financial agreement that Meyer had asked her to sign or that he'd promised to help her and Jan Holden become Hollywood producers and then hadn't come through.

Some of the more cynical NOW observers also guessed that Ginny had soon learned that her marriage was a political liability as well. Pointing to the predominance of lesbians in NOW leadership and particularly in California NOW, they said that in order to get ahead in NOW it was better to be a lesbian, and that Ginny might have realized that she'd lost political leverage when she identified herself with "heterosexual privilege."

"I don't think one has to convert to lesbianism to get ahead in NOW," said Karen DeCrow. "To my knowledge none of the presidents of NOW has been gay. Someone once wrote a so-called history of feminism and called me the first lesbian president of NOW. I wrote her and said I hoped that the rest of her history was more accurate. I wasn't upset to have anyone think I was gay, I wasn't threatening suit, but I did think she should get her facts straight since in fact I wasn't. I don't know of anyone who 'slept her way to the top,' although that may have happened somewhere. Of course, Betty

Friedan had often criticized NOW for being too preoccupied with the issue of lesbianism. When she changed her position in her speech at the Houston International Women's Year meeting in '77, we were all roaring, 'Nine years too late.' But my impression was that especially among the opposition to the Majority Caucus, we were identified as 'the lesbian faction,' which, of course, was ironic. A lot of the most lesbian-baiting, homophobic members were lesbians and were opposed to our group. Still, lesbian baiting, even among lesbians, isn't surprising. It's like members of black organizations having internal fights and calling each other 'niggers.' "

Ginny herself disputed the allegation that she had married Meyer simply for personal gain or to open doors for herself and Jan Holden as producers. And while the rumor that she had become a lesbian to get ahead in NOW was surprising, she said she thought it was indicative that such gossip could be used against her by women who were themselves involved in such relationships but refused to acknowledge them publicly. "It comes down to not wanting to upset those members like Betty Ford who they feel add power to the organization. They espouse issues, like prostitution and lesbianism; resolutions are passed at every national convention, but nothing is ever done publicly. That has to do with mainstream respectability. We can advocate stands about lesbianism but we certainly can't talk about the fact that half the leadership is. Yet people used it against me out of personal animosity."

After her annulment, Ginny returned to full-time feminist activism. Then, in the spring of 1981, Ginny, Shelly, Elaine Lafferty, and Jan Holden were considering opening a women's restaurant together. According to Mandell, Ginny raised the question of whether her past might prevent their getting a liquor license. "I thought she was referring to the Nevada arrest, which I knew had been dismissed. But she said we'd better check how her record looked before putting her name on the license application. I called someone in the city attorney's office, a friend of my brother's, and asked him to run a check. When we were about to make an offer on the restaurant, I bugged him. He said, 'Forget the liquor license, that woman was arrested for murder one.' I said, 'But that was dismissed.' He said, 'Yeah, that was dismissed, but it's still bad news.' I didn't tell Ginny, but he also said, 'Stay away from that broad'—he's that kind of guy. Still, I never saw a piece of paper, I never knew where he checked, and only much later was I told that he probably didn't have access to the big national computer, and all he got was the 1977 arrest in California on the Nevada charge, and the dismissal of it."

When Foat was told that the check had shown that the charge was dismissed, she apparently didn't ask if Mandell had seen a piece of paper, or to what charge Mandell was referring. It seemed rather that Foat believed or convinced herself that her friend's record check confirmed that no Louisiana charge or warrant still existed. In retrospect, Shelly insisted that she didn't know what she was checking for, and Foat hadn't told her specifically that she was worried about something turning up in Louisiana.

The restaurant idea came to naught, and Ginny and Jan Holden's production company, Anodos, which combined Ginny's catering expertise with Jan's show biz know-how to organize fundraisers in the area, wasn't a huge success either. Ginny was soon back to full-time work in NOW, although she was nominally unemployed. Having been administrative vice-president of the state chapter, she was in a good position to run for California state coordinator in the 1981 NOW election. But with her lack of income, she couldn't afford to take the position. What finally made it possible was NOW President Ellie Smeal's suggestion that the state coordinator be paid a salary.

Shelly Mandell had considered running for the position herself but then decided she'd rather go to law school. "I had dinner with Ginny and told her I'd support her," said Mandell. "I also warned her, though, that I wouldn't be able to be there for her all the time. Still, I thought she'd be a great person for the job, and that maybe she could go on from there to run for regional director, which would put her on the national board."

Foat also had the support of many chapters and individual members, and especially helpful were her ties to Toni Carabillo and the Los Angeles NOW chapter, the largest and wealthiest chapter in the state, whose fund-raisers had contributed significantly to the income that allowed the state to pay the salary of a full-time coordinator.

"My support helped her, of course," said Carabillo. "I knew she was going to run, and in a sense she was the logical person since she'd been administrative vice-president, the number-two spot, when Karen Peters was state coordinator. Then Judith Meuli and I worked out the by-laws change to make it a paid full-time job."

In 1981, Ginny's devotion to NOW, her long hours and unfailing commitment, were rewarded with a $24,000-a-year position.

The state coordinator of California NOW had previously been almost invisible. The state chapter was more a conduit to the national NOW office. It had never been as important in the NOW structure as the local chapters or specifically as the Los Angeles chapter, which had the most funds and attracted the most media attention with its annual walkathon and access to Hollywood celebrities who would lend their names and make appearances for the ERA. But with the combination of a full-time paid position and her own personality, Ginny set about changing this.

"Ginny was going to make the office into something," said Shelly Mandell, "and a lot of us helped her do it. When I'd been president of LA NOW, I got a lot more press than the then state coordinator, Karen Peters, and I realized that and sometimes I'd back off to give Karen and the state organization more visibility. So I was aware of the problems that made Ginny fight for more recognition. But it was also Ginny's own ambitiousness, and she began to say things that made me think that she was going a little weird. For example, when I was the political action committee member, I'd plead our cases in the Washington office and bring back checks. Ginny wanted to hand those checks out herself, and she said she wanted nothing under five grand. 'I'd be embarrassed to give less than that,' she said. I said, 'What the hell's wrong with you?' I don't know where she got it. For years, people in NOW said it was Kay Tsenin, not Ginny. But it also had to do with Ginny's wanting to make everything she did important."

After her election, one of Foat's methods of increasing her visibility was to visit chapters up and down the state, a change particularly welcomed by northern California chapters, since they'd long felt eclipsed by Los Angeles's power and direct ties to the national office. Her good friend Kay Tsenin was especially adamant on this subject, and soon Ginny, too, seemed intent on weakening the hold of the Los Angeles chapter over the rest of the state; most particularly she seemed to want to undermine what she perceived as the entrenched power of Toni Carabillo, who had long been regarded as not only a NOW founding mother but also, because of her editorship of *The National NOW Times* and enduring close friendship with President Ellie Smeal, a controlling force in NOW politics.

"I suppose the motivation was Ginny's personal ambition as much as it was a desire to change the state structure for the good of the organization," said Carabillo. "There were negatives to the attempt to make her position more visible. It's a nuisance to have conflict between the state coordinator and local chapters, or to have the state coordinator feel that the Los Angeles chapter is stealing her press. For that reason, in fact, the Los Angeles chapter has always felt it would be better for the state coordinator and her office to be based in Sacramento because her main job should be getting legislation passed. Still, when Ginny set about making her position more visible, she had to deal with the fact that local chapters are autonomous from the state chapter; she had to depend on the goodwill of chapters, and I think she neglected the coordination of the statewide efforts by chapters. She made her office more visible, but really only in the sense of statewide Democratic party politics, and that did not involve the chapters."

Whatever her political goals, it also seemed that she was focusing on Toni Carabillo personally, and while Carabillo herself did not consider it a feud, she immediately noticed that Foat seemed to want to lock her out. "In the first place people have always attributed more power to me than I actually have, I guess because of my friendship with Ellie, as well as Judith's and my editing of *NOW Times*. After Ginny was elected, I think in essence she saw me as a person competing with her for authority in the state. I went to two state board meetings, and I realized that I would have my hand in the air to speak and she just couldn't seem to see me. I had great difficulty being recognized. It became apparent that she intended to get into a fight—and we did have a couple of fights—but since we were just entering the ERA countdown campaign, my feeling was I didn't have time for it. She could do what she wanted, I just wouldn't go to state board meetings anymore. From my perspective, what she was doing was silly since not only had I helped her get the paid position but I also had no desire to hold any other NOW offices, so I wasn't in competition. I suppose, though, her feelings went beyond that, and what troubled her was my closeness to Ellie Smeal. She, like some other people, felt that the friendship puts me in a position of power because I can get Ellie's ear, and obviously it's an advantage. I think Ginny wanted a direct line to Ellie herself and thought of me as an impediment to a closer relationship with her. But Ellie was never going to say, 'Toni, forget it, I'm friends with Ginny now.' She would've included Ginny in, not excluded me out. That was an error on Ginny's part, and maybe it had to do with her turning things into a personal vendetta rather than seeing political differences as part of the process or another turn of the wheel. I always considered that a political shortcoming of hers, and I think maybe it was part of her insecurity about herself and her position. It was a kind of paranoia, even then, and she'd get upset when she saw friends talking to people she considered enemies. She also sees it as a series of confrontations during that period, when I wasn't aware of confrontations since I just withdrew at the state level. Later I realized that Ellie must have been hearing complaints from Ginny, because she asked me, 'Why are you and Ginny always fighting?' I asked her what she was talking about since I hadn't spoken to Ginny in months."

The Loyal Opposition, however, still regarded Foat as a sellout to Toni Carabillo, Los Angeles NOW, Ellie Smeal, and the national office. In retrospect, members of the dissident group admit they may have exaggerated Foat's allegiance to the establishment; at the time, though, they cited as examples of her sellouts her agreement to abolish task forces and her crusade, along with Toni Carabillo, to change her title from state coordinator to president. Toni and she argued that "coordinator" confused the press since it implied an administrative assistant even though it was meant to convey NOW's nonhierarchical, nonauthoritarian structure. Now her opponents felt Foat and "the team" wanted to undercut the feminist principle in the name of expediency and public image. As one critic put it, "Why don't we just call her 'Chairman' and get it over with."

Unbeknownst to the Loyal Opposition, though, Ginny still felt that Toni Carabillo was undercutting her importance. After all, she was developing her own constituency, not only in California but also in Illinois and Oklahoma where she'd worked in stepped-up ERA campaigns, and she soon seemed to feel powerful enough to challenge what she saw as the direct line between Ellie Smeal and Toni Carabillo.

When Foat discovered that Smeal had assigned national NOW funds to open an ERA campaign center in Los Angeles, which would be run by the LA chapter and Toni Carabillo, there was a major confrontation. "I complained to Ellie," Foat said. "By planning this with Toni, she had violated the usual procedure of going through the state coordinator. Toni always felt that the Los Angeles chapter should have certain privileges because of her closeness to Smeal. But

I believed in equality among the chapters and among the members, so I used my power as the state coordinator to make sure things didn't happen that put other members or chapters in a one-down position, and I won that struggle."

Toni Carabillo knew there'd be problems with the way Ellie had gone about planning the ERA office. Realizing that Ginny was, as she put it, "on an upwardly mobile course" and insistent on making her office important, she was aware that Ginny would be upset by what she agreed was a mistake on Ellie's part. "Part of protocol was that she should have notified Ginny first, and I was upset that Ellie hadn't made that call, especially since I knew Ginny was touchy and would be angry. But I didn't see it as a confrontation in the context of all we had to do for the ERA campaign. It was just another one of the damned irritants, and I had no problem with another ERA office."

Smeal didn't see the issue as a confrontation or a struggle either. "I thought it was a great compromise," she said, "since we got two ERA fund-raising offices, one in LA, one in San Francisco. I saw that as beneficial to the movement, not as a battle which Foat won."

At this point, however, Foat seemed to have focused on Ellie Smeal as another adversary, presumably because of Smeal's continued friendship with Carabillo. Any criticism of Carabillo, she suspected, was interpreted as disloyalty to the national office. "The sickness in NOW is that you have to agree totally with the national leadership if you want to be seen in a positive light," she said. "You get power by 'paying your dues,' not in terms of the work you do for the movement but in terms of 'gofering' for the leadership. But then they saw me becoming extremely successful without their advice and without their support. Toni was used to operating on her own, making the decisions, and all of a sudden I wasn't going along. She proceeded to try to destroy me with Los Angeles NOW members. It was all petty stuff, but her people believed me."

Foat thought Shelly Mandell was beginning to take Carabillo's side. Mandell denied it. Having been president of the Los Angeles chapter herself, she knew there was bound to be tension between the Los Angeles chapter and the state coordinator: "In fact, I was the person who suggested to Ginny that she call Ellie Smeal directly and remind her that as state coordinator she should be involved in the planning of the ERA countdown campaign office. This was after I'd gotten hysterical phone calls from Ginny asking what she should do about Toni Carabillo. I was in law school, I wasn't involved as much in the ERA campaign, but I guess that's when she and Toni got into battles. But I was Ginny's friend, and several times before, when I'd been president of the Los Angeles chapter, I'd taken her side in arguments against Toni. Still, we began to have differences of opinion on political things. Later people said she was always competing with me, trying to prove that she could make it without me. But the most I was saying then was, 'Ginny, you can't move the focus of the organization up north.' I also told her not to pick a fight with Toni with one hand tied behind her back. That is, she had to campaign for her turf in southern California, too, not spend half the week in San Francisco."

Mandell criticized Foat's poor judgment in trying to lessen Carabillo's power by aligning herself with Kay Tsenin and making San Francisco more important. She recalled that one of their first significant arguments occurred when, of all the ERA rallies up and down the state, Foat wanted Kay Tsenin's San Francisco ERA rally to be the biggest and the best. "Tom Hayden was running in a tough race in southern California," said Mandell. "He needed the exposure in the Los Angeles area, but Ginny wanted him and Jane Fonda in San Francisco. She said, 'He better do both,' and she was using her leverage as state president to force him to come north."

Ginny Foat and Kay Tsenin had other explanations for the growing tension between Ginny and Shelly. According to Kay, Mandell had expected privileges and favors from Ginny because of their friendship. "She wanted certain things for herself and her close friend Elaine Lafferty, and Ginny was growing weary of such requests, especially when Mandell was attending law school and was giving less and less attention to her NOW duties."

Mandell insisted that this was not the reason for their disagreements, and that in the spring of 1982 they hadn't yet broken with each other. She said she was still essentially on Foat's side although perhaps Ginny was annoyed that she had had to withdraw somewhat to concentrate on her law school courses. "I just couldn't be there for her all the time. I also began to hear from other people that Ginny was on a power trip, and I began to see things like that, too. I think the whole thing began to go to her head. She is an amusing, charming person and very loyal. But that spring she began to pull some numbers; she was really intent on making her office the most important office and herself the most important NOW leader. So she'd travel across town when I, as the NOW political action committee member, was presenting a check to Maureen Reagan, for example, just to make sure she got the publicity. I also noticed that she would take things too far, maybe make promises she couldn't keep, or step over the line by saying things like, 'Oh, by the way. I signed your name to this or that.' Friends would have to say, 'Hey, Foat.' Then she'd usually get a migraine, and we'd have to bail her out and clean up her act."

Elaine Lafferty had already begun to wonder whether Ginny's migraines were more conveniently placed than random. They seemed to occur whenever there was a difficult issue coming up: "Perhaps there might have been some timing involved, or perhaps it was just that they were stress-related so she'd get them when she was under pressure." But along with noticing the tension between Shelly and Ginny, Elaine also became more aware of "Ginny's numbers" before Shelly had herself. "Shelly tends to be a very trusting person and doesn't analyze people too much. Maybe as a writer I analyze things too much, but I began to see a little bit below the surface and wonder if Ginny were really a friend. Shelly was kind of tootling along the way she does, and it just seemed that Ginny had focused on working on Shelly in little political things. When Ginny gets projects, you really know it, and it seemed to me that undermining Shelly had become one of her projects."

Why she was doing this was another matter. People guessed that Ginny felt competitive with her friend because Shelly still had political clout in southern California and certainly in national NOW. Others linked it to Ginny's ambitiousness, that she wanted desperately to get to the top, and it didn't matter whether it was NOW or the Soroptimists or any other organization. It was not so much a question of feminist principles but an overriding desire to succeed; in that sense, Shelly Mandell was old baggage, a reminder of just how far she'd come with others' help and support. But despite some hints of tension, despite Elaine's remarks, Shelly said she still remained loyal to her old friend.

Toni Carabillo didn't see Ginny very much during this time, but she began to hear that people were dissatisfied with the way Ginny was handling the state office, and there were complaints about the "power trip" she and Kay seemed to be on. She also had one heated phone conversation with Foat herself. "I told her that I thought the things she was doing were destructive. I was very angry, but that was the call when I realized she had the ability to rewrite history. I'd seen it before, but that phone call really brought it home to me. She simply denied that any of it happened, took no responsibility for it, and seemed to believe that she had in no way caused any of the problems. It had all been done to her, she said with that whiny tone of hers, and it was as if we were all out to get her."

Jean Conger was still working in NOW's national office in Washington that spring and was well aware of the problems out in California, because, she said, Los Angeles politics couldn't be separated from what was happening on a national level: "Toni Carabillo felt she'd gotten Ginny elected as state coordinator and therefore Ginny owed her a certain allegiance. When Ginny refused to go along with their programs or took power away from the LA office, Toni and her chapter became disenchanted with her. As a result Ellie Smeal became furious because her good friend Toni was furious, and by 1982 the national office realized that Ginny would not go along with her old political allies. On a personal level, she challenged Toni and refused Shelly Mandell and Elaine Lafferty favors. But on a political level, she was questioning the unfettered power that the national leadership had assumed by ignoring the membership."

Ellie Smeal was aware of the discord in California, but attributed it neither to the personalities involved nor to the fact that it was the California chapter. "NOW never had a clear definition of what the state chapter should be, so state chapters were frequently seen as competitive with big city chapters. In California, the state president would seem competitive with the San Francisco or Los Angeles presidents. For example, what does the state president do vis-à-vis the president of the LA chapter in regards to the media?

"Like other state presidents, Foat saw herself as representing the smaller chapters. The LA chapter is so much bigger than other local chapters that it feels it carries much more financial responsibility. I don't think it was especially peculiar either to California or to Foat herself, but there was obviously discord during this period. I guess she saw things as confrontations that I didn't. I don't think Ginny and I ever really had knock-down, drag-out fights. I suppose the problem was that Toni Carabillo was and still is a very good, close friend. If Ginny and her supporters had a fight with her, they would think they'd had a fight with me."

Nevertheless, in 1982, Ginny Foat did focus on Ellie Smeal as the person who set NOW policy and was thus responsible for leading the organization "out of the revolution back into the mainstream."

"NOW leaders saw that each move they made toward the mainstream gave them more power," she said. "By 1982, Ellie Smeal had become more and more powerful, and I thought she and the national leadership had been seduced by power and the corporate image. After ten years of giving up everything for the ERA, we'd gotten nowhere because we were no longer addressing the real issues. The average homemaker or the woman in a factory still didn't know what the ERA could do for them. So I felt there needed to be a change."

NOW was scheduled to elect a new national president at its convention that October. Ginny was not alone in thinking that running for president provided the opportunity to change NOW's policies. Since Jean Conger had seen the problems at close hand, she also considered running and, resigning from her administrative position in NOW's national office, she told Ellie Smeal of her possible candidacy as well as Ginny's.

"When Jean Conger talked to me about Ginny's running for president," Smeal recalled, "I think she was worried. Although I hadn't known Ginny at the time of her '77 arrest, I'd heard that she'd been accused by an abusive husband in another state. But that didn't set off any alarms for me because it was my understanding she'd been cleared across the board. Jean was also thinking about running for president, but at the time I was trying very hard not to show any preference for any of the possible candidates, so I made no comment about either Ginny or Jean."

Despite the tension between them, Shelly Mandell thought Ginny's presidential candidacy was a good idea and urged her to run. "On a Sunday in early June of '82, we held a spaghetti dinner at her house and tried to convince other people to support her. Not everyone there was immediately enthusiastic; they said they had to think about it some more."

There were some who wanted to wait until Ellie Smeal had made her endorsement; others were also interested in another candidate, Jane Wells Schooley, NOW's national action vice-president, who was already campaigning in NOW chapters across the country. Still others, while admitting that there was no one yet whom they wanted to support, said they weren't sure that Foat had enough national experience. But no one at this meeting considered Foat's background an issue or a problem.

Ginny was already telling people that she was definitely in the presidential race. When Jean Conger heard from Jan Holden that Ginny had made the decision, she had two reservations. The first was the familiar political one: Since Ginny had not yet served on either NOW's national board or in a national office, did she have the administrative experience required to head a large organization with a substantial treasury? More troubling, though, was what Jean knew about her 1977 arrest.

"How is Ginny going to handle her background?" she asked Jan.

Holden said the question hadn't come up, and nobody wanted to press Ginny on it. This was a hazy area that even her closest friends were loath to raise as an issue. She herself had seemed to waver, sometimes insisting that the Louisiana case was resolved, at other times saying she was okay as long as she didn't set foot in that state. She said she assumed that the warrant had been dropped because two computer checks (the first by Shelly Mandell for their proposed restaurant's liquor license, another by Washington, D.C., police when she'd been stopped for a traffic violation) had both turned up nothing. While she acknowledged that Bob Tuller didn't actually have it in writing that the case was closed, she'd also been told that in 1978 John Sidote had been informed that Jefferson Parish was removing its warrant for him. Further, Tuller said that at the time of her release in Nevada a Jefferson Parish district attorney had told him he'd decided not to pursue the case against Foat since Sidote had refused to testify. That in itself did not guarantee the case was closed, but neither Tuller nor Foat requested a written statement. Whether this was carelessness on the part of Tuller or a naïve trust in the legal system, Foat couldn't be sure. But she insisted that it wasn't necessary for her to force Louisiana's hand by demanding a speedy trial. It was up to Louisiana to make the first move; that was her constitutional right.

In her friends' minds, however, the question was disturbing enough to cause alarm about her candidacy. Through her friendship with Jan Holden, Jean Conger had become close to Ginny by then, and in mid-June 1982, she again spoke to Jan. Since she, too, was thinking of running for president, Jean didn't want Ginny to think she was trying to force her out of the race by questioning the resolution of the case. Her concern, she repeated, was not a political one, nor was she worried that Ginny's background might give NOW a bad name.

"I'm worried that she could get creamed with it—personally hurt by it," she told Jan.

"A lot of people already know about it, it isn't a secret, so it doesn't have to be a problem," Jan argued.

"It's one thing to have it in *NOW Times,* but it's another thing to have it in *The New York Times,*" Jean replied, finally convincing Jan that someone should talk to Ginny about it for her own sake. Since Jan didn't want Ginny to question Jean's motives either, she agreed to do it herself.

Jan sat Ginny down to discuss "the problem." But when she mentioned Jean's anxiety, Ginny flared.

"If she's so concerned, why doesn't she call me herself?"

Her response was exactly what Jean had feared. "I suppose she didn't really want to deal with the question so it was easier just to get angry and accuse me of bringing it up for my own political reasons," said Jean. That was when she decided to speak to Ginny directly.

Ginny still sounded angry when in late June Conger reached her by phone in the Los Angeles NOW office. Jean again tried to explain that her question had nothing to do with her own candidacy.

"How are you going to handle the matter?" Jean asked at last.

"Why should I have to handle it?" Ginny said.

"Because of the kind of scrutiny people get when they run for NOW president."

"It's all resolved, it's taken care of, so I don't have to handle it," she repeated. But then she added, "I'll handle it like any . . ." She paused. "I was a battered woman," she said.

Jean didn't know exactly what Ginny meant by saying that she'd handle it as "a battered woman," but she didn't press her, because Ginny was still insisting that it wasn't a secret. Nor did Jean add what she was also thinking: If Ginny was hedging and it wasn't resolved, then she would never know when it was going to come up again. "I didn't know that much about the case," said Jean, "but I wasn't going to say either that she was lying, or, 'It isn't resolved because I can hear you're hedging.' "

"You have to consider how you're going to handle it, and we're going to have to talk about this again," Jean said finally, choosing to leave it at that for the moment.

Whatever Jean said to Ginny must have been more disconcerting than what Jean recalled of the conversation, according to people who were in the NOW office at the time. The room was filled with volunteers busily working on last-minute details for the June thirtieth ERA rally. Ginny was summoned to the phone—"Jean Conger, for you." She took the call in another room, then returned. Standing in the doorway for a moment, she looked stony and white-faced. As she passed Shelly Mandell and Elaine Lafferty, she said, "She's going to use it." Then she went and sat at her desk.

Shelly and Elaine could only guess what Jean had said, but their general impression was that with the upcoming presidential campaign Jean was going to "play hardball" and had threatened Ginny in some way.

Because Ginny still seemed so distraught, Shelly Mandell took her friend into the coffee room to have a private conversation. Whatever tension there was between them, Shelly still felt close to her and wanted to help.

Over a cup of coffee, Ginny said that Jean had asked her how she could run with her background. Shelly's primary reaction was anger—how could Conger pull this, essentially blackmailing Ginny to force her out of the presidential race? She assumed that Jean was referring to the 1977 arrest on the Nevada charge, and since she knew that was dismissed, she reassured Ginny, "People know what happened in 1977, the rumor won't go anywhere. This kind of stuff doesn't belong in NOW politics." Then she instructed Ginny that the way to put a stop to it was to go to her lawyer and get the documents that proved the charge had been dismissed. Ginny agreed she should do it, but still was quite dismayed that Jean should raise these doubts about her background. Suddenly it dawned on Shelly that whatever Jean was using to force Ginny out of the race must have come from Jan Holden. Jan had been close to Ginny, but with Jean's new friendship, perhaps she'd shifted allegiances. Shelly wondered if Jan was sacrificing her old friendship in order to give Jean's presidential candidacy a leg up. What that information was Shelly didn't stop to consider. She was just too angry at Jan and Jean. Besides, the problem solver in her came to the fore, and again she reassured Ginny that all she had to do was have Tuller provide the official papers that would render Jean's threat totally ineffective.

They went back to the office and tried to get some work done. But the phone call had cast a pall over them, and later Ginny said that she needed a drink. Elaine Lafferty had to run an errand, but she agreed to meet Ginny and Shelly at the Central Park Cafe in Brentwood. A fourth woman, another friend of Ginny's, would also meet them there. Shelly and Ginny drove the twenty-minute distance to the restaurant.

The restaurant is casual, with a large picture window, a bar in front, and an eating area with about fifteen wooden tables and cane chairs. It was supposed to be "New-Yorky," hence its name. But with its hanging plants and salads and quiches, its only resemblance to Manhattan eateries is its late hours. It wasn't crowded that night, and Shelly and Ginny and Ginny's friend took a table for four, with Elaine arriving a short time later.

The three women were already deep in a serious conversation focused on NOW politics and their indignation that Jan and Jean should have used this ploy to try to undermine Ginny's candidacy. Ginny was livid, too, but she could hardly believe that Jan would do this. "I'll never forgive her," she said. It was still unclear, though, what precisely Jean had said. It seemed vague, something about an unresolved problem in her background, and Ginny wasn't being very specific. While the three women concentrated on the effect this would have on Ginny's candidacy, Elaine still couldn't understand what Jean could have said that was so threatening. Back in the NOW office she'd asked Shelly. Shelly didn't really seem to know either and told Elaine she assumed it was the 1977 arrest on the Nevada charge. This, however, didn't make sense to Elaine. Since the charge had been dismissed, why was Ginny now referring to a problem that might be used against her?

Finally Elaine interrupted the discussion about NOW politics and what Foat should do. "Ginny, I don't see how we can help you unless we know what the hell you're talking about," she said. "All I've ever heard was that you were married to a man with possible Mafia connections who framed you for murder." Since that charge had been dismissed, Elaine wanted to know what the unresolved problem was.

Ginny took a breath. "All right," she said, then called the waiter over and ordered a glass of red wine. Once he'd served them, she took a drink, lighted another cigarette, and began to narrate her 1965 saga. She talked briefly about a first marriage in New Paltz, working at a boys' school, and then she described meeting Jack Sidote. He was a bartender and a singer, she said. He sang her a song, and she thought he was wonderful—a very dramatic, intense person who provided a great deal of excitement, sexual and otherwise.

The three women had never heard any details about this man before; as they listened intently, Ginny described what had drawn her to him. Elaine now recalled an ERA rally at which Henry Winkler had been one of the celebrities. She'd been surprised to see Ginny blushing and embarrassed, girlish, giggling, and fluttery in the star's presence. Elaine had asked, "What's the matter?" when Ginny hung back and, even as state coordinator, didn't introduce herself to Winkler. "I've always had a crush on him," Ginny told Elaine. "You know, the rooftop guys in New York? That was the kind I went for." Clearly she was referring to the "Fonz" character Winkler played, the "tough guys," the leather-jacketed gang members who carried on their liaisons on city rooftops.

Now, when Ginny was trying to explain Sidote's attraction, Elaine quipped, "Henry Winkler on the rooftops?"

Ginny laughed and agreed. He did indeed seem "heavy trade" to the other women, especially when Ginny mentioned he carried a gun in his car. She didn't say anything about Mafia connections—that wasn't part of her story—but she explained that when they decided to leave town and drive cross-country, her family was very mad at her and nobody in town would speak to her. Why her family and friends had had this reaction, none of the women asked, although Elaine suspected it was because he not only had a bad reputation but was married. For the moment, however, they just let Ginny talk on as she narrated a journey through several states. "He had friends here and there, and that's why we went to places—he thought those friends would give him jobs."

From the beginning of the trip, Ginny told her friends, Sidote was drinking a lot and acting crazy. The jobs wouldn't come through, or the ones he found never lasted, she said, and she would work as a waitress in bars and restaurants in the various towns they passed through. Ginny said she was also learning the ropes of bartending from him and she stressed over and over again that there were good times, that she was in love with Sidote, that this was the most important relationship of her life. Still, she conveyed the impression of danger and adventure, violence and hot, steamy nights. Sidote would get into bar brawls, she said, or she and he would get into arguments, and there was plenty of fighting. But, she implied, she could give as good as she got, slugging him when she could, and one time even managed to hurt him badly when she threw a vase at him.

Shelly and Ginny had often said they were friends because they came from similar backgrounds. But for Shelly, this was a new aspect of Ginny. Now she added a detail of their cross-country saga that took Shelly's breath away.

"We would always have to leave towns in the middle of the night," Ginny said.

"Why?" Elaine asked.

"I don't know," Ginny said.

"Didn't you ask?"

"No, I didn't."

"How could you be living with somebody and have no idea what was going on?"

Shelly interrupted. "You gotta understand, you just don't ask questions in those kind of relationships."

Elaine was willing to admit that, at twenty-six, she was from a younger generation that hadn't experienced the same force of tradition. She told herself it was possible that Ginny had been conditioned not to ask questions, and she realized that Shelly was accepting Ginny's explanation because she was thinking of her own first husband who'd also been domineering and demanding. Nevertheless, it also seemed to her that Shelly hadn't registered the implication of what Ginny was saying—that Sidote had gotten into some kind of trouble to require them to flee a town, perhaps to flee the police. But Shelly had precluded Ginny's explanation of why by insisting, "Of course, in that kind of relationship you just go."

Despite Ginny's allegations of violence, the man's drinking, his nuttiness, his jealousy, and the hints that he was up to no good, Ginny said she stayed with him. To Elaine, however, Ginny's tale did not betray the sort of passivity one associated with a battered woman's syndrome, except for the fact that she hadn't asked Sidote any questions. While Ginny said she was sometimes afraid of him, she also stressed the good times, the adventure, her sense that eventually they'd achieve what they'd set out for—a good job and making a lot of money. She was also, it seemed, in a position to leave had she chosen to. Her livelihood didn't depend on him; indeed she gave the impression that she was working more than he. There were no children, and at least two of the women at dinner that night had met her parents, knew they were warm and loving, and surmised they would probably have welcomed their daughter home at any time, their anger over her "elopement" with a married bartender notwithstanding.

Ginny rambled on with surprisingly detailed anecdotes about towns they traveled through, the hotels, people in bars, who said what to whom. At one point, she added that a third person, a waiter, was traveling with them and that in his jealousy Sidote accused her of having an affair with him.

For all these details, however, none of the women could yet discover where the problem was. If this was the background to which Jean was referring, it seemed tawdry and ugly, maybe stupid—"why did she stay with that creep?"—but hardly something to keep her out of the NOW presidential race. Still, it was as if the pressure had built up, and Ginny had finally uncorked the bottle; the words were flowing fast, the details, seemingly random and pointless, pouring forth, as she for the most part looked down at the table and lighted one cigarette after another. She took sips of wine but did not touch any of the food she'd ordered.

Shelly and Ginny's other friend were content to let Ginny talk. It was as if they knew she had to get this off her chest; in support and sympathy they were willing to listen. Elaine, however, asked questions when she didn't understand, when the saga seemed confused or the emotions seemed inappropriate or unanalyzed.

Finally, Ginny mentioned going to New Orleans, a town that, she added, she liked a lot. She said she worked in a bar there; she also explained that Jack would go out at night and she often stayed in the hotel and "did a lot of laundry." It wasn't clear whether this was a good time or a bad time in her and Jack's relationship. But suddenly she slowed down and then paused, as if to consider where she was in her story and what exactly to say. Finally, she announced, "That's where I think one of the things happened."

Since her narrative had been prompted by the question, What is this unresolved problem? the three women now realized that Ginny had come to the crucial part of her narrative. Indeed, suddenly she began to weep as she stumbled into her account, pausing and gasping. Shelly reached over and took her hand to comfort her.

Ginny now said that she had been in their hotel apartment one night when Jack came in. Once again he told her that they had to get out of town right away. But first, he said, she had to "go downstairs and clean out the car."

"I went down to the car, and the backseat was filled with blood," Ginny sobbed.

The three women were too stunned to react for a moment. Ginny was crying as she repeated over and over again how much blood there had been. She looked up and held Shelly's gaze, as she exclaimed once more, "You can't believe how much blood was in there!" Then she looked down again and told of having to get rags, then more rags, water and more water from the hotel apartment. She seemed focused almost exclusively on the act of washing the car, at one point mentioning that it was such a mess with blood and guts, adding, too, that their traveling companion had come down and helped her. She didn't seem aware of what her listeners might be thinking, nor did she address what might be logical questions.

Elaine had wanted to ask why, if the car was parked outside the hotel, nobody had noticed her or the car, especially since Ginny had implied that it took her over an hour to finish the cleaning. But she didn't want to interrupt as Ginny went on about "all the blood." Finally, however, Elaine could contain herself no longer.

"Ginny, what had he done?" she asked.

"I don't know," she said.

"What did you think the blood was from?"

"I didn't know. I didn't think about it."

Elaine alone pressed her, but Ginny was still crying copiously and continued to insist that she neither knew nor thought about why the car was filled with blood. All she'd done, she said, was clean up the mess as instructed; then she went upstairs, and after packing their belongings, the three of them drove out of New Orleans. She had now stopped crying and she continued the story of their travels. While none of the women expressed dismay, Shelly found herself tuning out; so shocked was she that she could barely take in what she'd heard.

Elaine was not listening carefully either, but for other reasons. She was startled, too, yet she was also analyzing what in Ginny's story didn't seem to make sense. If this was the problem in her background, what had come of it—an arrest, a warrant, or was it an unsolved murder? Besides, she had the uncomfortable sensation that Ginny had told only part of the story, or in a way jumbled her narrative because she'd decided precisely what she'd let them know. It was a catharsis, Elaine thought, but self-consciously constructed to tell her friends just one piece of the whole story, and in such a way that it wouldn't reveal too much.

Then, too, Elaine questioned Ginny's copious tears. She'd never seen Ginny cry before, or maybe just once. Sure, she thought, cleaning out a car full of blood and guts was awful and disgusting and maybe you'd cry a bit when you told how terrible your life had been. But Elaine had the impression that such nonstop, convulsive sobbing could only be prompted by guilt, grief, and terror. She began to wonder if there wasn't a hidden confession behind this rambling account of a blood-filled car. Moreover, she couldn't believe that the Ginny Foat she knew would block so insistently against the obvious conclusion that the man she was with had offed somebody. "She may be a lot of different things," Elaine thought, "but she's not stupid." She couldn't accept Ginny's self-portrayal that she'd sent her intelligence on holiday and not thought, "My God, he's killed somebody. I better get the hell out of here, or I'll be next."

Ginny only briefly mentioned Nevada, but then brought them to the part of the story when she and Jack bought a bar in California, and then Jack was convicted of shooting a young Samoan. Ironically, she talked about this as a "bad rap." It sounded to Elaine as if she believed that while Ginny suspected he might have committed other murders, this wasn't one of them. He was simply protecting the bar from a group of Samoans who were trying to rob him. In this case Sidote had been unfairly accused, she told her friends, and during his prison term she visited him faithfully. Then she described her job on the *Princess Louise,* having a friend named Bobbie, and meeting Ray Foat. He was married, she told her friends, a gentleman and very nice. Jack was now coming home on weekend passes and work furloughs, and she said that it was no piece of cake. She'd "had it" with the kind of life they'd been living, the financial pressure, the tension. That was when she realized she wanted to get away from Jack, she said, and told the women that they had one last fight when he tried to strangle her. Her roommate had then walked in. "If it wasn't for her I'd be dead," she said. (Elaine thought she said the roommate's name was Cheryl, but later it was a woman named Clare who would testify to this scene.)

From there her life had changed, Ginny said, and she married Ray Foat and started her own catering business. Then, in 1977, she told them, "these guys" came to the door of her home and arrested her. She said the cops accused her "of all these murders" and she didn't know about any of them. They told her that Jack had confessed to fourteen murders, and that she was under investigation in all of them, including "a body they'd found on Ventura Boulevard in the sixties." (Perhaps she was referring to the shooting of Richard Busconi, whose body had been found at the corner of Anaheim and Western avenues in San Pedro; she'd been questioned about this in 1969. But none of the women knew such details, and they were given the impression that the police had run wild with Sidote's confessions.)

"Then what was the Nevada charge?" Elaine now asked.

Again Ginny said she had "no idea." She'd been extradited—there was one police matron who'd accompanied her whom she'd liked. But then Jack had decided not to testify, and the charge was dropped, she said. Rather than offering any details of the Nevada charge, however, she turned back to the experience of being in Sybil Brand jail. She said she "went crazy," adding that she continued to have nightmares about it. She told them that she still often slept with her arm extended from the bed as prisoners were forced to do to show they were in their cells.

But once more there arose the question of what the problem was if the Nevada charge had been dismissed. Elaine questioned her again.

"I think there might be something in Louisiana," Ginny replied. But she added that she didn't know if Louisiana had dropped the charges, if they'd ever made any charges, what those charges could be, or if Louisiana had just been working with Nevada.

"You'd better find out," said Elaine. "It would make sense to find out what the hell's going on."

"Yes, I should," Ginny said dully.

Shelly agreed, but as was her wont, she was once more thinking excusively in terms of NOW.

"Call your lawyer," she said, "get the papers, show it's resolved before you go into the campaign."

Elaine was thinking along different lines. There'd been no mention of a warrant, yet that wasn't her primary consideration anyway. From what Ginny had said, obviously something had happened back in Louisiana. It seemed strange to her that, whether the police knew about it or not, whether charges had ever been brought or later dropped, this woman had lived with the knowledge of something about that night, something that had caused blood in the car. It was a devastating story, to say the least, and especially shocking when it came from someone who'd run a catering business, dressed in "power suits," and headed a respected and established political organization. "We all have different phases in our lives," Elaine thought to herself, "but Ginny must have been such a different person to live like that, and then carry the story around with her." Moreover, she wondered how Shelly could have been best friends with Ginny and still never have heard any of this before.

Just as bizarre, though, was the way the conversation ended. Ginny was once again calm as she and Shelly and her friend outlined what she should do in terms of NOW. First Ginny would call Jan and find out why she'd done this to her. Then she'd call her lawyer and "resolve" it. Shelly had been so shocked by the story that she was antsy to get back onto comfortable, "solvable" ground and then head for home. Here was a problem, and Shelly was a problem solver; without even acknowledging to herself the implication of what Ginny had said, much less how upset she was, she urged Ginny to take the necessary steps with her lawyer and then decide if she still wanted to run for president.

Ginny agreed, and she and Shelly talked for a few more minutes about how to deal with "it," whether it was "an unresolved situation in one of those states" or whether "the charges had been dismissed." Ginny said she would take this into account and would have to reconsider her candidacy. Nevertheless, since the earlier computer check had shown nothing, Shelly was optimistic that Tuller could easily stop Jean Conger's malicious gossip. Once again she urged Foat "to get it resolved, then go for it."

The women left the restaurant; it seemed that all but Elaine were thinking in terms of NOW or Ginny's presidential candidacy. With a kind of moral and legal obtuseness, the other women seemed not to have registered either what washing blood out of a car might suggest, or that, in fact, Foat might very well be in jeopardy—not in NOW, but with the police.

Nor did Shelly seem to share Elaine's dismay when Elaine phoned her later that night. It was as if she'd already blocked out the dinner conversation, Elaine thought, when Shelly replied to her exclamations only in monosyllables.

"Do you realize what she was saying? . . . Who the hell is she? . . . Do you think what I think?"

Elaine wasn't mincing words. Shelly was a good enough friend that she chould say anything. But when Elaine voiced her strongest suspicions, Shelly could only reply, "I don't know, I don't know." Clearly she didn't want to deal with it.

The evening had left the women with a lot to think about. Elaine began to reevaluate Ginny and their friendship and found herself growing cool. Shelly focused on the political—she still wanted Ginny to run for NOW president, yet she couldn't overlook the continued political numbers Ginny seemed to pulling on her.

What did Ginny Foat herself think about? Obviously, she'd have to decide if she should have Tuller take whatever steps were necessary to resolve the problem, to "handle" the difficulty. She'd also have to reconsider her candidacy. But one had to wonder if she also woke up the next morning and asked herself, "My God, what did I say last night? Will this come back to haunt me?"

Foat later implicitly denied that she had ever revealed such startling details about her past to her NOW colleagues. In her autobiography, *Never Guilty, Never Free,* she said that one of the persistent rumors circulating in California before her trial was that "I had confessed to both the Nevada and Louisiana murders in front of Shelly Mandell and Elaine Lafferty while having dinner at a restaurant in Los Angeles."

Whatever actually happened that night, it was significant enough, it seemed, to alter dramatically the waning friendship between Foat and Mandell.

THREE

Feminist
Protection

WHILE Ginny reconsidered her decision to run, Jean Conger went to see Toni Carabillo to discuss her own candidacy. Most national candidates made a point of stopping by Toni and Judith's home in Los Angeles to lobby for Toni's support, but Jean Conger said she was particularly surprised by Toni's reaction to her running.

"She told me that she didn't have any problem with my candidacy except that I'm a lesbian. I told her I didn't think it had to be a consideration since my background was strong enough to run on the issues. For the people to whom it's important to have a lesbian at the head of the organization, they would know that I am. Otherwise I didn't think it was important. But Toni said she thought it mattered because of NOW's image and the possibility that the press would know. Quite frankly, I believe that's one of the reasons that Ellie Smeal picked Judy Goldsmith as her successor. She was one of the few people in the national office who is straight."

Carabillo denied having this response, especially since she was intent on staying neutral until Ellie Smeal decided whom to endorse. "I was telling everybody who was thinking of running, like Jane Wells Schooley, who had also come by, 'Wonderful, the more the merrier.' I'd only heard that Ginny was also considering running, and I thought she was naïve to be aiming so high. She wasn't ready yet, she hadn't yet served on the national board, she should have run for that first. I supposed it was ego, so I wouldn't have supported her anyway. But that day Jean came to see me, she also told me and Judith Meuli, who was in the room, too, that she thought that with her phone call she'd convinced Ginny not to run because of her background. Jean seemed absolutely convinced that she still had a problem. I assumed she knew because of her close association with Jan and Jan's closeness to Ginny. I didn't really know what the problem was, it was a murky area, but I thought Ginny was crazy to think that she could become NOW president without its being exposed. It had come up once with the liquor license, I gathered, and I guess her saying that she couldn't set foot in Louisiana should have told me that there was still a problem, too. Nevertheless, even without knowing about the Louisiana problem, I felt that having just one murder charge dismissed against a candidate wasn't the best background for a NOW president. And it seemed as significant as anything else that this was coming from Jean Conger and that she had successfully talked her out of running."

Ginny soon told Shelly Mandell that she had decided not to run for president, saying that she didn't want either the move to Washington or the hassle of a campaign. For whatever reason, Shelly said she accepted her explanation and did not suspect that she was hesitant to resolve the problem in Louisiana or was frightened that her past might be revealed.

Earlier, Kay Tsenin had had her own reservations about Ginny's candidacy. Although she said she would support her, she also thought that Ginny should get on with her plans to finish her BA and go to law school. Otherwise, she'd be putting off what was in her own best interest for the sake of the organization. They had several conversations about this, Ginny at first deciding to work for her BA through Antioch Without Walls while running for NOW president, then planning a budget to save enough money so that she could go to law school after her term of office. Ginny also discussed with Kay the question that Jan and Jean had raised. Finally in July she told friends that she'd decided not to run for president after all. Then, a few weeks later, she announced to Kay that she would campaign for vice-president for action, the number-two spot in NOW's national office.

Wasn't she worried that the same thing might happen if she ran for or was elected vice-president? Kay asked her. No, Ginny said. She'd reasoned that a NOW vice-president wouldn't receive as much public attention as president. "I had to take it into consideration that even though the computer checks showed nothing," Foat recalled, "there was still the possiblity that the media would use the fact that I had been arrested. Since I wasn't interested in the presidency per se but in the direction the organization was taking, I could do that as well if not better as action vice-president without getting a lot of media coverage. Since my number-one interest in life was not to become president of NOW but in the more philosophical question of NOW's activism for women, I decided to run for vice-president."

"Besides," she told Kay, "I can't continue to live under this specter."

The specter she seemed to fear most, however, was media attention; that, after all, was her rationale for seeking only the vice-presidency—she would be out of the public spotlight. Nevertheless, wasn't she concerned about the effect on NOW if the story broke anyway? If so, then it would seem irresponsible, inappropriate, to say the least, for her to run for any NOW national office until she'd made sure that the Louisiana charges had been dropped. Even though she'd become a public figure in California politics, no one had delved into her background. Wasn't it naïve not to guess that the media might still investigate her past even as vice-president if there was any hint of scandal? And with several NOW colleagues and close friends referring to a "problem," with people coming away from the Central Park Cafe shocked and dismayed by her statements that night, wasn't she aware that her true vulnerability might lie with her sisters as well as the press? Didn't she have to worry that with one leak, one careless statement, someone might become intensely interested in what had happened back in Louisiana, whether there was a warrant in the system or not, whether or not she held a NOW national office?

But Foat seemed not to give this a second thought. She had her own constituency, particularly among California NOW members who agreed with her that Ellie Smeal had centralized power in Washington, D.C., and was too busy playing mainstream politics to pay attention to NOW's grass-roots membership. (Ironically, many of these were the same members who, as the Loyal Opposition, had criticized Foat earlier.) When Smeal endorsed Goldsmith as her successor, Foat heightened her attacks, arguing that Smeal had chosen Goldsmith so she could control her from behind the scenes. Confident that her criticism of Smeal and the national office would win votes, Foat began to organize her campaign and asked Jan Holden and Jean Conger to be her campaign managers. Whatever doubts Jean had about Foat's background for the presidency, she was persuaded by Foat's argument that a vice-president wouldn't receive media attention. Moreover, given Kay and Jean's own interest in and work on domestic violence, they began to prepare a paper that would explain the "background problem" in terms of Ginny's having been a battered wife. If the question arose at the convention, they'd circulate it at the caucuses. Further, Jean's earlier worries about something being unresolved were put to rest, she said, because Ginny was so insistent that it had been handled. For the moment the specter was banished from everyone's mind, including Foat's, it seemed.

The political became personal, too, as the lines were once more drawn between the factions in California. There were those who didn't see the political issues of northern versus southern California, or of a grass-roots versus a centralized structure, as significant. What they criticized was Ginny Foat's ambitious and willful desire for power. They felt her success had gone to her head; they believed that her close relationship with Kay Tsenin was motivating her to focus on San Francisco. More, even though she didn't make public pronouncements identifying herself with them, Ginny counted among her friends the more radical and dissident factions in NOW. What made them more radical on political issues was unclear, but the underlying message was that they were more rigorous in their feminism because of their openness about lesbianism. Their overriding theme was "a closet lesbian is not a real lesbian," and they formed alliances with the National Gay Task Force members who often criticized NOW for not taking stronger stands and for the homophobia that they felt was still endemic to the organization.

Most important, others in the organization thought Ginny Foat was making poor decisions and was ill-advised in her moves to consolidate her own power. Moreover, Shelly Mandell was upset that Ginny's desire to prove that she could succeed without her was sorely testing their friendship. Beyond that, it seemed to be prompting Ginny to take silly stands against both Shelly and Shelly's close friend Elaine Lafferty.

According to Mandell, the California state NOW convention in July of 1982 was a typical example of Foat's obsessive drive for power. "It became a joke, and everybody called that conference the 'Ginny and Kay Dog and Pony Show.' You could not walk into any workshop, any rap session, without hearing Ginny's voice, which is, of course, very noticeable because it's high and sort of whiny. I'd also known Kay for years, we'd been friends, too. Before, she hadn't been big in the organization. She was considered a gofer, but then she was in the limelight, trying to act the number-one adviser to Ginny. At the conference, it was the two of them together, taking everything over. They wouldn't let Jane Wells Schooley speak, because she was running for president, even though two weeks later, when Jean Conger finally dropped out of the presidential race, Foat threw her support to Wells Schooley."

Meanwhile, Shelly had decided to join Toni Carabillo and support Goldsmith, even though a large California contingent was lining up behind Wells Schooley. "In a sense, my people, the people I would have been with before, some I'd even trained, thought I'd deserted them by going to Goldsmith. That's where a lot of the later problems started, with that whole group ready to see me as the enemy."

In Foat's mind, however, the antagonism with Shelly was fueled by personal more than political differences.

"It had to do with Shelly's need to be involved in politics and my ability to do it successfully," she said. "But it also goes much more into a personal thing I'd rather not even talk about, regarding a relationship of hers and who that person is."

While Foat chose to be circumspect, others knew she meant Elaine Lafferty, but why Elaine and she had clashed was unclear. The real trouble, Kay Tsenin stressed, was that Shelly's repeated requests for favors for herself and Elaine had worn thin. "That summer of '82, Ginny let it be known that if she were elected to national office, she'd do everything she could to keep Shelly off the national political action committee. That was an appointed position and the only NOW office Shelly could hope to have in the organization since her visibility within the state had become so low. I'm sure those remarks got back to her."

While Shelly Mandell said that Kay's explanation was unfounded, she also agreed that the tension between her and Ginny was simmering all that summer. Ginny was letting her ego run rampant; before, Shelly had overlooked or ignored it or chalked it up to Ginny's personality, her insecurity, her need to be important and respected. But now she realized that there was growing antagonism, coldness, and aloofness from the woman who'd once been a close friend. That Ginny's hostility might have been connected to her anxiety about her revelations in the restaurant didn't occur to Shelly, however. She thought it was just Foat on a power trip, and considered the feud as more "a silent war than one big battle." But when still asked by Foat for her support on political issues at a national board meeting in July, Shelly had had it. She wasn't complying so readily, she said, and Ginny took her aside in the hallway for a private conversation.

" 'I don't want to talk politics,' " Shelly recalled Ginny saying. " 'I want to talk personally. I want to talk about our friendship.' "

"Ginny, there isn't any to discuss," Shelly replied, turning her back and stalking away without waiting for Foat's reaction.

Shelly was upset by the loss of their friendship, but to her it hardly seemed abrupt or unwarranted, given the tension that had been mounting. In the welter of motives on both sides, however, what seemed strange was why Foat had chosen to compete with or heighten the antagonism of Shelly and Elaine. Was it purely political—wanting to consolidate her own power while proving she no longer needed her old mentor? Was it simply a matter of resenting Shelly's inability to give as much of her time either to Foat or to NOW activities because of her law school courses? Was there even some jealousy that Shelly was now closer to Elaine, that she was listening to another New Yorker, a younger woman but one whose political experience and urban sophistication reminded Foat of what she didn't have?

Presumably there had to be a deeper level of motives. How else was one to understand what would later become Foat's almost obsessive suspicion that Shelly Mandell was the chief agent, Elaine Lafferty the prime instigator of a conspiratorial plot? Despite the tension of that spring and early summer, Shelly and Elaine had urged Ginny to run for NOW president; they'd also been two of the three women whom Foat trusted enough to tell part of her secret story. Had she awakened the next morning and regretted the intimacy, in a sense blamed Shelly and Elaine both for urging her to run for president (thereby raising the specter again) and for obliquely creating the pressure that had prompted her to confide in them? Perhaps then she'd exacerbated the hostility between them in order to keep them at arm's length, to deny the intimacy and trust on which she thought she'd have to depend. Having allowed herself to become vulnerable, having revealed to her friends a side they'd never seen before, did she then feel she had to erect defensive walls around herself? Not consciously, but unconsciously, had she used political moves as a way of shutting out the women she'd let get too close?

Alternatively, the political fervor and ambitiousness could have been a way of compensating for feelings of insecurity, helplessness, and perhaps fear. So absorbed with becoming successful at the national level of NOW, perhaps she did not even realize that she had antagonized Shelly to the breaking point. Shelly's remark in the hallway would then have come as a complete surprise. Moreover, for Foat, who drew distinct lines between friends and enemies, Shelly's dismissal could have seemed the kiss of death. With no friendship, with no trust between the two of them, Foat may have realized not only that she'd lost a friend, but that she'd provided an "enemy" with both the method and motive to hurt her.

But the thought of "getting Foat" hadn't occurred to her, Shelly insisted. Ginny hadn't even told her of her decision to run for vice-president for action. "Maybe it was her pride, maybe she was afraid I wouldn't support her," said Shelly. "Which I wouldn't have, but not because of our personal differences or because I'd reevaluated her after that night in the restaurant." It was a logical political decision, she argued, and not motivated by revenge. "I'd already told everybody that I was for Goldsmith, not Jane Wells Schooley, and since Ginny had tied herself to Wells Schooley, I would have been working against Goldsmith if I'd supported Foat. Still, I wasn't actively campaigning either against her or for the Goldsmith slate's vice-president–action candidate, Mary Jean Collins."

While behind the scenes Foat was linked to Jane Wells Schooley, her campaign stressed that she was running as an independent "off the slate." Her point was that it was necessary to challenge Goldsmith's slate of candidates, who, she said, were simply "handpicked puppets," selected to continue Ellie Smeal's policies of mainstream politics. Foat's campaigners even went further, describing Goldsmith as a "Smeal clone," "a song girl," another one of the NOW "oatmeal crowd, Midwest and mushy," who "can't think her way out of a paper bag."

Both Ellie Smeal and Judy Goldsmith insisted that Goldsmith alone was responsible for her slate. "I put it together, not Ellie," Goldsmith said. "Ellie was among the people I talked to about my candidacy and running with four other candidates for office. But I also talked to a lot of other people, both in the NOW national office and to activists around the country. Ginny puts it in terms of running 'against a team,' but that isn't the reality of the situation. The other four candidates and I chose to run together because we had a mutual agenda, programs or platforms for the organization, but no one was running against any individual per se. We perceived ourselves as running *for* the offices, not *against* anybody, and when Ginny saw herself as running against a team, she was perceiving a monolith where there wasn't one. As for our 'mainstream politics,' it's also not accurate. One of the fascinating things about NOW is that one end of the political spectrum attacks us for being hopelessly conservative and establishmentarian while the other end of the spectrum says we're wild-eyed, crazy, radical feminists."

Toni Carabillo also criticized Foat for calling Judy Goldsmith and her fellow candidates a Smeal conspiracy. Carabillo argued that Goldsmith was the logical front-runner for president, given her many years of experience and the long hours she'd devoted to the national administration, and the same was true of Mary Jean Collins. "Because of her support for Wells Schooley, Ginny was actually part of a slate, too," said Carabillo. "Even though she and her campaign managers said she wasn't, she and other candidates traveled around the country together and supported each other. A slate is a slate, no matter what monkeyshines you go through to say it isn't so."

Jean Conger insisted that Foat was absolutely not part of a slate. "I know that for a fact, because at one point she was considering it, and Jan and I said, 'You do that and we're pulling out.' " But as Ginny campaigned around the country, she won the votes of NOW members who were also antislate, those who saw the Goldsmith slate too dominated by Ellie Smeal and her administration's policies, and unofficially Foat supported other off-slate candidates as well.

"There were many delegates who didn't support Foat for the same reasons I didn't," said Carabillo, "and that didn't have anything to do with what Jean had told me or the 'rumors' of a problem. I'd seen her work as state coordinator when she'd taken unilateral actions without ever enlisting the chapters in a statewide mobilization on a project. That's exactly what the action vice-president has to do nationally, so I felt Ginny had neither the experience nor the competence for the job. Also some people believed that some of the credentials Ginny listed in her campaign literature were not her own. I doubt she's alone in that, but this tendency to claim an enormous background in NOW makes me uncomfortable. I've often said that the NOW nominating committee should do more than just check that a candidate is a registered NOW member. I'm in the minority, however, since the ethic that operates in NOW is that we don't check. But at the time, even though I might have been worried about Ginny's problem, I didn't feel it was important because I knew she wasn't going to win."

But Foat's supporters saw Carabillo's refusal to support Ginny as payback for Foat's criticism of her, Ellie Smeal, and LA's power.

"Sure, I had conflicts with Ginny when she was California president and I was the Los Angeles chapter president," said Carabillo. "But that didn't mean I wasn't speaking to her, or that we were out to get her. I was out to defeat her for vice-president, no question, because I supported Mary Jean Collins, who was part of Goldsmith's slate. But there were four people in the race for vice-president, and there were members who were supporting the other candidates besides Foat. That wasn't a conspiracy, though. Ginny had enemies just because you don't operate at any level in NOW, not as chapter president, not as state president, without making enemies as well as friends."

Although they'd heard inklings of a whisper campaign against her in Los Angeles, Ginny, Jan, Jean, and Kay were all fairly confident when the national convention convened in Indianapolis in October 1982. During the candidates' speeches, however, Jean and Jan were approached by one of the few members of the Los Angeles delegation who had helped with Ginny's campaign. She had lobbied Judith Meuli persistently to put Ginny's name second on the preferential ballot. If Ginny had any chance of winning, she needed to get into a runoff.

"Judith Meuli just asked me how I could work for Ginny when she has a murder charge still outstanding," she told Jan and Jean. "Do you know what she's talking about?"

"Yes, I can explain," said Jean, telling her about the 1977 charges and repeating Ginny's assurance that the case was closed.

Still, she was alarmed. Was Judith Meuli spreading these rumors? Was Toni Carabillo *that* eager to stop Ginny's candidacy? Jan and Jean went directly to Ginny and Kay and told them what they'd heard.

"Maybe you should bring it up in your speech," Jean suggested.

"No," Ginny said. "I don't want to deal with it now."

She'd been ready to distribute her "battered woman's" statement and talk about it at the campaign caucuses the day before, but it hadn't come up. Now with no real time for any questions or discussion, she felt it was too complicated to bring up in her campaign speech. If and when she was elected vice-president–action, she would make battered women an issue on which NOW should take a strong stand, and then would talk about her own experience. But so close was the election that she simply wanted to confront the women she held responsible for the rumors.

Ginny and Kay, along with Jan and Jean, found the Los Angeles member who'd reported Judith Meuli's remark and then marched on Judith.

"Why are you doing this?" Ginny demanded.

Judith could hardly deny making her remark in front of the Los Angeles member. "Besides, it's true, it's true," she said.

"No, it's not," Ginny flared. "Those charges are resolved."

"For your sake, I hope they are," Judith replied.

It sounded like a threat to Jean, and she turned to Toni, who had just joined them. This was, she remembered, the woman who'd written the essay "Toward a Feminist Ethic." "What are you doing?" she asked.

"I don't know what the hell *you're* doing," Toni replied. After all, she pointed out, Jean had been the person who'd convinced Ginny not to run for president because of an unresolved problem.

"Toni, I'm doing the best I can," Jean managed to mutter, the exchange having so boggled her mind.

In recounting the incident later, Carabillo said that she herself had heard no rumors on the convention floor even when she was lobbying for Collins against Foat. She was not present when Judith made her remark, but Judith described the incident to her. "I think she told me she said something like, 'Go ask Ginny if she can clear up the murder charge.' Maybe she said 'open warrant,' because really it's one and the same thing. But she didn't know anything more than what Jean Conger had reported to me and her that day when she talked about Ginny's background problem."

Carabillo had been in the back of the convention hall in the smoking area when she saw Judith surrounded by Ginny, Kay Tsenin, Jan Holden, and Jean Conger. "I walked forward to find out what in heaven's name was going on. They were in a heated conversation, accusing Judith of spreading rumors. Judith denied that she had, insisting she'd said it only to the one Foat delegate because she'd felt that Ginny should level with her own supporters. That's when Ginny said, 'It's resolved,' and, once more, if it came up at the conference she had a paper prepared to show she was a battered wife. Of course, in my own mind, I didn't think this disproved there was an open warrant."

Carabillo was also carrying on a cross-conversation with Jean Conger, reminding her that Jean, after all, was the person who had raised the question in the first place, indeed had given Judith the information on which her remark was based. At one point, according to Carabillo, Kay said to Judith, "If Ginny loses the election, I'm going to sue." As for Judith's statement, "For your sake, I hope it is resolved," Carabillo didn't think it was a threat. "I can see how someone might take it that way, but I think she really meant that she hoped it was cleared up for Ginny's own sake, not that she intended to do something about it. But Judith was unnerved by them, so it was all in how they chose to hear it. I could've killed her for making that first remark to the Foat supporter, but that's the typical kind of straight-arrow statement she'll come out with, with no hidden agenda and no sense of politics. But that was not the beginning of a conspiracy, and we did not spread the rumor."

Toni walked away, irritated that Kay was flexing her lawyer muscles. Jean was stunned that this would be used against Ginny by sisters in the organization. But Toni was not the only one having second thoughts about Foat's earlier admission that she was okay as long as she didn't go to Louisiana; after hearing the rumors in general or thinking that Judith knew something, some delegates were upset that Foat would run for a national office with the charges apparently less resolved than she had insisted. What would public exposure of the charge do to the movement? they asked. Toni felt it was a legitimate question, and at least not as simple as Ginny would like to have it.

Shelly Mandell wasn't present when Judith Meuli brought up the unresolved murder charge, but she soon heard about it. "Nobody can control what Judith says, not even Toni. Judith is so outspoken that she gets herself in trouble all the time. It was not a good thing for her to have said, but the next thing I knew, here come Foat and Conger and maybe Jan Holden, barreling down on me on the convention floor. It's true, there had been a blast of gossip from people across the country, and they'd been coming to me to ask me about it. Before then they wouldn't have dared to ask because they knew I was Foat's friend and very loyal. But once we'd broken, they asked me at the convention, and I simply said I didn't know. I'm sure Judith didn't know there was still a warrant either, but she's so proper, I suspect she thought that just the Nevada arrest and dismissal would've been bad enough for NOW. Plus there was the talk going around after Conger's call that Ginny might not have cleaned up everything in her past. Foat then confronted me with something like, 'Is it true you're responsible for this whisper campaign?' I said, 'Ginny, I didn't like it when Conger did it to you with her phone call, and I still don't like it. It's not my style, and I don't know anything about it or what Judith did.' I don't remember exactly when I asked Ginny, 'Is it not an issue?' Maybe then, maybe later, but she said, 'It's handled.' What was in my mind was, 'What a dummy I was to have pressed her about something being a problem if there was something there.' Still, when she said that, I assumed she meant that she'd finally checked with Tuller and it was resolved. I didn't start the rumor or spread it, but at that point there were enough people who had heard it that they were wondering about Ginny's past and putting herself in the limelight; they wanted to find out what the facts were. I don't know if anyone did anything about it then, but there was talk that Ginny shouldn't be running with that still in question.

"I admit, though, that I was mad at her, and my feelings were again hurt when she accused me of starting the whisper campaign. Still, given what I learned later, I do think it was irresponsible of her to run for a national NOW office. I suppose it was partly her personality. She has the ability to say, 'The room is pink,' and it is; by sheer force of will, she'll make it so. She won't deal with something if she doesn't want to. Because of the two computer checks, mine and the one in Washington, D.C., she wanted to believe it was resolved, even though most people later thought that in her heart of hearts, deep down, she knew something was there but didn't want to come to grips with it."

Elaine was standing with Shelly when Ginny, Jean Conger, and Jan Holden pulled her and Shelly aside on the convention floor. Accusing Shelly of starting the rumor, they demanded that she stop it, Elaine recalled. "Shelly said something like, 'I had nothing to do with starting it.' At that point I think I muttered something obscene. Shelly told Ginny that if she had a problem she should find out where it was coming from because it wasn't from her. But I don't think Ginny ever believed it. I hadn't yet heard about Judith's remark, but then, of course, everyone began asking everyone else, 'Gee, have you heard about this rumor going around?' So of course by then the rumor was circulating even more than it had before."

Later Shelly Mandell and Elaine Lafferty ran into Kay on the floor. Kay said they greeted her casually, as if nothing had happened.

"Fuck off," snapped Kay, sure that they'd spread the rumor. But they told her what they'd already said to Ginny.

"If you aren't responsible," said Kay, "then you can at least try to stop it." She turned away, refusing to speak to them, just as convinced as Ginny that they, with Carabillo, were using the rumor to defeat Ginny.

Rumors were common enough at NOW conventions, but one about a murder charge was bound to spread like wildfire. The question was how seriously the delegates took such talk that surely wasn't the usual NOW gossip. NOW members and leaders alike were bound to ask why Foat hadn't nipped it in the bud by making a statement or producing proof that the talk was unfounded. That she didn't only fueled speculation that there was still a problem. It was the Eagleton "skeleton in the closet" issue, which would naturally arise if in fact something in Foat's background would put NOW in a vulnerable position.

"I heard the rumor at the convention, and I knew it stemmed from the '77 incident," said Ellie Smeal. "There was always an undertone that there was a problem, but no one knew what it was; still, the rumor had nothing to do with a possible arrest, or at least no one spoke of it that way. Nevertheless, although some people said the rumor was a big deal at the convention, I never saw it that way. I was wearing the hat of the retiring president of the organization, and I was most concerned with creating a smooth transition, so even though in retrospect people might have thought Foat's vice-presidential race was the hottest because it ended up being the closest, I was most worried about the presidency. Besides, there are usually a lot of rumors at these conventions, even though we all try to discourage them. One of my strategies is to try to stop rumors, not to help carry them. At the '82 convention, I felt it was especially important because I was going out of office and I wanted the election to be focused on the issues and conducted on a high plane.

"Still, it didn't even occur to me to wonder if Foat was being irresponsible by running for office, because I didn't think there was any doubt about its being a closed case. I didn't know the New Orleans thing existed, and since I'm not naïve when it comes to the law, I would have presumed that with her high public visibility, an arrest couldn't have been a possibility in her mind. To this day, I still don't understand if she did or did not know that the case was still open."

That was the hazy area. When Karen DeCrow heard that Carabillo was upset at Foat for running with even the slightest hunch that the case might be unresolved, she agreed to some extent. But she also wanted NOW to take some responsibility, too.

"People in public life have certain responsibilities, of course. For example, I love to drive fast, but I wouldn't drive eighty miles an hour for anything because I'm aware I'm a public figure and I don't want to get picked up. But the organization also has a certain obligation to make sure it won't be embarrassed. I was angry at McGovern not to have found out about Eagleton's background, and I was angry at Mondale when he didn't ask Ferraro the right questions about a husband in real estate in Queens or rather in Little Italy—I am trying not to sound ethnic. Of course the person under scrutiny has a responsibility to answer truthfully if asked, 'Are there any skeletons in your closet?' But that person usually has such self-interest in forgetting the skeletons or interpreting the skeletons differently from the person looking for anything, that it makes sense to have an objective opinion about the possible problem."

Yet no such mechanism existed in NOW that would either have stopped the gossip or prompted a discreet suggestion to Foat that her candidacy should not proceed until the matter was resolved.

Three hours after Foat's confrontation with Carabillo and Meuli, the preferential vote was taken: Mary Jean Collins, of Goldsmith's slate, came in first, another nonslate candidate was second. Foat was third by four votes, and thus was eliminated from the runoff, which Collins eventually won. Foat and her supporters were convinced that the whisper campaign had cost her the election. If people hadn't changed their vote because of the rumor, she would have been in the runoff, and since the second-place finisher was also off-slate, the Foat camp reasoned that those votes would have gone to her and brought her a victory over Collins.

Carabillo and others argued that the election was neither lost because of the rumors nor as close as Foat was saying. "Ginny missed coming in *second* by four votes," said Carabillo. "Mary Jean Collins won the first ballot, and even if Foat had come in second, not all the other 'antislate' votes would have gone to her. So it wasn't close, and she certainly wasn't on the verge of becoming a national leader. She was farther away than that—one more candidate at least."

Foat was angry and disappointed, but she turned to the future. She would serve out her term as president of California NOW, would still criticize national NOW policies when she felt it necessary, and in January 1983 she would run for the southwest region's director-ship, which would put her on NOW's national board. She put the whisper campaign behind her and went on about her work.

"None of us thought anything would happen because of the conversation with Toni Carabillo, Judith Meuli, Shelly Mandell, or Elaine Lafferty either," said Kay Tsenin. "We felt very betrayed by what they'd done but I put it out of my mind, and I think Ginny did, too. Maybe I had some vague thought that perhaps they'd try to get some document from New Orleans saying that the charges hadn't been dismissed and use it against Ginny within the organi-zation. But I don't think Ginny or any of us really considered it a possibility."

After the conference, NOW members, particularly those in California, continued to raise the possibility of something still hanging over Foat. Some people were rumbling about asking the elections committee to check it out, or asking Ginny herself. But Shelly Mandell said that while she heard these rumors, they didn't enter into her thinking when she campaigned against Foat for regional di-rector. "No question, I was out to defeat her," Mandell admitted, "but that was because I knew she didn't support our new president, Judy Goldsmith, and wouldn't help her on the national board. I did the things that everybody does, I lobbied against her, I supported her opponent, I voted for the election conference to be held in Ar-izona because that wasn't where Foat's base was. So I was fighting her on the issues, and I knew I could beat her with votes. I don't believe personal stuff belongs in NOW politics."

Yet another confrontation between Foat and Mandell occurred in December 1982, one that Foat saw as the catalyst for Mandell's letter to Jefferson Parish. The California state Democratic conven-tion was to be held in January of 1983, and Ginny, as state coordinator, was responsible for naming NOW members to run as a part of a slate of coalition delegates headed by Tom Hayden. She had chosen to back Sandra Farha, a choice that ran directly counter to Carabillo's and Mandell's lobbying for Elaine Lafferty. Hayden received complaints about Foat's choice from Carabillo, Mandell, and Lafferty and decided to add Lafferty's name to the slate as well if Foat approved. Reached in Washington, D.C., at a NOW board meeting, Ginny gave her approval, then angrily sought out Mandell back at the meeting and told her she'd given her permission for Elaine to be added to the slate.

Foat was angry at the behind-the-scenes manipulation and undermining of her position. Mandell was equally angry, not only at Foat's attempt to keep Lafferty off the slate but at her high-handed statement about giving *her* permission. It seemed to Mandell that this was another one of Foat's competitive ploys to prove that her power was greater than Mandell's or Carabillo's. Still, Mandell insisted, neither the fight over the delegates nor her opposition to Foat's candidacy for regional director had prompted her to call and write Louisiana. "I was very sorry we weren't friends anymore," Mandell said. "That hurt, and, of course, I was angry about some of the numbers she was pulling. Still, my writing the letter was not done out of personal animosity nor because anyone else thought it was a way of 'stopping Foat.' "

At the time of Foat's arrest, however, no one except the police knew that Mandell's letter had revived Jefferson Parish's interest in her. During her first visit with Ginny in jail, Kay reminded her of Judith Meuli's remark at the convention. "That's when Ginny told me she had an inkling that Shelly Mandell was behind it," she said. "But I suspected that somebody had set Shelly up, and that Elaine Lafferty had something to do with it, too. I could imagine the scenario where Elaine said, 'Look, nothing's been done with her since 1977, so all you need to do is get a piece of paper from Louisiana, and you'll get rid of her, not only in NOW but in local LA politics.' There may have been others behind it, too, people with connections to the police, but I don't know that, so I can't say whether Shelly's letter just got out of hand or whether they expected an arrest."

There were those who had the same private suspicions that the Foat-Mandell feud was behind the arrest, a case of NOW trashing and Machiavellian infighting that led to dire consequences.

National NOW leaders had yet to make an official comment, instead sending a staff member from the Washington office out to California the day after Foat's arrest. "We sent a person out immediately so that we could have more direct communication," NOW President Judy Goldsmith explained. "That person got in touch with Foat's attorney Bob Tuller so as to ensure that nothing we did or said would inadvertently jeopardize her case." According to Ellie Smeal, NOW's attorney, Thomas Hart, also offered his assistance to Tuller, which Tuller refused.

But Foat and her supporters saw these visits as national NOW's first step toward dissociating itself from Foat. "The top aide came out only to make sure that California NOW didn't do any more support stuff for Ginny," Kay insisted.

The top aide was a source of anxiety for Toni Carabillo as well. She seemed too young, too inexperienced, and certainly too unfamiliar with California NOW politics to handle the ramifications of the situation, which had already become complicated for both Foat herself and NOW. If Carabillo had any criticism of Goldsmith's handling of the Foat case, it was her delay in coming out to the Coast to handle the crisis immediately, since the charges and counter-charges among NOW members were flying fast and furious; the divisions between the Foat loyalists and NOW loyalists were already threatening to break the organization apart.

Judy Goldsmith, however, remained in the national NOW office and continued to hold a series of meetings and conference calls to decide on NOW's official position. Midge Costanza was present when Jean Conger, still on the NOW executive committee, participated in one such call, during which national NOW leaders seemed ready to walk away from Foat.

Costanza was furious with what she thought the national office was proposing. "Give me the damn phone, I want to talk to them," she yelled at Jean.

Jean refused.

"You handle it your way, I'll handle it mine," she said to Jean, and continued to yell in the background until someone said to Jean, "We can hear Midge there."

Jean tried to quiet her. "Shhh, Midge, they hear you."

"Good," Costanza shouted back. "I want them to hear me say they're gutless bastards, and that I don't ever want them standing up for anything in my life."

Once California NOW and local chapters got wind of what national NOW was proposing, the antagonism between Foat supporters and national NOW supporters deepened. The California NOW executive committee called a meeting on Thursday, January 13, to discuss NOW's official position. Costanza was very vocal from the beginning: She told the gathering that she would have expected the people in the room "to support Foat unanimously, not only as a sister but as one of our leaders."

Shelly Mandell chaired the meeting, Costanza recalled. "She asked us to trust each other and discuss the situation openly. When she saw my hand go up, it was like a red flag, but she had no choice but to call on me. After I spoke, she replied angrily, something like, 'I sweated a lot to put NOW together, and what raises my hackles is when people dare to criticize this organization.' I wanted to say that any organization that cannot tolerate scrutiny or criticism from its membership should not continue to exist. But she would not call on me again."

Mandell seemed so defensive that some people in the audience felt that their private, seemingly paranoid suspicions about her were correct. But Mandell said nothing about her role in the case, instead only speaking in favor of separating Foat's case from NOW. Foat's supporters argued that she should be given a leave of absence and that the organization, if not recognizing her case as political, should at least give the appearance of support. The meeting came to no resolution, and so heated was the debate that the evening became famous in LA NOW circles as "the Thursday night massacre."

Later, Foat supporters would cite Mandell's participation in the meeting as another example of her duplicity. But Shelly insisted she had been asked to "facilitate" the meeting by Jan Holden and agreed, although Elaine Lafferty advised against it. Shelly didn't always follow her friend's counsel, and moreover, as a uniquely political person, she was able to compartmentalize the political from the personal; usually the political, especially when it involved NOW, took precedence. Sometimes, basing her decisions only on what was good for NOW seemed to blind her to consequences either personally or in the world outside the organization. Her presence at that night's meeting was a case in point. Aware that she was sitting on a powder keg, that although the police had promised not to reveal her letter it could blow up in her face any moment, she still was most concerned about what was happening to NOW. Since it had al-

ready become clear that the NOW national office was going to distance itself from Foat, it was rumored that "outsiders," people by
and large critical of NOW in any circumstances, were going to pack
the meeting and use it as an occasion to attack NOW again.

That was why Midge Costanza had jumped in with both fists
flailing, NOW loyalists argued. She and the others usually complained about NOW's structure, that it was too big, too middle-of-
the road, and yet still got all of the press. But now they were willing
to turn this meeting into a circus, said Toni Carabillo, just as they
turned Foat's arraignment into one. And this surely at the peril of
both Ginny and NOW, she thought.

"We were inundated by anti-NOW people," she said, "each for
her own reasons. Ivy Bottini has been hostile to NOW since 1969
when, she believed, there was a purge of lesbians in the Manhattan
chapter. I think it was more a question of style, that they weren't
comfortable with men's shirts or the like, and there were lesbians
on both sides in that fight. But at the Foat meeting, she was with a
large Gay Task Force contingent, and they were not only going after
NOW but some of them wanted to make Ginny's case a Task Force
cause célèbre. Meanwhile, of course, Ginny's lawyer was trying to
keep a lid on all this, but the atmosphere was so irrational, so heated,
so intense that a lot of NOW women were intimidated from saying
anything or trying to decide on the best approach to the problem
for both Ginny's sake and NOW's sake. That night was the first
time in my NOW experience that I left a meeting in tears. I was
convinced that between them all they were going to destroy the organization and hurt Ginny in the process."

Whatever the feelings about NOW and the official position it
seemed about to take, it certainly seemed misguided to have Foat's
most ardent defenders so publicly aligned with the National Gay Task
Force. Jean O'Leary and Jeanne Cordova were also at the meeting,
later made plenty of statements to the press, and were among those
prominently listed on Foat's first defense-fund committee. Robin
Tyler, the lesbian comedienne, didn't hedge her remarks either. It
seemed ironic that while they were criticizing NOW leaders for not
being sensitive to Ginny's plight, they seemed to want to portray
Ginny as a lesbian martyr brought down by the establishment. Since
Ginny had never presented herself this way nor had she openly agreed
that this was necessary to prove her feminism, it seemed unfair to
try to push her into such a position, one, when she was in jail and,

two, when the top priority was to not do anything that would jeopardize her should she go to trial in Louisiana.

But if feelings about the Foat case reflected attitudes toward feminism in the minds of the general public, they once again brought the various ideological disputes within the feminist movement to the fore. Some participants in the Thursday night meeting seemed to hark back to the old fights among straight, gay, and "closet-lesbian" factions, intent on proving their thesis that in order to be a good feminist, one had to be out of the closet. It was as if they'd forgotten that first and foremost Foat had to be gotten out of jail.

With the Thursday night meeting in such disarray, with NOW members unsure of what position was best for Foat and best for the organization, there was no consensus of opinion. The Foat partisans, however, were sure that both national NOW and the California executive board were trying to force Ginny into resigning.

The executive board held a conference call on Monday, January 17, to discuss the question of resignation. According to Kay Tsenin, national NOW had also suggested that it might be best if she resigned from the vice-presidency because of her close association with Foat.

Kay had had to fly to New Orleans that night to interview potential attorneys for Foat, and she suspected that her opponents waited for her to leave town before taking the final vote. With nothing decided that night, the meeting was continued in a 6 A.M. conference call the following day.

"I was a state board member then, and I took part in that call," said Priscilla Alexander, who from the beginning had supported Foat and considered her arrest political harassment. "I was also against putting Kay on leave because I felt there was no evidence that she couldn't handle the job while helping Ginny's case. Toward the end somebody said, 'There's an article in the *LA Herald* that's just been delivered—' Somebody interrupted her and said, 'We ought to vote on the resolution.' Somebody then started to say, 'Hey, it's just been on the news . . .' But someone else insisted we had to finish voting. I think the people who were saying, 'No, no, we have to vote,' knew what was in the article and realized that if the others learned what Shelly had done, the vote wouldn't be taken. So they voted to put Kay on a leave of absence—I was the sole vote against it— and it was only then we learned that Shelly Mandell had written the letter that had led to Ginny's arrest."

Despite Mandell's conspicuous silence during the previous week, Jefferson Parish Sheriff Harry Lee confirmed that she had sent the letter that revived police interest in Foat. Defending her action in a press statement, Mandell first said that she had been considering giving Foat's name to her employer, Los Angeles City Councilman Marvin Braude, for a vacancy on a city "human rights group," but to which group she was referring wasn't initially clear. She said she had made "a discreet inquiry to prevent possible embarrassment to Braude or to Ginny Foat." She was "stunned and alarmed" that her letter had led to Foat's arrest, she added. "I can't imagine how this happened. I just hope she's exonerated, that's all I can say."

While Mandell had used official city stationery, Marvin Braude's chief deputy announced that Braude had neither authorized her request nor heard her mention Foat for any appointment. The chief deputy also confirmed that Mandell's letter, of which Braude's office had no copy, was unofficial, especially since background checks were initiated only in the mayor's office once nominations had been submitted by a council member. The mayor's office had never been notified that Braude was considering Foat for a position, and it also wasn't clear that the nine-member Human Rights Commission even had an opening at the time she contacted Jefferson Parish. Just as puzzling was that Mandell's letter had cited the exact incorrect birth date (June 21, not Ginny's actual birth date of June 2, 1941) that appeared in the warrant—as if she'd been advised of the mistake in the warrant before she'd written. Further, Sheriff Lee said that prior to Mandell's letter he had received phone calls from someone in the New Orleans area asking about the Galluzzo warrant; to someone looking for a conspiracy, there was a definite impression that more than one person was trying to heat up interest in Foat.

Mandell soon left her post with Marvin Braude, and the rumor among Foat's supporters was that she had been fired for unauthorized use of official stationery. Mandell virtually went underground, refusing to offer any further reasons why she'd taken this step. Toni Carabillo, however, defended her. "I think she got a bum rap and she had terrible press. But she only did something many of us thought we should do after the rumors at the 1982 national conference: namely, find out once and for all if there was anything to worry about, and tell the nominating committee, 'Look, there's something in this woman's background that could be dangerous.' Although people had been speculating, nobody knew what to do with it. But Shelly's a 'can-do' person, and she took the initiative, and maybe because she's worked in law offices, she had some idea of how to get around the system."

Foat was aghast when she heard this justification for Mandell's letter: "If they felt it was my personal problem that I should've resolved, they should've approached me and asked me to resolve it, or even told me, 'If you don't resolve it, we're going to resolve it for you.' Instead they stepped in and invaded my privacy, and then they proceeded to lie about it. Sure, Shelly Mandell and Toni Carabillo are both 'can-do' persons, especially when it comes to destroying people."

Carabillo again defended Mandell's action. "It had nothing to do with revenge or the assumption that Ginny and Shelly or Ginny and I were political rivals. We really weren't. Shelly's a good person, an effective leader, one of the people who's helped build NOW. She was a chapter president, a national board member, and at first brought Ginny along in the organization. It's my understanding they had a falling-out over whom to support for national NOW president, and that split them. But Shelly never expected these consequences. She just wanted to get the information for NOW's benefit and for Foat's benefit. Since she'd been told once that the computer check was clear, she didn't expect to trip a live wire and have them come and arrest Ginny Foat."

Mandell became the villain of the piece in the press. Among fellow feminists she was called "Judas," a tipster, and once she'd given what seemed contradictory or at least garbled explanations of her letter, she clammed up and virtually disappeared. It was not until much later that she tried to clarify her actions and, indeed, tried to sort out for herself all her possible motivations, both personal and political.

She said that she'd been hired as an assistant by City Councilman Marvin Braude because of her political experience and high profile as a feminist leader in the Los Angeles area. Hers was a vague job description, but she believed she was supposed to increase his visibility in the community. One of her own goals, which she also thought would win him more support, was to bring as many feminists into city government as possible. "So I started looking for possible appointments. One day I got a letter saying there was a Braude opening on the thirty-five-member Human Relations Citizens Advisory Board—that is not the nine-member Human Rights Commission. I stress that they're two different groups because that's where I got killed in the press—except by Patt Morrison in the *LA Times* because she knew the difference. Yes, the appointment to the Human Rights Commission had been filled in December, but there *was* an opening on the advisory board, and they asked Braude to send names. I asked around about this appointment, what it entailed, and I thought of Ginny."

Despite her split from her, despite her campaigning against her for regional director, she thought of Foat? "Yes, I know people couldn't believe I could be so angry at her and still want to nominate her. But she had the highest NOW visibility, so there was a real chance Braude would agree to appoint her. Besides, even if I no longer was her friend, I knew she was a feminist and would be right on the issues."

As a result, Shelly said that she considered this a chance to "kill two birds with one stone"—resolve the rumors about Foat in NOW and clear the way for her appointment to the citizens committee. She didn't like not being Ginny's friend, and while she admitted that it was perhaps naïve, she thought that by clearing up everything, she could "make it nice" again. Also, since she had been blamed for the rumor and Ginny's defeat at the convention, she thought it was possible this would show that instead she was responsible for closing the rumor down. An all-clear piece of paper would make it impossible for the gossip ever to resurface. Campaigns for or against Foat would be conducted in terms of political issues. They'd be back on a high plane.

Her first step was to call her brother's friend, whom she'd asked for a computer check in 1981. She asked him if he'd actually gotten a printout saying, "No warrants, case dismissed." "He again told me that she'd been arrested but it was dismissed. I asked, 'There was nothing outstanding, was there?' That schmuck said, 'Hell, no! If there had been, I would have turned her in.' I practically had a heart attack—he could've gotten her into trouble back then. But he said he couldn't show me a piece of paper. I said, 'I have now heard that there might be something in Louisiana. Can you get into the big computer that covers everything to make sure nothing is happening there?' He said he couldn't, that I should write a letter. 'Where do I write?' I asked. He said, 'I don't know. Call.' Ergo, I called—first to Baton Rouge, then to New Orleans. Nothing either place.

I said, 'Good.' But then the New Orleans office told me that New Orleans was big and that there were other parishes. I didn't know about parishes, so maybe I asked what was closest, and they suggested I try Jefferson Parish, which I'd never heard of before. So I called that parish and was told I had to write them a letter, that they didn't give out such information over the phone."

Despite her explanations (it must be said that perhaps she didn't even know all her reasons or didn't want to confront what may have been unconscious motives), it was striking that she'd blocked out the Central Park Cafe dinner so extensively that she claimed she didn't recall that Ginny had spoken about an incident in New Orleans specifically. But whatever the psychological forces at work, Mandell had simply strayed outside routine procedure. Official protocol, much less common courtesy, should have dictated a phone call to Ginny Foat to ask if she would like her name placed in nomination and if she minded a background investigation.

"That's a valid criticism," Mandell agreed. "I should have asked Ginny first. It was dumb. I know people thought that Mandell was either vicious or dumb, and my background was not dumb, so I must have been vicious. But it was just plain dumb. I didn't ask Ginny first because my thought was I would never put her name in unless I was sure the record would come back clean. My major motive was to confirm in writing that there was nothing out there so that it could never be used as an issue, either inside NOW or elsewhere. It was absolutely not done out of malice."

But given what she'd heard from Ginny at the restaurant, why hadn't she suspected that there was bound to be a problem in Louisiana? Her main concern, however, seemed to be only what was in police records, not what was actually in Foat's past. It's difficult to understand the distinction unless one accepts what is Mandell's almost excessively political way of looking at the world. What mattered to her was a piece of paper that would make it impossible for a rumor ever to be used against Ginny in NOW or in a political office. The narrow focus seemed characteristic of NOW members in general; so devoted to NOW, they think exclusively in terms of the organization, and wear blinders when it comes to consequences in the outside world. Further, Mandell apparently suppressed so much of what she'd previously heard from Foat that she could insist she didn't connect the implications of Foat's story to what might be in the police computer. And, finally, again because she seemed to compartmentalize the personal, she could still say that the rift in friendship was in no way behind her letter; to her it was all politics. Besides, if anything, she seemed to have hoped that a letter proving once and for all that Foat was clean (and in her mind, as in Foat's, her brother's friend had reassured her that this was the case) might clear the air in the organization, convincing both her old friend and her supporters that she had not been "the bad guy" at the convention.

From Foat's side, it was easy to understand why she and Kay had suspected Mandell even before the letter was revealed. Ginny had put herself in a vulnerable situation, then been told "there was no friendship." In Foat's mind, her old friend had become the enemy, first at the convention, and then with the arrest. Because Ginny may have become aware of Elaine Lafferty's doubts or sensed her coolness after that evening in the restaurant, in Foat's scheme she would naturally become the instigator of the conspiracy, perhaps even the person who had found out the exact wrong birth date that appeared on the warrant.

Mandell, however, continued to chalk up the birth-date mistake to a weird coincidence. Since she, Jan Holden, Karen Peters, and Ginny were all Geminis, she said, she thought she remembered celebrating Ginny's birthday about a week after her own, which is June 13. She had tied the dates in her mind to two NOW meetings the year before, a week apart. Ginny had presented her with a cake; Mandell thought she'd then said, "You owe me, you do the cake next weekend." But it had been Karen Peters's birthday she'd been referring to, not her own. Shelly insisted her faulty memory was responsible, not an inside tip from the sheriff's office. Even though she'd put down the twenty-first, not the twentieth, which would have been a week after her own, and even though in some astrology charts the twenty-first does not even fall under the sign of Gemini, she said it was just a mistake. "I don't know why I came up with the twenty-first. I remembered that somebody was on the cusp, but I didn't know that date was on the warrant. I didn't even know there was a warrant. It was just weird, not at all sinister."

As for listing Ginny's name in the letter as Galluzzo, she said, "I put in her maiden name as an afterthought."

A few days after sending the letter, Mandell was phoned by the Los Angeles police. At first she thought it was a routine call for her to arrange an appointment with City Councilman Braude. "But when the cop said 'homicide' and 'Ginny Foat,' I went into shock, went blank, played dumb, and said, 'Gee, the name doesn't do a thing for me.' Then I got the hell off the phone and immediately called a lawyer, a feminist whose name I won't use because once things got hot she said she couldn't be involved. I told her about my letter and said, 'For God's sake, tell the police it's a big mistake, and I don't want to talk to them.' The lawyer phoned the police. They obviously knew who Ginny Foat was, and they said Louisiana was interested in her. My lawyer told them that they should go back and check their facts, that Ginny was a public figure. She also told them not to bother me at work but to call her. They then advised her to warn me not to contact Ginny or they would charge me with aiding and abetting a fugitive. A few days later, a cop, a good old boy, showed up in my office. I looked up from my desk, and my eye was level with bullets on his belt. I turned green. We walked outside the office, and again he warned me not to call Foat because I'd be charged, and since they knew I was in law school, they reminded me I couldn't afford that. He said that my connection to this was unimportant, that it would not be revealed to anyone. I told him to call Ginny's lawyer Tuller in Orange County, that I was sure he could clear everything up. Then the cop showed me a godawful picture, the horrible mug shot from her 1977 arrest, and asked, 'Is that Ginny Foat?' I said, 'That's not the Ginny Foat I know, but yes, that's Ginny.' He then hinted that the 'brass,' 'the big boys,' were aware of the case, meaning, I think, Daryl Gates, chief of police, and Gates's liaison to the city council."

It was this part of the case that Shelly later focused on when people talked about a conspiracy or an antifeminist plot:

"First of all, this dumbo here had caused at least a part of it, and I knew I wasn't conspiring. After all, I got hurt by this, too. I attributed it to stupidity—mine for sticking my nose in, Ginny's for not having taken care of this before. By the way, I always stick my nose in. When I was a little kid in the cafeteria, the teacher would say, 'Whose tray is that?' It wouldn't be my tray, but I'd still answer. I've never been able not to respond to a question. That's the part of me that always gets me into big trouble, just as it did with the press at first. But I do think that Police Chief Gates had his agenda, and this provided him with a chance to embarrass Foat and me, NOW, and the city council, all at once. There was no reason to arrest her at the airport with helicopters and rifles. He could have called her. I told him we were all going to the state Democratic convention the next week. As for me, I was a pain-in-the-ass feminist, I'd played hardball politics on issues, I'd gone up against city and state politicians. I had a high profile, and I think the police were glad to be able to set me up. That's why they leaked the letter. Because of my position with Braude, it was a perfect way to embarrass the city council, which was giving the police a hard time that year. I still believe the police must have had a conversation with Braude, and that's why he fired me. Even though his official reason for firing me was that I'd become too visible and too outspoken for his office, I'm sure it was because of the Foat case, not for unauthorized use of official stationery but because a lot of pressure had been brought to bear by the police. So only in that sense do I think there was anything like a conspiracy. Otherwise, when I heard all that talk about an antifeminist conspiracy, my thought was 'No, just two really stupid women.' "

Whatever Mandell's motivations and expectations, feminists inside and outside the organization were aghast that a NOW colleague was responsible for reviving police interest in Foat. Some, like Karen DeCrow, could hardly believe it was true. "Someone then told me over the phone that Shelly Mandell had written the letter," she said. "I knew her the same way I knew Ginny Foat, from California NOW when I was NOW president. When I was told about her letter, I listened with amazement, but I also wondered if it was true. Equally possible in the vicious NOW wars was that someone was just telling me this about a NOW colleague, and it would turn out not to be fact at all. It was never, quote unquote, confirmed to me. Then I think I heard that Mandell was a spurned lover. I didn't know about all the sides, but I couldn't believe that there was a NOW conspiracy to get Foat. Nor could I imagine Ellie Smeal telling someone to send such a letter."

Gloria Steinem seemed to want to believe the best of a fellow feminist. "I never quite understood Shelly Mandell's letter. I don't want to accuse her of motives that I don't know for sure since I gather she was in charge of investigating Ginny's background for an appointment. I was aware, though, that factionalism in California certainly played a role, although whether it was decisive, or whether she would have been pursued anyway, I didn't know."

California NOW factionalism did seem to have played a decisive role. As one southern California NOW colleague commented,

"A lot of people applauded what Mandell did—as far as the results of her actions. Although Shelly denies having done it purposefully, Ginny Foat and her gang had to be stopped one way or another."

Relatively distant from the feuding within California NOW, Ellie Smeal tried to adopt a more evenhanded perspective. "Of course, I was very surprised when I heard about Shelly's letter. I still don't think she did it to get Ginny, though, or to force her to reveal her background, or even that she thought it would cause her to be arrested. After all, she'd checked before and nothing had happened, so why would she think something would happen this time? Besides, how in the world would it serve her politically if she thought she would cause Ginny to be arrested? And why was there any need to 'stop Ginny,' anyway, especially when her term of office was almost up? I suppose that because Shelly knew Ginny very well, she may have been more upset by the convention rumors than I was, or anybody else was who was more distant from the situation. In that light her explanation that she wanted to clear it up for the sake of the organization seems reasonable to me. On the other hand, I can understand Foat's bitterness that she was not asked to resolve it herself. If you can understand one side, you can also have compassion for the other."

While Muriel Fox was well aware of feuding in California NOW, she couldn't believe that anyone had gotten Foat arrested to stop her rise to power. "There was and is very bitter infighting in California NOW," she said. "Ginny Foat's allies have also gotten in some vicious digs at their opponents, too, like some of the things that were said about Ellie Smeal and Judy Goldsmith. But I doubt this caused the arrest. I'd be willing to bet that what Shelly and the people in California wanted to do was clarify Ginny's past. After the '82 conference I'm sure everyone felt the air should be cleared, but no one dreamed that kind of charge would emerge, nor would they have wanted to do her harm or put her in jeopardy."

When Mandell stopped talking to reporters, they remained dissatisfied with her bland and sometimes contradictory explanations for the letter. It seemed too extreme an act to be simply the result of political differences. Perhaps for no better reason than the stereotype that all feminists are lesbians, the press began to speculate among themselves that the Mandell-Foat feud was less a matter of political rivalry than a lovers' quarrel. Given the gossip and innuendos that were usually rife in California NOW, it was all too easy for reporters to combine the one stereotype with an even older cliché, "Hell hath no fury like a woman scorned," and come up with the unfounded assumption that Foat had rejected Mandell, and that Mandell had written her letter as an act of revenge. The rumor that they'd been roommates also spread, despite all evidence to the contrary: Foat, Tsenin, Mandell, Lafferty, and any women who knew the parties involved denied it, and no public records confirmed otherwise.

Of course, such speculation revealed more about entrenched attitudes toward feminism than it did about Mandell's motivation. The gossip overlooked the way in which political alliances within NOW usually become personalized, as indeed political differences are then perceived as personal betrayals. Foat and Mandell had been political associates; they'd become close personal friends. Even if the source of their falling-out was political, it would still have been felt as a deeply personal rift and as such could have prompted Mandell's letter. The hostility seemed to come as much from Foat as it did from Mandell, and whatever Mandell consciously thought she was doing by writing the letter, one suspected that the shared enmity was strong enough to play at least a subconscious role in Mandell's action.

"It was quite clear that Shelly fingered Ginny and then felt terrible about it," *Rolling Stone* writer Grace Lichtenstein said. "I don't think her letter was as innocent or as naïve as she convinced herself after the fact. She did want to get her. Why she did, I don't know. In any case, none of the NOW people behaved very generously, to put it mildly."

From the Foat camp there were repeated accusations of a conspiracy among Foat's enemies in California NOW, with Mandell doing the dirty work for others, most notably for a cabal headed by Carabillo.

"I heard the rumor that I took the fall for what other people in NOW wanted done," said Shelly. "But to my knowledge I was not set up—other than 'Let Mikey do it,' and 'If there's something to straighten out, you can count on Mandell not to let it sit too long.' I didn't think or say, 'X knew this or Y tried to do that.' I wasn't going to hurt other people when I was the dummy who did it."

Nevertheless, in retrospect it seemed probably that Foat suspected Lafferty and Mandell of betraying her, of revealing what had been said in confidence over dinner. And given the factionalism within California NOW, given the feud between Foat and Carabillo, she may have thought that this information had gotten into the hands of all those whom she regarded as enemies, most particularly Toni Carabillo.

"When people suggest that I was behind or involved in a conspiracy to get Foat arrested, they're out of their minds," said Carabillo. "Sure, I'd heard about the problem from Jean; sure, I'd heard the gossip. I also thought that Ginny was irresponsible in not getting the question resolved before she ran for a NOW national office. Defeat Ginny for regional director, you bet. But not with gossip, and not by getting her arrested. Having spent so many years building up the organization, having been involved professionally in public relations, her arrest was about the last thing I wanted. After all, it played so well in the press. Great publicity for NOW—one of our leaders arrested for murder!"

Those who defended Mandell's action in terms of what was best for the organization did so with shaky logic and a myopic attention only to NOW. If "Shelly never expected to trip a live wire," why was it crucial to confirm in writing that the matter was resolved? If there was even a remote possibility that a warrant would be resurrected, how could it be kept secret within NOW without the authorities' acting on it?

Foat's approach to the situation was equally confused, however; if she suspected that Mandell wrote her letter simply to retrieve a document that would stop her within NOW, what did she think Mandell might turn up? If she'd said she couldn't set foot in Louisiana, didn't she have a hunch that there was still a problem? And if there wasn't, what did Foat think were the possible consequences in NOW of a statement that said the case was closed? Since this was the area that neither Foat nor her close friends seemed willing to confront before the 1982 convention, her own ambivalence may have sparked the rumors that led to an unauthorized background check. Certainly, her story in the Central Park Cafe would have led any reasonable person to believe there was something "back there." But if she was so sure that the case was closed, whatever the details of her saga, why hadn't she herself retrieved a document to that effect? That would have been enough to quiet her doubters and nip any gossip in the bud. But when she wouldn't or didn't, others may have inferred that there was good reason for hesitancy. Since it was known that she'd lowered her sights from NOW president to vice-president for fear of publicity, perhaps it was taken as a sign of vulnerability, which consequently aroused someone's interest, whether or not the interest was motivated by concern for NOW, antagonism toward Foat, or antagonism toward NOW. Even stranger, given the gossip, was why no one else had done what Mandell had done, but in a clandestine way. With talk about "so much blood," an anonymous tip to a crime-stopper hotline would have had the same effect as Shelly Mandell's signed letter. In this regard, it seemed that a number of feminists had conspired to protect her, not to get her, Mandell's "dumb mistake" notwithstanding.

If feminists inside and outside the organization were disconcerted by the Mandell revelation, there was even more debate about the steps national NOW chose to take during the week following Foat's arrest. On Monday, January 17, NOW President Judy Goldsmith finally went to California. Accompanied by NOW counsel Thomas Hart, she visited Foat in jail. Foat was bitter about the visit, resenting what she felt was both a lack of sympathy and an insensitive demand for her resignation. "Can you imagine the coldness of that person? She came in with some obnoxious statement of resignation when what I needed was support. There I was in jail, and she comes to me with that! But I refused to let her issue a statement saying that I'd resigned."

Judy Goldsmith said their meeting was very different from what Foat remembered. "I find it extremely painful that she saw it that way. When I went to see Ginny in jail, I had with me only one piece of paper, and that was a draft of the press statement I intended to release the next day. I wanted to check with Ginny and her lawyer that they found it acceptable. I was deeply concerned about Ginny, as we all were, and I certainly wasn't there to force her to resign. I would have found it repugnant to do that to someone in her position. In fact, though, it was Ginny who raised the question of taking a leave of absence. Perhaps because the circumstances for her were very strained—they were for both of us—it's possible that her perceptions could have been skewed so her characterization of what happened isn't accurate. I remember it as a very emotional experience. It was very difficult to see her in jail, but she was also concerned about California NOW and asked 'How's it going?' We chatted about that, and then at the end of the conversation we hugged. So to call it a 'cold' meeting is an absolute misrepresentation. Besides, I've never been cold in my life.''

Kay Tsenin insisted, though, that Goldsmith was there to force Foat's resignation. "After Ginny refused to go along, Judy appealed to me. She wanted me to issue a statement saying that Ginny had stepped aside. I told her to go to hell, that I wouldn't do it, and that's why later that spring they tried once more to run me out of office.''

Foat, of course, had been much more polite, and at first had found it hard to believe that NOW would actually dissociate itself from her. Then at a press conference on Thursday, January 20, Goldsmith, while making no mention of resignation, announced that NOW would not pledge financial or legal support to Foat. "What we have here is an individual's personal tragedy, for which we have great compassion." Feminists heard the emphasis on *personal* as an implied rebuttal to Foat's claim that her case was political; more, they couldn't believe that a feminist leader would forget feminism's first principle, that "the personal is political." But Goldsmith insisted that NOW was "not aware of any evidence that this was politically motivated," and urged NOW members to stop their squabbling and turn their attention from Foat to the "vitally important agenda of achieving women's equality and an end to sex discrimination in this country." She said that it was important for Foat "to pursue her defense with privacy, dignity, and without distraction.''

Although she insisted that the organization "was not abandoning anyone," adding, "reasonable people will understand that," many NOW members were upset by what they considered outright desertion of one of their leaders. It seemed a cowardly evasion at best, at worst a presumption of Foat's guilt and a condemnation of a woman's past. For all of Goldsmith's insistence that NOW wasn't abandoning Foat, her statement suggested that NOW was worried about the case tainting its image. Did political expediency rule the roost even in NOW? Was its rush to judgment against Foat the flip side of its earlier rush to advance her without considering the 1977 episode or her background?

Nevertheless, many feminists agreed that her case seemed to beg for a modicum of support, especially because of the role of a NOW colleague and NOW politics in it. Whatever the eventual verdict, the case added fuel to antifeminist fire, and NOW would have to face this head on, however much it tried to distance itself by calling it a personal tragedy.

Close to the case, Midge Costanza was horrified and condemned the organization in the press. "I'd always respected what NOW has done for women over the years. But when the national office took this position, I had to ask, 'If NOW can't stand up for one of its leaders, then how can it speak for *any* woman?' "

Speaking both as a reporter and as a feminist, Patt Morrison, the *Los Angeles Times* staff writer who'd been assigned to the Foat story, was surprised by the way national NOW chose to treat the case and its presentation of that position to the public. "I thought their deserting her was a fairly ungracious thing to do. As a feminist I felt being supportive should have entailed more than a press conference announcing that until her legal matters had been resolved, Foat was no longer California NOW president. Even though it was phrased as a 'leave of absence,' NOW officials didn't do anything to soften the impression that they didn't want anything to do with Ginny Foat, defendant. On the other hand, I realized that NOW had to be as attuned as any political organization to how best to get its message across. So another part of me realized that how the public would react to the Foat case had to be an overwhelming consideration. But I'm sure they were taken to task for that press conference which did, I think, seem abrupt and perhaps premature. When her attorney Bob Tuller wanted less publicity about Foat's connection to NOW, he was taking into account that she might be tried in a state that had suffered financially from the NOW boycott. Still, I think NOW might have put more time into investigating the case and deciding on a way to handle it that didn't seem to sever her completely."

At a further remove, feminists were at least perplexed by NOW's official position. Gloria Steinem thought that Foat's plight was an issue around which feminists could rally. "Her situation seemed to represent two important themes. One is that many of us have changed a very great deal in our lifetime, and Ginny's history was a tribute to the power of feminism, not in any sense a detraction from feminism. Also she had left a husband who continued to think of her as a possession and followed her around the country. But even though I supported Ginny, I wasn't criticizing NOW for its position. I was distant from the situation, but it seemed to me that some

of Ginny's supporters wanted NOW to make her case its total focus. That didn't seem fair to me either, since the organization had
to go on with its other activities and goals. So on the one hand NOW
was being criticized for its position, and on the other I was being
criticized for supporting Foat's legal-defense fund. In response to that
I said, 'She is like a family member, she deserves the best legal defense she can get and we should support her defense fund.' But by
that I was not implying anything negative about NOW. I simply
thought that Ginny was probably innocent and that in any event
you have to rescue individuals who are in trouble. At the same time
the general goals of the women's movement and NOW had to be
pursued. I didn't see anything contradictory in those two positions."

Foat, however, took Steinem's statements as public disapproval
of NOW and often cited the country's leading feminist when she
voiced her suspicion that Goldsmith's statement was based on a
presumption of guilt and disapproval of her past.

In addition to the many positions of leadership she'd held in
NOW since 1966, Muriel Fox had also served as president of the
NOW Legal Defense and Education Fund. While not involved directly with the decision about NOW's official position, nor in the
"middle of the fray" as she put it, she strongly agreed with Judy
Goldsmith's statement that Foat's case was a personal tragedy and
not a political issue that NOW should adopt as a cause. "Everyone
had tremendous compassion for her and hoped she would come out
of it successfully. But it had nothing to do with NOW's objectives
or NOW activities, and the fact that she was a California NOW officer was only coincidental to her personal tragedy. It's probably true
that if Ginny had not had the celebrity because of her NOW position, the case might not have gone as far as it did. At the same time,
however, that didn't mean that NOW had any greater responsibility to help her out. NOW had to weigh its priorities, and I think
NOW's real responsibility was to create a distance between this case
and the very serious political struggle that NOW is involved in on
behalf of billions of women present and future. We are running a
social revolution which some historians see as the most important
historical event of the twentieth century. It's true that women suffer
terrible abuse in our society, and to that degree Ginny's case could
be considered political, although I would call it more social. Nevertheless, her particular case wasn't a feminist NOW-related issue. It

was also important to stress that the case was unrelated to her NOW activism, and that actually NOW leaders and NOW activists do not necessarily live that kind of life-style. For the sake of NOW's worldwide, nationwide, and local activities and goals, we had to put that distance between us and that kind of life."

Not surprisingly, Toni Carabillo also argued in favor of NOW's official position. But in defending the decision she seemed to imply there was some truth to Foat's accusations that NOW was embarrassed by her background, that it was more worried about its image than about feminist issues that Foat claimed were at the heart of her ordeal. "It was a very difficult decision, but it had to be made in terms of what was best for the organization," said Carabillo. "Ginny didn't understand that NOW's responsibilities are multifaceted and couldn't just be solely to her. Besides, this was not a nice, clean case. Not only was she accused of rolling someone in a robbery, there was also all the rest about her background coming out. This is a middle-class organization, and it shocked a lot of people. People close to Ginny said everybody knew about it, but I'd known Ginny and worked with her, and I didn't know about that background. Most people in the organization across the country had no idea either, and it was very startling. Still, it was not a question of NOW presuming her guilty; it was a question of what was best in fairness to the organization, to the vast majority of members who'd known nothing about it."

President Judy Goldsmith, however, disagreed with her *NOW Times* editor, repeating that national NOW based its "difficult decision" after many long meetings not on what was best for the organization but on its deep concern for Foat: "It was Bob Tuller's position that a close identification between Ginny and NOW and the women's movement would jeopardize her case in Louisiana. He felt that the most important thing was for her to be able to pursue her case out of the glare of publicity. That was the main reason for our decision, absolutely not because there was any presumption of guilt on our part. Nor would I agree that NOW is a middle-class organization and that our members were embarrassed by her background. Certainly the news surrounding her arrest was startling, and the chain of events took people very much by surprise, but that's not the same as saying that members were either shocked by her background or disapproved of it."

Karen DeCrow confirmed that while NOW members she knew

in upstate New York chapters weren't terribly shocked by what they were reading about Foat's past, they also weren't upset by national NOW's position: "The official position was neither embraced nor denounced among NOW members in my area. Of course, I could see why Foat wanted NOW to defend her. But I could also understand why people who were concerned about the organization would've wanted to divorce themselves from the situation and might've liked an even milder statement than Judy Goldsmith made. In fact, though, I felt sorry for Judy. She'd just been elected that fall. She wasn't as highly visible a leader as Ellie Smeal had been, and this was the first time the press was going to meet her. A new president, a new image—talk about a test of fire. My God, what a way to start out with the media: 'We're not going to talk about equal rights, we're going to talk about a murder charge.' "

Having attended the initial meetings to discuss Foat's case, Ellie Smeal agreed with Goldsmith that everyone there had two primary concerns that they had to weigh—Foat's situation and the position NOW should adopt. "Of course, there was a very strong sense of responsibility for the movement. Maybe it's a strength, maybe it's a weakness, but we do tend to think of NOW and the feminist movement as interchangeable, so part of our consideration was wanting to protect NOW. But we also wanted to be responsible to Foat as an individual. Both sides were discussed at those first meetings, and in all fairness to Judy Goldsmith there was no ultimate or single decision made then and there. A few days later Judy went out to California, and I heard that Foat's lawyer told her that it was in Foat's best interest to keep her association with NOW low-profile. I really believe Judy was told that, and based on that, the reasoning behind her official statement made sense. In addition, we were hearing horrendous things about the Louisiana court system. We had to hope that she'd be treated as innocent until proven guilty and that the system would work. Nevertheless, we'd been told that the courts there don't have a reputation for fairness, and that indeed if NOW was more entwined with her case, Ginny's chances for a fair trial wouldn't be good. That was what both Ginny's lawyer and our NOW lawyer said, too, and I felt that argument was quite convincing. It was certainly one of the main reasons why Judy adopted the position that she did."

There were, indeed, conflicting messages coming from Bob Tuller and members of the Foat defense-fund committee. Tuller himself had even refused Tom Hart's offer of assistance because of his connection to NOW. Carabillo, who was present at the meeting, said that Hart's overriding concern was Ginny's rights and her ability to get a fair trial. But Bob Tuller was worried that the media emphasis on Ginny as a feminist leader would prompt detrimental pretrial publicity in Louisiana. National NOW's position made sense in terms of the line he was taking when he repeatedly asked everyone to be circumspect about what was said about Foat's feminism. Another of her California attorneys, Marcia Brewer, also talked of bureaucratic snafus, of warrants left in computers, but never of antifeminism. While Foat argued that Tuller wanted to distance her from NOW because of pretrial publicity, she also said that given the Mandell revelation, he feared that there were others in the organization who would try to hurt her or her case further. Whatever the reasons, Tuller and Brewer tried to depoliticize the situation while members of the Foat defense committee continued to call the case political and publicly condemned NOW for refusing to treat it as such. They argued that even if NOW's primary worry was a fair trial, such concern did not require a total dissociation, much less Foat's forced resignation.

Goldsmith and Smeal insisted that the national NOW office had never considered anything but a paid leave of absence for Foat. The pressure on Foat and Tsenin to resign seemed to be coming from within California NOW, because, they said, it had never been mentioned at any of the meetings in Washington that Smeal attended. "I don't believe the story that Judy or the NOW office pushed for Ginny to resign and that only later lobbying changed that decision," said Smeal. "From day one at the meetings I attended, everybody said, 'You can't jeopardize her income, she needs it now more than ever so she can defend herself.' It wouldn't have been proper to force her to resign, plus it would have been out of character for both NOW and Judy. She's just not that kind of person. So NOW did provide aid in the sense that it continued to pay her salary. Still, we also felt, and most people agreed, that we could not divert our funds to her and that her defense committee had to do its own special fund-raising."

With Foat still in jail, the California NOW executive board held an open meeting in Oakland, California, on February 5 to discuss what official steps should be taken. Enough NOW members who attended were opposed to asking for Foat's and Tsenin's resignations that they voted to grant Foat a paid leave of absence and to reinstate Tsenin not only as state vice-president but as acting president in Foat's absence. The meeting also censured its board for the poor way they'd handled decisions after the arrest.

In addition, the group passed a resolution requiring the *National NOW Times* to carry ads for the Foat defense fund and to publish an article about Ginny. The article was never published, however, and Foat complained that the ad was delayed two months because national NOW disapproved of her initial defense fund and its use of California NOW's Los Angeles address. A new defense fund was formed, which ran the ad with the acceptable address of Bob Tuller's law office. Still, Foat felt that Carabillo and *NOW Times* had carried out the meeting's resolution halfheartedly, since people were confused by the two fund addresses, and the ad, running only twice, raised a mere $1,800.

Toni Carabillo denied that *NOW Times* had been less than cooperative. "The ad ran three times and for free. Every time Ellie Smeal runs an ad for her Washington newsletter, she pays seven hundred and fifty dollars, and, God knows, Ellie has done fantastic things for this organization. But that's another example of the way NOW actually did things for Foat without publicizing it. I think everybody wished her well, but we were all very careful not to say anything detrimental. From her political friends to her political enemies, we were all silent." In that sense, she regarded Ginny as a bit of a "prima donna," who wanted it both ways. When it came to the trial she wanted to be dissociated from the organization; yet she still demanded NOW's acknowledgment that her case was political and exemplified a swing toward antifeminism.

Behind all the talk of antifeminist plot against Foat, it seemed that the real political conspiracy, the strategy for "stopping Foat and her gang" had its origins not in Louisiana's misogyny but in NOW's internal politics: wheeling and dealing for positions of leadership, name-calling, rumormongering, lesbian-baiting by lesbians, sisters accusing sisters of being alcoholic, frauds, even FBI infiltrators.

The background of Foat's feminist awakening, rise in the movement, and sudden fall exposed more the underside of feminist politics than a "climate of violence against women." This was the real "embarrassment," as tainting of NOW's image as Foat's background. Feminist consciousness seemed to have been shattered by delusions of power, by personal ambition. As NOW had grown larger, more acceptable in mainstream politics, women striving for office seemed to have adopted the strategies of the very organizations they criticized as hierarchical and patriarchal. Within the organization, who was elected, who wielded power, sometimes became all-important and justified whatever means assured these ends. More time was spent squabbling over power and positions within the organization than worrying about what little power women actually have in society at large.

Even worse, the Foat case revealed an ironic transposition of "the personal is political." The political was personal here, to an overwhelming degree, with wrangling, private feuds, and trashing masquerading as political concerns. It was disillusioning, to say the least, that feminism, as represented by the largest, most moderate organization of the movement, had come to that. Feminism had tried to obliterate the assumption that women can't get along and are always competing with each other, eager to stab each other in the back for personal gain. Yet here was the worn-out image, this time dressed-for-success and shoved center stage.

At first glance, the NOW factionalism behind the Foat case would seem to lend credence to the argument that such traits are determined by the x chromosome. But beyond the easy answer was the real cause: Women in politics are not immune to corruptions of power. And this was all the more disappointing in the case of NOW precisely because of feminism's idealism. When wholehearted personal commitments to the women's movement were twisted into petty rivalry, hurtful gossip, and vicious infighting, then it did seem worse than comparable power plays within "patriarchal" organizations.

Toni Carabillo, however, disagreed with this assessment: "We have the same controversies, the same problems with turf and fiefdoms as other organizations. We're neither different nor better than male organizations, and it's unfair to expect us to be."

But is it, given feminist principles?

Gloria Steinem refused to see the Foat case as emblematic, either of extreme factionalism within the women's movement or of the chestnut that women tend to personalize their disputes. "For that matter," she commented, "one might say it's characteristic of men to generalize them. I think we might be better off personalizing them. Perhaps that would get us into fewer wars. But I've never thought factionalism was worse in NOW than in other organizations. I've often felt we didn't disagree enough because we are so conscious of our stereotype of being unable to get along. We need healthy disagreement to work out tactics—that's necessary. Yet we know that when two women disagree people say they can't get along, whereas when two men disagree it's perceived as debate over an issue."

Nevertheless, feminists closer to the case couldn't help but conclude that political issues had taken a nasty personal turn. Grace Lichtenstein was particularly struck by it as she interviewed Foat's NOW colleagues for a story in *Rolling Stone.* "In West Hollywood, Westwood, and Beverly Hills, there are wealthy, educated, bright women, and frankly, there's a heavy dose of Jews. There are also plenty of Hispanic women in positions of leadership, and Hispanic women are just about the best feminists around. So you'd expect California feminists to be a little bit brighter and a little more with it. But what I discovered out there was more like 1955 attitudes. Factionalism is rife in every movement and has been from day one in the feminist movement, especially between gays and straights. Still, I'd never seen it quite as bad as those women out in California, who were just dying to do each other in. It confirmed the worst kind of sexist stereotypes to see women behaving like that. And besides, I was brought up to be more idealistic about feminist organizations. I do think we should be better than our male counterparts, or better than the organizations we criticize."

Midge Costanza was equally distressed by what she perceived as a lack of feminist principles in NOW's official handling of the Foat case. She argued that any feminist organization had to examine itself and remain committed to its feminist principles, even as it grew larger and more successful. "While structure is important," she said, "the principles and values around which you form that structure are even more important. The crucial role of both members and leaders is to remind each other of their basic beliefs. We're no better in the women's movement than those groups we want to change if we don't challenge ourselves continuously, even as we become more pragmatic and political. Becoming more politically savvy doesn't mean forsaking our principles and values. Myself, I've refused to let my experiences within a political party undermine my feminist commitment. If that means you have to stand up alone, then you have to feel alone. But we are not alone. The majority of the population agrees that equality is one of *the* main issues for women. Yet even as feminism becomes more acceptable, we shouldn't compromise our principles within our organizations for the sake of expediency or public perceptions."

Despite NOW leaders' explanations of their "complicated" decision, feminists inside and outside the organization began to wonder if feminist principles hadn't been sacrificed to success. Once NOW had become a strong national organization, with so many thousands of members that it was looked upon as the country's leading representative of women's concerns, had it forsaken the values upon which it had been founded? Was there something about the personal ambitiousness of individuals in NOW who aspired to leadership that made such factionalism and infighting inevitable? Had its history as an organization dedicated to bringing women "into the mainstream," i.e., into the establishment, sown the seeds for its role in the Foat case?

Then there was Foat herself and what her previously unknown background, feminist conversion, and rise in the organization revealed about certain strains in feminist ideology and the women's movement. To a certain extent, practical and psychological reasons accounted for few people knowing about her past. Yet the emphasis she (in her statement from jail especially) and her defense team placed on her feminist rebirth drew on what had become a dominant motif in the women's movement: Women weren't their "real" selves until they'd shed their earlier unenlightened selves, i.e., the masks that social stereotypes had forced them to adopt. But "the birth of a strong feminist" hardly answered the question that hovered over the case: Who is Ginny Foat?

In the face of concerted silence from Foat and her defense team, from NOW leaders both in California and in Washington, people wanted to know more; in particular, feminists who realized that her case would be presented as, indeed taken as emblematic of, the public's attitude toward feminism needed more information.

They had to wonder, too, if Foat's story, with its emphasis on an overnight transformation, wasn't indicative of California's brand of feminism. Despite the claim that Foat's rise in California NOW wasn't particularly rapid, from afar it looked as if her metamorphosis owed more to California quick-change psychology than to feminist awakening. Did the West Coast emphasis on weekend "getting-it's," the exploration of "the new you," and the marketing of "self-help" programs play a major role in Foat's story? Was the "California dream"—recent transplants nourished not by roots in native soil but by the warm baths of "sensitivity training" and hot tubs in Marin County—central to Foat's dramatic changes? With gold chains linking them to nothing but themselves in the present, with talk about "the Coast" as if the state bore no relation to the rest of the country, as if they were always on the verge of a new life, Californians often seemed willing, even eager, to obliterate their pasts. Had this California propensity exaggerated the feminist psychology of change, a feminist conversion in California offering an even faster metamorphosis than a weekend *est* marathon?

And, in turn, did this help explain how Ginny Foat emerged from jail in 1977 "a new woman," and rose to leadership in California NOW with no one stopping to ask about her past? Indeed, the California chapter was often perceived as "more radical" than the rest of NOW, more impatient for rapid change, and more demanding of total commitment. Many California NOW women prided themselves on this image, and what a woman brought to the organization was not who she'd been but who she was willing to be. Had this emphasis allowed Foat to become "who she is today" because identity in California NOW was defined only by feminist credentials, by NOW hours of activism, and among certain factions, a conversion to lesbianism? Had these California traits all combined to allow Foat to become a leader with no attention paid to her background?

Neither Toni Carabillo nor Ellie Smeal was comfortable with this suggestion. "I think it's chancy to say that Ginny could only have become a leader in California," said Smeal, "given what I know about the feminist movement in general and NOW in particular. NOW is a volunteer organization, and if you're excited, enthusiastic, and willing to do the work, then you move up fast wherever you are. That's the reality of it, because, my God, at the local and state levels it's all we can do to get people to take the jobs. One of the reasons I became a leader was that basically I did the work, even though people will attribute my position of leadership to this, that, or another thing. So I'm not detracting from Ginny when I say that was probably the reality of how she became a NOW leader."

From her many years of experience in NOW, Muriel Fox also wasn't sure if Foat exemplified a special brand of California feminism. "It's hard to say whether she would have become a leader in NOW in another state. I gather she did some things capably. On the other hand, with the way she dressed and spoke, she came on as quite a tough cookie, and I think that manner would've turned off a lot of the rank-and-file women in some other states. Still, I always liked her and thought there was a certain honesty about her that was very appealing. So probably she would have modified her manner to suit the requirements of the state where she was running and would have risen to office there, too."

Nevertheless, California NOW members did seem to have two special characteristics that became crucial in the Foat case. They tended to take each other at face value without spending the time to find out about personal lives. There was also more competition for turf and power in California NOW. These traits then combined with Ginny Foat's own personality to intensify the hostility and antagonism—from both "sides"—that came to play such a central role in her downfall. There was no getting around the impression that she was ambitious, she liked power, she wanted to feel important. It would seem, though, that her drive and her will to succeed had subsumed all other considerations, both personal and political. And, ironically, at first she had been rewarded for that in NOW.

In fact, it is possible that her climb to the top mirrored NOW's own overriding ambitions. That a quest for power on the part of both Foat and NOW caused them to let the ends justify the means. Had that in turn made her a sitting duck? Having used the tactics in which NOW had schooled her, why hadn't she stopped to consider either her own vulnerability or the possible repercussions her past might have on the public's perception of NOW? Had success blinded her to the reality of the politics in which she'd so excelled?

The past to which she rarely referred in detail legitimized her feminist identity in 1977. But it also provided the perfect ammunition to be used against her in 1983. Whoever wanted to "stop Ginny Foat" had only to find the most willing firing squad: John Sidote, the Los Angeles police, the Jefferson Parish sheriff's office and district attorneys, and the media. Yet, in another turn of the wheel, the Foat case raised a crucial moral question. For all Foat's charges of a political plot hatched by her NOW enemies, "feminist ethics" also protected her. If in moments of panic or desperation, Foat had herself supplied some of the ammunition, none of her "sisters" would own up to what in other circumstances might be construed as the ordinary responsibility of citizenship. Granted it was a difficult moral decision. Nevertheless, the social contract seemed secondary to the bonds of sisterhood; while expressing their hope that Foat would receive a fair trial, a good number of Foat's colleagues went underground. Whatever they'd heard, whatever they thought they might know, was to be kept "in the family." Outsiders met either invisibility and games of hide-and-seek or a defensive refusal to reveal, much less confirm, anything of substance about Ginny Foat's past. That, it seemed, was dangerous territory.

FOUR

The Rooster Crows

THE press, however, was as intensely interested in who Ginny Foat had once been as in who she had become. Because she and her defense committee were saying little about her past except for the rhetorical reference to "the death of a passive woman," reporters went to the other central character in the story—John Sidote. Sitting in his Nevada jail cell, he was becoming increasingly annoyed by the portrait of his ex-wife as a once-passive woman, the victim of his violent abuse, and now a respectable, almost matronly feminist and selfless political leader. Ginny's supporters had put it on the wire that he was a twice-convicted murderer, an alcoholic, schizophrenic wife-beater bent on revenge—in short, the villain of the piece. But the story was more complicated than that, he insisted: Ginny wasn't what she seemed, even what she claimed to be, and he himself wasn't the "cocky little drifter," the monster her defenders blamed for all her troubles.

He had his own story to tell: Back in 1965, Ginny had been more than willing to participate in their on-the-road saga. The year before, he had been working as a bartender at the Villa Lipani, a small vacation resort outside New Paltz, New York, in the Catskills. He'd worked there for three and a half years. The owner, John Lipani, and his wife were very fond of him, treating him almost like a son, and they'd even cosigned his loan for a new Bonneville convertible. Why? Because Sidote was a gregarious, popular man behind the bar. He would often jump up on the stage to sing along with the band, and his rugged good looks attracted women, even though he was married and had a baby girl.

But Sidote's version went further. Born October 6, 1938, he'd had an ordinary Italian Catholic boyhood. His father was a correctional officer at the Mattewan State Hospital. His mother, educated to the ninth grade, worked for IBM. There was an older sister, Angela, and although Sidote, Sr., had a drinking problem, the children had always felt well cared for. Jack had gone to church regularly, attended both parochial and public schools, and on graduation from Central High School in 1956, he joined the marines and returned to New York after a tour of duty in Texas and a brief look-see at California. In 1959, he married his wife Elaine; they had one daughter, and he soon bought a house near his parents' in Wappingers Falls, outside Poughkeepsie. It was altogether respectable, conventional—the son of working-class people establishing himself in the old community and finding work, usually as a waiter or bartender in local restaurants.

But at the Villa Lipani he was a success, even something of a celebrity. There were plenty of women, and the motel units to which he had access were readily available. He was also known as a "tough guy," able to handle himself, and Lipani put him in charge of depositing the daily receipts, sometimes lending him his car, where a gun was kept in the glove compartment. (He once was stopped by the police and booked on "illegal possession," but Lipani straightened it out.) Often, too, he could be found at the racetrack, with a friend who was the bartender at a nearby motel. A "new" Jack? Perhaps, but one unknown to his parents and wife alike.

Enter Virginia Galluzzo, who caught his eye when she arrived at the Villa's bar one night with a woman friend. Dark-eyed and voluptuous, Ginny was to return to the lounge alone two nights later, and Sidote spontaneously poured her a Cutty Sark on the rocks. Ginny had heard about his Don Juan reputation because from the first she'd made up her mind that she wasn't going to be just another of his one-night conquests, Sidote said. Still, she stayed in the bar until closing, and after they had coffee at a diner, they did, indeed, wind up in his room at the Villa.

To listen to Sidote, it was a *grande passion*. Of all the women he'd played around with, none had affected him so intensely. She was self-sufficient and independent, even a loner, he said, and "very stylish" to boot. Unlike other local girls, she didn't hang out in groups, and felt no compunction at showing up at the lounge both frequently and alone. Sidote, for his part, would jump over the bar, pick up the microphone, and unabashedly serenade her with "There Will Never Be Another You."

Soon the affair became serious, creating problems in Sidote's "respectable" life. The two would see each other every night after he got off work, with Sidote returning to his wife not until the early morning hours. Gossip about their affair reached John Lipani, who, according to Sidote, took him aside to offer paternal advice: Ginny was a schemer, and now that she was demanding a commitment, she would ruin his life.

But the passion held: Each and every time they'd break up, they couldn't stay apart. There were expensive dinners in New York City, evenings at the Yonkers racetrack, horseback rides at four in the morning. Sidote even arranged a weekend trip to Montreal instead of taking his wife on a promised vacation to Atlantic City. "Yeah," the bartender later told an interviewer, "what a sucker for a pretty face! I remember we both returned from Montreal with skinned knees! You know, rug burns!"

Still, he was worried that it was just "a blending of bodies," not something for which to leave his family. His wife suffered, his work suffered, and the whole thing was running him short on sleep.

Ginny's parents were upset as well. They had heard about Sidote, that he was married, and they were aware of the hours their daughter was keeping, the 3 A.M. phone calls and the all-night dates. Ginny had always been independent, but now she was breaking all the rules of their traditional Italian Catholic family; they saw her being led astray by this lounge-lizard Lothario.

Sidote himself, however, was furious that in later accounts he was characterized as the drifter and immoral seducer. After all, he'd been in the marines, spent years at the same job, had a wife and child, had bought a house. No, *she* was the one who had run through fifteen different jobs since high school, who'd been through a marriage and several boyfriends, and "was always looking for the gold at the end of the rainbow." It was Ginny, he insisted, who had done all the pushing. He tried to put off his decision, wavering, but finally couldn't hold back in the face of her ultimatum: "It's me or your wife." And in October 1965, rather than bedevil his wife any further or court the disappointment of his parents (it would be the family's first divorce), his plan was for them to leave town quietly and drive to Florida where he thought he could find work through a man who'd once stayed at the resort. Ginny agreed readily. But there was a problem. His license had been suspended for drunk driving—he was already drinking heavily during those months, he said, because of the tense situation—so he asked Wasyl Bozydaj to come along to help with the driving.

Wasyl was just out of high school and working at the Villa Lipani as a busboy. He'd told Sidote that he wanted to see the country, and when given the opportunity, he jumped at the chance, looking forward to a vacation. For Ginny, though, it was something more—a new life with the man she loved, and that night, after Sidote told her his plan, she informed her family. To no avail they tried to argue her out of it, and the next morning the three set off in Sidote's white convertible, Ginny's romantic fantasy but slightly tarnished by the presence of Wasyl.

Sidote said he wanted to stop in northern New Jersey to collect five hundred dollars owed him by a friend. The debt collected, he sat drinking ouzo with the friend's two Greek bosses, and by the time he was ready to leave he was thoroughly boozed, already trying to drown his guilt, he supposed. Wasyl drove all night, and by the next day, they reached Florida. Sidote had sobered up, and he was already regretting his decision. He'd left without telling anyone, and now he called his parents. Both were upset, his mother crying. Then he phoned John Lipani, who was furious and repeated his warning that Ginny would ruin Jack's life. To make matters worse, Sidote was unable to locate the man through whom he'd expected to find a job. Ginny was worried, too. Their money was quickly running out, and she agreed with Sidote's suggestion that they drive on to Baton Rouge, Louisiana, where an old marine buddy lived. In Baton Rouge it was another seedy motel, Ginny and Jack in one room, Wasyl in another, and within days Ginny was waitressing in a nearby restaurant, Wasyl working at a gas station. Jack, however, could find neither his marine friend nor work of any kind. Every night he sat in the motel room, he said, overcome with remorse for leaving his wife, putting away a fifth of liquor before passing out. As a Catholic, he confessed to Wasyl, he felt it was morally wrong to have left his wife and child, and the way things were going, it seemed that he was being punished for his sins.

One night in a diner they met a man who offered, in exchange for a ride to New Orleans, to introduce them to a bar owner who would give them both jobs. Ginny, Jack, and Wasyl moved on to New Orleans.

Located at the edge of the French Quarter on Canal Street, the Ponderosa bar was a dark, run-down joint, though not without a faithful clientele. It had been raided several times the previous year during New Orleans's 1964 crackdown on B-drinking (bargirls hired to solicit drinks from customers) and prostitution. Police also kept their eyes open for alleged gambling, and there had been an arrest for "lewd dancing." Foat and Sidote were introduced to the owner, Murphy "Happy" Ditcharo, who, Sidote recalled, took one look at Ginny and hired them both on the spot: she as a waitress, he as a bouncer. Waitresses were expected to do a little go-go dancing on the small stage behind the bar, Sidote said, and given the way Ditcharo had eyed Ginny's figure, Sidote, at 145 pounds, supposed he'd been hired simply as part of the bargain. Each was to be paid ten dollars a night.

With Wasyl working at a fast-food joint, the three of them took up residence in a one-bedroom apartment at the John Mitchell hotel, an old, gray hotel kept afloat by transient bartenders and dancers from the nearby French Quarter. Still, with their wages, the threesome could hardly find better, and after paying ten dollars each day for the apartment, they had only ten dollars left for food and cigarettes, and certainly no money for booze. It was a wearying grind, and it was then, Sidote said, that they decided they had to get themselves out of New Orleans and on to better things.

Which was why, he alleged, he and Ginny decided to "roll a guy," the consequence of which he would describe in graphic detail years later from the witness stand when he recounted the tire-bludgeoning murder of Moises Chayo. But back in November 1965, neither he nor Ginny spoke of it again, he said, as they fled New Orleans by plane, she later that night, he the next morning. Wasyl Bozydaj and a mutual friend of Wasyl and Jack's from New Orleans drove the white convertible to the Houston airport, where they all rendezvoused and proceeded westward to Carson City, Nevada. After a few weeks, however, none had found work and they were again low on money. Sidote drank and gambled, losing all but $40 of their funds at blackjack, including the $1,400 he said they'd stolen from Chayo. Again, he alleged, they resorted to rolling someone. He and Ginny, he recalled, pretended to be brother and sister and "chatted" with a man in a bar until Sidote went outside and fell into a drunken stupor in the Bonneville's backseat. Perhaps it was minutes, perhaps hours, but he was suddenly awakened by gunfire, and their robbery victim, Donald Fitting, a San Francisco hotel manager, lay dead in the front seat.

Just as before, he and Ginny never discussed the crime, Sidote said. Fitting had very little money, but they took his diamond ring, and as soon as Ginny had cleaned up the blood that had splattered the interior of the car, they hit the road, ending up in Hermosa Beach, a seaside town in southern California. There Sidote exchanged the foreign currency from Chayo's wallet, Ginny sold the diamond from Fitting's ring for two hundred dollars and went to work as a cocktail waitress. Wasyl, who was again working at a gas station, received his draft notice in early 1966 and took the bus home to New Paltz, his cross-country odyssey brought to an end.

Looking back, Sidote said he was struck by Ginny's lack of remorse, her steely control even then. By contrast, he continued drinking heavily, not just out of guilt but because he wasn't the boss anymore. It seemed that Ginny had taken over his life, maneuvered him into positions from which he couldn't extricate himself. She was his Eve. Seduced by her beauty, he felt he had been brought down by her ambition and willfulness.

Despite their later accusations against each other, in California they remained together. Both had taken jobs in a photography studio, and Ginny's diligence at soliciting customers had brought in a fair amount of money, enough so that when the photo chain went bankrupt, they bought a bar in partnership with another couple, Diane and Howard Monblatt. It was Ginny, too, Sidote said, who decided to marry him so that they could cosign the note for the new business, and over New Year's 1967, they took a quick trip to Arizona to legalize their union.

Located in Torrance, the bar was decidedly redneck, with country and western music and pool tables. Because it was known in the area, the new owners decided not to change its name, though for Sidote it was ironic that the two of them should have a place called "No Regrets." There were times, he said, when he wanted to climb up to the sign and paint out the "No."

Still, they lived day by day, making a go of the business. Sidote drank less, and they began to talk of having a family, this considerably distant from Ginny's later assertion that she stayed with Sidote only out of fear. Her picture of him as a wife-beating, domineering male notwithstanding, Sidote claimed that Ginny, in fact, liked his macho side, citing several examples of her urging him into fights with men who'd tried to pick her up. She enjoyed violence even in their sexual relationship, he hinted. He was tired of hearing her described as the hapless victim. During the first two years in California, he said, it was almost easy, putting the nightmare behind them, working, joking, making love. They were earning a good living, and Ginny had even called her parents, and despite their reservations about their son-in-law, the Galluzzos soon went out to visit.

The No Regrets seemed the answer to what Sidote called Ginny's driving desire to make something of herself. She was an achiever, but Sidote also felt that she was so intent on her own ambitions, so self-absorbed, that she would stop at nothing, including leaving him if a more desirable man came along. His love for her was mixed with trepidation. He sensed this even during their lovemaking: Her body responded, but her mind was her own. But he'd hit her only once, he insisted, and then only with a Scrabble board during one of their frequent interminable games when he was boozed, exhausted, and didn't want to continue.

The Monblatts, their partners, soon tired of running the bar, and Ginny and Jack bought them out. Meanwhile, the bar had begun to deteriorate, drawing a rougher and rougher clientele that was driving away the regulars. A number of Samoans had moved into the area, and Sidote was becoming nervous because of the recent riots in Watts. Indeed, his paranoia about blacks seemed at least in part responsible for his actions one night in August 1967.

According to his several accounts, Ginny was tending the bar when a Samoan got into a hassle with a regular customer over a woman. When Jack came in to relieve her, Ginny told him about the incident, then went home. The Samoan, meanwhile, had become drunker and drunker, and Sidote asked him to leave. After the bar officially closed, about three in the morning, there was a banging on the side door. Sidote, still drinking with friends, thought it was the police, but when the commotion continued he decided that someone was trying to rob him; that or the drunk Samoan had returned, and he went out into the side alley to check. Suddenly four men were standing in front of him, and one of them lunged at him. Sidote ran back into the bar for help, then returned to the alley; at the corner, three more men jostled him, knocking him down as they ran for their car parked across the wide boulevard fronting the bar. Sidote rushed to a friend's car where he knew a .25 automatic was stashed, his rationale being to keep the intruders from escaping.

The Samoans' car pulled away from the curb. Sidote ran parallel along the other side of the boulevard, shouting at them to stop. Threats were being yelled back. He raised the gun, and allegedly aiming over the car, fired what he later claimed was a single warning shot. Undeterred, the car sped off. Within the hour, however, Sidote began to worry. Back home, he asked Ginny to phone the local hospital to see if anyone had been admitted with a gunshot wound, and hearing that five men had brought in a seriously wounded friend, he returned to the bar—to get the night's take, he said—where he found three California Highway Patrol cruisers waiting. Taken to jail, he immediately confessed, offering up a labyrinthine tale of paranoia about blacks and shooting "into the air." But the interrogating officers hit him with the cold, brutal fact: His "warning shot" had entered the car and struck the driver in the temple, and Okeni Moe, a Samoan teenager, eighteen, was dead. Sidote was charged with murder.

Ginny was supportive throughout the trial, Sidote said, and his lawyer, Charles Crozier of Los Angeles, argued for involuntary manslaughter since Sidote hadn't weakened in his claim that he'd aimed high. Ginny helped in more material ways. She reported seeing the district attorney outside the courtroom coaching one of the Samoans to act out how Sidote had taken direct aim, and Crozier forced the witness to admit he'd been coached, with the result that the judge reduced the charge accordingly. Before sentencing, however, Sidote was ordered to undergo a ninety-day psychiatric observation. Subsequently, Jack Levitt, M.D., the examining psychiatrist, issued his report, in which he analyzed Sidote's "mental status":

> . . . This is a man with a previously good record who committed a homicide, evidently unintentionally, but in the course of the exercise of extremely poor judgment in the use of firearms. His motivation for firing the fatal shot can be described as weird and the passage of time has not given him better insight. The sequence of events by which he reached the conclusion to fire the shot sounds very much as if he were in a schizophrenic state at the time, although the diagnosis cannot be made at present. The diagnosis of schizoid personality would

seem most appropriate. Because of the seriousness of the offense and his failure to appreciate his own bad judgment, this examiner would be reluctant to release him into the community at the present time. There is insufficient evidence of current mental illness to justify a Mental Hygiene commitment.

PSYCHIATRIC DIAGNOSIS: (50.1) Personality pattern disturbance, schizoid personality (with acute schizophrenic reaction at the time of the offense). Prognosis: Unlikely to commit a similar offense in the future, but the small risk is too much to take in view of the seriousness of the offense.

During his stay at the Chino state prison—having pulled the liberal sentence of six months to fifteen years—Sidote underwent psychological counseling as well as treatment for his alcoholism. A year later, when it was time to apply for parole, he supported his application with a statement to the parole board, which was striking for its lack of remorse. Instead, the letter, handwritten by Ginny, rehearsed his explanation of the shooting, as if to justify again his garbled version of reality, and it was only the last paragraph that expressed any sense of regret or attempt to "change":

> To ask me to describe my feeling now is almost impossible. Everytime I see a kid his age or go past the scene I relive that night. There is nothing I can say to myself that takes that awful feeling away from inside of me. We will have to live with this. I only pray that God will forgive and help me to make another life for myself.

Given the later allegations from Ginny and her supporters that her life with Sidote had been a nightmare of alcoholism and abuse, one would have expected his imprisonment to be the final straw and her chance to escape. Instead, she was the dutiful wife, visiting every weekend, bringing her husband home-cooked meals, and in August 1969, when Sidote was about to come up for parole, she wrote a letter proclaiming her love and support, insisting that she found it "a very difficult and lonely life without him":

> When John was arrested I was both shocked and completely beside myself with grief. It became necessary for me to be under a doctor's care for sedation. . . .

During this last fifteen months he has become a changed person. He has taken advantage of his time to further his education both vocationally and academically. He has also been able to gain a full insight into the problems, the reasons and exactly what his responsibility was in the crime. He is also aware of the problems and grief he has caused to all concerned and is most repentant . . . , has developed a new outlook on life, and is ready to take his place in the community as a useful and law abiding citizen. As his wife and the closest person to his thoughts and feelings, I can honestly say that I feel that he is ready for probation and he is quite anxious to prove himself worthy of such consideration.

I love John very deeply and I am willing to give him any assistance that is possible to help him attain his goals and make a good and meaningful life for us and a future family. If probation is granted, I will do everything in my power to cooperate with John in meeting every provision of that probation. . . .

A letter from Mr. and Mrs. August Galluzzo, Ginny's parents, was also filed with the parole board, and whatever their doubts about Sidote's stability, whatever violence against their daughter they would later claim to have witnessed, they expressed only unequivocal support for his parole so that "he and our daughter may start their life anew":

This young man is sincere and has achieved a fine moral character with the help of the personnel at Chino. We flew to California and spent the month of December, 1968, with our daughter and visiting John. At that time, we found him truly sorry for his crime and anxious in some way [to] make up for all the grief and worry his mistake has caused. We know that if he is given the chance for parole his attitude and determination to make a new life for himself and our daughter would prevent him from ever being any trouble to the Court again.

We are praying that you will heed our plea and that of his parents, relatives and friends who know what a fine man he is. . . .

Hardly surprising was the letter submitted by Mrs. Michael Sidote, Jack's mother, at least not until compared with the style and syntax of the other two:

August 12, 1969

To Whom It May Concern:

When I was informed of the crime in which my son John was involved I found it almost impossible to believe. The reason being that John was never in trouble with the police before.

At the time I had just recovered from a serious malignant operation. The shock of John's involvement in the incident caused me to have a relapse and I have since been under the doctor's care. I'm taking tranquilizers as the days go by and I just don't know how much longer I can last under the strain of John's imprisonment.

Being John's mother, I feel that my son is ready to be considered for parole and ready to resume his life in the community. I received letters from him weekly and I have talked to both him and his counselor. Through his letters and our conversations, John has expressed and repeatedly told me of his desire to make restitution for his mistake. He has a deep regret for what happened and all the problems it has caused. He has, through discussions with his counselor at Chino, been able to gain a complete understanding of the mistake he made and what he should have done to prevent it. John is determined to return to the community and make every possible effort to repay society for all the trouble he has caused by becoming a useful and law-abiding citizen. He is also quite concerned with the welfare of his wife and the hardship he has caused her. . . .

The language of all three letters was strikingly similar, suggesting that Ginny had organized a campaign, recruiting letters that would answer the questions she'd been told the parole board was likely to ask. Incidents of alcoholic tantrums and beatings (which she would later allege) were nowhere mentioned. Then, too, there was the emphasis on "a good and meaningful life . . . a future family." Another letter from a social worker stressed that nothing was more important to Ginny than to be "reunited" with her husband, and whatever abuse she'd suffered at Sidote's hands she certainly hadn't revealed to this counselor: "The wife has undergone much hardship during the time of John's incarceration and John is eager for the opportunity to once again become a useful citizen."

An old family friend also wrote, attesting that theirs was an "excellent marriage" waiting only to be resumed: "Mr. Sidote has expressed a desire to make an honest living to provide a good home for his wife and resume an excellent marriage, so abruptly interrupted."

The parole board received letters as well from a priest and a police commander in upstate New York, as well as a joint petition from three dozen Torrance neighbors that stated, "Knowing Mr. Sidote, we feel sure he is incapable of committing bodily harm upon another person. We have found him to be a man of integrity and pleasant disposition. At no time have we ever found him to be a man of violence."

While Ginny was extolling his rehabilitation, marshaling support from every quarter, Jack himself had begun to feel that their future life together might be something of a question mark. With the bar sold, Ginny worked for the telephone company, then took a disability leave, so distraught was she, she said, over her husband's imprisonment. Later she found a job as a waitress on the *Princess Louise,* a floating restaurant in San Pedro, and soon she was boasting of the new people she was meeting, the restaurant's "select clientele." Nevertheless, according to Sidote and the police, one of her acquaintances soon proved to be a small-time hood, Richard Busconi, whom Ginny once brought to Chino along with a mutual friend and introduced to Sidote as "Blackie." According to Sidote, Ginny was later beaten by Blackie until her face was black-and-blue. When she missed her regular Saturday visit to Chino, however, Sidote said he was told she'd been in an auto accident. But two weeks later, he heard another story from two Los Angeles homicide detectives. One of them, John St. John, also known as "Jigsaw John," questioned him about the murder of one Richard Busconi, found dead of a bullet wound at 10:30 P.M., May 15, 1969. St. John said Busconi had gone to Finn's bar, a run-down waterfront joint in San Pedro. At 10:00, after two drinks, he left alone, and thirty minutes later his body was discovered at Anaheim and Western avenues. The police concluded that an unfired, holstered .357 Magnum found in a nearby trash can was Busconi's own, stashed there while he waited in the bar and available for use if necessary during his "meet." A spent 30-30 cartridge casing was also found, leading police to speculate that the use of a high-powered rifle meant a gangland hit, possibly a drug deal gone sour. But since they had evidence that Busconi was not only dating but, according to St. John, living with one Virginia Sidote, whose husband was in Chino, they also suspected Sidote of having hired a hit man. The motive? Revenge.

Ginny was questioned, not as a suspect but as a possible witness. She denied living with Busconi and insisted that he was only a casual friend, and while admitting that she had occasionally dated him, she claimed no knowledge of whom he was meeting that night or who might have killed him.

Sidote, however, was furious, since it was the first he'd heard that Ginny was "dating," much less living with another man while he was in the joint. He argued with St. John, trying to convince him that he hadn't been aware of Blackie's living arrangements, nor that Blackie's name was Busconi, and thus couldn't possibly have had any knowledge of the murder. He agreed to a lie-detector test and passed; still, the police were suspicious, and his parole review was postponed until the following August.

Hurt and angry, Sidote said he confronted Ginny, who denied everything, insisting that the police had fabricated the whole scenario. She complained that the cops had been hassling her, too, and tried to reassure Sidote that she'd never had an affair with Busconi and had only known him through Sidote's own friend. The police were at fault, she said, desperate as they were to close the case.

Peace was restored for the time being, enough so that during one of her regular visits, Sidote remembered discussing sex, or the lack thereof, in prison. He told her that homosexuality was widespread, although it was not for him. Then he asked what she was doing for "relief" since obviously she had the freedom to have affairs. She told him that what was more important was the close friendship she now had with a woman in Los Angeles who was kind and gentle and someone she could "talk to."

Then one day his confidence was shattered by his counselor, whom he'd grown to trust. The man called him into his office and showed him a letter written by Raymond Foat's wife. Sidote knew Raymond Foat was the manager of the *Princess Louise* and Ginny's boss, someone she often mentioned. Now it seemed clear to Sidote why her visits had become less frequent: Ginny was having an affair with him, and, indeed, the man's wife had enclosed a photograph of Ginny and her husband together. What she wanted, really what she was begging for, was Sidote's help in convincing Ginny to stay away from her husband.

Sidote confronted Ginny with the letter. Once again, she had an answer: The wife was a neurotic hypochondriac whom Raymond Foat no longer loved and from whom he was trying to separate. She was crazy enough to stir up trouble and blame her marital difficulties on Ginny. For Sidote, the story was so complicated that he was sure she was lying. Still, he told himself, let it slide—the most important thing was to get paroled, then everything would be all right.

In the spring of 1970, with the appointment of a new parole-board head, restrictions began to ease and Sidote was placed in a work-release program. He was still "institutionalized" but was allowed to drive back and forth to his job at a local body and fender shop. Every morning he'd stop by Ginny's apartment before work, but her hostility, he realized, was growing. Resentful at his waking her at 7 A.M. when she hadn't gotten off work until well after midnight, she wasn't interested in rousing herself, much less in making love. Still, he didn't say anything, figuring his best bet was just to carry on until his release.

But more and more he felt closed out of her new interests, he said. One Saturday she took him shopping for clothes at an expensive boutique, leaving him feeling patronized and vulnerable, put down for his lack of sophistication in a "hip" environment. She also introduced him to her new woman friend. Sidote liked her and found her attractive—blond, nice, and soft-spoken, but once again he felt excluded: Ginny and her friend talked while he, the outsider, sat in the living room watching TV. During another weekend furlough, Ginny took him to see Diane Monblatt, their No Regrets partner, who was by then divorced. But the women's conversation that day took a new turn, Sidote said: "It was anti-men, 'Who needs 'em?' That sort of thing."

Sidote was biding his time, reminding himself that things would work out. But the day before his release in July 1970, he arrived, as usual, early in the morning, and when Ginny refused to awaken, he couldn't stop himself. One thing led loudly to the next. All her games and bullshit were destroying him, he remembered yelling. Ginny's response was the cool, flat announcement that she no longer had a place for him in her life. That's when he blew, Sidote admitted, crazy as he was with sheer fury. He grabbed her around the neck, screaming that after all they'd been through together, she couldn't do this to him.

It was as if something had snapped, he said, but then he came out of it. He threw her to the floor and walked out, phoning two weeks later to demand a divorce. Ginny, however, had gone back to New York. Charles Crozier, his lawyer, filed for divorce, and on September 10, at her parents' home back in New Paltz, New York, Ginny signed the summons. An interlocutory judgment was entered on January 13, 1971.

Sidote remained in Los Angeles that year, living with a new girlfriend and working at the body and fender shop. The following year he went back to Wappingers Falls to visit his family and decided to stay. It was the beginning of a seven-year downward spiral. He was drinking heavily, and when he was able to find work the jobs were all temporary, like working in a garment factory or painting houses. He had no idea where Ginny was and couldn't have cared less, he said. Later he heard that she'd married Ray Foat in 1971, but then in 1973, at 6:30 one morning his mother called him to the phone, and he heard a slurred voice, "Wanna go out on a date tonight?" When he seemed confused, there was a teasing, "What's the matter? You forget your wives so soon?" It was Ginny, calling from California—3:30 A.M. Pacific time. He could barely make out her words and became angry.

"What the fuck do you think you're doing?" he demanded.

She said she just felt like talking. The conversation was screwy, he recalled, random, pointless, and he assumed she was drunk. Then silence, as if she'd passed out. He hung up. It was the last he heard from her, he said.

During the next few years Sidote's despair worsened, fed by his memories and at least a fifth a day. In his alcoholic stupors, the faces of Chayo and Fitting haunted him, he said, and he would relive the crimes over and over again in hallucinatory flashbacks. He had no one to talk to, he was no longer a practicing Catholic, he couldn't go to a priest. He couldn't talk to his parents either. He broke down and wept in front of his older sister one evening, but he was so incoherent that later he realized she'd had no idea what he was saying.

He continued to drink, every morning feeling that he was dying. It was a common enough cycle among alcoholics, and finally, in 1974, he admitted, he "flipped."

Inevitably, one of Sidote's problems had been money, and early one morning he awoke from a blackout to find himself in John Lipani's house. Lipani wasn't home, but Mrs. Lipani stood in front of him, her face bruised and bleeding.

"What happened?" he asked in a panic.

Mrs. Lipani told him that he'd broken into the house and demanded money, and when she'd refused, he'd struck her with a heavy glass ashtray. Sidote had no idea how he'd gotten there, nor did he recall hitting the woman. He sat down in a state of alcoholic bewilderment, and weeping told her to call the police.

Unable to meet bail, he was back in jail. His lawyer, Frank Martocci, argued with authorities that since he was no longer on parole in California, he should not be considered a predicate felon, and in December 1974 Sidote was released from prison to await the court decision that would determine his sentence. The case would be in the courts for the next three years, and Sidote continued his downhill slide; although he entered the Albany VA hospital alcohol-treatment program twice and several other clinics as well, he went back to drinking each time he was released. The nightmares continued, and he'd awaken shaking and sweating as he relived the murders. Still, he insisted, he wasn't thinking of Ginny. It was just his own personal hell, and nothing he did could put an end to it. To make matters worse, an operation on an arthritic big toe forced him to turn down the few jobs he could find, and he moved to a small apartment in Albany. Still drinking, about to face court sentencing for his attack on Mrs. Lipani, he said he realized he was suicidal.

It was this realization, he said, that prompted him to walk into an Albany police station and tell them of the two 1965 robbery-murders. Although he knew he'd be implicating Ginny, he insisted that he gave it no thought since he felt so compelled to confess to regain his sanity. He was sober when he described the killings, and police sent him home for a few days while they matched his statements to two unsolved murders. Then he was brought to the state police barracks in Highland, New York, where Senior Investigator Roger Gardner and Sergeant John Salters questioned him in greater detail. Coming down from a three-day drunk, Sidote was beginning to go into withdrawal and he told Salters he needed medication or at least a drink. According to a *New York Times* interview, Salters recalled, "He was going through the shakes, had the DTs. I bought him half a pint of vodka because he was gonna fall apart on me. He started telling us about two homicides that had been committed by him and Galluzzo. He had just had it, it was on his conscience."

Several weeks later and sobered up, Sidote repeated his testimony to the district attorney in two statements, the first on February 9, 1977, about the Nevada murder, the second on March 16, 1977, in which he recited what had happened the night in New Orleans:

> . . . in 1965 I left Baton Rouge, Louisiana, where I was looking for work with Virginia Galluzzo, on a promise of a job in New Orleans. This fellow we met one night at a restaurant said that he knew a guy by the name of Happy Decharo [sic] who owned a bar in New Orleans called the Ponderosa, and that I could probably get work down there; he was a friend of his. So, we arrived in New Orleans and were introduced to this Happy Decharo. He ran the Ponderosa Bar on Canal Street. After a short interview we started working for him immediately. We were making like ten dollars a piece a night. Virginia was working behind the bar and I was working out front. We did that for approximately two weeks, and we were living in a hotel off of Canal Street, I don't remember the name of it, and we were paying ten dollars a night rent, and subsequently we had ten dollars to eat and whatever. And as I stated before, all through this thing I was drinking quite heavily; probably half of the ten dollars went for a bottle every night. After a couple of weeks we just decided we couldn't make it on those funds. So, we decided that we would have to get some more money, and the way we decided to do this was Virginia was going to pick up — Let's say a subject in a bar on Bourbon Street. I believe this was a Friday night. Bourbon Street is a pretty good hustling area. We decided I was going to stay in the trunk of the car and she was going to drive this subject to a remote area and we were going to roll him. So, we proceeded to do that. She drove to Bourbon Street. We parked in a very small parking lot, and she was dressed very nicely, and she went—I don't know where,

somewhere on Bourbon Street, and picked up an individual. I was in the trunk of the car and I had a cloth, like to dust the car with; I had a cloth between the lock mechanism to keep the trunk slightly ajar, and I could hear muffled noises. I couldn't make out or distinguish them over the noise of the motor because of the traffic and what not, but I could hear two voices, one man's and Virginia's voice, and the car was moving; I have no direction which way we went, other than on the way back I remember some things. Anyway, it seemed we were driving quite a while, and apparently she hit a chuck hole and the trunk lid slammed shut. Finally the car stopped, and there was some mumbling; they were standing by the back of the car and I heard her say something. Virginia said that she felt ill or nauseous; she had some pills in the trunk of the car, medicine. She needed some reason to get the trunk open. When she opened the trunk door I came out and grabbed this guy, and that's the first time I had seen him. He was — Oh, I'd say about fifty years old. He was maybe a little shorter than I am, say five foot seven; very portly, very heavily built. A struggle ensued, and I just tried to knock the guy down. I had a tire iron. I wanted to get his money and leave. During the struggle Virginia was standing by the side of the car and she yelled, "He saw my driver's license. He knows my name. We got to kill him." I guess when the guy heard that he started fighting like desperately. He was a lot—I'd say he went about 210 or so, very stout, and I couldn't get my leverage; he was pushing me towards the back of the car. There were two lug wrenches in the car. I said to her, "You got to help me." At that time she grabbed a lug wrench and struck him on the side of the temple. He let go of me and he fell and then she struck him again, and at this time the guy was like passed out. I don't know what he was. Anyway, she grabbed his wallet and jumped back in the car and we left. On the way back I remember coming back into— I don't even remember how New Orleans is laid out. The main drag runs into— Canal Street runs east and west or north and south. I think it's east and west. We approached New Orleans from a westerly direction. We got back to the area of the hotel and my clothes were pretty well battered up, so she went upstairs and got me some fresh clothes. She had the wallet. We went some place on a dark street and I changed. The guy had fourteen hundred dollars in his wallet. We drove and got rid— Threw the lug iron away. I had a ripped shirt and my pants were ripped. I threw them away too. We went back to the hotel. That night Virginia flew to Dallas, Texas, from New Orleans, and I stayed there and I flew out the next day to Dallas.

Sidote was first extradited to Nevada to stand trial. There he learned that Ginny had also been indicted on the Nevada charge but was fighting extradition from California. Again, he gave a statement "in his own words and spelling," about the Nevada robbery-murder of Fitting:

This is my recollection of the incidents that took place on December 19, and the pre-dawn hours of December 20th 1965.

Virginia Foat and myself were living in Carson City at the time, and were in need of funds to get to So. California. We discussed the idea of going to one of the Casinos at Lake Tahoe, and getting a patron drunk and rolling him. At approx. 10 p.m. on the 19th we went to the So. Shore of Lake Tahoe with that intention. We went to a few of the clubs that were open, and had some drinks, and looked for someone. I recall I had a bottle of Canadian Whiskey in the car which I drank from so that we would not have to spend much of the little money we had left. At about 2 A.M. we went into the lounge at one of the casinos, and took a seat next to a man sitting alone at the bar. Virginia introduced herself, and then introduced me as her brother. She struck up a conversation with the man, who I later remember to be Donald Fitting, by telling him that we were traveling cross country on vacation. Virginia sat next to Mr. Fitting, and I sat next to her, so much of the conversation was lost to me. I made a few trips out to the car to drink, and started getting drunk. Finally around 3:15 I excused myself and went to the car. I had been drinking very heavy for the past two months, and particularly that day, because of what we had planned. At the time I left I had no idea of what Virginia intended on doing, because she was supposed to get the man drunk, and try to find out how much money he had. I must have fallen into a drunken sleep, because at times I could feel motion, and hear sounds. Then I heard loud noises. I thought I heard two, and vaguely recall seeing two figures. Then as I became more awake Virginia told me to help her get him out of there. It was at that time that I fully noticed a man sort of lying against the passenger side door. I got out of the back seat, and opened the passenger door. At that time the man sort of fell against me, and with the light going on I saw blood on the back of the seat. Virginia had come around from the drivers side, and helped me place the man at the side of the road. I remember her saying to get the ring off his finger, which I did. At that time I saw lights in the distance, and I was shaking all over with fright. I yelled some ones coming lets' go. I got back into the rear seat, and she drove, but I remember we were heading into South Shore again. She pulled into a side road, and we waited until a truck passed believing the lights we saw belonged to it. I took several drinks from the bottle I had on the way back to Carson City, to stop from shaking. Oh! Also when the front doors were open I noticed a gun on the front seat. On the way back to Carson I recall asking what happened, but was told "I don't want to talk about it." It was almost daylight when we got home, and we both went right upstairs. In a short time Virginia left to appearantly clean up the car. I just sat there for a time and drank I must have passed out, because when I woke up it was dark out again.

It seems that during the past 12 years I've tried to block all memory of what happened that night from my mind, because now as I try to recall it—it comes back to me in snatches. I didn't remember about drinking from the bottle in the car, but there was always at least a bottle of scotch and a bottle of Canadian in there, and I wasn't sure until now that we lived in an upstairs apt.

That night we left Nevada and went to So. California. When I got in the car to leave it was clean, as though nothing had happened. When we got to Calif. Virginia sold the stone from the ring Mr. Fitting was wearing in a jewelry store for $200.

I don't know where the gun that was used came from, or what happened to it afterwards. I don't recall any of the conversation or actions between them that led up to the shooting. Virginia and I never discussed what happened that night again.

Sidote's memory matched an unsolved murder described in police reports:

> The records of the Douglas County Sheriff's Office reflect that on December 20, 1965 at approximately 4:40 P.M., a person called the Zephyr Cove Sheriff's Office and advised that he had observed a body lying on the rocks west of the westbound lane of Highway 50 at the Cave Rock Tunnel. The crime scene was investigated and the body was removed to the Capitol City Mortuary in Carson City where it was determined the victim had been shot three times with a small caliber weapon. The ensuing investigation failed to turn up any suspects and the investigation was eventually abandoned and classified as an unsolved murder. . . .

Sidote was formally booked for murder on April 19, 1977, but according to his presentence report, it was stated that his pleas of guilty to the two felonies, voluntary manslaughter and robbery, were made in exchange for the following concessions:

(1) That the charge of First Degree Murder will be dismissed at the time of sentencing.
(2) That the defendant agrees to cooperate and testify in all proceedings in the matter of State vs. Virginia Foat, also known as Virginia Sidote, also known as Virginia Galluzzo.
(3) That the subject does waive preliminary examination.
(4) That the District Attorney will remain silent at the time of sentencing.
(5) That if the Parole and Probation Department recommends concurrent sentences, the District Attorney will go on record as not opposing concurrent sentences.

Had Sidote thought that confessing would mitigate the sentence on the Lipani burglary charge back in New York? By implicating his ex-wife, would he get lighter sentences on all these charges? Was he out to get Virginia, even at a cost to himself? The mind of an alcoholic and diagnosed schizoid personality, much less a "stir-smart con," works in mysterious ways. But in his March 19 statement, he'd insisted on explaining his motives:

The reason I walked into the police department in Albany and related these . . . twelve-year-old incidents, undoubtedly unknown to anyone other than Virginia and myself [is that] the past twelve years have been—well, like living in a nightmare because of my alcoholism, and I could see that I was killing my parents. . . . The reason I was drinking like that was because I was so disgusted with myself. This was my way of trying to escape or trying to kill myself, man, because I couldn't stand what I had become or what I had done. I guess . . . I will spend the rest of my life in prison, but I couldn't live on the streets anymore the way I was, knowing what I had done, having to live with that. . . .

. . . At first I thought it was for vengeance, to get back at Virginia for what happened when I was in prison, but the more I think about it, the more I realize I had to do it, not because of vengeance, but for higher, you know, I had to bare myself.

He didn't have the word for motives, higher or otherwise. But a psychologist might well ask why he'd had to deny the motive of vengeance if revenge hadn't occurred to him. Had he in fact been obsessed with Ginny all these years? Had he in his DTs seen her as a Medusa, a bitter fury who had destroyed him? Had he committed these crimes himself, and out of rage and anger and a pathological love for her not only placed her with him but put the murder weapons in her hand? Or could he be telling the truth, his hallucinations real memories? In his mind were the two of them locked together in a murderous embrace of shared guilt?

Whatever motives lay behind his confession, his obsession with Ginny seemed evident in his March 16 police statement:

She is about five foot five, I'd say, and she weighs about 135. She is a very well-built girl, very statuesque. She is a classic kind of beauty. She has high cheekbones, very straight nose. She has an olive complexion. She has a full, kind of sensuous mouth; black hair, and she usually wears a hairpiece with it to make it look fuller.

Sidote's February 9, 1977 description of her was even more lush:

She is about 5'5", weighs about 135. She has naturally dark brown hair, but always wears a hairpiece with it usually, nine times out of ten she would to make it fuller. She has olive skin, complexion, brownish; kind of aquiline nose, thin, slightly turned up. Her features are classic, high cheekbones, full mouth, full lips, sensuous looking, very statuesque. She is about like 38-24-36, something like that, very statuesque girl, very high fashion dresser, modelish type.

The girl of his dreams, the woman of his nightmares, so statuesque that he imagined her a *Playboy* centerfold. (Had he remembered that she'd once applied to be a bunny at the Playboy Club in New York City?) No wonder he'd insisted she was a go-go dancer in New Orleans. Her measurements, for Sidote, seemed paramount, her "statuesque" figure alive in his dreams.

Then, too, both statements were studded with jailhouse patois—the hip "man" and "terms of incarceration" and "what transpired." Cons seem to reach for the multisyllable jargon of the cop, and Sidote had done enough time to lapse into it easily. Moreover, he seemed well known to the New York State police, which raised another question about his motives. In September 1975, long before his two murder confessions, Sidote's attorney Frank Martocci, appealing Sidote's burglary case, had cited character references, one from the police department of Wappingers Falls, another from the sheriff's office of Dutchess County, New York, both giving a glowing background of Sidote in connection with "police work" in Wappingers Falls and Dutchess County. The nature of the police work was never mentioned. Had Sidote been a snitch? Was he well enough connected from his early years to be of use to local authorities? Had he perhaps decided to confess in 1977 because someone had discovered his past, leaving him little choice between cement shoes and a jail cell?

No one really seemed to know. While Sidote awaited sentencing in Nevada, Ginny was drawing another picture. She and her attorney Robert Tuller were fighting her extradition to Nevada, and at Tuller's request Ginny's parents wrote to describe the violence of their ex-son-in-law. Suddenly their feelings about Sidote had changed. Jekyll had turned into Hyde, even though they were referring to exactly the same time period when they'd previously extolled Sidote's virtue and great love for their daughter.

16 June 1977

To: Mr. Robert K. Tuller
    Atty-at-Law

In an effort to aid you in the presentation of your case before the Governor of California on behalf of our daughter, Virginia, we do have knowledge of and I was witness to the violence and threats upon Virginia, by one, Jack Sidote, and am relating the incidents as follows:

In the Fall of 1967, I visited Virginia and Sidote in Torrance, California. After I had been there several days, a discussion came up between them, about something, and Sidote started to punch Virginia. I came to her aid. I told him that, if I ever saw him do that again he would have to answer to me. Shortly after this incident, I questioned my daughter about this type beating and she told me that every time he lost his temper with her, he would beat her. I could tell she lived in fear of this man. From our discussion and what I witnessed, I have to presume that she was afraid to leave him, fearing that he would search and find her and inflict greater harm upon her.

I do not know for a fact that she stood by Sidote when he was confined at the Chino Penitentiary for killing a young man when they owned and operated the No Regrets Bar in Torrance, California.

In December of 1968, Mrs. Galluzzo and I went to visit Virginia, who was then living in San Pedro, California and while we were there we went with Virginia to visit Sidote at Chino. Even under those conditions, while they were walking around the recreation area, he slapped her. Apparently, the slap was severe as she came back to the table where we were sitting and we saw that she had been crying. On the way back to San Pedro we questioned her about the reason for her crying and she told us what had happened. That was the last we ever saw of Sidote.

I do know that Virginia continued to visit Sidote on the weekends, since she worked during the week. When he was told he would be paroled in 1970, Virginia told us she bought him a whole new outfit to wear home. Sidote apparently lied to her about the date he would be released as he came home a day earlier to the apartment in which Virginia was living, at the time, with her friend Clara.

Virginia was sleeping and Sidote came into the apartment, pulled Virginia out of bed, by her hair, and then commenced beating her black and blue.

Shortly after that Virginia came home to New York, her body was covered with welts and black and blue marks and stayed with us approximately five or six weeks. Shortly after that Virginia returned to California.

Shortly after Virginia left to return to California, we received a letter from Jack Sidote addressed to Mrs. Galluzzo and myself in which he called our daughter all the rotten things a woman could ever be called, and ended his letter with the statement that he would get even with our daughter, if it was the last thing he ever did.

Unfortunately and regrettably, I do not have that letter as I was so angry upon reading it and the letter was so vile that we didn't want to keep it in our home.

I attest the foregoing to be true and correct to the best of my knowledge.

August F. Galluzzo

Neither Tuller's argument that Sidote's accusations were the vengeful lies of an abusive husband nor the Galluzzos' affidavit could dissuade Governor Jerry Brown from extraditing Foat to Nevada. On August 27, 1977, she was arraigned in the Tahoe Township Justice Court. Her arrest and property record of August 25 from the Carson City sheriff's department listed her address as Canoga Park, and her marital status as married, her husband's name Raymond Foat. This was not, however, quite accurate: On February 8, 1977, she had filed a petition for divorce from Foat, in which she said she had been separated from him since November 1976. In his response, Ray Foat corrected her dates: They had been separated only since January 1977, and he supplied the correct wedding date, May 17, 1971. Ginny had listed the date as May 17, 1969, which would have meant that she had still been married to Sidote when she married Foat.

As it turned out, she was indeed still legally married to Sidote, not only when she married Foat in 1971, but at the time of the Nevada arraignment. A strange turn of events, which her lawyer argued disallowed Sidote's testimony against her on the basis of husband-wife privilege.

For Sidote, meanwhile, a surprise was in store, too. When he arrived in court for sentencing, the Douglas County district attorney handed him a note saying, in effect, "Accept both manslaughter and robbery charges or next week you're going up on first-degree murder." While nothing was in writing, Sidote had assumed that in exchange for his testimony he would be charged only with manslaughter.

District attorneys, however, can guarantee nothing. The probation department had discussed Sidote's case and, having reached the conclusion that his "extensive criminal record," the outstanding Louisiana murder warrant, as well as his involvement in this "wanton senseless crime" did not justify "further leniency by the court," it recommended that he be sentenced as follows:

> Count Number One—Voluntary Manslaughter, the defendant is to be confined in the Nevada State Prison for a term of eight and one half years.

> Count Number Two—Robbery, the defendant shall be sentenced to a term of twelve years in Nevada State Prison, with this sentence to run consecutive to Count Number One.

The court took an even harder line. Instead of the recommended total of eighteen and a half years, Sidote was given twenty-five—fifteen for voluntary manslaughter, ten for robbery, the sentences to run consecutively. Furious at the sentence, Sidote suddenly refused to testify against Foat.

Douglas County authorities nonetheless went ahead with Foat's preliminary hearing on September 22, 1977. Her Nevada attorney introduced a copy of her marriage license (objecting to Sidote's testimony on the grounds of the husband-wife privilege) and argued that his accusations lacked corroboration. Then Sidote was called, and he announced his decision for the court record:

> Due to the severity of the sentence I received last Tuesday in this case, I feel like justice in this matter has been duly served and, therefore, I choose to remain silent at this hearing. The only questions I will answer are those pertaining directly to my marital status at this time and to identification of the defendant in this case.

He said he resented the way the Douglas County district attorney had treated him, but more, he'd refused to testify because he insisted that all along he was not out to get his ex-wife but to "come clean."

The court noted his refusal, adjourned, and then on November 14, 1977, heard Foat's application for a writ of habeas corpus. Judge Michael Fondi ruled first on the defense's motion of husband-wife privilege, concluding that the "privilege does not apply . . . because the acts which are alleged to have been committed occurred prior to the time of the marriage of the parties."

The district attorney argued that, despite Sidote's refusal to testify, his written confession should be admitted as evidence. Judge Fondi, however, ruled that Sidote's statement had been "made out of the presence of the defendant," and hence wasn't admissible. Further, he concluded that the evidence offered by police officers, including a partial footprint of a woman's high-heeled shoe and the testimony of Wasyl Bozydaj, were insufficient to corroborate Sidote's testimony. All Bozydaj had testified to was that Ginny and Jack often went out at night together (whether looking for work or nightclubbing, he wasn't sure) and that one day they'd suddenly announced they were leaving for Los Angeles because they couldn't get work. The police officers investigating the crime had found the footprint near Fitting's body, but they had no weapon, no fingerprints, no witnesses. The district attorney had no case, the judge ruled, and on November 14, 1977, Ginny was released but then immediately rearrested on the Louisiana warrant. By the next day, when Louisiana had still failed to indict her, the judge again ruled that she was being "restrained of her liberty and continued in custody without charge or good reason." (Jefferson Parish authorities would later claim that since they knew Sidote had refused to testify, they hadn't a prayer of getting an indictment from their grand jury.)

Ginny returned to California and proceeded with her new life. For Sidote, it was the old life of prison. He was sent to the Nevada State Prison and placed in maximum security. He had never been in "max" before, and the rumors of riots and knifings were terrifying. He managed to stay clear of violence, though, and according to Carson City DA Bill Maddox, he became a model prisoner, completing an alcohol-rehabilitation program and successfully holding several outside jobs while in the prison's work-release program, one as a cook, the other working at a vinyl-products plant. He avoided trouble, no mean feat, and since he was accumulating "good time," he knew he'd soon be eligible for parole. Hence, he wanted to confirm the status of the Louisiana charge against him. During his hearings in 1977, Jefferson Parish District Attorney John Mamoulides had advised Sidote's Nevada attorney, John Kadlic, that the length of the Nevada sentence would determine what action Jefferson Parish might take, and when informed that Sidote had received a twenty-five-year stint, Mamoulides said he would ask the Jefferson Parish sheriff's office to remove the warrant.

In response to his 1978 inquiry, Sidote was informed that in fact the warrant had not been withdrawn. On the advice of his lawyer, Sidote filed for a speedy trial. In response to this petition, Deputy Steven Klein, supervisor of warrants and attachments in the Jefferson Parish sheriff's office, wrote to the Nevada department of corrections:

> Be advised that our Detainer #12-1655-65 dated 3-23-77 for one John J. Sidote, W/M, DOB/10-6-38, was withdrawn by our District Attorney's Office on September 27, 1977. Our District Attorney will not extradite in this matter nor will prosecute. Please return our warrant and cancel our detainer.

Sidote was relieved. The way was cleared for an early parole in 1981, after only four years of a twenty-five-year sentence. District Attorney Maddox said that Nevada parole regulations have been tightened since then, but argued that Sidote's record had been good enough to justify his release. "Murderers often make the best prisoners," he added wryly, "and after four years Sidote had both served the standard one quarter of his sentence minus his accumulated 'good time.' " He'd also been sober for four years, and now the prison gates opened. Sidote was assigned to a probation officer in Reno, the board reasoning that he could find work there more easily. It also added a "no drinking" condition to his parole.

Sidote had a hard time finding a job as a house painter, a cook, or anything else he went after. With an inevitability that could make all social workers give up their credentials, Sidote's life once again became a dreary round of TV-watching, and battling the bottle. The only bright spot was a new woman in his life. The Christmas holidays of 1982 were an especially difficult time, Sidote said. He was still unemployed, and the money he'd saved from his earlier work-release job wouldn't last much longer. His girlfriend was ill with pneumonia and had to be hospitalized. Alone and depressed, he decided to drive to Carson City to find a buddy, a guard at the vinyl plant where he'd worked earlier. Unfortunately, the factory was near a saloon. The temptation was too great. First it was one drink, then another, and another. Soon he was two sheets to the wind, and forgetting the friend, he hazily decided to drive back to Reno. Then there was a crash. He'd fallen asleep, the car was off the road, its bumper wrapped around a stop sign. Red and blue lights flooded his vision. A sheriff's deputy was standing by the car, peering in at him.

He was arrested at 1:30 A.M. and booked twenty minutes later at the Carson City jail. His bail was set at a thousand dollars, but his "convicted person's ID card" stipulated the no-drinking condition of his parole. With no question about his drunkenness, it was an automatic parole violation: He'd be held in the county jail until the parole board scheduled a hearing.

In his mid-forties, John Joseph Sidote's face was still roughly attractive but ravaged by the drinking, the difficult years, the serving of hard time. A long scar creased his forehead, the remnant of one of several car accidents. His dark brown hair, sideburns, and moustache were threaded with gray, and his brown eyes were inevitably tired. It was a coarse, masculine face, the face of a gypsy. At five feet seven inches and 150 pounds, the macho stance was exaggerated by his habit of rolling on the balls of his feet, giving his walk a certain kind of strut. By the same token, there was a decidedly basic illusion here, no more or less original in Sidote than in other jail-smart cons: Whatever happens, no matter what, somehow you'll get through.

Bill Maddox, the Carson City DA, was familiar with the prisoner, and he told Sidote he'd drop the drunk-driving and hit-and-run property charges if he simply admitted to the parole board that he had been drinking. No time would be added to his sentence, and the parole violation might cost him only six months. Sidote agreed, and a formal hold was placed on him until his parole hearing on January 18. Until that date, he would remain in the county jail.

On the morning of January 12, however, he was surprised to be led from his cell. He assumed one of his public defenders, Laura Fitzsimmons or Tom Perkins, was there to see him. Instead he was brought out to the sergeant's desk in the front hallway. Many people were milling around, some with television cameras.

"What's going on here?" he asked the sergeant.

"Reporters. They wanna talk to you."

"What, about hitting a stop sign?"

Now the sergeant told him: He was being booked for the 1965 murder of Moises Chayo in Louisiana. There was a warrant, and people from Jefferson Parish had come up to speak to him.

Sidote was even more startled to learn that his ex-wife had been arrested the day before, and soon one of the reporters told him that the case had the media hopping because she was president of California NOW. Having known nothing about her whereabouts or activities since 1977, he was startled by her celebrity as a feminist leader. But more, he had no idea what had led to the revival of the Louisiana warrant.

Shelly Mandell's letter was still unbeknownst to both Sidote and Nevada officials. Jefferson Parish Sheriff Harry Lee, after receiving Mandell's letter and taking renewed interest in the eighteen-year-old murder case, had felt stymied upon learning that Sidote, the principal prosecution witness, had already been paroled in Nevada. No Sidote, no case. But then coincidence, helped by computer technology, played its role—once Mandell's letter had prompted Jefferson Parish to reactivate the warrant for Foat, the Sidote warrant came "alive" in the computer since it bore the same number. When Sidote was arrested on the parole-violating drunk-driving charge, his name was routinely fed into the NCIC computer in Nevada, and much to everyone's surprise they were alerted to a Louisiana warrant for murder. As procedure dictated, Nevada officials notified Jefferson Parish authorities that Sidote was in custody, asking if they wished to act on their warrant.

Here was the real irony of the case, Bill Maddox said. With computer technology, no one could escape his past, and Jack Sidote and Ginny Foat were no exception. "Enlightened" law-enforcement people could talk about rehabilitation, but computer records were always going to haunt you. Not like the old days. He could remember—was it in the thirties or the forties?—a legendary district attorney in one Nevada county who ten years earlier had been convicted and served time for murder in the next county over. But he also figured that Foat's celebrity deepened Louisiana's interest. It was the "fish bowl effect." Once Foat's identity was known and her arrest exposed by the media, Jefferson Parish authorities would find it hard to back off, he thought. Still, as a humane man, he could feel compassion for Sidote. Maddox was sure he had not set out to get his ex-wife at this late date. His mistake—and dumb luck—was to get busted at precisely the moment someone else had resurrected an interest in Foat.

Louisiana authorities, however, insisted that it was not Foat's celebrity that had moved them to pursue the case. Simply put, unsolved murders never go away and District Attorney John Mamoulides just got the break he needed. The Los Angeles police had been notified of the warrant, they arrested Foat on January 11, and Jefferson Parish Assistant District Attorney G. Thomas Porteous flew to Carson City. There was, however, some indication that Sheriff Lee hadn't notified the district attorneys about the case before calling Los Angeles authorities or verifying Sidote's whereabouts.

"I did feel there were some problems with going ahead so quickly," Porteous said. "But in defense of Sheriff Lee, he did have an active and ongoing warrant which anyone can execute. Notified of our warrant, Los Angeles police decided to execute immediately, on January 11, and clearly, after her arrest and once we'd heard about Sidote's parole violation, my trip to Nevada had to occur instantly."

Sidote stood mute as the Nevada sergeant fingerprinted him and rebooked him on the murder charge. When brought in on January 4, he'd refused to sign anything, including the booking form; he'd replied "None" to "Next of kin," and listed only his woman friend in Reno. Now, as if realizing the gravity of the situation, he gave his mother's name, Grace Sidote, as well as her phone number, although he deferred his guaranteed call for a later time.

He did, however, agree to talk to the people from Louisiana. He wanted to find out what was going on. But before being introduced to Tom Porteous, he called the public defender's office to summon his lawyers.

Porteous is a sturdy block of a man, an ex–football player who took his law degree at Louisiana State University. With a fringe of dark-blond hair ringing his bald head, his face can turn from amiable friendliness to angry rigidity at a moment's notice, although his wry humor suggests a "heart of gold," a Lew Archer in a Ross MacDonald novel, say. But he is also a "tough guy," stern of manner and not a man to be crossed. Sheriff Lee had stated that he wouldn't know whether the Jefferson grand jury would indict Foat until they squeezed Sidote, and Porteous was the man to do it. Now he laid it out: Sidote was to come to Louisiana to testify. He pushed harder. Sidote was coming one way or another—either to be prosecuted himself or subpoenaed as the principal witness against his ex-wife.

Sidote's head was reeling. His lawyers still had not arrived, and Porteous wasn't interested in his plaintive insistence that the Jefferson Parish warrant had been dropped in 1978.

When public defenders Tom Perkins and Laura Fitzsimmons arrived, they didn't have documentation of the 1978 withdrawal of the warrant either. Besides, Porteous argued, it hardly mattered. The previous decision wasn't binding since murder has no statute of limitations. Jefferson Parish could proceed with its case, and he gave Sidote twenty-four hours to decide to testify against Foat or be prosecuted himself.

Sidote quickly tried to make a trade: his testimony in exchange not just for immunity in Louisiana but also for a dismissal of the Nevada parole violation. Bill Maddox called a halt immediately: Whatever deal Sidote worked with Louisiana was exclusive of his parole violation in Nevada, he said. All Sidote could hope for was a letter from the Jefferson Parish DAs notifying the Nevada parole board that he was cooperating. Sidote was stuck; he agreed to testify and signed an immunity agreement:

THIS AGREEMENT entered into on this 14th day of January, 1983, between the STATE OF LOUISIANA and JOHN JOSEPH SIDOTE hereby provides:

1. Presently there is a warrant for the arrest of JOHN JOSEPH SIDOTE for Murder and Robbery occurring in the State of Louisiana in November, 1965.

2. The State of Louisiana hereby agrees to grant immunity from prosecution to JOHN JOSEPH SIDOTE with respect to the above-described charges based on the following conditions;

A. JOHN JOSEPH SIDOTE agrees to voluntarily return to the State of Louisiana to testify before the Grand Jury.

B. The testimony before the Grand Jury must be in conformity with his sworn statement of March 16, 1977.

C. JOHN JOSEPH SIDOTE agrees to voluntarily appear and testify in any and all proceedings had in connection with indictments being returned on the above-referenced crimes; said testimony to be in conformity with any and all prior statements including, but not limited to the statement of March 16, 1977, and any and all testimony given before the Jefferson Parish Grand Jury.

D.   This agreement will not apply if JOHN JOSEPH SIDOTE commits perjury.

E.   This agreement will be void if any of the above-listed conditions are violated.

F.   JOHN JOSEPH SIDOTE agrees to the use of his testimony against him if for any of the above-stated reasons this agreement becomes null and void.

Then, hand-printed at the bottom, was the further condition:

G.   The State of Louisiana agrees to send a letter stating that John Joseph Sidote cooperated fully with the Louisiana Authorities if he testifies consistent with this agreement, said letter to be delivered to the Nevada State Public Defender's office on or before February 1, 1983.

After talking to Sidote, Tom Porteous said that while he tended to believe Sidote's story, he was also aware that he was a con. "That meant that I had to deal with him on a certain level. I would have preferred to charge him with the crime, too, even though there were potential problems with trying him, depending on what happened to him in Nevada and depending on how the 1978 letter from Jefferson Parish was interpreted. Still, I was prepared to roll the dice on that, and he knew it. Since he didn't want to risk being charged, he demanded immunity and although I preferred not to give it to him, it was ultimately not my decision. I just reported his position to the DA's office, and then received instructions to proceed with the immunity agreement. In Nevada I had to spend half my time getting Sidote to talk, and the other half negotiating with Nevada officials to allow me to bring him back to Louisiana. A guy can't just pop in and say, 'I'd like to take your prisoner.' 'For what?' they ask. So I had to sell myself to them in twenty-four hours, which I did."

Despite signing the agreement, Sidote continued to rail against Louisiana for going back on its 1978 decision not to prosecute. Louisiana had him, though, and he knew it. Jailhouse-smart, he sensed that the Nevada parole board would look unfavorably on his parole unless he continued to cooperate with Louisiana, and indeed, he was convinced he'd be kept in jail until Foat came to trial, even though he'd officially be eligible for parole the following August.

Meanwhile, Sheriff Lee was trying to answer the insistent question from the press, "Why—now—go after Foat?" His first line of defense was that in 1977 his office had thought that Foat was serving time along with Sidote on the Nevada charge, and that both were still in jail. It was Nevada's fault; they'd failed to advise him either of Foat's dismissal in 1977 or Sidote's release four years later. This wouldn't fly, though. Irritated by the implications of his remarks, Peter Demosthenes, a correctional services officer for the Nevada State Department of Prisons, produced the two 1978 letters to Sidote showing that Jefferson Parish had withdrawn its warrant and had no intention of prosecuting. Under the circumstances, Demosthenes said, Nevada was not obliged to notify Louisiana of Sidote's parole. Further, Louisiana must have known that Foat had not been sentenced to jail in Nevada: In 1977, when she was rearrested on the Louisiana warrant, Louisiana had issued no indictment and she was released on a writ of habeas corpus. With such evidence, Demosthenes was not about to let Sheriff Lee's explanation stand. "If they want to misrepresent the facts," he said, "we have everything here in black and white."

Louisiana authorities now changed their tune: They were proceeding against Foat because they'd just learned her whereabouts, plus they had "new evidence." Sidote himself had no idea what this evidence was nor what the prosecutors had besides his testimony. All he was compelled to do was repeat the confession he'd made in all his statements, including that of March 16, 1977. On January 14, a Nevada judge ordered him released to Porteous for transport to Jefferson Parish, and within twenty-four hours he found himself in isolation in the Jefferson Parish jail in Gretna, Louisiana.

The next day Sidote told his saga of eighteen years before. There were rumors of new witnesses, new circumstantial evidence, but the DA's office agreed: Basically their case depended on Sidote. His record wasn't terrific but they found him credible. Apparently the grand jury found him convincing as well, and along with Wasyl Bozydaj's testimony, they felt they had enough basis to return an indictment against Foat on January 18.

The indictment, of course, raised new outcries among Foat's supporters. The grand jury was all white, predominantly male, and willing to indict on the word of an alcoholic, diagnosed schizophrenic. The sexism was blatant, they claimed, but more, it was an attempt to get a feminist leader. Look at the South, they cried, it's always been antifeminist, and Louisiana especially, with its earlier unsuccessful suit against NOW. No matter that NOW itself had scheduled a meeting in New Orleans that very year; feelings had calcified.

In the face of charges of sexism on the part of Louisiana officials, parishioners wrote letters both to the Foat defense committee and to *The Times-Picayune* defending their district attorneys, citing John Mamoulides's work on behalf of welfare mothers and Assistant DAs Tom Porteous's and Gordon Konrad's sensitivity when questioning rape victims, and pointing out that Konrad's wife was herself a judge. Understandably, neither the DAs nor the citizens of Jefferson Parish liked to be portrayed as intolerant Southern rednecks. Law-enforcement officials were just doing their job, they said, what any police or district attorney's office would do when it found it could pursue an unsolved murder case.

Mary Landrieu, a Louisiana state representative from New Orleans and the chair of the governor's commission on women, read about the Foat case in the newspapers, then heard more about it from NOW acquaintances. As much as she sympathized with the woman's plight, she disagreed that the Jefferson Parish authorities were engaged in an antifeminist plot. She thought that a lot of the statements coming out of California were based on northerners' prejudice against the South, and she didn't think the characterization of Louisiana as a state eager to bring down a noted feminist "was true at all." "Besides," she added, "Jefferson Parish DA John Mamoulides is a friend of mine, and while I didn't personally discuss the case with him, I can't imagine that he would prosecute a case without some solid evidence. I'm sure he felt that the charges were serious enough to pursue no matter what her political position was. Often people will say I'm too defensive about women, so if I had sensed that it was unfair persecution of a feminist, I'd certainly say so. But in this case, I didn't think that was true, nor did I think John Mamoulides would try to attack the feminist movement. After all, it's said that people in Louisiana barely recognize the women's movement, so why would they perceive feminism as such a threat that they had to go after Ginny Foat? Why would they attack a feminist when there's hardly an identified feminist movement here? The community also thought these charges were well founded enough that she should go to trial. Most people here saw it that way, not as an attack on the women's movement either in Louisiana or nationally."

Kim Gandy, a senior assistant district attorney in Orleans Parish until 1979, when she went into private practice in New Orleans, is a regional director of NOW and was one of the contacts who recommended John Reed and Robert Glass to Kay Tsenin. As a feminist and an ex-prosecutor, she would have been particularly sensitive to the possibility of the DA's office going after a feminist. "I've never particularly worked with John Mamoulides, but I didn't have a strong sense that he was antiwoman to the extent that he was out to get a feminist. It's hard to say what motivates people, but I do think this wasn't antifeminism per se. The real problem was that from the *outside,* not the inside, it looked as if the prosecution had grounds to proceed because of the way the case was being played in the media. All the news stories allowed people to infer that the prosecutors had pretty decent evidence. But when I learned more about the case from Kay Tsenin and then began to pick up things around the courthouse, it seemed to me that these were only flimsy grounds on which to proceed. I heard things in the elevator or from other prosecutors inside and outside the parish, and it started sounding like there wasn't much substance. If I had been the DA, I would absolutely not have proceeded just on the basis of an ex-husband's testimony. Under Louisiana law, we don't need corroborative evidence of a 'co-conspirator's' testimony, but given the character of Sidote and given the fact he was an ex-husband, I would have wanted more. But I still don't know why John Mamoulides was willing to buy into it."

Lynne Renihan had just been elected president of New Orleans NOW, and at first all she knew about the case was what she'd read in the newspapers at the time of Foat's arrest. She was puzzled when she heard that a letter from a NOW colleague had set the arrest in motion. She was further perplexed, then annoyed by a telephone call from Judy Goldsmith, who provided no information about the case but instructed her not to comment to the press, not even to answer her phone. "We didn't know the details, but I believed somebody in California, in NOW or in politics out there, had it in for her. Some women here, not feminists but people I talked to in the street or where I work, thought she was probably guilty, one because she was a feminist, an activist and therefore aggressive, and two, because of the stuff about her past coming out in the news stories. It seemed to me, though, it had all started with someone in California who had wanted to get a powerful feminist, and then the Jefferson Parish prosecutors went for it, and the ball was rolling. That's typical of Louisiana politics, though. I'm originally from Iowa, and after five years in Louisiana, I realize that politics here are entertainment. The more outrageous you are as a politician, the more popular you are. Here it's like, 'Oh, great, we're going to have another show, this is going to be fun.' So with Foat, it was the circus atmosphere, the media attention more than anything else that seemed to be behind going after a feminist."

Those who were critical of the DAs' underlying motives for pursuing the case blamed it more on publicity surrounding the case than on deep-seated antifeminist attitudes. Sheriff Harry Lee was up for reelection, and it was said that perhaps he wanted the press coverage this celebrity arrest brought him. John Mamoulides is a powerful political figure in the area, and some suspected that he might have thought the attention focused on this "important" case with its national headlines would further his political ambitions. Still other attorneys who preferred to remain anonymous said that if one wanted to find antifeminism, one should look to the Los Angeles Police Department. They not only were the "real pigs" but a couple of cops out there "had had it in for Foat since her arrest in 1977." More, the women's movement was strong enough in the Los Angeles area to make a difference, and it was certainly lending vocal support to the city council's investigation of the charges that the police department's Public Disorder Intelligence Division (the official name of what had been called the "Red Squad" through the fifties), in defiance of a 1976 police commission order to destroy them, secretly retained intelligence files about city officials, other residents, and political organizations. Further, feminist groups had joined the ACLU's suits against the police department for unlawful infiltration and harassment of political groups.

While it could have been said that Sheriff Lee moved too quickly to advise the Los Angeles police that he had a warrant for Foat, the LAPD needn't have executed it in little over a week's time, nor did they have to arrest Foat in the midst of such media hoopla. It was that act, Louisiana loyalists claimed, that severely hampered the Jefferson Parish prosecutors in building their case, and the revelation about Shelly Mandell's letter, leaked by the police, essentially precluded a discreet investigation of what others in California knew or had heard of Foat's odyssey with John Sidote. Leads were drying up, people going underground, and that wasn't the prosecutors' fault, parish defenders said.

"If I had my druthers," DA Tom Porteous agreed, "I would not have proceeded at such 'breakneck speed,' for lack of a better term. No one was going anywhere, so we would have had time to organize beforehand, make sure we had everything lined up as opposed to after the fact. Nevertheless, I believed Sidote was credible enough to proceed, and obviously the grand jury believed that, too. The fact that she is a feminist didn't enter into it, and it certainly doesn't give her immunity, although it does make it more of a media event. Nevertheless, it was still a murder case, not a vendetta against a feminist. Nor do I think that the image of us and our state as antifeminist is accurate, but it takes coming down here to see that that's not true. But out in California I know we and those of us in our court system were being portrayed as Yahoos with chewing tobacco and pot bellies and Klan sheets in our closets who were just waiting to pick on 'radicals' and take them out and kill them."

But as much as sympathetic reporters, lawyers, feminists, and supporters of Foat pointed to southern attitudes or conservative tendencies or misogynist feelings, none could say for sure that anything more than a prosecutor's zeal for building and winning a case lay behind bringing Foat to trial.

"Sure, Louisiana law, Louisiana politics, all of that was intriguing," said journalist Grace Lichtenstein. "Sheriff Lee, the Chinese sheriff with his cowboy hat, that added to the story. And, of course, it's true that there's no women's movement down there, it's sort of backwater, and not exactly a bastion of feminism. Nevertheless, in the overall context of Foat's story, I don't think Louisiana law or its attitudes were particularly important."

Sheriff Lee—despite his cowboy hat—found himself revealing profeminist sympathies, while insisting that justice, even belated justice, required Foat's indictment. District Attorney John Mamoulides was equally perplexed, even a little confused. As far as he was concerned, Jefferson Parish was only doing what it would do with any unsolved murder case: with the evidence now available, prosecute. For Gordon Konrad, too, Sidote was convincing, a credible witness not only in his testimony before the grand jury but because there were no major discrepancies between his 1977 police and court statements and what he was telling them now.

Oddly enough, Sidote himself agreed with Foat and her supporters that Louisiana had it in for a feminist. After reporters had explained to him that his ex-wife was now a leader in the women's movement, he was certain that Louisiana was going after her for "political reasons." As for his own role, he continued to deny that he was out to get her. After all, he'd refused to testify against her in Nevada in October 1977, and had never done anything to jeopardize her since. Nevertheless, he felt the prosecution was relying too much on his testimony alone, and he gave Porteous names and information to investigate to build a stronger case.

"It's true that Sidote gave us leads," said Tom Porteous, "and we did follow up on some of the stuff he gave us. But I wouldn't put a whole lot of faith in his version of what we did or didn't do."

The lines of investigation the prosecutors chose to pursue were those that led to California, to Ginny Foat's friends—"contemporaries," Porteous called them. "What we had, I was sure, was a two-person crime," he said. "I didn't think there was any way Sidote could have gotten Chayo into that neck of the woods without some enticement or lure, or that the beating could have been done by one person. But the physical evidence was long gone, and all we had was the confession of one party while the other party stood mute. So we had to pursue leads that we had to people who, according to our information, had heard Foat make certain admissions."

These included, they thought, Danny Marcheano, Foat's ex-partner in the catering business, NOW colleagues, and, of course, Shelly Mandell. NOW colleagues tended to "evaporate," but Marcheano talked to investigators and later would be subpoenaed. Through her lawyer, Shelly Mandell let it be known she would not be interviewed, and virtually disappeared. The other person the prosecutors had high hopes for was Elaine Lafferty.

"I was convinced from the beginning that Foat had made admissions," said Porteous. "She couldn't live with it that long. Nobody's that much of an iron maiden. We then also got a bunch of anonymous letters from California, but we ultimately got to Elaine

Lafferty through phone calls and hooking up who knew whom. Our track to her was surrounded with cloak-and-dagger stuff, taking a little while to get to her, then setting up meetings."

"When the prosecutors contacted me the first time," said Lafferty, "it wasn't even clear that they had my name because they knew about my friendship with Shelly. I don't know how they had a lot of their information, but my sense was that somebody was supplying names. They also seemed to be going through NOW membership lists and were contacting NOW people whom Shelly didn't even know. They didn't mention the conversation in the restaurant, but they seemed convinced that I knew something. I told them only what I knew of Ginny Foat in California NOW and that I was considering writing a book on the subject. I was trying to interview them as much as I could to find out what they had, and that wasn't very much. The hottest lead they'd come up with was an elderly black woman who remembered seeing Ginny in a Gretna restaurant's women's room. She said Ginny was crying and told her that she was scared because her boyfriend had just beaten somebody up real bad. I'm not sure how they were connecting that to the alleged murder. Still, my impression from my own research was that there was evidence that they could have pursued but didn't."

"If that's the version Lafferty's happy with, then no comment," Porteous responded. "Still, writing her book was always the explanation for why she couldn't participate. She never showed me a book contract, but once she'd taken that position, maybe that was her way of getting it off her conscience."

Besides, leads in New Orleans like the older black woman weren't especially important, according to the prosecutors; all they did was confirm the "life-style" of Jack Sidote and Ginny Galluzzo in 1965, and they had enough proof that it was seamy and on the wrong side of the tracks. The reputation of Happy Ditcharo and his bar was well known to the police: There had been arrests for B-drinking and lewd dancing. Yet none of this nor 1965 acquaintances of Sidote and Galluzzo corroborated the alleged murder. That was what the prosecutors were after; meanwhile, it was said that the Los Angeles police were doing their own investigations and trying to link every unsolved homicide on their books to Foat and Sidote. But again this seemed pointless to the Jefferson Parish prosecutors, and offered no new evidence beyond Sidote and Bozydaj's testimony.

"I was aware that a certain segment of the case, not Louisiana, was trying to solve every homicide with Ginny Foat. It's true that she'd been around a lot of dead people—Busconi, that good friend of hers Bobbie [a waitress, who had been murdered in 1977 while Foat was in jail]. But I didn't care about those cases unless they had some ties to the murder case in Louisiana. They did not; all they served to do was break through her madonna image. But we could find no connections to our case, so in that sense there were no chinks in the armor, put it that way."

The press began to pick up on "a lot of bodies," too, and this especially upset Shelly Mandell. "I was just blown away by the article that talked about all the people Ginny had known who'd been murdered. People were terrified for me, and I sent my kid away. I also received a telephone threat that I was sure was from Kay, and physically Foat's friends went after me and tried to knock me down at a board meeting in San Diego. But I was shocked when I read those articles."

Mandell had already decided she wouldn't testify, had instructed her lawyer to inform the prosecutors the same, and told them again that she knew nothing when they happened to reach her by phone at the Los Angeles NOW office. "They threatened me with bad publicity, which was hysterical since I was already 'the bad guy' in every press story. Then I rented a car, left my house, lived other places, although I still went to work because nobody knew where my new real estate management office was. I was absolutely not going to talk to them or testify against her, because I didn't want to be the person who discredited Ginny Foat. I knew I would shake Ginny up bad if I testified, but I didn't want to be responsible for sending somebody to jail for the rest of her life. I didn't really know what had happened, and I just couldn't handle it, so I headed for the hills."

The prosecutors still could only hope that other Foat contemporaries in California would eventually agree to cooperate. But people seemed to have advance word of the investigators' and prosecutors' trips to California, and, as Porteous put it, "the earth just seemed to swallow them up, male and female alike."

For the most part, it seemed that feminists were closing ranks around her. "What we were fighting," said Porteous, "was the feeling that even if she did it, she'd changed so much—at least on the surface—that she didn't deserve to be prosecuted, didn't deserve this treatment any longer. Legally, I say if you commit a crime, you should be punished for it. Sidote isn't the equivalent of hard time. So she had to be tried for the charge, no matter that she'd supposedly changed. As for the morality of it, I say that's for priests, ministers, rabbis to determine. But I certainly don't believe that feminism grants immunity."

Feminists didn't see it that way, even those close friends who'd heard Ginny hint about her terrible life on the road with Sidote. In a sense they'd set themselves up as a parole board. Her hard work in the movement was the equivalent of rehabilitation, even perhaps her form of atonement. Whatever information people might have had about Ginny and her past, whatever Ginny, in moments of candor or difficulty, had told friends, was either rationalized away by the battered-woman's syndrome or was excused by her feminist conversion and devotion to NOW.

Tom Porteous was fully aware of the reasons for the reluctance, the stonewalling, he met with in California. "I know that people out there felt that they didn't want to be the ones to send Ginny Foat to jail. But that's the old cop-out. Still, if they were comfortable with it, then who am I to say it's an unconscionable position. I suppose there was the more general motive of not wanting to hurt the women's movement, although that may have been a convenient way of buttressing their individual reasons for not cooperating."

Elaine Lafferty agreed that it presented a very difficult moral issue, which she thought a great deal about and talked about with one other close friend. "The situation was profoundly uncomfortable. It was the same after her arrest when other people wondered what in fact they knew. The questions were: Did she do it, Did she not do it, What do *you* do? I know people were saying things like, 'It was a long time ago, she's made something of her life; if she was involved in it, she's not going to be involved in something like that again, so what do you do about it?' My feeling was that people decided how to best take care of their own lives. All I did was turn my friendship interest elsewhere and reevaluate my judgment of character. I felt misled, and I told myself, 'Wow, you better brush up, kiddo,' and I certainly learned something about how I perceive and trust people and let them into my life. Nevertheless, I didn't feel comfortable, even during that conversation in the restaurant and certainly never afterward, with the position, 'Even if she did it . . .' I don't think I find it acceptable to say it was only her way out of a bad situation whatever the real story is about that evening—which

I doubt we'll ever know. And I don't accept the argument that the point of criminal justice is to rehabilitate, and since she's been rehabilitated, she shouldn't be tried."

Meanwhile, Sidote sat in his jail cell. Any moral dilemma he had—whether to cooperate or not, whether to testify or not—was already out of his hands. Despite his insisting that he didn't want to testify, the prosecution had locked him in with the immunity agreement. And more, now that he was reading the stories about the new Ginny Foat, "who she is today," he was bemused by her conversion to feminism. In an unpublished interview with *Penthouse* magazine, he tried to counter her claims to martyrdom by insisting that she'd never championed anyone's rights but her own. Her rise to power in NOW he saw as another sign of her ambition, drive, and willfulness, which had been evident to him from the beginning: "She was always an opportunist, not just for monetary gain but a better life. With me, it was for more action; the racetrack, the trip to Montreal, the element of excitement. Ray Foat maybe offered a more monetarily rewarding future, a little more staid and another step upward. She's like a chameleon, changing her colors completely. Her life now is totally removed from when I knew her, but even when she started a new life with me, she cut everything off that existed before that moment. She thinks of her past as dead and buried. Maybe that's why she thought she could forget about the skeletons in her closet when she became a public figure. Maybe she saw being a leader in the women's movement as her way of covering up her guilt or blocking it out. Mine was drinking. But her way was to always latch on to a fast horse and ride it."

As skewed and self-serving as Sidote's statement was, Ginny Foat implicitly agreed that she'd been looking for a "new life" with the New Paltz bartender. Yet her rhetoric placed the responsibility for her ill-fated choice not on her own shoulders but on society's indoctrination of women, on the "myths" that women "internalized."

Had she really been carried off into the sunset, her whirligig trip to Florida with Jack a dream come true? "Oh, yes," she said, adding, "If I didn't believe in the First Amendment, I'd have *Cinderella* banned. But back then I bought the story that someday my prince would come."

FIVE

More Sinned Against Than Sinning

DESPITE the virtual media blackout imposed by the Foat defense team and her lawyers, the press was still going after the story. Interviewing her family, old friends, and, much to her distress, Sidote, reporters were trying to piece together the early life of Ginny Foat. The past that she had hoped to leave behind was now beginning to resurface in feature magazine articles, and the continual complaint from Foat's defense committee was that the press was "sensationalizing" her story.

Among the journalists who covered the Foat case extensively, several in fact came to it with a feminist perspective. Kate Coleman was writing a story for *California* magazine (May 1983), Teresa Carpenter for *The Village Voice* (April 5, 1983), Patt Morrison for the *Los Angeles Times* (in numerous articles and commentary), and Grace Lichtenstein for *Rolling Stone* (May 12, 1983). All four women had had their feminist "credentials" approved by the defense-fund committee. Despite beginning with some sympathy and not a little curiosity about a woman whose life seemed to signify extraordinary change due in great part to feminism, they soon found themselves running into the wall that had been constructed around Foat.

When their articles described what they had discovered about Foat's past, neither Ginny nor her supporters were especially pleased. Coleman emphasized Ginny's looks, her sensuality, her youthful "high spiritedness," and "a kind of wild blood." She quoted Ginny's comment (supplied by an unnamed friend) explaining her four marraiges, "I like weddings," and she dared to hint at a recent change in life-style: "Instead of flirting with men, Ginny 'interfaced' with women." But worse, Ginny's supporters said that, having interviewed Sidote, Coleman had obviously been "charmed by him" (she called him good-looking in a Charles Bronson way) and had repeated everything he said as if it were fact. To condemn Sidote and Coleman further, they pointed to his attempt to peddle his story as a book and said that she had agreed to help him.

California magazine lawyers had been scrupulously careful about her article (because of vague legal threats coming from Foat's committee). Coleman wasn't alone, however, in finding that neither Foat nor her friends would comment on what in her piece were clearly cited as Sidote's "allegations" or on information supplied by individuals in Foat's past life. She'd had her session with Kay Tsenin in San Francisco and been aware of being appraised for her feminism. But the clips of her articles, which showed a definite profeminist slant, failed to lower the defense committee's resistance either to talking to any reporters, except in proscribed ways, or to arranging an interview with Foat.

Teresa Carpenter, the Pulitzer Prize–winning *Village Voice* staff reporter, also approached the Foat story with initial sympathy. But like Coleman she found it necessary to raise questions rather than simply accept the image of Foat as a feminist martyr. Her innocence in a legal sense would be decided at her trial, but in her article Carpenter concentrated on Foat's "enigmatic character" and called her "capable of remaking herself again and again." That, indeed, seemed to be the source of the Foat team's disapproval of her article: that she'd given Foat an active role in the choices she had made, in the selves she had created and re-created as she moved from one phase of her life to the next. Carpenter had delved into her past through interviews with Foat's earlier friends and associates, not to mention Sidote, and like Coleman had come up with a portrait of a "high spirited," "conspicuously sensual" young woman who'd evidenced "precocious sexuality." Carpenter's collage of impressions showed very little resemblance to "the passive woman" described in Foat's statement from jail. There seemed to be an edge of doubt, too, when she described Foat's feminist "metamorphosis," her "amazingly quick ascent" in California NOW, the petty infighting among the NOW factions, and Foat's insistence on her case as a feminist allegory; as Carpenter pointed out, "she did not acknowledge the problems as her own but the scourge of womankind."

In order to answer the question of why Mandell had written the letter to the sheriff's office, Carpenter was one of the few reporters to talk to Shelly Mandell and Elaine Lafferty. Once again, Shelly had a hard time explaining her reasons. It would seem that she wasn't even sure about her motives, and so unnerved was she by what had happened, she didn't give a very clear account of her actions. One had to accept that she thought only in terms of politics, and yet it seemed that the rift between her and Ginny was deeper and more personal than perhaps even she had realized. Then there was the question of how she had known the exact wrong birthday that appeared on the warrant. Carpenter had herself discovered this, but when she confronted Mandell, her explanation was contradictory. First she said that Ginny had given her the birth date, but Ginny denied it. Then she said that perhaps Jefferson Parish had given her the date that appeared on the warrant when she first phoned. But according to Carpenter, the records department said it didn't give out that information. Only later did Mandell offer the explanation that she had confused Ginny's birthday with Karen Peters's. She had been so upset by the weird coincidence that she couldn't think straight, and she agreed that she'd "mucked up" her press interviews so badly that she finally decided to stop talking to journalists.

Because the defense team had closed down Foat's past to her, Carpenter couldn't answer key questions either. Yet she seemed to suspect that there was more to Foat than simply the perennial victim. She was as skeptical of the rendering of Ginny's life as a "Norman Rockwell print" or the self-portrait of "an ingenue swept into the Badlands" as she was of Sidote's presentation of himself as a "weakling at the whim of a vamp." Ginny's supporters couldn't be happy with either the complex questions she raised or her insistence that no one yet had the answers. At the close of her piece, Carpenter commented that perhaps only the various witnesses in Foat's trial "will reveal the source of her energy and the making of her several selves."

She had tried to find this source as well, but was frustrated, Carpenter felt, by people trying to manipulate her investigation of the story: "Bob Tuller wouldn't return my phone calls; Kay Tsenin was neither frank nor candid. Foat and her people wanted total control and tried to close down access to everyone."

As an experienced, well-respected journalist she couldn't simply adopt the feminist gloss that Foat's defenders were giving the story, her own feminism notwithstanding. "You always resent being press-managed," she said. "I didn't accept the simple explanation that this was an 'antifeminist plot' because the charges were too serious, the case too idiosyncratic for it not to have been pursued. It seemed NOW realized that as well. In 1977 when Foat had been low-profile in the organization, California NOW, or at least its newsletter, was willing to put it in a political context of the abusive male. But when NOW leaders heard how complicated the case was, they were unwilling to make such political points so easily."

Early on, Carpenter had realized that much of the story had to do with California NOW's infighting, and most particularly with a lesbian faction that was so strong in California. "Everyone knows that's part of the movement, but out there it was a subculture which no one wanted to deal with." It wasn't a matter of revealing people's private sexual preferences—all journalists, particularly feminists, took the position that it needn't be a part of a story if it played no role. But in the Foat case, it seemed to lead back to the question of the motives behind the intense animosity among the various players in the drama. Too, there was the initial hint that Foat was being adopted as a lesbian cause. Some of her early fund-raising was being organized by self-identified radical lesbians until her lawyers reduced their visibility. This was a part of the story that had to be explored, although Carpenter agreed that it was a ticklish problem. "It had to do with political alliances in California, but I didn't address it as directly as I might have. I also, of course, realized that Foat and her committee were terrified that any suggestion of lesbianism would prejudice the case in Louisiana."

Carpenter thought Foat's charge that the press sensationalized the story was unwarranted. The problem seemed to be not an exaggeration of facts but a paucity of facts, with every side, including the national NOW office, either refusing to comment or giving only set speeches. What journalists found was essentially "a self-serving tale, on the one hand, versus an unreliable witness on the other," she said. "The story called for an independent commentator but Foat didn't seem to want one. Even when she finally gave her interview to Rinker Buck for *Life,* it was little more than a photo opportunity. There was a lot to account for, but she didn't want to do it, and that was a real shame."

Patt Morrison, staff writer for the *Los Angeles Times,* had covered the Foat story since the day of the arrest. She'd pursued leads relentlessly, but like the magazine writers, she had felt stonewalled by Foat's colleagues, despite the fact that the defense committee thought her stories the fairest, the least "sensational" of any of the early daily reports about the case and Foat's background. When she was assigned to the Foat story, Morrison remembered feeling both shocked and sympathetic. "I had a sort of sick feeling that this was going to make people point fingers at feminism and say, 'Ah ha, I told you so.' "

Still, while she knew the story had to be handled with care, she was also a reporter going after information, and she soon found that California NOW people, both enemies and friends of Foat, were reluctant to talk. "I called the NOW office frequently to ask for both biographical information as well as information about her NOW positions and activities, what legislation she had lobbied for, what she had done as state NOW present. No one was willing to provide that sort of material, much less comment about the case. I got the feeling that they were all taken aback as well and were unprepared to deal with the questions that were coming. It was some time before they were organized enough to make a coherent statement. Then we heard about the factionalism behind the case and Shelly Mandell's letter. But Mandell also refused to talk, which was unfortunate because the story would have been furthered by an explanation from her. Finally, Ginny's associates started returning my calls when I asked for confirmation of things I'd come up with, but they seemed to fall back on rhetorical statements about the political nature of her case. The kind of information that was coming out about her past life demanded not a political line but a very human line. Yet there seemed great reluctance in her circle of friends to disclose those sorts of things."

Morrison was well aware that the wariness of journalists among Foat people was due to their condemnation of press sensationalism. "I've thought about that a great deal," she said. "But a lot of what they called sensationalism was simply confronting something unpleasant that Ginny was trying to shed. It was obvious that she had tried to overcome the problems she'd had in the fifties and sixties, and she didn't want to deal with that part of her life. Still, we had to write about it, and I'm sure that people reading the story were asking, 'How did this woman change, what was the motivation for living her life then, and what made her become something else?' So I originally thought of her story as a chronicle of progress and change, which I don't think did her an injustice. The problem was that we were all individually 'vetted,' and we couldn't get close to what allowed her to change because her early strengths were denied and the impression was that she'd changed overnight. But that's not the case with anyone. All our lives are a continuum, and there were things even early on in her life that gave an inkling of her ambition, which was not able to reach fruition during the difficult years. Plus, since both her friends and NOW people were unwilling to talk about her political activities, for example, what she'd done as a delegate to the 1980 Democratic Convention, we couldn't show the entire range of her life. So I don't think we journalists did her a disservice or were unfair because we wanted to know facts about both parts of her life."

While the Foat camp seemed to recognize that Morrison, as a feminist, was fairly sympathetic, they kept her at arm's length and attributed to her the widely repeated statement that Foat had been a go–go dancer. "That had been touted about by a lot of reporters. I've forgotten the source, but I don't think I was responsible for 'spreading the rumor.' Whether she was one or not didn't matter to me anyway, and besides, I felt that if you're talking about sisterhood, then you have to encompass women who may be forced to do that for a living. But I also thought it was indicative of her attitude about the stuff in her past life which she didn't want to come out. It wouldn't have changed the facts of what she'd done, but it would have been better to say frankly she'd done this or that, even though perhaps now she didn't like it and obviously she wasn't doing it anymore. Instead, all this was dropped in bits and pieces, there was no coherent story, plus there were a lot of discrepancies. Then when she finally gave her interview to *Life* it was framed to make the message clear. Readers can read Aesop without having to have the moral spelled out. Any reading of Foat's life all the way through, with her difficulties, then her political changes and successes, didn't require all that political frosting. To keep layering it on with the constant politicization of what was a very human, dramatic, and vivid story put people off to some extent. Even when I finally heard the 'horror stories,' it was very difficult to be drawn into that, especially for those of us who have been brought up 'gently' or were a different generation of feminist—what I call a 'mezzanine' feminist—for whom certain earlier major feminist struggles had happened before we were adults. Nevertheless, to hear the political rhetoric applied as an explanation for her life instead of a human explanation just didn't ring true for me or, I think, for a lot of other people."

Of all the journalists covering the Foat story, Grace Lichtenstein presented the defense committee with the most substantial feminist credentials. As a *New York Times* reporter she had covered the women's movement extensively, she was the author of *Machisma: Women and Daring,* and many of her articles were concerned with feminist issues. More, she had taken an interest in Foat's case out of a spontaneous identification with what she'd first heard about the woman's background. "Ginny Foat and I are exactly the same age, from Brooklyn, and from somewhat the same kind of background, and I first thought, 'Gee, there but for the grace of God.' She was someone who had traveled a classic road from nonfeminist to feminist awareness, and we could all identify with that."

Like her fellow writers, however, Lichtenstein also wanted answers to questions raised about Foat's background. Most of all she hoped to be able to speak to Foat herself. She thought that she, of any reporters, had the best chance of convincing the defense committee that she would not only be fair, but with her feminist approach, would be able to understand Foat's transformation in positive terms. Nevertheless, she said she felt strung along and misled by the people surrounding Foat.

Lichtenstein then went to friends, former husbands and boyfriends, and NOW colleagues for information. Soon she began to sense that there were "some pretty tawdry" aspects of Foat's past, not only the two alleged robbery-murders but other sordid events that Sidote told her about when she interviewed him.

"After I interviewed him," she said, "I went directly to the phone in Carson City and called Kay Tsenin. I told her I was near my deadline and that I wanted to give Ginny one last chance to reply to all these charges this guy was making. She said no. I went back again and again, and every time she said no."

Lichtenstein also had to decide how to cope with the rumors and gossip to which she had been treated by NOW associates in both the Foat and the anti-Foat camps. The most sensitive area was lesbianism, which feminists, surprisingly, didn't mind mentioning in their attacks on one another.

"To quote Rita Mae Brown, there is nothing worse than a lesbian in the closet," Lichtenstein said. "They use so much energy hiding between the racks that they lose perspective and have no energy for dealing with the real world. I'd thought the world, especially in California, was grown up enough not to care, so it was silly for them to try to hide it, because it wasn't something they could just sweep under the bed. Nevertheless, I was extraordinarily circumspect in writing about that aspect of the case even though what I'd seen went beyond the usual amount of bitching between gays and straights that exists in the women's movement, the deep division which has never been healed but which few people are willing to acknowledge. But the lesbian-baiting between lesbian and lesbian which I discovered in California was just plain bitching. What was germane was that at some point Ginny Foat may have rejected men, but other than that, the rest of the stuff was a smoke screen. So I threw a lot of the backbiting and lesbian remarks out the window, because that's the only way I know how to deal with it in the popular press without its being exploited. Teresa Carpenter, on the other hand, didn't have the same scruples. Maybe that's because she's a lot younger than I am, and I say, good for her. But I was spoiled when I covered feminism for *The New York Times,* because my friends were all at the barricades and they invited me along and told me things. So I guess I feel involved and sympathetic enough with what both the women's rights and gay rights movements have had to go through that I will do a certain amount of covering up for them when I probably shouldn't."

Having tried to be circumspect about both Foat and the women's movement, Lichtenstein was annoyed to hear the outcries of media sensationalism: "In the first place, they should've been pleased that journalists of our caliber and feminist sympathies were after the story. What I got were lies, and I know they were equally uncooperative with Teresa Carpenter and Kate Coleman. We're all aggressive reporters, and they knew we'd do the story anyway, but they wouldn't let anyone close. Jean O'Leary, with whom Ginny had lived at one point, and whom I knew from writing stories about the Gay Rights Task Force, was fairly straightforward with me; Midge Costanza, who should've known better, went through a lot of double-talk because she didn't want to tell me that Ginny's story had been sold to *Life*. Foat's spokepersons really did her a disservice in terms of the media. To say that I was angry is putting it mildly. No reporter likes being lied to, especially by people you start out being sympathetic toward. I know they were worried about the press, but it wasn't true at all that we were being too hard on Foat. Quite the contrary—the media made her into a heroine. We all did.

"As for the complaints about sensationalizing her past, that wasn't the case at all. It was a hell of a story, and if the press hadn't covered it the way they did, there would've been something wrong with American journalism. In fact, the press was relatively kind to her, given the stuff that was coming out. She and her supporters were furious with the coverage, but she ought to have kissed us all. Instead the people closest to her insisted on misleading us. I may be a feminist, but I'm a feminist *journalist,* and I hate being lied to. I wrote my article for *Rolling Stone* despite coming away from the story feeling that they should all roast. In a sense I think that their treatment of the press reflected their treatment of each other. They were not a pretty bunch, and the more I think about it, they got a better story out of me than they deserved.

"Still, I heard they were relieved when my piece came out, and Ginny said that she thought that of all the long feature articles, my story was the most 'generous.' But my feeling was that there was an untold story that we were never going to know. She seemed to have such weird paranoia about the press and our questions about her past, that you had to wonder if she was hiding something."

Nevertheless, other feminists insisted that the press was unfair to Foat by implying that there was something sordid about her life on the road with John Sidote, her jobs as a cocktail waitress, her four husbands, and her connection to a small-time drug dealer who'd turned up dead. "Classism"—disparaging women who had to work in such jobs—combined with "sexism"—condemning women whose sex life strayed beyond conventional bounds—cast a shadow over Foat, NOW vice-president Priscilla Alexander and Midge Costanza continued to insist. "There were all kinds of sexual innuendos behind the remarks about Ginny's past," said Costanza. "Plus the stories always implied some negative judgment of waitresses and barmaids, that they have some stigma attached to them, and as a result there was a presumption of guilt in the press because of Foat's jobs. The fact that she dared to have sexual activity in her life also allowed the media to portray her as a 'loose' woman."

Gloria Steinem agreed that the media had gone overboard, not because it had insinuated certain things about Foat's life, but because it had given her case so much exposure: "The media certainly focused an awful lot of attention on her story, even though she wasn't a nationally known figure and very few people outside of California had heard of her before. That was probably because of the so-called shocking background for a feminist, although it didn't seem shocking to me. I wasn't surprised when all the information started coming out about Foat's past, since I could've counted any number of women among my classmates in Toledo who'd had a similar past. If I had stayed there I might have, too. Second, while there was the implication that her background was not the usual one of a NOW leader, it seemed to me, on the contrary, that it had probably helped her understand what was wrong with women's situations."

As someone so experienced in public relations in addition to her longtime involvement in NOW, Muriel Fox had a slightly different take on the problem. "It wasn't necessarily that the facts of her past were exaggerated or not. It was more that an implied connection seemed to be made between all the lurid details and her being a high officer in NOW. I was unhappy about that, because I realized that a lot of women in Middle America would think 'So that's what those NOW women are like.' Being linked to a murder and to a life that Middle American women would consider unappetizing was especially unfortunate at a time when we were trying to reestablish the ERA fight and gearing up for a presidential election. On the other hand, given the terrible jam she was in, it was far more important for her to get through the charges, so I don't think anyone felt that she should be thinking primarily about NOW public relations. Nevertheless, the press seemed delighted that she was a feminist— that made it a more sensational story. I'm sure there were antifeminists who were especially delighted, but even if they weren't, there was the same sensationalism one sees when a rock star or a movie star is in trouble. But in her case, what made her a celebrity was the fact that she was a feminist leader. If she hadn't been, she would have been just another unfortunate woman."

Having read only a few of the articles, Ellie Smeal had the impression that journalists were digging up almost irrelevant facts from Foat's past and putting them in a most questionable light: "I know reporters had to go after the story," she said. "Still, having had experience with the media, I was skeptical of the articles. I didn't know that much about her personal life, but I'm sure she must have gone nuts reading those stories because they seemed so sensationalized to me."

Karen DeCrow, however, resisted drawing a simple conclusion about either prejudicial or sensationalized press coverage. "Again, I wear three hats when I consider the media's role in Foat's case," she said. "As a lawyer, which is the primary way I look at things, I would hope that the media wouldn't prejudice the disposition of anyone's case. But having worked as a journalist, I'm also sophisticated enough to realize that any reporter who didn't pick up on Foat's story would have been crazy. I'd fault journalists if they reported false information, but my impression was that neither the networks nor *The New York Times* nor the print journalists were being particularly irresponsible. Since I'm big on the First Amendment, I feel the press did what they should have been doing. They were having a field day, but why not? I mean, I admit when I read about her short fourth marriage, I thought, 'God, she really sounds like a nut.' Several people also told me after her arrest, 'If you think the press is having a field day now, God forbid that everything else about her life should come out.' They said that there was stuff in her story that I wouldn't believe. Of course, that was just hearsay, and I had no idea if she killed or participated in the killing of this guy. But after reading what the average person would read in the press, the only thing I faulted her for, so to speak, was that she had rotten taste in companions, lousy taste in husbands—sort of what I later felt about Geraldine Ferraro. Still, the press wasn't making that up. It happened to be the case. But finally, in my NOW hat, I would prefer that NOW members or leaders aren't indicted on criminal charges so that the organization doesn't have that kind of press attention."

That, indeed, was another complaint from the Foat camp: In every story she was identified as a feminist or a NOW leader. They were worried that her NOW affiliation, her political positions, her pro-lesbian and abortion rights stands, would prejudice prospective jurors in Louisiana; they wished that journalists would downplay her commitment to the women's movement and make only vague references to her "civil rights activities." The problem as Lichtenstein saw it was that Foat and her defense team were "looking at the case only from the perspective of going to trial. They weren't looking for total honesty. They were looking for help for their side."

Presumably, NOW itself would have preferred fewer references to Foat's position in the organization, too. After Goldsmith's first public statement, she and other NOW leaders became as taciturn as the Foat defense committee. The primary rationale of both camps was that the less said about the case, the better chance Foat had for a fair trial in Louisiana. But beyond that understandable motivation, the emphasis on public relations and public perceptions in both NOW and the Foat support group (obviously, the two weren't unrelated) seemed to blind them all to the fact that hers was a story to be covered, whatever the consequences. Freedom of the press had to be respected, even if, as Lichtenstein admitted in her case, some feminist journalists might be more circumspect to protect the women's movement.

While Foat sat in jail awaiting trial and stories about her were published, feminist spokespersons were discovering that while her case was seen as symbolic, the public tended to withhold judgment. In some ultraconservative corners there were antifeminist jokes, like the cartoon in a San Diego paper showing murder as a credential for a feminist leader. Similarly, in St. Bernard Parish, near New Orleans, a newspaper published a cartoon that showed Foat behind bars wearing a NOW button. The caption read YOU'VE COME A LONG WAY, BABY.

Lynne Renihan, president of New Orleans NOW, was furious about such remarks in local newspapers. Not only did she think *The Times-Picayune* was indulging in sleazy innuendos about Foat's past, but one day Renihan realized that she was being followed by one of the newspaper's reporters. "This woman was right on my tail at every public event, every meeting I went to, trying to pick up anything I said, anything that might have to do with the Foat case. Of course, I'd been told by national NOW not to comment, and although I was at first upset by their dissociation, I realized that it was probably better for Ginny not to say anything about the case. Still, it was pretty funny that while New Orleans NOW was no big potatoes down here, suddenly reporters were treating us like a major story. I suppose they were hoping to pick up some stuff about Ginny. Later I heard that the editor had told the two women reporters that this was a story they had to get, and assigned them to follow us NOW people to try to trip us up and get us to say something. Finally, I turned on one of them and said I was tired of it and told her to leave me alone. The next day *The Times-Picayune* misquoted me as saying I was 'tired of the Ginny Foat case.' So I know from my own experience that the press was terrible down here, much worse than the national articles. And because of the articles I think most people thought she was guilty."

"There were some really abhorrent, biased stories here," New Orleans NOW leader Kim Gandy agreed. "There was an article almost every day with major headlines. One reporter seemed to be particularly venomous. I don't know whether he wanted to 'get a feminist' or whether, like among lawyers, you'll find a few bad apples among reporters. It may have been that he was simply looking to get a little extra to make the story more sensational. But I think those stories allowed the public to believe that the prosecutors had a very strong case."

Such press coverage made Foat fair game for all the worst misogynist jokes. But in her area of upstate New York, Karen De-Crow found most references to the Foat case not only predictable but rather bland. "Since people knew of my connection to NOW, opposing counsels in court would say something like, 'We'd better not win this case or you'll get your NOW women to murder us.' It was a sort of gentle teasing from my male colleagues, and I decided to take all that in good humor. If a guy would win a motion, I'd say, 'Hey, Mike, you better watch out.'"

Gloria Steinem, too, discovered that the various groups she spoke to around the country naturally asked about the case but were more sympathetic than snide: "I didn't find rabid antifeminists making remarks, because no matter how judgmental they might have been about her past, they realized she had clearly lived a constructive life for years in between. I suppose there may have been a gleeful, 'Boy-have-you-got-trouble' kind of tone when some people brought it up, but they weren't really that firm about it. It was more like, 'Isn't this going to be used against women?' or, 'We're worried about how this will be used.' I did find a certain amount of subterranean glee on some people's part, but it wasn't terrible. Still, the level of interest in her was obviously much higher than it would have been had she not been a symbol of women's stiving for independence."

Costanza agreed that because of Foat's feminist transformation, people were eager to invest it with symbolic meaning: "I think some people did react with gloating—great, a fallen feminist—but for two reasons. The first was the general excitement everyone has about fallen heroes or public people. But in the Foat case, reactions reflected what the women's movement means to people in this country. That, of course, depended on who they were, where they were coming from, how they'd been affected by feminism before. For some, feminism has been a threat. For example, there are women who see Bella Abzug or Gloria Steinem, and react with envy, jealousy, or fear. They get scared and want the feminists to stop rocking their boats. 'How can I change my life if I've got four kids and my husband will react by leaving me? So I'm gonna stay where I am and be pleased with it, and I want Bella and Gloria to shut their mouths.' Others see the bright, articulate, knowledgeable feminists and react with a sense of pride that someone is doing what they wish they could do. Then there are men who are personally threatened and blame feminism for their divorces or unhappiness without realizing that the problems were already there. The women's movement is simply a support mechanism for women to achieve what they've always wanted to achieve. If not for feminism, the unhappiness would have manifested itself in other ways, like in alcoholism or changes in personalities. So people heard about Ginny Foat, and she became a magnet for all those different attitudes toward feminism, both negative and positive."

With Foat's story so invested with symbolic values, with the media so fascinated by the "juicy" details of the case, it wasn't surprising that there was immediate talk of books about her. Jack Sidote contacted both *Playboy* and *Penthouse* and offered interviews to the highest bidder. He told Teresa Carpenter that his story was "explosive enough, deep enough, passionate enough, to be a best seller." He was later annoyed when Kate Coleman, having circulated her interview with him among literary agents, failed to obtain a contract for his book. As other writers contacted him in the Nevada state prison, he continued to try to sell his side of the narrative.

Sidote wasn't the only principal in the case who was seeking a book contract, however. According to Los Angeles gossip columns, Shelly Mandell and her friend Elaine Lafferty were also rumored to be selling book proposals in New York. In fact, Lafferty had told her New York agent "to sit tight" while she explored what she sensed "was a fascinating story with all kinds of good Mafia stuff in it." Jan Holden was also telling reporters that she "owned the rights to Ginny's story" and that she was already discussing a possible TV-movie with the role of Ginny to be played by Patty Duke Astin, the actress who'd lent her support to the defense fund and over whose name the letter appealing for contributions had gone out. Kay Tsenin then spoke to several literary agents about representing Ginny's own book, finally choosing Peter Skolnik of the Sanford I. Greenburger Agency in New York.

Meanwhile, with all the stories about Foat appearing in the press, the defense committee decided that it was time for her to set the record straight. She would give one interview, and that to *Life* magazine. Despite rumors among journalists that she, too, had simply gone to the highest bidder, the strategy was designed to move her out of the feminist revolution into the mainstream. The rationale offered by Jan Holden and Kay Tsenin was that a widely circulated, middle-class, middle-of-the-road publication might help her in Louisiana. It certainly wouldn't hurt her as "left of center" or "hip" publications like *Rolling Stone* and *The Village Voice* might.

The article by Rinker Buck was published in May 1983, and was based on his interviews with Foat while she was still in jail. Although the banner headline SHE STANDS ACCUSED, A SORDID PAST CATCHES UP WITH CALIFORNIA'S LEADING FEMINIST seemed sensational, the specific "sordid" details were muted, and her feminism was reduced to noncontroversial references to her civil rights activism. It wasn't so much a matter of getting the facts straight, it seemed, but of explaining them in certain ways, of putting them in a "feminist" context. Nevertheless, even in this officially designated portrait, questions had a way of creeping in, and doubtless the shadowy parts of the story were startling both to NOW members and to *Life's* "middle-of-the-road" readership.

Buck's narrative was told from Foat's point of view with details and commentary provided by her in the interview. Her comments underscored what had been the defense committee's theme from the beginning: namely, that Foat's plight was an allegory for "every woman's ordeal," that with her arrest, "you, my dear sisters, also stand accused."

The shape of the narrative was constructed out of a series of events in which Foat was acted upon, constrained, but never herself in control. She was, the article implied, the victim of her small-town, Italian Catholic upbringing. Born in Brooklyn, the older of two daughters of August and Virginia Galluzzo, she grew up in New Paltz, New York, where her family had moved when she was in seventh grade. Second-generation Italians, her father drove a Wonder Bread truck, and her mother "kept house." Her parents' dream for her "was to marry early, raise children and never leave New Paltz," she told her interviewer, as if to suggest the pervasive and controlling influence of such provincial attitudes and all too common stereotypes imposed on young girls in the fifties. Whatever secret desires to rebel against these values, whatever seeds of ambition she had, Fred Schindler, her high school boyfriend, recalled that she "pretty much coasted through high school without a care." Although, according to Buck, old friends remembered her "streak of rebelliousness," the *Life* piece stressed the limitations imposed by her parents' attitudes: "Foat remembers 'coming home from school one afternoon after a career day. When I told my mother I had decided to become a lawyer, she burst out laughing.' "

The article also told of her early organizational ability. She "was a brilliant organizer of school clubs," Schindler was again quoted. According to her yearbook, her clubs were the Prom Committee, Hop Committee, Dance Club, Hugenot Staff, Mixed Chorus; she also appeared in a snapshot of the Chemistry Club, possibly because Schindler, who later became a chemistry teacher, was a member. While she was not identified as an officer in these groups, in her interview Foat seemed to have invested them with special significance, as if to convey a logical connection between her younger days and her emergence as a NOW leader noted for organizational talent.

The interview also touched on another aspect of personality that Foat seemed to feel linked her present self to her past: "a deep sense of compassion for anything that breathed." For example, she cried when her uncle shot a deer, a memory supplied by Schindler. The subtext of her story thus seemed to be that she'd fallen in love and stayed with Sidote out of her deep sense of compassion and desire to "save the world," even in her teens.

After graduation from high school, Foat worked as a stewardess for Allegheny Airlines in Cleveland, but then went home to marry a local boy. To explain her first marriage she seemed to suggest to Buck that she'd simply given in to others' (and by extension society's) expectations: "Her parents and Danny Angelillo, a handsome New Paltz football player, talked her into returning," and in 1962 her father "spent $6,000 on a church wedding and a catered dinner for 200 guests."

During her first year of marriage, she worked for the Wiltwyck School for Boys, "a State institution for the emotionally disturbed," the *Life* story continued, as she provided her interviewer with another example of how "her talent for organization began to emerge," an incident that also revealed her "instinctive ability to solve problems": "When the school wells ran dry, it was her idea to telephone nearby Stewart Air Force Base, which sent over two tank trucks of water in a matter of hours." This job also aroused her interest in civil rights, according to the story. "Many of the boys at Wiltwyck came from the ghetto, and Ginny, touched and indignant, became involved in the civil rights movement of the 1960s. She hired buses for Martin Luther King's 1963 March on Washington and sat transfixed as he spoke." This was, it seemed, the way by which she'd come to call herself in her 1982 NOW campaign, "Organizer for Martin Luther King March on Washington 1963."

Then, according to her narrative, her involvement in civil rights and her attendance at New York City weekend meetings of the Congress of Racial Equality caused the breakup of her marriage to Danny Angelillo. She also blamed social attitudes and stereotypes: "People in our family don't walk away from their marriages," she said, implying that she had rebelled against being a traditional wife, but more specific than "he was over there, I was over there," she didn't get.

By contrast, Danny Angelillo, now an art teacher and football coach at a Long Island high school, had told a different story to other interviewers. In retrospect he didn't remember her as passsive or weak: "She spoke her mind. . . . We didn't have a marriage where the male was the dominant figure. She would do what she wanted to do." Still, the annulment, he said, "was probably more my decision at that point, but there were no hard feelings. . . . I guess when we got married she wanted to have a family and a relationship that would last. I didn't want to. I wanted to pursue a career." Her going to Washington to participate in a civil rights march he mentioned proudly and refused to see their breakup as a result of his attempt to force her into a housewife's role. In his version, she was the one who wanted the traditional role. Nonetheless, she seemed neither a submissive wife nor a victim in his account, and the annulment seemed a realistic assessment by two people who knew their own minds. Even in Foat's own version for *Life,* it would seem that since she said she'd left him, she indeed, as her first husband recalled, "did what she wanted to do."

After the annulment, the first in the family, she said that in her parents' eyes, "I was a failure." Suddenly the *Life* portrait changed: She had succumbed to her family's attitudes, once again victimized and condemned to believe others' view of her. In the feminist parlance crucial to the drama, she had "internalized" her parents' image of her as a failure.

All this was prologue to Sidote, the suggested rationale that she was weak and not in control when she met him. In the *Life* article she had little to say about her motives except that she "loved the wrong man too long." Still, there seemed little connection between the Ginny Foat who could sit transfixed by Martin Luther King in 1963 and the one who in 1965 was transfixed by the bartender in a local resort.

Since Foat wasn't telling her interviewer, one had to look elsewhere. First, there was the photograph in *Life* supplied by ex-boyfriend Fred Schindler, of Ginny, posing as if for a fifties pinup, a small-town bathing beauty, her right arm cocked behind her head, her long black hair cascading down her back. What was the sense of self behind the pose? In a yearbook snapshot she leaned back against a rock, one leg drawn up, her chin up, in another imitation of a glamorous pose. The caption under it could serve for the bathing-suit shot as well: SIREN OF THE SEA. Popular with boys, as both her high school boyfriend and her first husband recalled, she seemed well aware that in her world, her attractive, voluptuous looks were her best credentials. As Schindler had told Carpenter, they "were not exactly the top-notch group in the world, but not the worst. We were a little bit wild in those days. In a fifties sort of way." And under her graduation picture, she was called IN AND OUT OF TROUBLE and FULL OF FUN. In other articles her friends and parents all remembered her high-spiritedness and sense of adventure. Such high school memorabilia were innocent enough, but nowhere in Foat's re-creation of her past for *Life* did she hint at what came out in the other articles about her based on interviews with these early friends: that she ran with a fast crowd and liked fun and adventure. Yet that side of her seemed more helpful in explaining why she'd fallen in love with "the wrong man": She must have been bored with her family and the small town, she liked the action, she also liked to be seen as beautiful and sexy. And perhaps she hadn't seen through Sidote's pretensions and grand delusions because in a sense he was holding a mirror up to herself, confirming her own illusions and desires for the fast lane.

No matter how sympathetic he was, Buck had to deal with other facts about her former life. Although he took it as given that Sidote was a wife-beater and that she'd stayed with a drunken, abusive husband out of guilt and fear, other details had to be mentioned. But these Buck handled delicately, with no comment added: During Sidote's jail sentence, Buck reported, "For a while Ginny was a dutiful wife, visiting the state prison at Chino every week. Then she began to date a small-time drug dealer. He was murdered." Period, end of paragraph, and Foat apparently had had nothing to add.

Foat's story continued with a brief reference to her "ask[ing Sidote] for a divorce" in 1970 (in contrast to Sidote's having filed for the divorce), his final beating, the flight home to escape, and her reunion with Ray Foat, whom she married in 1971, a marriage that "lasted nine years" (the first separation in 1977 wasn't part of the *Life* story's tally) but ended "because of her growing preoccupation with the women's movement." (In Buck's account, her fourth marriage to Jack Meyer lasted eight months, as opposed to other stories that reported a separation and a filing for an annulment just over a month after their European honeymoon.)

Then the interview moved to her feminist conversion. Foat told her interviewer that her feminist consciousness was raised, not when she was a stewardess, not at the bank when she applied for a loan, but because of her experience as a battered wife. Now she declared that her involvement with the women's movement begain in 1974 when she visited a shelter for battered wives in Santa Ana: "The awful memories of her marriage to Sidote returned. 'I suddenly realized I wasn't alone,' she says. 'There were thousands of other women who shared my shame.' " Then, she said, annoyed at being refused the bank loan, she joined the Orange County chapter of NOW. In another, later interview, however, she said that in the seventies in Los Angeles, she'd "stayed as far away as possible" from battered-women's shelters: "I couldn't deal with it. When I had the catering business, I would take food to the shelter and drop it off, or help raise funds, but I never involved myself. I could never deal with it." Again it was not so much a contradiction as a matter of stress; she seemed to be choreographing this authorized profile to make points for her defense.

Nevertheless, when presenting her credentials as she'd worked her way up in NOW, she hadn't announced a special interest in battered women. Given the fact that her first NOW chapter was in Orange County, that seemed strange. According to Del Martin's 1976 *Battered Wives,* the Orange County chapter of NOW was in the forefront of the NOW campaign to bring domestic violence to public attention: "Karen Peters, president of the chapter in 1975, spearheaded a task force that documented existing housing facilities throughout the country to ascertain the need for a shelter."

Something seemed slightly askew in Foat's self-presentation. If she'd realized, "I wasn't alone," and that "there were thousands of women who shared my shame," as she told her interviewer, why had she not "shared her shame" when the head of her local chapter was spearheading a movement for shelters, or even when Karen Peters became California NOW's state coordinator in 1979, and both Foat and Tsenin (herself a battered woman and active in a battered-women's shelter) were on the executive board?

In the *Life* article her memories seemed to cluster around rhetorical points to be made, and the cliché "shared my shame" seemed culled from numerous books on the battered-women's movement, particularly since, according to NOW associates, she'd certainly not "shared" with her colleagues in the women's movement the observation that her visit to a women's shelter was a feminist turning point. At the time she'd presented her awakening as more in keeping with the image of a professional, middle-class businesswoman who'd experienced discriminatory banking regulations. In fact, it was only her 1977 arrest that had revealed her experience as a battered wife, and then, as she rose in NOW, that past was left well behind.

Reconstructing her life to suggest a definite pattern, she had made it look too programmed, too sequential, as if it were a neatly wrapped package, all the loose ends tied into a feminist bow. She seemed to rehearse events in her life as an argument to buttress her accusations against Sidote, her feminist transformation, and what was undoubtedly her defense strategy. It was understandable that she had not wanted to be involved with the battered-women's movement because of her own scars. Yet in telling her story for the first time to the public, she appeared to be rewriting her history into a tale of a passive woman, creating an image that she thought would be more palatable than the image of a fun-loving, independent adventurer who one day became a feminist.

Foat may have had good reason for giving her autobiographical narrative a definite emphasis: It established the lines of a defense meant to appeal to "Middle American" values. Yet it also seemed that one of her personality traits was to talk about her life in a way that suggested that things just *happened to her*. It was what some NOW colleagues had noticed about her as she'd taken on more and more responsibility. She was seen as capable and a hard worker; still, when things went wrong it was generally someone else's fault and not her responsibility. She tended to rewrite history so that she was not the actor at the center but someone to whom things had been done.

"Ginny and I had discussions about her tendency to do that," said Shelly Mandell. "Even before any big fights but when our friendship was dwindling, I'd say, 'Ginny, why don't you be direct with me? I know you're angry at me.' She'd say, 'No, I'm not,' and when I'd insist, she'd repeat, 'No, I'm not.' Ginny never caused anything, she'd deny her responsibility; she was only reacting. I'll say, 'I did a dumb thing' but you'll never hear Foat admit that. It was dumb of me to send the letter, but it was dumb of her not to make sure the case was resolved, for her own sake and also for the sake of NOW. When I read the articles about her with all the details of her background, I was not only shocked; I was furious at her for what it might have done to NOW if she'd been elected. I felt terrible about the bad publicity NOW was getting and the part that I had in causing it. But Ginny didn't think in those terms, and when she finally told her own story, she had the same tendency I'd noticed in her before: 'They did it to me.' "

While this may have been a characteristic of Foat, her self-portrayal as a passive woman may also have been derived from, even sanctioned by, rhetoric that had held sway in the seventies. Consciousness-raising groups had emphasized a view of women's lives that made them passive hostages to social, economic, and psychological constraints. The passive verb was the mainstay of autobiographies, the heroine always acted upon and hence not responsible for her own choices and actions. Coupled with this narrative device was the talk of "internalization"; before their feminist awakening women were supposedly composites of myths, stereotypes, attitudes imposed on them and accepted as "selves." Foat's joking suggestion that she believed her prince would come because of the Cinderella myth was not an isolated self-justification. It had become a common theme in the women's movement, and indeed Susan Brownmiller's *Femininity* surprisingly harked back to this "you are what you read, see, or are told" ideology, despite its 1984 publication:

> [L]essons in the art of being feminine lay all around me and I absorbed them all: the fairy tales that were read to me at night, the brightly colored advertisements I pored over in magazines . . . , the movies . . . , the comic books . . . , the soap operas. . . . I loved being a little girl, or rather I loved being a fairy princess, for that was who I thought I was.

Aside from the tacit privileges behind her reminiscence, the lock-step pattern of such descriptions—"tell me I'm a fairy princess and I am one"—seemed a disconcerting way of talking about anyone's existence. Doubtless, social and psychological influences affect women's lives; still, women have cores of identity, centers of character. Like everyone else, they grow up in families, communities, and a society by which they are affected, to which they respond, and in which they develop their own complicated personalities. But they are certainly more than sponges that soak up what others tell them. Foat's remark too handily played on the "myth swapping" of consciousness-raising sessions and seemed too simple to explain why she'd gone off with John Sidote in 1965.

Besides, even granting her own explanation that she had been conditioned to believe that her prince would come, how could she have seen Sidote as her Prince Charming? It seemed unlikely that his downward fall, his years in jail, had turned *that* fairy tale upside down and produced a frog where once a prince had been. Wasn't it more probable that like many women, she had been attracted to the wild side, the Peck's Bad Boy in Sidote, not the princely side? He must have been handsome but coarsely so, even then, and his sturdy machismo and his reputation as a ladies' man were more than likely appealing. He was a high flyer—a cool dude of the late fifties, her James Dean (according to Lichtenstein's article, a friend remembered that Dean's death had devastated her). And as she later confessed to NOW colleagues, she'd had a crush on Henry Winkler, "the Fonz," because he reminded her of Sidote, the type of tough guy she'd always gone for.

Everyone, male and female alike, makes mistakes with mates. James Baldwin once said, "We don't choose our lovers, we accept them." Nevertheless, the first step, if not a conscious choice, requires a realization of what in oneself is drawn to the other. Even in her authorized *Life* interview, Ginny didn't say why she'd found herself so attracted to Sidote, preferring to blame social stereotypes. She seemed especially reluctant to acknowledge what seemed likely, that something in her had led her to choose him for his devil-may-care, rebellious side, the slightly sinful, "outlaw" aura about him. Hence, it would seem that Ginny Galluzzo was more than the passive woman when she fell in love with Sidote and allowed herself to be carried off by her white knight in his white convertible that autumn morning in 1965. She had chosen him not just as a Prince Charming, but as a prince of darkness, too.

Foat did concede that she'd fallen in love "with the wrong man." Even that phrase, though, implied it just happened, as if she'd slipped on a banana peel and fallen head over heels in love. The message was that she bore no responsibility for it. Yet hadn't she convinced herself that Sidote was a way to climb out of a boring, small-town existence? Hadn't she leaped to the conclusion that this was an important man? Her perception of Sidote then said something about her character, her judgment or lack thereof. Even granted the parochialism and provincialism of her upbringing, didn't she have a clue that this was a vulgar man? To be serenaded in a bar with "There Will Never Be Another You," to have 3 A.M. phone calls and dates, to hear he was a local Lothario despite his marriage, weren't these signs of a man's questionable character?

"Well, she certainly had lousy taste in men," said many feminists who read about her earlier years. That, of course, didn't prove her guilty. Nevertheless, judgment of character has to rely precisely on such questions of taste. Why not make such judgments in Foat's case? Perhaps it had to do with the peculiarly contemporary reluctance to do so, a tendency that Diana Trilling criticized in *Mrs. Harris*:

> In the style of life that any of us chooses there's contained a psychological, social, and moral message. . . . Suddenly I was filled with rage at our present-day unwillingness to connect esthetic

and moral judgment. The bad esthetics of a society *matter* and so do the bad esthetics of the individual within the society; . . . style is a moral mode, a mode in morality.

Even allowing for Ginny Foat's romantic dream of a Prince Charming, she could still be held accountable for her lousy taste, poor judgment, or even "bad esthetics." (Could one hear so often about the song "There Will Never Be Another You"‑ without cringing?) Still, in her case it seemed that contemporary diffidence in the face of moral judgment was exaggerated by her feminist colleagues who applied the rhetoric of early consciousness-raising to excuse her questionable judgment. Because women new to feminism often depicted themselves as victims to whom everything just happened, they tended to embrace the notion of inauthentic or invalid selves, masks that society had forced them to wear before their feminist identities emerged. Therefore, they were not responsible for anything that had happened to them before their clicks of awareness, before their "new" selves were born. Ginny Foat's first description of herself from jail, "the death of a passive woman named Ginny Foat before the birth of a strong feminist by the same name," had tapped into the same rhetoric. Speaking of oneself in the third person implied another identity, one outside oneself before the birth of the real self, the strong feminist.

The paradigmatic example of this mode of thought could be found in Marilyn French's novel *The Women's Room.* At the beginning of the book, the first-person narrator establishes that the story is about the victimization of a character named Mira, who sees a sign in a bathroom, SOME DEATHS TAKE FOREVER, and takes it as symbolic of her own life. The narrator then recounts in the first person what happened to Mira; this she does in flashbacks from her own isolated existence in Maine, where she lives alone, "enjoying my pain." The narrative stance thus leads the reader to assume that Mira is another character. But "the revelation" at the end of the book is that Mira and the "I" narrator are one and the same woman, exiled to teach at a community college near the coast of Maine, where I/she walks the beach every day, drinks brandy every night, and wonders if I/she is going mad.

Perhaps French intended to hint at madness with this device; nevertheless, the ideological subtext suggests that the "I" narrator is a "new woman" who has re-created herself to such an extent that she is as distant from her old self, Mira, as she is from another person. Hidden behind such rhetorical stances was a message of disassociation: Who women are has nothing to do with who they were, since they had just accepted all they were told that women should be. As French explains "Mira lived by her mirror as much as the Queen in *Snow White*. A lot of us did: we absorbed and believed the things people said about us."

The Queen in *Snow White*, however, had power over her mirror and could demand a confirmation of how she wanted to see herself. Of course women are influenced by social definitions and stereotypes of feminity (as men are by masculine images). But with the wholesale denial of individual responsibility and choice, women tended to depict themselves as having been only weak, mindless, helpless victims before they came to feminism. By savoring that chestnut, women bought into the very stereotype feminism was supposed to be fighting.

Beyond sympathy for Foat's plight, her case raised the very real question of whether women were more than simply victims, and that in turn made a telling point about feminism in the eighties. Certainly, most feminists have now recognized the need for expanding the appeal of the women's movement beyond a privileged class that could enjoy the luxury of extolling their daily victimization. The writer Alice Walker once remarked that she could never understand white, middle-class feminism's emphasis on weakness and incompetence. The women she'd grown up with had been strong and competent; they'd had to be in order to survive, even to triumph over the very real economic and social difficulties in their lives. As feminists begin to reconsider the implications of seventies rhetoric, they must realize that women are indeed conscious before they reach feminist consciousness. Feminine stereotypes had denied women's minds, identities, and moral priorities. But women do have identities, despite the stereotypes; what in fact makes feminism so potentially powerful is the force of the varied personalities that women bring to the women's movement, not vice versa. Feminism doesn't create a self out of whole cloth, nor does it fill an ethical or moral vacuum; it provides a philosophical underpinning, indeed a confirmation of experiences, perceptions, and judgments from which a sense of choice, will, responsibility evolve.

As sympathetic as she was to her friend's ordeal, Midge Costanza had to admit that will and choice were involved even in what she had called "a metamorphosis." Comparing her own background to that of Foat's, she could identify with what had happened to her. Yet the difference was evident in her active verbs and her acknowledgment of the choices she'd made: "The pressure points in our lives must have been similar," she said. "As daughters of Italian parents, we were expected to get married and have kids. But suddenly you reach an age when you realize, 'Wow, I can do what I want to do,' and you go nuts. I went through a period of testing how late at night I could stay out and still function the next day. I'd wanted to go to college, but we couldn't afford it. My family's attitude was that college wasn't really necessary for me, though if we'd had the money they would've supported me in my decision. Still, my teachers told them they'd do anything to help me get into college, but I was having too much fun dating, cruising down Main Street. That was my sense of suddenly being free. You go wild with it, and you feel you are making decisions. And if someone had come along, I'd have gotten married, because I used to say, 'If just the right person came along and said they'd take me away from all this, I'd go.' Then I had a job with a real estate developer. I liked it and I stayed with it for twenty-five years, and started to learn the business. But I also reached a point when I wanted something more out of life than just my job and dates. I began to ask myself, 'Where do I stand? Who am I?' I didn't want to be a one-dimensional person. That's when I went into politics.

"Of course, that involves a certain amount of willpower. The first step is to ask questions—that's part of natural personal growth. Then you go forward, you make choices. When I went into politics, I became dissatisfied with a structure that was not opening up to women or minorities, so I went through another change. I resigned as vice-chairman of the county Democratic committee; I did it in the name of justice—feminism wasn't a recognizable name for what I was then feeling."

Foat, however, seemed to diminish the role of will or choice in her life. On one level, it was part of her defense strategy: Portray herself as a passive victim of an abusive husband and people might accept more readily that Sidote was making wild and vengeful accusations. Nevertheless, feminists, while understanding why she might present herself this way to win a verdict, had to wonder whether this sense of self carried beyond the courtroom. If it did, then it was necessary to question what this position meant for women in general.

"I use the argument that women are just victims of social stereotypes all the time in my cases," Karen DeCrow conceded. "Not in criminal cases, but in employment-discrimination cases, which I do a lot of. For example, I'll argue, 'This woman didn't make demands earlier in her employment because she'd been raised not to.' Nevertheless, I'm not sure I believe it. That's neither here nor there inside the courtroom, but outside the courtroom, I don't really accept the rhetoric of women's total victimization. While women are affected by social attitudes, all people are responsible, with some exceptions—say people who have a brain tumor, or are drugged, or who are very young. But when someone becomes an adult, female or male, they're responsible for their actions. For example, if a woman burns down the house with her husband inside because he was beating her, the prosecutor will ask, 'Why didn't you leave instead of burning up the house with him in it?' She'll say, 'I couldn't, I was so under his control.' Then a feminist therapist will get up and describe how the more women are beaten, the more they come under the husband's spell, and they can't leave, and so on. Any defense lawyer will want to raise that to try to get her off the hook, even through logically one has to ask, 'If she can burn down the house, why can't she just open the door and leave?' Beyond the courtroom, though, I think that position is utter nonsense. To argue that women are not responsible for their actions undercuts their dignity as individuals. I can understand Foat wanting to use that line in her defense. But when in her statements outside the courtroom she implied she wasn't responsible for marrying that bartender, I say, pish-tosh."

According to Ginny Foat, however, her ordeal was happening to her because she'd been nothing but a cipher before her feminist conversion, Ginny on the road to NOW headquarters; hence, she could hardly be held responsible for her earlier life.

Men have often been "stepping-stones" upward for women. Ginny Foat's "mistake" was her extraordinary misjudgment of the man she had hoped was her ticket to freedom. More disturbing was her later refusal—as a feminist—to acknowledge the role she'd played in her own miscast drama. Every statement about Sidote seemed an excuse, derived from a feminist formula: It wasn't my fault because

I wasn't "my true feminist self," as if feminist consciousness obliterated conscience. Even more startling was the way she seemed to blame her parents, especially her mother, though consciousness-raising had tried to help feminists avoid these tendencies.

Grace Lichtenstein guessed that living in California had enabled Foat to see herself as if she'd "emerged like Botticelli's *Venus,* pure out of a clamshell." She was disappointed since she'd hoped to find in Foat a feminist leader whose story could be meaningful to other women. "But she was presenting herself as a woman with no past, or she'd chosen to deny it and didn't want to deal with it. Maybe there was a lot to cover up. She had become the most important feminist politician in the most important political state of the union, she'd almost become NOW vice-president, yet with all her talk of victimization and passivity, I could no longer find the feistiness, the charisma, the self-awareness, of the sort that one would expect from someone who'd become a feminist leader. As somebody who has covered the women's movement from day one, I simply couldn't put her in the same league with the likes of a Gloria Steinem or Betty Friedan, a Bella Abzug or a Gerry Ferraro, any one of the leaders from any point along the feminist spectrum. She didn't seem to have the brains or the perceptions to hold a candle to any of those people, whatever one thinks of their individual politics. Bella Abzug, for example, is one of my heroines. She may be hated by a lot of people, but she's honest as the day is long. She's smart, she's a lawyer, and she certainly wouldn't have gotten into the mess Foat did.

"Still, I thought Foat would have a great deal to tell women about going through dramatic transformations in the last two decades because of the women's movement. But she didn't want to tell that story at all. Unfortunately, the symbolism of her story was better than the reality, precisely because she tried to erase her past."

Other feminists were drawn to the symbolic value of Foat's narrative. Yet her case prompted some moral judgments that in any other circumstances would have been highly suspect. They were not unlike the feminist "excuses" for Jean Harris: She wasn't guilty or shouldn't have been punished, because she wasn't responsible for her actions—she was drugged, or the Scarsdale Diet doctor drove her to it (the old cliché, "her man, he made her do it"), or the social attitudes she'd internalized forced her to the desperate act.

Foat's case was slightly more complicated and required an extra convolution. If it turned out she was guilty of the 1965 murder, then

Sidote must have forced her to do it, so passive and abused was she that she had to obey her torturer's demands. But even if she was guilty, she'd suffered enough. Five years with a wife-beater was the equivalent of "hard time" for murder.

Ginny Foat received several letters expressing the same sentiment: They didn't care if she was guilty or not, they'd still support her because of her work for the women's movement. One woman added that if Foat had murdered someone, she was glad the victim was a male.

Nevertheless, it was startling to hear that even Gloria Steinem believed that since Foat had made such a "useful life" for herself in the feminist movement, the alleged 1965 crime no longer mattered.

"Yes, I did say that even if she were guilty, it didn't matter, given her new life," Steinem agreed. "By that I meant that her story was a confirmation of the transformational powers of feminism, and that Ginny should be paid tribute for her socially useful life all those years. I'd say the same thing about woman who have similar cases, and I'd apply it to men as well. It's like the 'I-was-a-victim-of-a-chain-gang' story. He lived a productive life after he had commited one crime. Then they took him to jail, and he actually became a criminal. The main point is that people change.

"I'm not implying that women are not responsible for their actions. But I do think that with women and men, but with women especially, you have to take into account what they're responding to. If a woman has been beaten for ten years and she kills her husband, even if it's true he didn't threaten her life directly, she's responding to an intolerable situation. Although the essence of feminism is you take responsibility for your own life, the battered-wife syndrome is more like the political-hostage syndrome, in which even after a day or two hostages become dependent upon and attached to their imprisoners. That has now become understood, even though when Patty Hearst was on trial, it wasn't, and it's why her defense lawyers and the general public gave her short shrift. But the much deeper phenomenon of battered wives may not be understood fully yet. Such women have children with these men and they have no other means of survival or dignity, plus it's similar to the hostage syndrome because of the psychological phenomenon of what happens to these women in isolation."

Nevertheless, Ginny Foat wasn't just pointing to the battered-wife syndrome to explain why she'd stayed with Sidote. In her presentation of her history, she was using feminist rhetoric to suggest that social attitudes and stereotypes had forced her into certain situations throughout her life. That was the most disturbing aspect of raising her story to the symbolic level, and indeed ran directly counter to what should be the starting point of feminism: that women are not second-class citizens, are not helpless children, but like all human beings, have an active role in determining their own fates. As Simone de Beauvoir insisted in *The Second Sex* (undeniably one of the classics of feminist literature): "I shall place a woman in a world of values and give her behavior a dimension of liberty. She is not the plaything of contradictory drives, she devises solutions of diverse values in the ethical scale."

It was a useful exercise when considering the meaning of Ginny Foat's story. Placed in a world of values, she had devised a solution in 1965: Whatever her "contradictory drives," she took up with Jack Sidote, she traveled with him, she settled with him in California, she worked to support him, she married him, she stayed with him even when he'd been sent to jail for manslaughter and diagnosed as schizoid, she wrote letters supporting his parole and proclaiming her love. And finally she'd left him. That was, in rough outline, the life she'd made for herself. Whatever the reasons for not leaving him sooner, her brand of feminism seemed to preclude a judgment about the life she'd chosen in 1965. If it was a matter of "taste," it was still a matter of choice. Yet her bad taste, poor judgment, or even basic ignorance could hardly be blamed simply on a lack of feminist consciousness. It seemed more a lack of consciousness in general, or, in de Beauvoir's terms, an extremely narrow ethical scale.

Foat's failure to see Sidote for what he was involved more than falling in love with the wrong man. Choosing Sidote, she wasn't acting only out of passion or a sexual obsession, she also seemed to have seen him as her chance for a new or better life; no matter that he was already married, no matter that they were practically sneaking out of town, that her parents objected, or that all the messages she received—his carrying a gun in his car, his mysterious trips to New York for his boss—should have told her the bartender was bad news. But it seemed she'd put all other considerations aside when she chose to see him as the man who could rescue her and give her a better life. And those considerations were ignored not because she didn't have a feminist consciousness. It seemed more likely that she was ready to take on a new identity and throw all caution to the wind. No, she wouldn't be the traditional wife of her first marriage; she'd be the girlfriend of the high flier, the star of the Villa Lipani. She'd have her ticket to freedom.

Journalists indeed went after Foat's story, and the biographical facts they discovered indicated less a passive woman than someone who, for whatever reasons or goals, had changed herself dramatically several times during her life. Her metamorphoses seemed to occur at turning points that didn't just happen, but that Foat herself chose, often coinciding with a choice of mate. In that sense, even her feminist conversion had the look of a love affair, her life suddenly given over with the same passionate intensity to the romance of sisterhood, her identity totally redefined with her new commitment. These involvements in her life had roused her to new roles, much like the pattern of the narcissist who, as Norman Mailer describes in *Pieces and Pontifications* (*pace* feminists), "must alter that drear context in which one half of the self is forever examining the stale presence of the other. That is one reason why narcissists are forever falling in and out of love, jobs, places, and addictions."

Foat readily talked about herself in the third person, denying a connection to her earlier self and her previous lives; yet she reconstructed her past to insist that she'd not only taken an 180-degree turn and found a new identity but was not responsible for past roles or actions. She was, after all, no longer "herself"; yet as Mailer points out, as the narcissist takes on different roles and re-creates the self in response to surroundings or other people, "confusion is great" and one's "passivity feels pervasive."

Whatever the internal motivations for the way Ginny Foat chose to see herself and her past, it was also quite possible that she presented herself in her first interview as a modern-day Sister Carrie to counter the negative publicity that she felt Sidote, in league with unsympathetic or unscrupulous journalists, had prompted. Keenly aware of public perception and the importance of image, she may simply have taken on the mantle of the hapless victim to elicit sympathy from those who would regard a strong feminist with skepticism or suspicion. Whether she believed in her tale of passivity and miraculous rebirth was another question. Not until her trial would she reveal how assiduously she clung to this sense of herself.

SIX

The Slow Dance
of the Law

IN one very real sense, Foat was indeed the "passive woman." Like anyone charged with a major crime, she had to wait for the slow turn of bureaucratic wheels. Denied bail, she remained in Sybil Brand throughout January, February, March, and most of April, 1983.

In January, Kay had flown to New Orleans and hired John Reed and Robert Glass as Foat's defense attorneys. They were to be responsible for muting the defense team's anti-Louisiana and political harassment rhetoric, even though they themselves came highly recommended for their liberal credentials and civil rights work. Both northerners, Reed from Rhode Island, Yale- and Harvard-educated, Glass from Philadelphia and a University of Pennsylvania Law School graduate, they'd gone south in the sixties as legal-aid lawyers, handled controversial cases, including defending Black Panthers, and in the seventies went into private practice together. Listed among the country's leading defense lawyers by Harvard Law School in 1983, they were known to be sympathetic to the women's movement and more liberal than most of their Louisiana colleagues. Kay Tsenin had found them by asking associates in feminist and legal circles for suggestions, and every response included Glass's or Reed's or both names. In 1977, when Bob Tuller had thought Foat might be tried in Louisiana, he'd been referred to Glass as well.

Kay had considered trying to find a woman lawyer through the close-knit feminist legal network. (One woman was suggested, but then she was appointed to a judgeship.) Nevertheless, Kay also saw the advantage to having two men defend a feminist, comparable, she thought, to the psychological advantage of having a woman defend a rapist.

Kay was particularly concerned about the choice of defense lawyers after having met the Jefferson Parish district attorneys just before the January grand-jury proceeding when Foat was indicted. She and Bob Tuller had brought Sidote's psychiatric evaluation from Chino in the hope of convincing DA John Mamoulides that Sidote was crazy, his story an alcoholic hallucination and hardly the basis on which a prosecutor would want to proceed. In Kay's eyes, Mamoulides seemed aggressively intent on prosecuting Foat, and he wasn't interested in the psychiatric evaluation. "He sat back with his hands behind his head, leaning back in his desk chair, as if he were Big Daddy or Daddy Warbucks," she said, "and I realized they wanted to go full bore on this case. All he did was to try to pump Bob Tuller and me for information."

Sidote's testimony before the grand jury was actually delayed, according to DA Tom Porteous, because the prosecutors had received word that Kay and Tuller were arriving to talk to them: "We waited for them, but they didn't come in with new information. All they were waving in front of us was self-righteous indignation. 'Why are you going ahead with this? Why don't you dismiss it?' We said, 'This is why we're holding up the grand jury?' But they went on with, 'How can you do this?' "

In addition to thinking that the prosecutors would never listen to reason, Kay was equally alarmed when she heard that because of Mamoulides's political clout in the parish, any parish jury would more than likely be proprosecution. One other lawyer who'd been recommended seemed more tied to the old-boy network and Louisiana political structure, so she suspected that when push came to shove he might "sell Ginny out." Although she was worried that Reed and Glass's liberal reputations might alienate a conservative jury, it seemed better to go with lawyers who were more outside the power nexus and who "would be more attuned to nice causes."

Ginny Foat could only rely on Kay's impressions, and from her jail cell she agreed on the choice of Reed and Glass. She had several telephone conversations with them about her defense, should she come to trial; during the following three months, however, she and her California lawyers were concentrating on fighting her extradition. They had only a slim chance of winning but it gave Reed and Glass more time to conduct their investigation of the case and to prepare their defense strategy. Although Governor Deukmejian had already signed the extradition papers on March 6, 1983, Judge Michael Tynan granted Foat's lawyers a month to make their argument that discrepancies in Louisiana's papers as to the date of the alleged crime invalidated the extradition order.

On April 2, however, Los Angeles Superior Court Judge Ronald M. George rejected the Foat challenge, concluding that the challenge was "hypertechnical" and "somewhat esoteric," although he then stayed her extradition so that her lawyers could appeal his decision. On April 25, the California State Supreme Court upheld George's ruling without comment; nevertheless, since Justice Stanley Mosk had written separately that he felt more hearings should be held, Robert Tuller announced that there was a basis for seeking a federal court decision on his argument that the extradition order violated Foat's right to due process. A day later, however, he abruptly reversed himself. Ginny Foat had decided not to fight the extradition order any longer. "She's anxious to get down to Louisiana and get the trial on so she can return to California," he said, and the next morning she appeared for the last time in Judge Michael Tynan's municipal court to announce that she had no further challenges to extradition.

Judge Tynan, softening his stern judicial demeanor, twice wished her good luck in the future and commended her for exemplary conduct in the courtroom. Foat's friends applauded, and Tuller appreciated the remark, perhaps feeling it would play well in the press. Ginny herself was furious, and as Kay Tsenin saw it, the remark betrayed the irrational biases against feminists. "What had Tynan expected her to do, take off her bra and burn it right there in the courtroom?" Still, Tuller again struck an optimistic note outside the courtroom. He was confident that she would be admitted to bail in Louisiana and eventually would be acquitted, despite supporters' fears that she could not get a fair trial in Louisiana. He was taking the line suggested by Reed and Glass. Now that she was on her way to Gretna, she would announce her faith in the decency of the parish citizens.

Nevertheless, Foat's supporters got in a few last digs at Louisiana, accusing Jefferson Parish once more of "overkill" by sending one of its district attorneys along with the police officers to accompany Foat on the plane.

"When I first got to the court, reporters walked right past me," said DA Tom Porteous with a laugh. "I guess they expected to see somebody in 'shit-kicker' overalls and cowboy boots, and they didn't recognize me in a three-piece suit. I know that our so-called excessive force that went out received a tremendous amount of attention. But I went simply as a legal arm, because we didn't want our deputies to get out there and have one more snag. Of course, California kept reassuring us it couldn't happen, but there's no such thing as 'can't happen' in the law. It takes only twelve seconds to type up a temporary restraining order or in some fashion delay the extradition. We were advised that the extradition had been ordered, flew out, and planned to bring her back the next morning. The LA authorities then wanted us to wait another day. I said, 'I'll not have any part of this, we're leaving tomorrow morning.' "

On April 25, Foat was returned to court for formal extradition; she once again blew kisses to her supporters, who stood and cheered her. She was then handcuffed, driven to a police helicopter, and whirled away to the airport. Porteous met her on the tarmac at the rear of the plane, introducing himself, and told her that she was now the prisoner of the Jefferson Parish sheriff's office. He said, "No one will try and question, or even talk to you." She had already been searched, and he told her she would not be handcuffed and that she should try to be as comfortable as she could.

She was accompanied by a female detective from Jefferson Parish. Tall and blond, with a cheerful, attractive, strong face, Susan Rush could easily have appeared on *Cagney and Lacey;* having once lived in southern California, it seemed especially ironic that she should be perceived as another one of those dumb-hick retrograde southerners. Besides, she was only doing her job, which was to provide a female police escort for Foat on the plane back to New Orleans.

"Ginny was seated by the window," said Porteous. "Susan was next to her, and I was on the aisle. She and Susan talked, just general conversation. One of Ginny's major concerns was whether she could wear her makeup to court. That was one of her initial inquiries, but I didn't listen or try to overhear what was essentially between Ginny and Susan. My impression was that her lawyers were concerned about the makeup, but I didn't pay much attention."

Accompanying Foat was Bob Tuller and his wife as well as a slew of television and print reporters. If Foat was thinking of herself as a celebrity and having to concern herself with her makeup, the press was treating her as such, too. Every minute of her flight into unknown territory, every reaction that registered on her face, was being monitored.

Little celebrity marked her routine processing at the Jefferson Parish correctional center in Gretna, a two-story, modern concrete building across the street from the courthouse. Foat was booked, led to a holding cell, and provided with the jail uniform, a bright red-orange jumpsuit. The next morning she was led across the street to Judge Robert Burns's courtroom for her arraignment; her trial was scheduled for October 11, and her bail was set at $125,000. Since a property bond was required, however, she had to wait in jail until it was arranged that Dr. Norma Kearby, a fifty-five-year-old New Orleans physician long associated with NOW and feminist circles, would post her French Quarter properties.

Known as Niki to her friends, the slim, blond-haired, gentle-voiced southerner had received a telephone message—"Someone from California is calling to talk to you about Ginny Foat." At first she hadn't recognized the name, but was told that she was in jail in California and about to be extradited to Louisiana. Kay and Bob and John had Dr. Kearby's name from a mutual lawyer friend as someone who was both a feminist and a property owner. "It boiled down to who called," said Kearby. "Because of what the lawyer whom we both knew told me, I thought it sounded like someone was putting the screws to Ginny Foat. She was someone in need, and I came to her need. So I got in touch with John Reed and Robert Glass and agreed to put up my property."

While Glass had told her that the bond would become a matter of public record, Dr. Kearby certainly hadn't expected the publicity surrounding her participation in the case. After filling out the necessary forms at the courthouse that afternoon, she returned home to find a TV newsman with a camera lurking by her doorway. She ducked into a neighbor's and waited until he gave up and went away. But the news was out, and with the 5 P.M. television broadcasts, she heard the details of her property recited, plus vague insinuations about the bonds of sisterhood that had prompted her to come to Foat's aid.

Later, at dinner that night with Kay and Ginny, she would be surprised to hear that there were rumors of lesbianism surrounding Foat's case and she admitted to having second thoughts. She was especially dismayed to hear at a later date that Foat and her lawyers were discussing a defense that was open about a commitment to lesbian rights. Although active in the feminist movement and supportive of gay and lesbian rights, Kearby wasn't pleased that the Foat case prompted such gossip. "At fifty-five, I can say that I didn't live my whole life for her defense strategy to put my medical practice in jeopardy." But apparently the Foat team revised their decision, and while the innuendos were bound to continue, attention on Dr. Kearby gradually subsided. She received two negative phone calls, one at home, one at her clinic, but finally most of her friends and patients, instead of being embarrassed, accepted her act for what it was—a gesture of kindness. "Now I can say I'm glad I did it," she said. "But at first I thought, 'I don't need this.' I'd never been as scared in my life because of all the publicity."

As a result of Dr. Kearby's help, Ginny Foat was free on April 26. As she walked out of jail, she kissed Bob Glass on the cheek, and embraced Kay Tsenin. Both women were in tears, Foat losing her composure in relief. They went to the lawyers' downtown New Orleans office, and the next day she held a press conference. For the first time local reporters who'd been writing about the "notorious feminist with a sordid past" saw her in the flesh, and they were taken by surprise. This was no heavy-duty, leather-wearing, aggressive female. She was gray-haired and conservatively dressed, and her speech, though forceful, was not strident. Suddenly their clichés weren't appropriate, and Foat's lawyers and supporters were pleased to see that she was charming them. She explained that while she could not discuss the case, she wanted to assure the New Orleans community that she believed she could receive a fair trial. But she also pleaded with the reporters not to accept as fact everything Sidote and the district attorneys told them, like saying she had been a go-go dancer, "which I never, never was," she insisted. This had become emblematic to her of the way the press accepted and repeated Sidote's accusations without confirmation; her denial of this allegation had become as vehement as the protests of her innocence.

Judge Robert Burns had scheduled a pretrial hearing for July 22, and Foat hoped that in the next few days he would rule favorably on her request to leave the state.

Waiting for the judge's decision, she spent the next few days in

New Orleans meeting with her attorneys and the private investigator, Gary Eldridge, they had hired. Ginny had felt relieved after meeting Reed and Glass initially, and now as she spent more time with them she was growing even fonder of them. "They walked in, John in his cowboy boots and jeans, both of them laid-back and wonderful, and we fell in love," she said. Still, Kay was slightly perturbed that instead of an immediate political reaction to the case, they concentrated more on the facts of the alleged crime. "But after spending those first few days with Ginny after her release, I think they got politically attuned rather quickly," said Kay. "At first they took the attitude that 'our poor DAs got caught up in the press attention to the case and now they can't get out of it. They have to go ahead with it to save face.' But then they realized that the DAs were blocking us every step of the way, for example, with our speedy-trial motion. Plus we asked John Reed to imagine if Ginny was a man and Sidote a woman, then would the case have been brought? Would they have accepted the woman's accusation as easily as they accepted that of a man? John identified with that exercise very quickly, and since he believed her innocent from his own sifting of the facts, he came to see how political her case actually was."

Foat herself was immediately enthusiastic and threw herself into preparing her defense as intensely as she'd committed herself to day and night work for NOW. She had the impression that neither Reed nor Glass had experienced such active involvement by a client. "We became not attorneys and client but a legal team. At first there was some hesitation about my and Kay's involvement. But then later they weren't protective of their position, and we had actual group meetings and went through group decision-making processes. It was wonderful, and we became even like a family."

Foat's lawyers immediately confronted the critical question of how much the case should be presented as political both in the courtroom and in the media. Difficult decisions had to be made as they found themselves walking a narrow line between politicizing the case and arousing antifeminist prejudice. "We talked about 'How much do we compromise our beliefs?' " said Ginny, "and that was real hard. For example, in another case John and Bob wouldn't have had any hesitation about filing a writ claiming that since the Jefferson Parish grand jury had no blacks on it, it was not a jury of my peers. We had a long philosophical discussion, but then decided it would be better not to file a writ that would bring to light my civil rights involvement. Then somebody suggested a joint fund-raiser for the Ginny Foat Defense Fund and Amnesty International." Again, the decision was negative; they did not want to be perceived as too liberal. "But every time we made that kind of decision," said Foat, "there'd be a long silence, and we'd go back and talk about how important was winning the case versus compromising our values."

Foat was also treading on slippery ground with NOW members in the New Orleans area. Lynne Renihan and other members of the local chapter put together a reception for her; yet they took pains to stress that it was not a fund-raiser to avoid seeming to flout national NOW's directive. Such apparent schisms within NOW would have given the New Orleans press another occasion to depict Foat as a strident feminist who'd been abandoned by her leaders and colleagues. "So the reception in New Orleans was a 'come meet Ginny Foat' sort of thing," said Kay. "Everybody who meets Ginny for any length of time immediately falls in love with her. That's what happened down there, and the guests kept saying, 'What are they doing to this woman? And how can we help?' As a result we were able to line up a group of volunteers to assist us during the trial."

The connection to New Orleans NOW had initially been made through Dr. Kearby. Because of national NOW's official position, Foat could never be sure what attitude local chapters would adopt. She had received letters of support from individual members all over the country but wasn't sure whether New Orleans NOW was strictly adhering to the national office's policy. When Lynne Renihan read that Dr. Kearby had posted the property bond, she wrote her a note saying she was "thrilled" by her action. Renihan had never met Dr. Kearby, although she was listed as a NOW member: "Niki then forwarded my note to Ginny to show her she had support from New Orleans NOW. Then after Ginny's release, I helped plan the get-together as a low-key, private fund-raiser. We wanted it laid-back and comfortable. We wanted to meet her, but didn't want her hounded by the press. We didn't let anyone outside know that Ginny would be here, and we had it in a private home. Still, we had a really big turnout and helped raise money for her defense bills."

One of the outcomes of this get-together was the California contingent's reassessment of the Louisiana women. "When they first got here, they seemed a little hostile or wary of us," said Renihan. "I had the feeling they expected us, even those of us in NOW, to be running around in hoopskirts. As a northerner I had a bit of the same attitude when I first moved to New Orleans. But I learned that women were doing fantastic things down here, too. So when the California people got here, they had to cool down. At first it was as if they thought they were on another planet. Of course, they were upset about the case, but I kept having to say, 'Hey, we're trying to help, too.' "

Soon new stories and rumors about Foat surfaced, and she blamed the more favorable newspaper articles for provoking the prosecution into passing negative comments to cooperative New Orleans reporters. At least that was the defense's hunch when they began to hear gossip around town about Foat's sexual proclivities. The photographs of Kay and Ginny hugging after her release from jail were pointed to with smirks; stories circulated about her drinking and dancing at lesbian bars and discos. "That was really stupid," said Kay, "because we kept Ginny at the Royal Orleans in the French Quarter. If she wanted to drink, that's where she drank, right there in the hotel lobby's bar."

Equally damaging was a report on May 8 in *The Times-Picayune* that Wasyl Bozydaj would testify that he'd heard Foat and Sidote "openly discuss the crime" and that she "might have disposed of bloody clothing afterward." Foat and her lawyers attributed the story (it was untrue, they insisted) to the prosecutors' desperation and publicly denounced the pretrial publicity as prejudicial to Foat's right to a fair trial. Judge Robert Burns was also furious and threatened a press ban. But the Foat team privately wondered if the prosecutors had dropped the Bozydaj information in a reporter's lap to provoke just such a reaction, even a gag order, from the judge, since the media tide seemed to have turned in Foat's favor.

Given permission to leave Louisiana until her trial, Foat and Tsenin flew to Los Angeles for a reunion with friends and supporters. From there they would fly to San Francisco, returning to Kay's hillside home in Marin, where Ginny planned to stay until her trial in October. But in Los Angeles she received word that her father had been taken to the hospital in New Paltz and was in a coma. After only a few days in California, she rushed to New York.

Spending most of her time in New Paltz with her family and at her father's bedside, she also joined her New York City literary agent to interview potential ghostwriters for her book. Her first choice was a writer who spent the next four months interviewing Foat and working on the project, but eventually found the conditions im-

posed on her—total control by Foat, her lawyers, and her agent—
too constricting. After she quit, the Foat team hired Laura Foreman, an ex-*New York Times* reporter who lost her job after an investigation by the *Philadelphia Inquirer,* her previous employer, into
alleged unprofessional behavior and conflict of interests. According
to the *Inquirer's* report, she had been having an affair with and receiving gifts from State Senator Henry (Buddy) Cianfrani, whom
she covered and used as a source when she was the *Inquirer's* political writer. She later married the man, but her reputation as a journalist had been tarnished. She would say later that her experience
gave her special insight into Ginny Foat's ordeal of being unjustly
accused. Foat herself said Laura was an appropriate choice because
she understood how the male establishment will try to bring down
successful, powerful women.

But this choice and the prospect of a book and a TV-movie were
kept secret until after her trial so as not to stir up negative publicity.
For the same reason, Reed and Glass also told her they were worried about plans for nationwide fund-raisers. Two had already been
scheduled in California, one by Patty Duke Astin in Los Angeles,
the other by Lia Belli (president of the California Democratic Council
and the wife of lawyer Melvin) in San Francisco. Reed and Glass
reminded Foat of her "image problem," pleading with her to keep
a low profile. Not only were they worried about the trial itself, but
they knew that Judge Burns might even revoke her permission to
leave Jefferson Parish if too much publicity preceded the pretrial
hearing scheduled for July 22.

Ginny finally returned to Kay's home (while she'd been in jail,
Kay had moved her things out of her Silver Lake apartment and
brought them up to Marin). From there they consulted with Reed
and Glass on the legal steps to be taken in Louisiana over the next
two months. The lawyers had filed a dismissal motion, arguing that
Foat's right to a speedy trial had been violated, since Jefferson Parish had ignored or failed to act on previous opportunities to arrest
and indict her. As a result, they argued, the defense was "impaired"
because some witnesses could not be found, and four others who
could have confirmed beatings by Sidote were now dead. Among
these four was the woman named Bobbie, the close friend who had
been killed while Foat was in prison in 1977. She had substituted
for Ginny at the *Princess Louise* when she was too battered by Sidote
to go to work, Foat's lawyers said. Later DA Tom Porteous would

cite this as another reason for his cynicism: "Ever notice how many bodies there were around Foat? Like Busconi, that was another unsolved murder. But before the trial Reed and Glass were saying Bobbie would have helped her case!"

Reed and Glass argued that Foat's father, who had recently died, would also have been able to verify beatings by Sidote. While he had given a statement to the Nevada court in 1977 testifying that his daughter "lived in fear of this man," he could have said much more if still available as a witness. Further, according to Reed and Glass, hospital records indicating treatment for the injuries received in the beatings were difficult to find and in some cases missing.

The secondary part of their motion concerned Louisiana's failure to pursue the case in 1977. While both Foat and Nevada authorities asserted that Louisiana had been notified of her release, Jefferson Parish DAs argued that Sheriff Harry Lee's office had never been notified of it or her return to California. Reed and Glass then had to document that Foat had been held for a day in Nevada on the Louisiana warrant in 1977 and that only after an exchange of phone calls between the Nevada district attorney's office and the Jefferson Parish sheriff's office, with no indictment forthcoming, had she been released. Foat's attorneys included both the record of her "hold" for Louisiana on November 14, and the telephone records showing numerous phone calls between Nevada and Louisiana authorities.

Another aspect of the speedy-trial argument relied on Bob Tuller's memory of conversations he'd had in 1977 with one Shirley Wimberly, a Jefferson Parish assistant district attorney who'd since retired. Tuller insisted that after Ginny's release on the Nevada charge, Wimberly reassured him (orally but not in writing) that he was not going to pursue the case. But now the retired DA insisted there'd been no such conversation, and Foat's file showed no notes to the effect that he had decided not to prosecute.

Tsenin was outraged at the ex-prosecutor's "stonewalling" and the current DAs' excuse that they had not prosecuted in 1977 because they either thought Ginny was serving time in Nevada or hadn't known where she'd gone after her release: "Wimberly had a big lapse of memory when he was called to testify to this. It also cost us mucho bucks to prove that Louisiana had known that Ginny was released in 1977. They could easily have acknowledged it, but they wouldn't until we retrieved all the files and the phone records. A good DA sees himself or herself as an officer of the court in search of truth and justice and honesty and will lay out the facts they have because they're interested in convicting guilty people, not innocent people. But with Mamoulides there was a total lack of cooperation. We had to fight tooth and nail to get information, even the original police's missing-persons report filed by Chayo's son, which was important because it differed from the description of the victim in Sidote's 1977 confession. It was their lack of cooperation, in fact, that finally convinced John and Bob just how political this trial was."

The defense felt that they were being blocked every step of the way by the prosecutors and pointed to this as further proof of a vendetta "to get a feminist at any cost." The district attorneys, however, saw it strictly in terms of legal maneuvering, as a necessary strategy in reaction to the defense team's demands.

"The problem for us was again their self-righteous indignation," said DA Porteous. "They marched in and wanted everything, even though they didn't need everything for their speedy-trial hearing. What they clearly wanted was open discovery. So we decided that since they were trying to get everything, we'd give them nothing; we'd simply let the judge tell us what we *had* to give them. We weren't blocking them, it was just tactical. We were not acting irresponsibly or blocking them because we were out to get her. We did what any prosecutors would do when the defense makes the claim that they need everything. In fact, she got a fairly quick hearing on the speedy-trial motion. I can guarantee that if she'd been tried in California, she would not have been arraigned in April and scheduled to come to trial in October.

Foat's defense lawyers named other witnesses who were unavailable: a) the man who had found Chayo's body, who would help confirm that Sidote's 1977 description of the victim and the locale of the crime fit neither Chayo nor the place where his body had been found; b) Happy Ditcharo, the owner of the bar where Foat and Sidote had worked, who had suffered a massive stroke twelve years before but could have testified to Foat's work hours; c) Sidote's own sister, Angela, who could have testified to Sidote's alcohol problems but had since died; d) finally, the young man who was supposed to have traveled with Foat, Sidote, and Wasyl Bozydaj from Texas to Nevada in 1965 but had still not been located. The prosecutors also wanted to find him but had been as unsuccessful as the defense. He became known in the press as the "missing witness," a pawn used by both sides.

Oddly enough, Foat's lawyers enlisted Sidote's help to buttress their contention that Louisiana had chosen not to prosecute in 1977. Sidote gave the court a statement claiming that Jefferson Parish had never asked him to testify against his ex-wife before 1983. While he supported Foat's argument that Louisiana had failed to pursue its case in 1977 when the opportunity had presented itself, he also emphasized his present willingness to cooperate. Again, Sidote was having it both ways:

> At no time in 1977 did any Louisiana official ask me to testify against Virginia Foat in connection with the death of Moises Chayo in Louisiana. In fact no Louisiana official in any way contacted me concerning the possibility of testifying against Virginia Foat in Louisiana until after I was rebooked (I was already in jail on a DWI charge) on the Louisiana charge in January 1983. . . . However, based on what I was presented with by the District Attorney's office in 1983, had those same alternatives been presented to me in 1977 I believe I would have testified for the State of Louisiana against Virginia Foat.

When Reed and Glass presented their motion, they argued as well that the unresolved murder charge had adversely affected Foat during the intervening years. Their goal was to convince Judge Burns that the Louisiana charge had curtailed Foat's free speech and movement and that her rights had been jeopardized by the delay in prosecution. Ginny Foat took the stand to explain that while she thought the charges were resolved, she was also afraid that they hadn't been, and as a result had been limited in her political actions and achievements. Glass tried to show that Foat might have been elected president of NOW but hadn't run for that office because of the charges, that she then wasn't elected vice-president because of these charges, and also hadn't run for elected public office because of the ambiguity of her situation. Judge Burns, however, interrupted this line of questioning abruptly, announcing that this was not a political trial and he wouldn't allow it to be turned into one.

Since Foat had often stated that the charges had been resolved, it was questionable how far Reed and Glass could have pursued this line of reasoning. Foat's testimony at the two-day pretrial hearing would be limited to the personal effect of the unresolved charges, and these remarks seemed to reflect the same ambivalence she had expressed to friends and NOW colleagues. On the one hand, she insisted that her life had been destroyed since her release in Nevada. "I have lived every day of my life since 1977 worrying about what Louisiana would do," she said, adding that her marriage, business, and political ambitions were destroyed by the pending murder charge. Which marriage and which businesses weren't specified, and it was difficult to see how her political ambitions had been destroyed, since she'd gone as far as she had in the organization. The reasons she'd lost the vice-presidency were open to dispute, and just as ambiguous were her motives for not running for the presidency—whether it was the threat of publicity or of prosecution that had given her second thoughts. Shaping her testimony to support the dismissal motion, she once again strayed into the blurry area that her own friends had noticed. Although she insisted she'd worried every day, she also said, "I was lulled into a feeling that maybe Louisiana wasn't going to prosecute me and I had to get on with my life. I didn't know I was a fugitive."

After the two days of testimony, Judge Burns denied the defense motion, ruling that deceased witnesses and missing evidence about her beatings were not relevant. He took under advisement the question of delay impairing her defense or causing her undue anxiety, but scheduled her trial for October 11. Reed and Glass immediately took the ruling to the state appeals court. That court, however, refused to rule on Burns's decision. Having returned to California, Foat received the bad news by phone. With Kay on the extension, they all found themselves weeping. Then Ginny stopped and tri- to cheer Kay and her attorneys by reassuring them, "We're stor- up all our good luck for the end."

That became her slogan. Yet they all knew that Judge B- rulings during the hearing didn't bode well for what he wo- low at the actual trial. The fact that he considered her invol- and leadership in NOW irrelevant to the case was the lea- defense's worries. Burns's pronouncement that this was n- ical trial could in some ways benefit Foat, since she didn'- prosecution to use her feminism against her either. M- some was his ruling that witnesses and evidence to pr- battering were irrelevant. This was the crux of Foat's just how strict Burns chose to be would severely affect her court-room strategy.

Reed and Glass then decided to take the appeals-court ruling on the speedy-trial motion one step higher, to the Louisiana Supreme Court. A recent U.S. Supreme Court decision indicated a strong basis for forcing a ruling before Foat actually went on trial. They also believed that their arguments met the criteria for such motions as established by the Supreme Court in 1972: length of delay, reason for delay, the defendant's assertion of his right, and whether or not the defendant had been prejudiced by the delay. Their primary hope was that a favorable decision would make a trial unnecessary; meanwhile, they started planning her defense.

That summer Foat had found herself facing another trial, this one held by NOW colleagues in southern California who brought formal grievances against Kay Tsenin for mishandling of funds and a failure to perform the required duties of acting president of California NOW. Further, they argued that Kay's personal relationship with Foat perpetuated the public perception of a close association between California NOW and the case and jeopardized the organization; Toni Carabillo wrote an addendum to the grievance charges, citing the "public relations" problems Tsenin had caused.

Foat concluded that the grievance procedure against Kay was simply another attack on herself and an attempt to undermine her support among individual members. When Kay had initially refused to resign in January, Foat and Tsenin had heard a spate of rumors about themselves, all designed, they felt, to alienate NOW members' support. Such rumors were incredible and hard to believe, but resurfaced in the summer of 1983, and were brought to a Los Angeles feminist lawyer, a friend of Foat's, to convince her that Tsenin should resign. She was told that Louisiana had resurrected the charge because, in exchange for her release in 1977, Foat had agreed to become an FBI informant in the women's movement. She had done as directed, pushed herself forward and become prominent. Upon losing her 1982 bid for national office, however, she was no longer useful to the FBI, and as a result the FBI convinced the Louisiana authorities to go after her in 1983. Shades of sixties paranoia, it even extended to Kay—that she had known Foat was an informant and had sanctioned it because of their close personal relationship.

The lawyer was aghast. Not that she believed a word of it, but she told Kay she probably should resign. The very fact that NOW members were talking this way scared the hell out of her. If they were willing to go to such lengths to impugn Foat and Tsenin, indeed to tarnish Kay's personal character and destroy her as an attorney, then Kay would be wise to give them a wide berth.

Kay refused to be frightened into resigning, prompting the official grievance procedure. The most serious charge was tampering with funds, but the real crux of the complaint seemed to be in Carabillo's "Supplementary Statement" in which she argued that Tsenin's refusal to distance herself from her friend had caused a close identification between NOW and the Foat case, which was a clear conflict of interests:

> The issue of interests in conflict—Foat's best interests and NOW's best interests—arises out of the overlapping of roles Kay Tsenin assumed after Ginny Foat's arrest. . . .
>
> The harsh reality is that the very nature of the charges made against Foat almost immediately made it essential in NOW's best interests to be separately represented to the public. Tsenin clearly—because of her close association with Foat—could not easily make the distinction between the cases of Inez Garcia and Joanne [sic] Little and the Foat case; both Garcia and Little killed in self-defense, but Foat was not charged with killing the husband she has alleged beat her—she was accused of killing a victim that she and her husband had allegedly robbed.
>
> Tsenin's loyalty to Foat, arising out of their close relationship, did not permit her to believe for one moment that Foat could participate in such a crime, but the general public, viewing the case dispassionately, had no such reserves of intimacy to draw on, and could only be shocked and alienated at the nature of the charges.
>
> While it is appropriate for Tsenin, as a close friend, to be loyal to Foat and publicly defend her, NOW, as an organization vital to the interests of many thousands of women, cannot afford such blind loyalty. . . .

Carabillo's primary concern was the public perception of NOW's close ties to Foat because of Kay Tsenin's position in the organization. That was hardly the grounds for a grievance procedure per se.

Instead, Carabillo listed the occasions on which she felt Kay had slighted her NOW duties for the sake of her intense involvement in Foat's case. These included unauthorized press statements proclaiming NOW's unwavering support of Foat; failure to control Foat supporters' demonstrations and prevent their wearing "Go Foat" T-shirts (publicly identifying Foat with NOW) during the California extradition hearings; neglect of her NOW duties at the California Democratic convention and at the women's caucus while making an unofficial fund-raising pitch for Foat at the convention's dinner; while publicly identified as acting state coordinator, involving herself in actions such as retaining attorneys in Louisiana, assisting in arrangements for bail, welcoming Foat on her release from jail in Louisiana. As a result, Carabillo concluded, Tsenin's personal interests were in conflict with NOW's interests and in conflict with what her responsibilities should have been as acting state coordinator.

Foat and Tsenin saw Carabillo's charges as yet another attempt to control California NOW, since they considered the young woman who would succeed Kay, although once Foat's roommate, less forceful and experienced and more easily manipulated by the Carabillo faction. While the grievance procedure would consider the specific charges against Kay for financial mismanagement, Foat and Tsenin circulated a strongly worded rebuttal of Carabillo's supplementary complaints about Kay's conflict of interest and public perception of her role in the Foat case:

> . . . Throughout this diatribe she condemns the organization and then condemns Kay Tsenin for following the directions of the leadership and membership of the organization. She uses terms such as "injurious to the organization" but gives no evidence of such injury. She talks about potential conflict, public perception, appearances, but gives no evidence of fact in any instance except personal opinion. . . . Clearly, all the evidence that has been presented proves that Kay Tsenin was following the direction of the Board of Directors of California NOW and the Executive Committee in her dealings with the Foat matter. . . .

Foat and Tsenin went on to cite their evidence that Kay had simply followed the policies of the California NOW board of directors and the executive committee; yet they were most incensed by the distinction Carabillo had drawn between Foat's case and the Garcia and Little cases, which had drawn dramatic nationwide attention from feminists.

> She further damages her credibility by using the example of Jo-Anne [*sic*] Little and Inez Garcia, stating that Tsenin could not see the difference. In her own words, she states that Foat is accused by the husband who "allegedly" beat her. But Little and Garcia killed in self-defense. Would Ms. Carabillo have us believe that we should disassociate from Ginny because we, as a feminist organization, believe on the one hand the word of two women that say they acted in self-defense, but on the other hand do not believe one of our own when she professes her innocence to a crime. Ms. Carabillo obviously wanted us to believe a three-time self-confessed schizophrenic murderer, Foat's exhusband, John Sidote. The membership of Cal NOW does not believe this, and Kay Tsenin followed their directives. . . .

Foat and Tsenin included the many articles about the Foat case in which Tsenin was quoted to indicate that she had been careful to distinguish between her NOW position and her closeness to Foat; they argued that the problem was not public perception but Carabillo's personal opinion, not based on fact. In conclusion, they blew the lid off the whispered charges made by one NOW faction behind closed doors and explained why Bob Tuller had wanted Foat distanced from NOW for her own sake:

> . . . In reality, Attorney Tuller was concerned only about jeopardy to Foat from other NOW members, and not with her association with the organization. Tuller perceived that he had a client that had just been betrayed by a person in a leadership role in NOW. He was concerned about further damage to his client by her feminist sisters. Unfortunately, we found there was basis for his fears, as evidenced from [another attorney's] testimony regarding conversations with the grievants and their blackmail attempts and threats to further harm Foat. . . .

The lawyer's testimony about remarks by the grievants was quoted directly:

". . . it was basically an ultimatum to Kay that if she did not resign her office, that action would be taken against her and against Kay . . . I'm sorry . . . and against Ginny, basically to impair Ginny in her lawsuit in the criminal action against her, that things would be done to harm her in that and things would be done to impair her as a feminist, to impugn her as a feminist and that things would be done against Kay to . . . grievances would be filed against Kay, that action would be taken to remove her from office if she did not resign from her office by 3:00 P.M. the next day. . . . I would say 10 or 12 items were mentioned, things that would be gone through and mentioned, such as the PAC account and that there were various things, several of which I consider defamatory and I don't wish to repeat. . . ."

As a result, the lawyer said, she had advised Kay to resign because she was "being blackmailed through Ginny," and there would be an attempt to "impair Ginny both in her criminal suit and as a feminist." Although she admitted she found these threats "absolutely ludicrous, totally unbelievable and without any foundation, a matter of fantasy on the part of God knows who," still she told Kay she thought she should resign, because "this was scary stuff [and] people were out to get her and . . . Ginny."

After rebutting Carabillo's attacks point by point, Foat and Tsenin concluded by reasserting their anger at the way Carabillo and other NOW leaders had treated the Foat case from the beginning.

In Carabillo's closing paragraph she sums up by telling us her magic answer to what is in NOW's best interest. Her self-possessed authoritative air tells us that in NOW's best interest Kay Tsenin, California NOW, and the membership of this organization should desert their feminist principles and should violate the Constitution of the United States and adopt a posture that anyone who is charged with a crime is guilty until proven innocent. If we follow Ms. Carabillo's line of reasoning we have in essence provided the opposition to the women's movement the most valuable weapon they could ever possess. Accuse one of us of a crime and the rest of us will run with our tails between our legs so that our image is not tarnished—so that public perception is not jeopardized. It is sad that Ms. Carabillo does not see the damage that her perspective is doing to the women's movement. Over and over, Kay has heard the question, "If one of your own can't count on you, how can the women of America expect more"—but then, maybe that is Ms. Carabillo's new feminist ethic.

The lines again had been drawn, and the grievance hearing at the Westwood Holiday Inn in late June 1983 brought the pro- and anti-Foat factions out in force. Pro-Foat members spoke openly about "a kangaroo court," and handed out fliers with a picture of a kangaroo on them. As one woman said, "Some NOW leaders are so opposed to Foat that if Louisiana doesn't get her, then they will."

Carabillo was well aware that she was perceived as the ringleader of the anti-Foat contingent. Nevertheless, she said she herself hadn't instigated the grievance procedure. "The charges had been compiled by a group of NOW people who were very concerned that Kay could not function as both acting state coordinator and spokesperson for the Foat defense committee. In the process, they felt she had mishandled NOW, and they came to me for my signature. But that was absolutely not 'my plot' to get either Ginny or Kay. I did write the addendum about mishandling public relations, and I also went to the grievance procedure. My mother went, too, and when she saw Ginny, she hugged her, because she felt very sorry for what Ginny was going through. Ginny hugged her back, but neither she nor Kay spoke to me. They still didn't realize that I felt sorry for her, too, but my other concern was NOW, and that's why I'd written my addenda. I did think it was interesting that they didn't put me through the cross-examination that they put everybody else through. I certainly didn't like the flavor of the Foat camp rhetoric. I also think I would have convinced people there that in fact what Foat's defense committee wanted NOW to do in terms of public statements would have seriously hurt her chances for a fair trial in Louisiana."

Despite Carabillo's expression of sympathy, she was perceived as anti-Foat by the pro-Foat forces. After all, she defended Shelly Mandell, the argument went, and had always been eager to stop Ginny once she'd become powerful in her own right and no longer bowed to Carabillo's wishes.

Shelly Mandell also attended the grievance procedure, and, of course, her presence deepened the antagonism between the two factions. "I'm not a chicken," she said, "and even though I was very hurt and very depressed and frankly didn't want any more of it, I still went. I felt terrible about the dumb thing I'd done and what had happened, but I agreed that Kay's behavior had been incredible. Since this is my organization and my movement and I love NOW, nothing is going to keep me away when I think it's being jeopardized. But during the hearing Ginny's supporters stuck chairs in my way; they'd say, 'Oh, excuse me,' and hit me with a chair."

For obvious reasons, nothing could have lessened the antagonism between the two factions; aside from the personal animosity, both groups thought of themselves as representing what NOW should be, what the organization's position should be, not only in terms of the Foat case itself, but in terms of what in NOW policy the case had come to symbolize for both sides.

Other NOW members who fell into neither camp also attended the session, because they were appalled by the escalation of animosity among the membership. Even more than the Foat case, this was jeopardizing their organization and hurting the women's movement. Representatives from chapters throughout the state turned out, and whatever their opinions about NOW's policy toward the Foat case, they were willing to testify that Tsenin had performed her duties as acting state coordinator adequately, even admirably.

Foat was so outraged by the attempts to remove Kay from office that, despite her own concerns, she went to the grievance hearing to testify on her friend's behalf. She was cheered by the favorable reaction to both her and Kay: "I certainly didn't find that I was being persecuted for testifying on Kay's behalf. The membership in the audience was clearly supportive and outraged by the charges. They saw how much it was costing the organization because of the political feuds behind it."

Carol Schmidt and Norma Hair were also astonished at the charges brought against Kay and stayed for the grueling session, lasting all day and into the morning hours of both Saturday and Sunday. They were astounded to hear the basis for some of the grievances, especially since Hair was a bookkeeper by profession and had long been involved with NOW finances. "Norma and I knew that, in fact, a lot of the things they were accusing Kay of were actually Ginny's doing, but they were no big deal," said Schmidt. "For example, the fact that checks had only one signature recorded was no different from what California NOW always did. Officially, checks require two signatures, but one person signs a thousand checks and the other person then makes them out and signs them when needed. So in effect it's one signature, only one person approving the check, but it's a common method in NOW to save time." She also learned that a NOW state treasurer, herself once under scrutiny for mishandling funds, had joined the Carabillo group, and had charged that Kay had failed to file quarterly tax forms for California NOW's political action committee. As a result, the CPA's statement that the books weren't in order had become the primary grievance. Schmidt said she also watched with shock as Kay's accusers brought in a male lawyer, a male CPA, and a male court reporter, and at the recess she heard a woman say to Kay, "How dare you put Ginny on the stand? Hasn't she gone through enough?" Schmidt was furious and defended Kay: "Ginny has to be here because this is another attempt to get her. It isn't Kay, it's her enemies who are putting her through this."

Later Kay produced all of the tax reports, and in her testimony Ginny said, "[These complainants] wouldn't recognize a quarterly report from a profit and loss statement." As it turned out, they either hadn't recognized them or hadn't seen them; once the CPA scrutinized them, he announced that if he'd known such reports existed, he wouldn't have charged mishandling of funds or concluded that the books weren't in order.

Kay was cleared of all charges and remained acting president. Her term of office was almost up anyway, since the California State NOW convention was scheduled for July 16 and 17 in Oakland, and there a new president would be elected.

Although she was still on a leave of absence, it was rumored that Foat might resume her position as president to lead the two-day convention. A number of local chapters hoped she'd do so, but Foat was worried that her participation would attract too much publicity and detract from the meeting. In statements to the press, Kay herself emphasized what she saw as the discontinuity between national NOW's disassociation and individual members' support for Foat: "The basic majority feeling is that she's innocent until proven guilty. By and large, she has broad-based support [from within NOW ranks] in California." Another NOW spokeswoman, Jaqi Asghedom, directly contradicted Judy Goldsmith's official NOW statement that Foat's case was not political, although she qualified her remarks by saying it was just her own opinion. "Personally, I believe the only reason she was arrested on a seventeen-year-old case is because she's a strong feminist leader. They're out to get her." She then went on to counter Toni Carabillo and others' statements that many members were so shocked by the Foat story that they'd resigned. Asghedom said, "We had a lot of new members join after reading about Ginny. They felt she was being railroaded."

Kay Tsenin and other Foat supporters were also angry that the California executive board had scheduled NOW President Judy Goldsmith as the convention keynote speaker. Kay thought it was a direct slap in the face. "I was even more furious than Ginny that other NOW members didn't object, or at least voice their opposition at the convention to Goldsmith's disassociation. Sure, a lot of members supported Ginny personally and sent money—that didn't go against NOW policy. Very few of them, though, had the guts to stand up to Goldsmith and say, 'We won't tolerate this, we don't like the stand you took.' Priscilla Alexander, for example, could have included support for Ginny as part of her campaign for vice-president, but she didn't. Neither did Sandra Farha when she was elected to succeed Ginny, even though it was Ginny who as president had brought Sandra along in NOW and appointed her to positions despite opposition from Carabillo and Mandell. But when Sandra was elected president, she didn't criticize national NOW's position because she didn't want to do anything controversial that would spoil the appearance of unity. I ranted and raved about Goldsmith's being invited; other friends did, too. We wanted to organize a demonstration, but the board didn't want that because they didn't want to be embarrassed."

Finally, Ginny chose not to lead the conference, but she did attend. When she came to the podium she was given a bouquet of roses; when she finished, she received a standing ovation, and many women in the audience were crying. During her brief speech she made only oblique remarks about her ordeal: "Today is not the place or time" to say anything more, she said, but thanked members for their support, which "has made it possible for me to survive." She explained that she had decided not to lead the conference because she felt "too physically and emotionally drained." Moreover, she wanted the focus to be "on women's issues" and not on herself.

The press, however, knew where the story was that weekend. They covered her, not the speech by Goldsmith, which announced

NOW's primary goal for the year—to remove Ronald Reagan from office. Foat was scheduled to lead a workshop on "The Building Blocks of Feminism," but the room was packed with eighty NOW members and over a dozen reporters and photographers. The press people were told to leave, the doors were locked, and the curtains on the windows drawn. But having already seen the circus inside, Foat decided not to lead the workshop, since she was receiving so much media attention.

Although Foat didn't want her presence to detract from the issues, she was also wary of negative publicity about herself: "My attorneys worried that if anything came up around a controversial issue, if, for example, my authority was challenged by even a small minority, the headlines in Louisiana would read FEMINIST MOVEMENT DESERTS FOAT. As it was, what came out in the press was positive stuff—that I got a standing ovation."

Foat was accompanied throughout the convention by Annabelle Hall, the Nevada attorney who'd worked on the documents from the 1977 charge there and who was now interviewing Sidote. "She stayed with me all the time, and it was really because she was so worried about the press that I canceled my workshop," said Foat.

Toni Carabillo argued that exactly this kind of notoriety at the conference justified NOW's decision to distance itself from Foat's case. It happened all the time, she said, and was undermining the work NOW had to do. Even if Foat wasn't physically present at a NOW function, she was what the reporters wanted to talk about. "The Foat case created problems with our public meetings," she went on. "We had planned fund-raising events, but how could we have them when we knew that reporters were undoubtedly going to ask the attending celebrities, 'What do you think about Ginny Foat? What do you think about the latest development in her case?' It was taking away from the issues we were supposed to focus on. I didn't go to the Oakland conference, but I heard it happened there, too. Judy Goldsmith gave one of her best speeches, and it got no coverage. Ginny Foat's appearance received all the media attention."

Marney Delaney, elected president of LA NOW in 1984, added that Foat's notoriety had also hampered the everyday running of Los Angeles NOW. She had been working full-time in the office in 1983 but felt frustrated by the publicity hoopla surrounding Ginny Foat. "My usefulness was being undermined, I really couldn't function in terms of the press or in terms of fund-raising. That's when I decided to go back to my regular job because the Foat case had set back the agenda for what had to be done in '83 to get ready for '84 and the campaign against Reagan. As it turned out, it wasn't as bad as I'd predicted, though, and we were pretty well set up and organized."

"Yes, but we were set up *in spite of* it," Carabillo added, and Marney Delaney agreed. "We had a bit more to do in terms of making up for a couple of fund-raising events which we lost because of the celebrity given to Foat, and in the short term, it kind of paralyzed me personally."

Speaking less personally, Carabillo said that in general the Foat case "had a chilling effect on NOW's public events. We had been planning a major fund-raising dinner and had been talking to various fund-raisers in Los Angeles. When the case broke, suddenly their schedules were too full to deal with it. Now we don't know if their schedules were actually too full or they just didn't want to handle the PR that Foat's case would create for such an occasion." Nevertheless, despite the dissension within NOW, despite her own antipathy for Foat and the way she and her supporters had handled the case and its publicity, she put an optimistic gloss on it: "NOW is certainly not falling apart because of it. We're hunkering down and seeing it through, although we had some real testing during those months."

At the time Foat was still awaiting a ruling on her motion that her right to a speedy trial had been violated. But then on September 3, John Sidote filed a petition of his own in the First Judicial District Court of Nevada in which he alleged that his right to equal protection under the law had been violated as well. He argued that Jefferson Parish Assistant DA Thomas Porteous had coerced and intimidated him into agreeing to testify against his ex-wife and had illegally ignored the 1978 Jefferson Parish documents that had assured him the case was closed and the warrant removed. Claiming that the deadline imposed by Porteous during their first conversation had hampered his lawyers in documenting the 1978 withdrawal of the charge, he requested a hearing from the Nevada court.

At first Thomas Porteous only read about Sidote's petition in newspaper accounts, and from the sound of it, "It seemed like a typical 'jailhouse lawyer's' suit. Besides, I was with him alone for only five minutes before we got lawyers in from the public defender's office. In those five minutes I simply laid out the options to him. If I could coerce and intimidate him in five minutes, I must be a mighty effective DA."

On the face of it, however, Sidote was less disturbed by Porteous's alleged intimidation than by the Louisiana DAs' subsequent failure to support him as strongly as he expected at his Nevada parole hearing in August 1983. Initially, his parole had been revoked for only six months. Despite a letter from Porteous confirming Sidote's cooperation in the Foat case, in August the parole board returned him to jail for at least another six months. His suspicion was that he would be kept there until he'd testified at the trial, and he was damned angry. Feeling that the Louisiana DAs could have been more forceful, he couched his anger in legalese, putting the DAs on notice in the hope that once more he could avoid testifying or at least force them to effect his release from prison.

Assistant DAs Porteous and Gordon Konrad took a hard line. Telling him that he could be prosecuted for the Chayo murder did not constitute coercion by their lights; Sidote might have had a legal point because of the 1978 letters, but he might also have been incorrect and therefore would still have been subject to prosecution. "It was a roll of the dice for him, and he knew it, so he chose immunity," said Porteous. But since Sidote's attempt to renege on his immunity agreement reminded them all too well of his 1977 Nevada turnabout, they had to be worried. Konrad then issued what amounted to an ultimatum when he described Sidote's petition as "an unusual tactic," and added, "If he's not happy with his immunity agreement, he can simply choose not to abide by it and not testify. [But] he'd be right back where he was before the agreement was entered into." Without spelling it out, he was also putting Sidote on notice, "Decide not to testify, and face prosecution yourself." Porteous was equally adamant that even if Sidote refused to testify, he could be brought to Louisiana as a witness without immunity, held in contempt if he didn't testify, and even prosecuted as well.

In California, Foat and her friends took Sidote's petition as a sign of hope. While she and her lawyers waited to see a copy of the petition, her supporters felt it confirmed what they'd believed all along: Sidote *had* been squeezed by the DAs, and in his usual attempt to barter an easier jail sentence, he'd agreed to testify. Jan Holden, speaking for the Ginny Foat Defense Fund, said, "It was good to finally hear John Sidote acknowledge that he was coerced into testifying against Ginny Foat."

Despite Konrad's implied threat, Sidote didn't budge, forcing District Attorney John Mamoulides to accompany Porteous and Konrad to Nevada "to straighten out Sidote's confusion." Foat's lawyers alleged that the Louisiana DAs were sweetening the deal by promising to get him paroled to a job in Louisiana, although the Nevada parole board denied that such promises were made. All Mamoulides did, they said, was repeat to them in person his statement that Sidote was cooperating. Still, it was enough for Sidote to drop his petition and sign a second immunity agreement that he and his lawyers worked out with Mamoulides. Dated the sixteenth of September, 1983, it made a few significant changes in the earlier one. The January 14, 1983, immunity agreement stated that he would "voluntarily appear and testify in any and all proceedings held in connection with indictments being returned in the above-referenced crimes." In contrast, the September 16 agreement read that he would "be subpoenaed to testify in the trial of Virginia Foat for the homicide of Moises Chayo in November of 1965." The change implied that Sidote wanted to stress that he was not testifying voluntarily. It was probably a more important point to him than to the prosecutors—that he had not chosen to go after his ex-wife.

In the January 14 immunity agreement, Sidote's testimony was required "to be in conformity with any and all prior statements, including but not limited to the statement of March 16, 1977." In the agreement of September 16, it was required that he only "testify truthfully, and consistently with his sworn statement of March 16, 1977." It seemed that Sidote was worried that discrepancies in his various court and police statements would come back to haunt him in the form of perjury charges. Indeed, the first immunity agreement had stated: "This agreement will not apply if John Joseph Sidote commits perjury" and he "agrees to *the use of his testimony against him* if for any of the above-stated reasons this becomes null and void." That was the threat: He could be prosecuted for the murder on the basis of his own previous statements and confessions if he were charged with perjury. With his second agreement he had reduced the possibility of a perjury charge and even if that were to occur, according to the second agreement, the consequence would be only a perjury charge, not prosecution for the Chayo robbery-murder.

In the second immunity agreement, Sidote also left the way open for a suit against the State of Louisiana for its disregard of the 1978 letters: "John Sidote specifically reserves any claims and defenses he may have as to the original charges and the processes employed by the State of Louisiana in connection therewith, including, but not limited to, claims and defenses based upon his right to a speedy trial."

With Sidote's writ withdrawn, the Carson City district judge signed the order extraditing Sidote to Jefferson Parish's custody for the duration of Foat's trial. Mamoulides, Konrad, and Porteous flew home to Louisiana, reassured that their principal witness was still in place.

In the midst of these Nevada negotiations, Foat lost her appeal in the Louisiana Supreme Court. On October 3, in a 4–3 decision, the court ruled that Foat's right to a speedy trial had not been violated because the reasons for the delay in prosecution had been beyond the State's control and had neither impaired Foat's case nor affected her life. She was ordered to stand trial on October 11 as scheduled.

There were more tears on the telephone, more brave reassurances between Foat and her attorneys. She was disappointed, true, but in another sense she and Kay both felt relieved. Now she'd get this over and done with; the case would finally be tried by a jury, not in the press.

On the evening of Monday, Octoter 10, the day before the opening of her trial, the press took what to many observers seemed an outrageous liberty. The late afternoon edition of *The Times-Picayune* blared in boldface PROSECUTION CAN'T FIND WITNESS WHO HEARD FOAT TALK OF SLAYING. Written by James Gill, the local reporter whom Foat's lawyers suspected of having a direct line to the DA's office, the story stressed that it was only the prosecutors' "belief" that the missing witness had overheard Foat and Sidote discuss the murder. Still, television news coverage that night repeated the headline as fact: "One prosecution witness is still missing. The hitchhiker who allegedly overheard Foat and Sidote discuss the murder can't be found." The rest of the coverage with its films of the matronly Foat and the handcuffed Sidote seemed a dramatic enactment of the trial's theme—respectable woman versus the disreputable ex-con. But the publicity about the missing witness was damaging.

The next morning, local and national reporters dutifully went through the tedious process of applying for press credentials and having their photographs taken in the Gretna jail next to the court-house. Nevertheless, most thought it a pointless exercise. With last night's headline, how could any judge proceed? To many of the veteran courtroom journalists, a postponement was more than likely, a change of venue a distinct possibility, too.

Outside the modern steel and concrete courthouse in Gretna, the civic center of Jefferson Parish, a crowd had gathered, drawn by the TV cameras and the news vans drawn up at the curb. A few minutes later Ginny Foat arrived in a car driven by Bob Tuller. A deputy opened the door for her and as she stepped out the TV crews mobbed her. John Reed and Bob Glass quickly moved to one side of her, Reed taking her elbow.

Reed has a long, thin face accentuated by a receding hairline and high forehead, a patrician look except for his brown lupine eyes. Bob Glass is taller, heftier, and has dark wavy hair, striking blue eyes, wide, full lips, and a large nose. He presents himself as more the New York, "street-smart" aggressive lawyer than Reed, who has a more diffident, aristocratic air. Visibly annoyed by the reporters, Reed waited for Bob Tuller to take Ginny's other elbow, and together they pushed the throng, forcing two cameramen back against a nearby car. Foat and her attorneys had perfected this "game" during her public appearances, giving each other points for knocking cameramen or reporters off their stride, two points if one was backed into a car or another person.

Ginny wore one of her standard dress-for-success suits but without its jacket, and looked slightly chilled in the pink-and-beige-print puffed-sleeve blouse with a matching bow tied at the high collar. The gray skirt was a plain A-line, a little tight at the hips, and her shoes conservative dark pumps. She wore no jewelry except pierced gold-hoop earrings, a watch, and instead of the several rings she'd worn in her photographs, she had on the fourth finger on her left hand one plain gold band with a small jewel.

She stared ahead with no expression on her face as she climbed the courthouse steps. Kay Tsenin had led several reporters to expect a statement, but she and her attorneys continued their "no comment" litany. Just as she disappeared through the door, a black woman in the crowd shouted, "Good luck, Mrs. Foat." Ginny leaned back around the door and flashed a smile. "Thank you," she said in a demure voice.

Inside, Foat was swarmed by the press as she waited for the elevator. At the rear of the defense entourage stood Jan Holden, her uniform a blazer and trousers; two gold chains hung around her neck, one of them with the letters "ERA" dangling from it. She chatted amiably with those members of the press she deemed sympathetic, like Patt Morrison of the *Los Angeles Times*. However, Holden turned cold and aloof, adopting her professional "dealing with the media" mode, when asked if the trial was going to be postponed. "I can't comment on that," she said, her glance toward Ginny convincing reporters that she knew it would be.

After greeting some of the acceptable journalists with a warm "I'm so glad you're here," Ginny joined her attorneys in the waiting elevator. Her face turned inexpressive again as the elevator doors closed. The third-floor button pushed, the car gave a hiccup upward, then stopped. "Oh, God, stuck forever in the Gretna courthouse elevator," Foat said to Reed and Glass.

"Yeah, and having to look at that same damn graffiti," said Bob Glass, pointing to the spray-painted announcement on the door: MICHELE LOVES JOHN.

"I wonder if Michele still loves John," sighed Ginny.

While Reed and Glass disappeared into the judge's chambers Ginny sat beside Kay Tsenin in the first row reserved for guests of the defense. Next to Kay was Annabelle Hall, the Nevada lawyer. She was a small, thin, nervous-looking woman with short blond hair, almost swamped by her matronly gray suit and a high-necked ruffled white blouse. Ginny said not a word to her, and except for a few whispered remarks to Kay, she stared straight ahead, the masklike quality of her face accentuated by the peeled look of her plucked eyebrows and high forehead. A few minutes later a deputy sheriff brought her a telegram. "This came for you, Mrs. Foat," he said, like all the deputies, treating her with deference.

The courtroom was crowded with spectators, for the most part women. One young woman, who carried a sleeping infant, and a blond companion were pointed out as New Orleans NOW members, the blonde being chapter president Lynne Renihan. Asked if she was there as a representative of NOW, she said warily, "I'm here as a private individual," thus adhering to the national NOW directive that the organization must not be closely identified with the case. Still, it was safe to assume that among all the women in the room, some were from the local NOW chapter, others were recognizable as Foat supporters from California who had attended the extradition hearings.

Soon Reed and Glass returned to the courtroom, and Ginny moved to the defense table, where the three whispered together until the courtroom was called to order by Judge Robert Burns. The one Republican judge in the parish, he was rumored to be pro-prosecution and a strict disciplinarian who kept tight control over his courtroom. At thirty-nine, his dark hair was already receding, and his large, horn-rimmed glasses masked any emotion on his face. His eyes were small and hard, and his pale skin was rough and slightly scarred by acne. He moved quickly to the large chair behind the bench, and cast a stern look at assistant DAs Tom Porteous and Gordon Konrad, who were still talking. District Attorney John Mamoulides was not with them, yet another clue that the trial would not begin that morning.

Which indeed it didn't. Judge Burns immediately announced that he had ruled in favor of a joint prosecution and defense motion for a continuance. With yesterday's *Times-Picayune* headline, he said, "it would be unnecessarily difficult to select a jury unaffected by recent publicity." In addition, he acknowledged that because of the defense attorneys' appeals on the speedy-trial motion, they'd had only six working days to prepare to go to trial. "It would be an injustice to both sides to proceed today," Burns concluded, and postponed the trial until November 7.

Then he imposed a "restrictive order," very carefully insisting that this was not to be interpreted as a gag order. While he ordered the prosecution, defense, and any court personnel not to make statements to the press, he also qualified his remark: "The press, of course, is free to write what they want." A superfluous statement given constitutional guarantees, yet the publicity surrounding the case seemed to have made him especially anxious that one false move would provoke reports about a "backward" or "prejudicial" parish judicial system. "We want this case decided on the basis of the evidence presented in court, not on what is developed in the press," he intoned, glancing toward the reporters.

Bob Glass rose abruptly, his face flushed, his voice strident with anger. "Since we are putting everything on the record," he proclaimed, "I want to state our position about the headline and the so-called missing witness. That is the witness we've been looking for.

We believe that witness would exonerate Mrs. Foat and blow the prosecution's case right out of the water. We've made gargantuan efforts to find that witness, but we've had no success at all. For the prosecution and the press to imply that this witness would prove Mrs. Foat's culpability is inaccurate." (No feminist "Ms." for his defendant, not even the sound-alike, but more drawn-out, southern "Miz.") He concluded his impassioned speech by adding diplomatically, "We've always felt that Mrs. Foat can get a fair trail in Jefferson Parish, but this kind of pretrial publicity would prejudice anyone."

Neither Judge Burns nor the prosecutors replied, although they all looked somewhat annoyed by Glass's speech. After all, the judge had already ruled in his favor. The glances exchanged among the four attorneys were enough to betray their mutual hostility. In a month they would all be ready to come out swinging.

SEVEN

Masks of Conformity

THE noise in the courtroom subsided the moment Ginny Foat walked down the center aisle on Monday morning, November 7. She wore a dark blue-gray skirt and a beige silk blouse that was high-necked and yoked with tiered ruffles. The suit's jacket was draped over her shoulders, and she removed it now as she stopped to talk to friends who had arrived from California.

The removal of her jacket was important; she needed to soften the image of a feminist, which the National Jury Project had found was an area of prejudice among potential jurors. Since they would find it harder to believe that a strong woman had been the submissive victim of a wife-beater, even her outfits were chosen to hide signs of strength. She was aware that a suit jacket conveyed the impression of authority and power, and she immediately swept it over her arm. Instead the jury would see only more feminine, soft-colored, high-necked, and ruffled blouses.

By 10:00 A.M. the courtroom's pews were filled with reporters and spectators, who all rose as Judge Robert Burns took the bench. Robert Glass, pulling Ginny's chair back for her, seated his client at the defense table between himself and John Reed. Here was another touch: Ginny was to be treated like "a lady." Despite the feminist injunction against chivalry, it was now revived for the courtroom drama, as if to say, "A real lady could not be guilty."

Judge Burns looked serious as he now called the attorneys into chambers, his demeanor announcing that he would brook no misbehavior in his courtroom. He'd doubtless never had to deal with a "celebrity" trial before and hence would insist even more stringently on courtroom decorum. He seemed to share the attitude common among the courthouse personnel: What was all the excitement about? This was an ordinary murder trial; Ginny Foat was simply the defendant, not someone who rated national media attention.

After the in-chambers conference, Judge Burns announced his rejection of one of the defense's pretrial motions, a decision he had deferred until this morning. He was satisfied that the State had proved Jefferson Parish the likely venue of the alleged crime, and the trial would proceed as scheduled.

John Mamoulides was in attendance this morning. Tall and imposing with gray hair, he seemed confident. His two assistant prosecutors looked relaxed, too, as the voir dire procedure now began. Ignoring the NO SMOKING signs, Tom Porteous lighted up, having received a dispensation from Judge Burns for his chain smoking. Ginny, too, was an addicted smoker, yet she refrained.

Two hundred people had been called for the jury pool this morning, and the first forty whose names had been drawn were brought up the center aisle. They looked uncomfortable, glancing at the press section and the courtroom artists, already aware this was a special case. Terry Waller, a tall, curly-haired woman from the National Jury Project's Oakland, California, office, was now seated at the defense table, ready with her checklists. The defense was pleased as they scanned the first group of jurors: Among the forty were several black men and women, unusual by Jefferson Parish standards. Many looked like blue- and pink-collar workers from the Gretna area on the west bank of the Mississippi, as opposed to the more common jury pools of middle- and upper-middle-class residents from the Metairie area across the river.

As soon as they had the list of potential jurors, Jan Holden coordinated volunteers from the New Orleans NOW chapter to do "drive-bys." This had also been suggested by the National Jury Project. From their surveys, according to Kay Tsenin, they concluded that "the people who were going to hang Ginny were housewives or wealthy white men." They were also told not to expect many blacks, and since the first jury pool included several, they felt lucky. Still, the drive-bys might reveal something further about the forty possibilities. "We were looking for signs," said Kay, "like a swastika or an American flag or a National Rifle Association emblem on their houses, something negative that was revealing. A drive-by isn't that determinative, it won't give you the perfect juror. Still, if you find something significant, you can take that into account. But, in fact, we didn't find anything negative or positive during our drive-bys of possibilities."

The prospective jurors were meanwhile sneaking looks at Ginny Foat and the journalists, as Judge Burns announced that the case of "Mrs. Foat, otherwise known as Ginny," was one "of national importance." This made it doubly necessary, he said, that they not discuss the case among themselves or with anyone outside the courtroom. "At lunch, you'll be free to move about in our local restaurants, but if anyone asks about the trial, you are not to talk about it. The case may be a topic of conversation," he added with a smile toward the press rows, "but it's more likely that yesterday's Saints' victory will be what's on people's minds."

The forty were sworn in together; most looked surprised when told that if chosen they would be sequestered at a local motel, probably for nearly two weeks. Then they were led from the room, and the voir dire proceeded with the bailiff drawing names of prospective jurors to be questioned in groups of three. It would be a long, tedious process, taking just over three days. In the course of it, the prosecution and the defense would disclose the crux of their arguments and the style each had chosen to adopt. More revealing, though, were the attitudes toward the women's movement in general and specific feminist issues evoked from the questioning. If feminism was on trial in the Gretna courtroom, most prospective jurors were barely familiar with it.

The voir dire of the first three candidates, two young men, one white, one black, and a middle-aged white woman, set the tone of the legal teams' two different approaches. Executive District Attorney Gordon Konrad, a tall, handsome, blond man with alert blue eyes, a ready smile, and a lilt of a southern accent, stressed "common sense" as he focused on the law under which Foat had been charged: The jury could find her guilty of murder if the crime was intentional, or guilty of manslaughter if committed unintentionally, "in the heat of blood," or in the perpetration of another crime such as simple armed robbery. To explain "in the heat of blood," he described a man coming home, finding his wife in the arms of another man, and shooting him.

The spectators murmured their disapproval at this example. In the hallway, the joke became "What if a man found his wife in the arms of another woman?" Still, Konrad's repeated use of this anecdote during the day's voir dire revealed the prosecutor's attitude. Told from the man's point of view, the story implied that the woman was guilty, the instigator of the crime, and by extrapolation provided the motive for murder.

The defense lawyers also had anecdotes to explain their points, but they chose to use the more politically correct, neuter word *spouse*. "Does one spouse always know where the other one is?" Reed often asked. Yet he was almost always referring to the female spouse's point of view: When a spouse is having an affair, "isn't *she* the last to know?" In the defense's examples, despite their enlightened, non-gender-marked language, it was clear that they pictured the woman as the victim and, ignorant of her husband's deeds, she was by implication innocent of his sins, or, in this case, unaware of his crimes.

Nevertheless, some consciousness-raising occurred over the next two days. Soon DA Porteous began to speak of "the spouse" as well in his voir dire. This hardly marked a change in his view of Foat. Rather, he seemed sensitive to charges of sexism behind retrogressive language and was attempting to counter the "male chauvinist" image with which the Foat defense committee had saddled him. Later, however, he said he'd been unaware of his language and certainly hadn't felt pressured to adopt "acceptable wording."

Reed and Glass were equally circumspect about their language. They talked about "women's rights" and "women's organizations," but the term "feminism" as well as specific issues of feminist politics were avoided.

The State's voir dire continued to be fairly pro forma, with the prosecutors asking candidates their age, marital status, children, employment, and clubs or organizations. As was repeatedly the case throughout the first day, Konrad seemed content with the noncommittal replies of the initial three prospective jurors. He then went on in his relaxed, almost chatty tone, to what was bound to be the problematic area of the State's case. Because John Sidote was a convicted felon, an ex-con, and a confessed co-conspirator who had received immunity, would the jury find it possible to believe him, or could they decide on the weight of the evidence? The woman and the black man gave acceptable replies, but the other man, young and white, strayed from the litany: "I don't think I could believe him." Konrad pushed harder: If the State proved the defendant's guilt beyond a reasonable doubt, then could he decide? He nodded, but then repeated his wariness of Sidote's immunity agreement and prison record. Yes, the manslaughter-robbery conviction in Nevada would definitely affect his impartiality, he added. This would become the usual basis for the prosecution's dismissal of prospective jurors. Either their prejudice against Sidote was so great that the Court had no choice but to excuse them for cause, or enough negative reactions were expressed that the State used peremptory challenges to eliminate anti-Sidote jurors.

Still, these first three candidates, like those who followed them, surprised the courtroom spectators and attorneys alike with how little they knew or confessed to know about the case. The woman had read a few news stories, admitting she'd noticed something even in this morning's paper, because—she hesitated, as if afraid to say something wrong. Konrad helped her. Was it "normal curiosity"? Yes, she replied. Yet most prospective jurors didn't betray even an inkling of such normal curiosity. For all the concern about pretrial publicity, over the next three days jury candidates continued to insist they knew little and remembered less about the case.

Once Konrad had finished his questioning, John Reed startled the courtroom by escorting Foat over to the prospective jurors. As she smiled at them from only a few feet away, Reed introduced her as "Ginny," explaining that he wanted them to see her up close, not just "tucked away across the room." Konrad and Porteous were visibly annoyed. Still, it was what had been hinted at all along. Her image was crucial—an attractive, gray-haired, respectable woman, friendly, standing three feet away and smiling sweetly—how could such a figure be guilty of a bludgeoning murder?

Repeated in every round of voir dire, the strategy had originally been Reed and Glass's idea, with which Foat had concurred as a compromise to her own suggestion of being put on as a "co-counsel" and conducting some of the questioning herself.

"Maybe it was self-centered, and it certainly wasn't a very legalistic theory," she said, "but I felt that once jurors talked to me they couldn't possibly believe the charge against me. The Jury Project had advised me to avoid the appearance of strength, so instead of doing any of the questioning, I just went over to be introduced so that they could identify with me as a person and a friend, as somebody they knew prior to my taking the stand. Perhaps they'd resent a vicious cross-examination or at least, after that closer contact and after having to look into my face, they'd have a tougher time lying about their real feelings during the voir dire."

"Feelings" were, in fact, what the defense was after in its voir dire, in dramatic contrast to the State's emphasis on common sense. Reed began in a quiet voice. He reassured them that he knew they must be nervous. "But I'm nervous, too," he said, his tone slightly patronizing as if he were coming down to the jurors' level in a gesture of camaraderie. He explained that he wanted to find out if they had "any feelings" that would make it hard for them to be on the jury. For example, he said, because he had two young daughters he would be unable to judge someone accused of molesting a little girl. In one quick allusion, he had established himself as a family man (to counter the stereotype of feminism being antifamily) and simultaneously underscored the theme of the defense—that Ginny Foat was an innocent girl molested by an evil man.

Once again, he tried to relax them: He'd be himself, they'd be themselves, and all would be fine. Nevertheless, throughout the defense's voir dire, the jurors seemed reluctant to be themselves. It seemed not a question of inauthenticity or lying; rather, like everyone else involved in a courtroom drama, they seemed intent upon playing a role. Despite their insistence that they knew little about the case, they were certainly aware of its national importance and the presence of the reporters and courtroom artists crowded into the pews. Whether or not they'd heard explicit remarks about backward southerners or antifeminist "rednecks," they were certainly not going to allow the national media to see them as anything less than tolerant, upstanding, respectable citizens.

With this in mind, expressions of support for "women's equality" signaled middle-class values more than heartfelt beliefs. Just as it became unacceptable to make derogatory statements or jokes about blacks, so it seemed that the women's movement had become respectable enough, at least in one manifestation. When questioned by Reed or Glass about feminism, every prospective juror agreed that he or she was in favor of equal pay for equal work. The defense couldn't afford to go near the more controversial aspects of feminism. Thus prospective jurors could give "high-minded" civics-class answers that hid their less than tolerant attitudes toward more specific issues. Still, as Reed proceeded to question the first three candidates about their knowledge of the women's movement and Foat's involvement in it, a pattern began to emerge, one that indicated as much about the role of feminism in their lives as it did about its significance in this case.

It began to appear that feminism or the women's movement had as little to do with them as the latest styles out of Paris. Maybe they'd noticed it, maybe not, but it certainly didn't affect them. During the first voir dire, the woman, who'd given her age as thirty-nine (with her weathered face and tightly curled gray-brown hair she looked older), seemed slightly more informed than the two younger men when she replied she knew Ginny Foat "was president of NOW, but I don't know what NOW is." Her admission, plus her pronunciation of N-O-W as separate letters, not as an acronym, drew laughter from the spectators as well as the judge, who stole a look at Foat. She, too, was laughing, and the woman was perplexed, earnestly adding the acceptable refrain that the women's movement was "good for equality, for getting jobs" and "for not being discriminated against because you're a woman." Reed ignored her next comment, "Some are going overboard," although this became the usual waiver to the tolerant approach. As the young white man said a few minutes later, he was glad that women were "making advancements," but he thought there would be problems when women "took away men's jobs."

The "personal is political" in a trial as much as in the women's movement, and the defense attorneys concentrated on the details of private lives to uncover more about the candidates, so much so that the prosecutors often objected, and the judge often sustained, cautioning Reed and Glass that they were getting "too personal."

What they were seeking were facts that fit the Jury Project's checklists, which Terry Waller and Ginny Foat repeatedly consulted during the voir dire. They were already pleased by the information supplied by the woman: She'd worked for twenty years as a secretary but was now studying at night to become a court reporter because she wanted "advancement." She had two children, eighteen and fourteen, from her first marriage, had been married for five years to her second husband, who often had to be out of town on jobs (so, yes, she said, she understood the old adage that "the wife was the last to know").

Then Reed came to the crucial matter for the defense—attitudes toward wife abuse. While not couched in feminist language, his questions indicated what he was looking for—responses that most closely reflected both the current analysis of why women do not leave battering husbands and Ginny's explanation for why she hadn't left Sidote.

"Are you aware of domestic violence?" he asked the woman.

"You mean a husband and wife fighting?"

"No, wife-beating," he replied.

The women nodded. She'd read about it and had heard about clinics for battered wives.

"Are there some women who like it?" he asked, leading her on.

"They've gotta be nuts if they like it!" she snapped back.

"Then why wouldn't a woman leave?"

"Insecurity," she answered. "But I wouldn't hold it against her because it takes time to figure things out." For that she received a smile of approval from Reed.

The young black man's answer to the same question was non-committal. At first he said he'd heard of it happening but didn't understand why a woman stayed. When pressed, though, he echoed the woman's reply, "Insecurity," also earning himself a smile from Reed. Reed's sudden barrage of personal questions about his first marriage and divorce, however, surprised him and he remained mute as Judge Burns sustained the State's objection and called the attorneys to the bench for a side bar, his look of irritation betraying his annoyance with this line of questioning.

Reed concluded his voir dire by once more calling Ginny over to the jurors. This time, however, Judge Burns sustained Konrad's objection and told the defendant to remain seated. Still, Reed ended on an emotional note, setting the tone for the trial: "Look at her! Look at Ginny! Will you give her your word that you will give her a fair trial?"

The jurors nodded somberly, slightly self-conscious, as Ginny smiled in their direction.

Only two of these first three were chosen, the State using one of its eight peremptory challenges to excuse the young white man because of his anti-Sidote prejudice. After a prolonged consultation among Foat and her attorneys as well as the Jury Project expert, the defense accepted the young black man, not so much for his opinions (of those he had few) but because, despite his youth, he gave the impression of "having been around"; from Pensacola, Florida, he was less likely than a Jefferson Parish native to be proprosecution and, according to most jury studies, as a black he was more likely to be sympathetic to the defendant.

The woman was selected as well, again not so much because of her pro–equal rights statements or middle-class tolerance, but because of her "life experience," which the defense guessed was not as middle class as she implied.

This became the watchword for the defense throughout the voir dire. A strange tension set in: With prospective jurors resolutely projecting their respectability, the defense team was probing for hints that their lives had been neither as conventional nor as untroubled as they claimed. With Ginny Foat in a sense on trial for a "sordid past" as well as for an alleged murder, they wanted to find those jurors whose own backgrounds might make them less judgmental about her life on the road with Sidote. Oddly enough, though, their profile effectively precluded the younger women who seemed potentially more profeminist, whose opinions were strong, and who, while not calling themselves feminists, had been affected in positive ways by economic and social changes directly attributable to the women's movement.

During the second round of voir dire one woman in her late twenties spoke self-confidently about the way she'd worked her way up in her company despite having only a high school diploma. While she said she had "no feelings one way or another" about the women's movement, she was proud of the fact that she had been promoted to a managerial position in which she was responsible for hiring and firing, and she said she hoped to climb even higher. All the while Glass let her know he was pleased with her answers; here was someone who would understand Foat's ambition, her desire to make something of her life.

Ginny, though, didn't seem enthusiastic, and later, during the defense team's consultation, she shook her head adamantly about this young woman, forcing the defense to use its first peremptory challenge. The young woman was upset that she hadn't been chosen, since, as she said in the hallway, she thought she'd given "good answers." The answers, however, had struck Foat as too good. "I was afraid of her because of her age and strength. We wanted older people who'd experienced life, who'd had marital problems, who'd supervised others at work and seen firsthand when their employees couldn't come to work because of beatings or drinking. Although the first young woman wouldn't call herself a feminist, we felt she was a feminist at heart, and yet because she was so young and competent and opinionated, I was afraid she wouldn't understand what I'd gone through."

Hence, during that round of voir dire, only one juror, an older

white man, was chosen (the State having excused the third prospect, an older woman, because of her prejudices against Sidote). A
retired electrical engineer, he had worked in a supervisory position,
was among the most educated and knowledgeable of prospective
jurors, and living in a New Orleans suburb across the river, he didn't
have to cultivate a respectable image. Perhaps because he was firmly
entrenched in the middle class, he seemed to feel no pressure to voice
his tolerance of women's rights, since he said he knew nothing about
either feminism or Foat's NOW affiliation. This was surprising, since,
unlike other jurors, he kept up with current events by reading *Time,*
newspapers, and *Reader's Digest.* Nevertheless, he was unwilling to
let Glass reshape his replies with feminist interpretations. Asked about
his wife's job, he said that she was a secretary for a doctor and took
care of his office.

"You mean she runs the show?" Glass said.

"No, not all of it," the man replied firmly.

Still, the defense took him for his age and his quiet fortitude; he
would make up his own mind and not be easily swayed by anyone
else on the jury.

The last juror to be chosen the first day was a woman who initially seemed even too malleable for the defense. In fact. Kay Tsenin
argued against her, slipping notes to Terry Waller and Foat as the
woman responded to Glass's questions with noncommittal answers
and self-conscious giggles. (Like Reed, he tried to reassure the jurors with the by-then rote opening, "If you're nervous, I'm nervous, too.") She'd lived in the area all her life, worked for the
Department of Transportation, was married, and had two daughters, fifteen and eighteen. She knew nothing about the case, read
neither newspapers nor magazines, belonged to no organizations,
political or social, and while she said her Catholicism was an important part of her life, she was no more involved in the Church
than weekly attendance at mass. As for feminism, she'd heard a radio program about the women's movement, but she hadn't "thought
about it."

"I read there is one," she added, as if she were talking about a
technological invention, a microwave oven; yet she insisted that her
distance from it implied no antagonism. "I don't know anything
negative about it," she said.

As if he thought this unlikely, Glass tried a new tack, hoping to
slip by her reticence. Would she object if her daughters became in-

volved with the women's movement? After Burns overruled Porteous's objection, she giggled again and with a coy, sidelong glance replied, "Well, I think they're kinda young for it," as if she were referring to sex. This remark was the closest she came to venturing an opinion, and her repeated response of "I don't know" and "I haven't thought about it" exasperated Kay, especially when the woman shrugged "I don't know" to Glass's question about why wives stay with abusive husbands.

Once the State had accepted her, Kay leaned over the front pew and whispered to Ginny and Terry, "too weak, too weak." The defense did not challenge her, though, and she became the fourth juror.

Terry turned to Kay with a apologetic shrug. "We had to take her," she mouthed. The defense had been afraid to use another peremptory challenge on an almost indifferent juror when they might need it later for a more prejudiced prospect. Besides, given her flirtatious gestures toward Glass, he might easily sway her to Foat's side.

Tuesday, the second day of voir dire, concluded with five more jurors chosen. Again, the State was troubled by prejudice against Sidote; it seemed that anyone who'd read anything about the case and formed an opinion had severe reservations about the prosecution's main witness. It didn't bode well for the prosecutors when anyone who'd heard about Sidote's previous record and his immunity agreements admitted they'd find it hard to believe him, even under oath.

The defense, however, rejected people with strong opinions as well, especially young women who conveyed their ambitiousness and desire to get ahead. Instead, they were looking for older women, perhaps not as pliant or diffident as the first day's choice, but women who would listen to Ginny's story much as they'd enjoy a soap opera. Without making judgments about her past, they'd sympathize and become absorbed in the emotional drama more than they'd worry about the logic or common sense of the narrative.

At first, the next female candidate seemed an unlikely prospect. In her early forties and wearing a dress-for-success suit much like Foat's, she gave her occupation as a "self-employed image-and-management consultant for women in business." Wearing her blondish hair in a modified beehive, she spoke carefully, often using unnecessarily long words and complicated phrases. The middle-class assumptions behind the defense's questions like, "Do you want to get ahead?" "Do you supervise others?" had confused some of the prospective jurors. This woman, however, rose to the occasion, as if the questions confirmed her upward mobility. Unlike most prospective jurors, she was a member of several professional organizations, including the New Orleans Press Club, and a few church-related groups. Still, there was some initial concern about possible conservatism and antifeminism when she explained that her image-and-management consulting business was about to produce a bridal fashion show in California.

The defense soon warmed to her, though, as she described her background. She'd grown up in Houston, met her husband at LSU, and with him in the navy, had moved thirteen times before returning to the New Orleans suburb of Metairie. She was now divorced, and Reed gently probed her feelings about it. There were some hurt feelings about it, she said, but she and her husband were still friends, even though they'd "grown farther apart." She and her husband "lived apart well," she added, but she could imagine bitterness in other divorces.

When she was later asked about domestic violence, however, the defense team was alerted by her pause before she said she'd only heard about "battered wives"; yet she readily provided reasons why women might stay with abusive husbands: fear, financial insecurity, concern for the children. "No, they're not masochists," she said, supplying the psychological term when Reed asked her if women stayed "because they liked it." Terry Waller and Ginny Foat nudged each other and ticked off a line on their checklist, the woman revealing more knowledge of domestic violence than the other prospective jurors.

Given her upward mobility (she'd recently upclassed herself by changing from the Presbyterian to the Episcopal Church), her comments about the women's movement were in keeping with her presentation of herself as a competent businesswoman and educated citizen. In more extended replies than those of other jurors, she said she was pleased "by what has happened in this country" with the women's movement, especially because it has brought to people's attention "women's work for less pay."

"But I am not an advocate of some of the principles that have been challenged," she announced. What this meant wasn't clear, nor did Reed ask her to explain.

"It's been too long in coming for women," she said, but while conceding "you have to go to extremes to get change," she was glad that "there's been a return to the middle of the road from the more activist part of the movement."

"What is too extreme?" Reed ventured bravely, verging on controversial areas.

"Gloria Steinem is an example of going to an extreme." she said.

Murmurs among the defense supporters and the spectators grew even louder as she said that the ERA was also "too extreme," because "if you read the intricate wording of ERA very closely . . . it would actually hurt women."

"Intricate wording?" said Kay, turning back toward the first press row and quoting, "Equality of rights under the law shall not be denied or abridged by the United States or by any State on account of sex." It was the position so often taken by the anti-ERA movement, that the amendment "would actually hurt women." Nevertheless, her response seemed emblematic of the prevalent attitude at the trial that equal rights meant "equal pay." She, like so many women of the eighties, was talking from the pocketbook. She wasn't afraid of being denied her rights as a woman so much as being refused a place in the bourgeoisie.

Despite the woman's anti-ERA statements and her ambitiousness, she seemed to be more on Foat's side, especially since she was older and seemed to hint at an earlier, different kind of life. She might sympathize with Foat's transformation and admire her success and her celebrity, the signs of achievement with which she would want to align herself. The patrician gentility of John Reed and the sophistication of Bob Glass would entice her as well, much more so than a John Sidote, who smacked of the loser, whose story was a downward spiral. With her respectable image, she wouldn't associate herself with an alcoholic, wife-beating ex-con, either in public or in the deliberation room.

Another woman chosen the second day fit even more closely the profile of a woman who would be sympathetic to Foat's story. Middle-aged and overweight, with large blue eyes often watering from asthmatic coughing, she was less intent on presenting an image of respectability and spoke her mind, often giving speeches when a simple "no" would have sufficed, and looking at Foat for her approval. When the prosecution asked if she'd heard about the case, she replied, "My daughter said maybe I'd be on this case. She told me that she's the lady extradited from California and charged with murder. But I don't look at any news on TV." Then she gave Ginny another smile. She was in fact the only jury candidate to greet Ginny aloud when she had as usual been brought over to be introduced.

Later, when asked about the women's movement, this woman again speechified. She had no "strong feelings" about it and didn't know about NOW: "But I'm for a woman getting up in the world. A woman can hold a man's position if she's smart enough. As far as equal rights go, I don't get into it that much," she added, but she opposed the ERA because, as she explained in a lengthy monologue, it would "force women to pay men child support."

A Baptist who attended church regularly, she mentioned a first marriage, another mark in her favor. She'd worked all her life, too, in clerical and kitchen jobs, and the impression that she'd probably had a hard time of it suggested an identification with the defendant, even though the defense lawyers were apprehensive about her talkativeness and her strong yet often uninformed opinions.

Not Ginny, however, even when the woman insisted she'd have trouble deciding the case if she heard only Sidote's side of the story.

"The defendant has the right to remain silent," Judge Burns reminded her.

"But if someone was talking about me, I'd be the first to get up and say 'It's not so,' " she argued. "Let the public hear my side of the story. Of course, if she don't want to give me no evidence, then I have to decide on what the State gives me."

Could she presume the defendant innocent if she didn't take the stand? Glass pressed.

She looked bewildered. He rephrased the question.

"You're over my head," she said, challenging him with a stare.

"She's wonderful," Ginny whispered over her shoulder toward Kay and Annabelle. "I love her."

As if she were aware of Foat's praise, the woman used Glass's routine question about domestic violence as the occasion for another story: Of course she knew about it, and in fact, her daughter's neighbor used to beat his wife. Although the daughter called the police on him, the wife would always say it was a happy marriage, she added, so she could understand a woman staying, though she wouldn't herself. "Once my husband shoved me. I told him I was leaving, and he apologized," she said, rambling on about showing him who was boss. Porteous tried to object to no avail, and as the spectators' laughter grew louder, Judge Burns had to resort to the gavel. Ginny, too, was laughing: "Oh, she's wonderful!" she repeated several times, and during the discussion of the three prospective jurors, pushed hard for her in the face of her attorneys' and Kay's reservations about the irrepressible talking. "She likes me, I like her, so she's gonna hold out for me no matter what," she later told Kay, and finally, with no challenge from the prosecution, the talkative woman was accepted.

The other juror chosen from the same group of three was a middle-aged black woman. The defense team had been especially happy to see her. They wanted minorities, but after selecting the young black man in the first round of voir dire, they'd run into trouble. One older black man questioned had been a reporter for a major black newspaper before taking a job at the post office. He was excused when he admitted that he'd read a great deal about the case and already formed some conclusions (even though he said he knew that reporters were usually only 75 percent accurate, prompting laughter from the press and a nod of agreement from Foat).

Another young black woman, while giving an acceptable answer about the women's movement ("From what I've heard it's doing a great job"), seemed too young, too shy, and too easily swayed by others' opinions. Reed had also tried to raise her consciousness when she told him that she worked as a bricklayer. Yes, she said, she knew that few women were bricklayers.

"Isn't that because twenty years ago women didn't think they had the strength to be bricklayers?" he sermonized.

She looked befuddled, even more so when Reed rephrased his question after a sustained objection from the prosecution.

"Can you imagine that fifteen years ago Ginny Foat didn't have the strength to go out on her own?"

A second sustained objection stopped her from giving an answer. Nevertheless, a few minutes later, she all but removed herself from consideration when she said that while she'd heard of "domestic violence," she'd never be in that situation. "Why would I stay with somebody who beat me all the time?" A minority or not, a young woman who couldn't understand Ginny's story wasn't acceptable, and the defense excused her.

Finally, another black candidate repeatedly said that Foat had been "convicted" when he meant indicted. The prosecution and the judge were ready to excuse him; Reed, however, undertook to "rehabilitate" him, only confusing him more and in the process embarrassing him even further. Finally Judge Burns intervened, dismissing the man, who was humiliated by the laughter that Reed's prolonged questioning had provoked.

With the voir dire of the middle-aged black woman the second day, the defense was especially hopeful when they heard she was a full-time reading and math tutor. She was impressive for her earnestness, the attention she gave to the questioning; her hint that she'd left her husband because of his problems, coupled with her sympathy for women who were afraid to leave, made her a good prospect for the defense.

The DAs, however, had doubts about her. Konrad had talked about "co-conspirators" being "equally guilty." If that was so, she asked (the math teacher in her coming to the fore), why wasn't Sidote being prosecuted? Konrad explained that while they were considered equally guilty, the State had granted him immunity in exchange for his testimony. She shook her head, but didn't ask the next logical question: Why him and not her? Instead, she backed off and said she'd listen to Sidote and weigh his testimony. The State was reassured enough to accept her, and she was added to the panel.

In the last rounds of voir dire the second day, the prospects were all men. Among them was a young white student whose ultraconservative views brought an almost immediate challenge from the defense. Another man was in his early thirties, with a pleasant face and longish black hair combed into a modified Elvis-like pompadour. He often glanced at the floor self-consciously, earning him high marks from Terry Waller for sensitivity. Even more in his favor was his openly talking about his divorce (he said his first wife had falsely accused him, and Ginny nodded enthusiastically). He said he knew women were sometimes afraid to leave violent husbands and was aware of the existence of battered-women's shelters. One of the few prospective jurors who supported the ERA, he also bragged that his union, the Brotherhood of Railway, Airline and Steamship Clerks (BRASC), was among the first to pass an equal-pay-for-women clause and had enforced rules against discriminatory hiring. Although he said he knew little about the case, he called Foat "the head of a feminist group out there," and used the word "feminist" casually and naturally. The State chose not to use a peremptory challenge, despite what seemed to indicate a positive response to Foat and a more than neutral attitude toward feminism. Too, he seemed to have been around and might be well enough aware of Sidote's type to have some doubts. Yet since he had insisted that he would listen to the evidence, the State had no objection to him, and the defense had found another juror very much to their liking.

But the next prospect gave them problems, much as they hoped that as a black he would be a prodefendant juror. He was middle-aged and self-employed as a gardener, and he immediately tried to have himself excused because of the hardship two weeks of jury duty would impose. The judge refused, and he went through his voir dire apologizing that he knew "nothing about the law." He said he was a Baptist, and raised even more concern at the defense table with his remarks about sinful and evil people when asked about alcoholism and domestic violence. The hellfire and brimstone language of his replies was troubling, and worse, he said that if a woman stayed with a wife-beater, "she must like it."

Still, the other candidate in this round was just as questionable—an engineer who seemed to have a private agenda for getting on the jury (his replies were guarded, and he constantly repeated questions before he answered). Ginny wasn't pleased, and the defense team took an even longer time consulting. Afraid to use two more of their eight peremptory challenges when they didn't know who remained in the jury pool, they finally excused the engineer and accepted the middle-aged gardener, hoping, it seemed, that a black juror's prodefendant bias would outweigh the man's strong fundamentalism.

The third day of voir dire, Judge Burns seemed especially impatient with prolonged questioning and anxious to fill the three remaining openings on the panel. But the day dragged on with several prospective jurors excused for either hardship or explicit prejudice against Sidote. The defense also had to use peremptory challenges to excuse more young women who, while commenting favorably about the women's movement, seemed too ambitious, proud of their accomplishments, and often suggested that it was the woman's fault if she stayed with a violent husband. The State also challenged one young black woman who had seemed too easily swayed by Reed and had enthusiastically said, "I love the idea of women's rights" as she grinned in Ginny's direction.

The one woman who finally pleased the defense was older, a grandmother who spoke in a low, gravelly voice. Cheerfully complaining that her car had been towed, she seemed neither intimidated by the voir dire nor concerned about her image, and soon she became as much of a crowd pleaser as the talkative juror the day before. Although she'd worked as a secretary for many years, she explained that she now loved to spend time with her grandhild, and her answers were couched in homey examples. Asked if she'd ever been falsely accused, she replied, "When I was a kid, my mother would accuse me, and I'd say, 'Nah-hh, it wasn't me.' " She read *Consumer Reports* and *Better Homes and Gardens,* but hadn't heard much about the case and didn't know that Ginny Foat "was a feminist." She had "no feelings whatsoever" about ERA, she said, "no knowledge" of the women's movement, and "no opinion about women fighting for political change."

"I do enjoy a man opening the door for me or lighting my cigarette, those kind of manners," she added, "but that doesn't affect my feelings about the ERA."

Ginny liked her, her diffidence about the woman's movement and her remark that women should get out of violent marriages notwithstanding. What convinced the defense to choose her, however, was the woman's admission (the first of all prospective jurors) that she knew about the problems of alcoholism "personally" and was aware that alcoholism caused problems "in the family."

When Glass asked if she'd "ever heard the expression 'mean drunk'?" she went him one better. With a knowing look (as if to say, "You young whippersnapper"), she replied, "Of course. Like Dr. Jekyll and Mr. Hyde."

Her place on the jury was guaranteed, and once the prosecution had agreed to her, the defense, while excusing two young women in the same round, readily accepted the good-natured grandmother.

Female candidates, young or old, were few and far between this last day, and the defense found itself trying to find the "most sensitive" of the men who were called. These tended to be younger, like the twenty-year-old accountant, a clean-cut, preppy type with glasses and a moustache. The defense team became interested in him when he said he read newspapers, subscribed to an accounting magazine, and someday hoped to open his own accounting firm. His attitude toward feminism was the standard response of the voir dire: "I don't have anything against equal rights, but I'm against the ERA because you shouldn't change the Constitution." Beyond this, Reed didn't go, hampered as he was by Konrad's continued objections to questions like, "How do you think Ginny is feeling?"

Judge Burns sustained the objection, but Reed repeated it, and the judge interrupted him. He was losing patience, he said.

"You should have a little patience after eighteen years," flared Reed.

"Not if you're going to go on forever," Konrad shouted into the fray.

Judge Burns called them to the bench. After the side bar, Reed looked petulant but turned with an ingratiating smile to apologize to the young man.

"Did you feel attacked, were you upset?" he asked.

"No," said the accountant, although he'd seemed unnerved by Reed's performance, as if he'd seen the mask of the gentle, sensitive young lawyer slip too easily.

Nevertheless, the defense was reassured, and once the State had approved the young man, Reed acceded as well, assuming that it was safe to accept the college-educated, unmarried accountant.

In fact, though, they were lucky in the final voir dire of the afternoon. Of the three prospects, one was a handsome blond man in his twenties, a salesman for an oil company, who, coincidently, had been a fraternity brother of the accountant's. Like the union man the day before, he made a good first impression with his pleasant smile and nervous glances down at the floor. Although his initial responses were bland, he indicated more diverse interests than other jurors (he subscribed to *Sports Illustrated* and a psychology magazine, and liked to jog and play racquetball), and soon revealed a sensitive awareness of domestic violence. He explained that his wife was a nurse and had told him about treating children who'd been beaten. Over the four and a half years he'd known her, his wife had told him about "things she sees in her job," including, he said in an emotional voice, mothers who came to the hospital with injured children who themselves had black eyes or other signs of beating.

He was circumspect when asked about the women's movement: He didn't know enough "to form an opinion" he said, and wasn't "for or against the ERA," although he said he paid attention "to whether or not it's voted in or out." Nevertheless, Ginny liked him, especially when he said forcefully, "I think wife-beaters should be locked up." Ginny nodded to Terry, then at Kay, when he added that although a woman might stay in such a marriage "out of love," he wouldn't blame her or say she asked for or liked the beatings. "Maybe she hopes he'll stop or will get help," he said, convincing the Foat team that despite his youth, he would understand Ginny's explanation for not leaving Sidote. He was accepted by both the State and the defense and by late Wednesday afternoon, the twelve Foat jurors were selected (two alternates were chosen, one that evening, one the following morning).

The grueling process and the prospect of the actual trial soon beginning seemed to have taken a toll on Foat and her lawyers that afternoon. Reed and Glass both had lost their tempers several times when the prosecution and the judge had objected to their personal, repetitive, and often argumentative voir dire; Ginny had also succumbed. For the preceding two days she'd seemed unflappable, cool and efficient. In the hallways, she talked to reporters easily, announcing that she was "heartened by the objectivity of the prospective jurors." In the courtroom, passing notes to Terry Waller, conferring with Reed and Glass, she seemed more a lawyer than the defendant in the case. But Wednesday afternoon, as she listened to the last round of voir dire, something gave way.

One of the prospective panelists, a middle-aged wife and mother of three, told Konrad that she might be prejudiced by Sidote's immunity agreement, because "he doesn't have anything to lose."

Konrad explained that since Sidote wasn't granted immunity from perjury, he couldn't lie on the stand.

The woman stared back, as if to say, "How can you be so naïve?" Then she demanded, "Do you really think he's going to come in here and tell the truth?"

The spectators laughed, and Ginny, too, was laughing. Suddenly her laughter dissolved into sobs, and she slumped in her chair, her shoulders shaking. Then she turned away from the jury box and while John Reed moved to shield her from view, she dabbed at her eyes with a lace-edged handkerchief. Bob Tuller hurried to squeeze into the front pew behind the defense table and leaned forward to comfort her, his hand on her shoulder. Ginny turned slightly and gave him a shake of her head, as if to indicate that she didn't want him to call attention to her tears.

Previous prospective jurors had made similar comments about Sidote, prompting their dismissal by the State but never upsetting Foat's poise. Today, however, she seemed fatigued, her face drawn, as if she'd come face to face with the stark realization that the trial would begin the next day. That, or indeed the pressure of the trial, had inflicted a migraine headache.

With the final round of voir dire, jury selection was no longer an abstract legal or sociological exercise. These people did, after all, hold her fate in their hands.

That night, too, she was worried. Kay Tsenin, Jan Holden, and Jean Conger all tried to reassure her. Still, none of them could avoid trying to second-guess the jurors. Jean had written about the problem of an "ultraconservative jury" in her article about the trial for the bimonthly newsletter *Southern California Women for Understanding*. Yet she was cheered, because potential jurors had asked during voir dire, "Why is she being brought to trial now?" "It was a victory that people said they had trouble with that issue," she said, although in fact, most of those candidates had been excused.

Kay Tsenin was bothered by the jurors who said they didn't have an opinion about anything and she was particularly worried by the woman who'd giggled but never revealed her true feelings. Even though she held a job, she called herself a housewife, and in the National Jury Project test groups conducted that summer, every housewife had voted to convict Ginny, and Kay was worried that when push came to shove, this juror would condemn Ginny for her life-style. Although she was somewhat relieved that more of the prospective jurors hadn't been like the young conservative student, she was even concerned about the jurors she thought might be good. "They said so often they had no reactions, say, to alcoholism, that I just couldn't believe it. So I really had nagging doubts the night before the trial because although we did a much better job on voir dire than the DAs, we still weren't sure what the jurors' real attitudes were. My impression was that a lot of their reactions just didn't come out, and I didn't know whether they lied or we just didn't ask the right questions."

Kay looked at it from a lawyer's point of view—how could the voir dire have been better? How could deeper feelings or prejudices have been brought out? Ginny was in a state of panic, however. "We were able to do all the things we wanted to do," she said, "and we got the kind of people the Jury Project profile thought would be best for my jury. We'd been successful in the sense that there were six women, three blacks, several divorced people; most were older and some of them had supervised others on the job. But I was in an absolute panic because I had never listened to so many people who said they never belonged to an organization, never read newspapers, never watched television, and didn't have an opinion on anything. I was saying to myself either 'These people all want to get on the jury because they need to convict me,' or 'These are people who want to get on because they think I'm innocent.' I couldn't believe the latter, so my paranoia let me hang with the first reason. I was sure the twelve people fooled us, and I had a terrible anxiety attack the night after the jury was picked."

EIGHT

"The Way She Was Brought Up"

THE six men and six women of Jefferson Parish expressed nothing more than earnest solemnity as they filed into the jury box after lunch, Thursday, November 10. They'd had to wait for their second alternate to be chosen that morning. Now they were ready, holding themselves rigorously alert, to listen to opening arguments. Ginny Foat seemed as impatient as they to get on with the trial itself; her eyes blinked rapidly as she glanced several times at the press rows, as if she were aware that the focus had now turned from the jurors to her. More reporters, these from the television networks and national news magazines, had filled the pews, and an even greater number of spectators had arrived at six in the morning to claim the limited number of seats.

Judge Burns entered and took his seat in front of the Louisiana State seal, a pelican feeding its young, the Christian symbol of confession and atonement an especially appropriate backdrop for the next days of testimony. He now called on the State for its opening argument. Of the three DAs, Gordon Konrad had been selected to present the prosecution's case, and as he had in his voir dire questioning, he adopted an impersonal, matter-of-fact tone as he explained how Ginny Foat happened to be on trial.

In the summer of 1965, Konrad began, John Sidote was living in upstate New York. His was an "ordinary life" with a wife and child, he was buying a house and a car. He repeated this expression several times, as he conveyed the impression that Sidote's job as a bartender was an ordinary, respectable man's employment, which provided the occasion for meeting "the then Virginia Galluzzo" that summer. She was divorced from her husband, a friendship developed, and early in November 1965 they decided to leave New Paltz and travel to Miami because John Sidote thought he could get better employment there. Konrad implied no judgment or criticism as he narrated his account. Explaining that Wasyl Bozydaj, a seventeen-year-old who was working as a busboy in the bar, also went along, he said this was an ordinary turn of events, the three of them setting out in Sidote's white Pontiac convertible. Unable to find work in Florida, they then drove to Baton Rouge, where Ginny Foat found work as a waitress. A few weeks later, they met a man who said his friend could give them work in New Orleans. Konrad now paused, then told the jurors that the Ponderosa bar had been located on Canal Street next to the old Joy theater. While he simply provided this information, he was also reminding anyone who knew the area that it was a seedy part of town; he also seemed to convey a double message with his bland statement that Ginny and John got work at this bar, he as a bouncer, she as a barmaid and "dancer."

Ginny was sitting between Reed and Glass with her head lowered. But the reference to her as a "dancer" brought her chin up, and she shook her head at the jury. She had repeatedly denied being a go-go dancer, even more strenuously than the murder charge, it seemed. But Konrad appeared to be insinuating something more to any juror familiar with the Ponderosa or other bars in the area that had been raided by the police for B-drinking and dancing.

In the same vein, Konrad said that Sidote, Foat, and Bozydaj rented a room at the John Mitchell hotel, a block away from Canal Street. He didn't characterize the hotel, and only jurors who knew it could be aware that it was a somewhat seedy hotel for transients. Konrad was choosing not to lard his matter-of-fact speech with adjectives, but was letting the jurors draw their own conclusions.

He now turned to a second narrative line: In October and November 1965, Raymond Chayo, aged twenty-three, was in a New Orleans hospital undergoing treatment for phlebitis. His father, Moises Chayo, an Argentine businessman, had come to see his son two weeks before Saturday, November 20. He'd rented a room in a hotel across the street from the hospital and, "as the son will tell you, he visited every day." Then on the nineteenth or twentieth of November, having learned that his son would be released on Sunday the twenty-first, he made sure to have the cash to pay the hospital bill. On Saturday, Raymond Chayo said good-bye to his father, expecting him to return the next morning to check him out. When he failed to arrive on Sunday, the son called the police. They investigated his hotel room, but no missing-person report was filed, since there was nothing to indicate foul play. Then three weeks later the police discovered the body of Moises Chayo in a ditch in Metairie, a town outside of New Orleans.

"Now we go back to Sidote and Foat," Konrad continued, almost conversationally. The two of them "hatched a plan to commit a robbery" to get money "to get out of New Orleans." The defendant, "a young, attractive woman," would go into the French Quarter, find a prosperous-looking man, lure him into their car, and drive to an isolated area. There Sidote would get out of the car's trunk and the robbery would be committed.

"Moises Chayo was the unfortunate individual lured into the car," he said after a pause. He was driven out to the West Napoleon Canal. There the defendant got out of the car, Chayo got out of the car. Sidote is small, Konrad explained; he was riding in the trunk, and when he got out there was an altercation. After an exchange of words between Sidote and Foat, she picked up a tire iron to break Chayo's hold on Sidote. She struck another blow, then Sidote hit him, too.

This was in contrast to Sidote's other statements in which he'd said only Foat had wielded the tire iron, and indeed, as Konrad continued, "The victim was dragged to the canal," "his money was taken," the passive verbs became important since he seemed to want to avoid saying who actually was doing what. In fact, though, it didn't matter who struck which blows, since the prosecution insisted that the defendant and Sidote were equally guilty under the law. Together they drove back to the John Mitchell hotel, according to Konrad, where they told Wasyl to drive the car to Houston. They would meet him at the largest hotel at the airport there. Foat and Sidote would fly in separately.

Meanwhile, Konrad explained, they'd picked up a fourth person whom "the State has not located." Foat and Sidote left New Orleans on November 21, met up with Wasyl, and eventually, at the suggestion of the fourth person, they drove to Carson City, where they stayed a month. (He was careful not to mention the Nevada murder charge, since the defense had won a pretrial ruling to exclude all references to Sidote's implication of Foat in the Nevada crime.) Then they drove to Torrance, California, where they bought the No Regrets bar and were married, Konrad continued, his voice now flattened to match his simple sentences and abbreviated outline of the event in the narrative that might give the jury pause about Sidote's character. In 1967 Sidote was in an altercation in the bar, he said, then shot into a passing car, and served three years for manslaughter in Chino prison. While he was in jail, Foat remained his wife, and when Sidote was on a work-release program, he would visit her. But a week before his permanent release in 1970, they had a fight and separated. Then between 1970 and 1977, there were two calls from the defendant *to* Sidote.

Konrad was beginning to lose the jurors. Remaining unemotional, he chose not to explain why certain facts, like phone calls from the defendant, were important. He'd stripped his account of so many details that he wasn't calling the jurors' attention to the State's contention that Sidote's motivation for implicating his ex-wife was not revenge but a desire to relieve his conscience.

Konrad described Sidote's voluntary confession in 1977 in equally bland terms: Those seven years (from 1970 to 1977) were not "a good time for him," he was an alcoholic and his "life was gone because of what he did," hence the confession to two 1965 crimes, one in New Orleans, the other in Nevada. At the time, Konrad emphasized again, Sidote had no connection to Foat. He pleaded guilty to manslaughter and received a twenty-five-year sentence in Nevada. He also made statements to indicate he wouldn't testify against Ginny Foat in Jefferson Parish. (This wasn't precisely accurate—Sidote had said he was never asked to testify in Jefferson Parish—but it served to answer any question from an alert juror about why Louisiana hadn't indicted her in 1977.)

In 1983, Konrad concluded, Jefferson Parish received an inquiry about an outstanding warrant for Virginia Galluzzo or Foat from an "official with the Los Angeles City Council." His remark elicited groans from Foat's supporters in the courtroom, since they believed the letter from Shelly Mandell was hardly the official procedure he'd implied.

Konrad also couched his explanation of Sidote's immunity in guarded clichés: It had been granted "because he solved the crime which would otherwise remain unsolved. He has already been punished and is serving time. If he didn't get immunity, the other defendant would never be prosecuted." Then to counter the suggestion that the State was relying only on Sidote, he listed other witnesses to be called: the investigating officer; the coroner; Wasyl Bozydaj, "who will confirm the trip west." He added that, based on this testimony, the State would corroborate Sidote's testimony. Under Louisiana law, it wasn't necessary to introduce corroborative evidence of a co-conspirator's testimony. Nevertheless, it was a meager list, Bozydaj the only witness named who might confirm any part of Sidote's testimony.

Konrad had taken no more than twenty minutes to frame his straightforward "logical" story while avoiding the tangled motivations and the more complicated aspects of the case. It was the barest sketch as provided by Sidote's confession, and with little emotion or dramatic impulse behind it, the DA's account seemed unlikely to entice the jury as a good story would.

In contrast to Konrad's calm, reasonable tone, Reed's voice was taut with emotion as he began his opening argument. After he warned the jury that things were not always what they seemed or what the State said they seemed to be, his voice took flight: "In July of 1970, after five years of living in a cage that John Sidote had fashioned . . . , a cage made at first of love and Virginia Foat's extreme insecurity, and a cage later of fear and terror, Ginny Foat, then Ginny Sidote, made a decision to get out and to leave that man . . . forever. And when she made that decision, that man beat her as he had never beaten her before. He beat her in the face, he beat her in the breasts, he beat her in the arms. He grabbed her by the hair, he put his hands around her neck, he squeezed as hard as he could and he almost killed her, and she thought she was dying."

The connection between the beating and the motives behind Sidote's later accusations Reed now made explicit. During the last beating Sidote had threatened her, he said: " 'I'll kill you, I'll kill you if you ever leave me. I'll make you pay for my crimes if you ever leave me, and I'll see you behind bars and rotting in jail like me if you ever leave me.' " And that was what happened, Reed went on: In 1977 Sidote, "a broken-down, suicidal alcoholic, at the pits of his life," carried out his threat. "Not caring about himself or anyone else, he took out his revenge on Ginny Foat. And he put Ginny Foat for a while back in a cage, this time a cage with bars." But that time, he explained, Ginny was allowed to go free.

Reed was alluding to her imprisonment in 1977 but didn't want to refer to the Nevada arrest specifically. Still, he had captivated the jury; they were leaning forward in their chairs, as if waiting for the next turn of plot, and seemed not to notice the quick leap from 1977 to January 1983, when, Reed said, "someone dusted off John Sidote," when he was sick and again suffering from his alcoholism, and "gave him no choice but to repeat what he said back in 1977." Otherwise, Reed explained, Sidote would have to go back to jail himself for the rest of his life.

At this Porteous shook his head slightly and glanced at Konrad and Mamoulides, irritated at the insinuation of improper legal conduct. But Reed took no notice and now introduced the story line that would become the central motif of the trial. Since "these were not just two ordinary folks in an ordinary relationship," he would explain why Ginny "got to know and got to like John Sidote, what their relationship was like and what those threats were like." He also promised to tell the jury something about John Sidote so that they would understand why in 1977 he'd carried out the threats he'd made in 1970, and why he had no choice but to repeat these lies in 1983. And finally, he would tell them who Ginny Foat was in 1965 and how she could have taken up with a man like Sidote.

She was born in Brooklyn in 1941, Reed began, the daughter of second-generation Italians. Her mother was at home, the father worked hard, and the mother was totally dependent on her husband until his death in April, he said, as if to emphasize the stereotyped expectations imposed by the parents and society, "a traditional Italian Catholic family" in the small town of New Paltz, New York. After high school, he continued, Ginny worked as an airline attendant, but then in 1962 she married Danny Angelillo, since "that was the way she was brought up." Yet a year and half later the marriage was annulled, said Reed, "in the eyes of many because Ginny was not wifely." It seemed that she did things like "attending the March on Washington in 1963," and as a result of the first divorce in her family (there were "no divorces in Italian families") at twenty-two she was made to feel a failure by her parents and friends.

Suddenly Konrad asked for a conference at the bench to present the expected objection to the introduction of Ginny's "biography" to the trial. The prosecutors had known it was coming, and their argument was that all of this background—of which they, too, were well aware—was irrelevant to the alleged crime. Reed countered that the defense argument, as indicated in its pretrial motions, required such background to buttress its claim that Sidote's accusations were part of a pattern of abuse and threats, that his testimony was an act of revenge. But to do so, Reed and Glass had to show how Ginny had fallen into her relationship with Sidote, how she had been victimized by this violent man. Judge Burns listened intently to Reed. Even in whispers, his voice betrayed the intensity of his arguments, and finally Judge Burns conceded: objection overruled. He agreed with Reed's contention that it was necessary to hear about Ginny's earlier life for them to be able to judge Sidote's motives and credibility. There were sighs of relief from the defense pews. Later Kay Tsenin agreed that this was the most important ruling of the trial. Yet she wasn't sure on what legal grounds the judge had accepted Reed's argument. "It was almost like someone watching a soap opera or a miniseries on television," she said. "It was as if the judge didn't want to miss the next episode. He got so caught up in the story that he wanted to hear what happened next."

Now Reed turned back to the jury with an air of triumph. He spun out a causal connection between Ginny's "sense of failure" after her annulment and what he'd already implied was a crucial turn in his narrative of Ginny's life. She seemed aware of what was coming. She sat with her head lowered, her eyes squeezed shut, and Glass grasped her shoulder more tightly as Reed said: In 1963 Ginny had "an encounter with a man. Whether it could be called a rape or whether she got in over her head, it was a sexual encounter in which she felt she was not fully consenting." As a result she became pregnant, and "the change she felt was enormous." Gasps from Ginny's supporters filled the courtroom. She kept the pregnancy secret for six or seven months, she concealed it from neighbors and parents, Reed continued, and then, telling her parents she was going to stay with friends, she drove to a distant home for unwed mothers.

Stressing the "shame and guilt" with which Ginny was burdened after giving up her child for adoption, Reed set the scene for Ginny's meeting with Sidote a few months later at the Villa Lipani, "a nice resort in the Catskills" filled with "nicely behaved, nicely dressed people," which in turn, he implied, led Ginny to perceive Sidote as equally respectable, and an "important man" as well. Important in what sense Reed didn't say, although he added that Sidote was thought of as a "white Sammy Davis, Jr.," for his singing.

Reed now re-created their romance as a courtship in which "John Sidote swept her off her feet." When she first met him, she ordered a Scotch; when she returned a second time, he gave her a Scotch without asking and jumped over the bar to sing "There Will Never Be Another You." "But we have to understand why she came to cling to a kind of man like John Sidote," Reed continued. It seemed that John Sidote showed her another kind of life: He took her down to New York City, he took her to the racetrack. Because he was a favorite of Mr. and Mrs. Lipani, he was an "important" person at the resort, and as a result, Reed announced emotionally, Ginny "felt special, important, and loved."

Reed countered the State's suggestion the Ginny had been the instigator in the affair, pushing Sidote to make a choice between her and his wife. Instead, Reed insisted that Ginny thought Sidote was separated from his wife in Poughkeepsie because he seemed to be living at the resort.

Further, when Sidote said he had a job opportunity in Florida, he didn't say what it was, "just as he always kept things under his control." Although her parents were opposed, she decided to go with him, said Reed, so that she wouldn't be "left a failure in New Paltz." But, he added, she "missed a message" that she should've picked up along the way: Sidote had told her to "borrow some money," which "she did because he demanded it." Then the morning of their departure, she was surprised to see Wasyl Bozydaj in the car. "That didn't fit" her romantic notion either, said Reed, "but she made explanations to herself." On the way to Cocoa Beach, Florida, she missed another message, too, Reed added, when Sidote first showed his violent side. Outside Washington, D.C., Ginny asked Sidote a question about money. He ordered Wasyl to stop, then took Ginny out of the car and slammed her against the trunk. " 'Don't ask questions like that,' " Reed quoted Sidote. " 'Otherwise you can take your bags and get out.' "

Ginny agreed to stay, according to her attorney, since she felt she couldn't go back to New Paltz.

But Sidote became even more violent in Florida, Reed said. Not finding the acquaintance who might give him a job, he "lashed out" as he always did "when things didn't work out."

In response to Ginny's question, " 'What are we going to do?' " he beat her, said Reed, and threatened her by telling her he had once brutally tortured and killed a woman. Ginny responded, " 'No, it isn't true, Jack. It isn't true,' " said Reed.

Foat was weeping, as were many of her supporters, while Reed explained what Ginny thought of Sidote's abuse. She told herself,

" 'You don't leave. You think it's a sickness, like epilepsy. You work it out. You don't go back and admit you're a failure again.' "

Instead, she went on to Baton Rouge, then to New Orleans, where she worked as a barmaid at the Ponderosa but *never* as a dancer. (That was a "figment of John Sidote's sick imagination," he added.) Sometimes Ginny had the night off but was often left alone in their room; some nights she worked alone in the bar because Jack, the bouncer, wasn't needed, he said. Then he told two stories to remind the jury of Sidote's violence. Once Ginny was hassled by a drunk customer. She called Jack over, and he took the man outside, beat him until the police came, and then told her she should let him know if it ever happened again. As instructed, she later pointed out another drunk who was bothering her. Again, Sidote took the man outside and didn't come back for a long time. The next night Ginny asked him what had happened with the drunk the night before. Sidote became angry, said Reed, and shouting that she must never question what he'd been doing, he beat her again and told her: " 'I take drunks into alleys and put a knife through their kidneys.' " Later he repented and told Ginny "it wasn't true, that he was sorry, that he wouldn't do it again."

Once again Reed paused in his narrative to explain why Ginny stayed with this violent and seemingly crazy man. She couldn't go home "as a failure," he repeated, but this time added that Ginny believed "a woman must change the man somehow."

With Sidote's violence and Foat's steadfastness established, Reed described the night of the alleged crime: John Sidote came back that night to the hotel room, excited and scared, and told Ginny he'd cheated a man at cards, a man who was important and would come after him. It was not his usual rage, Reed explained, but more like repentance. Then Wasyl came in, and Ginny thought, "Things will be better because Wasyl's here." But Ginny didn't ask what had actually happened, Reed said, because of Sidote's rage and violence when she'd questioned him before. " 'Just don't ask questions. Be a good wife and make this marriage succeed,' " Reed described her thoughts at the time, apparently ignoring the fact that Foat and Sidote were not yet married. Hence, he said, she knew nothing about what had occurred that night. All she was certain of was that she neither met Moises Chayo nor was aware of what happened. She knew only that Sidote had to get out of town.

Reed skipped quickly to the couple's arrival in Torrance, California, omitting the details of their flight to Texas, their drive to Nevada, and their hurried departure from that state. In 1966, Reed said, they worked in a telephone soliciting business, and "when that didn't go well, Ginny was beaten." In January 1967 they were married and opened the No Regrets bar, but when that started to fall apart, "there were more beatings, some worse than others." Still, he emphasized, Ginny had her dream of love and romance, of setting up a home. Because of love, she wanted the marriage to succeed.

Reed now told the jury about the shooting in California, but unlike Konrad's version, his was told from Foat's point of view: One night Ginny called Sidote to come and take over for her in the bar because she'd been sick. Sidote was drunk and refused, and later when he finally did come in, he was angry. "Ginny knew she'd gone too far," said Reed. She'd pushed him and because she was afraid of what he'd do when he came home, she didn't get undressed or get into bed. But that night, Reed said, "Sidote's rage was taken out on someone in the bar," a young Samoan. When he returned and told her about the shooting, he looked the same way he'd looked that night in New Orleans: not in a rage but fearful of what might happen to him.

In the period before going to jail in June 1968, he got meaner and meaner, because, Reed alleged, he was afraid that "Ginny would escape his cage." The beatings became worse, and he threatened her: "Visit me every week, stay away from men, or I'll kill you or I'll accuse you of crimes I have committed."

Reed described Ginny's reaction. She blamed herself, she thought it was her fault, and she told herself, " 'I shouldn't have pulled him out to the bar, I shouldn't have insisted.' " But she also thought that jail might make him better, with psychiatric counseling and no drinking. And that, Reed declared, was "the same kind of persistence as what makes her who she is today."

Sidote was happy at Chino, said Reed, and as an "important" person, a trusty, he "had the run of the grounds," so that he and Ginny could visit in private and he "could hit her in private." Meanwhile, she told him that she was "succeeding" in her new job on the *Princess Louise* and making new friends. This made Sidote angry, Reed said, and in June and July 1970, when Sidote was on work release, he beat her, brutalized her, made her do unmentionable things, and when she threw up, he laughed at her. Finally she realized she couldn't take it anymore, that she didn't love him, she would have to get out.

Reed had come full circle to the final beating with which he'd begun his opening argument. He paused, then announced dramatically: When Ginny took one bag and got on a plane and left, "she was free at last," and from 1970 to 1977, she "became herself." Without mentioning the women's movement or a feminist conversion, he explained that when she heard that Sidote had had his parole transferred to New York State, she flew to Vancouver "to be free." Then returning to California, she ran a successful catering business and was married to Ray Foat from 1971 to 1980. That didn't work out, Reed said matter-of-factly, and they separated, then got back together, but finally split up. "It's not surprising her marriages didn't work, given five years with Jack Sidote," Reed commented, but while referring to "marriages," he omitted mention of Foat's fourth marriage and its brevity.

The narrative continued but Reed seemed to be running out of steam as he responded to points made by Konrad. Yes, it was true that Ginny had telephoned Sidote's home in 1973, but not to speak to him. He just happened to be there when Ginny called to ask about Jack's mother's mastectomy.

As for Sidote, said Reed, he was going downhill, he was an alcoholic, and he went to the cops because he didn't care if he went to jail; in fact, he liked jail because "he was a big man there." But then his confession put Ginny "back in a cage, almost in the same jail, until she was allowed to go free because she could not be prosecuted on his word." This was a sketchy explanation of what had happened in Nevada in 1977 since, for obvious reasons, he didn't want to make very much of the earlier arrest. But then in 1983, Reed continued, "John Sidote was dusted off. If he didn't stick to the deal he'd made, he could go to jail for the rest of his life," so "he has to say what he said in 1977."

Reed's voice now rose dramatically as he told the jury that the verdict came down to a choice between Ginny Foat and John Sidote. Forgetting his statement that after 1970, "Ginny became herself," ignoring the portrait of the helpless victim he'd drawn, he proclaimed: "There's been only one Ginny Foat these twenty years. She's the same person who's always doing good things. The Ginny then is the Ginny now." In contrast, "There are two John Sidotes": "the sober one who speaks well, who can charm you as he charmed

Ginny Foat; or John Sidote the drunk, who savaged Ginny Foat, who threatened her with murder, who was alcoholic and suicidal." With his voice again tremulous, Reed faced the jury and instructed them: "Look at Ginny Foat, look into your heads and your hearts," and "do justice."

The courtroom was silent; then came scattered applause from the spectators, which provoked a scowl from Judge Burns and a short recess. Reed's emotionalism had certainly won out over Konrad's "common sense." As James Gill, the *Times-Picayune* reporter whom Foat's team had considered the most proprosecution of the local reporters, conceded, "If the jury voted now, they'd vote to hang Konrad."

Out in the corridor, Kay had her arm around Ginny's shoulder as friends came up to congratulate her and John Reed on his forty-five-minute performance, completed without notes.

"Your mother's taking it well," Jan Holden said, having just returned from phoning Mrs. Galluzzo. The defense team hadn't wanted Ginny's mother to hear about her daughter's baby for the first time on the television news.

Reed's opening argument had not only set the tone of the defense, it had also established how Ginny would be presented. While her feminism was never mentioned explicitly, the implication of Reed's melodrama was that her feminist consciousness had evolved from her suffering. The jury was not to hear about her emergence as a strong woman but only about her passive victimization: the way everything had happened *to* her, the roles that had been imposed on her and internalized by her because that was "the way she was brought up." Like the *Life* article, the language of Reed's story stressed this: With no mention of the fun-loving, adventurous, risk-taking girl portrayed in her yearbook and by early friends, Reed characterized Ginny as someone who was made to feel a failure, made to feel guilty, made to feel special, important, and loved, and finally made to feel controlled by Sidote, and either too faithful to the stereotype of "the good wife" or too scared to leave him even when he was in jail.

Of course, the defense was creating a drama to convince the jury that there was no suspect motivation—like shared guilt—for her having stayed with an abusive, violent, schizoid husband. But the calculus of female stereotypes and social oppression was close enough to the narrative told in Rinker Buck's story to suggest that this was the way in which Ginny Foat had reshaped her history according to her feminist awakening.

Feminists as well as journalists writing about the case had predicted that the Ginny Foat trial would be a litmus test for feminism. But apart from the voir dire, the jurors weren't being asked to respond to the women's movement or NOW per se (Reed's opening argument mentioned neither). They were seeing only the woman-as-victim and they were being told that the woman is not responsible; Foat and her lawyers had constructed a drama, the expected strategy of any defense, and indeed one that had become quite common for women accused of killing their abusive husbands. Among the defense team and her friends and supporters in the corridor, Reed's narrative was taken as a feminist morality tale, and they almost seemed to congratulate Foat on her suffering. But Reed had invested his characterization of Foat with no spirit, no energy to struggle out of her victimhood, and no strength to resist either the social forces or the misguided options thrust on her. Reed's pronouncement that Ginny was the same person then as she is today could only confuse the jury. In his drama she had no identity except that of the passive woman. What in her character, what in the women's movement made her "who she is today" were lost to the bathos of Reed's tale. The real test of feminism would be found in the jury's ability to understand and even intuit what lay behind the transformation of the passive woman into the strong feminist. But so far, they had been given no inkling of "who she is today," and Reed had offered no indication that they would ever be told in the following days.

Compared to the emotionalism of Reed's opening argument, the rest of the day dragged on with the prosecution's scant forensic reports, police testimony, and circumstantial evidence. Cross-examination compared Sidote's 1977 descriptions of the victim and the scene of the crime with the description of Chayo in the missing–persons report and photographs of the locale, thus chipping away at the prosecution's case by finding discrepancies. The personal belongings inventoried and collecting dust on a shelf for eighteen years were introduced. Dr. Thomas Farris, the pathologist who had performed the autopsy, read his conclusions from the report he had filed in 1965: The body had been in "an advanced state of decomposition" with the face and abdomen markedly swollen and the skin extensively bloated. He estimated that the man had been dead two or three weeks, even possibly sixteen to eighteen days, given winter temperatures. The only significant wounds found were two lacerations on the front of the head, two on the right side, and one more on the left side. These were about two inches long, deep enough to break the skin but not the skull. The brain had liquefied, not from the injuries but from the two or three weeks of decomposition. He could only presume that Chayo had bled to death, although it was possible that he had drowned. The lacerations alone couldn't have caused death, he concluded, since they weren't deep enough, but they were "not incompatible" with wounds from a tire iron.

Bob Glass cross-examined the elderly man and became antagonistic as he asked if there weren't other tire irons with a different width, ones that were bent or had pointed ends.

"I'm not familiar with tire tools," the doctor replied.

Glass became more aggressive: Why had the doctor measured the wounds "by eye," not "by ruler"?

"I don't need a ruler to measure," the doctor bridled.

Now Glass suggested that other objects might leave the same marks: a wrench, the barrel of a pistol, a rifle? Finally he reached for the absurd: a microphone? gesturing to the one in the witness box.

No, the edge would have to be sharper to cause a laceration, the doctor said.

Still, Glass had made his point: The police and DAs were relying only on Sidote's testimony to identify the weapon used. Further, on redirect, the doctor admitted that it would take "a pretty strong side-arm" to break the scalp if one of the blows were struck by a person standing at Chayo's side.

After a recess to record the exhibits, court was back in session at 4:15 with Raymond Chayo called to the stand. A tall, handsome man in a blue-gray suit, he looked grim, his face gaunt and drawn, his deep-set eyes shadowed by fatigue. He glanced at Foat several times, but she flipped through papers and didn't look up as Chayo gave his name and his Davis, California, address. As Konrad took him through his story of how he, then twenty-three, and his father had happened to be in New Orleans in November 1965, his voice became tremulous, his eyes tearing. Even during the mundane explanations of his treatment for phlebitis at the Ochsner Foundation Hospital in New Orleans and his father's arrival from Buenos Aires, he was sobbing and overwrought. Ginny now looked up at him from time to time, but his tears seemed to have little effect on her, even though his testimony in no way suggested her guilt but only established the circumstances of his father's death.

Some of his story was already familiar from newspaper articles. According to a *Times-Picayune* article of October 1983, Moises Chayo was born in Aleppo, Syria, in 1903, the youngest child of a large, poor family. He married, moved to New York City, and opened an import-export business. In 1950, after their two daughters and their son had been born, he moved the family to Buenos Aires, where he started a successful vacuum-cleaner factory. The family was prosperous, with servants and chauffeurs, and became part of the wealthy, elite society of Buenos Aires. The photograph accompanying the article showed a middle-aged, heavy, almost completely bald man with a bulbous nose, dark eyes, a ready smile, and a sleek look of prosperity about him.

In the article Raymond Chayo seemed to know little about the alleged crime, but stressed his father's respectability. While Sidote had said that Ginny had lured a prosperous-looking man from a bar, Chayo seemed to deny any possible sexual interest on the part of his father. He said he "trusted people too much" so it "could be in his nature to get in a car with two strangers." It seemed he couldn't admit that his father might have been looking for a woman, but instead suggested that his father might have wandered off with Foat and Sidote for a friendly chat. To underscore his father's respectability, Chayo added, "He wasn't a playboy or anything like that but he was very social, very friendly. . . . He could have stopped by for a drink. . . . His only fault, if you could even call it a fault, was that he was overly friendly [and] very trusting of everybody."

After identifying the round, gold Omega watch, the heavy-frame glasses, the belt with the Buenos Aires shop label, the gold pen as looking familiar and "what his father would carry," Chayo was subjected to Glass's cross-examination. The attorney's voice was hard and angry, as if he were moving in for the kill, and soon the tears of a grief-stricken man gave way to a defensive and defiant tone as he was questioned about his father's habits and comings and goings in New Orleans.

"Were the evenings your father's own time?" asked Glass.

"I'd have dinner with him but the late evenings were, yes."

"But sometimes he went into New Orleans to eat?"

"Yes, but I don't know where," said Chayo with a shrug.

"Didn't your father have a soft spot for card playing?"

"He played bridge," said the son. "Both my parents were champion bridge players."

Glass was trying to establish a basis for Foat's story that Sidote had said they had to get out of town because he'd cheated a man at cards, the implied scenario that Sidote had lured Chayo into a card game, then robbed and beaten him.

Didn't Moises Chayo gamble? Glass pushed.

"Not that I know of," replied his son. "I never saw money on the table."

He insisted that his father looked for bridge games not because he liked to gamble but because both his parents simply enjoyed playing. For example, when his mother visited him in California, she always sought out bridge games as well.

Glass was feeding out the line, ready to reel him in as soon as he'd forced Chayo to admit that it was possible that his father had looked for bridge games in New Orleans.

Hadn't he ever warned his father about such games? Glass asked.

Chayo's voice was now hard and indignant. "My father was a man of the world, he traveled all over the world," he said. "He spoke four languages. Everybody loved him. He was not a person to tell, 'Dad, be careful.' "

"He could handle himself?" Glass said.

"Handle himself doing what?" Furious at Glass's insinuation, he added, his voice again breaking, "Sometimes he'd find a bridge game. What was there to warn him about? I didn't realize it was such a dangerous city."

Glass waited a dramatic moment, then adopted a momentous tone as he asked, "Was Moises Chayo Jewish?"

Surprised by the question, the son said that yes, he went to temple twice a year.

Glass looked pleased with himself as if he were savoring a secret triumph, but didn't explain the significance of Chayo's Jewishness. It was a time bomb set to explode during Sidote's testimony. Now he only completed his cross-examination with the son's description of his late father: he was sixty-two years old at the time of his death, was about five feet eight, weighed 170 pounds, and was bald with a fringe of gray hair.

With no redirect from the prosecutors (not even a question about whether his father, as a man of the world, had liked attractive women), Judge Burns adjourned for the day.

Later DA Porteous conceded that Ray Chayo was definitely a problem and had lent more credence to the defense's argument that it was more likely that Sidote had lured the man into a card game than Ginny Foat had lured him into the car for sex. "He couldn't admit that his father might have been looking for a woman that night," said Porteous. "His father was dead, there was no further need to hurt him, and he didn't want to hurt his mother either. So even though we were sure his father was a 'Continental' type, 'a man of the world,' we didn't try to get him to say, 'Oh, sure, my father might've been looking for a woman that night.' It was too difficult for him."

It rained during the night, and Friday morning, November 11, was gray and steamy. Even more people were clamoring for seats, yesterday's "juicy" revelation about Ginny's child as well as the announcement that Sidote was slated to take the stand bringing out the crowds. As if in anticipation of Sidote's appearance, the bailiff was now sitting between the witness stand and the defense table instead of next to the jury box, perhaps to intercede if there were any outbursts either from or against Sidote.

Before getting under way, however, Judge Burns called the attorneys into chambers. Out in the corridor Ginny was holding an informal press conference. Although she'd have to face Sidote today, she seemed calm and collected as she explained to the reporter from *Newsweek,* "The reason John was so effective is that my attorneys know my life so well. They're so moved by it that John couldn't help but move the jury."

Another reporter asked her how much she'd participated in her jury selection.

"Sometimes John and Bob thought I participated too much," she said, but despite her laugh it was apparent that she attributed a great deal of importance to her contribution.

Finally court was called into session. Ginny, it seemed, had forgotten the courtroom etiquette (was it fatigue, tension, or self-absorption?), and Bob Glass had to remind her to stand as the jury filed in. Judge Burns had yet to make a ruling about which of Sidote's various statements and confessions would be admissible, the topics of this morning's in-chamber discussion, and instead asked the State to call its next witness.

Wasyl Bozydaj now took the stand.

Tall and thin with sandy-brown hair, he affected a "mod" look with his moustache and gold wire-rimmed glasses. Still, the tan polyester suit, blue shirt, and "coordinated" tan-print tie betrayed his working-class background. In a tense voice, he gave his name and address in upstate New York and stated that he had been married for twelve years, had two children, and worked as an auto mechanic. Glass repeatedly objected to the phrasing of Konrad's questions—stating facts, then asking Bozydaj to confirm them, but Judge Burns overruled; Konrad wasn't so much leading the witness as dispensing with "vital statistics" as quickly as possible.

Finally, Bozydaj recounted his story of the 1965 trip. He was eighteen that summer and as usual employed at the Villa Lipani. He'd worked there since he was fifteen, part-time during the school year, and full-time summers and then the year after he'd graduated from high school. A kind of "handyman," he did odd jobs in addition to being a busboy in the restaurant and lounge. In 1963 or 1964 he met John Sidote (he called him "John," not "Jack," perhaps to distance himself from the old friendship), who was the bartender in the nightclub. In 1965 he also met Ginny Foat, two or three months before they all left for Florida. But he couldn't remember the specific date of their departure: "John Sidote called that morning and said he and Ginny were going to Florida for two or three weeks and he wanted to know if I wanted to come along. He picked me up, then her . . ."

Konrad interrupted to ask about Sidote's marriage.

"As far as I knew he was happily married," Bozydaj replied, then looked perplexed by the laughter in the courtroom, unaware of the humor in his description of a man "who was seeing girls on the side," then leaving town with his girlfriend as "happily married."

He continued: They left in Sidote's 1965 Pontiac "white convertible with a blue interior" and, stopping only once, drove straight through to the Fort Lauderdale area, where they stayed in an "efficiency cabin." They all drove at one time or another, he said, and didn't remember if he drove more than the others. His statement contradicted Sidote's 1977 confession explaining that he'd lost his license and asked Wasyl to come along to help with the driving. Too, it was at odds with Foat's insistence that it wasn't easy for her to leave Sidote since she never drove during this period.

No, there were no unusual incidents or fights between Sidote and Ginny during the trip, Bozydaj said, but conceded that when Sidote couldn't reach his friend about a job, "he got upset." Still, he wouldn't call it a "fight" with Ginny. On they went to Baton Rouge, where they stayed in a motel room "for a couple of days" with "none of them working"; again he remembered no unusual incidents or fights. Then to New Orleans, where they took another efficiency apartment—a kitchen, one bedroom, and a living room with a sofa bed—in a hotel, the name of which he couldn't remember. He worked as a soda jerk somewhere and John and Ginny worked in "a saloon on Canal Street" (again he couldn't remember the name), John as a bouncer, Ginny as a barmaid. Once again he said there were no incidents, "no problems as far as I could see."

He'd been speaking in a peculiarly flat monotone, as if he were trying to control his apparent nervousness. But as he neared the crucial part of his testimony, his voice became breathless. He couldn't remember how long they'd stayed in New Orleans, "perhaps two or three months," but "I lost track of time as I was traveling." He did, however, remember the way they left New Orleans because it was "different" from the rest of their trip.

"They told me to drive to Houston, and they said they would meet me there," he said. He explained that Sidote had told him he'd been in a fight in the bar and had to leave town fast. But whether he'd left that night or on the following morning, Bozydaj couldn't recall.

Konrad now led him back to the earlier part of the evening. Bozydaj explained that at first Ginny and Jack had had the same working schedule, but later they'd had different ones. But that night, he said, they went out together and came back together about eleven or midnight.

"Ginny came in first, like they'd had a fight, and walked into the kitchen. John came in the second entrance, the kitchen door," and Bozydaj, who was in the living room, said he heard them talking in the kitchen, but had not gotten out of bed because he was in his underwear. Then John came into the living room, gave him instructions to go to Houston, and handed him a one-hundred-dollar bill. The explanation for the hurried departure—that Sidote had had a fight in the bar, or they were unhappy with their jobs—was hazy. But he said, "it sounded good at the time."

How were the two of them dressed that night? Konrad interrupted, almost as an afterthought.

Bozydaj replied that they were "dressed up" to go out, Sidote in a white shirt and black slacks, she in "a blouse and slacks." Yes, she looked "pretty," he agreed, and Konrad left it at that, going on to ask about their meeting at the Houston airport.

Bozydaj said he didn't remember the exact instructions of how to find Ginny, or whether he'd left that night or the next day. But Ginny was at the airport motel when he arrived by car, he said, and Sidote arrived one to two hours later, "accompanied" by "another friend of his and mine."

This fourth person (the man who'd become known as "the missing witness"), he explained, had been Sidote's friend whom he himself had later met. He glanced nervously around the courtroom, aware of the courtroom murmurs but unaware of the discrepancy between his testimony and the story Sidote had repeatedly told. According to Sidote, the fourth person, the "missing witness," had been Wasyl's friend, not his, and had accompanied Wasyl on his drive from New Orleans, much to Sidote's surprise turning up in the car. Now Bozydaj was insisting that the fourth person was not only Sidote's friend but had flown with him rather than driven.

Bozydaj continued: From Houston the four of them drove to Las Vegas, then to Carson City. Leaving the fourth person in Nevada, he and John and Ginny then drove to California. Asked if there were any unusual incidents or fights along the way, he told the story about which the prosecutors had been hinting in their remarks to the press. As they were driving to Nevada, he said, Jack (he'd now shifted to the nickname) was in the backseat of the car. He was rambling, sick, talking to himself. Suddenly he screamed, "You shouldn't have hit him so hard."

The story had an effect on the jury. Up to then they'd looked bored, since, not knowing the details of Sidote's statement, they were unaware of the problems that Bozydaj's testimony would later present.

In Carson City, the "fourth person left us," Bozydaj said. There he saw no physical fights, no "smacking or hitting," but he did think there was "more tension." Ginny was crying a lot, he said, and they did a lot of arguing in their room.

Konrad avoided any mention of what else happened in Nevada and simply asked about their arrival in California. There they all lived together in an efficiency, Bozydaj said, and he worked in a gas station for two or three months, perhaps less, perhaps until around Christmas, when he had a letter from home telling him that he'd missed two draft notices and if he missed another, "they'd come after me." He used his own money to get home. Since that day, he said, he had never spoken to Ginny Foat, John Sidote, or "the fourth person," nor had he written to or received any letters from these people.

Konrad was finished, and now there was a slight pause as the State offered State Exhibit 13 into evidence: Sidote's March 16, 1977, statement to the New York State Police. While the jury read the document, Ginny stared directly at Bozydaj. During his testimony he'd kept his eyes riveted on the district attorneys; now he still refused to look at her, staring into space or at the bailiff or at the ceiling, anywhere but at her directly. But she seemed worried. The man seemed credible, since there seemed no reason for him to lie about Sidote and Foat coming back to the hotel together.

Still, he was nervous and coughed, prompting Ginny to take a drink of water. Catching the movement out of the corner of his eye, he now cast a sidelong glance at her and since she'd already turned away, he continued to stare, his eyes seeming to narrow in anger, for what reason it was hard to fathom.

Glass began his cross-examination in a matter-of-fact tone, but then turned snide as he asked Bozydaj for his impressions of Jack Sidote in 1965.

Glass:	Was he a popular guy?
Bozydaj:	Yeah.
Glass:	Sometimes he sang?
Bozydaj:	Yeah.
Glass:	Didn't he sometimes jump over the bar to sing?
Bozydaj:	I've never seen him do that.
Glass:	Didn't he like to sing when he got drunk or had a few drinks?
Bozydaj:	He didn't drink that often in the beginning.
Glass:	Didn't he have a little authority at the Villa Lipani?
Bozydaj:	Not really. He was an employee.
Glass:	Wasn't John Lipani in the lounge a lot?

Bozydaj: At the time he and Jack had a good relationship.
Glass: Didn't some people think that John Lipani thought of Jack Sidote as a son?
Bozydaj: I didn't have that impression.

Glass was trying to buttress the defense story that Ginny fell in love with Jack Sidote because he was "an important man" at the Villa Lipani. Still, since he had so much contempt for Sidote, he also undermined the point of John Reed's narrative. The subliminal message was that Sidote was neither a knight in shining armor nor a star of the resort.

"Didn't you know he had a way with women?" Glass continued. "Didn't he often stay in the motel unit with women despite having a wife and child at home?"

Bozydaj: Sometimes.
Glass: Did he sometimes go elsewhere?
Bozydaj: I didn't follow his life story.

Glass seemed to have forgotten what point he wanted to make. Implicitly he'd prompted Bozydaj to confirm that Sidote was known as a ladies' man and also known to be married, even though Reed had said that Ginny thought he was separated, and was unaware of his reputation. Similarly, Glass cast doubts about Ginny's version of her romance when he asked Bozydaj why he chose to take Sidote's offer of the ride to go to Florida.

"When we left it was an opportunity to take a vacation," he said. "I'd never had a vacation, I'd always worked summers and after school, so it looked like a break for me."

"So on a moment's notice, you leave?" Glass asked, his voice thick with sarcasm. An eighteen-year-old who went off on a lark for a vacation hardly deserved such cynicism, especially when it might well be turned against Ginny for leaving, "on a moment's notice" with a singing bartender, notorious ladies' man, and unfaithful husband.

"Back then I looked up to him," Bozydaj tried to explain.

Glass rephrased his remark: "Didn't you look up to him as a mentor? Didn't you look up to him for things that men knew?"

Konrad's objection was overruled, and Glass asked if he looked up to him "for his way with women?"

"No, that didn't impress me," he said, eliciting laughter from the spectators as well as the jurors.

Glass:	Did you look up to him for the way he sang?
Bozydaj:	No. [It was said with such genuine disbelief that again there was laughter.]
Glass:	For the way he tended bar?
Bozydaj:	Yes, he had a real style, a real knack.

Again, laughter, this time embarrassing the witness. Now he seemed to realize that Glass was ridiculing him for looking up to Sidote. Glass seemed to enjoy his mockery of both Bozydaj and Sidote without realizing that such snobbery bespoke more about Ginny's love for the singing Don Juan than it disparaged an eighteen-year-old's admiration for a man who "had a way with words" and a "class act" as a bartender.

"Had you ever before seen him as upset as he was in Florida when the job fell through?" Glass now pounced.

No, he hadn't, he admitted.

"Was it frightening, obsessive?"

"A little bit."

"Did it scare you off?"

"I stayed."

The answer was bland but again provided a tacit analogy to Ginny's behavior. If Bozydaj "stayed," then perhaps Sidote's behavior wasn't as frightening as Reed had alleged in his opening argument.

Bozydaj provided a few details about their weeks in New Orleans. The place he worked was some distance from the hotel so he would take the car to work, while Ginny and Jack would walk to their jobs at the nearby bar. On his nights off, he'd sometimes go to the bar, which was where he met the friend of Sidote's, the so-called missing witness.

"Didn't you look at pictures in an effort to help the prosecution?" Glass asked. "Wasn't there a special act performed to help you remember?"

The "special act" was a hidden reference to hypnosis, but it was only later in the trial that it became clear why Glass was loath to use the term. Bozydaj, however, denied both accusations, although showing him photographs might well have been routine police procedure.

"Isn't it true that the police stopped your car in New Mexico and found a gun in the fourth person's possession?" Glass continued.

"That's what I was told."

Since it was a significant incident, hadn't he tried hard to remember? asked Glass. Yes, he had tried, said Bozydaj, but all he remembered was that the man's name was John or Tom and that he had blue eyes and brown hair.

Besides, he added, he didn't really remember the incident, because, "I didn't see no gun."

"Aside from knowing about a gun, did you ever see John Sidote with a gun?" asked Glass.

There was a long pause. Then Bozydaj sighed. "I saw John Sidote with a gun two years before we left but not on the trip."

Glass tried to push him, but he insisted he was sure. There'd already been the implicit suggestion that Chayo's wounds were caused by the butt of a gun; Glass was allowing the jury to think that Sidote might still have had the gun on the trip south. That Sidote had a gun two years before in New York came as no surprise, since his police record showed a 1965 arrest for illegal possession of a gun, a charge that was later dismissed.

Glass returned to the details of the night of the alleged crime. Bozydaj stuck to his story, now adding that he couldn't hear what Ginny and Jack were arguing about in the kitchen because there was water running. Konrad hadn't brought out this important detail, even though Sidote had said in his 1977 confession that he was cleaning up in the kitchen.

Glass, however, seemed aware of the implication of water running and moved quickly to Sidote's instructions.

All Bozydaj remembered was that he'd been given a hundred-dollar bill and instructions about leaving town.

"He told you to go to Dallas?" asked Glass.

Glass was implicitly referring to the fact that in all of Sidote's earlier statements he'd talked about meeting in Dallas. But Bozydaj said he thought he was told Houston.

No, he then replied, he wasn't suspicious about the explanation Sidote had given him.

"Was there anything about the explanation that should have made it suspicious to Ginny?" Glass asked.

Konrad's objection that it called for speculation was sustained; Bozydaj started to reply, referring to their explanation for their speedy departure. Now Glass insisted that "they" meant Jack, and Bozydaj agreed, "Yes, Jack."

Glass wheeled: "And you still don't remember whether it was Dallas or Houston?"

Konrad objected, "argumentative," and was sustained. But Bozydaj shrugged, as if to say, "No big deal," either large airport in Texas would seem the same, especially after eighteen years.

Despite Glass's repeated questions, Bozydaj refused to agree that Sidote was either a maniac or "volatile." "He'd get mad like anybody . . ." he said, but "he never got violent in front of me." Sure, he'd heard Ginny and Jack arguing, but when Glass asked, in a weird turn of phrase, if there were any "products" of their arguments, Bozydaj replied, "Crying and swollen eyes were about it." No, he repeated, he was unaware of "physical violence," and he hadn't noticed "any bruises on her."

Wasn't he interviewed by Roger Gardner (a New York State Police investigator) in March 1977 about the trip? Glass countered, prompting an objection from Konrad and a side bar at the bench. Glass was then allowed to ask his question but without introducing Bozydaj's statement into evidence.

"When you spoke with Senior Investigator Gardner on March 23, 1977, did you not tell him one of your reasons for leaving California was because Jack Sidote was continually beating up Virginia and you did not like the situation and wanted to leave?"

Bozydaj paused. "I said—"

"Did you or did you not say that, first?"

"I might've."

Glass turned on his heels and walked back to the defense table. "Tender the witness," he said with a smile at Ginny as Bozydaj tried to modify his remark.

"Let the witness explain," Porteous objected. Judge Burns only motioned him to proceed with his redirect, and Porteous began by asking Wasyl what he had wanted to say.

What he meant, he said, was that in California there was underlying tension. Although he'd never seen Sidote hit her, it was possible, even obvious, that he might have.

"Did you see him hit her in Louisiana?" Porteous pushed harder.

Bozydaj: No.
Porteous: In Florida?
Bozydaj: No.
Porteous: In New York?
Bozydaj: Once I seen her beaten there.

The remark was surprising; equally so that Porteous left it at that. In the defense's picture of their romance, no one had mentioned an early beating as another "missed message," even before she'd been "swept away" to Florida. Although Porteous wasn't asking explicitly, it was clear that Bozydaj didn't remember Ginny Foat as either passive or a victim.

"Did you ever see how Ginny Foat operated in a bar?" Porteous now asked.

"She was a typical barmaid, you know," Bozydaj replied. "She wasn't as good as Jack. He had it down to a science. But she knew how to handle herself in a saloon, she knew what she was doing."

Porteous seemed to be looking for a comment about her go-go dancing or talking to men. Bozydaj, however chose not to elaborate, as if he were disconcerted by the derisive laughter at his remark "He had it down to a science." He seemed relieved when Porteous chose not to continue, and he stepped down, looking awkward and self-conscious, probably all too aware that the laughter was for his bad grammar and naïve adulation of a bartender.

The prosecutors weren't pleased with Bozydaj's performance. They'd run into the same problem they had with Ray Chayo. Each for his own reasons, they felt, hadn't told the whole story. Before, Bozydaj had given them his account in greater detail, with "more specifics." "Everybody seemed to have a cloudy memory when it came to points they just didn't want to talk about," said Porteous. As if they'd known Bozydaj felt vulnerable, whether or not he actually was, they'd granted him immunity. "I think he was very scared," Porteous conceded. "While legally immunity protected him, it was a fairly moot point. I don't think he had any involvement in the offense, but the basic problem was that we couldn't give him immunity from public criticism, from the press, or from attacks on him that brought up this stuff from his past. I couldn't give him any assurance that people wouldn't look at him after the trial and say, 'Oh, you were with a murderer.' There was no way I could convince him that his friends would still be his friends when the trial was over. He'd been a kid at the time, he was sorry that the damned thing ever came up again, and there was no way we could get over that hump. He wasn't recalcitrant, he just wouldn't tell *the* story. He'd give pieces of it and then just wander off. I think he never really did tell the entire story. Even though I doubt that Wasyl had any firsthand knowledge of the crime itself, the parts started not fitting together at all well. Wasyl's information was essentially about the circumstances after the crime. There was the one detail about hearing water running. But the jury seemed to forget about that or lose interest, especially when he seemed to clam up."

After the lunch recess, Ginny entered the courtroom, this time escorted by Reed and Glass on either side, who then seated her between them at the defense table.

She was upset, her face ashen and drawn, as she turned in her seat and, searching the defense pews, asked, "Where's Jan, where's Jan?"

Kay tried to calm her. Soon Jan pushed into the crowded front row. Ginny smiled in relief but quickly turned toward the front of the room as she heard from behind her the crowd's excited whispers, "He's here, he's here!"

In the rear wall a small window allowed a view of the courtroom from the foyer leading into the hallway. There in the window was Sidote, his face framed like a mug shot.

Reed and Glass each took one of Ginny's hands and clasped them tightly as Judge Burns asked the prosecution to proceed.

Konrad called for Mr. John Sidote.

Ginny bowed her head as her accuser strolled up the center aisle.

NINE

"I Struck Her, But I Never Beat Her"

JOHN Sidote's hands were clasped in front of him as if he were coming forward to receive communion. Perhaps he was simply used to wearing handcuffs. He rolled on the balls of his feet in a strut of a walk, and short and stocky, he wore his slightly long, graying dark hair combed back from his forehead and tucked behind his ears. His extended sideburns and full moustache were well trimmed. A long, ropy scar accentuated his high forehead and receding hairline. Although the blue blazer, gray slacks, light blue shirt, and red-striped tie were eminently respectable, the jurors seemed suspicious, especially the men, who exchanged sidelong glances as Sidote took the stand.

Ginny kept her head lowered until he was sworn in, then she looked up at him. He ventured not even a glance in her direction, and concentrated only on Gordon Konrad as he answered the perfunctory opening questions: He was forty-five; he'd been twenty-seven in 1965; he'd finished high school, worked in a truck body shop until he had a car accident, went into the marines in 1957, and was honorably discharged in 1960. He'd lived in California for a few months, then returned to Wappingers Falls where his parents lived, about twelve miles from New Paltz. As if he felt compelled to explain the scar on his forehead, he added that on the day he returned to New York he'd suffered mulitple lacerations and a concussion in another car accident.

Jack Sidote was a talker, incapable of replying without elaborating on one irrelevant fact with three or four more. If Konrad offered too few details, Sidote provided too many. After explaining that he'd been the bartender in the three-hundred-seat Driftwood Lounge nightclub at the Villa Lipani, he began to breathe heavily, his deep, gravelly voice faltering and breaking: In 1965, "Virginia Galluzzo" had come into the bar with a group of women. He was tending bar, and he asked a friend who she was. After that she occasionally came in by herself, they finally met, and they began dating "on and off." He was "still married and living with his wife," but he knew Virginia had had an annulment, when, as Konrad put it, their "relationship became more than casual dating."

"We had a tremendous physical attraction to each other," he volunteered. Always referring to Foat as "Virginia," "the defendant," or "Mrs. Foat," he described himself as "being drawn more and more" to her.

> Konrad: In the fall of 1965, did you decide to leave New York?
> Sidote: Yes. I was having trouble at work.

Once more the judge instructed him just to answer the question.

Konrad now asked, "Why?" and Sidote elaborated: "The attraction I had for Virginia was becoming insurmountable." He saw his life much as Ginny saw her own, but in his version, he'd been the passive partner, swept away by her and unable to control what was happening. And like Ginny, he recited social values and family attitudes to explain himself: They together (not he alone) had decided to leave the area to "save my family the disgrace of divorce."

Bozydaj was brought along to help with the driving, but Sidote insisted that he had discussed this with her. In October 1965 they left—"me, Mrs. Foat, and Bozydaj"—and went to Florida because of a man he'd met at the Villa Lipani "in the computer field" who'd talked about jobs in his hometown of Cocoa Beach, Florida. What in 1965 qualified Sidote for a job in computers seemed dubious, but Konrad didn't ask him to explain.

After stopping in Newburgh, New York, because "Virginia said she knew someone there who could loan us money" (this was the "message" Reed had said she hadn't read—"he told her to get some money and she did"), they went to New Jersey "to see some men who owed me money." Then they drove to Florida, where "the fellow [from IBM] wasn't listed so I made no contact."

Without being asked, he volunteered an explanation for his temper tantrum in Florida. "I had been drinking, and . . . I realized what I had done. I called my parents, I called Mr. Lipani also. It was bad. There were a lot of harsh words over the phone. Mr. Lipani didn't want me to leave. We'd had arguments about my relationship with Virginia before."

He then described moving on to Baton Rouge, where they'd met the man who introduced them to Happy Ditcharo, a bar owner in New Orleans.

"I was hired to keep an eye on the job," he said.

"You mean a bouncer type?" Konrad clarified.

"I guess that's how it would be termed," said Sidote, adding, "Virginia was hired as a barmaid and go-go dancer."

At this Ginny, Kay, Jan, and Annabelle all shook their heads in unison, but Sidote's eyes only flickered as he noticed the reaction but didn't look in Ginny's direction.

Since they were paid only ten dollars each per night, after two weeks in New Orleans, "we were short of funds, ends just weren't meeting, and we'd exhausted everything else," he said. "Virginia and I talked about the possibility of rolling a man to get sufficient funds to leave the area."

Konrad asked what he meant by "rolling."

"You take someone by some means to an area and beat him and steal his money," he said. But when describing that evening, he made the woman's participation central: "Virginia would be dressed up and on a weekend night would go into one of the bars in the Bourbon Street area and lure an individual to leave with her and by any means possible to go with her into the car. At that time she was supposed to drive to a remote area somewhere. I would be concealed in the car, and then she'd get the individual out of the car, and I would come out of the trunk and strike the individual and take the money and leave."

Konrad asked him what actually happened.

"We executed that plan."

Unaware of his macabre pun, he began to sob and gasp and stammer as he described the night of November 20: He had climbed into the car's trunk as soon as he saw "Virginia come down the street with a gentleman." He used a piece of wire wrapped in cloth to hold the trunk open and keep it from rattling, and during the drive the car "must have struck a bump or a hole in the road, and the trunk slammed shut. It seemed like an interminable time," he said, "perhaps a half hour or forty-five minutes," and he was having trouble breathing because "I'd exhausted the air supply." After the car came to a stop, he said he heard voices near the trunk, then "the trunk came open," and he stepped out: ". . . there was a man before me, and I started struggling with him. I guess I had a tire iron in my hand, and I apparently made a motion to strike him, and he grabbed my arm and I grabbed his arm and we were struggling . . . I remember him yelling 'Madre Dios' [sic] or something like that. And we were locked like that, and he was shorter than I was but he was a very strong man, he was very, very powerful."

Then he heard a scream, he said: " 'He knows who I am, he knows who I am. You've got to kill him.' "

Tears were running down Sidote's face, but he kept his hands clasped in his lap as he explained that he couldn't break the man's hold, and he panicked and said, " 'You've got to help me, you've gotta do something.' " Then: ". . . there was a blur, it came from the side, from like over my right shoulder . . . or from my right side." He heard a grunt, and the pressure was released on his wrists. "And then I struck the man also. . . . I don't recall how many blows. . . . The man fell to the ground."

Sidote explained that he'd fallen to his knees and was gasping for breath until Virginia pulled at his jacket, gestured toward the ditch, and said, " 'We've got to put the man in here.' " They then dragged the body, he said, and together they placed the man in the ditch.

"The two of you?" Konrad confirmed.

"Yes," said Sidote. But then he turned to the passive construction as if to avoid identifying who did what: "The wallet was taken, that was all," and "after removing the wallet, we got in the car and Virginia drove us back to the hotel."

As Sidote recounted the part of the story to which Wasyl Bozydaj had already testified, the jurors exchanged knowing looks, some of them nudging each other when the statements of the two men didn't agree at several points. According to Sidote, since he was filthy, "Virginia went up to the room" alone to get clean clothes, then came back down and drove around the corner, where he changed his pants. Then they returned to the front of the hotel, and Bozydaj came down.

Sidote added that Bozydaj had known nothing "about what was being planned," but they had told him to stay home from work that night. They gave him money and told him to leave town right away, because they didn't want the car seen. While Bozydaj had said that Ginny and Jack came in together to the hotel room at about 11 or 12, Sidote placed their conversation in front of the hotel at about 9:30. Then, he said, Bozydaj left and he and Virginia went upstairs and "extracted the money," $1,400 and "some foreign currency" that "was later exchanged for thirty-seven dollars."

Again, there was the confusion of their meeting place in Texas. "I believe it was Houston," Sidote said. "It may have been Dallas." That morning Bozydaj had said he believed it was Houston; in his 1977 testimony in a Nevada court he'd said "Houston or Dallas." Sidote's March 1977 statement had said only Dallas.

But the most glaring inconsistency was Sidote's testimony about the missing witness. "Virginia took a plane out to Houston that night," he said. He drank most of the night at a bar and then flew to Houston the next morning, where Wasyl met them at the airport. They now had "a new member of the party," he said, "a fellow Wasyl had met who'd expressed a desire to go to Carson City," who had driven with Wasyl from New Orleans (not, as Bozydaj had testified, a friend of Sidote's who'd flown with him to Houston).

Once again Sidote was sobbing about drinking "very, very much" as Konrad led him through his account of their trip to Nevada, then on to California, their marriage, their purchase of the No Regrets bar, and finally the incident that sent him to prison in California. Suddenly Sidote was no longer weeping as he told his convoluted tale of shooting the Samoan teenager. Like his letter to the parole board, it was full of illogic and self-justification, and his lack of remorse was in striking contrast to his tears and grief over the death of Moises Chayo. Konrad let him ramble on to explain how he's shot a bullet in the air to get the car to stop. "The ballistics expert said," he began, but Glass objected, fortunately for the prosecutors, although the jury had already seen the strange machinations of the man's mind.

Finally Konrad asked Sidote about the event that resulted in his separation from Virginia in 1970. "During the period of time in 1970 that I was on work release," he said, "I was in the habit of stopping by the apartment and then proceeding on to work. . . . Our relationship was strained at that point," because "incidents occurred while I was in prison that led to tension in our relationship." Without asking about the nature of these "incidents," Konrad asked Sidote to describe their last fight.

"I went to the apartment," he said. "Virginia and I had a very severe confrontation. It had become apparent to me that there was no future for us, but no reasons were ever stated why this was happening . . . I confronted her with what was happening, and it developed into a terrible scene. . . ." He paused, then prodded by Konrad, he said, ". . . I grabbed Virginia in the area of the throat and I started shaking her. We were both screaming at one another. It was a chaotic scene, and I was choking her. Suddenly I stopped and she was coherent. . . . I pushed her and she slumped to the floor and I just thought, 'After all this, it's not worth it,' and I left."

It wasn't quite the beating Reed had described, but bad enough, and Konrad had wanted to get it out of the way. Indeed, now he asked Sidote to remind the jury that it was Ginny who later phoned him, "on two separate occasions," once when he had moved in with a girlfriend, and Ginny had said, "It didn't take you long to find a new girlfriend, did it?" The second time occurred when he was back in New York in 1973, "At six A.M. New York time. My mom answered the phone and said it was for me. It was Virginia. She said—"

Konrad stopped him, abruptly asking why had he gone to the police in 1977 and voluntarily confessed to two crimes, one in Louisiana, the other in Nevada?

"I felt I had to," Sidote said. "My life during the twelve-year period, 1965 to 1977 . . . became pure hell. I had become an alcoholic. I couldn't function normally. . . . The guilt from my participation and the fear and the self-hatred . . . had just consumed me. In some way I had to try to absolve my guilt."

Even though it might mean spending the rest of his life in jail? Konrad asked.

"It didn't matter compared to the life I had been leading." Once again he was sobbing.

Judge Burns watched him closely, and he seemed to find the man's tearful rambling distasteful. When Konrad asked, "Were you extradited to either state?" Sidote took a deep breath as if to begin a new narrative. The judge interrupted, his voice filled with impatience: "The answer is 'Yes, I was.'"

Sidote repeated the answer, but added, "to Nevada," and went on to say he pleaded guilty and received ten years for manslaughter, fifteen years for robbery, but stressed it was a consecutive sentence. Still, he insisted that the twenty-five-year sentence was not the reason he'd refused to testify against "Mrs. Foat" in 1977. Instead, he'd simply realized, "I didn't want to harm her. . . . I felt that justice had been served, I was willing to take my sentence and let the incident drop."

Finally he was asked to explain that he was once again in jail because he'd been arrested for drunk driving in January 1983, and "as a consequence my parole was revoked." But this hardly suggested how Ginny Foat had come to be arrested in 1983, since it was true, as Sidote now said, he had done nothing to bring the charges against her at that time. Konrad chose not to continue and only asked Sidote to confirm that he had requested and received immunity.

After an hour and fifteen minutes, Konrad tendered the witness. It seemed an abbreviated questioning of the man on whose testimony the State had built its entire case.

After a fifteen-minute recess, Bob Glass began his cross-examination. Standing at the defense table, he was forcing Sidote to make a concerted effort not to look at Ginny.

"In 1970, Ginny left you, or you left Ginny?" Glass asked.

"I walked out of the apartment," Sidote said.

"In 1977 you told police you'd killed some people and then you told the story about Virginia?" Glass went on.

"Vir—"

Now Glass interrupted angrily: "All the accusations you made are against *Virginia*, not against Ginny!"

Judge Burns sustained Konrad's immediate objection. Glass persisted: "In fact *Virginia* is a figment of your imagination."

Another sustained objection, but Glass again wanted to alert the jurors. "In fact you haven't looked at Ginny," he shouted, Konrad's sustained objection too late to counter the effect on the jury.

During the next half hour Glass focused on the discrepancies between Sidote's account of the crime today and his prior statements, as well as the differences in Bozydaj's and Sidote's testimonies. His voice was filled with contempt as he addressed him as "Jack" and turned his words against him. Asked why Bozydaj had not been at work that night, Sidote explained they'd told him to stay home that night, that they'd planned it that way. But in his nervousness and his way with words, he replied, "it was preordained."

"Preordained?" Glass said. "By God?"

Sidote rolled his eyes and shook his head, as if confused and embarrassed by the laughter in the courtroom.

The defense now introduced into evidence the two immunity agreements, the first dated January 14, 1983, and signed by Tom Porteous, the second dated September 16, 1983, and signed by Mamoulides, thus reminding the jury that Sidote's testimony had to be consistent with Sidote's March 16 statement. Then he pointed out that on page 10 of the earlier statement, Sidote claimed to have flown to "Dallas," not "Houston," nor to "Houston or Dallas."

Sidote: It was Dallas or Houston, I don't remember.

Glass: Does Dallas or Houston change? Does the truth change over the course of six years?

With Konrad's sustained objection, Glass rephrased the question: "Does *your* truth change over the course of six years?"

Konrad now fairly exploded: Glass was "speechifying" and "argumentative," he contended. The objection was sustained but the defense attorney kept at it: Wasn't it true that he and Ginny had gone upstairs at the hotel and argued (as Bozydaj had also testified)? Wasn't it true that the fourth person was Sidote's friend and flew with him to Houston or Dallas?

No, Sidote insisted, none of that was true.

"You're making it up, aren't you?" Glass lashed out, earning a sustained objection. But he continued to push at the discrepancies in Sidote's various statements.

"Do you ever talk to yourself?" he suddenly asked, " 'Jack, stop drinking. . . . Jack, don't do that . . .' "

It was possible, he said, that he talked to himself about his drinking. But no one had ever told him that he talked to himself, even when he was, as Glass put it, "wrecked on alcohol."

"You're really a bad alcoholic, aren't you?" Glass sneered.

"At times," said Sidote with a sigh.

"For twenty years?"

"No, that's false," Sidote flared.

Glass was peppering him with disjointed questions and hostile accusations in order to provoke an outburst. But Sidote remained unflappable (corridor rumor had it that heavy doses of Valium were suppressing his volatile temper).

Once again Glass went back to highlighting the discrepancies between his and Bozydaj's testimony about the night of the alleged crime.

Glass: The plan required her to dress up and put on a fancy dress?
Sidote: Yes.
Glass: High heels?
Sidote: I don't recall.
Glass: The plan required her to get dressed up. She couldn't lure a man if she were wearing a plain blouse and slacks?
Sidote: I don't remember. That would be making an assumption.

Perhaps he really didn't remember. Perhaps because of Glass's emphasis on blouse and slacks, he realized that Bozydaj must have testified to that, and he now did a fast shuffle; one might not remember how a woman was dressed on a night eighteen years ago. But the inconsistency seemed to have an effect on the jury.

Glass now concentrated on the difference between Sidote's 1977 description of the scene of the crime as near a warehouse, "a rough, stony, flat area," with no mention of a ditch, Glass pointed out.

"Perhaps in that statement I didn't," said Sidote.

Wasn't he shown the photographs of the grass, weeds, and ditches in the area, Glass asked, and didn't he change his story accordingly?

Yes, he'd looked at pictures, but he'd said only that it was possibly the scene of the crime, not that it was a memory. His 1977 description was his recollection of where the striking occurred, not where they'd dragged the body, he insisted.

Sidote's 1977 description of his victim was equally at odds with Chayo's actual appearance: "To the best of my recollection he had dark hair, dark features, and later on [Ginny] told me that the guy was from South America"; he was "about fifty years old, stood about five foot seven," and was "very portly, very heavily built . . . about two hundred and ten or so, very stout."

The police report and the son had indicated that Moises Chayo was sixty-two years old, six feet tall, weighed about 170 pounds and, most important, was bald with a fringe of gray hair.

Sidote seemed unaware of this, and Glass now set him up. Hadn't he said in 1977 that "the guy had dark hair and was dark-complected?" Sidote agreed, but then hedged, "Under the conditions that prevailed at the time, he appeared to be dark."

Glass now moved to within two feet of Sidote and, leaning forward, asked if he'd heard the victim say, "Madre Dios."

Sidote: Something to that effect.
Glass: This *Jewish* man was saying "Madre Dios"?

Glass turned with an air of triumph as Sidote lamely added, "It appeared to be that."

It was unclear whether the jury would understand Glass's insinuation that Sidote either had robbed and beaten another South American who cried "Madre de Dios" or had embellished his story to fit what he'd heard about Chayo. But Foat and her supporters in the front pews were jubilant. Sidote had fallen into the trap. No Jewish man would have used that expression, they whispered conspiratorially to the reporters behind them.

Buoyed by his victory, Glass railed at Sidote: "You never called her Virginia until you made that statement in 1977. Then you had to change her name to Virginia because your accusations were about someone who was a figment of your imagination. From the moment you walked into this courtroom you haven't looked at her. You *can't* look at her, can you?"

Despite two sustained objections, Glass had persisted. The emotional pitch was high, and Judge Burns, seemingly irritated at Glass's defiance of his rulings, called a fifteen-minute recess.

It was already after five when Sidote took the stand again and admitted "there may be a discrepancy" in his January 1977 statement about the time of their return to the hotel. He asked to see the statement and read it, the pages trembling in his hands. "The fact that Ginny flew out that night leads me to believe that it would have had to have been before eleven P.M.," he conceded finally.

Now Glass was taunting him with his jailhouse language. Sidote had said he had been "incarcerated," and Glass repeated, "Incarcerated?"

Not hearing the sarcasm, he replied: "Yes, sir, I was incarcerated in Chino . . ."

Glass: So you learned the ropes?
Sidote: Anyone in prison has to adjust.

Glass wanted to show that Sidote was jailhouse-smart and asked him why he'd had to serve only four years and eight months of a twenty-five-year sentence in Nevada. Sidote cited his various jobs and good behavior, his "No write-ups," but Glass continued to taunt him. No, Sidote said, it was "people who worked their butts off," "people who accomplished what I had," who got out early, not people who, as Glass suggested, "knew how to work the rules," or "play the system." Weren't the immunity agreements another example of Sidote's ability to "play the system"? he continued, and won the round when Sidote conceded that of course he wanted to get out of jail.

Sidote admitted he'd been angry at Konrad the previous August when his Nevada parole request had been denied.

"I'd hoped for more cooperation than I got," he said, and yes, he had phoned Mr. Konrad and "expressed—you could call it displeasure."

"You yelled?"

"There were words exchanged," Sidote hedged. "Yes, all right," he yielded, he had filed with the court a petition claiming that DA Porteous had "coerced and intimidated" him. (Sidote's "Petition for a Writ of Habeas Corpus" was entered as Defense Exhibit 4.) Now Glass pointed out the revisions in Sidote's second immunity agreement of September 16, 1983, rewritten when Mamoulides, Konrad, and Porteous had come to visit him. Glass now accused Sidote of holding out for a better agreement; Sidote argued that his lawyers (Tom Perkins and Laura Fitzsimmons) were only protecting his right to raise legal issues later, including his right to a speedy trial.

With Sidote's rambling about legal matters, the jury had been snoozing. But now they looked alive as Glass went to the heart of the matter. Yes, Sidote said, Mr. Mamoulides had spoken to the parole board the very day the second immunity agreement was signed and had discussed transferring Sidote's parole to Louisiana.

Wasn't the Nevada parole board told that there would be no problem with the Louisiana parole board because the DA had influence? Glass asked. The insinuation outraged Mamoulides, but Sidote didn't understand the implication.

"I don't recall that," he said. "Only that they would assist me in transferring, because my life would be in jeopardy after testifying."

"Your life?" Glass shouted. "Ginny never beat you! You beat her!"

Konrad's objection was sustained. Sidote, however, hadn't flinched. If anyone was succumbing to the pressure, it was Glass. And Ginny, too. She was slumped in her chair and shaking her head as Sidote repeated calmly that his life would be in danger because of testifying. He didn't say from whom, although in an interview he'd said he feared that NOW had a lot of powerful contacts. His fear of feminists seemed paranoid; on the other hand, snitches are always vulnerable in prison.

After letting Sidote cheerfully talk about a friend in prison who told him about "off-shore catering" jobs in Louisiana, Glass again became aggressive, accusing him of agreeing "to lie" to get a better deal from the DAs.

Sidote: I'd hoped to get help from them, but nothing that I
         would get from the DA would make me lie.
Glass: When do you lie?

"That question is like asking someone, 'When did you stop beating your wife?' " Konrad objected. An unfortunate example, it provoked muffled laughter and someone in the defense pews quipped, "He still hasn't," as Burns sustained the objection.

Glass: Do you lie to save your own skin?
Sidote: No.
Glass: Didn't you lie when you told about what happened with
         the eighteen-year-old Samoan?
Sidote: Anytime I've been on the stand, I've told the truth.
Glass: You've only been on trial once, in California.
Sidote: I consider this a trial.
Glass: [with indignation] Your trial?
Sidote: The way you're approaching it, it is.

He wasn't far wrong. There were two defendants in this courtroom. In order to find Foat innocent, the jury had to find Sidote guilty of bad character. Yet Sidote was trying to retain a shred of dignity, even when Glass began to question him about his alcoholism. He admitted his drinking problem, and when asked if he was an alcoholic in 1968, he replied that it was hard to define an alcoholic, but he had "drunk a lot on and off for two or three years." (Ginny was once more avidly involved, passing notes and whispering to Reed.)

Wasn't there an alcohol problem in his family? Glass now asked. Hadn't his father been an alcoholic?

"That's not true," shouted Sidote, for the first time losing his composure. Glass could call him names, and he'd take it. But besmirch his dead father's reputation and he flared, even though his presentencing report in Nevada had mentioned his father's drinking problem.

After another fifteen-minute recess, Glass continued to berate Sidote for his "alcoholism." Konrad objected to this line of questioning as irrelevant to 1965, but Judge Burns overruled him, much to the relief of the defense. Admitting that in his own mind he was an alcoholic in 1974, Sidote gave what sounded like the rote Alcoholics Anonymous definition of an alcoholic: "Once you come to realize you're an alcoholic, you're one the rest of your life even though you're sober."

Glass: Did you ever have hallucinations?
Sidote: It happened to me once that I can relate to.
Glass: 1977?

Everyone laughed at Glass's reference to his 1977 confessions. Although Sidote was flushed with anger, he said calmly, "No, it was in 1974 in New York. But I'd like to explain what brought it on."

"Sure," replied Glass, with a sarcastic edge, as if to say, "Sure, go ahead, hang yourself."

Sidote detailed his attempts to quit drinking at home, his hallucinations when he was "coming down" and taking tranquilizers, his stays in detox clinics where, yes, he'd had DTs. He had also joined AA, he added, then recited what seemed an AA speech: "There are fifty million alcoholics. Like cigarettes, even though they'll kill you, you don't stop."

Porteous sat with his usual lighted cigarette as Konrad objected.

Judge Burns called for the "next question," casting a mild glance in Porteous's direction as Glass asked if Sidote had learned at the VA hospital treatment center that alcoholics make up excuses.

Sidote: They make up excuses for their drinking.
Glass: For *their* failure?
Sidote: The only answer I can give to that is that alcohol is the excuse for the failure.
Glass: Don't alcoholics make up alibis?
Sidote: I don't know what you're referring to.
Glass: Isn't there a pattern of blaming your failure and your alcoholism on other people?
Sidote: [loudly and emphatically] No.

Glass kept hammering away at his alcoholism until he made his point: Wasn't he drinking at the time of his 1977 confession to the New York State Police?

Yes, he was, said Sidote. "But not to the point where I didn't know what I was doing."

Glass: You'd just gotten out of the VA hospital [one of several treatments Sidote had admitted undergoing]?
Sidote: Yes.
Glass: And you went right back to being a drunk?

Sidote bridled, then drew himself up in his chair. "Sir, I am an alcoholic." His response was not without dignity, and although it was an AA member's standard statement, it still had some force in the face of the defense's attempts to diminish him.

Whispers and nudges in the defense pew accompanied the next question.

"If records from the VA hospital show how you were during the period preceding the 1977 statements, wouldn't that information be of help to you?"

Sidote said that he thought so, although Konrad was already on his feet objecting that a witness could not rule on the admissibility of evidence.

Glass sprung his surprise anyway. Addressing Sidote directly, he announced, "We have subpoenaed those records from the VA hospital, and we have a lawyer and a custodian of those records here with them. The only way we can have those records released is if you give your permission."

A young woman had come to the defense table with a box of files.

Sidote looked stunned as Konrad roared, "Remove the jury."

Sidote wanted to step down to examine the records and make his decision. Glass declared that Sidote should not be counseled by the DA.

"Are you ordering me not to speak to John Sidote?" Konrad asked indignantly.

"I'm not ordering you to do anything," Judge Burns interrupted their exchange. But even as Konrad and Sidote left the room, Glass shouted, "I object if any advice is given by the DA."

The real mystery was why the prosecutors were surprised that the defense was trying to introduce these records or hadn't themselves subpoenaed them to show that the 1977 confessions were not the product of an alcoholic fantasy.

As it turned out, however, the VA hospital records themselves were not a surprise. "It was just that they made it such a theatrical presentation," said Porteous later. "They were trying to get them in without getting them in. We'd seen the records, we knew what was in them. The suicide attempt was, of course, there, but we weren't going to bring it out."

It was left to Glass to disclose Sidote's "self-destructiveness" when, not surprisingly, Judge Burns ruled the records inadmissible under any circumstances.

Hadn't he thought of suicide before 1977? Glass asked Sidote.

Sidote: My self-worth was then very low. I can't remember a specific incident when I contemplated suicide.

Glass: In 1976 or 1977, didn't you try to commit suicide with a gas stove?

Sidote: I don't think it was a suicide. It was a drafty apartment. The window was open, there was a screen door. It didn't work.

He admitted he'd turned on the gas, blown out the light, and stayed in the room until somebody walked in. "But I don't believe it was a sincere suicide attempt," he hedged again.

Hadn't Sidote confessed to the crimes in 1977 because jail was better than dying? Glass insisted.

"Jail was not the reference for this feeble attempt at suicide," Sidote replied awkwardly, adding even more clumsily: "From 1965 to 1977, the frame of reference, any reference to self-destruction was because of what I had been involved in during that time. It was a period of low self-worth."

Glass then asked, "Do you think it was a period of high self-worth for Ginny Foat?"

Sidote replied, "No," to the rhetorical question. In point of fact, though, the period between 1970 and 1977 must have been a period of "high" self-worth for Ginny Foat compared to Sidote's downhill slide. She was married to Ray Foat, ran a successful catering business, lived a well-off suburban life, and joined the Soroptimists and NOW. If anyone had succumbed to social pressures and a sense of failure, it was Sidote. But Glass had implied that Sidote was to be blamed for Foat's "low self-worth," and that somehow her sense of self was more important than his. The scales of justice were weighted with self-esteem as if this were the moral currency by which to decide guilt or innocence.

Glass now reminded Sidote of his 1977 description of Ginny in which he'd said she was "beautiful," "statuesque," with "full sensuous lips, an aquiline nose," "a classic beauty."

Glass: Is that the way you thought of her in 1977 when you walked into the police station?

Sidote: I've never changed the way I thought of her features.

Ginny shut her eyes and put her hand to her forehead, as if Sidote's words were a physical violation.

Having suggested Sidote's "obsession" with his ex-wife, Glass was once again hammering away at him with accusations. But Sidote still insisted that he'd gone to the police in 1977 only to "purge" himself, the word allowing Glass to mock him further. Was he raised a Catholic? he asked.

Yes, Sidote said.

"Aren't there a lot of Catholic churches in New Paltz and a bunch of priests?"

The question was put so snidely as to be offensive, especially to the Catholics on the jury. His contempt for Sidote had made him seem sarcastic.

"Weren't there priests to purge your soul?"

Sidote: It's been done.
Glass: So if you wanted to *purge* your soul, why go to the police station, not to a priest?

Konrad's immediate objection was sustained, but Glass looked pleased with the dramatic note on which he'd been able to end this arduous day. Yet it seemed a low point, evoking more hostility for him than for Sidote. Most of the jurors had started out disliking Sidote. But watching a man humiliated, scorned and practically spat upon, their hate might become mixed with pity. What Glass didn't seem to realize was that the jury could find Ginny innocent without watching the defense draw and quarter a witness, much less a man who was already down and out. For all the feminist talk about victimization, the trial recessed late Friday evening with Sidote seeming the more battered and weak and pitiful partner.

Saturday's session began at 12:30 in the afternoon with Glass again trying to provoke Sidote. His argumentative questions and angry exchanges with Konrad over his objections (most of which were sustained) required the frequent removal of the jurors. They were beginning to look tired and annoyed as Glass taunted Sidote about "running out on your car loan cosigned by John Lipani," the man who'd "trusted you almost like a son," or flying "into a rage when the Florida job fell through." Yet Sidote managed to remain calm. No, he was only "emotionally upset" in Florida after his phone call to his parents; no, he hadn't "put it all on Virginia" in his March 1977 statement, as Glass insisted. Indeed, in his confession Sidote had said that Virginia struck the first blow, but admitted he had a tire iron as well and had "tried to knock the guy down." Still, while he might understate his role in the murder, he was neither denying it nor flying off the handle.

The men who were losing their tempers today were Konrad and Glass as they argued the admissibility of Sidote's various statements in police and court records. During these heated exchanges, with the jury hurried from the room, Sidote sat back in his chair and watched Glass and Konrad as if he were at a tennis match.

With Judge Burns ruling that the police report of Sidote's first oral confession was inadmissible, Glass resumed his questioning. He asked Sidote about the breaking-and-entering charge of 1974. It was a result, Sidote said, of an alcoholic blackout when he'd tried to steal money from Mrs. Lipani. Like his ex-wife, Sidote seemed to enjoy playing attorney; in great detail he explained how his breaking-and-entering case had been on appeal from 1974 to 1977 because he was fighting a longer sentence "as a predicate" felon. This was what Glass seemed to be looking for: Hadn't Sidote made his first confession to the police on January 22 because he was going to be sentenced for the breaking-and-entering charge on January 26?

The logic of this seemed flimsy—Why confess to two robbery-murders, which would necessarily bring a longer sentence, to avoid a breaking-and-entering sentence? Sidote held firm, and while flushed and sometimes weeping, he repeatedly denied confessing to get a better deal.

Finally, Glass wheeled on him. "Who was the fourth guy who flew with you to Dallas or Houston?"

"I don't remember," Sidote replied, not denying that the fourth guy *flew with him.* Glass glanced at the jury with a smile.

He'd been trumpeting these allegations across the country, from coast to coast? Glass now contended.

Sidote said he had given stories to *Rolling Stone,* to West Coast and Chicago reporters, and to *The Village Voice.* But Glass asked, "Weren't the reporters all women?" hinting at some sexual innuendo behind the fact that women reporters, as Sidote said, "were the ones who called." It seemed that Glass had forgotten that it was Ginny the NOW leader, not Jack the charmer, who made it more likely that women reporters and writers were covering the story.

Glass went on to accuse Sidote of giving interviews to make himself "look bigger," to "feel good," despite repeated objections from the State. Finally, Judge Burns ruled that he would allow him questions only about possible financial benefits from such interviews.

Yes, Sidote admitted, he'd written to *Playboy* to try to sell his story.

Glass: It's true, Mr. Sidote, that you have been in ongoing negotiations with *Penthouse* magazine for your story for the past six months?

Sidote: The negotiations were completed.
Glass: Couldn't you work it out?
Sidote: *Penthouse* purchased it from me.
Glass: For how much?
Sidote: Three thousand dollars for an article on myself and Ginny Foat.

Ginny raised her hand to hide her face in a gesture of shock and dismay and turned away in disgust as gasps filled the courtroom. But surely she and her lawyers had heard about the *Penthouse* interview, and this was a show of righteous feminist indignation. More, the defense wanted to suggest to the jury how appalling it was that Sidote should sell "his side of the story," even though it was common knowledge that Ginny's ghostwriter, Laura Foreman, was in the courtroom every day and that both Peter Skolnik, her literary agent, and Marvin Minoff, the TV producer who'd bought the rights to her story, would soon be arriving to hear Ginny's testimony. Since the prosecutors were either unaware of this fact or chose not to bring it to the jury's attention, the defense could enjoy the holier-than-thou attitude implicit in Glass's next question: Didn't Sidote tell *The Village Voice* that his story was "deep enough, explosive enough, and passionate enough to be a best seller"?

The spectators laughed, happy to join Glass's mockery. Ginny was staring at Sidote with disdain. The irony, of course, was that neither Ginny nor Jack would have a story to sell without the other.

Glass now returned to Sidote's alleged abuse, as if his attempt to sell "his side of the story" had been yet another example of his brutality. Hadn't he beaten Ginny during their five years together? Konrad's objection forced Glass to be more specific.

"Did you ever beat her before you left New York?"

Sidote said, "No, sir."

In Florida? In Louisiana? Glass continued. No, twice more. Then: "In Hermosa Beach?"

"No, I never beat Virginia Foat. I struck her, but I never beat her."

Despite outraged mutterings and indignant laughter among the spectators and shakes of the head among the jurors, Sidote tried to explain. He'd struck her only three times: once on the head with a Scrabble board; once he'd pushed her face into a wall; and finally during their last fight.

Hadn't his mind snapped? Glass asked.

No, Sidote said. He'd just realized that he didn't want to harm her any further. So he left.

Hadn't he almost killed her in 1970, didn't he leave her close to death?

"She got on a plane that night," Sidote replied.

"You threatened to say that the killings you had committed, you'd put on her if she left you?"

Sidote was sobbing again: "I don't recall that, sir."

"She's not the only woman you've beaten, is she?" Glass shouted.

He replied, "The only other woman I have ever touched" was Marie Lipani. He'd broken into her house, he said, but that was because he'd suffered an alcoholic blackout. Still, he wouldn't allow Glass to say he'd "attacked" her. "I don't know what you mean by 'attacked.' I forced Mrs. Lipani in an attempt to get money. I know that later she had a scratch on her face."

"Scratch on her face!" shouted Glass. "I show you a photograph of her—"

With Konrad's furious objection, the jury was quickly sent out. Of course the photograph was disallowed, but the jurors had already seen black-and-blue eyes and swollen features and were aware of Sidote's potential for violence when drunk.

Glass and Konrad were sniping at each other again as Glass became even more argumentative, repeatedly accusing Sidote of harboring thoughts of revenge and having alcoholic reveries about Ginny.

Sidote said no, but then, weeping, he began to answer Glass's repeated accusations with "I don't recall." He didn't recall having periods of hate for her between 1970 and 1977, and when asked, "Didn't you write a letter to her parents saying you'd get her if it was the last thing you ever did?" his "I don't recall" seemed more an admission than a denial.

Glass left this subject quickly—the letter no longer existed—and instead quoted again from the March 16, 1977, statement in which Sidote had voluntarily brought up the motive of revenge in order to deny it. " 'At first I thought it was . . . to get back at Virginia for what happened when I was in prison,' " Glass read aloud, " 'but the more I think about it, the more I realize I had to do it, not because of vengeance, but for higher, you know. I had to bare myself.' "

Sidote stood by his statement, despite Glass's argument that this was the one time he'd told the truth, that vengeance had indeed been his motivation.

"Weren't you a big man when you ran away with Virginia Foat?" Glass now asked. "Weren't you an important bartender? Didn't you know how to treat a woman right?" Konrad's objections were sustained, even as Sidote repeatedly answered no. Yet Glass's sarcastic remarks undercut Reed's opening argument. The defense was building its case on the conventionality of the love affair and Ginny's desire to "stand by her man." But with Glass demeaning Sidote, mocking "the important bartender," the jury might suspect more questionable motives for her failure to leave him.

Didn't Sidote blame Ginny because in his mind he'd done it to get money for her? Glass then asked.

"I blame myself for all the problems I have had in my life," Sidote announced.

Glass paused. He walked behind Ginny and placed his hands on her shoulders.

"John Sidote," he intoned, "you look at Virginia Foat. You look at Ginny Foat and tell her that she did what you say she did!"

Sidote's eyes only flickered in Glass's direction. Konrad objected. But before the judge could rule, Sidote replied, "Mr. Glass, I don't want to be here to testify to begin with. I feel badly enough I have to do this. I'm not following your instructions to look at Virginia Foat and tell her that this is the way it has to be."

Glass shouted, "You can't do it, can you?"

Sidote bowed his head and began to weep.

Reed hugged Ginny in triumph, as if he were sure that the strategy had convinced the jury that the man was a liar. Yet in this instance, Sidote's refusal seemed more an attempt to retain some self-control, his weeping more out of sorrow at having to testify than guilt for his lies. Indeed, as he left the stand, he clamped his jaw shut to try to stop his tremors, and later the news spread in the corridor that he spent the fifteen-minute recess in an office sobbing.

Court resumed at 2:50. Sidote was back on the stand for redirect but the next half hour was tedious, the attorneys arguing about the admissibility of another 1977 statement by Sidote. Finally, after much citing of legal precedents by both sides, Judge Burns ruled it admissible, and copies of the twenty-two-page document were handed to the jurors. A half hour later the documents were collected. (Louisiana court procedure required the jury to rely on its memory; no exhibits could be reexamined during its deliberation.) Now they were given Sidote's two immunity agreements. The jurors seemed pale and exhausted from the emotional afternoon, and the hour of reading was taking its toll as well.

Judge Burns, himself nodding off while watching the jurors slowly turn the pages, grew impatient. Once they were finished—and it wasn't even clear that all the jurors were through—he recessed the proceedings until Monday at nine in the morning.

By 8:30 Monday morning, Novermber 14, Ginny Foat was already in the courtroom, and the attorneys retired for a conference with Burns in his chambers. At two minutes past nine the court was called to order, a prompt beginning, as if Judge Burns wanted to hasten the trial after Saturday afternoon's torpor. He looked grim as he took his seat, called for the jury to be brought in, and nodded at Gordon Konrad to begin.

"Your Honor," Konrad intoned, "the State is not going to put Mr. Sidote back on the stand for any redirect. The State will rest its case at this time."

The courtroom was in turmoil, with reporters and the defense team scrambling over each other to get to the phones in the hallway. The jurors sat stunned and open-mouthed. What had happened to John Sidote?

No one could say. Nor would the DAs confirm the rumor that he'd broken down the day before and was unfit to take the stand again. Later, however, the prosecutors denied that Sidote had caved in on them. It was simply a tactical decision, they said, and they saw no reason to resubject him to yet another cross-examination. "What was he going to rebut?" said Porteous. "I'm never a strong advocate of rebuttal unless it's got some meat in it. All Sidote would have done is retell what he'd already told, and that's not rebuttal."

With the repeated exclamations of, "Is that all the State has?" the courtroom hallway was again filled with rumors. There was talk of other "big" witnesses to be brought in, rumors of Shelly Mandell and Elaine Lafferty having arrived at the last minute. (Danny Marcheano, Foat's partner in her catering business, had been scheduled to testify, too; later the prosecutors claimed that he'd reneged on what he'd told them during questioning in California. Upon his arrival in New Orleans, he told the DA he knew nothing more than what he'd read about the case in the newspapers, and the State lost another witness.)

But the major question was whether Ginny herself would take the stand. With the State's case seemingly so weak, with the jury less than impressed, it would seem, with Sidote's character and credibility, would she decide not to testify? That was certainly her right, but not her style, most of the reporters felt. Odds were running high among journalists, spectators, and even the prosecutors that she needed to tell her story. The more cynical said that she wanted the stage; the more compassionate said she must want to set the record straight after all that had been written about her.

Ginny herself seemed amazingly calm, and whatever decision she and her lawyers had made was, for the moment, her secret. She stood in the hallway smoking a cigarette and chatting with reporters. She wanted them to know "how supportive" the people of New Orleans were being. For example, she said, the evening before the trial began a local Marianite order of nuns had held a prayer service for her. "They sang, they said prayers, and it was so beautiful that I blubbered the whole hour. Then they anointed me with hot scented oil."

In fact, this order of nuns was known for its feminism; one of its members explained that they had not only removed all references to "God the father" from their prayers but worshiped only the Virgin Mary in their nonpatriarchal order. And yes, she said, they'd had a prayer service for Ginny and anointed her with scented oil. It was the writer Barbara Grizzuti Harrison who discovered what fragrance had been added to the oil: It was called White Shoulders.

When Ginny Foat took the stand, she seemed to surround herself with a similar aura of innocence.

TEN

The Birth
of the Passive Woman

THE defense first called several witnesses to buttress its presentation of Sidote as a vengeful, alcoholic psychotic. Dr. Thomas Smith, a thin, red-haired psychiatrist from San Francisco who had trained at Louisiana State University and interned in New Orleans, was an expert on alcoholism. His effectiveness on the jury was undermined, however, when he was asked to name a few of his publications. "Art Therapy and Alcoholism," he said. He paused, as if he'd drawn a blank, then blurted that he'd published an article about gay male alcholics.

The jury was tittering among themselves even as he made a few telling points: Yes, an alcoholic can harbor resentment for a lifetime, blame others for his failure, and will boast and lie. But once again his testimony became less than effective when Glass asked for an example of the way in which alcoholics come to believe that the lies they tell are actually the truth. The man fidgeted. "My mind's gone blank," he said, sighing loudly and repeating, "My mind's gone blank." During a brief cross-examination, Konrad forced Smith to admit that although an alcholic may blame somebody for something, he may also be telling the truth.

The defense then called Dr. Jack Levitt, the doctor who'd conducted the psychological examination of Sidote after the 1968 shooting of the Samoan teenager. An older man, he listed his credentials as a psychiatrist employed by the California Department of Corrections at Chino prison from 1967 to 1977, adding that he had been retired for six years. Although Konrad accepted him as an expert witness, he immediately objected to the defense's attempt to introduce the psychiatric report on Sidote as an exhibit. The jury was led from the room, and after a heated exchange between the lawyers at the bench, Judge Burns sustained the objection. Dr. Levitt left the stand, and while he freely distributed copies of his report in the hallway, the jury returned, puzzled by the doctor's disappearance. They could only suspect the worst, that a psychiatrist would call Sidote crazy, whereas in fact the report said only that he had suffered a schizophrenic episode (as distinct from the defense label of schizophrenic) and was not an inherently violent man: "It would be unlikely that he'd commit a similar offense in the future."

The head of central records of the sheriff's office was now called to present the missing-person's and investigation reports, the defense again highlighting the differences between Sidote's 1977 description of his victim and the scene of the crime and the actual appearance of Chayo and the police description of the locale of his body. After lunch, two witnesses were called to support, albeit obliquely, Foat's story that Sidote's reason for having to get out of town fast was that he'd cheated an important man at cards. The subtext of their testimony was that Chayo was more likely looking for a card game than a woman. With the DAs' cursory cross-examinations, coupled with Chayo's son's testimony, the defense had certainly raised the possibility of a card game as Sidote's lure, not Ginny.

The next two witnesses introduced the dominant theme of Ginny Foat's own story: John Sidote's beatings. First Clara Sparks took the stand. A woman in her late thirties, in 1970 she had been Ginny's roommate when they'd both worked as cocktail waitresses on the *Princess Louise,* and Reed asked her to describe what happened the day that Ginny went back to New York.

Suddenly Konrad objected. It was a little late for the prosecutors to claim that the 1970 fight was irrelevant to the 1965 crime, and Judge Burns overruled him, accepting Reed's argument that he should be allowed to show Sidote's pattern of brutalizing and threatening Ginny, which "he began in 1965 and has continued until today."

With tears in her voice, Clara said that day she heard Ginny in her room choking and moaning, gasping for breath, and crying for help. She said she'd heard those sounds before when Jack Sidote was in the house. This time she went up to Ginny's bedroom and saw Jack Sidote leaning over her and choking her.

Then, she said, "he came towards me, and he was yelling . . . and screaming at me . . . 'I'm going to kill her, I'm going to get even with her if she leaves me.' " He had a crazy look in his eye, she remembered, but she'd said nothing to him, since "when somebody's in a crazy rage like that, you can't."

After Sidote left, she saw Ginny "partly on the floor and partly on the bed, and her face and her eye was all swollen and her lip was all puffy and blood was draining from it, and she had her hand around her neck and she was moaning and gasping for breath." That's when she decided, Clara said, to put Ginny on a plane home to her mother and "safe . . . away from Jack." She called her then boyfriend, John Boyd, and asked him to help.

This was not an isolated incident, Clara testified. Whenever Jack was in the house, she'd hear gagging and vomiting sounds coming from Ginny's bedroom. She never assisted Ginny when Jack was there, but when he left she would help her "finish being sick, and we would brush away the loose strands of hair that were . . . coming out in gobs." Yes, there were days that Ginny was unable to work because of black eyes and bruised arms resulting from Jack's being home on weekend passes or even from Ginny's prison visits. With no objection that she was drawing a conclusion, she also recalled that the times she had driven Ginny to visit Sidote in Chino she seemed frightened. Asked to describe Ginny in those days, she said, "She was always nervous, very meek, timid, and withdrawn around Jack Sidote. Otherwise she was always happy, an outgoing, friendly person."

Clara's remark brought Ginny to tears again, and weeping could be heard in the rear pews as well as from the defense rows. Several of the women jurors looked stricken.

The prosecution had a narrow line to walk. Although they wanted to suggest that the 1970 beating had no relevance to the murder charge, they also had to indicate that Ginny's alleged infidelity enraged Sidote without condoning his brutality. It would be tricky, and surprisingly Mamoulides was assigned to the task. The one time he'd questioned prospective jurors during voir dire, he seemed careless and random, and his cross-examination today wasn't much better. When he asked Clara if she knew Raymond Foat and she replied noncommittally, "He was the manager of the restaurant," he accepted her answer. Nor did he press her when she denied knowing the name Richard Busconi, and he failed to ask about other boyfriends or Ginny's social life. He only wanted to know why the police were never called during all these beatings.

"I never would call the police, sir," said Clara. Mamoulides left it at that.

After Reed's brief redirect examination, he called John Boyd, Clara's ex-boyfriend, to confirm that she had called him for help after the fight. Ginny was "very badly bruised and beaten about the face," he said. "She looked like she'd been used as a punching bag in the face. One eye was already starting to completely close, like a fighter's eye. . . . Her lip was very badly cut and bleeding. It was very hard for her to talk. Her neck had bruises on it and she had a great deal of upper body discomfort. . . ." He added that "she was on the verge of emotional collapse," and since "it was very difficult for her to keep her mind on any one thing for one moment past another," he said he "had to put her on the plane like a small child."

When asked if she'd been beaten on other occasions, he replied that she'd missed work because of being beaten. (Surprisingly, the DAs still weren't objecting that the witness was drawing a conclusion, since he hadn't actually seen any beatings.) He also testified that those evenings after Ginny had visited Jack in jail, she was so emotionally upset she'd need a drink to calm down to go to work. (Again, no objection.) This was unusual, he said, because she was "always very competent, very intelligent, and a very kind person," his remark moving Ginny again to tears.

Konrad cross-examined Boyd, pushing a little harder than Mamoulides had but without making it clear what he was driving at. When asked, "Wasn't it true that Raymond Foat was a married man?" Boyd sidestepped: Raymond Foat got a divorce in the 1970s. But no, he didn't know that Ginny had dated him and, like Clara, he also said he hadn't known Richard Busconi.

"Didn't you know that the defendant was going out with Richard Busconi while Sidote was in prison?" Konrad insisted. The defense objected, but Judge Burns overruled the objection, reminding Reed that this was after all a cross-examination. Ginny stared angrily at Konrad, incensed by his questions, but the DA had moved on to another topic: If Ginny was so badly beaten, why hadn't Boyd sought medical assistance? Boyd replied that she wanted to get to

New York as fast as she could, "because she was afraid for her life."

Why hadn't the flight attendants noticed or been astounded by Ginny's appearance if she was so badly beaten? Konrad pushed, his disbelief at the severity of the beating, however, making him seem callous.

Boyd's reply that she was wearing sunglasses seemed inadequate to explain how sunglasses could hide a face that he'd said looked as if "it had been used as a punching bag." But wisely Konrad didn't persist.

Ginny Foat's sister, Emilia Guigi, followed Boyd to the stand to describe what Ginny looked like when she returned to New York. Her face, she said immediately, "looked as if it was used as a punching bag." Coming directly on the heels of Boyd's testimony, the cliché seemed rehearsed, and her description of black-and-blue marks on Ginny's "upper body" was the same clinical phrase chosen by Boyd.

Still, she was a sympathetic witness as she wept softly. She was younger than Ginny but looked older, her face softer, less defined, not only because she was heavy, but her prettiness was also obscured by thick framed glasses. She wore a nondescript print dress, a matronly outfit suited to her life as a wife and mother of four children who had lived in New Paltz most of her life. This was the sister, it seemed, who had not sought adventure, who had been the "good" daughter and lived the life that Ginny implied she would have been condemned to had she stayed in New Paltz. What had she thought of her sister's ambitions and her success, her emergence as a feminist leader in California political circles, especially when Ginny's remarks about being condemned to that life implicitly demeaned her choice?

Now Virginia Galluzzo, Ginny's mother, was called to the stand. Short and round-faced, she was pretty. Her large blue eyes behind her glasses twinkled, and her smile was warm and pleasant. Her hair was bobbed and gray, combed much like Ginny's own, but framing her face so tightly it had to be a wig. As she walked to the witness stand, she took something from her mouth and dropped it into a planter at the side of the room. Burns at first looked shocked but then laughed along with the jurors. Mrs. Galluzzo laughed, too. She'd endeared herself by discarding the lemon drop she'd been sucking on. No, the courtroom didn't intimidate her; she would just be herself, a refreshing change in this trial, and in contrast to the previous witness, her comments (slightly accented and awkwardly constructed) sounded more like her own.

Ginny wept as her mother told what she knew of Ginny's life with Jack Sidote. Which, in fact, was not very much. She remembered the day her daughter left in 1965, because she and her husband asked her not to go: "I wanted to keep her home with me because after her divorce from Danny, it made her very, very upset." She explained that Ginny's was the first divorce in the family; on one side alone, she added proudly, ninety people had the same name. So, she said, "The first divorce, it was very bad."

She and her husband were sick about her leaving with Sidote "because we loved her. We wanted her to stay with us. Her dad didn't want her to go. He didn't like that man. He struck her and said, 'You gotta stay here.' "

The ease with which she mentioned August Galluzzo striking his twenty-four-year-old daughter was shocking. In a trial whose dominant theme was battered women, did Mrs. Galluzzo find it acceptable that her husband had struck Ginny, by then a grown woman? Had he done the same to his wife when she crossed him? Had Ginny been reared in a world in which she accepted that men struck women, and had she therefore accepted Sidote's first beatings? On the other hand the subtext of Mrs. Galluzzo's description of their argument in 1965 was also the father's exasperation. Had he had enough of Ginny's rebelliousness? Had he seen too often where her headstrong nature had led? To a divorce, to an aimless series of jobs, to 3 A.M. dates with a man whose reputation was notorious? Why else did Ginny say, as Mrs. Galluzzo now testified, " 'I'm going, I'm going,' " as if to say, "You can't tell me what to do, you can't keep me here. I don't have to listen to you." Hadn't this been the taste of freedom that Sidote had seemed to offer?

Mrs. Galluzzo admitted she hadn't known about Ginny's baby until the other day when she was told. Then Reed took a leap forward in time: It was only when Ginny and Jack were married in 1967, she said, that she went to California with Jack's parents and "Gus went out later." When Jack was in Chino, she and her husband went out again and accompanied Ginny on a prison visit. "She brought a fully cooked meal, and they ate out in the prison yard." Then Ginny excused herself and went off to talk to Jack alone, Mrs. Galluzzo continued. "When she came back she was holding her face and crying, but she dried her eyes because she was afraid her father would see her." She told her mother that Jack had hit her. Mrs. Galluzzo remembered saying, " 'Honey, come home, come home.' " But Ginny told her, " 'I have to stay a little longer to help him through this.' " This comment implied that she was already planning to leave, although it was also about this time when Ginny and her parents had written their letters to Jack's parole board attesting to his rehabilitation and their hope for their future as a family.

Mrs. Galluzzo's description of Ginny's appearance when she arrived home in New York in 1970 was an abbreviated version of what the court had already heard: "I saw welts on her face and neck, and her neck was so bad. That night I saw her arms were bruised, and all day she was holding her arm down."

Ginny had stayed home for a while but then, according to her mother, she'd decided she wanted "to go on a trip." Presumably this was the trip to join Raymond Foat; Mrs. Galluzzo, however, didn't seem to realize where or why Ginny was going.

The prosecution now challenged the admissibility of Mrs. Galluzzo's testimony about a letter from Jack Sidote in 1970, with Konrad arguing that since it no longer existed—"if it ever existed," he snidely added—Mrs. Galluzzo's testimony would be only hearsay. Reed argued that since Sidote was available to be questioned about it, Mrs. Galluzzo should be allowed to talk about it. (Konrad's problem, of course, was that Sidote had said he didn't recall writing such a letter.) But Judge Burns was convinced by Reed's argument about Sidote's availability, and even though "at first blush" he said he'd thought it was hearsay, he overruled the State. Konrad was fuming.

With the jury back in, Mrs. Galluzzo said she and her husband received a letter from Sidote in 1970, but "the language . . . was so vile" that they tore it up, because "we just didn't want it in our home." Sidote had written, she said, " 'I'll get even with your blank Virginia"—he called her a bad name, she said—"if it's the last thing I do, I'm going to kill her."

Tom Porteous cross-examined her gently: After all, he would say later, the mothers were not on trial here.

After Ginny had left in 1965, Mrs. Galluzzo admitted, she didn't hear from her: "I waited and waited, I don't know how long"—maybe six months or a year, she said. When Ginny finally called, she said she was going to marry Sidote. Mrs. Galluzzo remembered saying, " '*Please,* come back. Don't marry him.' " Once again Porteous stressed that Ginny hadn't been in touch with her parents during this time, and Mrs. Galluzzo agreed, forgetting that her mother's lament didn't particularly play well for the defense: "She never called, she never wrote."

Mrs. Galluzzo again confirmed that Ginny left with Sidote against their advice, but added a remark that the prosecution had been hoping for. In contrast to the defense's portrait of Ginny as malleable and helpless, Mrs. Galluzzo said: "She made her own decisions. After her divorce, she was upset and wanted to get out of town."

Mrs. Galluzzo stepped down, and the defense asked that she and her daughter Emilia be "excused from sequestration." Permission granted, Reed now moved several of the defense supporters into the second row so that Mrs. Galluzzo and Emilia could sit in the first row, in full view of the jury, to watch Ginny testify. Hence, the stage was set for Ginny's testimony. Although there had been rumors of more defense witnesses, experts on battered women, character witnesses from California, or even a few New Orleans residents who claimed to remember Ginny from 1965 and her whereabouts the night of the crime, it was Ginny Foat whose name was next called.

Because the prosecution's case seemed so weak, Ginny Foat might have chosen not to testify. But she'd long ago made up her mind that no matter what, she wanted to take the stand. "Both the Jefferson Parish district attorneys and the press had talked about me as if I were schizophrenic," she said. "Since I didn't want people thinking there were possibly other personalities that could have committed the murder, I wanted them to know that the same strength and commitment I once gave to John Sidote are the same strength and commitment I now give to the women's movement. I wanted people to realize that Ginny then and Ginny now are the same person, except with more understanding of her options."

Reed had stressed this theme in his opening. Yet from her cell, Ginny had described a more dramatic transformation: the death of a passive woman" to the "birth of a strong woman." But it was only "the passive woman" who was resurrected on the witness stand in Gretna that day. The woman who had faced audiences of thousands, who'd given strong political speeches on women's rights, and who'd also taken an active role in passing notes, arguing for and against prospective jurors, as well as "handling" the press in the hallway, had disappeared. In her place sat a woman shrinking in the witness chair, her shoulders hunched, her hands clasped in her lap, as she gave her name as "Ginny Foat" and her address as 5625 Lafayette, West Hollywood, California (where, in fact, she no longer lived). Her whispered response to Reed's first question completed the physical regression.

Reed: Did anybody ever call you Virginia?
Foat: Sometimes, when my mother is mad at me.

Whether it was a conscious courtroom ploy or an unconscious expression of self-pity and feeling of victimization wasn't clear. But the effect, while perhaps evoking sympathy, conveyed the image of a woman as helpless as a child.

Reed matched his tone to her image; he became a concerned parent, so gentle and filled with consolation that the jurors could barely hear him. That this was a style contrived for the occasion became obvious with Konrad's first objection. Then Reed flared suddenly, speaking loudly, the "sensitivity" driven out of his voice by anger. He then turned back to Ginny and once more adopted his quiet, whispery tone.

Konrad had objected to Reed's questions about Ginny's arrest in 1983. Judge Burns allowed her to answer a few of these questions, and she explained that she was at the Burbank airport when several police cars stopped her, and both plainclothed and uniformed policemen arrested her. "There was also a helicopter," she continued, but Konrad finally won the ruling that this was irrelevant. Similarly, Judge Burns overruled Reed's questions about Ginny's position as president of California NOW and the size of the organization. The defense wanted to suggest that the airport arrest had been given maximum media exposure and that Ginny was on trial only because she was a well-known feminist. The objections had brought Reed up short, however, and the jurors looked blank, unaware of what these references to her NOW position or media attention implied.

Now Reed asked her about the 1977 arrest. At the time, she said, she was married to Raymond Foat, although separated from him, and living in Canoga Park. She added that after her arrest they were together again, but neglected to say that they were subsequently divorced and that she had been married and divorced a fourth time.

Prior to her 1977 arrest, she said she'd been the owner of a catering company, run a food concession at a tennis club in Woodland
Hills, California, and been successful. Reed confirmed that she was
in jail three months and was then released.

Ginny's voice had been high and weak, as if he'd been limber-
ing her up before asking her about what he'd already outlined in his
opening argument as the crucial part of her story: What happened
when she and Sidote parted in 1970. Ginny lowered her head and
squeezed her eyes tightly shut as if to cry, but they seemed to be
tearless tears as she gave her account in choppy, run-on sentences:
"He tried to kill me. He went into one of his rages, and he started
to punch me in the body and he twisted my arms behind me and
he punched me in the face and he kicked me. And then he started
to strangle me." She had told Sidote she was leaving, that she couldn't
live with him or his violence anymore. "And he told me I couldn't
go, that he would see me dead before I went. And if he couldn't kill
me, he'd see me rot in jail the same as he did."

Reed's technique was that of a psychologist eliciting "her feelings," and surprisingly the DAs had no objections.

Reed: How did you feel in 1965 to 1970?
Foat: Shameful. It was terrifying. But I never told any-
       one . . .
Reed: Can you tell the jury?
Foat: I don't know. I'm so ashamed.
Reed: What for?
Foat: I'm ashamed of having loved him, I'm ashamed of hav-
       ing stayed. I'm ashamed of my own stupidity.

The cadence of her reply, one that would be repeated at several
of the climactic moments of her testimony, had a stylized quality.
The public speaker had won out over the little girl. And yet her
"confession" had a strange ambiguity to it. While seeming to take
responsibility for her past, she had stressed shame, not guilt, giving
her speech a heavy dose of self-pity.

Reed asked her to tell what happened in 1965. The jury was now
leaning forward, eager to hear what she would say about the night
in November. But she was a long time getting there as she continued with only a few interruptions from her lawyer. In 1965 she was

living in New Paltz with her parents, she said, working as a cock-tail and food waitress. She had just "gotten through" with her mar-riage and she'd just given up a child. Reed interrupted to ask what the end of the marriage had meant.

"My mother and father both cried," she said. "It was a dis-grace." They were an Italian Catholic family, she explained, and she was the only one to get a divorce. It also meant excommunication from the Church, and no one had done that in the family. (In the testimony from Ginny and her mother, the fact that her marriage was annulled seemed to have been overlooked, but perhaps the em-phasis on excommunication was for the benefit of the Catholic-dominated jury.)

"I felt like a failure," she went on. "Somehow I wasn't able to be the wife I was supposed to be."

What had she done wrong? Reed asked.

"I'd been too independent," she said. "I'd gotten involved in things outside of him. I'd helped organize a march on Washing-ton." She had also been promoted in her first job, she said, and since she was putting her husband through school, it didn't allow for much time with him.

It was a common enough story of husbandly jealousy and wifely self-sacrifice. She also gave her explanation a feminist gloss: She said she was too independent, not "the same kind of wife my mother had been to my father."

When she was pregnant, did she share it with anyone? Reed now asked.

"No, not at the time I didn't," she said, adding, "I just couldn't bring further pain to them."

"Whose fault was it?" Reed asked.

Konrad's objection was sustained, but the question would later become a refrain and the prosecution, either out of fatigue or for-getfulness, wouldn't object. Then Ginny would say: "It was my fault."

Ginny said that after she had the baby, she returned to New Paltz. Now Reed and Ginny were practically whispering to each other in a private conversation at the witness stand. Not for the first time several jurors waved at the judge to indicate they couldn't hear.

Reed tried one more time to ask, "How did you feel before you met Jack Sidote?" This time Judge Burns sustained the State's ob-jection to vague questions about feelings. Ginny was allowed only to describe the way she met Jack Sidote. With her head bowed, she still hadn't looked up at the jurors, and a few of them seeemed impatient as they strained to listen to her breathless testimony. She had gone to Villa Lipani with a friend of hers, she said, and when she ordered a drink at the bar, Jack Sidote gave it to her. Then friends introduced them. "I was very attracted to him," she added, prompting Ginny's mother to exclaim, "That rat!" Ginny's sister quieted her, but she shrugged, hearing giggles from the defense rows.

The next night she returned to the Villa Lipani, Ginny continued. "It was a long way from the door to the bar," and the drink she had ordered the night before was on the bar waiting for her. "Then Jack took the microphone and sang, 'There Will Never Be Another You.' " She stopped, as if to let this sink in.

But had she known Jack Sidote was married? Reed prompted her. She had heard he was, she said, but he told her he was separated from his wife, and then she "asked a friend who said—"

Konrad objected, and although the objection was sustained, she went on anyway, "I didn't believe him to be married. There were too many women around." Ginny now repeated what Reed had emphasized in his opening argument: "Before I met him I felt a failure. I was awfully depressed." But then he made her "feel beautiful and important," she said. "He treated me like I was special. He took me to New York. He had a special seat at the racetrack," he had connections with people at the Villa Lipani, and so "he made me feel important again and whole again."

How had he made her feel important? she was asked. Because he seemed important, she replied. People went to the Villa Lipani just for him: "He was the star of the Villa Lipani. I was his girlfriend, I was *his* star."

She was weeping again but still dryly. She seemed to believe in the language of romance; indeed even in NOW she'd needed to be made to feel special and a star. But back then, she suggested, her only mistake was to believe that Sidote could grant her such self-importance.

Her remarks about the trip to Florida emphasized that she felt she was duped, not by her own taste or values or needs but by him. He had told her that he had a job offer, a partnership in a restaurant or something like that, something "more than just a bartender's job." She'd never heard until yesterday's testimony anything about a job in computers, she added. But she decided to go, because "I wanted to leave New Paltz." She wanted to stop being "a burden" on her family, she wanted to escape her "dead-end jobs," and she loved him and thought she could be his wife.

Wasyl's presence was yet another surprise to her, she continued. All Jack had said was that they couldn't go unless she got some money. She announced this with a self-righteous air; Reed had called it a "message she had missed." But seeing Bozydaj, whom she hardly knew, in the car upset her, too: "This was a romantic trip with the man I loved. There was something wrong with Wasyl's being there."

Her father saw something wrong in the trip, too, she admitted. She'd had arguments with him about the way she was seeing Jack, like the phone calls at four in the morning to ask her to go horseback riding. "He thought he was a hoodlum," Ginny said, and when she told him she was leaving with Jack, he hit her and told her she was acting "like a whore." Perhaps the fight about Sidote was only the last in a series of arguments in the Galluzzo home, with Ginny viewing the Florida trip as a way of asserting her independence and escaping her parents. But now she said she'd wanted to atone for the pain she'd caused them: "I thought we'd make it up to him—we'd have a nice home in Florida where my parents could come and visit in the winter."

Her fantasy of "a nice home" must have faded quickly. Her voice became even more whispery and childlike as she detailed the beatings she received during the trip. Outside Washington, D.C., she said, she asked Sidote about their plans and also about the money she'd borrowed and given to him. He or Wasyl pulled the car over to the side of the road, and Jack ordered her out of the car and around to the trunk: "The palm of his hand came at my shoulder." He hit her so hard that she fell back against the car, she said, and "he told me I was along for the ride as long as he wanted me along. He told me to get my suitcases out of the trunk and leave right then if I wanted to leave." She said she got scared and knew she should go home, but couldn't, since "I'd just had a fight with my parents."

Reed stopped her: "Whose fault was it?"

She replied in a singsong voice: "It was my fault. I shouldn't have nagged him."

Ginny's voice became even more halting and whispered as she

supplied further examples of what Reed called Sidote's "other rages." The cadence was much like that of a child "tattletaling"—And then he did this, and then he did that, and then he did this again. Reed was practically leaning into the witness stand as he continued to whisper, "What happened next?"

Ginny said that she and Wasyl were in the Florida motel room when Jack "came home in a rage." He was saying all these "curse words," but mainly to Wasyl, and she realized that the job deal had fallen through. "I didn't listen to that, I was thinking more about me," she said. "Everything was falling apart. There was no money, no job."

"Did something happen between you and Jack?" Reed asked.

"Wasyl was getting nervous and scared about the way Jack was acting," she began. At last Konrad objected, and Judge Burns ordered her to respond to the question.

What did Jack Sidote do in the bedroom? prompted Reed.

"I went into the bedroom," she whispered. "He came into the bedroom, too, and I started to get undressed to get into bed. I said to him, 'What are we gonna do now? Maybe we should go back to New York.' The next thing I knew, he grabbed me by the shoulders and turned me around and was punching me. He was punching me in the stomach. Then he put me down on the bed and he told me, 'It's not your place to ask questions. I make the decisions.' "

Then he was sitting on top of her and was hitting her in the breasts: "He had this crazy look. He took his finger and drew a line around my breasts. He said. 'You're a whore, just like the whore I killed. Her breasts weren't as big as yours, but I cut hers off when she didn't give me the money. It'll take longer, your breasts are bigger.' "

She said she cried, " 'Don't say that. It's not true.' "

She'd already said she *always* believed him, but apparently didn't then, even when Jack insisted it was true. Still, the testimony had had an obvious effect on the jury: One woman was crying, another seemed on the verge of tears, and several times jurors glanced at Ginny's mother and sister, who were weeping, their arms around each other. Robert Glass's eyes were red-rimmed as well, and he turned back to the first row to take Mrs. Galluzzo's hand.

Sidote then stopped, Ginny said, and began stroking her hair. He told her that it wasn't true. "He'd never do it again, that I wasn't a whore, I was beautiful." Then he fell asleep in her arms. She "figured it was about the job and everything" and that "he'd been drinking."

"Whose fault was it?" Reed interrupted.

"My fault," Ginny said. "I figured I had to find a way that these things wouldn't happen. He was under too much stress. I needed to figure out how to make things easier for him. He'd left so much, I'd left so little, so it was easier for me to make things better."

During the fifteen-minute recess, Ginny stood with her friends and supporters in the corridor. Once again she seemed an entirely different person from the woman on the stand and less distraught than her supporters, whose eyes were red from crying. Anyone listening to her testimony was, of course, outraged at Sidote and sympathetic to her. Yet the "my fault" litany and "I'd left so little" seemed excessive, as if the defense were trying to align the battered-women's syndrome too closely with these first incidents. After all, they had occurred after only a few days together. Once outside of New Paltz, had she immediately become the weak woman she appeared to be on the witness stand? Had she been "stalemated," as Del Martin put it in her book, *Battered Wives,* by her helplessness and fear on the one hand, her "oh-but-he-needs-me" attitude on the other, combined with the acculturated belief of women that "the failure of a marriage represents their failure as women"? The key to these rationalizations was guilt—and according to Ginny, she felt it deeply—"it was my fault." Yet it seemed that the defense was trying to touch all the bases, infusing these first incidents with the emotions that were more cumulative than instantaneous in the stories of other battered women's lives.

Back on the stand, Ginny had more points to make. Yes, she conceded, they did have some good times, like stopping to run and play on the beach. But no, she hadn't talked to him about that night. She wanted to, but he had said he was sorry, and he was so down about everything, she never had "the time or the opportunity." This, too, Del Martin explained in the same terms: "Many wives live from one of these good moments to the next, doing their best in between to suppress the knowledge of their husband's cruelty and their own crippling passivity."

Reed, however, was shaping his questions to move from one bad moment to the next. During the Baton Rouge phase of the trip, "Did anything happen?" he asked.

"Anything that happened" referred only to beatings, it seemed, and she replied, "He swung his hand back and I got a bloody nose. He said it was an accident so I guess it was an accident."

She said that most of the time he was drunk, and although "sometimes rages took over more than drunkenness, most of the time it was drunkenness." In Baton Rouge, she continued, he told her they were low on money, and although he didn't work, he picked her up at the Italian restaurant every night where she'd gotten a job as a waitress, and she'd give him her tips. But when she was at work she didn't know what he was doing, and she didn't ask, she said, setting a pattern for the night of the alleged crime.

As her story neared that night, she frequently repeated that she couldn't remember dates or events (this in contrast to the detailed memories of the beatings): "I keep going over these things, but I don't remember." But she did know that going to New Orleans was "Jack's decision," and after two or three days of seeing the French Quarter and sights of the city, "Jack said we were gonna go over and get this job, and I needed to go with him." Since Jack had introduced her to a man named Happy Ditcharo, she assumed that they'd met previously. Ditcharo hired her only as a barmaid behind the bar. She'd never been a dancer or a go-go dancer, and with a nervous giggle she added, "I'm not even a good dancer."

Now she recounted more of Sidote's atrocities, all of which Reed had mentioned in his opening argument but which Ginny now described in excruciating detail: the drunk pestering her, whom Jack had taken outside and beaten until the police came.

So Jack was jealous? Reed asked.

"By the time we left New Paltz, I was isolated from all my friends, I couldn't go anywhere myself. If I went to the grocery store and was ten minutes late, he'd come after me." And how did that affect her? "I thought he loved me."

Konrad now objected to Reed's question about what Sidote had done to another drunk Ginny had pointed out in the bar. The attorneys were called to the bench for a side bar; with the judge's ruling, Foat was allowed to describe only what had happened when she asked Jack what he'd done with the man.

He just laughed at her, she said, and then that night they had a good time dancing at a place in the French Quarter. Then they walked back to the hotel. Ginny paused, as if unable to continue.

Reed: Did you go up to your room?
Foat: Yes [with a long sigh].
Reed: Was Wasyl there?
Foat: No, he wasn't there [another long pause].
Reed: Did something happen?

Another long pause and a sigh preceded her account: "I remember being happy and laughing and having a good time." Then she turned toward Jack and saw that look on his face. " 'What did I do wrong? What's wrong?' " she asked him. "He said, 'Take off your clothes—' "

Ginny buried her face in her hands.

"What is happening?" Reed whispered.

Her face contorted, she continued. After she took off her clothes, he hit her. "He grabbed me by the hair and pulled me back onto the bed. He pinned my hands down and said, 'Don't you ever ask me where I've been. I don't have to answer to you. You're not my mother, you're not my wife, you're not anything.' Then he said, 'Remember all those drunks you pointed out—' "

Konrad objected angrily. This was all irrelevant, he argued, and she looked up dazed, as if surprised by his presence.

While the jury was hustled out, Ginny became herself, glaring at Konrad for his objection and watching Reed intently as he argued that he was trying to show that Sidote abused her not only physically but psychologically.

Finally, with scattered applause from the spectators, Judge Burns ruled that since he was allowing testimony about their relationship and Sidote's physical abuse, he would also allow testimony about alleged psychological abuse.

Konrad had lost. Burns had stuck with the defense, going even further than most judges in trials of women charged with killing their abusers.

"Do you remember where you are?" Reed whispered to Ginny, as if he were putting her back in a trance.

"In the room at the John Mitchell," she said. "He told me, all the drunks I'd pointed out to him, he'd taken outside . . . and taken a knife and stabbed them in the kidneys to drain out the alcohol and then threw their bodies into the dump behind the bar."

"What's happening now?" Reed asked.

"He hit me a couple of times. I said I knew he wasn't telling me the truth. He said, yes, he was. Then he had intercourse with me, and then he was crying and saying he was sorry, that he didn't mean it, that he'd been mad at me, but he wasn't mad anymore."

"What are you feeling, Ginny?" Reed asked.

By this time the prosecutors had stopped objecting to such phrasing. They'd been overruled every time and now felt it was futile. "We got our heads kicked in with that, so what was the point?" Porteous said later.

Ginny said she held him and she "was feeling bad. Here he was, a bouncer in this town, and he had so much more talent than that. And things were so bad for him."

Reed didn't ask what talent that might have been. Instead, he wanted to know why she had stayed.

"I stayed because I loved him. I hoped things would go back to the way things were in California—I mean New York." She had thought if she made changes, changes in herself, "maybe it wouldn't happen again." What kind of changes she didn't say, but it was another commonly reported justification of women who stayed with battering husbands. Once more she didn't talk to him about the incident since "everything was fine the next morning, and I just didn't want him to be mad at me again."

Finally, Reed relinquished his quiet, solicitous tone to ask matter-of-factly, "Do you have any recollection of the night you left New Orleans?"

At first her answers were brief: "I remember being at the hotel and sleeping." No, she didn't remember the time. "I just remember being there. I think I was by myself. Wasyl wasn't there when I was. I was reading a book and I fell asleep."

Then Jack was shaking her awake. " 'We have to get up, we have to leave.' " "He had this look on his face," she added. "Not a look like I was gonna get hit but more the look he had after—" she stopped then: "It was the look of a little boy who'd done something wrong. He said he'd been in a card game or arranged a card game and he'd cheated someone. And this person was important and would come after him."

She paused and sighed, repeating again, "It's so hard to remember," as she went on to explain that Wasyl came in and Jack talked to him about the card game and having to leave. "I've tried so hard to try to remember it, but I can't," she said, insisting that she had no recollection of leaving New Orleans that night and recalled nothing about flying to Dallas or Houston: "The next thing I remember is driving through the dry counties of Texas looking for something for Jack Sidote to drink."

The whispers in the press rows caused Porteous to cast a glance back over his shoulder. He knew the reporters were finding it hard to believe that she couldn't at least remember flying during this one leg of their cross-country journey.

The defense must have realized that this would be a problem for the jury, too. Reed confirmed again that she couldn't remember flying or flying alone that night. Then she explained why, in what sounded like a speech prepared for this difficulty:

"I've put a lot of walls up around those years over the years. It's hard to reach back and get everything, the insignificant things, the things that didn't have pain in them. It's hard to remember the good parts. They just aren't there."

Examined closely, the rhetorical flourish seemed contradictory. Even if she only remembered the "things that had pain in them," wouldn't his panic have alerted her, causing her to remember that they'd been forced to flee New Orleans in the middle of the night for fear that something bad might happen to them?

Reed concluded by asking her about Moises Chayo.

"I never met this man. I've never robbed anybody. I've never killed anybody," she announced, her voice suddenly strong.

Before the jury was brought in the next morning, Ginny was at the defense table, tearing up paper into smaller, note-sized pieces. She was competent, all business, but twenty minutes later, back on the stand, she'd regressed again. The defense committee, however, in its usual evening assessment of the day's testimony, had apparently been concerned about the jury's reaction to her lowered head and closed eyes.

Reed: Yesterday you were looking down. Can you look at the jury now and tell them why?

Foat: [addressing the jury directly] Because I never talked to anyone about the shame and the embarrassment of my life with him. I couldn't look at you. I couldn't look at anybody.

Her voice fell to a whisper. "I don't know if I can today."

Reed now led her through a few mundane, unemotional questions to arrive at the next beating, this one in Carson City, Nevada.

Ginny said, "He punched me a lot of times in the stomach, in my arms, in my breasts, and then he kicked me . . ." Then she looked down again. "I can't keep going through this."

This was a moment of great concern for the defense team. She had worked with a therapist for two weeks before the trial to break through her resistance to talking about these events. Had she blocked again, unable to go on? But once she'd calmed herself, she said, in response to Reed's usual questions, that she blamed herself, today qualifying the answer with "at the time I thought it was my fault, because he didn't have anything, he couldn't find a job, he'd left New York."

Now Reed tied up some loose ends, like her first phone call home. "I kept waiting to tell them the good news," she said, "but then there was never any good news to tell them. In Carson"—she corrected herself—"I mean, Hermosa Beach, I couldn't wait any longer."

When Wasyl left because of a draft notice, she felt envious but she stayed and got a job as a barmaid in Torrance. Jack was not working, and most of the time he was drinking heavily, although he occasionally picked up relief work at one of the bars down by the pier.

Stopping to ask for a drink of water, she seemed to be preparing herself for describing another beating. Judge Burns stared at her hard, as if he, too, wondered if she was hypontized; Reed's voice had become even more incantatory as he placed her back at this scene in California.

Foat: He came in. He was drunk. I saw the look that by that time I knew.

Reed: What look?

Foat: [bowing her head, her eyes shut] Crazy anger.

Reed: What's he saying?

Foat: He asked me why I was going out all painted up like that.

Reed: Were you?

Foat: No, I was just regular. I said I was going to work. He said . . . [she paused, looking up at Reed from under her lashes] I can't say the word.

Reed: [his voice a whisper] You have to. What's he saying to you?

Foat: He said . . . Oh, I can't . . . He said, "You're going out there all painted up because you're . . . you're . . ."

Reed: It's all right—

Foat: [blurting the words, weeping] "You're going to suck somebody's cock."

Once more she said to him, " 'No, that's not true,' " but he went on: "He said, 'I found this drunk on the pier and cut off his—' " (she couldn't repeat the word again) " 'and I was going to bring it home and you would've liked that.' "

Again she said, " 'No, Jack, that's not true.' But he kept saying it. Then he threw me down on the bed, pulled my hair and punched me and said, 'I want you to do this to me.' "

A few of the women on the jury seemed shocked, the rest only somewhat embarrassed. Even the judge seemed slightly uncomfortable as he cast a sidelong glance at Ginny.

"Then when it was all over," she continued, "I told him I would quit my job, I'd find another job. And he started to cry," and "told me he loved me so much he couldn't stand me being out there with other men." She quit her job "so he wouldn't have cause to worry," even though she'd "never given him cause to say those things."

Her weeping subsided as she answered Reed's brief questions about their jobs in a telephone soliciting office for a chain of photography studios, and their later purchase of a bar with their friend Howard Monblatt. "Howard put up most of the money and I guess Jack borrowed money from his parents," she said. This was a good period, it seemed: "The bar was doing very well. We had a nice family clientele. It was fun. We got a beautiful apartment on a golf course, and we got married. . . . Everything was starting to come true, everything I'd waited for—a successful business, a house, marriage," and so her parents finally came out to visit.

Then things began to go wrong. The bar was being run poorly, the area was changing. With a large Samoan population, a lot of regular customers weren't coming in. Jack then bought the partner out (she didn't say where the money came from), but once the bar wasn't doing well, Jack was often drunk and depressed, and she'd have to work both day and night shifts. "That's when it started to get real bad again. The beatings started again."

Specific beatings were not described this time but were a prelude to Sidote's shooting of the Samoan teenager. Like Reed's version in his opening argument, she described the episode from her point of view. She'd had the flu but Jack still refused to take over for her in the bar. When she threatened to close the bar, he finally came in. "The minute he walked in I knew that night was going to be another one of those nights." She'd gone home but kept her clothes on so that she could run—"at that point I'd started running"—and since most of the beatings happened in the bedroom, she lay down on the couch.

At two or three in the morning, Sidote was shaking her. "I didn't want to open my eyes because I thought I was gonna get hit again. He said, 'I've just killed somebody.' I said, 'Don't start it again. I don't want to hear another story.' But then I opened my eyes and saw the little-boy look like he gets when he cries . . . the look I'd seen when he'd woken me up in New Orleans . . . I knew it was another one of those times."

Asked her reaction when he was arrested, she said, "I remember being hysterical that I was gonna lose him, that they were gonna take him away."

Judge Burns called a recess; he had a knack for doing so at dramatic moments. Before the jury had filed out Ginny had returned to the counsel table and wept with her head in her arms.

Out in the hallway, Kay Tsenin heard her name shouted. She turned and found herself face to face with Elaine Lafferty. She had been handed a Louisiana subpoena the moment she stepped off the plane in New Orleans and been kept at a Gretna motel, where she repeatedly told the DAs that she wouldn't testify. Then they had brought her to the courthouse to give the defense team a glimpse of her presence in an attempt, she thought, to make them—and especially Ginny—nervous. Today she'd run down the hallway and called to Kay. The bailiffs tried to separate them, but to no avail. Despite Kay's personal animosity toward her (she still suspected that she was part of, perhaps even the instigator of, the "get Foat" plot), she told Elaine that a Louisiana subpoena had no jurisdiction over her and that she'd find a lawyer to get her released from it. Meanwhile, Jean Conger escorted Elaine into the courtroom and found her a seat next to Norma Hair, the NOW colleague and unofficial treasurer of the Foat defense fund, and instructed Norma to keep her there.

Porteous laughed when he heard the machinations of the defense team to "keep Lafferty from testifying." The DAs had already decided to release her, he said, since she still refused to take the stand. He also explained that Lafferty refused to cooperate because she said her publisher had warned her not to jeopardize her book. Elaine in fact didn't have a book contract and later denied using this as her reason for refusing to testify. Nevertheless, Porteous insisted that for whatever reason, she'd dug in her heels and reneged on what she'd told the DAs before, testimony that he felt would have greatly strengthened their case.

Lafferty said she'd gone to Louisiana only to observe the trial for her possible book, never to testify. She told that to the prosecutors from the beginning, she said. When they picked her up at the airport and took her to a Gretna motel and basically put her under lock and key, she was damned angry and even more adamant about not testifying.

She knew that the DAs had a very weak case. Whatever their suspicion about what Ginny had or had not admitted to her, Elaine was not going to help them. She was legally astute enough to realize that no prosecutor would put her on the stand without having an inkling of what she might say. "Still, they shlepped me through the hall for two days," she said, "with the hope that Ginny, who was then on the stand, would think I was going to testify and would get rattled and change her story. They were playing brinksmanship, and it was dumb. That's when I broke loose and told Kay I wasn't there to testify. Maybe if I'd thought they were competent prosecutors I would have taken the stand. On the other hand, since they had so little, I couldn't believe that they felt the case rested on me. I suppose I would've hurt Ginny's credibility, but I wasn't going to put my ass on the line when the DAs didn't have anything else. I wasn't going to testify when you had a bunch of dingdongs who couldn't make the case."

With Lafferty released from her subpoena and sequestration, the defense team still had to worry about Mandell. As far as anyone knew she'd never been served with a supoena in California, and her lawyer had told both Reed and Glass as well as the prosecutors that she wouldn't testify. Her reasoning was similar to Lafferty's with the added consideration that she was already seen as the villain of the piece, and her political and personal life was in disarray from her "dumb mistake." Meanwhile, according to Mandell, Ginny was sending her messages—"We'll talk when I get back. We can't while the trial is going on, but afterwards . . ." In her more cynical moments, Mandell thought this was a way to try to assure her continued noncooperation with the prosecutors. Still, she had a glimmer of hope that perhaps after the trial they would indeed be able to sort the mess out, that she could convince Ginny she'd never meant to do her harm. She considered her refusal to testify proof of her basic goodwill and good intentions, no matter what the defense team or the press said about her.

If Ginny was aware of the incident in the hallway, if she was at all disconcerted by Elaine's presence, she didn't show it when she retook the stand after the recess. She said she was now forty-two, having been born in 1941, that she was twenty-four in 1965, twenty-six in 1967. No, her hair hadn't been short and gray but dark and long in 1965. (This was to allay any suspicion aroused by the original police report in which one witness said he had seen Chayo that night with a woman whose hair was short and gray.)

Then Ginny went on: While Sidote was awaiting his trial and sentencing, the beatings again became more frequent. She gave several more descriptions, and said that one time she went to the hospital because she thought he'd broken her nose.

The defense introduced its one hospital record in which the attending doctor had reported that her nose was swollen and tender (the X rays showed no break) and prescribed ice and Empirin.

Why had she told the doctor that she'd tripped and hit her face against the wall? Reed asked.

Ginny explained that she couldn't tell anyone about the beatings then, and she was also afraid to say anything while Sidote was awaiting sentencing because "he'd get in trouble." Yes, she had called the police before, once in Hermosa Beach, twice in Carson City, she thought, but felt "it was a waste of time; they'd come and they'd talk to me, and it didn't matter what I looked like, what condition I was in, it was just not something they wanted to be involved in."

Despite her admission that his beatings became worse and more frequent as his imprisonment neared, she said she was "getting real scared of having to be by myself. I didn't know what I was gonna do without him," she said. "I loved him. I didn't know if I was gonna be able to survive without him . . ."

Again, Reed adopted his "hypnotic" method to elicit a description of yet more violence. "Do you recall being in the bedroom?" he asked.

"Yes, . . . he . . . he started . . ." She paused, her head again bowed, her eyes squeezed shut.

Reed: Where are you?
Foat: He started to make me do things again and again sexually and he'd say he wanted to make sure that while he was in jail I wasn't going to be out whoring around.
Reed: [in a whisper] What's he doing?
Foat: He hit me again. He started to threaten me . . .

He told her, she said, that if she was with anyone else or if he heard she was, or if she left him, that he'd kill her. He told her that she "could never live without him," that "he would never give up control of my life." Then he told her, " 'Remember all those drunks you sent out of the bars,' " the ones " 'I put in trash cans,' " or the drunk he said he'd mutilated in Hermosa Beach? This was the threat, she said, the one that lay behind his accusations of her: "He said, 'I'll tell them you did it and they'll believe it, because you're such a whore.' "

Ginny's response? " 'I don't believe you, Jack,' " she remembered saying. " 'Don't start again.' " But she still rationalized: "I didn't believe he really meant it. I thought he was just getting through . . . the trying time of having to go to prison."

With Sidote in Chino, she worked at the telephone company, then took "emotional disability" because "I was having a hard time adjusting to being by myself. . . . It was a whole new world." As Sidote had insisted, she went to Chino every visiting day unless she was sick, brought him hot home-cooked meals and clothing for him to wear, and stayed till the end of visiting hours.

Judge Burns was leaning back in his chair, staring up at the ceiling, as Ginny detailed her arduous but faithful prison visits. The jury seemed equally bored and showed no reaction even when Ginny said that Sidote would slap her around when they took walks alone in the prison yard.

The change in her life occurred, she said, when she began to work on the *Princess Louise*. Not only was she a cocktail waitress, she sometimes waitressed for the catered banquets and soon began to get more involved "in the actual planning of banquests." She began to describe the five-hundred- or six-hundred-seat affairs she'd planned and run. "I felt proud—"

Konrad objected. Reed flared: He would show it was relevant.

Burns sighed. "It seems not to be relevant, but I'll give you the chance to put it together."

Reed's point was to show that Sidote had denigrated her success: "He told me it was all a hoax on my part," Ginny said, "so that I would get to meet all these bartenders . . . and that it was a waste of time to put something together for prostitutes and bums. Then he got real angry again and he hit me again, and he told me I couldn't do it anymore . . . that I shouldn't start feeling that I could do things without him . . . or exist without him or he'd see me rot in jail."

Reed had brought her to the turning point in her story—how she had changed from the weak oppressed victim to the woman who finally stood up for herself. This had been attributed to her feminist conversion in her interviews and in the defense committee fundraising letters. Her subjugation had been so drastic, her passivity so dramatic on the witness stand, however, the jury would find it difficult to understand this transformation, with or without the mention of feminism.

In fact, according to her testimony, not the women's movement but her growing friendship with Raymond Foat accounted for her "finding" herself.

Reed had already set the stage by asking her when she met Ray Foat, at the same time countering the State's suggestion that Sidote's anger was justified by her infidelity. Although she'd met Foat in 1969 when he came to work at the restaurant as its manager, she insisted that at first they were just friends, "confidantes," and that she hadn't yet made the actual decision to leave Sidote. But once he'd been scheduled for release in June and July 1970, she said, "I was real afraid of his coming home. . . . I dreaded the day. . . . I couldn't live with his sickness anymore."

How had she come to realize that she felt this way? Reed asked. The moment of transformation seemed extraordinarily flat: She'd been meeting people, doing things, and she also thought "Raymond helped."

Now Reed asked her bluntly, had they had an affair?
"I went to bed with Raymond before Jack came home."

Reed: How did he help?
Foat: Because he was—he still is—a kind, gentle, loving person . . . who had recently been through an experience with his wife which involved some craziness. And we sort of cried on each other's shoulders.

He also, it seemed, encouraged her ambitions. As the restaurant manager he helped her get more involved in banquet planning because he believed "I wasn't just a cocktail waitress."

After she again stressed the initial innocence of her relationship with Foat (Sidote's jealousy and the letter from Mrs. Sidote both irrational responses to their friendship, she claimed), Reed asked the question that had hung in the gap between the passive victim and the strong woman: Who gave her the confidence to make the decision to leave?

"I gave it to myself," Ginny said, her voice suddenly firm. She did not elaborate.

The momentary strength in her voice soon gave way to her halting whisper as she repeated that she had felt she had "to stick by" Jack Sidote until he got out of jail: "I wasn't gonna leave him in there." Because of his work furlough, he was able to visit her every morning on his way to his job. "The first time he tried to put his hands on me, I couldn't stand it. I couldn't stand for him to touch me. I tried to force myself but I couldn't do it." There were more beatings, more forced oral sex, and still he made his repeated threat, " 'I'll see you rot in a jail cell.' " Finally she couldn't take it anymore, she told him she "couldn't live with his sickness anymore," and "that was when he tried to kill me."

She had come full circle to the beating with which both Reed's opening argument and her testimony had begun. Once more she sobbed convulsively as, adding details to the brutal scene, she now emphasized his threat of sending her to jail for his crimes. Still in question was what crimes she thought he could possibly accuse her of. He said, " 'You did all those things,' " she testified, then gave as an example his threat to accuse her of "cut[ting] off that drunk's"— she paused, now unable to say the word—"in Hermosa Beach." She seemed confused about which "crime" he meant, especially since she'd said she didn't believe such stories. Now she took a handkerchief from her lap, dabbed at her eyes, and looked at Reed plaintively: "It's all blurred together now. I just knew I had to go."

She then flew home to New Paltz.

"What did you feel?" Reed asked again.

Like the end of the previous day's testimony, her reply had a rehearsed quality to it.

Foat: I felt like this great weight had been lifted off my shoulders, like I wasn't a little girl anymore. My mother had fixed up my room . . . and I felt like I was being born again. I had left, I was free.

Reed: Are you free now, Ginny?

Foat: [with tears brimming her eyes] No, I'm still living with John Sidote.

Reed then upped the emotional ante: "When you leave this courtroom will you be free?"

Burns sustained Konrad's objection but Reed looked pleased with his rhetorical triumph and tendered the witness with a confident air, as if he'd already won a not-guilty verdict.

The prosecutors' cross-examination was bound to be grueling given the gaps in Foat's testimony. While the defense had concentrated on the beatings, the stitchings of her narrative had to be unraveled. The State's primary concern was how to respond to the image of the helpless little girl on the stand. Would they play to that role, or would they try to evoke the strong, competent woman?

From the start, however, the tearful, rambling, confused victim with her head bowed became a stalwart, almost taciturn woman, her chin thrust out and her voice firm, as if indignant that she should be questioned at all.

Konrad chose to ask his questions in his "commonsense" tone. While his cross-examination betrayed a hint of snideness, it was not in his tone but in what his questions implied.

As the afternoon progressed, it seemed he didn't want to come on too hard, fearful of appearing either to "batter" a victim or persecute a feminist. Instead of probing her story more deeply, he tended to let her repeat her testimony without insisting on more details that might expose discrepancies or suggest a scenario quite different from her story of Sidote's repeated and continuing brutality and threats.

He began by calling attention to her name. "Mrs. Foat," he said. "Is that what you prefer to be called?"

"Virginia Foat or Ms. Foat," she replied, pronouncing it as the shortened feminist *Ms.* as opposed to the drawled "Miz."

Hadn't she remarried after her divorce from Raymond Foat? he countered.

Reed's objection was overruled, and she looked annoyed as she replied, "I just retained the name Foat and my last marriage was annulled."

Without asking if there was a reason for not taking back her own name, Galluzzo, Konrad questioned her about her four marriages by simply letting her chronicle them: the first to Danny Angelillo, with whom she stayed for "a little bit more" than a year, then the marriage was annulled; John Sidote, whom she married in 1967 and from whom she thought she received a legal divorce in the beginning of 1971; her marriage to Raymond Foat in May 1971, from whom she was twice separated, reconciled, and then divorced "in '79 or '80"; finally, her fourth husband, Jack Meyer, whom she married in 1980 or 1981. How long did it last? Konrad wanted to know. About a month, she told him, and then it was annulled under California law.

In contrast to her extended replies to Reed, Ginny's answers were now one-liners, and her lips were pressed tight with anger, especially when Konrad asked her for her present address. She gave the Hollywood address she'd stated when she was sworn in. What was the address in Marin County? Konrad challenged. A residence? She was fumbling, and Kay, too, looked worried. Konrad's insinuation was clear—by confronting her with a reference to Kay Tsenin's house, he was hinting at a possible relationship between Ginny and Kay.

"Where is your own home?" he repeated.

"I do not have my own home," she said. "Some of my friends moved me out of my apartment when I was arrested. So I live in either of those two places."

But Konrad didn't ask who owned the second place, the Marin house, or the nature of her relationship with Kay. Behind the scenes, as both Kay Tsenin and Tom Porteous later confirmed, Konrad had already told Judge Burns that he wanted to question Ginny about her "life-style." In chambers the judge had refused to allow it. Later

Konrad expressed his bitterness at this ruling, pointing out that while Burns had allowed questions about her relationship with Sidote, his alcoholism, and his life after 1970, the State had been prevented from asking her about her life. What Konrad hoped to gain from such veiled allusions was questionable. Perhaps he wanted to stress her independence from men and at the same time arouse antilesbian prejudice; nevertheless the tactic might well have backfired, even with a conservative jury, as Porteous himself agreed. He'd thought Judge Burns's ruling the correct one.

After several questions about the many jobs in her earlier years, he had Ginny bridling again by asking where she went to have the child.

"I would rather not say," she replied with hauteur in her voice.

"There are many things you might not want to say," Konrad snapped.

In her anger she'd missed the point of his question; he wasn't forcing her, as she put it, "to give [the child's] identity away." In a series of short questions and answers Konrad brought out that she drove to the Midwest *alone,* was gone about three or four months, stayed in a home for unwed mothers there, gave up the child at birth, then drove herself back to Cleveland, where she met another friend, who rode back with her to New Paltz.

Konrad had tipped his hand: He was trying to undermine the weak, passive image by bringing out her strong, independent, willful side, the woman who came and went as she chose with little regard for the consequences.

He now returned to her meeting John Sidote, again having to pull from her brief replies and "I don't remember" many times. He was met with a stolid silence when he pointed out that if she'd known Sidote six months before leaving for Florida, as she'd said, then she must have met him as early as March 1965. She insisted that she knew Sidote was "still legally married," when she met him, but again didn't answer when Konrad asked when their affair began. Konrad rephrased the question awkwardly: "How long did it take to cultivate the relationship?"

"Two weeks, a month," she replied.

Did they see each other every day?

They saw each other "as often as two people in love could see each other," she declared.

Two people in love, but one of them married, Konrad insinuated, by asking if she at no time was aware that Sidote was still living at home.

"When he called me at four A.M., he was calling from the Villa Lipani," she said, seemingly unaware that even this brief response hinted at the furtiveness of the affair.

Once again she portrayed herself as the naïf, swept away, as she insisted that she had nothing to do with the planning of the trip to Florida. He'd just told her that he wanted to go to Florida because of a job opportunity in a bar-restaurant operation, she said.

"Didn't he leave because he'd fallen as deeply in love with you as you with him?" Konrad asked, throwing her own romantic language back at her.

"Are you asking me to speculate as to why he left?" she said, now angry enough to adopt lawyerly language.

He was trying to suggest that while Sidote had seen the trip to Florida as a romantic elopement, she had seen it as a chance to escape her family and New Paltz. But meeting her resistance, he then tried to cast doubt on the saga of repeated beatings. Why hadn't Bozydaj been aware of her bruises?

"I wore clothes," she replied.

Still, the frequency or severity of such beatings was hardly the issue, and Konrad's doubt might make him seem callous to the jurors. His implication that she was responsible for Sidote's guilt and alcoholism, and that she had worked in a bar and had heard about B-drinking laws was hardly the point either. The heart of the matter was why she couldn't remember how she'd left New Orleans, why Sidote had threatened to see her rot in jail, and why she hadn't left him while he was in prison.

Finally Konrad seemed about to take up the question of Sidote's threats. With all his stories about stabbing drunks in the kidneys, had she believed him? "Did the police find bodies behind the Ponderosa?"

At first she'd believed him, she said, "but then it was too . . . ."

"Preposterous?" Konrad filled the blank. "Did you believe he'd killed all these people?"

"No, sir," said Ginny.

Konrad now challenged her amnesia the night of the alleged crime. She held fast. No, she couldn't remember if it was her normal routine to work weekend nights, and, no, she and Jack had not decided together to take the night off. She'd simply been home alone, reading a book, and fallen asleep until awakened by Sidote. Beyond that she could remember nothing about their departure. Asked the time of Sidote's return, she adopted her indignant tone to repeat what she had often said in her own defense: "Mr. Konrad, this day has no significance to me other than the fact that I left New Orleans after that night."

"When did you go blank?" Konrad asked.

"I started packing when Jack went over and told Wasyl we were going to leave. That's all I remember. I've tried to remember."

Konrad again backed off, even though "starting to pack" was a new detail. Nevertheless, Konrad had rattled her slightly. Doubtless her failure to remember was the strangest aspect of her story, and she said in an almost whiny voice that there are "all these stories," and that Wasyl had said that she and Jack "went together." Konrad corrected her. No, Wasyl and Jack both remembered that she and Jack left on separate planes and that Wasyl drove. Reed objected, but he was overruled; Ginny was now backpedaling: She'd read in a statement that she and Jack left together. "Then I remembered him saying that I left first, he left later."

"May I see that statement?" Konrad pounced. "If your attorneys have that statement . . . we're entitled to see it."

What statement this could possibly be, no one knew. Ginny's attorneys were confused, too, and denied the existence of such a statement. Konrad asked if she thought there was such a statement.

"I don't know where I heard it from, I don't know where I read it," she stammered. She tried to suggest that everyone's memory of the departure was cloudy and contradictory, but Konrad now took a different approach. Had she ever been hypnotized? he asked.

Foat: When I had my teeth fixed.
Konrad: In this case?
Foat: No.
Konrad: Who was Miss Waller?

Reed objected, but Judge Burns overruled him. In fact, Konrad was barking up the wrong tree. He knew or suspected that a psychologist had prepared Ginny to testify but had mistakenly assumed that it was Terry Waller, the Jury Project expert. Still, when Ginny insisted that Terry Waller had only helped with jury selection, Konrad challenged: Didn't she know that she was a psychologist?

"I don't know her degree," Foat hedged. She seemed worried about revealing either that she'd worked with a therapist or that a psychologist had helped pick the jury.

Konrad now returned to the striking contrast between her detailed memories of so many other events and her total blank about the New Orleans departure.

"I've tried to remember it, because I'm the only one who can't seem to remember it," she replied, indeed making the prosecution's point.

A few minutes later Konrad took up the same theme when he reminded her that she'd described Sidote's "little-boy look" after the Samoan incident as the same as the one he'd "had in New Orleans." She remembered that expression but not how she left town? he asked, incredulous.

"Yes, sir," she said.

Konrad moved on to questions about money. Sidote sometimes seemed to have money, sometimes not, she said, but she didn't know why. Nor was she made curious by the sudden appearance of hundred-dollar bills.

Now the DA seemed to be running out of steam as he consulted his papers and then randomly took up loose ends. Amid these loose ends, however, he blurted the crucial question: With the many, many incidents of beatings, why hadn't she left? Couldn't her parents send the air fare? Wasn't she just "a phone call away"?

She admitted that was true and that she'd been jealous of Wasyl when he left.

"Couldn't you have gone back, too?" Konrad pressed.

"Logically, but not physically or emotionally. I was dependent on him."

This should have been the hardest and the most significant part of his cross-examination, since it was unclear why she'd been dependent on him, especially when he was in jail. Moreover, why had she been frightened by his threats of "seeing her rot in jail," which she again insisted he'd made more than two or three times ("I didn't touch on all of them")?

But Konrad was trying to impugn her character rather than probe the motivations for her failure to leave Sidote. His accusation: that she had had an affair with a married man. It seemed beside the point, except that her response was exactly her defense for taking up with Sidote. Raymond Foat was separated from his wife when they'd started their affair, she said, overlooking the fact that she had still been married, even though physically separated from Sidote. Still, it seemed unlikely the jury would convict her for bad character or lack of judgment.

Konrad now suggested that she'd always been afraid of the police. When she was arrested in 1977, why had she given her name as Meg Austin? he asked. (Meg Austin was her sister-in-law's name.) She said that when the four or five men came to her door, she didn't know they were police officers. Then after they were in the house she told them her real name.

Wasn't it true, Konrad went on, that it was *she* who'd contacted Sidote in two phone calls between 1970 and 1977? The first, she agreed, was shortly after their separation to discuss their divorce. The second, in 1973, was actually a call to his mother. Again Konrad didn't challenge her by asking the time of the phone call, and if 6 A.M. Eastern time, 3 A.M. California time, was the usual time for condolence calls.

As it later became known, Mrs. Sidote was sequestered in the courthouse, ready and willing to testify that Ginny had asked to speak to Jack when she'd phoned at 6 A.M. More, that at the time she had suffered no recurrence of cancer, which Ginny had said was the reason for the call. Nevertheless, according to Tom Porteous, Mrs. Sidote was so angry at Ginny, blaming her for her son's downfall, that they were loath to call her to the stand, even though her testimony might support the State's argument that if she had feared Sidote's revenge, she would not have contacted him, nor even his mother.

In fact, Konrad now reminded her, in her 1977 twenty-two-page police statement, she hadn't talked about beatings, much less threats to see her "rot in jail" for his crimes.

"I tried to tell the police how scared I was," she countered, then asked to read her statement. During the fifteen-minute recess she looked stricken as she read the statement, but with the jury back in, she seemed to forget the question at hand. Instead she went back to explain it was in this statement that she had read that, according to Wasyl, she and Jack had flown together from New Orleans.

Konrad was no longer interested, however. Had she told the police in 1977 about Sidote's threats? he pushed.

"I told them he had threatened to kill me, that he was crazy," she said. "But they didn't seem interested in that. . . . I had the feeling that I was cut off by them."

Konrad wanted a yes or a no: Had she mentioned the threat of false accusation?

No, she allowed with a sigh, not in this statement.

The cross-examination seemed to have run its course as Konrad returned to earlier questions almost randomly. Foat admitted that Sidote wasn't in a rage and didn't threaten her when she spoke to him in 1973. He seemed cold, but she didn't remember the conversation, she was just "real surprised to get him on the phone." No, she hadn't called anyone to complain about the beatings from 1967 to 1970, not even anyone back East, no, not even Angie Armstrong, Jack's sister.

Konrad then returned to the crucial question of her final decision to leave Sidote. Hadn't she decided to leave him before the last incident?

"Yes, shortly before." She hadn't told him yet, though, because she "wasn't going to leave him until he was out."

But hadn't she told him on one of his furloughs, when he was still in fact locked up? asked Konrad.

"Yes, sir," replied Foat.

Letting the illogic speak for itself, Konrad paused and consulted his notes for several moments. Then he looked up at the judge.

"No more questions," he said.

Judge Burns did a double take, then stared at the prosecutors. The jurors gaped, too, as Ginny looked up, seemingly stunned.

Reed's redirect examination was brief, but it provoked one last battle among the attorneys. He asked if Ginny had talked about Sidote in other 1977 statements. Yes, she had, it seemed, but immediately Judge Burns sent the jury out and called the attorneys to the bench. Reed was referring to a 1977 statement in which both the Louisiana charge and the Nevada charge were discussed. In his pretrial decision, Judge Burns had ruled out allusions to the Nevada charge. Now Reed argued that those segments that bore on Konrad's cross-examination should be excerpted and allowed in. Konrad was unyielding: The statement could be admitted only in its entirety. Judge Burns agreed, and since that would acquaint the jury with the Nevada charge, he excluded the entire statement. Reed noted his objection again, arguing that because he could not excerpt from the statment he couldn't rebut the State's inference that Ginny had made inconsistent statements. Judge Burns remained firm and had the jury brought back in.

Reed tried to come in the back door. Suddenly, he began to read from Ginny's statement: "page thirteen: Look at Mr. Scott's response: 'A man will never turn in his woman out of revenge—' "

Konrad was on his feet objecting. The statement had to be entered in its entirety, he shouted, on the verge of referring to the Nevada charge.

"This is grandstanding," Reed shouted frantically. "Remove the jury! Remove the jury!"

The jury was finally removed, and while Reed and Konrad continued to shout at each other, Burns seethed. Not only were the attorneys virtually ignoring him during their shouting match. Worse, Reed had flown directly in the face of his ruling, and then challenged his authority by demanding, "Remove the jury!"

Courtroom decorum was at a low, and Burns finally called a recess. "I want to see you in my office!" he said to Reed in an ominous voice, much like that of a father promising a trip to the woodpile.

After the recess, Reed returned with a sulky look but continued to argue that the State should agree to excerpt the statement. Konrad refused, and Burns repeated his ruling that since the defense could introduce the statement only in full, he would exclude it. Once again, Reed noted his objection and glanced over his shoulder at Kay, who was blinking back tears.

Realizing that her excuse for giving the police an alias in 1977 sounded flimsy, Reed now asked her to elaborate. She had given her name as Meg Austin because with the four to six men outside her door, "I thought they were people who . . . I was having a very nasty battle with Raymond about the business. It involved attorneys, and I didn't want to be the first to be served."

Once more she clung to her explanation for the 1973 phone call to Jack's mother, that she'd heard she was ill again, and she called "out of respect for her."

Finally, to dispute Sidote's impression that she had been drunk and incoherent on the phone, Reed asked how her life was going in 1973. Her life was going very well, she said, since she was the catering manager of the Hilton, "right next to the Nixon California

White House. A lot of White House people came in there, and I was doing very well."

Reed seemed to be preparing for another rhetorical flourish. Konrad, however, disrupted his rhythm with an objection to his first question, "How difficult is it to go back to events eighteen years ago?" But finally he was allowed to ask what she had to do to dredge up these memories.

"I have to make myself naked in front of everybody," Ginny said, once again adopting the little-girl voice. "I have to make myself talk about things I've never talked about to anyone."

Could she talk about these things to four police officers? Reed reiterated.

"No," she said simply without elaborating.

"How difficult is it to talk to us?" he asked, as if he were prompting her to another emotional crescendo.

Konrad's objection precluded any reply.

"The defense rests, your Honor," said Reed. Weeping again, Ginny returned to the defense table.

For all the talk about the district attorneys' insensitivity and persecution of a feminist, Ginny Foat had been handled with kid gloves.

ELEVEN

The Strong
Feminist Reborn

CHAOS reigned the next morning, Wednesday, November 16, when even more spectators showed up, informed by the evening news that on this, the ninth day of the trial, the case was about to go to the jury. The courtroom was locked, and the bailiff was checking press badges before letting reporters inside. Spectators were moved into an orderly line to await admittance one by one. Ginny, her lawyers, and her mother and sister arrived. But before they could be escorted into the courtroom, Nancy Konrad, Gordon Konrad's wife and herself a juvenile court judge in the same building, approached Ginny's mother. Handing Mrs. Galluzzo a small blue copy of *The Pieta Prayer Booklet,* she said, "My thoughts are with you."

Mrs. Galluzzo smiled and showed her the rosary she had entwined in her fingers. For all the defense team's derision of her husband, Mrs. Konrad said she understood what any mother must be feeling at a time like this.

With everyone crowded into all the available seats, the session began with Judge Burns ruling against most of the defense's requests for special instructions. He did, however, agree to raise the venue issue (where the body was found) as something the State had to prove; he would also instruct the jury that if they thought a witness had willfully deceived, then they could disregard his entire testimony. Reed then moved that the manslaughter alternative be stricken from the jury's charge. Konrad argued that the jury could reach a verdict on the lesser charge, and Judge Burns agreed.

The jurors filed into the jury box. They seemed extremely serious, aware that today was their day, and Judge Burns's instruction to "pay particular attention to the closing arguments" seemed almost superfluous.

John Mamoulides led off the State's closing argument and focused almost exclusively on the question of Sidote's credibility. His tone was unemotional as he told the jury that the defense had in effect put John Sidote on trial by bringing out his alcoholism, violence, and prison record, all of which "was elicited to determine whether he was telling the truth." Still, while the talk "about beatings, alcohol, and state of mind" went to the credibility of the witness, John Sidote was not on trial. He directed the jury to consider what someone "had to gain or lose by testifying," and pointed out that while Foat claimed not to recall the night she left New Orleans, Bozydaj and Sidote remembered their departure with only minor discrepancies. His was the commonsense approach adopted from the beginning of the trial; indeed, he concluded by asking the jury to analyze the testimony and use its common sense to determine whether "both or three or one are telling the truth about the night Moises Chayo was killed." By both he meant Sidote and Bozydaj; by one, Ginny. But all three was illogical. By trying to seem fair he'd blurred his crucial argument: Two people tell virtually the same story about the circumstances of that night; one person says she can't remember. If the jury believed Sidote and Bozydaj, then it would have to believe Sidote was credible and telling the truth about the crime as well.

Porteous followed and came on strong. While also stressing logic and common sense, he cast doubts on the image of Ginny Foat as a passive, weak, vulnerable victim and called her testimony about Sidote's threat of "seeing her rot in jail" and his motive for revenge "a recent fabrication." Admitting that Sidote was an alcoholic, Porteous reminded the jury that he had been on the stand five hours without changing his story. Also, he asked, how could he be out for revenge when he hadn't communicated with her from 1970 to 1977 and it was she who had phoned him twice? And why had he refused to testify against her in 1977 if he was so bent on revenge?

Porteous became sarcastic when he reminded the jury that while the defense had tried to portray Moises Chayo as a gambler, his own son didn't know he gambled and the man with whom he played cards in New Orleans had never seem him play poker. Besides, he added, "Can you picture John Sidote walking into the New Orleans Athletic Club?" The jury laughed, realizing that the club was fairly proper; at the same time, however, they'd betrayed their attitude toward Sidote, which was the prosecution's greatest liability.

Now Porteous disputed the frequency and severity of Sidote's beatings. This seemed the weakest strategy. Still, he had an effect on the jurors when he called attention to Wasyl's statement that he hadn't seen any bruises, and disparaged Foat's explanation that she'd concealed such marks with clothes. " 'We had fun running along the beach,' " he quoted her, adding, "In what, long-sleeved blouses?"

Now he came to what he called her "blackout," lasting from the night she left New Orleans until the dry counties of Texas. Reed's technique, "Where are you now? What is he saying?" had elicited a great many details. " 'Then he did this, then he did that,' " he mimicked in a staccato voice. " 'And then he came in and he had that little-boy look.' But when asked, 'How did you leave New Orleans?' she said, 'I don't remember, I built a wall.' I'll tell you why she built a wall," Porteous said, his voice rising: "She and Sidote left New Orleans separately, because together they killed Moises Chayo. And it is only when they are back together in Texas that the defendant gives lots of details again."

At last Porteous had introduced emotion into the State's appeal to common sense. Of the three prosecutors he argued most forcefully that Foat had reshaped her history, not only for her defense but in the way she presented herself to the world. While there were inconsistencies in Sidote's various statements, he said, they were understandable given the length of time that had passed. By contrast, the defense had tried to make everything too consistent to fit the image of Ginny Foat as only "a passive lady reborn after she left Sidote."

He argued that the details of Foat's earlier life indicated a more complex and willful person. After all, he said, how could a passive woman hold so many jobs, drive to the Midwest alone, and finally just pick up and leave with a man, contrary to the advice of her parents? Nor was she so passive the five years she was with Sidote, he continued. Of course, he said, modulating his voice with some sympathy, Sidote did hurt her (although his tone also suggested some skepticism about all the "lengthy talk" about the beatings). Nevertheless, he concluded, his voice vehement: she "was not *that* weak.

I do not condone what Sidote did, but the defendant was not that passive."

Ginny seemed stricken by his remarks and was blinking rapidly. For the first time the prosecution was on the attack. Porteous argued, She would have you believe that for six months she was passive while Sidote was nice to her, and then once they'd left New York and he began smacking her, she also just accepted it passively. "But she has to tell it that way to make [the story] flow."

It was a crucial point, and the jury seemed to be looking at Ginny's portrait in a new light.

After attacking the defense's argument that Sidote confessed in 1977 to two robbery-murders because he was going to be sentenced for burglary (is it reasonable that someone would trade a possible one-to-four-year sentence for two life sentences?), Porteous returned to his main point that Ginny Foat on the stand was a recent fabrication as well. While he conceded the violence of their last fight, he argued that Sidote had no motive of revenge, since after their separation they'd not had contact; their past together had been left behind. "But the past," Porteous said passionately, "is the one thing Virginia Foat cannot hide from any longer. She cannot build walls around her past anymore. We have laid out Ms. Foat's past to you. Ms. Foat's past is her downfall. Ms. Foat's past has *caused her to be here today*. She must be held accountable for her crime. She must be punished for it."

Robert Glass's closing argument began with the same assumption: that Ginny's past had caused her to be here today. Yet he would praise her for it, not punish her for it. "There are only two truths here," he said. "Ginny Foat is innocent, and John Sidote is a crazy person and a liar." His voice became emotional: "You saw Ginny glowing in the glow of innocence and you saw in Jack Sidote the red glow of the devil." He turned and addressed Ginny directly. "I listened to you, I heard you get naked in front of the jury, in front of your mother and sister. You told things no human being of pride would want to tell. Therefore, I know you're innocent."

The jury must hold John Sidote to be a truth teller before it could find Ginny guilty beyond a reasonable doubt, he said. Therefore, he would lay out the true nature of the man's character "to prove Jack Sidote is a liar." Yet he preferred to talk about Ginny Foat first, he said, since her life, her truth, is "uplifting" while Jack Sidote represents "degradation and death."

Once again he recited how Ginny had "come to be" with Jack Sidote. That was the central question, especially if Sidote was as vile as the defense had implied. Even though Glass called him "that word merchant, charmer, women's man, bartender," he blamed Sidote, implying a concerted deception. Not only had Ginny been "very low" and vulnerable in 1964 and 1965, Sidote "knew a glimmer of class and substance, and he went about showing Ginny Foat that he was the man for her." He made her feel important and he could show her a good time because he was the man "who could take the horses out at two, three, four in the morning." Then he explained the attraction as a function of Ginny's innocence. She'd been conned because "at the center of her core are good things, love, loyalty, helpfulness, kindness." These virtues were the "seeds that bloomed and blossomed over the years," he said. In contrast, "Jack Sidote had a hole where conscience should be," and "that hole grew and grew so what you saw was a frame without a core, a shadow without a substance." But Ginny "was the same Ginny then as the Ginny now."

"Ginny now" hadn't put in an appearance, but the jury might still wonder whether her attraction to Sidote or her failure to leave him was explained either by her essential goodness or the implicit feminist gloss with which Glass excused her from any sense of responsibility. She had been conditioned to stand by her man, he said: "She couldn't get away from the tradition that made it the woman's fault if something was wrong." So she stayed "for good reasons," he repeated, not wanting to alienate the jurors who thought the tradition acceptable, but at the same time blaming Ginny's life with Sidote on "the feminine mystique." While admitting that the yoke that bound her to Sidote was "her doing in part," he implied that the tradition had been forced on her. She looked back "with the pain and shame which you saw," he continued, but she had "the will and the trust to share with you the things she went through."

He was indignant that the DAs had suggested the jury hadn't seen "the true person," since Ginny Foat had been on the stand for four hours telling about "the patterns of beating and subservience" and could have been cross-examined on these things. "But Mr. Konrad sat *down* there" (Glass pointed to the counsel table, as if to stress Konrad's bad manners in not standing for a lady) and asked only about Sidote's threat to put her in jail. And how dare the prosecutor doubt the beatings, he said. "Will he say Mrs. Galluzzo lied?

Was her sister lying when she said 'her face looked like a punching bag'?"

After a few more remarks about Sidote's lying, a brief recess was called. The respite seemed to have calmed Glass as he began in a more subdued voice to list the discrepancies between Sidote's testimony and that of the State's only "corroborative witness," Wasyl Bozydaj. Then he turned to Ginny's failure to remember the night she'd left New Orleans. "If she doesn't remember, it's because it wasn't important to her," he said, not because she is lying. After all, a plane trip wouldn't have been so important to someone who had been "a flight attendant." Besides, he argued, if she were lying, she could have said, " 'Jack said to go and I went,' " since "independence was knocked out of her." Or "she could have made up a story." What she remembered was only "the little-boy look." "*That* was important to her," he said, not her "means of transportation."

Now Glass turned his attention to Jack Sidote, arguing that the jury had seen only his Dr. Jekyll side and insisting that Sidote not only consciously lied but lied without knowing it, changing things over time "to make himself look as good as possible, to accept as little responsibility as possible . . . for what he'd done. . . . He's a phony human being," Glass shouted, "with no sense of right or wrong or of what is nice or kind." Still shouting, Glass repeatedly called Sidote a liar, and reached his emotional peak as he cited Sidote's revolving-door drinking and prison sentences: "He's not like any human being, he's an animal, a snake!"

After detailing more discrepancies in the State's evidence and suggesting an alternate version of that night (Sidote and the fourth man rolling Chayo after a card game), Glass returned to the main theme of his argument. "Why does a man like Jack Sidote make up a story about Ginny Foat?" he asked. His answer: Because of his irrationality, hallucinations, and psychotic breaks, and because in 1977 he'd just come out of a treatment center but was back on a fifth of whiskey a day, and was suicidal. He mimicked what Sidote might have said to himself in 1977: " 'Jack, you're gonna go back to jail anyway. Why am I like this? Because Ginny left me in 1970. . . . I stole the money for her because she needed to be with a person with money. I did it for her. Goddamn, she's gonna pay for it, too.' "

His "last graceful act," said Glass, returning to Sidote's motivation, could be seen in the final paragraph in his March 16, 1977, statement when he admitted, " 'At first I thought it was for vengeance.' " That was "a little beacon" of truth, said Glass, proving that the man had been obsessed with Ginny, suggesting even that he was still in love with her. Perhaps he thought his 1977 confession would be only "an inconvenience" for Ginny Foat, Glass told the jury. He would "bring her down, humiliate her, and then release her like he did before, when he made up stories and then said they weren't true, when he beat her and then said she was beautiful." But now his "demonic evil" had come back to haunt him and he was "stuck with it."

Glass listed more examples of Sidote's lies. In August the defense committee had heralded Sidote's court petition as his first moment of truth; but now Glass presented Sidote's allegation of coercion by Porteous as another lie. That charge of intimidation had brought Konrad, Mamoulides, and Porteous back to Nevada, Glass said, "at the taxpayers' expense." They were forced "to do additional things for John Sidote," because "that charmer had talked them into believing him. They had made their beds, they were stuck with him, so they went trooping out west" and told Sidote "they'd help out." Glass's contempt was obvious, and Judge Burns seemed as indignant as the prosecutors at Glass's innuendos of unprofesional behavior.

Glass went on to excoriate Sidote as the man "who's invited every woman to tell his story," from *Rolling Stone* to *The Village Voice* and four hours on CBS, and who tried to sell his story to *Playboy* and *Penthouse*.

Then he reached his rhetorical climax: Someone once wrote that the masses are more easily deceived by "big lies," he said. "You can tell the most impudent lie and something always remains from it." The author of that book? Hitler in *Mein Kampf*. But his analogy, that Sidote was Hitler, Ginny Foat like the Jews, persecuted for being who she was, a woman and a feminist, was probably a bit complex for the jury, since her feminism had been scrupulously excluded from the trial.

Glass concluded, "It makes me feel ugly to talk about Jack Sidote. Maybe he's to be pitied, but he's certainly not to be credited." He'd rather talk about Ginny Foat, he said, "about life-serving people, not death-dealing. Ginny is innocent. . . . Jack Sidote is a crazy person and a liar." Now he paused and repeated the direction with which the defense had begun the trial: "Look at Ginny and say, 'Ginny, I've heard you and I believe you . . .' "

Others would look at Jack Sidote, he added, and say he cannot be believed. But Ginny, he ended in a declamatory voice, was kind, loyal, loving, industrious. Those qualities were there back then, they are still in her today, and are the reason why she "got out from under on her own and made herself who she is today."

Scattered applause came from Ginny's supporters as Judge Burns called another short recess. After the break, Reed continued the defense's closing arguments, returning to the melodramatic emotionalism of his opening argument and, like Glass, asking the jury to concentrate on "looks" and "feelings." He reminded the jurors that during the voir dire he had brought Ginny up to meet them, one by one, because he had wanted them to meet the woman he'd met eight months before. But the woman they later saw on the stand was not the woman who'd brought all these people to the courtroom, he said. Instead, they saw the woman in Sidote's cage of four or five years. Brick by brick the walls were torn down, the walls, he explained, that "protected her from who she was twelve years ago."

Once again his rhetorical flourish had confused the point. For all the "walls" and "cages" of this trial, it was hard to decide where the real self existed. Authenticity for him, though, had to do with "standing naked," showing herself completely in a way "you never do even with loved ones": "She relived the experiences she'd gone through when she lived with Sidote, and you saw the woman who loved, cared, and endured . . . You saw the face of a good, fine, wonderful person who endured because of the qualities she had then. You saw not the face of a murderer but that of a wonderful, fine woman."

He had returned to the defense's leitmotiv—her "looks." "Look at her," he now cried to the jury. "Tell Ginny she need not be ashamed anymore, that she need not fear Jack Sidote anymore. Jack Sidote made her bare herself, just as he beat her and made her stand naked."

Sounding close to tears himself, he bade the jury, "Tell Ginny he can't beat her anymore . . . , tell Ginny that it is over, that she is out of the cage, that he can't come back . . . , that Jack Sidote isn't going to haunt her for the rest of her life. . . ."

Reed and Glass held Ginny's hands as Gordon Konrad gave his rebuttal. His voice smoldered with angry sarcasm as he, like Porteous, tried to undermine the image of the passive, innocent victim.

He reminded the jury that there was only one source for this portrait of Sidote as crazy and monstrous, the defendant herself. But
she stayed with him! he exclaimed. Then more calmly, he said he'd
been around sixteen years as a prosecutor and he felt the descriptions of the beatings were horrible, "So I know they must have been
horrible for you." He paused. "But she didn't leave him!"

This was not a dependent woman, Konrad argued. She drove
alone to the Midwest, she was an airline stewardess. But "to hear
her describe it, she was living with Charles Manson." Implying that
she stayed with Sidote not "out of loyalty" but because of their
mutual guilt, he cited her three other marriages, all of which she
left easily, including the fourth in all of a month. The defense was
really saying, he continued, "Don't look at the facts. Look at the
monster. Then look at the little lady" (his voice was heavy with
contempt) "so good, so pure of heart," who says she stayed with
one man even though she easily left three other men. She "left a
child after one hour," but she "couldn't leave Jack out of loyalty."

Ginny bowed her head and began to weep as Glass clutched her
shoulder. Konrad might very well question her "dependence" and
"passivity" by the trip alone to the Midwest, but to use the detail
of the child seemed heartless, especially since the usual procedure in
such homes was to remove the child from the mother as quickly as
possible. More, the cheap shot might alienate the jury as it had the
spectators.

Yet he seemed unaware of the outraged murmurs in the courtroom as he argued that Ginny was the stronger partner. "Whose
cage was who in?" he asked, insisting that Sidote had been leading
a successful life before he "fell for the defendant for some reason."
Then when they ran out of money, he went on, they decided to rob
someone, maybe with no intention of murdering anyone. But those
years were bad years for him, too, "even though Mr. Glass would
have you believe he was a man of no conscience." Yes, Konrad
conceded, in 1977 he was drinking again, but not when he went to
the police and bared his soul. "A rational man can do just that. It
happens all the time in law enforcement."

The suggestion that Ginny was the evil force behind Jack's
downfall brought muted jeers and laughter from the spectators.
Konrad paused a moment but seemed to ignore the hostility around
him. Once more his goal was to convince the jury that Sidote's 1977
statement was truthful, given voluntarily to relieve his conscience

and not to get the defendant. A statement "against his own interest should be given the greatest veracity," he said, suddenly switching to legal language. That is why, he concluded, if the jury found his reasons for confessing believable, then it must find his story believable.

Again he repeated the prosecution's main argument: Why could she remember not having to work that night, that "she stayed home and read a book," and yet could give "no explanation of why she refuses to tell us why they got on a plane separately?"

His other main point was that she hadn't told the police in her 1977 statement about Sidote's weird threat "to see her rot in jail." "A weird threat," he repeated, supposedly made on three or four occasions, and she'd never mentioned it to the police? Logically, wouldn't that be the first thing you'd tell the police? he asked the jury.

The State had proved its case beyond a reasonable doubt, Konrad concluded, because it was reasonable to believe that the statements of Sidote "made on his very own" and that "would put himself in jail for the rest of his life" were the most truthful kind of statement. Wasyl Bozydaj also confirmed parts of his statement. The defense, he said, had needed to create an aura of craziness, had needed to accuse Sidote of despicable deeds. Ending on a peculiarly flat, unemotional note, he said the State had proved that the defendant was with Sidote the night of the murder.

Judge Burns's instructions to the jury were equally straightforward, cutting through the emotionalism of the defense: The jury was to decide on the basis of the testimony and evidence alone. To find her guilty, they had to conclude that the State had proved its case beyond a reasonable doubt. The defendant, however, did not have to prove herself innocent.

Nor was the jury to be influenced by public opinion. Given the obvious media attention, the rows of journalists and courtroom artists, that, of course, would be hard for them to do. Further, they were not to be swayed by sympathy or compassion; another tall order when the defense had built its case on stories intended to arouse precisely these emotions.

Ginny had been staring at the jurors, blinking, blinking, blinking. Her face looked heavier, as if she'd folded in on herself, especially when Judge Burns listed the charges that the jury was to deliberate: Find the defendant guilty of murder, find her guilty of the lesser offense of manslaughter—a homicide committed in a sudden passion but without intent to kill or in the course of a criminal act, or find her not guilty on all charges. And finally he announced that there were a few details of "housekeeping" to be taken care of. In a trial punctuated by references to women's "traditional" roles, it seemed ironic, and as if he were aware of the trial's subtext, when he gave a nod toward feminism by instructing the jury to choose a "foreperson."

The jury was ushered out at 1:45. They would begin their deliberations over lunch. The principals in the case adjourned to a nearby restaurant. There Ginny Foat took it upon herself to apologize to the woman proprietor behind the bar for Konrad's "insult" to all waitresses when he'd implied that there was something sordid about Ginny's stints as a barmaid. Tom Porteous had taken Reed aside on the way out of the courthouse and apologized for Konrad's remark about the baby. A decent gesture, but Foat seemed ready to use that against the prosecutors as well when even before the verdict she had shifted to pronouncements about the prosecutors' male chauvinism.

At 3:35, just under two hours later, the bailiff ran down the courtroom hallway where reporters had settled in for a verdict watch. "They're coming in, they're coming in," he shouted.

A deputy was sent across to the restaurant to summon Ginny and her attorneys, plus the group of supporters who had joined them for lunch. With the jury in so quickly, they were confident, laughing and hugging each other and Ginny. They pulled Mrs. Galluzzo along as they hurried back to the courthouse and pushed through the crowds into the courtroom.

John Mamoulides looked angry and dour as he entered the courtroom. The three DAs were well aware of what a speedy verdict betokened. Bob Glass and John Reed approached them, extending their hands in the attorneys' ritual of wishing each other good luck. Gordon Konrad fairly hissed at them and turned away. Glass and Reed looked stunned, but they returned to Ginny with triumphant smiles on their faces. They sat again, each clasping one of Ginny's hands. Ginny's eyes were once more blinking uncontrollably.

Finally Judge Burns beckoned to the bailiff. Ginny remained standing, still holding Reed's and Glass's hands, as the jurors filed in with somber expressions, none looking in her direction. It was courtroom legend that a jury with a "guilty" verdict will not look at a defendant. But then as Judge Burns called on the young blond man who'd been chosen the jury "foreperson," another man winked, and there were hints of smiles from two of the older women.

The clerk took the slip of paper from the foreman and handed it to the judge. There was total silence as Judge Burns looked at Ginny and read, "We, the jury, find the defendant, Virginia Foat, not guilty."

The spectators burst into cheers and shouts. Ginny slumped as if she were about to faint. Reed and Glass held her up and embraced her as journalists, spectators, friends, and jurors all surged toward her.

"Thank you, thank you," cried Annabelle Hall, the Nevada lawyer, to the jury above the general pandemonium. Like many of Ginny's supporters, and even her attorneys, she was in tears. Judge Burns didn't try to restore order but swiftly exited to his chambers; the DAs also hurried out unnoticed.

Several members of the jury—four of the five were women—pushed forward for Foat's autograph to be signed on napkins and placemats from lunch. John Reed praised them, "You were a wonderful jury, you were just great. This is why we have juries." Then in his excitement he raised his fist in a sixties salute and shouted, "All power to the jury."

The talkative older woman with the large watery eyes and asthmatic cough now approached Ginny.

"I didn't know if you knew about talking with your eyes," she said.

"Oh, I could see it in your eyes," said Ginny. Then she inscribed the cloth napkin the woman had placed before her, "My love and appreciation for your eyes. They're a measure of your heart."

Bob Tuller, her California lawyer, stood quietly by as reporters interviewed Jean Conger about Ginny's "return to the women's movement."

"Ginny can't ever leave the women's movement, just as the women's movement can never leave her," Jean announced.

Bob Tuller winced and later spoke his thoughts aloud: "For her own sake I hope she stays far away from those women, or they'll try something else."

But Jean had continued enthusiastically. "She's free, she's free! She has a fabulous future wherever she wants to go. She can do whatever she wants for the rest of her life. Just give her a few minutes to realize that she's finally free!"

Ginny Foat hardly needed those few minutes. John Reed had announced a press conference at ten the next morning. Ginny, however, clutched his shoulders and said, "We'll miss the news," and Reed rescheduled for six that evening.

Kay had finally reached Ginny's side. "This shitty, shitty year is finally over," she cried as she embraced her. Side by side they made their way out of the courthouse with Reed and Glass, as well as Mrs. Galluzzo and the defense committee, following close behind. Outside, a crowd had gathered and as Ginny came down the front steps, it sent up a cheer, "Who Dat Dey Say!" It was the New Orleans Saints ritual chant, shouted for Ginny Foat's moment of victory.

The law library of Reed and Glass's New Orleans office was packed with reporters and TV cameras. There Ginny Foat, the passive woman on the witness stand, was suddenly transformed into "the strong feminist by the same name." With only a few notes in front of her, she spoke firmly and without hesitation into the microphones and cameras. "It's as if she's prerecorded her speech and simply pushed the 'play' button," said one journalist.

Foat lashed out at the prosecutors' sexism, not only for taking the word of an alcoholic, schizophrenic, violent man over that of any woman, but for robbing women of their dignity with the "sexist perspective" that informed their cross-examination about the things in her life that "were most painful."

Announcing her case as symbolic, she proclaimed her verdict "a victory for all women whose plight in life it is to have to stay in a position because of social mores. When they choose to move on, they run the risk of being prosecuted." She said she was being prosecuted for her marriages ("Who could have a good relationship after living with a Sidote?" she asked), and either for being able to leave him finally, or for "not leaving somebody when I thought I could help." Although she'd "hid for a long time," she "wasn't hiding anymore," she said, and she hoped her story would help other women—"and some men, too, I might add"—who are in the same situation.

She then established her role as a feminist spokesperson by reminding everyone that in the midst of her trial, no one had noticed that Congress had defeated a new ERA measure that very morning. When asked about "blaming anyone in the women's movement," she also played politician. A vendetta in NOW had led to her arrest, she insisted, but she had "no personal animosity," even though that seemed unlikely, given her and Kay's remarks about Mandell and Lafferty. Instead, she used the occasion to criticize NOW. "It used to be a grass-roots organization but now it's too worried about its corporation image." While individual members had supported her, national NOW leadership had backed away, "because I became something that tarnished the corporation image. They could have used my case as a rallying point," she insisted, "because of what it symbolizes," because she had become "vulnerable as a leader of that organization, not as a private citizen."

Obviously, Foat's bitterness toward NOW's leaders had not dissipated. It was unclear whether she would in fact go back to that organization. She said that she would be using the money from her movie—to be produced by Marvin Minoff of Group W—and her book to be written with Laura Foreman to establish a defense fund for women in situations like hers. "You get as much justice as you can pay for. That changed my outlook quite a lot." She was especially concerned about minority women in prison ("White women don't usually go to jail"), but implicit in her remarks was the same notion that had surrounded Jean Harris's trial—that women were often not responsible for their crimes or they had been forced into a criminal act by social mores and therefore did not deserve to be in jail.

She talked more about her victimization at the hands of the prosecutors, the press, and an abusive husband. Asked, "Are you now free of John Sidote?" she replied that she hoped he'd be put out in the ocean to work on an oil rig. "I've always feared for my life with him," she said, now explaining that the reason she had moved to Canada and "changed" her name was to "escape Sidote" (presumably when she'd married Ray Foat in Vancouver).

Once again the story seemed to have changed, or at least she'd altered the stress she was giving to certain facts. Thus it seemed ironic when she said that before the trial Mamoulides had offered to reduce the charge to accessory after the fact. The prosecutors later denied any plea bargaining, but at her press conference Foat said, with a laugh, that she had told them she would "plead guilty only to wearing a mask on a day other than Mardi Gras—which is a crime in New Orleans."

Soon she brought the session to a close, but with the telecast of her statements on the news that night and subsequent interviews, members of the jury began to wonder if she wasn't in fact guilty of wearing a mask. They were astonished by her feminist rhetoric, her insistence that she was a symbol for all women. Theirs was only a reasonable-doubt verdict, they said, not a victory for women's rights. They had decided among themselves not to talk about their deliberations; however, once they saw Ginny Foat on all the morning TV news shows as well as *Nightline,* they began to talk.

Ginny Foat's declamations about her trial ran roughshod over their sense of themselves and their understanding of their experience in the courtroom. They agreed with the district attorneys' assessment—it was a classic reasonable-doubt verdict, because "it all came down to Sidote." They'd been suspicious of him from the moment he walked into the courtroom. "A gut reaction," they admitted, but they'd taken an immediate dislike to "his cocky strut of a walk," to "the way he clasped his hands in front of him like he was handcuffed," to "his jailhouse lawyer talk about 'incarceration,' " to his "alcoholic weeping" and "his self-pity when he cried he was on trial, too." They distrusted him for his self-confessed alcoholism, his prison record, and his two immunity agreements, and they had only cynical laughter when he denied physically abusing Foat by saying, "I only struck her, I never beat her." Since there were several discrepancies in Bozydaj's testimony, they felt he hadn't offered enough corroboration. While admitting that the State had raised some significant questions about Foat's "amnesia" the night of the crime, their impressions of Sidote were uniformly dubious, and it took only one vote to reach their not-guilty decision. As the jury foreman said, "After we saw Sidote, Ginny Foat could've taken the Fifth on everything and it wouldn't have mattered."

But it did matter to Foat; she wanted to tell her story, yet the image she and her attorneys had presented was designed more to elicit sympathy and "feelings" of protectiveness for what one juror called "the helpless little lamb." Like many of her fellow jurors, one woman thought Foat had also seemed hypnotized. Still, she said, "when I heard about all the beatings my heart went out to her."

While most jurors did sympathize, some suspected that her beatings had been overdramatized, her descriptions overrehearsed.

"It got to be like a recording," remarked the young union man, "and we thought it was overplayed. We wondered why she couldn't look at us and show her anger instead of just looking at the floor and crying. With Mr. Reed's whispering and all the hits and bruises, we asked, 'Why go through all the dramatics?'"

Besides, a number of jurors argued, if she had really been as passive and helpless as she appeared on the witness stand, perhaps she'd been under Sidote's control and been forced to participate in his crimes. Nevertheless, their doubts about her litany of beatings, her failure to remember leaving New Orleans, the discrepancies between her and Bozydaj's testimony (why hadn't he seen any bruises?), weren't enough to counter their suspicions of Sidote. For that they blamed the prosecutors; they hadn't "drilled" her hard enough, hadn't pressured her "except about the child" and then they'd "pushed too hard." In their minds, neither her suffering nor her feminism made her immune from a tough cross-examination. They asked, Why hadn't the prosecutors brought out things about her life in the same way the defense attorneys had to make Sidote look so bad? (His trying to sell his story to *Penthouse,* for example, had affected them, they said, and they wondered why the prosecutors hadn't revealed what Foat announced only at her press conference, namely that she, too, was "selling her story" and that a TV-movie was to be made of her trial.)

More, they were particularly astonished to hear Ginny Foat's televised accusations of a "political trial" or "political persecution." Once they heard that charge, they not only were angry, but they began to sense that Ginny Foat had been treated kindly by the prosecutors precisely for "political" reasons. Having finally heard the background of her arrest and the charges of antifeminism, several jurors thought that the State had treated Ginny Foat more gingerly than the usual defendant for fear of looking insensitive or seeming to confirm the stereotype of retrograde feminist-hating southern men.

Still, they insisted that Foat's feminism had played no role either in their impressions of her or in their deliberations. They were quite aware of Reed and Glass's emphasis on her looks and their feelings. Most jury members had been astonished when Ginny had been brought over to meet them during voir dire. "It shocked me real bad," said the grandmother of the group. "I didn't feel comfortable with their introducing her like 'Here, I want you to meet a friend.' I thought she was a real nice-looking woman, but that didn't come up in our talk, and neither did her women's lib stuff."

The union man, however, liked the idea of bringing her up to the jury box. "It made me think, could I look this woman in the eye and say she's guilty? I thought she was attractive and nicely dressed, but I wasn't going to judge her on that or on what women's movement organizations she'd belonged to. I couldn't have sat on the jury if I was just going to think, 'She's very pretty, she looks so innocent, how could she have done anything like Sidote said she did?' "

The jury foreman reported that the jurors were well aware of the media attention to the Foat trial but disputed the prosecutors' impression that the jury had felt that because of the case's notoriety, they needed more evidence to convict Foat than a jury in a less celebrated case. Nor did he feel that they had needed more evidence than usual to convict because of Foat's image of respectability and attractiveness.

"Sure, I thought she was pretty, so did the accountant who was a fraternity brother of mine, and we got real curious about what she'd looked like at twenty or twenty-one. We thought she must have been a very good-looking lady back then, but we also felt that even with all the ruffles and high-necks, she wasn't as innocent as she tried to come across. We caught on that Reed and Glass were doing a number on her image, telling us to look at her, standing up for her whenever she got up from the defense table. We didn't miss that but we kept it out of our deliberations."

And even the irrepressible woman, the most pro-Foat juror from the moment their eyes had met ("the staring of her eyes," she called it), insisted that she hadn't judged her on her looks or her "nice, pretty clothes," or because she resembled someone she knew, "almost a twin sister."

For all their insistence that neither Ginny's image nor her feminism nor the contrast between the stereotype of an aggressive feminist and Ginny's "feminine" attractiveness and ladylike respectability had swayed them, the jurors had been affected by her image of helplessness and passivity. In this respect, the defense's voir dire had accomplished what it had set out to do: find jurors whose "life experiences" would enable them to understand and sympathize with what Ginny had been through. Not only did they sympathize, but a few of the jurors called on events in their own lives to help answer some of the questions they'd had about Ginny's story.

In particular, they suspected that she was hiding something when she said she couldn't remember leaving New Orleans. But one woman, the grandmother, offered an explanation based on her personal experience with alcoholism. She told the other jurors that her father had been an alcoholic and had often lied (hence she suspected Sidote was lying); she said she also understood "blocking out" bad times in one's past. "I thought about it a great deal, and I told the other jurors that sooner or later you push things into the back of your mind, like my brothers and sisters and I did with things we wanted to forget about our father. That's why I thought maybe she had, too. With all that fighting back then, she could've blanked out that whole day and night and not remembered flying out of town." (Of course, Foat had said she'd blocked out that night because it was so ordinary; she remembered only the worst times.)

One of the jurors' major doubts was why she had stayed with Sidote so long if he'd been so violent and abusive; indeed, they considered if the motive had been shared guilt or her fear of his turning her in. The grandmother once again came to Ginny's defense: "I told the others about my mother staying with my father for twenty-five years, even though he was alcoholic. That kinda opened up all the rest of them and they started talking about what experiences they went through." One woman told of staying in a bad marriage until her mother died because she didn't want her mother saying, "See, I told you he was no good." Another woman admitted that she herself couldn't have gone through what Ginny had gone through, yet she told her fellow jurors, "I've been around people who have taken beatings or put up with alcoholics out of love. My own mother lived with my father, who was a drunk, a gambler, even a mental patient, until he died, which was when I was quite small."

Of the men, the union man most often agreed with the women, adding that he also believed that Sidote might have been out for revenge. Although he'd been slightly annoyed by the defense attorneys' personal questions about his divorce during voir dire, he found himself telling the other jurors about his ex-wife's false accusations and her repeated attempts to haul him into court to get even.

With such empathy for what Foat had suffered, why were jurors then "aggravated," "angry," or simply "shocked" at Foat's proclamations on television? In the first place, they were annoyed by what they saw as the manipulation of the story. They realized that the defense had created a narrative of victimization for the purposes of winning the case. Yet they insisted they had stalwartly deliberated "only on the facts." For her to misrepresent what had happened in the courtroom, for her suddenly to transform herself into a feminist and her case into a symbolic triumph, offended them. The foreman was particularly upset, the televised news conference prompting him to speak out.

"When she started talking like every one of us signed up for NOW, I got mad," he said. "Sure we asked for her autograph but that was out of our sense of jubilation that the trial was over. The fact is we listened to her and to a certain extent believed her and sympathized with her, even though my gut reaction—which others had, too—was that she knew more than she was saying and, like Sidote, had a convenient memory. And I especially began to wonder about that when she changed so quickly from the helpless victim to the women's rights leader. Two hours after the verdict I watched her and her supporters announce that it was a victory for feminism. That's when I said, 'Bullshit!' "

Ginny Foat's proclamations evoked more hostile attitudes toward feminism from the jurors than they had expressed during their voir dire. Whereas they had adopted the tolerant "I'm all for equal rights" or "equal pay for equal work" positions earlier, once they'd seen Foat on television, they were willing to express the antagonisms that had lurked beneath the surface of the trial. Even though feminism hadn't entered into their deliberations, they had been aware of Foat's supporters in the courtroom and had betrayed their attitude by joking about lesbianism among themselves. One juror said they thought that most of the spectators were Foat's "NOW associates from Los Angeles" and suspected that most of the women "fighting for the real hard-core women's rights" fit "that mold": "The visible NOW people seemed very butch and if they weren't gay, they were very masculine, and that led to the suspicion that was the way all of them were. Because there were two Davids on the jury, one with the nickname "DC," we started calling the other David AC, so AC/DC became our joke. It was our feeling that her whole support team was that way. In fact, I have the impression that the whole women's movement is like that, and that's why it's failed. When you get down to it, equal rights and equal pay for equal jobs are fine, but most people don't want all that stuff about gay rights. It's not just a life-style, like they say, but something that the bible frowns upon, and I think it's gross and disgusting.''

What seemed to lie at the heart of the jurors' antagonism toward lesbianism—and by extension, the hostility toward feminism—was the feeling that certain aspects of feminism demeaned or distorted or ignored what was important to their own lives. Most significantly, they condemned any facet of feminism that seemed to undermine what was central to their existence—their families. Abortion rights also fell into this category, the jurors admitted, and Foat had won points with them for having put her child up for adoption.

"I know women want their rights," said one woman, "and I'm all for that. But I cherish the way I live, and I'm not gonna do without my family because my family is my happiness. A husband will light your cigarette or open the door for you whether you have equal rights or not; he'll do it out of respect for you and because he loves you, just like you do things for him. And it has nothing to do with women going out and working. I'm all for women doing that, because if they've been housewives for twenty-five years and their husbands pass away, they'll have to be able to do something."

The source of the jurors' anger and irritation at Foat's post-verdict proclamations was similar to the reason for their anger and irritation at the women's movement: Both reshaped or re-created their own interpretation of their experience and discounted what they felt was important in their deliberations and in their lives. They had brought solid values from their families and communities to her trial, ones that they would embrace long after Foat had announced that the verdict "was a victory for all women."

"Well, I didn't elect her to speak for me," the grandmother complained. "It wasn't a victory for women at all, because being a woman had nothing to do with it. This trial certainly doesn't change my opinion that women's lib is bunk. They've gone too far, making men and women the same. We're not the same, but if in a marriage you don't try to make one another happy, then one of you is goin' out the door. My husband and I have always tried to do for one another. To me no man is better than what I am, and I'm not better than what he is. So when Mrs. Foat said we were all going out to join the women's movement because of her trial, I said, Banana friddles! As far as I'm concerned they can take the women's rights organization and run it out of town. As for the extremes, the gays, they oughta take them out and shoot 'em. So I don't want her making this into a women's lib thing. That organization is outrageous, and those women ain't doin' nothin' but cutting their own throats."

The jurors' confusion and resentment at Foat's instantaneous transformation made it impossible for them to see the trial as political. Having heard about and sympathized with only "the passive woman," they had no basis on which to perceive or understand her sources of strength. It looked too much like a quick-change artist, "the strong feminist" a new pose adopted for the occasion. "The defense had made a big point of how Ginny Foat was the same Ginny Foat back then," the foreman commented. "But she didn't seem the same to me. Other women who've been beaten don't automatically become NOW leaders or even NOW members. She was acting like she'd become a martyr for the cause, and for that reason I don't trust her. Seeing her on television, I wanted to tell people, 'Hey, we found Ginny Foat not guilty, we didn't find her innocent.' Ever since then I've had to wonder, who is the real Ginny Foat?"

Did Ginny Foat know herself? Once more her public role, her persona, had changed overnight in an almost visual reenactment of the dramatic transformation described in her first statement from jail. At the time, that statement had seemed ideologically clichéd but perhaps understandable, even acceptable, given her duress and her defense team's desire to rally support for her case. Yet during the trial and especially in her post-verdict comments, she seemed to adhere to the same kind of rhetoric. Continuing to talk about herself in the third person, it was as if she sought to put a great psychological distance between her present self and her past self, even as she insisted that the two were the same. "I had to go back to being Ginny Galluzzo with the same insecurities and vulnerabilities that she had," she said, describing her performance on the witness stand. "As Ginny Foat, I would have told them as a feminist, with much more insight into why and how it happened. But we felt it was important that I tell it as I had experienced it. So I guess on the stand I was not Ginny Foat, I was Ginny Galluzzo. But I was still the same person."

But the jurors hadn't thought so, since there was too much disparity between the two images. They had a "you can't get there from here" reaction, and indeed their "commonsense" impression was instructive for feminism in the eighties: A victim did not necessarily a feminist make.

To understand Foat's transformation, to understand what feminism meant for women, the jury had needed to hear about the sources of strength, the reserves of character on which Foat had drawn to escape Sidote, to struggle toward a new life for herself— those same traits of personality that she had brought to the women's movement and that, in return, the women's movement sanctioned, confirmed, and helped develop. But the way Foat had told her story, both in her pretrial jail statements and in her testimony, relied too much on the notion of "the click of consciousness," made famous in *Ms.,* perhaps to the detriment of the women's movement. The jurors had implicitly recognized the limitation of such rhetoric of instantaneous conversions; every feminist (let alone any individual, gender notwithstanding) knows in her heart that one's identity, or call it self-knowledge, is formed in a long, hard pull, a struggle every day in one's private and public lives. Statements such as Foat's were too similar to codas of miraculous conversions not to raise doubts about authenticity. In that sense, one strand of feminist rhetoric had been on trial in Louisiana, and the jury's reaction foretold a deeply ingrained suspicion of the refrain of "new selves" born out of a feminist metamorphosis.

In one respect, though, Ginny Foat did seem the same person before and after her conversion. Announcing herself as a symbol for all women as she toured the country and went on television, she was still the victim and still shaping her statements to emphasize her victimization. Now she seemed to feel that the Louisiana prosecutors' insensitivity, her scars of persecution, had granted her the status of a symbol, and once again history was rewritten. Instead of the litany of beatings from Sidote that she'd described at her trial, she insisted that the prosecutors had "sensationalized" her 1965 cross-country trip with Sidote when she "was only doing what everybody else was doing in the sixties." Further, the jury had seen the unfairness of the prosecutors' asking her about what she described as "the different things that all women have in common," and she included in this list her four marriages. On a segment of Hodding Carter's *Inside Story* devoted to the power of the media, she added the press to her persecutors, and she presented herself as a victim of overzealous reporters who'd "pieced the story" of her past together from interviews with "old lovers and family friends," "with old husbands and old boyfriends." As a result, she said, "Emotionally it was awful. . . . I spent three months in the county jail reading the newspaper every day, reading about myself, realizing that the world was reading about me. . . ."

Earlier she had said that she hadn't read any articles "after the first long one, because I couldn't deal with being incarcerated and reading them." Now she'd changed her version subtly to make her point about the media's "power to destroy or create" and its "persecution" of her. The media had, however, created her public platform, had allowed her to present herself as an emblem of all women on television shows and speaking tours, so much so that the New York *Daily News* listed "Ginny Foat on battered women" as one of the country's top women speakers during the year following her trial.

After her remarks on *Inside Story,* Hodding Carter asked reporter Bob Woodward, "Was Ginny Foat crushed by the press?"

"No," was his realistic assessment. "She'll go back and have her private life."

In truth, she would go back and have her public life; she would continue to extol the symbolic meaning of her trial by citing the tears among women in the courtroom, including those of a few members of the jury, as proof of "her victory for all women." "They didn't feel that way because of a person named Ginny Foat but because I became a symbol. When you have the March of Dimes, a cause like that, you march out the little crippled kids and people can identify and give money. When we battle as feminists for rape victims or for spousal abuse victims, we don't say, 'Here we have four battered wives. Look at the blood, look at the black-and-blue marks!' So I became a visual symbol in so many different ways because there were so many parts of my story that related to feminist issues. A feminist is usually not somebody who grew up with a silver spoon and has never seen pain. I think that what makes a feminist is being in dead-end jobs and experiencing the inequities, the unfairness of life, and how women suffer differently and so much more severely than men do. If anything, my life was the pattern of how somebody becomes a feminist. Take my dead-end jobs, take my life with him, it all led to feminism. Either that or suicide."

In order for her to become a symbol, people had to "identify" with what was being represented. But since Foat represented her victimization and persecution as the basis for her feminism, one had to accept her "everywoman's" morality tale of wrongs done to women in order to perceive her ordeal as emblematic. Yet, like her interpretation of her verdict, her insistence on this source of feminist awakening seemed to distort women's sense of themselves, the complexity of their experiences and their disinclination to see themselves as simply victims or passive hostages to a "feminine destiny" or social forces. Like the young women among the prospective jurors, a number of women weren't going to buy into weakness as a prerequisite for joining NOW. Whatever obstacles or inequalities they faced, they also recognized and valued their energy, competence, and intelligence; they made as much of their triumphs as of their defeats. Ginny had feared putting them on the jury because they wouldn't have understood or accepted her story of complete passivity. But ironically, the older women on the jury had had the same reaction once they'd seen Ginny Foat the strong feminist emerge. Sympathy for Ginny Foat's plight in the courtroom had brought no feminist clicks of transformation to them either.

What the jurors had needed to see were the sources of strength, independence, and energy that had been part of her character from the beginning. While that would have meant taking a chance on their attitudes toward feminism (although the defense seemed overly cynical and unwilling to trust the grass-roots common sense of these people), it also might have provided the jurors with a greater understanding of what feminism meant in one woman's life. They needed to hear how Ginny Foat changed, not overnight, not in an instantaneous metamorphosis, but in the intermediate small steps, the incremental advances as she struggled toward making a life of her own and confirmed her developing sense of autonomy. A progression over time, a translation of experience into self-awareness might have been perfectly recognizable, if not in feminist terms, then in human terms. And yet with the quick shift from "It was my fault" for the bad years with Sidote to (when asked, "Who gave you the confidence to leave him?") "I gave it to myself," the jury wasn't privy to how she could have given herself such strength. The self was the currency of her story, first self-pity, then self-congratulation. Both implied virtue unrewarded, lending her an aura of long-suffering martyrdom. Yet the jurors and most of the spectators at the trial weren't able to accept the symbolic value with which she'd invested the verdict. For them feminism hadn't been on trial; only a woman against whom the prosecutors didn't have a strong enough case.

Patt Morrison covered the trial for the *Los Angeles Times,* and she was equally dubious of the feminist victory that Ginny Foat publicly proclaimed. "When she made her political statements, my professional skepticism had to come into play. Then I talked to the jurors. I always like to do that because whenever the door closes on the deliberation room, it's as if some secret Jeffersonian quality comes out. I really believe their insistence that they dealt justice without any political considerations. Their empathy was personal, for her, but they never saw her as a feminist. As a result I think that Foat's statement claiming that the jury vindicated not just her but her politics ascribed motivations and feelings to the jurors that they really didn't have. Besides, it's also hard to know what exactly her case means for feminism, especially for feminists of my generation. Her case was so extraordinary that those of us who have never gone through that kind of abuse find it hard to think of ourselves in those terms. While you can admire someone who comes to political clarity as a result of that background, it's hard for us to identify with her as the victim or to see ourselves in Ginny Foat as she is today."

After the trial New Orleans NOW President Lynne Renihan felt that Foat's case had brought new attention, even new respect to NOW. "I found a lot of women, especially in the suburbs, who, of course, had heard about the trial—it was a big topic for a while—who didn't even realize she was connected to NOW or even what NOW is. I had to raise their consciousness about that. But they seemed to feel good about the verdict and were upset that she could have been wronged like that. They didn't even know that the NOW administration didn't support her, but when they heard what she'd done in the movement I think they were impressed. It's also true, though, that they were amazed when they saw her as a strong feminist on television. The prosecutors had dragged out so much of her personal life and all her tragedies at the trial that women could relate to her, 'Oh, that poor woman.' Some women I talked to could understand, because they'd been battered, too. That was how they came to it, and they were outraged by what they heard about the court proceedings. So our chapter received phone calls from women who were interested because of the battering. But I know there was also the feeling that Ginny on television was not the same woman as she was at the trial. They only felt for her as a victim. It was almost like, 'You can do this, but you can't do that.' "

The problem among local Louisiana women, as State Representative Mary Landrieu saw it, was that while her case was a topic of conversation in feminist circles, it didn't seem to have much effect on other women in the area. "It really didn't seem to touch me or them in a personal way, and I never went as far as thinking that she was in trouble because of her feminism. There was probably some sympathy for what she'd gone through, but I wasn't aware of women adopting her as a role model."

At a further remove, Muriel Fox concluded that the verdict was a victory for women only "to some degree": "Women are so abused in our society, and that includes the way they're treated in the criminal justice system, that it was helpful to women that she won. If she had lost it would have been a tragedy and a step backwards for women. But the fact that she won was only a minor victory, not one of our historic triumphs of all time."

Other feminists who hadn't been at the trial, however, continued to invest Foat's trial with symbolic meaning. Not surprisingly, two women who had donated their names and time to Foat's defense fund, Patty Duke Astin and Midge Costanza, spoke at a reception in Los Angeles to welcome Ginny back to California. "I think that every woman in this country felt like she was set free because . . . we were on trial with her," Costanza shouted amid the cheers for Foat.

Like the complicated reaction to Foat's arrest, attitudes seemed to vary not according to the facts of the trial but according to individual responses to feminism. Ginny Foat is a feminist, and she was found innocent; therefore feminism had triumphed—that seemed to be the argument, even though it overlooked the fact that neither a feminist nor feminism was visible at the trial.

"I saw Foat's verdict as a triumph for women," Gloria Steinem agreed, taking the same line. "First of all she fought, she didn't just slink away or try to escape. She stood up for her rights and her experience; she was believed and she won, so I would call that important for all of us."

Despite Foat's open suspicion that Ellie Smeal had aligned herself with her friend Toni Carabillo, Smeal herself believed that the verdict was a victory for women: "In the first place, Sidote's word didn't stand up to hers, and he didn't triumph over her just because a man made those accusations. Second, it was a victory in the sense that despite feminists' fears, her association with feminism was not a liability in a southern court. In our paranoia we're sometimes led to believe that there are places in the country where people automatically believe we're bad and tainted. But that didn't happen, and in fact her feminism may have been an obvious plus. I've lately come to believe that as feminists we are in a majority opinion and we have a good reputation, and the verdict seemed to indicate that, too. And third, there was sympathy for her as an individual and, beyond her, for all women. She made a nice appearance for her case and for women. Too often we suspect there's general hatred for women, but that turned out not to be true because her situation as a battered woman was stated in a manner that people could identify with. In those senses it was a victory. But since I didn't see it as a political trial, I don't think of it as a political victory. And since, as I was told, she appeared as much more a victim than a feminist leader, feminism was never on trial, only the victim."

How was one to know whether the jury—or the general population—would have identified with her as a feminist, a woman who'd changed her life and been a winner as well as a victim? Grace Lichtenstein was convinced that Foat's case received less attention than it warranted and seemed less important in the public's mind than, say, the Jean Harris case precisely because she hadn't been a victim. While it was certainly not a universally held opinion that Jean Harris was only a victim, Lichtenstein portrayed her in this light for the purpose of her argument: "Ginny Foat had taken hold of her fate, whereas Mrs. Harris was never anything but a victim and paid for it. Because more women can identify with Jean Harris than they can with Ginny Foat, the Foat case was 'undercovered.' It's why *Ladies Home Journal* has a larger circulation than *Ms.* But the other problem is that Foat's basically an unsympathetic character, and I also think people felt there was something fraudulent about her."

That indeed seemed to be what the jury had felt—that there was something inauthentic about her. Not that feminism itself was unacceptable or intolerable or terrifying, but that they'd wanted to hear and judge the whole story, not just sympathize with her suffering. Similarly, to accept or understand her feminism, they'd wanted to hear more than complaints about the oppression of all women. Feminism made sense only when it included the strengths of women as well.

Gloria Steinem saw the possibilities of moving beyond the woman-as-victim mentality to a more complex form of feminism in the eighties. Doubting that women want to identify with victims or with a Jean Harris more than a Ginny Foat, she said, "I think we've had it with women singing the blues. We already know how to do that, thank you very much. After all, in the middle of the blues were wonderful, bawdy, sexually aggressive songs, but they weren't commercial. We never wanted to be seen as only victims, we were just pointing out our victimization. But while we still struggle against inequality, we're also seeing our triumphs. Take the popularity among young women of *Flashdance*. That was clearly a sign of rejoicing in a young woman who was on her own, who had an ambition which she followed, and who lived a free life sexually and economically. Perhaps the problem for Foat's jury was that we're only acceptable when we sing the blues. But we need both sides of the picture, not only women's victimization but their strength to escape (though we can't blame the victim when she doesn't escape). If we have to remain victims to get justice, we're not getting justice. If we have to remain in a powerless position in order to be allowed to survive, then we're in a different kind of prison."

Other feminists were less willing to invest the Foat case with symbolic value, either in what it said about women or in what it indicated about NOW and feminism. Speaking as both a lawyer and a feminist, Karen DeCrow was hesitant to grant more profound meanings to the case precisely because so many women with different voices, personalities, backgrounds, viewpoints, had come to the women's movement in the last few years. Since NOW was neither a monolith nor a fragile structure, she argued, one individual could neither represent it nor cause its collapse: "To say Foat's verdict had to do with a victory for feminism is like saying that a black man's acquittal for a jewelry-store robbery is a victory against race discrimination. In both cases, it simply has to do with a lack of evidence to convict. I certainly didn't feel this was a victory for women or for feminism or for NOW. And even if she'd been convicted, I wouldn't have felt it was a repudiation of feminism or that NOW wouldn't have survived the blow. We don't have to be so careful about our image or reputation anymore now that we are such a large, strong organization. NOW is here to stay, so we can handle these internecine wars. We can even handle convicted murderers, although that wouldn't be my first choice."

NOW was certainly big enough and was most probably "here to stay." But Foat continued to criticize the organization after her verdict, proclaiming that NOW's official distancing from her case only confirmed what she had been saying the year prior to her arrest: that NOW leaders had forgotten its grass-roots members and concentrated too exclusively on mainstream politics. Once again the political was personal, however, even as Foat talked about herself and her case as emblematic of NOW's excessive concern with image.

But beyond that, she was bitter that she hadn't received a personal message of congratulations from NOW President Judy Goldsmith. With Foat's first press conference's condemnation of NOW leadership and continued critical remarks, though, one wondered why she had expected anything more than Goldsmith's public statement saying that she "was extremely pleased" with the acquittal and adding that she hoped Ginny "can now pursue her feminist activities free of the glare of this publicity." California NOW President Sandra Farha also annoyed Foat by wording her congratulations in almost the same way. Foat heard this as NOW's continued refusal to see the political significance of her case.

Judy Goldsmith said she simply hadn't thought a personal message particularly appropriate. "I knew relatively little about Ginny except for a couple of very brief meetings during a period of a few years. Since then I'd had no direct or personal contact with her. So it's difficult for me to say whether the fact that ours certainly has never been a close relationship made it inappropriate for me to send a personal message or whether I was affected by the comments that were coming very steadily from her and her partisans. Moreover, I didn't agree at all with the way she was describing NOW. It didn't square with the reality I've seen in NOW, and to me it was not an accurate representation when she said we were becoming too middle-of-the-road while she was going to lead us out of the mainstream."

What leadership role Ginny Foat could have in NOW was questionable to Muriel Fox, not simply because of her background but because of the criticism she continued to make of NOW national policy. "Her celebrity might help her, she'll have name recognition, so in that sense the publicity has put her in a position to be a spokesperson. On the other hand, her past life may continue to upset some people. But what will hurt her most is the fact that she has aligned herself with the 'nonmainstream' elements in NOW. Most of our members believe that NOW has to move within the realities of the American mainstream to win the hearts and souls of women and men. If she continues to be part of the 'out of the mainstream, into the revolution' group, it's not only difficult to see where in fact she thinks she would take the organization; she is then also removed from the main trunk of NOW membership and NOW thought. NOW members are generally liberal, but they're not radical."

Although Foat had fastened on Toni Carabillo as one of her enemies, Carabillo stressed her sympathy for the situation Foat had been put in and the difficulties of her past life. Nevertheless, her first loyalties were to NOW. She couldn't understand "a mentality that would risk all the work we've done to make NOW what it is today." Nor was she certain whether there was a place in NOW for Ginny: "I think she has a tremendous amount of rebuilding to do if she's going to resume a leadership position. She'll also have to put a lid on the remarks she's made about the organization, although I'm not sure she has the self-discipline for that. She seems to want to continue to see herself as a victim not only of the male establishment but of NOW, and I'm not sure how long that's going to play. In the eighties we'll have to get beyond her kind of rhetoric, and I've never thought her understanding of feminist issues runs very deep. She picks up language easily, but she hasn't completely done her homework, which is one of the reasons why she had trouble with the media. When questioners start to probe for a deeper understanding she gets uncomfortable. I'm not sure she'll change, though, because she has a group of devoted supporters, mostly in California, who accept her as the leader of a dissident faction which thinks they'll bring NOW 'back to the grass roots, back into the streets.' While they announce themselves that way, I don't see an ideology or a philosophy that makes them more radical. It's just rhetoric to be used within the organization, and I doubt it will get them very far."

It seemed unlikely that Foat herself or the moral derived from her case would push NOW out of the mainstream. Nevertheless, the Foat case had affected NOW in several ways. Toni Carabillo said that a vast majority of its members had been shocked and had worried about a decline in membership or a diminishment of public support. But NOW leaders, both on the national level and in local chapters, didn't find that happening. Obviously, it had prompted negative perceptions of NOW in certain hostile quarters before the verdict, a kind of "I told you so" about feminism, when antifeminists read unfavorable accounts and even after the verdict made snide jokes, like the man who said to Midge Costanza, "Boy, you feminists really do get away with murder!"

Still, most NOW leaders agreed that the Foat case had had its most negative effect within the organization and on feminists' perceptions of NOW. "There were a goodly portion of feminists, within NOW and outside NOW, who thought we did not behave in a proper manner," said Ellie Smeal. "They took Judy Goldsmith's statement as not supportive and criticized her and NOW very vocally in the press. In the long term we probably lost more on that. On the other hand, while I can understand Ginny Foat's bitterness, I wish she didn't criticize NOW for what was a very complex decision. Who knows if it was the right decision, but it wasn't made because we've become 'too mainstream.' It was the kind of situation where you couldn't do anything right. Judy and the other NOW officers were worried about Ginny, but they also had to worry about the organization and the impact the case would have on it. There's nothing bad about that, they had to be concerned, but as humanists they also cared about the individual involved. It was a terrible situation for Judy, she'd just come into office, and it seemed that whatever she said, something could be read into it. So all of us are a little uptight about the Foat case, even to this day. But that in no way means that Judy and the others weren't trying to act out of compassion and understanding while being concerned about NOW, too. Everybody can have a theory in retrospect, but it was such a damned unusual situation that no one person can know confidently what should have been done. Nor should people be judged too harshly on it."

Other feminists, however, were inclined to judge more harshly, feeling that NOW leadership had helped make a bad situation worse.

"I don't know how Smeal would have handled it," said Lynne Renihan, "but I was very displeased with the way Goldsmith didn't support Ginny and didn't give our chapter any help with handling a difficult situation. First there was Judy's directive to me, 'Don't talk, don't even answer your phone.' Then a lot of us were upset by the NOW statement that was just fluff. They were treating Ginny like dirty laundry that they didn't want around; or maybe they hoped that if they ignored it, it would go away. So I was very critical of the NOW administration. They not only left Ginny high and dry, they left us high and dry, and I told that to some poor woman in the national office when she called me about some other issue a month or so after Ginny's arrest. I'm not an angry person, but when she phoned, I yelled at her, 'Do you know the name Ginny Foat? Well, this is Louisiana you're calling, and I won't talk to you.' Then I apologized—it wasn't personal—but it certainly ate in my side enough to affect the way I felt about the Goldsmith administration."

Grace Lichtenstein was critical of both sides. She thought that the ways the case was mishandled both in NOW's national office and in the Foat camp were predictable and interrelated. In a sense they all seemed to deserve each other. "NOW was always the bourgeois wing of feminism and never in the forefront of the movement," she added. "I thought Ellie Smeal had been an especially good leader, and for a time the radical and moderate streams of feminism became one when with the slogan 'Out of the mainstream into the revolution,' the revolution became the mainstream. I don't know where either is today. Yet with the Foat case, NOW leaders were mealymouthed when the logical thing for them to have done was to defend her and presume her innocent. Like Foat's people, they handled it very badly from a public-relations standpoint. From a political standpoint you have to question how effective an organization NOW is when such people become its leaders. Maybe it's symbolic of a trough, an emptiness in the leadership of NOW. And I also wonder what it says about NOW that Ginny Foat almost became one of its national leaders. I started out sympathetic, but then I realized that none of these people were wonderful representatives of the movement. It certainly wasn't a great episode in feminist history."

That the issues and complex questions of the Foat case would force NOW to take a long, hard look at itself was doubtful. At least no one was publicly saying that it was definitely time for some honest self-appraisal. Some feminists inside and outside NOW suggested that after the Foat case, NOW should be more careful about investigating the backgrounds of its candidates for national NOW offices. Yet no one in NOW was sure they wanted to adopt that measure since it seemed to smack of elitism. "You should know people better, there's no question about that," Smeal admitted. But both Goldsmith and Smeal agreed that in a volunteer organization like NOW, there wasn't time to do the kind of checking other organizations might find necessary. Smeal added that she wouldn't want such background checks to keep women with, say, "life experience" credentials from seeking a NOW office. "You have to decide what matters as a qualification. We're trying very hard to be a movement of all women, so we don't want to make it necessary to have certain credentials. On the other hand, if there was intentional fraud in the way someone presented her background, that would be a problem. So we should have a way of knowing about someone, and as long as persons are who they say they are, then that should be enough."

Without some checking, it would be difficult to know if persons are who they say they are. In fact, the lack of verification or confirmation seemed to be the reason why rumormongering is prevalent, as most NOW members readily agreed and about which they often complained. Yet no one seemed able to remedy it.

"It's so easy to smear somebody," said Smeal, "but I've always thought it was our responsibility to stop rumors, not to spread them. Most of us feel that way, and we tend to fight these campaigns on the issues themselves." That was the line NOW leaders wanted to take—that factionalism and trashing were no worse in their organization than in others; everyone was committed to the struggle for equality, not to the accumulation of personal power. Yet the facts of the Foat case belied such high-minded principles and would seem to have warranted some housecleaning, even some consciousness-raising, once the Machiavellian maneuverings behind the scenes of the Foat case had been revealed. Instead, NOW insisted that it had to focus attention on its number-one priority—defeating Ronald Reagan in the 1984 election.

Foat, too, turned to the future. "All my friends have been taking care of the women's movement. Now I'm back to help them," she announced on her triumphant return to California, and she listed the need to revive the ERA campaign and the defeat of Reagan among her feminist goals.

That she would do so as a NOW member was dubious; she would be traveling around the country lecturing about her experiences as a battered woman to raise money to pay her legal expenses. She would put off law school for another year, but someday, she said, she hoped to become a lawyer and run for public office. Meanwhile she founded Legal Advocates for Women, a group dedicated to bringing justice to women who "are unfairly accused," and organized a women's prison network. She and Laura Foreman were completing her book about her ordeal, and her TV-movie *The Death of a Passive Woman* was in the works. Oddly enough, its producer had already announced that in his "Ginny Foat story," "the feminist angle won't be stressed." But it would be Foat's own choice if she was portrayed and perceived as only a victim. Then the hard-won struggles, the energy, strength, and ambition that must have been part of her character from the beginning would be lost to the public, just as they were to the Louisiana jury. Indeed, if there is a moral here for feminism in the eighties, it is to be found in the response of her jurors: The woman as victim may evoke tears and sympathy but she rarely wins votes for women's rights.

TWELVE

Epilogue

FEMINISM was again on trial—this time in the 1984 presidential election. While Ginny Foat had proclaimed her verdict as "a victory for all women," the vice-presidential nomination of Geraldine Ferraro was a very real triumph, breaking the gender barrier of the country's highest political offices. Yet despite the argument that the "gender gap" would elect the next president, the female voters did not achieve a victory for the Democratic party ticket. The defeat, it seemed, could have been predicted from the jurors' responses to the Foat case.

The National Organization for Women played a crucial role in this test of feminism as well. Soon after the Foat case concluded in November 1983, national NOW held a meeting in Washington, D.C. There, Democratic presidential hopefuls spoke to NOW representatives from across the country. NOW President Judy Goldsmith announced the organization's number-one goal of defeating Ronald Reagan; as a result, NOW would endorse a presidential candidate for the first time in its history. Some members were critical of this decision, including Ginny Foat. Wasn't this yet another example of NOW becoming just an arm of the Democratic party, of concentrating exclusively on "mainstream" or Washington, D.C., politics?

"Not at all," said Toni Carabillo. "We had to fight against Reagan. Another four years of him was going to be another four years of setbacks for women. I don't care what cosmetic approaches the Reagan administration takes. From day one they've attacked the fabric of every single piece of legislation we've passed to ensure women's rights. They either don't enforce it, they don't fund it, or they appoint people to positions who are philosophically opposed to our goals. At this point, you'd have expected at least superficial respect for what seemed to be generally accepted principles, but there is none. Not only does the administration make antiwomen jokes, but doubtless their policies would become even worse if he was reelected because then he would be home free, and not just on women's issues."

Leading the list of women's issues, of course, was the "feminization of poverty." While Republicans talked about economic recovery, studies showed women headed 16 percent of all families in 1983, and nearly half of those families living below the poverty line were headed by women. Republicans argued that this statistic indicated a change in "life-styles"—more divorces and a higher out-of-wedlock birth rate. Yet as more and more documentation poured forth, it was revealed to be a shaky excuse: Forty-six million women, 53 percent of all adult females, are in the labor force, they earn sixty-four cents for every dollar earned by men, and only 10 percent earn more than twenty thousand dollars a year. An ad hoc coalition of eighty women's groups, including the Women's Legal Defense Fund, the National Women's Political Caucus, and the American Association of University Women, issued its analysis of the impact of the Reagan administration's budget cuts on women. Called "Inequality of Sacrifice," it showed that cuts in federal aid most dramatically affected women by reducing funds in such programs as federal aid for dependent children and the Legal Services Corporation; and, of course, since women and children are 85 percent of all food-stamp recipients, they felt the effect most forcefully of the almost five-billion-dollar reduction in funds during 1982 and 1983.

Still, the gender gap widened not so much because of specific women's issues but as a result of the "umbrella" issues of the economy and the national defense. A *New York Times* poll in November 1983 showed that only 38 percent of women, compared to 53 percent of men thought Reagan would be reelected. Forty-one percent of women believed the recession was over as opposed to 47 percent of men, but most significantly, 49 percent of women but just 33 percent of men feared Reagan would get the country into a war.

At their meeting on December 9, 1983, NOW representatives heard the various candidates explain their positions. Many expressed interest in Gary Hart and Jesse Jackson, and some were explicitly lukewarm to Walter Mondale, either because of lingering animosity toward President Carter's ineffectual support for the ERA or insistence that Mondale was a sure loser to Reagan. Nevertheless, since Mondale already had extensive labor-union endorsements and a large campaign treasury, he seemed the sure winner of the Democratic primaries. With the number-one priority of defeating Reagan, the argument went, it made sense politically for NOW to endorse Mondale. While he had not publicly guaranteed a female running mate, as Jesse Jackson had, Goldsmith announced that the price of the endorsement was a female running mate.

There were feminists inside and outside NOW who believed that the organization had jumped the gun. Or at least, they argued, NOW should have waited until some of the primaries were over, the results giving them more leverage to insist on a female vice-presidential candidate. Those who defended NOW's decision did so in terms of party politics—the Democratic party would recognize not only what energy and commitment NOW members would bring to their candidate, but also that their valuable hours of campaigning would be doubly guaranteed if Mondale chose a female running mate, especially one known for her strong support of feminist issues.

Ann Lewis was the political director of the Democratic party in 1984, and as someone extensively involved in both party politics and NOW politics, she strongly disagreed with the argument that NOW had endorsed Mondale "too early." "Maybe that was a risky choice, but it was the right one for several reasons," she said. "In the first place, people throughout the political process learned that NOW was a source of people, of commitment and follow-through. Those connections would not have been made if NOW had waited to get in after the convention. That recognition could come only from NOW's work in the primaries, not in the general election. Second, the nomination of a woman vice-president would not have happened if the women as typified and exemplified by NOW members hadn't rolled up the chips that they had throughout the first half of the year. And finally, the members of NOW got the opportunity, the challenge, to get into the campaign early and in a substantial way. In the course of it, they learned how good they were at the political process and that the skills they'd used in developing NOW worked as well in forming alliances in the primaries and talking to voters."

Despite the "chips" NOW had accumulated, Mondale seemed to waffle on a female running mate once his nomination was secured in June of 1984. He went into retreat in Minnesota and began to interview candidates, including San Francisco Mayor Dianne Feinstein and New York Representative Geraldine Ferraro. But he was by no means indicating that he was strongly leaning toward a woman.

At the end of June, NOW held its national convention in Miami Beach. There, President Judy Goldsmith announced that with NOW's five hundred delegate seats, there would be a floor fight if Mondale failed to choose a woman as his running mate. NOW passed a resolution calling for the nomination of a woman from the floor "if necessary"; Goldsmith took an even harder line, insisting that NOW would not be placated by a Mondale pledge of posts half-female cabinet or women nominees to the Supreme Court. The three-day conference focused almost exclusively on this issue, and while some delegates favored backing Ferraro as their choice, most decided that a general resolution was more effective. Mondale himself addressed the convention. When his speech was interrupted by chants of "Run with a woman," he said, "We'll get around to that in a moment," but never did. Later, at a press conference, he seemed almost surprised by the demand. According to a *New York Times* report, he recalled that when NOW had endorsed him in December, it had not required a female running mate, only a feminist. "They asked that women be included in the process, and that's what I'm doing," he said. The defensive tone was unmistakable.

Mondale went back to Minnesota and continued his "affirmative action" interviewing, including Los Angeles Mayor Bradley and Philadelphia Mayor W. Wilson Goode, both of whom "are feminists," conceded Goldsmith, adding that a black candidate would avert the floor fight. But NOW's public ultimatum brought opposition from both feminists and antifeminists. While many feminists agreed that a woman would be the strongest running mate against Reagan, most women in public office tempered NOW's resolution, reluctant as they were to make threats the month before the convention or to jeopardize the image of strong party unity. Both Ferraro and Feinstein said they would not let their names be placed in nomination from the floor, and Representative Pat Schroeder, who had been Hart's campaign manager and supported him as a possible vice-presidential candidate, pointed out the impracticality of the resolution.

While Ann Lewis sympathized with the feelings behind the NOW resolution, she was aware of the backlash it provoked both inside and outside the Democratic party. "If I could rewrite history, the only thing I wish had been done differently was the language of the resolution at the Miami Beach NOW convention. In itself it wasn't meant to be harmful or negative, but it came at a time when people were looking for ways either to prove that there was something wrong with 'interest groups' or that Walter Mondale was a wimp. Of course, the latter was absolutely sexist—the remarks that Mondale was so weak he was being pushed around by a bunch of feminists. But there was the real political world and public perception to consider. In the political business, there's a difference between delicately hinting, conveying, or implying without, in a sense, 'putting it in writing.' The same message can be sent indirectly as effectively and it won't be used against you. If you put it in writing your friends have to dissociate themselves from it, and your enemies get to chortle over it."

One of NOW's loudest and most perpetual critics, the antifeminist columnist Patrick J. Buchanan (who in 1985 was appointed White House communications chief) came out swinging after hearing NOW's resolution. To him it wasn't just a matter of bad strategy; comparing the Democratic party to a subsidiary of Ringling Brothers, he took feminism as the primary example of how "out of touch with the times and with the country" the party was: "The heyday of Bella Abzug and Betty Friedan is as much in the past as that of Bull Connor and Lester Maddox."

Rather than seeing NOW's endorsement as a boost for Mondale, he called it an "albatross about [his] neck." The reasons he asserted were the old shibboleths about feminists: "mannish stridency of language, a conscious lack of femininity, an impatience and almost visceral hostility when the role of wife and mother is broached." Listing examples of feminism's extremism, he included two NOW resolutions: one citing "homophobia as a form of sexism" that "perpetuates heterosexual privilege"; and one that barred anyone who opposed legalized abortion from speaking at any future NOW convention. And finally he announced as his would-be coup de grâce: "Ginny Foat, the California NOW leader lately acquitted of beating some john to death with a hammer, received a cheering ovation." Then he exclaimed, "This is Mainstream America?"

Why had Ginny Foat turned up in his diatribe? On one level, the insinuation was exactly what feminists had expected from antifeminists—that the story of her past, the saga that had brought her to trial, was caricatured as the expected or authentic background of feminists despite their claims to respectability. It was what NOW leadership had most feared: The distasteful details of her earlier days tainted the organization in the public's mind. In Buchanan's scheme of things, there was something decidedly "off" about an organization that would give Ginny Foat a standing ovation when, to mainstream America, Ginny Foat was not only *not* a heroine, but unacceptable, her not-guilty verdict notwithstanding.

For all Buchanan's ranting and raving, however, he'd also touched a nerve, both in NOW politics and in the response of the general public to the women's movement of the eighties. Ginny Foat attended the NOW convention in triumph, and yet she also seemed to be there both to remind NOW leadership what they had done, or failed to do, and to symbolize her "victimization" at the hands of abusive men and the male establishment. Ginny Foat represented one significant strand in NOW's politics. Her claim to a "more radical stance," her attempt to move the organization "out of the mainstream, into the revolution," was now symbolized by both her abuse and her persecution. That, indeed, seemed to be her message, symbolizing the more extreme factions of NOW— that men were the enemy. Ginny could be the poster girl for the victimization of women. Buchanan was in one respect correct: It seemed unlikely that women outside this faction, women "in the mainstream," just plain women across America, would accept a symbol that insisted that men were the oppressors and that women would remain the victims as long as they "perpetrate heterosexual privilege." The subconscious meaning of the more radical NOW workshops as well as Ginny Foat's standing ovation seemed to suggest that women had to denounce or leave their ways of life, their heterosexual privileges, or, actually, their families, if they no longer wanted to be treated like women, that is, badly.

Foat, however, still felt she had her own constituency among NOW members, if not among NOW leaders. "During the convention, I came face to face with Judy Goldsmith. She had not said anything to me, I hadn't said anything to her, and she went out of her way not to speak to me at the convention." Foat seemed to want it both ways, however. Goldsmith was genuinely pleased that Foat had triumphed over her personal difficulties; nevertheless, she could hardly be sanguine about Foat's continued criticism of NOW, not only for its dissociation from her but for its early endorsement of Mondale without a guarantee of a female vice-presidential candidate. Foat herself interpreted NOW leaders' snubs or avoidance of her to their wariness of her potential role in the organization. "National NOW leaders were constantly on the lookout to see what I was up to. They were convinced I was going to run for president of NOW at the next election."

Once again NOW leaders criticized Ginny Foat for investing herself with too much importance. The priority at NOW's 1984 convention was developing a strategy to ensure a woman vice-presidential candidate, to organize delegate strength behind several crucial feminist planks in the Democratic party platform, and finally, to plan ways for NOW members to mobilize voters to defeat Ronald Reagan. The 1985 NOW presidential election wasn't high on the agenda compared to the 1984 national presidential election.

Beyond that reality, however, it was staggering to think that Ginny Foat considered herself a viable candidate for national NOW president. Despite her verdict, despite her "triumph for women," it seemed unlikely that either the press or the public would ignore her background if she again placed herself in the limelight. As Grace Lichtenstein exclaimed, "Ginny Foat run for national NOW president? As we say in New York, 'What a pair of cojones!' " Perhaps not cojones, but Foat seemed to forget how the press had treated her story; the facts were once sensational, they would be treated that way again precisely because she was a celebrated feminist. It wouldn't be a matter of "retrying" her case; instead Foat herself had set the terms that would force such reexamination. Her feminist credentials, indeed her notoriety, political or otherwise, were presented in terms of her suffering. Was that an adequate qualification for office, either in NOW or in party politics?

Moreover, questions were still going to be asked about her character, her sense of herself, even her questionable taste. No feminist gloss could wipe the slate clean. Nevertheless, since Foat was announcing herself as a spokesperson for women precisely on the basis of her victimization both as a battered wife and as a persecuted feminist, it seemed unlikely that women would simply accept her as their symbol. As one woman at Ginny Foat's trial commented, "It's a sad day for women when Ginny Foat is adopted as a national heroine, if women have to choose between her and Phyllis Schlafly." It wasn't just a matter of stereotypes. Instead, it was a question of how the general public perceived women who announced themselves as representatives of their sex.

Finally Walter Mondale took the brave step and named Geraldine Ferraro as his running mate. Why not make a little history while trying to win the election? Women seemed to have a new heroine; it was a moment of jubilation. Ferraro's outspokenness and humor were refreshing, a welcome relief to the stiffness of Mondale's "Norwegian wood." Perhaps the gender gap would make a difference as crowds of women turned out to cheer her, taking pride in her accomplishment, a significant advance that doubtless wouldn't have been possible without the achievements, small and large, of the women's movement during the previous decade.

As with any heroine or symbol or celebrity, the public wanted to know more about her. Like Ginny Foat, her past came under extensive scrutiny. Coincidentally, and even perhaps with some deeper meaning, Geraldine Ferraro and Ginny Foat not only shared the same initials but also similar Italian Catholic, upstate New York backgrounds. Yet with the first published minibiographies, Gerry Ferraro's journey to success and accomplishments seemed especially instructive. An Italian immigrant, her father had been a prosperous restaurateur in Newburgh, New York, until his death when his daughter was eight. The family's reduced circumstances prompted her mother Antonetta to move the family to the South Bronx and to go to work in the garment district. It must have been a work a day struggle, but even with the "traditions" of such a background, this GF won scholarships to Marymount School and Marymount College, and while teaching fourth grade in a Queens public school, worked at night for her law degree at Fordham University. Three years older than Ginny Foat, she might have been even more susceptible to the mores of the fifties "feminine mystique" and her Italian Catholic upbringing. Yet she made certain choices—working hard, winning scholarships, and three days after her bar exam marrying John Zaccaro, a real estate developer. In the next six years, while raising three children, she still remained involved in local politics and community activities.

One read between the lines of her "story" just as one had with Ginny Foat's. The same question was crucial: Could feminism explain her decisions, her energy and ambition combined and, indeed, melded with her "traditional roles" or her "oppressed" circum-

stances? But feminism as it had evolved in the seventies had no answer as to why one GF had passed the bar and the other had hit the
road with a bartender; no retrospective feminist analysis could reduce the emotional, ethical, and aesthetic complexities to social forces
or historical circumstances that had determined the life of either
woman. It was the domain of novelists—character, in both senses
of the word—that might convey why one woman "succumbed" and
the other one didn't. The feminist moral imagination could easily
have perceived both GFs as controlled and defined by their environment. Yet one had fallen victim, the other hadn't. The analogies were
there, but the "moral" of this everywoman's story was quite different. Geraldine Ferraro's achievements pointed out the deficiencies
of a feminist gloss that portrayed women's lives as a series of passive acceptances, not active choices. In Ginny Foat's case, feminism
was used to explain away everything; in Geraldine Ferraro's, the same
interpretation explained nothing.

But soon, with so much press attention, Geraldine Ferraro was
asked to explain a great deal. Just as Ginny Foat had been forced to
expose her past and her ex-husband, Geraldine Ferraro was confronted with questions about her past and her husband. At first it
seemed the press had done what Foat had criticized them for—gone
after a feminist with a vengeance. The *New York Post,* most notably, began running long "exposés" about her and her husband's financial statements, her parents' history in Newburgh, and her
husband's real estate business in lower Manhattan. Given Rupert
Murdoch, the *Post*'s publisher, and his great love for Reagan, it
seemed a not very subtle attempt to "get" a Democrat, and a woman
to boot. Equally, there were those commentators who, opposed to
a female candidate, took special joy in the brouhaha surrounding
Zaccaro's questionable real estate dealings in Little Italy. With the
reports of suspect tax returns and "Italian" connections, antifeminists had a field day. Less than enamored with Ferraro's candidacy,
they accepted the news stories as the gospel truth and accused her
of "sinking the ticket." Feminists, however, pointed to the press
sensationalism. It wasn't fair, and indeed many of the stories did
seem hyped. The *Post* dredged up information that Ferraro's father
had run a gambling operation out of his restaurant in Newburgh.
That was emblematic of attributing the worst to any fact: It might
well have been true, but given the time and the circumstances, it
was common enough among Italian immigrant communities to be

forgivable, hardly meriting the sinister insinuation that Ferraro came from a Mafia family. Everyone loves Ellis Island sagas but not for political candidates, it seemed. Only WASPs need apply (although Rockefellers, too, had skeletons in their family closets), and Italians were always smeared with such innuendos of mob connections.

Ferraro was also criticized for failing to list her husband's business interests on congressional financial disclosure forms. This accusation appeared to be another example of antifeminists going after her unjustifiably. After all, it seemed preposterous that Mondale's staff hadn't made sure there were no problems in this area. The hints of financial irregularities sounded as insubstantial as the silly report that one of Zaccaro's buildings housed a pornography distributor. The press was latching on to anything to counter the excitement her candidacy had injected into the campaign, and this, too, was hyped and exaggerated. Ferraro soon announced that she would set the record straight with a full disclosure of her and her husband's financial matters.

Then came the first stunner. John Zaccaro refused to make public his tax records. Ferraro looked silly, then put her foot in it: "Well, you know how stubborn Italian men can be." An alarm went off once she started to make excuses. Wasn't she having it both ways, too? A feminist, a woman who insisted on her own career, whose ambition and diligence were supposed to be a model, and she was not only talking about the dominance of a husband, but also calling on the sterotype of "macho" Italian men. Finally Zaccaro gave in, leading to jokes about the "henpecked" Italian husband. Ferraro held her marathon press conference at which she admitted that "mistakes" had been made and won that round with her spirited handling of the reporters' questions. The "mistakes" were one thing, but she was still left with the failure to list her husband's business holdings on her congressional disclosure forms. She had claimed no financial interest in his business, and yet had been on record as one of its officers.

Soon it was also revealed that Zaccaro was under investigation for his guardianship of two estates from which he'd made loans to himself and his business. Further, there were reports of real estate transactions that lifted some eyebrows in addition to more reports of sales and rentals to "mobbed up" clients. Anyone familiar with New York City real estate wasn't terribly shocked, however. What company with holdings in Little Italy wouldn't have on record sales or rentals that through third or fourth parties or by innuendo could be made to seem "dirty" or Mafia-connected?

Mondale's people remained conspicuously silent during the controversy over Ferraro and Zaccaro's financial disclosures, as if they'd been taken by surprise. A feminist interpretation in this instance did indeed explain their quandary: They hadn't known about these matters because of reverse sexism. Having chosen a woman, they'd considered her spouse like a "wife." Negligible as wives are, there was no need to look into Zaccaro's background or business. He was just the "little man" behind the powerful woman. In this case, however, the spouse turned out to have a life and business of his own, which had come back to haunt the campaign.

That was a comfortable argument as more revelations about Zaccaro's business affairs and his loans to his wife's congressional campaign hit the newspapers. Added to this explanation, though, were cries of outright sexism. Ferraro and her supporters also insisted that this sort of press coverage of her was more rigorous because she was a woman. But it was here that a feminist analysis fell short, given political reality. What, after all, had she expected? In the first place, any politician had to foresee such public scrutiny. Certainly some of the stories about her were sexually marked—no profiles of male politicians concentrated so heavily on clothes, grocery shopping, or what was in a candidate's refrigerator. Still, she was cooperating in this sort of coverage, as if to make sure the voters realized that she was a good wife and mother, not one of those man-hating feminists. (Joan Mondale had done her bit, too, when asked about her first meeting with Ferraro: "Oh, what do women talk about? She liked my new red dress. I was so surprised that she could still think in feminine terms. That's what's so wonderful! She's not jaded and sour and crabby.")

Nevertheless, while some of the articles about new campaign etiquette (should she be kissed, how she should be addressed?) were trivial, it also became clear that many of the financial and business disclosures required further probing. It wasn't just the *New York Post* going "after" her: *The New York Times* and *The Wall Street Journal* were now questioning the candor, forthrightness, and integrity with which the couple's financial affairs had been handled. Then Mondale's campaign chairman admitted that he and his staff had spent only forty-eight hours going over Ferraro's records and that things were now coming out that "were not picked out in the review."

That admission fueled public criticism of Mondale and his staff for lack of judgment. But what seemed more important was what it said about Ferraro. Since her campaign would "make history"— indeed, she'd been picked not just because of Mondale's commitment to women but because her presence would bring more attention and perhaps more voters—hadn't she realized she'd receive extraordinary media coverage? Again she seemed to want it both ways. She had been chosen because she was a woman. Now she was complaining of "special treatment."

She also charged that if not for her candidacy her husband would never have been investigated so extensively. That wasn't quite true. Zaccaro had already been under investigation for his conservatorship of two estates from which he made loans to his own business. (In September 1984 it was revealed that he had been under investigation for the falsification of a purchase price to arrange a loan for an associate's real estate deal. In January 1985 he pleaded guilty to a misdemeanor charge, but without corroborative evidence he was not charged with arranging $25,000 in kickbacks to officials of the Port Authority Credit Union in return for an improper $550,000 loan to the same real estate associate.) But even while Ferraro was being interviewed by Mondale, she must have known about the investigation of the estate loans, since Zaccaro himself had asked for a postponement of the hearing. Why hadn't Ferraro told Mondale that an investigation was in progress? Whatever the outcome of such investigations, their existence was bound to be made public.

Amnesia had struck again. It was reminiscent of Eagleton's failure to mention the skeleton in *his* closet, his shock treatment for depression. And too close as well to Ginny Foat's own failure to recognize that the murder charges in her past would place NOW in a vulnerable position if she should be elected president of the organization.

At least Mondale had the good grace and courage to remain loyal to his candidate (though he did so mainly in silence), while McGovern and the Democratic party as well as NOW had rushed to dissociate themselves from their embarrassments. But what were the motivations of three people who put themselves in the public eye without considering their liabilities? Certainly ambition had to be at the core of such omissions. Yet in the case of the two women, it's likely that feminism had also spurred them onward. For good reason, yes, since each woman saw herself as doing something for women. But there were questionable motives as well. Perceiving themselves politically, as emblematic of all women, they seemed to have suppressed the complexities of their individual, private, or personal lives. Committed to the greater good, they'd transcended themselves and existed only on a public level, their ethical judgment suspended for the sake of feminist symbolism. How else to explain their surprise when details of their private lives came back to haunt them? Their shared condemnation of the press's intrusion or excessive "muckraking" because they were women was not the point. The press had pursued the stories exactly for the reason that they were public women, held up as symbols or images of Everywoman.

In the seventies, feminism had seemed mired in the personal. With the motto "the personal is political," discussion of both important and trivial examples of daily oppression was meant to politicize through consciousness-raising. But as everything became political, the personal somehow dropped away to the extent that moral ambiguities and ethical choices, so uniquely individual and crucial to the formation of character, were overly simplified and even obliterated. Feminist ideology sanctioned it with its reshaping or even its denial of the past, with every click of consciousness heralding a "symbolic" new woman. And yet when the whistle was blown, the dime dropped, the criticism made, the excuse became, "It's happening to me only because I'm a woman, and besides, I am not responsible for the mistakes of my past."

Ferraro later objected to a question from Phil Donahue about her reaction to certain news stories: Had she cried? he asked. "Certain things are personal," she replied. But when the personal was invested with so much political importance, that was a lame excuse. The movement's motto had come back to haunt feminists.

Geraldine Ferraro was not immune as she continued to resort to this explanation. Not only did she feel unfairly treated by the press during the campaign, but after the election when she made the dubious decision to advertise Pepsi Light, she charged she was criticized more harshly because she was a woman. Yet in both instances, her sense of herself as a symbol for women had obscured an ethical judgment. (Feminism didn't guarantee good taste, after all.) While at the same time indeed proving that she was a fully qualified and strong, independent-minded candidate, she lapsed into what seemed an all-too-easy accusation: that she was being given special treatment because of her sex.

Well, of course she was. Wasn't that what her campaign was about? Yes, she was the "token" woman on the ticket, and almost everyone was glad for it. As Ann Lewis declared, "The selection of Geraldine Ferraro changed politics, changed history, and changed the way every woman feels about her future." Yet a Gerald Ferraro from Queens with the same credentials would never have been selected by Mondale. Even if he had been, the financial irregularities of his spouse, his questionable claim of an exemption from congressional financial disclosures, and derived benefits from his spouse's business would also have been subjected to intensive press coverage. Granted, in earlier years this might not have been true—then the wife of a politician was less likely to have either her own career or her own financial affairs. But given the change in women's status and attitudes toward them, a spouse of any politician was going to be held accountable, as the investigations of, for example, Antoinette Hatfield (a real estate agent married to Senator Mark Hatfield), Marion Javits, and even Attorney General Meese's wife, Ursula, make quite clear.

Hence it was a disappointment when Ferraro seemed to imply that while she was proving women were equal, she couldn't take the rough-and-tumble treatment by the press. Her complaints that the media had been especially aggressive because she was a woman prompted the cynical thought, "If you can't stand the heat, go back to the kitchen." No one was asking her to be Caesar's wife, only the equal of Caesar.

What was most disturbing was the way in which feminism was too easily adopted as a ready-made alibi—"because I was a woman." It was the flip side of no, you can't do that "because you're just a woman." The brass ring of equality had become a loophole. As the movement became mellower, less revolutionary, and more generally accepted in the public consciousness, feminism seemed to drape an aura of innocence and suffering around every woman. When it was convenient, the most disparate people quickly donned the victim's wrapper like a folded plastic raincoat. Jeane Kirkpatrick, for example, suddenly announced that she'd been discriminated against by "classical male sexists" in the Reagan administration. What should have come as no surprise seemed to have astounded her. Instead of seeing a connection between the obstacles she'd faced and the administration's policies that dramatically affected women's lives, she went right on supporting Reagan. The "feminization of poverty" mattered little compared to the "feminization of policy" in her brand of feminist awareness. More, feminism had nothing to do with her achievements, only her failure to receive a new White House appointment she'd wanted. Female victims were sanctioned to proclaim their oppression at the most opportune moments.

The cliché of the seventies women's movement—the woman as victim—seemed to be the form of feminism that had become most acceptable in the public consciousness. Ginny Foat and Geraldine Ferraro were linked by the rationalization "because she was a woman" or "because she was a feminist." While polls showed a general recognition of inequities between women and men (a majority of voters supported the ERA despite state legislators' failure to ratify it), women themselves seemed loath to identify with victims or to announce that they were defined simply by male oppression. As Muriel Fox was quick to point out, "Just because someone is a woman doesn't make her a feminist victim."

After Reagan's landslide reelection, commentators asked what had happened to the so-called gender gap with Reagan having in fact increased his vote among women. Even stranger was an ABC news poll that found 85 percent of Mondale voters said Ferraro "made no difference in their votes." *Newsweek* also quoted Kathy Wilson, president of the National Women's Political Caucus; like NOW, her organization had given Mondale its first presidential endorsement, but she said, "I hope we never do it again." In his usual rhetoric, Patrick Buchanan gloated that "the feminist element has become a millstone about the neck of the Democratic party. Judy Goldsmith of NOW is the Typhoid Mary of American politics."

While many voters might not have wanted to admit that a woman on the ticket made a difference, it's doubtful that Goldsmith or Ferraro or feminism per se had turned voters away from the Mondale ticket. In the first place, it was predominantly an economic vote. If the economy was improving, either by one's own account or according to television, then men and women alike stayed with Reagan. The excitement generated by Ferraro wasn't translated into votes, most simply because women were voting from their pocketbooks. However misguided voters were to think that Reagan guaranteed a strong economy, they backed away from the specter of a return to a Carter-like recession. To them it didn't seem to matter that the gap between the haves and have-nots had widened, and that this gap affected women and minorities most directly. Those who realized this, either out of their own experience (they were the have-nots, they knew it, and things were getting worse) or from reading economic reports, were going to vote for Mondale anyway, whether Ferraro was on the ticket or not. Perhaps they did so with more excitement, with more hope that a Democratic victory was slightly more possible with Ferraro. Yet when the votes were counted, Ferraro's candidacy remained a watershed moment in history while Reagan had his landslide.

The political mood of the country had changed, commentators insisted before the election, and despite the grim economic statistics, voters were more likely to support President Reagan, in whom they had trust and confidence. Why? He was, of course, "Teflonized," in Congresswoman Pat Schroeder's apt description. Voters failed to see the connection between what was happening in the economy and his administration's policies. Yet it seemed that there was more than willful self-deception or ignorance at work. With all the talk about "have-nots" and "victims" of Reagan's policies, fewer voters were willing to identify themselves as part of this group. While the crowds turned out for Ferraro, while Mondale had a few gains in the polls, in the voting booth people seemed unwilling to cast their lot with "losers."

What did this say about women? Ferraro had predicted a "surprise vote by women," those women who sent small contributions to her campaign but "didn't want their husbands to know" or who didn't let their husbands know what they were going to do in the privacy of the voting booth. But these "surprise" votes didn't materialize. It seemed that while commentators were using the occasion of Reagan's victory to draw conclusions about the Democratic party, the failure of Ferraro to attract the predicted female vote, to widen the gender gap, said a great deal about the future of the women's movement in this country.

In the public's consciousness, feminism had been diluted to lamentations about the inequality of women, to litanies of day-to-day oppression. These were decidedly middle-class complaints of who did the dishes, vacuumed the rug, "parented" the child, or accusations of "negative" images perpetuated by television commercials and pornography. The message at its most extreme was interpreted as "women are simply slaves, victims, nonentities, an oppressed class, even whores." Yet how many women agreed that social and economic conditions had cast them in such roles? They were struggling day by day with their lives as they were leading them. Making dinner after coming home from a hard day's work in a restaurant or behind a typewriter was not a matter of weakness but a given, an economic necessity, and as such it was equally a matter of strength and resilience as it was of victimization. Outside the movement, awareness of feminism amounted to hearing statements that seemed to denigrate or deny those very reasons why women could take pride in themselves or feel they were somebody, at least to their children, at least to their families. It was as if they didn't want to make too much of those dirty pots and pans—"it's a messy job but somebody's got to do it"—and they certainly didn't want to be made to feel "unliberated" or retrograde. That, however, was the message middle-class feminism had managed to convey to them over the last fifteen years. While they might admit it was true that women were discriminated against in the job market (by 1984, equal pay for equal work was noncontroversial, equal pay for comparable work not so easily accepted), few women outside the movement felt comfortable or identified with the stereotypes of victimization at the hands of men and oppression in their homes.

They still deciphered in feminism the earlier battle cry of abolishing the "patriarchal" family as the bastion of capitalism and sexism. In her book *The Second Stage,* Betty Friedan recognized the perils of this emphasis when she called for feminism to relinquish antimen and antifamily statements. Still, there was the suggestion of "bringing the message" to uncommitted women, and while accepting the reality of the family, proposing architectural, financial, and legal measures to bring "gender-role equality" to the family was hardly the point. How little these solutions for getting men to share the housework had to do with those women who were, either with or without men, eking out their existence. Their families, however they were patterned, weren't the last bastion of capitalism or sexism; rather the family was a fortress against a sense of defeat, helplessness, or invisibility in a modern, technological, and bureaucratic society. In the midst of fatiguing and disillusioning rounds of work and insignificance, the family was the locus of whatever pleasure, sense of competence, and control one could hope to have in this world. And if feminism would abolish that, would run roughshod over women's experiences with redefinitions and re-creations of family life, what was left? NOW conventions could pass resolution after resolution about "heterosexual privilege." But more and more it seemed such privilege wasn't what most women were protecting when they said that feminism had little to do with their lives. Instead, they were guarding the complexity, all the goods and the bads of that part of their life from which they drew whatever love, esteem, and sense of identity they expected to have.

When Mondale and Ferraro recited statistics about the feminization of poverty and the larger group of have-nots, women could accept the statistics but not the solution of voting for Mondale. To do so meant identifying themselves as losers, and just as they'd refused to do so when the women's movement promulgated the image, they refused to call themselves victims in order to vote for Geraldine Ferraro. It wasn't her doing, however. If anything, her candidacy meant a triumph for women, as her highly charged audiences suggested. It was the suggestion, sometimes implicit, sometimes made explicit by feminists, that women would vote for her out of an awareness of their discrimination or oppression. Not so. Women, like men, voted for the "winner." They could cry joyful tears for Ferraro's nomination, but like most men, they saw no recognition of their own realities in the Democratic party's worn-out appeal to the "disadvantaged" or "disinherited" groups.

After the election commentators could only agree that Ferraro had neither helped nor hurt the campaign extraordinarily. Looking back, however, it seemed that the response to her candidacy was predictable from the experience of the Ginny Foat jurors. While they'd heard hours of testimony about her degradation and seen a dramatic reenactment of her passivity and victimization, they refused to accept her as a symbol of women, her plight an Everywoman's tale. Her dramatic transformation into a feminist after the trial had alienated them, and they disputed her attempt to characterize her verdict as a "victory for all women." What her statements did were in part what the women's movement had done for years: denied the reality of the experience that each of those jurors lived through, not only in viewing her but in living their own lives. More, by holding herself up as a symbol of women, she had insisted that every woman was a victim, oppressed by violent, misogynist men. While the jurors, particularly the women, sympathized with her plight, they were not about to characterize their own experiences in the same terms. Nor did they understand how a woman of such weakness and passivity could become such a strong, ardent feminist. They'd felt duped in a way, an emotion that was the common reaction of such women recruited by the women's movement. Appealing to them on the basis of their weakness, oppression, or passivity, feminism seemed to ask them to bring to the movement a sanctioned sense of self-pity and beleaguerment. Whatever the strength, competence, or resilience of their pasts, they were all but denied if they didn't fit an acceptable feminist mode. Male dominance was the theme; hence, ironically, feminists portrayed themselves as weak and more passive than they'd actually been in order to proclaim their total transformation.

With the reelection of President Reagan, the women's movement has an especially full agenda to achieve economic, legal, and social equality of women. As the largest feminist organization in the country, NOW has an uphill fight on its hands with the administration cutting away at so many social programs and legal guarantees that have advanced the cause of women's rights but are now in jeopardy. On that, all feminists could agree. After the achievement of a female vice-presidential candidate, a triumph in which NOW had played a major role, the organization had to define its course of action for the future. It wasn't so much a matter of goals but of strategy, and in 1985 the membership was once again divided, a division that would reach its culmination with the NOW presidential election in 1985.

A number of members felt dissatisfied with Judy Goldsmith's tactics of mobilizing around diverse feminist issues and lobbying on Capitol Hill. They argued that the Reagan mandate for the conservative view of women's rights, traditional family values, and opposition to affirmative action and civil rights programs called for more dramatic, larger-scale, and more attention-getting actions. Within the organization, these members felt that the activist impulse, the energy and commitment with which NOW had begun and which had reached its culmination in the ERA campaign, had been lost. Local chapters were less successful in both recruiting new members and bolstering a level of involvement when there was no major public campaign around which to organize. A number of these local and state representatives believed that a change in leadership was necessary. They sought a candidate who could mobilize hundreds and thousands of women to convince the public that women's rights and feminism were not, as Patrick Buchanan had said, passé. Of all their possible candidates, there seemed but one choice. They turned again to Ellie Smeal, the previous NOW president who had served from 1977 to 1982, had organized the massive ERA campaign, and during whose term NOW membership had increased from 35,000 to over 220,000 members and NOW's annual budget had burgeoned from $500,000 to $10 million.

Smeal was approached by several NOW delegations who eventually convinced her to run against Goldsmith. (This seemed especially ironic given the earlier charges that Goldsmith was simply a Smeal puppet.) With the announcement of her candidacy, newspaper stories appeared that predicted a "catfight" in NOW and quoted remarks presumably from Goldsmith supporters that Smeal was running because she couldn't stand being "out of the limelight."

Of course, the remarks about a catfight were the predictable sexist description of a debate between women. Smeal was careful to stress that her candidacy was not a personal attack on Goldsmith, nor was it either a condemnation of what Goldsmith had done during her term of office or a dispute over policies. "The debate centers on tactics," she said a month before the July 1985 convention. "I agreed to run because there was concern about the lack of visibility and lack of growth in the movement. With Reagan's days at their height, I agreed we needed larger and bigger activities. The only way we can bring about a change is to create a climate to bring about such change. We have to return to big rallies and demonstrations and marches in order to take center stage again. We must focus on a few major programs to bring them to such prominence that we can show that we have momentum again, rather than concentrating, as Judy has, on multi-issue programs."

It wasn't that Smeal didn't think such issues were important; nor did she disrespect or criticize Goldsmith's contributions. She also didn't expect the election to be a catfight, especially since Goldsmith and she had remained friendly colleagues. Her strategy, however, was to bring more public attention, for example, to the civil rights restoration act. "We're about to lose Title Nine" (the pivotal legislation against sex discrimination) "and although we're lobbying for the bill, we're doing it so quietly that few people know about it. Therefore, it's necessary to express our outrage and show that we can mobilize people who won't tolerate losing their civil rights."

A second priority was, of course, ensuring guarantees of pro-choice in the face of the growing, energetic, and well-financed antiabortion crusade, and especially once the Reagan administration's Justice Department had pushed for a Supreme Court reassessment of the historic *Roe* v. *Wade* decision. Once again Smeal believed large demonstrations were necessary to show the public that the women's movement hadn't lost momentum on this issue, but could in fact retake the "moral high ground" the pro-lifers "were insisting was their terrain." And finally, Smeal promised to revive the Equal Rights Amendment campaign, not only because it was in her mind the most crucial and all-embracing feminist cause but also because, in NOW's experience, the ERA campaign had brought more members to NOW than any other issue.

From the outside, the July 1985 NOW election seemed to promise an amicable but necessary airing of differences in strategy, and such differences seemed to be the only things that set Goldsmith and Smeal apart. Otherwise, their goals were the same and the distinctions between them seemed related to their personal styles: Goldsmith the more low-key negotiator, perhaps bespeaking her experience as a college teacher; Smeal the more flamboyant, the more media-minded, perhaps indicative of her long years studying and being involved in politics. Both came from poor, working-class backgrounds, Goldsmith from Wisconsin, Smeal from Pennsylvania. Each woman had her loyal supporters, the delegates whom they had rallied in their visits to NOW local chapters across the country in the months before the national convention.

Muriel Fox was attending the convention, but because of her position with the NOW Legal Defense and Education Fund she was not a delegate nor could she express support for either candidate. Nevertheless, she predicted a peaceful convention unlike the intense battles at other elections, such as the famous 1975 Philadelphia meeting. That convention was historic not only because the "out of the mainstream, into the revolution" faction won, but because of the charges, countercharges, and investigations of voting fraud and irregularities. After the convention, Betty Friedan had loudly lamented the takeover of NOW by radicals like DeCrow and Smeal. (Friedan also criticized Smeal's candidacy in 1985, fearing that a major election battle would hurt NOW's unity at a crucial time for the women's movement.)

Muriel Fox, however, foresaw no such cataclysmic upheavals in 1985: "Ellie and Judy are very close in their objectives," she said. "I really love and admire them both, and I think it will be a healthy competition between them which can only end up being good for NOW. Their candidacies do not represent a schism like the ones NOW has had in the past. Still, when you think that NOW is *the* organization which represents the aspirations of most American feminists, it's amazing that we've held together at all because obviously there are people who feel very differently about our objectives. But this will not be one of the big ideological battles we've had before."

Although the July 1985 NOW convention promised only an extensive debate about tactics, it betokened one other aspect that, if it wasn't cataclysmic, was at the very least ironic. For all the talk at the time of the Foat case about Louisiana as antifeminist, misogynist, and retrograde, and despite the earlier ERA boycott of the state, NOW scheduled its convention at the Fairmont hotel in downtown New Orleans.

Among Foat devotees, there were murmurs of slaps in the face to Foat, of locating the convention in a place that would make it extremely painful for Foat to attend. Nevertheless, even Lynne Renihan disputed this impression, despite her continued loyalty to Foat: "We lobbied extremely hard for two years to have a NOW convention here. Or at least we wanted it in the Deep South to show that not all women wear hoopskirts down here, that we're not all redneck or backward, and that we are doing fantastic things down here. It had nothing to do with the Ginny Foat case either way."

State Representative Mary Landrieu agreed that it was very important that NOW hold its convention in New Orleans. In the first place it would show the people in the area what a legitimate and major political force the women's movement had become. But the convention could also introduce feminists from other parts of the country to southern women; perhaps it indicated a reexamination of the way in which feminism could encompass women from diverse backgrounds and various feminist approaches. "It seems that NOW has reassessed its position and realized that we are one country, that the South is not a separate unit," said Landrieu. "A lot of good things are happening in the South. The number of women in elective offices is still low, five percent in the legislature compared to the national average of thirteen percent. But we've been getting better, and there are other states that are worse. The polls also show that the citizens of Louisiana support the ERA, but the problem is that the legislature hasn't passed it. Plus people forget that in a popular vote New Jersey and New York didn't pass the ERA either. But the most important thing in the South, as I learned at a recent southwestern regional conference of state women's commissions, is that women's greatest concern is the pay equity issue. 'The feminization of poverty' is not an abstraction here; it's very real and means a great deal to women in the South, because there are still many, many poor people in the South. White women understand that, black women understand that, it cuts across racial lines, because wages are low and opportunities are low, and that will be the issue that rallies the South more to the forefront of the movement. So I think it's especially important that NOW held its convention in New Orleans. It may encourage women to take stronger stands in Louisiana; they've been doing things for women, too, but maybe now they'll realize they can call themselves feminists and be proud of it."

It certainly seemed that NOW had taken a different approach, not only in the location of the convention but in the implicit theme chosen for the meeting. Called "Organizing for the Future NOW— One Fine Day," the three-day program included speakers who were considered "breakthrough" women. From astronaut Sally Ride and Olympic volleyball silver medalist Flo Hyman, to Blandina Cardenas, U.S. Civil Rights Commissioner, and Eleanor Holmes Norton, professor of law and previously the first woman to chair the Equal Employment Opportunity Commission, all of them stressed triumphs as much as losses; organizing for the future meant building on victories, not miring women in their victimization. *Cagney and Lacey,* Tyne Daly and Sharon Gless, sent a videotaped message (their show had been rescued by a strong outpouring of support from women viewers, in part organized by NOW). And Geraldine Ferraro sent a filmed speech from China, which prompted a standing ovation. The mood was upbeat. Despite the setbacks of the Reagan years, despite his reelection and the retrogressive attitudes of his administration, the NOW convention had an aura of optimism. With such accomplished women speaking to the delegates, there was a sense that it was women like these, strong, proud of their accomplishments, and aware that their victories affected other women, who symbolized the important turn the women's movement was taking in the eighties.

* * *

Yet beneath the surface of optimism and hope, of unity and progress, simmered the antagonisms of a NOW election convention. The predicted polite, high-minded debate about strategy soon degenerated into accusations, name-calling, charges and counter-charges of dirty pool, rumormongering, and backroom deals. Granted, Smeal and Goldsmith both tried to keep the campaign on the higher plane of debates over issues; nevertheless, hints of acrimony began to creep into their voices as they explained their programs at the various board meetings, regional caucuses, and press conferences.

Goldsmith charged that Smeal's overzealous commitment to a "one-issue" approach—the ERA campaign—had wreaked havoc with NOW's budget, leaving her administration saddled with high debts and draining loans to be repaid. Smeal was put on the defensive, and at her press conference found herself explaining the intricacies of matching funds, donations, and loans, which, she asserted, would not have depleted the treasury if Goldsmith had maintained the high level of membership recruitment that her leadership had inspired. She hit back with the charges that Goldsmith had adopted programs that had reduced NOW's previously high profile in both the media and the public's mind. Legislative lobbying didn't work anymore, she said, and NOW needed to regain its "independent political voice": "When the right wing is so visible and such a clear danger, NOW ought to be rallying its people. It ought to be a highly visible critic every time the Reagan administration has taken steps that hurt women." She cited as an example the revision of the tax structure that would eliminate tax breaks for working couples and reduce child-care credit. "I would have been out there immediately explaining its impact on women, but NOW didn't make it a big enough issue." It wasn't too late, she said, but it depended on NOW leadership's bringing public attention to yet another setback for women.

She was most defensive, however, when she was questioned about her "one-issue" focus. She had never been and never would be a one-issue candidate, she said. While the ERA perforce had had to receive the most attention, she argued that under her leadership NOW also spent a good deal of time working on such issues as abortion rights, sex discrimination in Social Security, the gender gap, and pay equity.

The candidates, however, were much less adamant and antagonistic than their supporters. With the political again personal, there were angry disputes on the convention floor and in the hotel hallways with bitter name calling and damning gossip. One of the main activities of the two days before the election was lobbying delegates for their votes—not only for the presidency but for the candidates for other offices who had aligned themselves with either Goldsmith or Smeal. Yet it was difficult to find any uncommitted delegates among the 2,500 who were registered. Everyone seemed to be totally committed, and they argued as if their very lives depended on who was elected. Workshops were packed with a candidate's supporters if her opponent happened to be on the workshop panel. Their tactic was to position themselves by the microphones, hoard them, so that they could dominate the discussion period, not with questions about the issues at hand, but with ones designed to embarrass the candidate.

Journalists who had covered both national party conventions and the meetings of other organizations were alternately amused and annoyed. The overriding suspicions of dirty tricks and unscrupulous tactics created an atmosphere of rampant rumors and paranoia. It was difficult enough to confirm the truth of rumors, but some delegates suspected that the press was out to get them, forgetting that more media exposure was exactly what NOW needed during a time of reduced visibility. Delegates refused to be interviewed or quoted; a tape recorder set down in a meeting room during a cigarette break immediately came under suspicion. "Has that been going the whole time?" someone shrieked, making to grab for it as if to tear out the cassette.

In this instance, the press was extraordinarily generous and circumspect, concentrating on the issues that most of the reporters seemed to think were serious and significant. While it seemed that Goldsmith and Smeal, whatever their differences, were addressing the realities of the world outside the convention, the hotel had also taken on an aura of unreality. The intensity and personal animosity between factions was hard to fathom: Did it really matter that much who was elected president to the point that women were in tears, or physically struggled over possession of a microphone, or tripped each other as they tried to make statements from the convention floor?

The culmination of this kind of behavior occurred once after the nominations of candidates Friday, July 19, the night before the election, and once during the voting on Saturday night. Lois Galgay Reckett was the incumbent vice-president–executive in the Goldsmith administration. While she had remained officially neutral, her incumbency led delegates to assume that she was in Goldsmith's camp, and because everyone felt she'd served NOW well, she was running unopposed. Suddenly, after the nominations were closed, she announced that after long and hard deliberation, she was endorsing Smeal. Not only had she had profound misgivings about the way Goldsmith's administration was run, and no less the decline in new members, but she also found herself agreeing with Smeal's agenda for the future and the strategies that she thought would reinvigorate NOW and the women's movement. It was not a question of personal antagonism, dirty tricks, or a betrayal of Goldsmith that impelled her to change her endorsement, she insisted. It was a question of her own analysis on the basis of her feminist commitments and beliefs. She cited "feminist ethics," but subsequently, she was treated to another version of feminist ethics: She was physically assaulted twice, once with a slap, once with a blow that was warded off by a friend who stepped between her and her attacker. Delegates were appalled, especially so when they heard that one of the attackers was a young, paid staff member in Goldsmith's administrative office. The next night, when Reckett gave her campaign speech before the voting began, she was close to tears and her voice shook. What did feminism mean if not standing up for what one believed in, if not ethical responsibility and fidelity to one's beliefs? she asked. And for remaining true to her sense of feminist ethics, she'd been assaulted by her sisters.

With feelings running so high, it seemed that some delegates lost sight of both feminist issues and feminist behavior. No less, they forgot that just outside the hotel entrance a real world existed. But equally, as some NOW members agreed, given the nature of the organization, given the way NOW accepted or welcomed any woman at face value, it was bound to become a haven for what Toni Carabillo admitted were a few "crazies." "They have no standards, and they always go after the bizarre. Still, the majority of NOW people are sane and sensible, live in the real world, and are offended by unethical or underhanded things."

Ex-NOW President Karen DeCrow agreed that there was a strain in the movement that led to some of the more extreme and irresponsible stances. "What I find most terrifying, most distasteful, is anti-intellectualism. I don't want us to be guilty of elitism, yet I do want us to adopt values that are associated with the elite. I'm appalled when feminists don't read anything. They're into tarot cards; they stay away from science because they say 'it's male.' Someone has cancer, and they sit in a circle and chant for you. They don't know anything about civil liberties or about the Constitution. And if you happen to mention Simone de Beauvoir, they think it's a wine!"

If anything linked such various examples of bizarre or strange behavior, it was a denial of consequences in the real world, the same kind of denial or evasion that certainly played a major role in almost every facet and on almost every side of the Foat case. Yet at the NOW convention several other aspects of the Foat case were repeated as well. Lesbianism was a taboo subject; the press for the most part avoided any reference to it, aware how it could be misused now against NOW and feminism just as it might have been used against Foat in Louisiana. Antifeminists had always denounced the women's movement as a horde of rabid lesbians. Outside the Fairmont hotel pro-life picketers marched up and down protesting NOW's pro-choice campaign. Two men "who spoke for God" carried a scaffold from which an effigy of Judy Goldsmith was hanged (Lynch Judy Goldsmith but don't kill embryos, seemed to be their Christian message). Another man carried a fetus in a bottle, and one woman carried a poster reading LESBIANS PLUS COMMIES EQUAL MURDERERS.

Yet inside the hotel, some lesbians seemed to think that the convention gave them license; they seemed to ignore or care less about the impression they might be making. It was understandable, of course. Discriminated against in society, fighting for their rights, having finally forced NOW to examine its homophobia and to adopt lesbian rights as part of its platform, they had made NOW their refuge. They could act and dress however they chose. Still, one strain of lesbianism seemed to proclaim that this was the be-all and end-all of feminism. Their commitment was announced in a uniform of jeans, men's shirts with tails out, and heavy shoes. They carried with them an air of arrogant defensiveness toward straight women or even other lesbians whom they considered less "out-front," and therefore less radical, their feminism not as pure or strong as theirs.

No one was asking them to return to the closet or to disavow their sexuality or life-style. Nevertheless, since NOW had become large enough and significant enough in the public's eye to attract media attention, and indeed was intent on gaining more visibility, their actions seemed inappropriate. They didn't have to suppress their lesbianism or their commitment to lesbian rights. But why indulge in behavior that was sure to alienate the public? More and more Americans were willing to say that individuals' sexuality was their own business. Nevertheless, lesbian couples necking during debates on issues or kissing in the lobby seemed excessive. What possible political gains could be made by selling in one of the stalls in the exhibition hall envelopes whose back flap read "This envelope licked by a lesbian"? Just as there was a kind of myopia at the initial Foat defense-committee meetings when some Gay Task Force members wanted to make her a lesbian cause, so there seemed to be a stubborn insistence that a commitment to lesbian rights sanctioned such silliness.

The other extreme that manifested itself at the NOW convention was a group led by Andrea Dworkin, the antipornography crusader. Her presence at the NOW convention, the meetings and lobbying she organized, had one goal: to convince NOW to adopt her antipornography plank, one that supported her campaign for municipal antipornography legislation based on the argument that pornography is an infringement of civil rights. It was a complicated position, an approach that many NOW members thought raised more issues than solved the problem of pornography, which by and large they, too, opposed.

The basis on which Dworkin argued her position both in her book *Pornography, Men Possessing Women* and at the NOW convention was similar to the central motif of Ginny Foat's explanation of her feminism. In this analysis, women are as delicate and easily manipulated and bruised as fragile blossoms. The "degradation" of women in pornography requires the lock-step causal argument that since women are perceived by men as whores, women perceive themselves as whores (the quick leap was based on the etymology of *pornography* as meaning the depiction of women as whores). The cumulative effect, feminist antipornographers argue, promotes rape, wife abuse, and violence against women; yet they conveniently ignore other studies that contradict their assertions by disproving causal connections between pornography and violent sex crimes.

With her latest push for antipornography laws, Dworkin seemed to believe that women were as compliant and masochistic as their portrayals in pornography. No woman could walk past such pictures on a newsstand or outside a theater without feeling insulted and demeaned, the antipornography crusade insisted. Demeaned from what—the virgin? The perfect woman? You had to buy into the madonna-whore stereotype to feel affected. Not so surprisingly Phyllis Schlafly had long been spouting the same line: "Porn is the degradation and subjugation of women. It has an enormous effect on sexual crimes and in the way men view women. And I think it's a major cause of domestic violence."

Both the far right and the Dworkins of the feminist movement implicitly seemed to insist that what counted most was how men viewed women, not how women viewed themselves. Women who have strong senses of themselves don't faint dead away in some kind of swoon if a copy of *Penthouse* is flashed before them. Leaving aside the very real First Amendment rights that the new antiporn legislation blithely ignored (censorship had always depended on who had the power to say what was offensive to whom), this arm of the women's movement had regressed to the ideology of man the oppressor, woman the infantilized victim, and was resorting to a form of "protectionist law," long used to proscribe women's freedom. But, ironically, only the acceptance of the stereotype of female weakness and passivity guaranteed a feeling of being victimized either by pornography or men in general.

Nothing seemed either as tragic or as indicative of women insisting on their own victimization than the young woman who doused herself with gasoline and set herself on fire in a Minneapolis pornographic bookstore. Perceiving herself as nothing but a victim of pornography, she had done herself more violence than the pornography she was protesting.

Pornography may indeed be a symptom of second-class citizenship; first things first, however. If women have economic and social equality, pornography can hardly be symptomatic of women's slavery, nor can it reinforce it. Economic equality, not the wholesale censorship of pornography, would be the major step toward combating degrading images of women, wherever they are found.

Andrea Dworkin, however, came to the NOW convention with what sounded like an ultimatum: "Support my position, join my fight for antipornography legislation, or you're not the feminists you claim to be." When NOW members did not agree that hers was the position to be adopted as a NOW policy, she became angry. Holding an impromptu caucus in the back of the convention hall during a lunch break, she lambasted NOW for its failure to care about women, for its wishy-washy politics, for, quite simply, its cowardice. Suddenly her microphone went dead: A NOW member stood by her side, livid with rage. Dworkin could propose and lobby for her position, she said, but NOW would not provide her with either an audience or sound equipment just to have her "bad-mouth" the organization.

"Let her speak! Let her speak!" Dworkin's supporters shouted. The microphone was turned back on. Dworkin continued in tears, railing against NOW once more for refusing to see that "pornography creates inequality" at a time "when we are living at the beginning of a holocaust against women." She called for NOW members to "make those bureaucrats responsible for their politics" and she sarcastically denounced the organization's concern for the First Admendment with "all the freedom of speech and the democracy we see expressed here." Her emotional speech concluded with calls for legislation that would stop the exploitation of women, particularly poor women, so that "we can't be used as pieces of dead meat." Then she announced a march on Bourbon Street to protest its rampant pornography.

That night, after the NOW campaign speeches, just as the balloting was begun, Dworkin's march set out in the hot steamy night. Bourbon Street was alive with its carnival atmosphere, music blaring, sex heavy in the air. Into this atmosphere came the antipornography march. Was anyone upset? No. Was anyone suddenly aware that all the usual French Quarter revelry—straight, gay, you name it—was exploitation? No. It was just a hoot, the antipornography parade another part of the circus. With Andrea Dworkin in her jean overalls shouting through her bullhorn, the demonstration became entertainment. The crowds applauded and laughed, but not maliciously. For all anyone knew, the New Orleans Chamber of Commerce had staged it to add to the excitement of Bourbon Street. The next time they'd have a band playing "When the Saints Go Marching In."

The call went out from the hotel, however: Bring the delegates back. Whether they were marching or not, if they'd voted before 9:30 that night, they had to return to the hotel to vote again. There'd been a foul-up in the polls. A sample ballot provided by the Smeal campaign had placed candidates' names on the wrong line. Since this was the first year NOW used computers for its vote tallies, it was argued that delegates might have simply marked off their sample ballots, line by line, then duplicated their marks in the voting booth without glancing at the name beside each box.

Charges and countercharges flew fast and furious. The Smeal people insisted it was an honest mistake, but they accused the election committee (dominated by Goldsmith staff people) of waiting until a large number of Smeal delegates had already voted to call attention to the mistake. Goldsmith's camp countered with charges of election irregularities. The result was a "woman hunt" in the streets of New Orleans—get the voters back. It became an all-night vigil, and the polls were kept open until 6:30 the next morning. But even with the computer tabulation, the results of the election were still not forthcoming by midmorning. NOW had already lost media coverage of its presidential election in *Time* and *Newsweek*. With the added delay, reports of the election wouldn't appear until Monday's newspapers. It had the feel of the McGovern debacle, when the voting took so long that he didn't appear to accept the nomination until the early hours of the morning. The announcement of the NOW results was further delayed by the democratic, "nonhierarchical" tradition of announcing all the election results at once since it shouldn't seem that the presidential race was given preferential treatment; meanwhile, journalists with deadlines were trying to convince both Goldsmith and Smeal that they were there to cover the presidential election. The impression conveyed, said several of the most cynical, was that "the ladies can't get their shit together." Just when NOW wanted higher visibility, they'd forgotten the effect on the press and were stuck with the image of ineptitude and incompetence within their organization. Finally, just after lunch, reality broke through, and the new president of NOW was announced.

Ginny Foat was not there to hear it. Even though Smeal herself had phoned her to ask if she would attend, Ginny declined. There had been some talk that she might indeed enter the presidential race. It was rumored that she had attended a meeting earlier that year with the thought in mind that, given the division in the ranks between Goldsmith and Smeal, she would be turned to as the logical alternative. Except to her loyal supporters, though, this notion seemed a pipe dream. She had done nothing to endear herself to NOW members with her continued criticism; further, she'd burned her bridges, first by criticizing Smeal in 1981–82 for returning NOW to the mainstream, then by calling Goldsmith "a Smeal puppet." More, she seemed to have a personal animosity against Goldsmith for the way she had treated her after her arrest, and she seemed to hold her responsible for NOW's official dissociation from her case.

The Foat case had in some respects affected delegates' feelings about Goldsmith. Those NOW members who'd criticized her for her handling of the case were by and large Smeal supporters. (They either didn't realize or chose to overlook that Smeal had participated in a few of the early meetings and agreed with Goldsmith's difficult decision, the one that attempted to juggle Ginny's needs with those of NOW.) Nevertheless, some delegates agreed that while it wasn't their primary reason for voting for Smeal, Goldsmith's position on Foat provided another reason for supporting Smeal.

Among the large contingent of Smeal supporters from California were Toni Carabillo, Shelly Mandell, and Elaine Lafferty. Although Carabillo had resigned from editing *NOW Times* the previous year, she was still very active in NOW and was especially enthusiastic about returning her good friend Smeal to the presidency. She agreed wholeheartedly with Smeal's criticism of Goldsmith's low-key, lobbying strategies. The Foat case was well behind her and behind NOW; the organization could move on to developing a large activist campaign around the high-priority issues.

For Lafferty and Mandell, the issue was slightly more complicated. Both kept a low profile. While this was the usual stance for Lafferty at NOW conventions, it was foreign to Shelly's political nature. She worked tirelessly for Smeal behind the scenes but wore neither a Smeal T-shirt nor any campaign buttons, and she wasn't registered by name in the hotel. "It wasn't just because of the Foat case that I didn't wear any badges," Mandell explained. "It also went back to the previous election when the California delegation felt I'd deserted them and their candidate Jane Wells Schooley to support the Goldsmith slate. So even though most of the California delegates were for Smeal, and so was I, they were still angry and, of course, the Foat thing had been the clincher. So I didn't want to publicly align myself with Smeal since I didn't know if I would hurt her chances. I'm still very political, and I didn't want to be visible and take the floor because I really believed that the future of NOW and the movement hinged on whether Smeal resumed the presidency."

The reasons for Ginny Foat's nonattendance must have been complicated. The official reason was that her schedule didn't permit it. It had, indeed, been a busy year. Not only had she been speaking about battered wives on the lecture circuit and working on her women in prison network, but she and Kay Tsenin had filed a five-million-dollar lawsuit against Shelly Mandell and twenty-five unnamed people for invasion of privacy and emotional distress. She was also working on her book with Laura Foreman. Both the lawsuit and the book required more interviewing in an effort to expose the conspiracy against her. Foreman interviewed the Jefferson Parish prosecutors. Having been elected a district-court judge in 1984 (no, the Foat case obviously hadn't turned voters against him), Tom Porteous was quite willing to talk. Again he insisted there was no conspiracy or antifeminist plot, although he allowed that Elaine Lafferty had been one of those important parts of the case that fell away. Gordon Konrad had also left the district attorney's office, moving into private practice, but not because he felt driven out by the bad publicity surrounding the Foat case. He, too, was unwilling to renege on his insistence that the Foat case was neither political nor the result of a conspiracy. Still, there was the rumor that Sheriff Harry Lee, hearing from LA that Foat was a feminist leader, had initiated her arrest before notifying the DA's office. But he was not talking, finding himself again under siege in the community. His release of a convicted rapist on a work-parole had prompted a recall drive, with New Orleans NOW in full support; his latest action was in their minds only another example of his disregard for women.

Still, Kay Tsenin proceeded with the Foat suit against Mandell and others (three times having been instructed by the judge to resubmit her complaint if she wished to have it accepted into the courts as a legitimate civil suit). Foreman completed writing Foat's story, and by the time of the NOW convention, the book had gone into galleys. Foat was preparing for tours and interviews, which prevented her attendance at the NOW convention. More cynical observers quipped that since she'd become so talented at entrances and exits, an appearance at the NOW convention might have brought her useful publicity.

Beyond the snide remarks, however, there was a sense in which NOW's organizing for the future had left her behind. Smeal had been announcing a return to "grass-root organizing" to mount large-scale demonstrations around abortion rights and the revival of the ERA campaign. Furthermore, her campaign speech stressed going back into the streets, back onto campuses, recruiting women from all backgrounds, and using confrontational tactics. It wasn't that different from Foat's position when she'd criticized NOW's policies. While Foat had dismissed Smeal and Goldsmith's "mainstream, corporate-image politics," at first glance, Foat's view of NOW policies seemed little different from Smeal's 1985 campaign.

Yet there were profound differences, as Foat's rendering of her life story made quite clear. Ginny Foat obviously had had to do what was necessary to stage an effective defense at her trial. Yet in her book, the narrative followed almost exactly the same lines as her defense, with similar descriptions shaped by the passive tense, the internalization of Cinderella myths, and the enforced "traditional stereotypes." Even her explanation for her five years with Sidote had a helpless ring—"I loved him." The language of the beatings and references to the battered-wife syndrome, which had sounded familiar and rehearsed during her trial, were repeated, but in her book she made explicit reference to Del Martin's study in *Battered Wives*. She talked about Ginny Galluzzo and Ginny Foat as two separate people, just as she had both in her statement from jail and during her testimony. Her narrative also examined the psychological preparation for her trial, in which she placed herself apart from her previous incarnation and screamed at her for what she hated. (Only later, she said, did she manage, with the aid of her therapist, to find "the good parts" of Ginny Galluzzo that allowed her attorney to argue that "Ginny then was the same as Ginny now.")

Yet, for all the splitting off of the two selves, they had more in common than in fact Ginny Galluzzo Sidote Foat Meyer was willing to admit. She had been enamored of Sidote's "There Will Never Be Another You." For her wedding to Ray Foat, music again was important: "Bridge Over Troubled Water" and "I Never Promised You a Rose Garden" were her choices, a detail she added with no self-awareness of their tastelessness. Ray Foat, like Sidote, made her feel special—he treated her "like a lady," she said; she had her hair done in the same shops as Vancouver society women, and she thought her design for her wedding dress—a long skirt split up the front to reveal hot pants—was so high-style that she had a miniature replica of it made for the doll atop her wedding cake. When in 1975 she almost haphazardly attended a NOW meeting she found herself out of place, she thought, because of her clothes, flouncy wig, and long fingernails. As a result she went out and bought herself a new outfit at an army surplus store and read a few of the feminist classics. The image and the language were transformed to fit the new context.

Just as her lawyers and her own testimony insisted, in her book she fell back on the rationale that social pressure had defined who she was: "I remembered her growing up, a child of her times and circumstances, feeling so guilty and confused because she wanted things those times and circumstances didn't allow." In her own telling of her story, her conversion to feminism was similarly determined by external forces. Equally, the theme of her book was again that it had all been done *to* her. When a situation cried out for an explanation or analysis, she adopted the same pattern that had been apparent at the trial. "I didn't think about it; I pushed it away; I tried to forget; I can't bring back what I've walled off or blocked out," she repeated whenever the complexity or the bizarreness of an event begged for interpretation. Furthermore, her narrative seemed to suffer from the same amnesia she'd experienced during her testimony. For example, Richard Busconi was nowhere mentioned in her narrative, and, of course, she had no memory of either people she knew in New Orleans or when and how she eventually left town in great haste. The point of her book, *Never Guilty, Never Free,* was to depict her as the innocent victim, the young tomboy who never seemed to get her life together, who because of internalized stereotypes, traditions, myths, and expectations had become a passive woman.

Aside from Foat's busy schedule, aside from having no place in an election when the two candidates were the leaders she had so vehemently criticized, her own strand of feminism might have worn thin. Based as it was on a reshaping of her past life to insist on her victimization, it may indeed play a small role in the revitalization of feminism in the eighties. Her jurors could view her abuse with sympathy, but could see no connection between her passivity and her feminism. So, too, was NOW realizing that women came to feminism with a sense of strength, not simply out of helplessness. The women's movement needed an injection of the willfulness, sense of competence, and individuality that many of such hardscrabble women found in the circumstances by which they were supposed to be only oppressed. It would be hard to translate the plight of Ginny Foat into a parable for women that would bring them into the women's movement. If she continued to portray herself as a victim to whom everything just happened, those parts of her identity that existed long before her feminist conversion would be obscured to the public, just as they'd been to her jury. And that denial severely undermined her effectiveness as either a "role model" or a feminist spokesperson.

The recognition of women's strengths—and the acceptance of their diverse identities and circumstances—is an important turning point in feminism. Smeal's promise of increased membership and large, highly visible actions was posited on reaching out to women from diverse backgrounds with complex identities and personalities. Finally, it seemed, the women's movement had come to recognize that when its ideological message was stalled in "the woman as victim" mentality, it alienated a large number of women who could bring their power, strength, and commitment to the struggle. Feminism doesn't confer instantaneous identities; women bring individual characters, pasts, loves, hates, emotional ambiguities, private and public needs, and multiple concerns to feminism. But they will only come to the women's movement when feminism doesn't deny or obliterate or rewrite as "correct" the lives from which they've forged those identities.

Too often feminism has seemed a monolithic crusade of "new selves," "instant identities" cut off from their pasts, their private lives politicized out of existence, their public lives filled with hostility, petty jealousies, and Machiavellian maneuvers for power. Women are more and better than that, and NOW indeed wants to mobilize that force. It will, too, when it relinquishes the propensity to cast women in the mold of inept, passionless, joyless, passive hostages to fate. Feminism will only be strengthened by those women who refuse to be "symbolized" or defined by equally unrealistic stereotypes, by women like the feisty grandmother on the jury who heard Ginny Foat's "feminist" proclamation of a victory for all women and announced, "I didn't elect her to speak for me."

* * *

In July 1985 NOW elected the woman who would speak for it: Ellie Smeal defeated Judy Goldsmith by a wide margin. With a rallying cry of "Let's give 'em hell!" Smeal announced a new phase of feminist activism and mobilization. Ginny Foat received two write-in votes for NOW president.

Index